Sunset

Western Garden

Problem

Solver

By the Editors of Sunset Books and Sunset Magazine

SUNSET PUBLISHING CORPORATION • MENLO PARK, CALIFORNIA

A northern California garden

Sunset Books
VP, Sales & Marketing: Richard A. Smeby
Editorial Director: Bob Doyle
Production Director: Lory Day
Art Director: Vasken Guiragossian

Staff for This Book
Managing Editor: Sally W. Smith
Assistant Managing Editor: Valerie J.Cipollone
Contributing Editors: Suzanne Normand Eyre, Lance Walheim
Sunset Magazine Senior Editor, Gardening: Kathleen Norris Brenzel
Assistant Editor: Tishana Peebles
Production Coordinator: Patricia S. Williams
Writers: Mia Amato, L. Patricia Kite, Rosemary McCreary, Carol B. Moholt,
    Janet H. Sanchez
Chief Copy Editor: Carolyn McGovern
Copy Editors: Julie Harris, Elinor Lindheimer, Judith Dunham
Proofreaders: Desne Border, Melinda E. Levine, Mary Roybal
Indexer: Thérèse Shere

Art Director: Alice Rogers
Computer Production: Linda M. Bouchard
Photo Editor: Pamela K. Peirce
Map Design and Cartography: Reineck & Reineck, San Francisco
Illustrators: Jenny Spreckels, Margaret Robinson, Charlotte Coqui,
    Mimi Osborne, Jane McCreary, Catherine Watters
Iconography: Elisa Tanka

Cover photograph (digitally altered): *Honeybee on* Gaillardia grandiflora,
    Richard Shiell
Title page photograph: *Geranium budworm,* Ron West
Foreword illustration: *Life stages of a monarch butterfly*
Endpapers photograph, hardcover edition: Acer palmatum, Pamela K. Peirce

Second printing April 1998

Foreword

The battle against garden pests is ever changing. Until a few decades ago, dusts and sprays made up our arsenals. One blast of a potent chemical and whole colonies of aphids would vanish—at least temporarily.

Then scientists and, eventually, the Environmental Protection Agency, began reevaluating the safety of some chemicals, and recalling others as unsafe. Concerns mounted about substances that harmed children, pets, and wildlife, or left residues in our crops, soils, and water. We began turning to less hazardous alternatives, such as soaps and barriers. Still, most of us acknowledged the need for occasional dusting or spraying, when infestations became too heavy.

In the late 1950s, scientists at the University of California introduced a method of using natural pest controls in combination with the timely use of chemicals. In the 1970s, this practice became known as Integrated Pest Management (IPM). Because IPM complements Sunset's philosophy of working closely with nature in the garden, it is the method highlighted throughout this book.

An important principle of IPM is the need for a certain tolerance. It is impossible to permanently eradicate garden pests—their survival systems are too strong—but with thoughtful management we can reduce their numbers to acceptable levels. We do best when we view the garden as a balanced ecosystem. Even the smallest patch of planted ground is filled with organisms of all kinds, most of which are better kept alive. Among other things, these essential creatures pollinate plants, hasten the decomposition of organic matter in the soil, and even feed on the insects that cause real damage.

Prevention is another key to IPM. After all, a well-tended garden—with appropriate plants, healthy soil, and a balanced ratio of beneficial insects to pests—rarely, if ever, needs heavy-handed pest control. Over the long haul, your best hope for winning the battle against pests, diseases, and weeds is simply good gardening—amending the soil, proper irrigation, crop rotation, routine cleanup, and the like.

When plants do show signs of damage, however, this book can help you identify the culprit and find the right solution.

Gardening, after all, is a gentle pursuit. Tend your plot of ground with a light touch, and it will reward you in more ways than you ever thought possible.

Kathleen N. Brenzel
Senior Garden Editor, *Sunset Magazine*

CONTENTS

GARDENING IN THE WEST

SOLVING GARDEN PROBLEMS

PROBLEM SOLVING BY PLANT TYPE

SYMPTOMS AND CAUSES AT A GLANCE

Gardening
IN THE WEST

*S*unset divides the West into 24 climate zones. Knowing the characteristics of your zone will let you create a
*healthy garden by selecting plants that will thrive in that zone's soil, temperature range, and natural humidity
and moisture, augmented by the irrigation you can provide. This chapter explains the zones and describes western
garden conditions, starting you on your way to developing a garden that is naturally resistant to insect pests,
diseases, and weeds—the easiest way to solve garden problems.*

THE WEST: A DISTINCTIVE AND DIVERSE LANDSCAPE

Imagine you're gazing down at Earth from the perspective of several miles up. As the planet rotates below, you'll soon find your eyes drawn to the western part of the North American continent. The high ranges of the Rockies and the Sierra Nevada—with many peaks towering above 10,000 feet—are the first thing to catch your attention. Then, as you look a bit closer, you'll see some of the jewels in nature's necklace: Yosemite Valley in California, Yellowstone Park in Wyoming, Monument Valley in Arizona, and Utah's Bryce and Zion canyons. You'll see deserts high and low, the Great Salt Lake of Utah, California's spectacular Lake Tahoe, and rivers—the mighty Columbia, the lengthy Colorado, the remote Salmon. Major topographic features include California's Death Valley, the Grand Canyon in the Southwest, the string of northwestern mountains from Rainier to Hood to Shasta.

An aerial perspective would also reveal the abundant plant life of the West, both naturally occurring and human-created: conifers (including bristlecone pines, among the oldest plants on Earth) covering the mountains, the surprisingly varied desert vegetation, the temperate-zone rain forest of the Olympic Peninsula, and alpine meadows sprinkled with wildflowers. Among these natural wonders are the wheat fields in Montana, the apple orchards in Washington, the bountiful Willamette Valley in Oregon that supplies the nation with its ornamental trees and shrubs, and the grapes and food crops in California's Central Valley.

Like the landscape, gardens of the West reflect the many climate zones that dot the region, as well as the many gardeners who tend them. The West's distinctive and diverse natural features unite gardeners in the challenges they face and the successes they claim.

CLIMATES, MICROCLIMATES, AND ECOSYSTEMS

With such varied topography, western gardeners are always dealing in diversity. For instance, there's no such thing as "the western climate." Ask someone to describe it, and you'll hear of Seattle's rain, Los Angeles' heat and smog, the southwestern deserts' scorching summers, and the Rocky Mountains' cold and snowy winters. There are some broad patterns—the mountainous states of Montana, Wyoming, and Colorado share a similar climate, with many under-100-day growing seasons. But you can find almost every one of the West's 24 climate zones in California's 800-mile length. Climate zones nestle so close together—the growing region at the base of a coastal canyon is entirely different from the one at its top—that "microclimate" is often the most accurate description.

Wherever you garden in the West, learning about your zone is the first step in becoming a successful gardener. Rocky Mountain gardeners may spend much of the winter indoors, perhaps reading seed catalogs and figuring out new ways to artificially extend the growing season, but the rest of the West, for the most part, enjoys mild winters. And though it's true that the rain along the Pacific Coast keeps gardeners out of the garden for a few months each winter, many westerners garden year-round. That's a mixed blessing. As a western gardener once said: "The good news is that we garden all year round. And the bad news is that we garden all year round. Occasionally, I'd enjoy one of those snowy winters so I could have some time for planning gardening rather than doing it!" Figuring out how to keep the garden attractive and inviting most of the time does take extra effort.

In many parts of the West, the natural landscape dominates. Red cedar *(Thuja plicata)* thrives west of the Cascades in Oregon and Washington. Long before European immigrants came that way, this tree had an important place in the culture and lifestyle of the Native Americans who lived there. Its bark provided clothing, its timber became canoes and containers, and it played a significant role in many ceremonies and celebrations. Today red cedar, along with spruce and firs, continues to dominate the ecosystem near northern coastal gardens.

Travel to Tucson, Arizona, and walk through dense stands of saguaro *(Carnegiea gigantea)* at the Saguaro National Monument. This plant, branching into an almost human shape, lives for several

Many gardens in the West reflect their zones (clockwise from top left): the aspens and meadows in cold-winter areas, plants in California from the far corners of the earth, the elegant shape of the Northwest's vine maples, and the dramatic structure of desert plants in the Southwest.

hundred years and can reach 50 feet in height. The beautiful yellow flowers that it displays each spring symbolize the richness of the plant material found in the desert ecosystem—hundreds of different grasses, flowers, cacti, shrubs, and trees. These desert plants, like the red cedar of the Pacific Coast, sustained the peoples who lived among them. If you can't travel to saguaro country, you can still experience desert plants just by getting off a plane at the Phoenix airport. There you will see palo verde trees (covered in yellow flowers if you're lucky enough to be there in the spring) and the golden barrel cactus *(Echinocactus grusonii)* growing dramatically around the terminals, with the whiplike ocotillo *(Fouquieria splendens)* forming a backdrop.

For these gardeners on the Pacific Coast and the Sonoran Desert, the natural environment dominates the landscape and nearby gardens. For many other western gardeners, however, the natural environment is much less easy to find. The original oak-dotted grassland of Northern California was replaced in many areas by cultivated crops. California's Santa Clara Valley (just south of San Francisco) used to be called "Valley of the Heart's Delight" because its lush farmland, ringed by gently rolling hills, was filled with cherry, plum, and apricot orchards. Now humans have altered it again, replacing crops with housing developments and high-tech research parks. The few orchards that are left are preserved in public parks as historical relics. And as land prices soar each year, lot sizes for new homes decline to the proverbial size of a postage stamp. The garden consists of perhaps one tree, three or four shrubs, a square lawn, and a container or two filled with flowering annuals or a tomato plant. Gardeners in these new urban and suburban homes—whether in the Santa Clara Valley or the emerging suburbs of Las Vegas—have perhaps the greatest challenge.

The Many Landscapes of the West

Whether natural features, such as the Olympic National Forest in Washington (upper left) and Saguaro National Monument in Arizona (lower right), or human-made ones, such as the apple orchards and wheat fields of Washington State (lower left and upper right), the grandeur of large-scale landscapes dominates the West.

The Varied Western Garden

Plant diversity in the West ranges from lilacs that need winter cold (far left) to the blackbrush acacias of the Southwest that thrive on warm temperatures year-round (below). Throughout the entire West, whether warm or cold, old-fashioned roses brought by settlers have thrived over the years. 'Harison's Yellow' (left) blooms against a rough-hewn wall in a high-country Oregon garden.

PLANT DIVERSITY

One factor that unites the gardens of the West is the multitude of plants that can be grown in so many of its locations. Apples, pears, and lilacs thrive in cold-winter areas. Berries of all types abound in Oregon's western valleys, from Portland south to Medford. Gardeners near San Diego fill their gardens with fragrant gardenias and other sweet-scented tropical plants.

Because so much can be grown in the West, it's always tempting to experiment. Many a gardener considers the statement "It can't be grown here" to be not a fact, but a challenge. Tomato varieties chosen for their ability to withstand Colorado's cold and ingenious devices for warming the soil and air enable some gardeners to harvest baskets of tomatoes right in the shadow of the Rocky Mountains. Drive through parts of Northern California where some gardens are framed with lush perennial borders, and you'd think you were in England. Visit a busy nursery in the West on a spring morning, and you'd find plants from the four corners of the earth and every imaginable climate. It has been said that a greater number of different plants grows in Oregon's Willamette Valley than in any equivalent square-mile acreage in the entire world.

The horticultural variety of the West is enriched by a comparable human diversity. Many gardeners come to the West from other parts of the country and the world, bringing their plants and gardening styles with them. Walk into one western garden and you'd think you were in Japan, not Portland. Or visit a garden tucked into a San Francisco backyard and find a little piece of Southeast Asia, where the gardener has carefully sought out plants that re-create the essence of the jungle climate he left behind in the Philippines.

Where so many plants can be grown, it's sometimes easy to become a bit cavalier, to select a plant just because you fancy it, even though it may not be happiest in the setting you can give it— the summer heat is too much, or the salty ocean spray isn't appreciated. Under such conditions, a plant is more likely to become a candidate for a pest or disease infestation. As many western gardeners come to understand the good sense of suiting the plant to the location, more and more of them are including plants in their gardens that will naturally fit that particular climate and topography— these plants simply aren't as fussy. You'll find gardeners along California's coast patiently surveying seed lists from the Canary Islands or asking at their local botanic garden about plants from Australia or Chile (other places with a similar Mediterranean climate). In the Rocky Mountain states, gardeners are learning about plants from Turkey or Central Asia and adding them to their high-elevation, short-growing-season gardens.

At the same time, gardeners are taking a cue from the "natural gardens" in their area. A downtown Los Angeles gardener with a garden full of lush subtropicals, for example, observes the plants he sees on a drive up and out of the Los Angeles basin. Membership in a native plant society follows, and a subtle change begins to occur in this gardener's landscape. The garden begins to reflect the natural palette of California and the nearby Channel Islands. The coffeeberry *(Rhamnus californica)* and Catalina cherry *(Prunus lyonii)* give the garden form. The native bush poppy *(Dendromecon rigida)*, with its bright yellow flowers, is joined by St. Catherine's lace *(Eriogonum giganteum)*, its silvery leaves and white lace cap blossoms adding elegance to the late-summer garden.

In the Pacific Northwest, the native salal *(Gaultheria shallon)* is finding its way back into the garden. With year-round glossy foliage and white-to-pink bell-shaped flowers in the spring, it's an excellent foundation plant in the acid soils of Northwest gardens. As an added attraction, local birds enjoy feeding off the late-fall berries. Drive along the Columbia River in the fall, and you'll find vine maples *(Acer circinatum)* providing swatches of orange, scarlet, and yellow color among the evergreen forests. This fast-growing plant has many uses in the garden: it can be a multistemmed shrub in a partly shady location or a straight-trunked tree in the sun.

THE ARID WEST

One reason that western gardeners are turning to native plants and plants from similar climate areas in other parts of the world is that, once established, these plants are easier to care for and less likely to succumb to many pests and diseases. They provide important habitats for beneficial insects, birds, and other creatures that help keep the garden free of pests. These plants also have relatively low water requirements, an important consideration in many areas. For the most part, the western states just don't get a lot of water, and periodic droughts bring the point home.

If you ask gardeners in the eastern United States about their irrigation systems, you may anticipate hearing stories about success with the latest drip emitters just installed, but that's not what you're going to get. Instead, you'll hear something like this: "Well, we get about 25 inches of rain here each season between the first of May and the end of October. I put out a hose sometimes if we're having a heat spell, but most of the time the rain takes care of the irrigation needs."

Not so in the West. Sunset editors, studying rainfall patterns in the United States, published the following statistics in 1997, vividly demonstrating the huge differences in summer rainfall experienced by the eastern and western parts of this country (the dividing point is the 100th meridian, which runs north to south from North Dakota to Texas).

Average rainfall between May 1 and October 31 in these eastern cities is as follows:

- Miami, Florida — 43.89 inches
- Norfolk, Virginia — 25.44 inches
- Omaha, Nebraska — 21.72 inches
- New York, New York — 21.32 inches
- Atlanta, Georgia — 21.27 inches
- Duluth, Minnesota — 20.66 inches
- Chicago, Illinois — 20.02 inches
- Boston, Massachusetts — 19.57 inches
- Cleveland, Ohio — 18.91 inches
- New Orleans, Louisiana — 18.47 inches
- St. Louis, Missouri — 18.47 inches
- Dallas, Texas — 16.40 inches

Compare their rainfall with that in some of our western cities in the same period:

- Colorado Springs, Colorado — 11.85 inches
- Seattle, Washington — 10.42 inches
- Portland, Oregon — 9.8 inches
- Billings, Montana — 8.78 inches
- Salt Lake City, Utah — 6.61 inches
- El Paso, Texas — 5.33 inches
- Boise, Idaho — 4.15 inches
- Phoenix, Arizona — 2.71 inches
- Reno, Nevada — 2.29 inches
- San Francisco, California — 1.95 inches
- San Diego, California — 0.94 inch
- Los Angeles, California — 0.86 inch

Clearly, the West is significantly more arid than the East. In the cold-winter states—Idaho, Montana, Colorado, and Utah—and the mountainous parts of other states, it is not possible to garden in the winter. During the short summer growing season, the scant summer rain is the only natural irrigation available. Coastal Oregon, Washington, and many parts of California do receive winter rain, which allows gardeners in those regions to grow vegetables in the winter and enjoy many winter-blooming flowers. In the summer, though, they must rely on irrigation to sustain a garden of any type.

Irrigating in the Arid West

This vegetable garden benefits from the versatility of two irrigation systems. Soaker hoses provide drip irrigation for the corn, and the belowground system, with its raised spray heads, supplies overhead water for a late-season crop in the same bed.

This lack of summer water means that western gardeners must become masters of irrigation. A timer-based system is one way to garden throughout the year and waste little of our precious water resources. In a well-equipped garden, you're likely to find a system that includes the following elements:

Controlled-drip emitters and flexible tubing. These emitters have pointed ends that are inserted into the flexible tubing (often called "spaghetti tubing" because it looks somewhat like black strands of spaghetti). The tubing can be looped around plants, so the individual emitters can be placed just where they are needed. The emitters have flip-top lids, making them even more versatile: if a plant is getting too much water, the lid can be flipped shut, cutting off the flow.

Miniature sprayers and misters. These watering devices are similar to the sprinklers commonly attached to the end of hoses. They attach to rigid headings on spaghetti tubing, or to stakes that connect to the tubes, and deliver water to a small area. They are useful for plants that require high humidity, or in areas of ground covers or turf.

Soaker hoses. These rigid plastic hoses with factory-drilled holes along the surface are most often used to water a vegetable garden or an area of foundation planting.

Porous polyvinyl tubing. At high pressure, this tubing produces a fine spray of water; at low pressure, it emits small droplets that slowly irrigate plants.

The controlled-drip emitters and miniature sprayers are attached to spaghetti hosing, which in turn is plugged into rigid plastic tubes (usually ½ inch in diameter) that are buried in the soil. This kind of system is especially useful in a bed with permanent plantings. It can be installed when the bed is planted and needs only minimal adjusting over the years. These systems are also great for container gardens. The plastic tubes can be either buried underground or placed along the rear of a deck or patio, and the spaghetti tubing goes directly into the container. When the system is on a timer, the container plants get regular watering.

Irrigation Choices

Soaker hoses (left) and polyvinyl tubing (below, left) are easy-to-install irrigation options. Either hoses or tubes are laid out on top of the soil to deliver water directly to plants. Tubing is more versatile: it can deliver either a slow drip or the fine mist that is beneficial to plants that prefer high humidity and overhead water.

Soaker hoses and polyvinyl tubing lie on the ground surface (although you can cover them with a light mulch) and can be attached to outdoor faucets or included in part of a larger system. They're good alternatives when you don't want to install an underground system, or if you want to move them to accommodate different plantings in an annual flower garden or vegetable plot.

Rigid sprinkler systems with fixed-location heads are common in older gardens, and many gardeners find this type of system helpful in maintaining lawn turf. Most, however, are reducing the area in their garden devoted to lawn so as to minimize water use. Kits are available that let you convert some or all of an in-ground irrigation system to drip irrigation.

An irrigation timer can be as simple as a kitchen timer set to remind yourself to turn the water off. Or it can be complex enough to accept programming for up to a two-week period. Some of the more sophisticated timing mechanisms let you water for a series of brief periods over several hours, especially useful if you're watering lawn and want to avoid runoff in claylike soil or on a slope.

When you can deliver just the right amount of water to each plant, your garden will be healthier. Irregular watering, overwatering, and underwatering cause many of the problems that gardeners face—and may interpret as diseases. Rather than needing a fungicide, you may merely need to put together a consistent watering program. Such a system not only helps conserve our precious water resources, but also makes for a healthier garden.

SPECIAL CHALLENGES

Western gardeners face other challenges. Those living in outlying areas in this arid land face the danger of fire. Not a summer goes by without at least a few houses burning to the ground. Keeping trees and brush trimmed back and eliminating highly flammable plants may be the difference between saving and losing your home.

The high cost of land in many parts of the West means that there are gardeners who don't have a traditional garden to call their own. Some garden on rooftops, others on the decks of apartments and condominiums. For these gardeners, learning effective ways of container gardening isn't just an option, it's the only way they'll be able to grow trees, bushes, flowers, and vegetables. And for those lucky enough to be able to move into a new home with a yard, the soil is often abysmal. Many new homes are now being built on marginal land on sites that wouldn't be the first choice of the homeowner who planned to garden—what topsoil that may have existed is frequently scraped away during the construction process. In such places, gardening begins with a lengthy soil-building process. In other cases, homes come with built-in landscaping, but lacking good soil, the new plants and lawns often languish and fall prey to every pest and disease in the vicinity. These gardeners often find themselves starting over after several difficult years.

Where they do have land, westerners may still face challenges. In many places with hot, arid summers, soil is mostly clay. While rich in many nutrients, this soil becomes bricklike during the dry season. Unless the gardener amends it regularly, garden plants languish, choked off from air and summer irrigation water. In some desert areas, the high alkalinity makes growing plants difficult. And because it's hard—and expensive—to amend it, gardeners with this type of soil often keep the plant palette simple, frequently sticking to the plants native to the area. When they want to grow non-natives, or perhaps a vegetable garden, they construct raised beds and bring in topsoil.

The ocean is a garden neighbor along the northern Pacific coast. Gardeners in this region have found good choices for foundation plantings among native plants, which are adapted to the salty spray and highly acid soils that are common along the coast. They also make sure that other plants they choose are happy with ocean air and acid soil.

Weather, of course, can unleash powerful forces all across the West. In the Rocky Mountains, gardeners face tremendous problems caused by wind. Winds not only break off limbs of trees and shrubs, but they also dry out the soil so that the plants must face both chilling winter cold and lack of water. In the summer, hailstorms wreak havoc in many of the mountain states, utterly destroying a flower garden in a matter of minutes. Savvy gardeners have learned to include many native plants in their flower beds because they have adapted to the hail and will revive almost as soon as the storm passes.

Even with its problems, the West is well loved, both by those who live here now and by those who wish they could. Whether you are looking at the West from an aerial vantage point, or driving through it in your car, it's impossible to forget that this is one of the most utterly beautiful and geologically diverse spots on planet Earth. While this book focuses on solving the problems that western gardeners face, it is also a reminder of how fortunate we are to inhabit this extraordinary land.

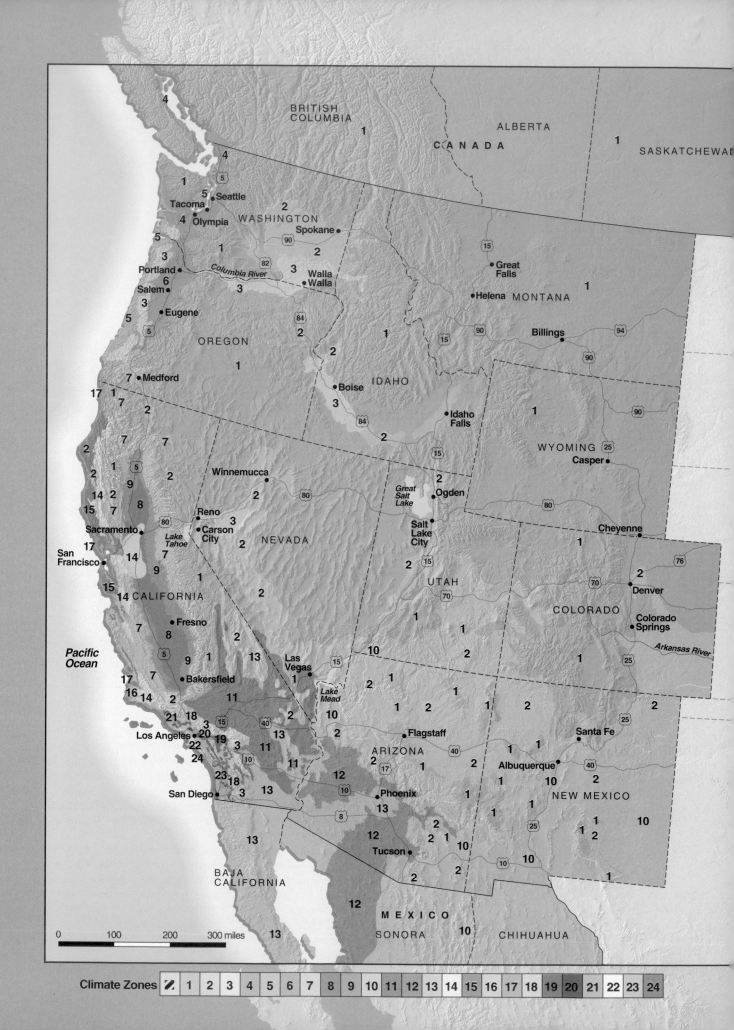

SUNSET'S *24* WESTERN CLIMATE ZONES

To garden successfully in the West, it is essential to understand the attributes of the climate zone in which you live. Sunset classifies 24 western zones, numbered from harshest (Zone 1) to mildest (Zone 24), and organized by region from north to south. Throughout this book, a plant's climate adaptability is indicated by zone numbers. The boundaries of each of these unique zones are a function of six geographic and climatic factors: latitude, elevation, ocean influence, continental air influence, mountains and hills, and local terrain. Taken together, these factors determine what will grow well in your garden and what won't; knowing them makes clear any extra steps you may need to take to make sure your plants thrive.

Latitude. Generally, the farther a spot is from the equator, the longer and colder are its winters. And moving toward the poles causes length of daylight to increase in summer and decreases in winter. Gardeners in northern latitudes face a shorter growing season and find that the number of plants they can grow is restricted to those that withstand cold.

Elevation. High gardens get longer and colder winters, and lower night temperatures all year. Gardeners in high elevations face short seasons, punctuated by stormy, windy conditions.

Ocean influence. Weather that blows in off the Pacific Ocean tends to be mild and laden with precipitation in the cool season. It's a major factor in keeping coastal gardens lush and green throughout the year. In the north, heavy winter rainfall is common. In summer, the jet stream keeps the rain away from California, making fog the major influence.

Continental air influence. The interior of the North American continent originates its own weather, which—compared with coastal climates—is colder in winter, hotter in summer, and more likely to get precipitation at any time of year. The farther inland you live, the stronger this continental influence is. However, gardeners who live near coastal mountains can expect to experience dramatic shifts in weather conditions.

Mountains and hills. These land formations determine whether areas beyond will be influenced most by marine air or by continental air. The Coast Ranges take some marine influence out of the air that passes eastward over them. The Sierra-Cascades and Southern California's interior mountains further weaken marine influence. East of the Rocky Mountains, continental and arctic air dominate. This air, flowing from the interior westward to the coast, is affected first by the Rockies, then by the interior ranges, and finally by the Coast Ranges, each of them reducing its influence on the zones of the West.

Local terrain. South-facing hillsides get more solar heat than flat land; north-facing slopes get less. Slope also affects airflow: warm air rises, cold air sinks. Because hillsides are never as cold in winter as the hilltops above them or the lower ground around them, they're called thermal belts. Lowlands into which cold air flows are called cold-air basins. Gardeners a few miles from each other may wonder why, for example, one can't grow oranges, yet the others can. Learning about thermal belts helps you understand differences in local growing conditions.

WHY DON'T WE USE USDA CLIMATE ZONES?

The U.S. Department of Agriculture employs a climate zone scheme based on winter minimum temperatures. It provides a useful plant-hardiness index, but it has some important drawbacks; for example, it puts the Olympic rain forest into a zone with parts of the Sonoran Desert. Our zone scheme considers winter minimums, too, but it also factors in summer highs, length of growing season, humidity, and rainfall patterns to give a more accurate picture of what will grow where. Our thanks to the University of California and the many people and institutions who helped us create and refine it.

Springtime in Montana

Spring-blooming tulips and lilacs, a welcome sight after a long winter, punctuate this urban garden. Colorful early bloomers—flowering plants that can withstand cold—are a good choice in the West's cold and snowy zones.

UNDERSTANDING THE ZONES OF THE WEST

The overall theme of the problem-solving techniques in this book is prevention—keeping a problem from happening in the first place. An important element of prevention is to choose the right plant for the right location. Plants properly situated will be healthier, less prone to disease, and better able to fend off and survive a pest infestation. The following sections discuss the West's climate zones, providing you with guidelines that will help you choose plants appropriate for your garden, and explain special zonal considerations that will help keep your plants free of pests.

THE COLD AND SNOWY ZONES: 1, 2, AND 3

The snow-covered peaks of the Rocky Mountains and the Sierra Nevada are the dominant features of the West's coldest zones. And while the mountaintops hardly lend themselves to gardening, the high valleys and plateau areas of Montana, Wyoming, Colorado, Utah, and parts of Idaho support both agricultural crops and home gardens. The mildest of these three zones, found along the eastern Columbia River and extending into Idaho, is an area of great agricultural importance, with crops including fruit trees, vegetables, and the famous Walla Walla onion. Oregon's Hood River valley and northern Washington produce apples and other fruit-tree crops.

The short growing season means it's critical to get a garden off to a good start in these zones. Unlike parts of California, where a vegetable garden can be replanted if decimated by an onslaught of hungry caterpillars, here every day of the growing season is important. Mulching, both to keep the soil warmer in early spring and to protect plants from winter's cold, is vital in these areas. Using tree and shrub hedges to protect the more tender plants from cold and drying winds is a common practice.

Because much of the area in these zones has a dry climate and high altitude, roses aren't as likely to be bothered by the diseases that plague them in lower-altitude zones with high humidity. If you grow roses here, purchase plants that can withstand the lowest temperatures in the area. They'll be more likely to thrive than their tender cousins, and thus more resistant to pests and disease.

While some insect pests, like the whitefly, don't overwinter in these zones, they can hitchhike a ride into the garden on six-packs of flower and vegetable seedlings from commercial nurseries. When you bring home any plant, inspect it carefully for pests and remove them immediately. Grasshoppers and other insects common to the grassy plains will be a problem each summer. The codling moth is a serious pest of apple and pear trees. And a disease associated with the coldest areas in this zone, snow mold, can infect many ornamentals. Yet, whether it's grasshoppers, codling moth, or snow mold, gardeners here follow the same Integrated Pest Management (IPM) techniques as others do in the West. Focus on prevention and management as described in the encyclopedias of pests, diseases, and weeds common to the West. Also check with your cooperative extension office. The agents there are the best source for information on problems of local areas and for suggestions on solving them.

Zone 1. Zone 1 includes the coldest areas of the West—all of Wyoming and portions of the states surrounding it: Montana, Idaho, Utah, and Colorado. Zone 1 is also found along the Sierra Nevada range of California and Nevada.

This zone has the shortest growing season of any in the West, between 75 and 150 days. And because frosts can occur any night of the year, gardeners in this zone employ a variety of techniques to protect plants from cold and wind. It's especially important here to choose plants that can withstand the cold. While some marginal plants may live, they'll be susceptible to disease and pests.

Zone 2. Zone 2 differs from Zone 1 primarily in the coldness factor—average winter lows are slightly higher. Zone 2 areas cover much of Colorado and Utah, parts of eastern Oregon and Washington, and western Idaho. The high plateaus of New Mexico and Arizona, and parts of Nevada and the high country in California are also Zone 2 areas.

Sandstone Cliffs Shelter Orchards

Orchards thrive in warmer portions of the cold-mountain zones. The red-rock formations of Utah's Capitol Reef National Park contrast with the green stands of fruit trees. Visitors can pick fruit in summer and fall or enjoy flowering trees amid wildflower meadows in spring.

GROWING VEGETABLES IN WYOMING

Wyoming's Zone 2 climate makes for a short growing season—so short, in fact, that vegetable gardeners there have found some ingenious ways of trapping heat for growing crops.

Even used tires have been put to use as planters for this purpose. The tire casing provides wind protection and absorbs sun warmth, slowly giving it off to the plant or two inside it. The casing can also be filled with water to hold heat for release during the nighttime hours. These are just two of many ideas put to work by Wyoming gardeners.

The growing season in Wyoming ranges from 20 to 130 days, depending on location. And even during the growing season, daytime, nighttime, and soil temperatures are lower than most plants desire. This means that great care is taken in choosing which vegetables to grow. For example, the tomato variety of choice is named "Sub-arctic Maxi." A number of mail-order seed companies specialize in vegetables for northern climates. They include varieties that grow and produce very quickly. While tomatoes, melons, cucumbers, celery, sweet corn, and similar crops need at least 100 days to produce, other vegetables do well in short growing seasons and cool weather—radishes, leaf lettuce, and green onions among them. Other cool-weather crops are chard, broccoli, cabbage, cauliflower, head lettuce, spinach, beets, carrots, and peas.

Wyoming gardeners take care to find a south-facing location for their gardens. In addition, some choose to garden in raised beds or along ridges; in both cases, the elevated soil warms faster than ground-level soil. Savvy gardeners have learned another reason to amend heavy, clay soil and make it more loamlike—in addition to being a better growing medium, loam soil warms up faster than clay. Windbreaks are also important, whether made from board fences or living trees and shrubs.

While successful vegetable gardeners everywhere pay attention to the health of their soil and the need for fertilizers, it's critical to do so in areas with short growing seasons. A gardener here can't afford to let poor soil or lack of nutrients slow plant growth. Adding organic matter helps lighten heavy clay soils and make them healthier. Fertilizers help vegetable crops mature rapidly. To maximize growth, look for one with higher percentages of essential nutrients.

Vegetable gardeners throughout the West start many plants indoors and transplant them later to the garden. Wyoming gardeners take this process one step further by accelerating the seed germination process itself. Some seeds are soaked in water overnight. Others are kept warm and damp, but not wet, in a shallow layer where they can get plenty of air. When new growth is ½ inch long, seeds are carefully transplanted. This method can save up to two weeks for seeds such as parsley and carrot that germinate slowly.

But back to that old tire. It's just one of many ways to protect plants and provide warmth. Plastic is also widely used. Clear plastic is placed on the beds early in the spring, often raising the soil temperature by 10–15°F in just a few days. (It's removed for planting, or the seedlings are planted through holes in it.) Clear plastic is also placed over furrows: plants grow in the bottom of the furrow, protected from cold wind by the furrow walls, and are kept warm by its plastic "roof." As leaves grow, the gardener makes slits in the plastic so the leaves can slip through. Rigid plastic is also widely used, including everything from plastic jugs over individual plants to sheet-plastic row covers in various forms. (All these methods do mean extra attention is required—covers may need to be removed in the heat of the day to prevent scalding.)

If you'd like to learn more about cold-weather gardening in Wyoming, contact one of the cooperative extension offices in the state. Tips such as these are included in several bulletins. You can learn about choosing the right vegetable, including details about which ones handle early frosts and which late frosts. Specific directions for seed germination and indoor starts are included. And many ideas for how to locate a garden to maximize warmth are carefully spelled out. While it may take a bit of extra work, a garden with a view of something like the Grand Tetons is worth every bit of effort it takes.

This Cheyenne vegetable garden is protected from the wind by both a surrounding wall and a dense cotoneaster hedge behind it.

Winter Blanket Fit for a Rose

The bud graft on this standard rosebush is high off the ground and susceptible to cold damage from sudden drops in temperature. To keep the rosebush warm, a cold-zone gardener has insulated the graft with padded burlap.

The growing season here is usually 150 days per year (though in some areas it is 200 days). The longer season, along with slightly milder temperatures, makes it possible to grow a few more plants. In many locations, by planting windbreaks and mulching heavily, you can grow plants that would otherwise perish from the effects of wind, cold, and winter sun.

Zone 3. This is the mildest of the three snowy-weather zones in the West. It includes the fruit- and crop-growing areas along the eastern Columbia River and portions of Idaho near Boise. This zone also extends along the eastern side of the Sierra Nevada range, encompassing the Reno area, and it includes the Coast Ranges of Oregon and Washington.

The growing season here is usually 160 days (although 220 days can be usual around the Walla Walla region of eastern Washington). On the east side of the Cascade Range and the Sierra Nevada, the drying winds of winter exacerbate the cold by dehydrating plants growing in frozen soil. And along the Coast Ranges in Oregon, the heavy winter rain, occasional snow, and rugged terrain combine to limit the plants grown. This zone includes the Tillamook Burn area, an open scrublike area visible for miles as you drive along Oregon's coastal mountain range. This area is especially plagued by Scotch broom, a notorious plant pest found along the coast of California, Oregon, and Washington.

THE RAINY NORTHERN ZONES: 4, 5, AND 6

Mention the Pacific Northwest, and visions of rain come to mind. And while rain does dominate the winter and spring seasons, the area also boasts one of the longest and mildest summer and fall growing seasons in the country. This is one reason it's such a prolific producer of fruits, berries, vegetables, and other edibles, as well as a major supplier of nursery trees and shrubs.

While some months are very rainy (in many winters, Seattle receives around 50 inches of rain), the long, dry summer and fall make the area very different from the East Coast of the United States and England, whose landscapes appear similar. And while many plants from those geographic areas do well here, they must receive summer irrigation to thrive. Occasionally drought comes to these zones, threatening the beautiful stands of rhododendrons and other foundation plantings that aren't irrigated as a matter of course.

Microclimates within gardens and neighborhoods factor large in the Seattle area and western portions of northern Washington. Zone 4 cuts right through many Seattle neighborhoods, bringing with it a much colder climate than the neighboring Zone 5. Nearby Sequim, on the Olympic Peninsula, receives only half the rainfall of Seattle, meaning irrigation needs must be more carefully considered to keep a garden healthy. If you don't put the right plant in the right location, your plants may not do well and will become susceptible to various pest and disease problems.

A great deal of the soil in this area is acid, one reason the rhododendrons and azaleas thrive. It's often rich with humus and other decaying matter, so if planting beds aren't well drained, various molds and soilborne diseases can be a serious problem. Likewise, plants native to hot areas with alkaline soils will be more prone to disease and pest infestation than those that are happy with "wet feet."

Tulips Abound in Washington

Zone 4 winter temperatures chill the ground enough to ensure that tulips thrive—as they do in this field near the town of Mt. Vernon—making the northwest corner of Washington a major bulb-producing area.

Characteristic Gardens of the Northwest

The Pacific Northwest climate provides all the ingredients for lush and beautiful gardens. A cottage garden thrives in the rich soil of the Willamette Valley (below). Along Seattle's Lake Washington (bottom), a garden is filled with rhododendrons and azaleas, signature plants of many Northwest gardens. The Portland Japanese Garden (left) uses native conifers and maples in its design.

Some of the largest weed pests are problems here. The blackberry can be especially difficult to eradicate from the garden, often taking several seasons. Dandelions in lawns need to be controlled early in the season or they can crowd out the grass and destroy the entire lawn. And while this area isn't overrun by the brown snail that plagues California, slugs, earwigs, and other pests are problems in many gardens. As with any area that grows food crops, careful monitoring is needed to control the many caterpillars, borers, and other insects that feed on tender leaves and stems.

Because the rain leaches nutrients from the soil in all three of these zones, it's important to add amendments regularly to keep plants healthy and disease resistant. Organic mulch, which can be worked into the soil each fall, is a choice of many.

Another problem to be aware of in these zones is camellia petal blight: at the first hint of this brown disfiguration on petals, remove and destroy all infected blossoms.

Zone 4. Many people know this zone for the miles of tulips in the Skagit Valley. In fact, this area has more spring bulbs under cultivation than all of the Netherlands. The slightly colder winters of Zone 4—compared to those of Zones 5 and 6—help induce dormancy in the bulbs. Zone 4 extends into the greater Seattle area.

Zone 5. Zone 5 includes the coastline areas of Washington and Oregon that are famous for lush vegetation. While it's not particularly warm in the summer (it's hard to grow tomatoes in some areas), the long growing season favors flowering plants, such as fuchsias. Native plants of all types, including salal and Oregon grape *(Mahonia aquifolium),* make for pest-free gardening in this zone.

Zone 6. Zone 6 includes the Willamette Valley and the areas around Portland/Vancouver, and follows the Columbia River a few miles both upriver and downriver from Portland. It's been said that more plant varieties are grown in the Willamette Valley than in any comparable acreage anywhere in the world. Drive Interstate 5 from Medford to Portland, and you'll see orchards and farms that are growing fruit trees, berries, hops, vegetables, and many ornamental trees and bushes.

Sitting right below the Columbia River Gorge, Portland and its surrounding areas often experience periods of freezing rain and ice storms, which can kill fragile trees and shrubs. Check with local experts and your cooperative extension office to find out what to do if an ice storm hits. Plants damaged in such a storm are often very susceptible to disease.

THE NORTHERN AND INTERIOR-VALLEY CALIFORNIA ZONES: 7, 8, 9, 14, 15, 16, AND 17

Mild climate and fertile soils make much of Northern California and the Central Valley a gardener's paradise. This widely divergent area encompasses seven separate zones, all of which can be found within a 50-mile radius of San Francisco.

Zones 7, 8, and 9 cover much of the Central Valley of California, from low hills in the south to hilly pine areas in the north. This area includes the agricultural communities of Bakersfield, Fresno, and Merced. It skirts Sacramento (which, being more influenced by the ocean, is in Zone 14), and continues up through Chico and into Red Bluff. You'll see cotton and grape fields in the southern part of this set of zones, fruit trees and crops of all types in the central area, and almonds and rice in the north. A Zone 7 valley is also found near Oregon's Rogue River.

Zones 14 through 17 comprise the lands around the San Francisco and Monterey bays, extend inward to Sacramento, and follow a thin band of the coast from Eureka to Santa Maria. This area's many zones make it very diverse, ranging from the chill of the Northern California coast to the heat of a summer afternoon in Sacramento.

This is an area that gardeners from all over the world describe as being close to paradise. With the exception of some of the coldest portions of Zone 7 and the warmest parts of Zones 8 and 14, you can choose almost any type of plant you like for your garden.

Because there are so many zones and even smaller microclimates close together here, nurseries stock plants for a wide variety of conditions: you're likely to find a rhododendron right next to a desert-loving plant from the Southwest. You need to do your homework to find out which plants will thrive in your garden, but you don't need to worry as much about freezing in winter as you do about providing plants with the correct amount of sun or shade, warmth, and water.

With such diversity comes an equally diverse group of pests. You're likely to find fireblight and mildew, water molds and wilt, all kinds of weeds, and pests that specialize in eating every fruit crop, vegetable, or flower you want to grow. And to top it off, the ubiquitous common brown garden snail munches on everything. Practicing good prevention techniques, such as soil preparation; using fertilizers correctly; mulching; and routine cleanup are essential here. And because so many leaves stay on the tree or vine, and annuals don't know when to die, you need to take special care to clean up the garden each fall, getting rid of all spent plants and diseased leaves.

In the Central Valley zones, irrigation is a must. Proper plant choice is an issue here, too. For example, it isn't practical to attempt growing large-scale citrus groves in the somewhat cold Zone 8, even though they thrive just a few miles away in Zone 9. Wonderful cottage gardens abound in the Gold Country, a Zone 7 area in the foothills of the Sierra Nevada. Yet water conservation and other concerns are causing many gardeners to include more native plants in their gardens there. Since natives require less summer water than nonnatives, fungal and bacterial problems due to too much water can affect the natives—oak root fungus especially is a problem for overwatered oaks.

Northern California Vistas

Nothing so typifies California valleys as springtime poppy fields studded here and there with stately oaks (right). Northern Californians exuberantly mix plants in their gardens. The garden above features wisteria with succulents, desert-loving plants, and grasses—an unusual and effective combination.

Summer in the Central Valley

California's central valleys experience intense summer heat. The bright pink of the summer-flowering crape myrtle is also a Central Valley signature, blooming throughout the California interior from Redding to Bakersfield.

Zone 16. Zone 16 is considered by many to be one of the finest gardening climates in California. It includes thermal belts, which means it gets more heat than areas right next to the coast (Zone 17), but warmer winters than those in Zone 15. It can grow more subtropicals than 15 with less danger of winter frost. It includes areas around the greater San Francisco Bay Area, and portions near the coast south to Santa Maria.

Zone 17. Zone 17 is fog country. It's of this zone that someone (not Mark Twain) said that the coldest winter he ever experienced was a summer in San Francisco. In its cool, moist air, fuchsias, brussels sprouts, and artichokes thrive. There's rarely any freezing weather in the winter, and summer temperatures mainly stay in the 65–70°F range. In addition to the San Francisco and Monterey bays, this zone extends in a very narrow band up the coast to Crescent City and south to Santa Maria.

Zone 7. Zone 7 is found in Northern California and Oregon's Rogue River valley. While the summers are mild and ideal for many crops and gardens, the growing season is shorter than in neighboring Zones 8 and 9. The winter is also somewhat colder, making this an excellent climate to grow plants that need some winter chill to thrive, such as peonies and flowering cherries. The region is noted for its pears, apples, peaches, and cherries. Pests that bother fruit trees are a major consideration, and mulching against the cold is often necessary.

Zone 8. The center of the Central Valley is Zone 8, noted for its cold-air basins. The crops that thrive here are those needing some winter chill (similar to Zone 7). You'll drive by miles of orchards that require the cooler winter to set fruit. You'll also see many heat-loving plants, though mostly those that handle the cooler winters.

Zone 9. While cool air flows downward into the valley, where it gets trapped, the surrounding low-elevation foothills are warmer. This is Zone 9. Zone 9 is safest for heat-loving plants like citrus, hibiscus, melaleuca, and pittosporum. The weather can be cold in the winter, including long periods with thick tule, or ground, fog. During extremely cold periods, air blowers are needed to keep the temperature from dropping too low and killing the citrus crop.

Zone 14. Zone 14 covers the small Napa and Sonoma wine-growing areas of California in its cooler and marine-influenced section, and the rich farmlands of the Sacramento–San Joaquin River delta area in its warmer inland area. (Some similarly zoned areas extend down the coast almost to Santa Maria.) Fruits that need winter chilling do well here, as do shrubs needing summer heat.

Zone 15. Like Zone 14, Zone 15 favors plants that need some winter chill to succeed and has warm, sunny summers. Yet because of its proximity to the ocean, its atmosphere is more moist, and it has cooler summers and milder winters. It is found slightly farther from the ocean and from San Francisco Bay than 14, extending up and down the coast from Mendocino to Santa Maria. Like Zones 16 and 17, it has nearly year-round growing conditions.

Stately Redwoods

Marine-influenced Zone 17 is the natural habitat of the coastal redwood—here combined with pink rhododendron and other plants that like their climate cool and tempered by fog.

Beverly Hills or Southeast Asia?

Because frost rarely touches gardens along the coast of Southern California, a wide variety of tropical and semitropical plants can be grown there. In this Beverly Hills hillside hideaway, each plant has been carefully chosen for its contribution to the jungle ambience. The sculptured elephant and the Asian-influenced architecture complete the effect.

THE SOUTHERN CALIFORNIA ZONES: 18, 19, 20, 21, 22, 23, AND 24

If you're gardening in one of Southern California's seven zones, you need to pay attention to average winter low temperatures. These lows are a major factor in determining whether your neighborhood can grow citrus or avocados, whether tropical ornamental plants will freeze, and in general, which plants will thrive.

The greater Los Angeles basin, along with the warmer-climate areas that surround San Diego, is among the mildest-temperature parts of the West. It joins Florida as one of the greatest citrus-producing areas in the United States. Because it supports many subtropical and tropical plants, garden designs often feature lush jungle-like plantings. Some inland areas are hotter and drier, bearing a resemblance to the drier areas to the east and reflecting southwestern desert influences. Here, you will find warm-weather grasses, succulents, and cacti thriving along with other plants that prefer a warmer and drier climate.

The zones in Southern California aren't always consistent, particularly in areas that are influenced by both the ocean and the interior winds. One day your garden might be marine influenced; the next day it might be warmed by Santa Ana winds. It's important to know the full temperature range of your zone, including these fluctuations.

Drive a few miles in any direction from central Los Angeles and you will come across each of the region's seven zones. As in Northern California, local nurseries sell plants that thrive in several or all of the zones. It's up to you to determine which plants will actually do well in your own front and back yards, patios, and balconies. Plants that aren't good matches for your zone are more likely to be stressed, due to either too much or too little cold.

Again as in Northern California, the warm climate and wide variety of plants grown mean that many pests and diseases will also be present. And since many areas rarely "go dormant," you'll need to pick off old and diseased leaves and get rid of spent annuals. Some Southern California gardeners declare part of the Rose Bowl weekend as the time for stripping all leaves from all the rose bushes in

A Glory of Western Gardening

Traffic stops when the jacaranda tree (*Jacaranda mimosifolia*) blooms. Its vivid flowers are a treasured benefit of the mild-climate zones of the West.

their gardens—the only way to force the roses into some semblance of dormancy and also get rid of old leaves, often covered with rust, black spot, and other problems.

Mulching the ground to minimize the drying effects of Santa Ana winds helps keep plants healthy in many of the Southern California zones. Much of the soil here is alkaline and claylike; amending it with organic matter improves its quality and the vigor of plants growing in it. Zones near the coast can be plagued with mildew. Selecting plants that aren't susceptible to mildew is one avenue of defense; another is a program of preventive spraying, using mixtures of baking soda or oil with water. And yes, the common brown snail is often a problem in many gardens in this area.

Any big-city area can experience smog, but the Los Angeles basin has been especially bothered by this problem. While there isn't a lot you can do to prevent smog damage to plants (other than working to reduce the causes of smog), it's helpful to be able to recognize the difference between smog-caused problems and others. See page 242 for information on air pollution damage.

Zone 18. Zone 18, located inland from the ocean, was traditionally an area of apricot, peach, apple, and walnut orchards. Now it's mostly filled with suburban communities. Zone 18 areas are usually found on hilltops and in cold-air basins, where winter lows can range from 28°F to 10°F. While it's too hot, cold, and dry for fuchsias, you can grow many of the hardier subtropicals here.

Zone 19. A warmer version of Zone 18, Zone 19, with winter temperatures that range from 27°F to 22°F, is located next to Zone 18. It is one of the Southern California areas famous for citrus

Desert Hallmark

Perhaps no plant symbolizes the dry desert zones of Southern California as does the Joshua tree *(Yucca brevifolia),* here silhouetted against the snow-draped San Gabriel Mountains. Underfoot is a carpet of spring wildflowers and other newly green desert plants.

Like Zones 18 and 19, Zones 20 and 21 are viewed as a pair. Zone 20 is the cooler of the two. In general, they're both likely to be influenced by the ocean part of the time and by the inland climate at other times. This means that your garden may sometimes feel the effects of the hot Santa Ana winds, and sometimes the cool breezes of the Pacific Ocean.

Zone 22. Zone 22 is a special zone that covers Southern California's coastal canyons. Influenced by marine air, these canyons have somewhat colder winter temperatures deep in their clefts and on their hilltops. While winter temperatures in general are mild along the coast, in Zone 22 canyons you can find average annual winter lows that range from 24°F to 21°F (although they rarely fall below 28°F). If you garden in this area and include subtropical plants, you can protect many from frost damage by planting them under building overhangs or the canopies of trees.

Zone 23. Zone 23 is one of two coastal zones in Southern California and the one more favored for growing subtropical plants. (Zone 24 is the other coastal zone.) This is the best zone for avocados, and while it isn't as hot as inland valley zones, it is warm enough to grow warm-weather plants like gardenias. In some winters, the temperatures can drop significantly, with lows ranging from 38°F to 23°F. Along the open hills, warm summer days favor the growing of cacti and warm-weather grasses.

Zone 24. If Zone 17 in Northern California represents the typical San Francisco climate, Zone 24 exemplifies San Diego. And while it, too, runs along the coastline, and both are marked by cool marine climate and many foggy days, the San Diego zone is warmer. As in San Francisco, fuchsias thrive here. But you'll also find many tropicals that grow nowhere else in the western states, including rubber trees *(Ficus elastica)* and umbrella trees *(Schefflera actinophylla),* both sold as house plants in most of the West.

groves. You can grow macadamia nuts and avocados here, as well as many tropical and subtropical plants. Zone 19 is also an inland-valley area, only minimally affected by the ocean.

Zones 18 and 19 are viewed as a pair, with the major difference that 18 is cooler. They are both more influenced by inland climate factors than by the ocean.

Zone 20. Zone 20, while not on the coast, is influenced by the ocean more than Zones 18 and 19 are. Its winter temperature lows range from 28°F to 23°F. Because of the marine influence, you'll find you can grow a wider range of plants in this zone than in some neighboring ones. For example, birch, jacaranda, fig, and palm trees all thrive in this zone.

Zone 21. Also influenced by the coast, Zone 21 has the mildest winter temperatures of Zones 18 to 22. Winter temperature lows range from 36°F to 23°F, rarely dipping below 30°F. Along with Zone 19, it, too, is a prime citrus-growing area.

If It's Southern California, There Must Be Oranges

This part of the West is legendary for its orange groves. Although acre after acre has been swallowed up by housing developments in the last several decades, there are still many orange trees growing here. This thriving grove is in the Pauma Valley, near San Diego.

THE SOUTHWEST DESERT ZONES, FROM CALIFORNIA TO NEW MEXICO: 10, 11, 12, AND 13

Zones 10 through 13 make up America's Southwest, stretching from the edge of the Los Angeles basin out through Death Valley, Palm Springs, and the Imperial Valley; reaching over to the Las Vegas area of Nevada; and continuing eastward throughout the states of Arizona and New Mexico. They include hot low-desert areas, and colder high-desert areas that abut nearby snowy and wintry mountain areas. This part of the country has saguaro cacti, date palms, and grapefruit trees. It's also an area with huge vistas over ground covered with low shrubs that have adapted to harsh drying winds and weather extremes. This is the desert that bursts into bloom with miles of wildflowers each spring; it is also the desert that can defy the home gardener who struggles to break through hardpan and amend alkaline soil.

In this part of the West, you need to be aware of the best time to plant—or even to attempt to work in your garden. In this zone, timing is the secret to a healthy garden, one less prone to pest infestation. In Zones 10 and 11 (roughly covering the high-desert areas of Arizona and New Mexico and the medium-to-high desert of California and southern Nevada), follow gardening practices similar to those in Zones 1 through 3: plant in the spring, taking heed of late frosts, and finish your gardening before the harsh winter sets in. In Zones 12 and 13, which include Phoenix and Tucson in Arizona and El Centro in California, the best planting season begins in September or October. In the warmer areas within these zones, fall and winter are the only times of year you can successfully harvest a head of lettuce. Many gardeners in Zones 12 and 13 don't garden at all in the heat of summer except for necessary watering to keep established plants alive.

Facets of the Desert

The landscape of the Southwest desert is one of contrasts. In Arizona, the Sonoran Desert is warm all year round; here (upper right), it's lush with springtime greenery and flowers. Yet the desert, when close to the cold and snowy zones, also experiences winter chill, as in this New Mexico garden (right). In California's desert valleys near Indio, the year-round warmth is perfect for growing date palms (above) and harvesting honey-sweet dates.

One of the biggest problems for southwestern gardeners is struggling to maintain a garden with material that just isn't appropriate for it. With water made available by municipalities, and nurseries full of flowers from other parts of the country, you might be lured into attempting lawns, flowers, and ornamental plants that just are not meant for the desert. These plants are stressed by such conditions, making them susceptible to pest invasion. And in trying to compensate for soil differences, you may resort to heavy doses of fertilizers to help plants survive. If you use many pesticides and fertilizers, the natural balance in your garden will be disturbed, bringing with it more problems. To break this cycle, Southwest gardeners are increasingly turning to native plant materials, including cacti, shrubs, and trees, for use as landscaping. Subtropicals such as bougainvillea lend color, as do heat-loving native perennials, such as the various penstemons and mallows.

Dormant season cleanup is important here, especially if plant diseases are likely to survive the winter. You'll want to remove all spent plants and leaves, assigning them to either the compost pile or the trash. As in any western zone, check with your cooperative extension office for pamphlets and expert advice about local gardening practices. While the range of pests is similar to many areas of the West, you may want to keep a close lookout for the palo verde borer. It can be a problem for the many native palo verde trees used extensively in gardens as shade trees and accents.

In the colder desert areas, you'll want to provide adequate mulch in the winter for frost protection and in the spring to shelter young plants from spring frosts. This protection improves their overall health and makes them less a target for a later pest infestation.

Zone 10. Zone 10 is found just below the mountainous regions of Arizona and New Mexico and in southern Utah. It also covers most of eastern New Mexico and parts of southern Nevada. This high-desert zone has a definite winter season; temperatures drop below 32°F from 75 to more than 100 nights each year. With such cold winters, this zone's gardening season runs from spring through fall; plant in spring. While similar to Zone 11, it receives just a little more rainfall (an average of 12 inches per year, with half falling in July and August) and has a little less wind.

Zone 11. Like Zone 10, Zone 11 has cold winters. On the other hand, Zone 11 also is like Zone 13 in having intense summer heat. Gardeners in this zone are among the most challenged in the West. They must contend with hot summer days, cold winter days and nights, late spring frosts, and drying winds. In the Las Vegas area, there are more than 100 days each year when the temperatures are higher than 90°F. Keeping sufficient water on garden plants is especially important—the drying winds and the bright sunlight often combine to dry out even normally hardy evergreen plants, killing or badly injuring them.

Zone 12. Zones 12 and 13 are similar, the main difference being winter cold. While the average winter low temperatures are comparable, Zone 12 has more cold days. Frosts can be expected some of the time during the four winter months. In Zone 13, frosts usually occur only one month in the winter and not at all in some locations. Zone 12's desert area is lush, comprising a highly diverse palette of plants, many of which can be included in the home garden. The best season for cool-weather crops, such as salad greens, root vegetables, and cabbage family members, starts in September or October. A typical Zone 12 area is greater Tucson, Arizona.

Zone 13. Zone 13 includes the Southwest's low- or subtropical-desert areas. You'll find it in diverse locations such as Death Valley, California, and Phoenix, Arizona. Summer temperatures range from 106°F to 109°F, occasionally peaking higher. Here, the gardening year begins in September and October and extends through March and April. Summer rains help established native plantings survive throughout the summer, although most plants will require year-round irrigation. Many gardeners consider the summer months the dormant season, and if they work in their gardens at all, do so shortly after dawn or in the evening twilight. This is the zone famous for grapefruit and date palms.

Where Water Is Scarce

A xeriscape garden, which requires little summer water, replaces traditional turf in one Phoenix yard (below); a palo verde tree in full spring bloom dominates the landscape in a second (bottom). Both illustrate the trend in urban gardens of the Southwest toward native plants, as well as those from other desert areas around the world.

PESTS ON WHEELS

In decades past, you probably had a good idea about what type of pest was likely to find its way into your garden each season. You grew plants from seeds or bought them a few miles down the road from nurseries that propagated the plants themselves. And while you had your share of insect pests and problems, they were for the most part local to your particular climate zone.

Times have changed. Now you're as likely to bring a plant into your garden from a supplier thousands of miles away as to grow it from a cutting given to you by a fellow gardener down the street. Nonetheless, those out-of-area suppliers follow inspection procedures to make sure their plants are free from pests, so you're unlikely to acquire plant problems from them.

It's the dreaded amateur plant-toters that cause us all grief. They bring "just one little plant" home in a suitcase after visiting an out-of-state gardening friend. Or they tuck away some fruit from the tropics in an airplane carry-on bag—a special treat for a friend back home.

Deliberate importation of plants for money-making purposes has overrun California with *Helix aspersa*, the common brown garden snail. Recent smuggling is the reason for aerial pesticide sweeps that attempt to kill the Mediterranean fruit fly, which devastates citrus and other fruit crops.

States with climates similar to California's don't want brown garden snails to overrun their gardens, either. So if you're a California gardener, think twice before digging up an agapanthus plant (referred to by some as snail apartment complexes) and driving it to your niece in Georgia.

Rather than resorting to hiding a plant and possibly unleashing the next decade's Mediterranean fruit fly on an unsuspecting population, get your plant checked by an inspector and obtain a certificate so that you can transport it safely in or out of your local area.

While the inspecting agency and the process may vary a bit state by state, the best place to find out exactly what you need to do is your local cooperative extension office. Ask the extension agent how to contact an agricultural commissioner. Tell the commissioner what plant you have and where you'd like to take it. If it's a question of only a small plant or two, you are most likely to be asked to take it in to a nearby office for a check. On the other hand, if you're moving 20 years' accumulation of large potted ornamental plants to your retirement home, you can make arrangements for an inspector to come to your home. If the inspector finds a problem, you're permitted to spray or fumigate, then request another checkup. Upon clearance, you can travel with good conscience—a certificate of inspection sitting on the car seat, right next to that agapanthus.

Mediterranean fruit fly

HOW TO USE THIS BOOK

One of the most difficult tasks a gardener faces is diagnosing a problem. You come across a plant with disfigured leaves and don't have a clue what caused it. Sometimes it isn't even apparent if the damage is due to an insect pest, a disease, or a cultural condition such as a watering problem.

Because understanding and managing garden problems can be complex, information in this book is organized and presented in several formats. If you're experienced enough to recognize a lawn webworm when you see one, and you just want to know the best way of dealing with this pest, go straight to the "Encyclopedia of Damaging and Beneficial Creatures." There, you'll be able to learn about the webworm's life cycle and read various suggestions for managing this unwanted pest. There are similar encyclopedias on plant diseases, cultural problems, and weeds. Note that included with the insects are beneficial creatures—those we want to attract to and keep in our gardens. You'll want to be able to recognize these "good guys" so that you don't accidentally get rid of them along with the pests.

On the other hand, if you want to understand general principles about a commonsense approach to pest management, start with "Solving Garden Problems." There, you'll find out about Integrated Pest Management—IPM for short—the foundation of the com-

monsense approach advocated here. Simply put, the goal of IPM is to prevent problems from occurring in the first place. The chapter follows the principles of IPM, with information on basic gardening practices that will help keep your garden healthy and free from pests, diseases, and weeds. When you do have a problem, this method encourages you to start the process of managing it with simple approaches that don't upset the complex ecology in your backyard. Sometimes, however, you may find that a pesticide might be the best solution to help bring a problem back to a manageable level. This chapter helps you consider the risks and benefits of pesticide use and gives you straight talk on safety, so that if you make the decision to use a pesticide you will be able to do so correctly and appropriately.

Between the general instructional material about IPM and guidelines for applying its principles to your own garden, and the encyclopedia entries for specific problems, this book contains two other sections to help you identify problems. "Problem Solving by Plant Type" helps you understand the needs and problems of each type of plant. You'll find sections here on everything grown in the West, from trees to lawns, annual flowers to vegetables, berries to ground covers. Here, the most common problems are discussed. You can then refer to the encyclopedia sections for information on how to manage the problems you've identified.

You'll also find "Symptoms and Causes at a Glance" valuable. Organized by symptom, it offers possible diagnoses for problems such as holes in leaves, bare patches in lawns, and rotting fruit.

No matter where you start in this book, you'll find advice that suggests that one way to avoid having problems is to choose the right plant for the location. This is the best method for keeping your plants healthy so they can withstand a stray disease spore that wafts in on the afternoon wind, or a marauding group of insect pests that decide to make your garden a pit stop as they cruise the neighborhood. To find appropriate plants for your garden, refer to the *Sunset Western Garden Book*. Not only do its many entries include descriptions and drawings of the plants, with height, width, and distinguishing features, but you can also learn whether a plant thrives in your area (you first look up your location on a zones map, then check to see if your zone is listed next to the plant you are considering). You'll find out whether a plant thrives in sun or shade and how much water it takes, and whether there are special conditions, such as a requirement for acid soil. Keep it next to a stack of mail-order catalogs, and take it in the car when you visit a local nursery or plant sale.

Another companion book is *Sunset Western Landscaping*. It focuses on creating a beautiful garden and shows you hundreds of ways that western gardeners have interpreted the word "beautiful" and applied it to their particular setting. Whether you live in the hot Sonoran Desert or the high Colorado Rockies, you'll see just how attractive a garden can be in your area. And, because the ideas in this book keep in mind natural conditions in the West—such as heat and cold, soil type, amount of rain, and microclimates—you'll learn more about choosing the right plant for the right location, ensuring a healthy garden. In addition to the garden design ideas, *Sunset Western Landscaping* gives you many practical ideas about constructing a garden. You'll find good tips for installing an irrigation system—so crucial to gardeners in the arid West—along with information on constructing decks, patios, and paths, and many other landscaping topics.

These three books—*Sunset Western Garden Book, Sunset Western Landscaping,* and *Sunset Western Garden Problem Solver*—are tools that can support you as a gardener in the West, perhaps the greatest gardening area on planet Earth.

A Western Garden

There is no typical Western garden; each reflects the climate and geography of its location, as well as the individual style of its owner. However, many share an informal, naturalistic feeling that is exemplified by this one with its grasses and loosely structured plants.

Solving
GARDEN PROBLEMS

Every gardener encounters problems—aphids on the roses, yellowing leaves on the lemon tree, dandelions in the lawn. The way to deal with these setbacks is to take a commonsense approach. The first step is to work toward a healthy garden, because many pests can't get a toehold in a garden made up of plants that are right for their location and nurtured with proper care. When problems do appear, the best response entails restraint. Simple management methods—and patience—are often all that is needed to rid the garden of unwanted visitors. If a problem persists, however, the answer is to attack it knowledgeably, appropriately, and in a way that's safest for the gardener, children, pets, and the environment.

THE COMMONSENSE APPROACH TO PEST, DISEASE, AND WEED MANAGEMENT

Thinking about gardening usually summons up images of the lovely landscape you'll create, the pleasure of harvesting homegrown produce, moments of quiet contemplation while watering with a hose, planting bulbs on a crisp autumn day, and the excitement of seeing them bloom in the spring. You don't immediately think about pests and diseases—not, that is, until you find that a prized vegetable bed has been eaten overnight, or discover that a favorite tree has been ravaged by a life-threatening disease.

Finding out exactly what causes such problems and how to cure them can seem like an overwhelming task.

The encyclopedia sections of this book will make it easy for you to isolate a problem and solve it. And while the many entries may lead you to believe your plants don't stand a chance, it's actually possible for you to have the garden you're dreaming of. What it takes is a commonsense approach to pest, disease, and weed management.

PREVENT PROBLEMS IF POSSIBLE, MANAGE THEM IF YOU NEED TO

Sunset's philosophy on garden problem solving starts with trying to prevent problems from ever finding their way to the garden and follows up by attacking problems that do turn up with simple measures. These management tools are often inexpensive, take only a few minutes to work, and have a minimum impact on the natural balance in your garden.

If you encounter a severe problem that doesn't lend itself to simple methods, the Sunset approach calls for educated interventions. Such methods, including the judicious use of pesticides, can be effective tools when used appropriately.

Prevention. Many pest and disease problems can be prevented from occurring in the first place, and prevention starts with a healthy garden. Fertile soil—along with the right amount of fertilizer, water, and sun or shade—is the basis for plant health.

It's all too easy to make an impulsive buying decision when you see bright blooms at a favorite nursery. However, if you don't take the time to prepare the soil for these additions, water them regularly until you plant them, and monitor them through their postplanting transition, you're adding stress to those plants and leaving them vulnerable to pest infestation or disease.

Learn to ask questions about disease resistance when you make a purchase. For example, certain tree varieties are more resistant to fireblight than others. While that doesn't mean there's a guarantee, it does reduce the likelihood of your losing a mature tree to this disfiguring and eventually life-threatening disease.

And finally, a diverse garden with different types and sizes of trees, shrubs, flowering plants, and ground covers will have fewer problems than one made up of just one or two different plants. In a monoculture garden, one severe pest infestation can devastate the entire landscape as it spreads rapidly from plant to plant. In a diverse garden, however, even if a severe infestation comes through the neighborhood, some plants are likely to have greater resistance than others and survive.

Management. Preventing a problem is the first line of defense in keeping your garden free from pests, diseases, and weeds. Managing problems through early intervention—or with simple techniques—is the backup plan.

Often a simple barrier will solve a problem. If you live in deer territory, you may resort to fencing those parts of your garden that contain plants known to be deer favorites. Or you might place a row cover over a bed of lettuce to prevent flying insects from eating tender leaves.

Consider adding elements to your garden that will attract pest-eating allies. Certain flowering plants attract beneficial insects,

This collection of western gardens includes (clockwise from top left) a cottage garden of brightly colored blooms, a kitchen garden that combines vegetables and flowers, an individualistic garden that reflects the artistic creativity of its owner, and an alpine garden well suited to its high mountain site.

which in turn consume plant-eating pests. Daisy family members are among the best at attracting helpful insects. A summer annual, such as sweet alyssum, can be another such ally. A simple bat house, and an overturned pot near a water source to attract toads, are other possible offensive tactics: bats eat several hundred insects per hour, including mosquitoes, and toads help out by consuming small slugs.

Sometimes you'll find that a problem has taken hold in your garden and physical controls won't manage it. A range of products is at your disposal for reducing or eliminating problems, products that have varying impacts on you and your family, beneficial insects, and the environment.

Some of these are biological controls. Tiny nematodes, for example, feed on many kinds of soil-dwelling and plant-boring pests. (These are different from the nematodes that attack plant roots.) Previously available only through specialty mail-order suppliers, nematodes are now carried by some garden centers and hardware supply stores. To use them you just mix the nematode package with water and apply to the soil with a watering can.

Bugs by the Bushel

Managing pests the commonsense way may mean plucking handfuls of tent caterpillars from a tree branch or picking hornworms off a tomato.

Other controls are simple sprays that reduce or eliminate common pests and diseases. Baking-soda-and-water solutions that you make yourself or a lightweight oil-and-water mixture will manage many outbreaks of mildew. Soap-and-water solutions (which are commonly sold as insecticidal soap spray) will rid a plant of a variety of invading pests.

If a problem requires a more stringent solution, you will find a wide variety of pesticides available. Before you buy, make sure you have the right one for the job. Read its label carefully, and follow all directions exactly.

Plant Protection

Many pests are a problem for only a short time, most often when plants are young and tender. It's a simple task to cover a bed with gauzelike cloth during this critical time. The gauze keeps out flying and crawling pests while letting light reach the plants.

Sometimes, even with the best of care, a plant simply won't thrive in your garden. Have you ever heard gardeners talk about shovel pruning? This isn't a fancy gardening technique but a tongue-in-cheek way of saying, "Dig up the plant and get rid of it." Experienced gardeners may give a plant one or two seasons—perhaps even move it to a new location—but if it doesn't thrive, there comes a time when it's best to consign it to the compost heap.

LESS RELIANCE ON PESTICIDES

Gardens such as Los Angeles's Victorian Rose Garden, which uses no pesticides (see box, page 29), are becoming the norm rather than the exception. Individuals, organizations, and governmental regulating agencies have all realized that pesticides may not always be the most appropriate method of management.

Note: "Pesticide" is a general term for a broad range of products that will kill or repel pests of all kinds, or at least minimize their impact. Some common pesticide types include insecticides, designed to kill insects and other small living creatures, such as spiders and centipedes; fungicides, for killing diseases, such as mildew and molds; and herbicides, for killing weeds.

One reason pesticide use is falling out of favor is that even if you succeed in making your own garden a pest- and disease-free zone through the use of pesticides, it's only a matter of time before other pests and diseases will arrive from neighboring areas. In addition, the spraying, dusting, and baiting process constantly needs to be repeated, becoming an expensive and time-consuming obligation.

More important, in the long run many pesticides don't work. Most insects carry enzymes that help them overcome the naturally occurring toxins in the food they eat. These same enzymes make it possible for a few insects in the population to resist the poison in a pesticide. Mating, these survivors can rapidly reconstitute the population—with a strong resistance to the pesticide used to eradicate their fellows.

This lesson was first learned after large areas were sprayed with DDT. When it was introduced in the 1940s, DDT seemed miraculous because it rapidly eliminated typhus-spreading fleas and malaria mosquitoes. Yet within just a few years, researchers found new populations of these same insects that were resistant to DDT.

Another discovery was that some pest populations that were not a problem at the time of spraying became a problem afterward. Sometimes the natural predators of these pests had been eliminated, allowing them to thrive. In other cases, the circumstances were more complex. For example, in one instance an herbicide used to kill nearby weeds subtly changed the chemical makeup of another plant, making it more nutritious for pests and thereby boosting their life expectancy.

Finally, the popularity of pesticides is decreasing as we learn more about their long-term effects on the environment. The experience with DDT is a good example of how our understanding of the complexities of pesticide use has evolved. Early tests indicated DDT was harmless because it rapidly disappeared in water. Only later,

IPM Tools

Sweet alyssum provides food for insect allies, copper strips keep slugs and snails out of the garden, and nematodes kill lawn grubs.

when flocks of birds suddenly began to die, was it understood that DDT was being stored elsewhere—in bottom mud, plants, and even other animals that the birds were consuming. As a result, the pesticide was concentrating in the birds' bodies to fatal levels over time. As years passed, other long-term problems were attributed to DDT use, such as the thinning of eggshells, damage that endangered entire falcon and eagle populations.

The Integrated Pest Management (IPM) approach. Over the past 40 years, increasing numbers of people in the gardening and agriculture community have moved away from the notion of pest and disease *eradication* and focused instead on the concept of *management*. The central ideas are to prevent problems by choosing appropriate plants and giving them good growing conditions and to minimize pest populations rather than annihilate them. This approach has a formal name—Integrated Pest Management; it is commonly referred to by its acronym, IPM.

Since its introduction in the 1950s, IPM has been gaining acceptance among commercial growers—especially in the greenhouses. The concepts are also becoming popular in home gardens, even though home gardeners might not know or use this term.

When action against a pest is warranted, IPM suggests first using physical and biological controls. Physical controls let you suppress a pest by mechanical devices, such as traps and barriers; biological control involves releasing natural enemies and disease-causing microbes that attack pests. Pesticides are used only as a last resort. From this description, it should be clear that IPM is a commonsense approach that can work well for all of us.

Research in IPM methods takes place at private nonprofit organizations, universities, and various state and local government agencies. Turn to the "Resource Directory" of this book for groups that provide information on pesticides and alternative management methods.

A cautionary word about "organic" pest and disease solutions. Just because the word "organic" is used to market a naturally occurring pesticide, don't think that product is inherently safer than its synthetically derived cousins. For example, certain pesticides are derived from plants, lulling some gardeners into a false sense of security. "After all," you might think, "if this is made from flower blossoms, what harm can it do?" The pesticide's origin isn't the key factor—what's important is its state when formulated for use by the gardener. Some naturally occurring pesticides will dissipate rapidly, making them a potential choice to use when pests are infesting a vegetable garden. Yet they can be just as dangerous as a

A SPECIAL ROSE GARDEN

Most gardeners have brought home a rosebush or two that attracted every insect on the block and caught every disease on the afternoon breeze. Many believe that it's impossible to grow roses without inviting plagues that require pesticides. However, a special Southern California public rose garden is proving this isn't so. The Victorian Rose Garden at the Arboretum of Los Angeles County is jam-packed with visitors from March through November.

Yet this gorgeous rose garden requires no pesticides. Prevention is key. For one thing, copious amounts of organic material were worked into the soil before the roses were planted, and additional organic mulches and fertilizers are added throughout the year. Another preventive measure is found in the roses themselves—all strong, disease-resistant varieties. They include the popular David Austin types, the old garden roses, and early hybrid teas. By eliminating susceptible roses from the garden, its managers have gone a long way toward reducing the need for disease and pest control.

HOW THE GARDEN STAYS HEALTHY

In the spring and early summer, gardeners control aphids by knocking them off the roses with streams of water. Hosing is done often to keep this insect population under control (100 percent of aphid offspring are female, and they are born pregnant). Later, naturally occurring ladybugs keep the aphid population in check. In late summer, water is also used to knock off spider mites. The grasshoppers are caught by hand—not hard to do, volunteers say, once you get the hang of it.

Overhead watering early in the day keeps most mildew under control; hand-spraying with a water-and-baking-soda mixture handles severe problems. If a rose is attacked by black spot or rust, its leaves are stripped off, diseased leaves are carefully picked up, old mulch is replaced, and the plant is sprayed with a summer-oil-and-water mixture to prevent recurrence.

Thrips—difficult to control even with a pesticide—are few, and their damage is slight, so no attempt is made to eradicate them. The lack of thrips is attributed to the choice of roses and to the soil, fertilizer, and mulches that keep them in good health.

If you look at individual bushes, you will find some rust, mildew, and evidence of insects. But you have to look closely. Step back just a few steps, and what you see is a healthy and beautifully blooming garden.

'Desprez à Fleur Jaune' (climbing Noisette rose, France, c. 1830) at the Victorian Rose Garden

New Products Attack Old Problems

Neem-based pesticides, which dissipate rapidly and are safe to use on food crops, are an effective tool in managing hard-to-control pests like the leafhopper. This magnified photograph shows the damage leafhoppers can inflict on grape leaves.

chemical-based pesticide if you spill them on your skin during the dilution process, or if they wash into streams, where they may kill fish. When you use a pesticide, no matter what its origin, read the label and use the product exactly as directed.

Looking to the future. Researchers are reaching out in previously unexplored directions to learn more about environmentally safe pest management methods. For example, *Azadirachta indica,* the neem tree, has long been known by herbalists to protect humans from various bacterial infections and to keep harvested crops from pest infection. Recently, pest management experts have introduced neem products. Some are growth regulators, which prevent immature insects from reaching adulthood; others prevent the adults from eating. Sprays made from neem tree oil have been effective in controlling certain plant diseases as well. With low acute toxicity and no known long-term adverse effect on mammals, neem products are examples of appropriate solutions.

Researchers are also exploring the world's rain forests. There, multitudes of plants and animals live in balance in a complex system. By learning how their natural chemical self-defense mechanisms work, researchers hope to find solutions to horticultural problems that can be duplicated in our gardens.

TAKING THE COMMONSENSE APPROACH

Chances are you've already begun your own commonsense approach to solving problems in the garden. Each time you take a morning stroll through your garden, sit on a bench to admire the view, or do routine weeding and pruning, you're in the process of observing what's going on. With a little practice you can improve your observational skills and easily spot changes—the first step in managing a pest, disease, or weed problem.

Improve your observational skills. One useful gardening skill is recognizing the relationship of pest, disease, and weed pat-

terns to the overall climate in your region, taking into account yearly weather variations. An unusually cold winter often means fewer pests in your garden in the spring. And a mild and wet spring brings with it a greater number of weeds. You probably recognize these patterns with no difficulty. But others may take closer observation and analysis. An example is the seasonal spider mite problem. These mites usually show up in the latter part of a warm summer. If you note their arrival date one year, you'll be ready the next to take preventive steps to manage them. Spider mite infestations can usually be minimized by hosing them off plants as soon as they appear. But if you don't start intervention right away, the troublesome mites can decimate entire plants in just a few days.

Another highly useful habit is to routinely make a detailed check of both permanent and seasonal plants on a regular basis. Think of it as the plant equivalent of an annual checkup, only one that is done more frequently. A good rule is to match it to the watering cycle: pick one or two plants from those you water weekly, those you water monthly, and those that require little water.

With each plant, scratch away a little of the dirt around its base and check for pests. See the "Encyclopedia of Damaging and Beneficial Creatures" (page 148) for photographs of common garden pests to help you identify what you find.

Next, work your way up the stem or trunk, looking for crawling insects such as ants. Ants are probably harvesting nectar from

Prospecting in the World's Rain Forests

Many plants and insects have natural defense mechanisms that keep enemies away. In the rain forest, with its multitudes of plants and insects surviving in balance, scientists are seeking to learn more about such defenses, hoping to turn new discoveries into useful pesticides for farms and gardens.

A Pound of Prevention

Get in the habit of checking the plants in your garden regularly. This practice will help you make sure pests aren't getting the upper hand. Look for obvious signs, such as holes in leaves, flowers, or fruits, as well as overall decline in health.

aphids, soft scales, or whiteflies. To maintain this food source, the ants protect these pests from their natural predators, and as a result the pest population can get out of control and jeopardize the plant's health. If you find ants on any plant trunk or stem, you must assume that the plant is harboring a pest population. If it's a tall tree, an ant trail up the trunk may be the only way you'll know that pests are in the top branches. Check the leaves for damage and insect presence, looking at both the tops and the undersides.

If you have a lawn, step back and take a good look at it. Is it yellow in spots? Are raccoons digging it up or is there evidence of moles? Either spots or holes might mean you have lawn grubs (the grubs eat the grass roots). To check, use a sharp knife to slice a section of turf, and peel it back. If the roots are discolored and shriveled rather than healthy and white, or if you see white larvae among the roots, you probably have a grub infestation.

Some of your observations should be done at night. One successful gardener lists the flashlight among her five favorite gardening tools because she spends time in the evening looking for evidence of snails, slugs, and earwigs—among the worst problems in western gardens. During nightly forays, you'll be able to hand-pick many snails and slugs and get rid of them, either by squashing them or by dropping them into soapy water. If you see earwigs, roll up several newspaper sheets into a funnel shape, slightly dampen them, secure with rubber bands, and place them on the ground near where you've seen the pests. Earwigs will crawl into the paper funnels, and you can dispose of it early the next morning.

A hand lens is another good tool. Botanists and entomologists rarely go outside without one. These compact, powerful magnifiers help them easily see tiny flower parts and insects. Hand lenses can be found at nature supply and outdoor recreational retailers. Or you can use the type of magnifying lenses often found at bookstores; they will magnify sufficiently for you to view many plant parts and insects in good detail.

As you observe your garden for a full season, you'll recognize the insects most common to your area. If your garden is healthy, you can surmise that the creatures you're seeing are beneficial, or kept in check by natural predators and your current gardening practices. If, in future seasons, you find severely damaged plants,

you can look for unfamiliar pests in the garden, then use the reference sections in this book to pinpoint the problem.

Regular observation will also help determine the severity of a problem and whether it's bad enough to warrant intervention. If you usually have rust at the end of the summer, you'll know when to expect it and whether it's particularly bad. If it shows up at a different time or seems more severe, you'll want to monitor it more carefully. If leaf-cutting bees regularly "borrow" a few round circles from rose leaves to make their nests, you will probably be willing to share. On the other hand, if all your tomato bushes are suddenly filled with hornworms, you will need to intervene right away and get rid of every one of the pests.

Complexity and tolerance. Controlling some pests can be straightforward. If snails are a problem, for example, you follow a simple routine of setting traps for them or you can hand-pick them on a regular basis.

At other times, the decision to control pests is more complex. When a pest has infested a wide area of your garden and is small and numerous, it isn't as easy to come up with a solution that kills only the unwanted creature. For example, if you spray a broad-spectrum insecticide on open flowers early in the morning to rid them of a troublesome pest, you may also kill the beneficial honeybees that drink nectar from the same plant later that morning. This would be particularly unfortunate because bees are on the decline throughout our country.

You might choose instead to postpone spraying until the plants have stopped blooming. Or you could spray after sunset, when the bees have left the garden, using an insecticide that will dissipate by the time they return in the morning.

There are some biological controls that kill only a specific type of insect. One such control is *Bacillus thuringiensis* (BT), a poison that paralyzes and destroys the stomach cells of insects that consume it. It may take a few days for the insect to die, but once it has eaten a leaf or plant part coated with BT, it will stop eating.

Nevertheless, BT is not appropriate in every instance. One of the formulations, BT caterpillar toxin, is widely used to rid gardens of destructive caterpillars. But the same product will kill caterpillars at the stage when they are turning into butterflies.

This can leave you in a quandary: do you protect your vegetables with the BT and put at risk your future butterfly populations? Savvy gardeners have come up with several solutions. They grow an extra row of vegetables so there is enough for both humans and caterpillars. Or, in an area away from the vegetable plot, they grow other plants that caterpillars eat and move the caterpillars to those plants. Because butterflies are so popular, you'll find many articles and books about them. These sources will tell you which butterflies are likely to come to your garden and the plants they feed on at their caterpillar and butterfly stages.

White-backed garden spider

Fearful of insects? Let's face it: most people aren't very comfortable around insects. You may be kindly disposed toward ladybugs (ladybird beetles) and perhaps the brightly colored dragonfly or the delicate lacewing, but it's not likely you'll be pleased by many others that live in the garden. You may have decided "Not me!" as you read the previous sections about scratching around in the dirt to look for insects, or using a magnifying glass to examine them close up.

Knowledge can help overcome such fears. For example, information about bees, wasps, and spiders—types of insects that distress many gardeners—may help you be more comfortable with their presence in your garden.

As we've all been told, most bees and wasps sting only in self-defense. When working in the garden, give these insects space as they visit your flowers. Some are pretty easygoing, especially the bumblebee, which seems to be quite tolerant of gardeners and very interested in hanging around when you are hand-watering. The black or brown solitary wasps that live in the garden are important pollinators, as are honeybees and bumblebees. Some of them even hunt and eat other harmful pests.

Such desirable wasps may be confused with yellow jackets, which are responsible for most of the bee and wasp stings reported each year. Yellow jackets are easily identified by their characteristic yellow-and-black—striped, elongated bodies. Their communal nests are built in the ground, and you'll want to have them removed by a professional, if you find them in your garden.

Spiders are among the most important natural predators in the garden, ridding it of many pests harmful to plants. You don't want to indiscriminately kill spiders.

Most spiders you encounter will rapidly flee from you, so they're of little concern. However, two spider types are dangerous to humans: black widow spiders, which have shiny black bodies with a red hourglass on the abdomen; and brown recluse spiders, which are matte brown with a darker brown, violin-shaped mark on their heads. The bites of these spiders are serious and require immediate medical attention.

In general, it's a good habit to wear gloves when you work in your garden. You'll be less bothered by the occasional grub, worm, or slug if you have the protection of a glove between your hands and the insect. (Note: Many gardeners prefer latex gloves—like those worn by medical professionals—because they allow greater dexterity. However, some people are reporting topical skin allergies to the latex. If you prefer close-fitting gloves, you may want to look for some made of nonlatex materials.)

You may not become good friends with all the insects in your garden, but knowing how to identify the ones that can cause harm will go a long way toward increasing your comfort level.

KEEPING YOUR GARDEN HEALTHY

Keeping your garden healthy is the first step toward controlling pests, diseases, and weeds. To find helpful information, consult the "Practical Gardening Dictionary" section of the *Sunset Western Garden Book*. It's a wealth of facts about major gardening topics important to the health of your garden.

Here's a list of topics you'll want to consider:

- Understand the soil types in your garden and what may be needed to make them productive.
- Learn how to amend soil in a new garden, or what you can do annually to improve soil in an established garden.
- Determine what type of irrigation system is most appropriate for your location and the kinds of plants you're growing.
- Be sure your irrigation program accounts for seasonal changes.
- Become knowledgeable about garden nutrition basics and what types of fertilizer you need for plant health and productivity.
- Mulch your garden to protect plants from temperature extremes, improve soil texture, and keep weeds under control.
- Weed, thin, and prune to help plants thrive.
- Undertake routine cleanup and maintenance throughout the year, in addition to seasonal maintenance tasks such as winter spraying and pruning.
- Understand planting basics, including how to germinate seeds and transplant plants of all sizes.
- And finally, determine each plant's water needs. This critical skill is gained through observation, practice, and asking others for advice. It isn't unusual to become convinced that a plant is suffering from a disease or a pest only to find out that the problem is caused by either too little or too much water.

Dragonflies (above) and katydids (below) are common garden insects.

LEARNING FROM THE WHITEFLY

Gardeners want pest solutions that work, but given a choice they prefer those that are quick and simple. However, sometimes a quick and simple solution causes more problems than it solves. Attempts to eradicate the whitefly with pesticides illustrate how knowledge of a particular pest—and patience—can be a better pest management tool than a quick spraying.

The whitefly is one of the top ten pests in every part of the West. Disturb the leaves of an infested plant and hundreds of tiny white insects will fly up and swarm around you—these are whiteflies. Although named for their adult shape and flying habit, these insects are actually more akin to aphids, and—like aphids—they weaken plants by sucking juices from the leaves. Heavily infested plants lose vigor and turn yellow. The honeydew secreted by whiteflies attracts ants and causes black sooty mold to form. Ants protect the flies from their natural enemies, and mold harms the plants further by blocking light to the leaves.

The whitefly has four life stages; only the adults and young nymphs are susceptible to commonly used insecticides.

The fluttering white insects that rise from infested plants are the adults. Except when disturbed, they remain on the underside of plant leaves, sucking juices and, eventually, laying their eggs on the leaves. Their damage to plants is minimal.

Soon after hatching, whitefly nymphs begin to feed. Examine an infected leaf, and you'll see small, slightly flattened ovals firmly attached to the leaf. These are the nymphs. The nymphs suck plant juices and secrete the honeydew that attracts ants and causes sooty mold.

In time the nymphs change to nonfeeding pupae. Also attached to the back of the leaf, the pupae are thicker and rounder than the nymphs. The adults emerge from the pupae, and the cycle starts all over again.

Most commonly available insecticides of all types are ineffective against the mature nymphal and pupal stages of the whitefly. A few adults are killed by insecticide sprays, but most escape during the spraying process. However, tiny parasitic (or more properly, parasitoid) wasps found throughout the West *will* kill nymphs and pupae. These wasps, the most common of which is *Encarsia formosa*, drill through the pupa or nymph outer shell with their ovipositors, and lay their eggs inside. The eggs hatch and eat their host.

The common mistake is spraying to kill the adult whiteflies. Doing so merely kills these wasps and eliminates the allies needed to break the whitefly cycle.

REDUCING WHITEFLIES IN YOUR GARDEN

What's really needed is a way to reduce the whitefly population using methods that won't affect the wasps. Here are methods that will help.

First, if a particular plant seems very susceptible to whiteflies, eliminate the plant from your garden. Or pick off and destroy heavily infested leaves from a plant you want to keep.

Second, try killing the adults through other means:

- Hang or post yellow cardboard squares covered with sticky substances (sold at garden centers) near the infested plants. The yellow color attracts whiteflies, and the sticky material traps them.

- Protect the plants with row covers. This tactic is especially effective when the whiteflies are infesting low-growing vegetables and young flower seedlings.

- Spray the infested plants daily with strong bursts of water. This may drive some adults away and even kill a few, and it will also wash off the honeydew, preventing ant infestation and sooty mold buildup.

- Use nitrogen fertilizer sparingly; whiteflies reproduce more vigorously when the plants they're feeding on contain high levels of nitrogen.

- Attract beneficial insects to your garden by providing a healthy overall environment. (Lacewings and ladybugs also will eat whiteflies.) The encarsia wasp is common throughout the West, although it may appear a little later than early outbreaks of whitefly. You can also purchase these insects from various mail-order suppliers.

- For a heavy adult infestation, spray with an insecticidal soap before resorting to a stronger insecticide. Insecticidal soap solutions may not be as harmful to beneficial creatures. Try to target the application to just the infested plant, at a time when there's no wind to carry the spray.

Remember that absolute control isn't needed, since plants can withstand moderate infestations. Whiteflies have many natural enemies; they'll often gradually disappear when you stop using insecticides.

In the coldest areas of the West, whiteflies may be killed during the winter and the cycle broken. However, new infestations are introduced by plants that come from greenhouses. To minimize reinfestation, check carefully for whitefly evidence before you buy plants.

SEVEN STEPS TO PEST, DISEASE, AND WEED MANAGEMENT

When you detect a pest, disease, or weed problem in your garden, follow these steps to address it:

1. Correctly identify the problem. If you mistake rust pustules for whitefly nymphs, you won't be able to solve the problem.

2. Decide whether the problem needs to be corrected or if you and the plant can tolerate it. If every leaf is being stripped and the plant's survival is in question, you must take immediate steps or lose the plant. On the other hand, a few chewed leaves may not be worth the effort required to eliminate the chewer.

3. If the problem needs attention, use physical control methods first. These include trapping and removing insects like snails and earwigs, hosing aphids off plants, putting up row barriers, and so on.

4. When other steps are required to eliminate the problem, determine whether biological controls might work. For instance, you may be able to eliminate lawn grubs by soaking the lawn with a nematode-laced solution.

5. If you determine that a pesticide is required, read the labels carefully and choose a product that has been identified as the most effective with the least risk to you or the environment. For example,

some gardeners will try insecticidal soap as their first choice for ornamental-plant pest control. It kills many insects outright, has minimal impact on plant tissue, and dissipates right away. You might not think of it as a pesticide, but it falls under federally regulated pesticide classification, and its label contains the appropriate information required by law.

6. Sometimes a stronger pesticide—or one formulated specifically for a particular pest or disease—may be the only way to manage a problem. You must, of course, follow its label directions exactly. In addition, be very judicious about the area you cover. Spray only the affected plant or area rather than the whole garden. Or, if you're using a bait-type product (such as those formulated for snail control), place it in just a few locations, away from where children or domestic animals will encounter it.

7. And always follow carefully all directions on the label for mixing and applying. Any product with the word "Caution" or "Warning" on its label must be handled exactly as directed.

PLANNING TO PREVENT PROBLEMS: CREATING THE HEALTHY GARDEN

It's frustrating to lose prized plants to pests and diseases. Sometimes it seems that all you do is battle these problems. It can take hours of time and may consume a great deal of money, and even then the plants may die.

Seeing a favorite—such as a potted camellia that graced the front porch for years—become a scraggly shadow of its former self due to severe aphid and sooty mold infestation is devastating. Fortunately, there are techniques you can learn to prevent the problem from reaching such a stage.

Because your camellia is in a pot on a covered porch, you may not always remember to water it regularly, especially during cool and rainy weather. Irregular watering has probably weakened its natural defenses. One solution is to attach the pot to a drip irrigation system so that a regular amount of water is delivered at all times. Nutrients in the original potting soil will deplete over the years, weakening the plant. You can buy a fertilizer especially formulated for camellias and add it to the soil once or twice annually.

In addition, you can mulch the camellia by adding 1–2 inches of well-aged compost to the soil surface. Mulch helps protect roots from variations in temperature. And finally, you can spray the garden area near the camellia each winter with a dormant-oil spray to minimize the number of aphids in your garden.

The pages that follow cover the prevention aspect of Integrated Pest Management, with suggestions such as the ones above to help prevent pest, disease, and weed problems from invading your garden. Some may be familiar to you as general good gardening techniques, but here their pest-, disease-, or weed-prevention aspects are emphasized. You'll be able to identify the links between certain gardening basics and problem prevention so that you can create and maintain a healthy garden.

Planning for Color All Season Long

Planted the previous fall and late winter, this California garden is awash with pastel blossoms by mid-April (above, right). Hidden among these spring blooms are vegetable seedlings, fast-growing annual vines, and vibrant flowers that thrive in summer heat. All three come into their own in late July (right).

MAKE TIME FOR PLANNING

Planning is one of the most important things you can do to keep a garden healthy. No matter where you garden, there comes a time when most activities slow down or stop. For many, the dormant period occurs in January, when seed and plant catalogs begin to arrive. The catalogs stimulate thinking about what worked and what didn't work last year—and what you might do differently this time.

Before you begin planning for an upcoming season, do a walking inventory of your garden. Make notes as you go, recalling what happened in each area and planting bed. Perhaps your peaches were afflicted with peach leaf curl, aphids wreaked havoc with your roses, or spider mites caused problems in the dwarf conifers. These pest infestations can be remedied by preventive techniques during the dormant season, followed by prompt attention as they first become apparent next spring. If you kept a journal or made a few notes during the past season, refer to them to remind yourself which management methods worked.

Some problems might require structural solutions. Perhaps last season's cutting garden was a failure because a layer of hardpan just below the topsoil prevented proper root development. You make a note to construct raised planting beds to remedy this problem. Or you see some struggling shrubs and jot down a reminder to order soil amendments next spring.

If you have a vegetable and herb garden each year, you may decide to rearrange it, breaking up one large plot into several smaller ones dispersed throughout the garden to take better advantage of microclimates. If you have particular pest problems with a certain vegetable, you might diversify its planting among the various beds so that pests don't spread from one plant to another. In many western climate zones, you can also let some herbs, such as lavender and rosemary, do double duty as foundation shrubs.

Another aspect of planning ahead is preparing for later pest prevention. For example, if you lost an entire flat of transplanted vegetable seedlings to cutworms or earwigs the day after you planted them, make a note to start stockpiling milk cartons now. This season, surround each seedling with a cutoff carton at the time you plant. The carton will prevent cutworms from getting to the plants and eating them. (Make sure there's at least 1 inch between the outermost plant leaves and the edge of the carton and that the carton extends 1 inch below soil level and 2 inches above it.)

Taking inventory and doing advance planning doesn't mean that every task in your garden must be strictly governed by rules. In fact, a great deal of gardening's popularity is due to its relaxed nature—a refreshing change from the busy lives most of us lead. But your garden will be healthier and you'll be able to enjoy it more if you pay timely attention to a few key tasks.

DORMANT-SEASON CLEANUP

Removing all diseased plant material, along with spent annuals and vegetables, is key to preventing diseases from recurring season after season. In most areas of the West, this cleanup is done in late fall.

Until just a few years ago, it was generally recommended that the garden be stripped bare. While that ensures the most protection from recurring disease, it may make your garden uninhabitable for creatures you want to protect during the dormant season. Some unkempt areas may be just what's needed for birds, small mammals, and other attractive or beneficial creatures to find shelter in the cooler months. Of course, you should remove anything that's badly diseased or has completed its life cycle. But otherwise, moderation is a good rule of thumb. Chemicals sold for "total soil cleanup," for instance, are highly toxic and their use should be avoided.

One task you should plan on completing during the dormant season is dormant-oil spraying. Spraying trees and shrubs with an oil-and-water solution will kill many pests in their dormant stages; it will also prevent some diseases from occurring the following spring. Dormant-oil spraying is one way of keeping next season's aphid, scale, and mite populations under control. (You might want to limit this spraying to those plants that had the greatest infestations in the prior year. Widespread spraying may have the unwanted side effect of killing beneficial creatures.)

Some commercially available oils contain disease-preventing components—sometimes the only control that will prevent certain diseases, such as peach leaf curl, from occurring later during the growing season. Consult your cooperative extension agent to learn details about winter spraying of ornamental and fruit trees.

Oil sprays are sold in two formulas. Those applied during winter are heavier and better able to coat tree and shrub branches, suffocating insects in their dormant states. Summer oil is lighter weight. If you apply dormant-oil spray during warmer seasons, it puts too heavy a coating on leaves, making it difficult for them to breathe and making them more vulnerable to burning from sunlight reflected by the oil. As with any material you purchase to spray on your garden, be sure to follow the directions on the label exactly.

If you're growing roses in a mild-winter area, you'll find their leaves don't drop naturally. While the task can seem daunting, you must strip off all old leaves—sometimes you can knock off the majority with a broom—and dispose of them. By winter the leaves have lost their vigor, and most are harboring some evidence of black spot or rust. If you don't remove them, the disease spores will rapidly infect the new leaves next spring. Once you've removed the leaves, do your regular winter pruning and then spray the entire bush with dormant-oil spray.

In colder-winter areas, most rose leaves will drop naturally. However, remember to spray your rosebushes with dormant-oil spray after their annual pruning.

In both types of climates, dispose of rose leaves with the trash, not in the compost. Disease spores will survive in compost, even in a pile that generates high temperatures.

Harvest Lettuce Nearly Year Round

While other vegetables are just getting started, the first batch of late-winter lettuce is harvested in a California garden (above, left). Additional lettuces (left) are also being planted for late spring and summer salads. With planning, mild-climate vegetable gardens yield crops over many months.

WHAT IS SOIL pH AND WHY IS IT IMPORTANT?

It sometimes seems there's a lot to know about gardening. Just learning the basics about the zone you live in can be daunting. In addition, there's general information about clay and sandy soils, fertilizer types, and irrigation methods—all time-consuming topics. If the question is then raised, "And just what is the soil pH in your garden?" you may begin to feel overwhelmed. But the answer does matter.

Soil pH can be a complex topic. However, you need to understand only a few fundamentals.

The term "pH" refers to a soil's relative acidity or alkalinity. It's measured on a scale from 0 to 14, with neutral point at 7. A pH value lower than 7 is acidic, while one higher than 7 is alkaline. "Good" garden soil usually has a pH between 6 and 6.8, the range in which the vast majority of plants thrives.

The right acidity or alkalinity in the soil makes it possible for plants accustomed to one of those soil types to extract nutrients from it. Thus, if you plant an acid-loving rhododendron in highly alkaline soil, it won't flourish, even if you've met its temperature requirements and you give it sufficient water, fertilizer, and shade. The only way it will grow successfully is if you amend the soil to be more acidic.

The norm in western zones that receive little rainfall is slightly alkaline soil. By amending such soil with compost and similar materials, you can move the pH closer to the desired 6–6.8 norm. However, if the soil in your garden is moderately to highly alkaline, bringing it to neutral or slightly acid levels is an expensive and complex process; just adding soil amendments won't do it. A better choice is to garden instead with plants native to your zone, or with plants from other areas of the world that also tolerate alkaline soil. Examples of alkaline-tolerant plants include acacia, bottlebrush, date palm, dusty miller, eucalyptus, oleander, olive, pomegranate, and thyme. If you want to include vegetables in a garden with highly alkaline soil, a practical alternative is to grow them in raised beds, filled with a prepared soil mix.

Acid-rich soils are associated with high-rainfall areas, such as the rainy coasts of the Pacific Northwest and Northern California. Acid soils can be moved toward the neutral level by adding lime. However, if the soil is highly acidic, you may prefer to stick to acid-tolerant plants. In general, any plant that likes filtered or morning sun and thrives in moist soil that's rich in decomposing plant matter is acid tolerant. Plants in this category (growing successfully in soil with a pH of 5–6.8) include azalea, blueberry, heather, hydrangea, and rhododendron.

To determine soil pH, you can use a purchased test kit or have a professional do the testing. If you do your own testing, it's important to gather samples from several different locations throughout the garden. You can also send the samples to a lab for complete analysis. To find labs that do professional soil testing and analysis, contact your local cooperative extension office. You may want to get professional advice on the soil amendment process as well.

Acid-loving and Alkaline-tolerant Plants

Rhododendrons and camellias prefer moderately acid soil (top). Thyme and cinquefoil (*Potentilla*) grow in neutral soil (bottom) but also tolerate high alkaline levels.

GROWING HEALTHY PLANTS

Learning about the soil in your garden and taking steps to improve it are key to plant health. You also need to understand the water requirements of different plants, when and how to use fertilizers, and why mulch is important.

Soil types. Soil is a mass of mineral particles mixed with living and dead organic matter. There are three kinds of soil: clay, sand, and loam. In clay soil the particles are small; in sandy soil they are large. Loam contains midsize particles. Loam is the most desirable kind of soil because it's rich with nutrients and easy to work, but few gardens are so lucky. Most tend to be either claylike or sandy.

You know you have clay soil if it sticks to your spade when it's wet. Squeeze a handful together, and you'll get a gummy mass that doesn't break apart even if you tap it with your shovel. When the soil dries, it tends to crack, and it often becomes hard enough to deflect a pick. The density of clay soil means it suffers from lack of air, and water drains through it poorly. On the plus side, it's usually full of nutrients.

The properties of sandy soil are exactly opposite those of clay. No matter how often you wet it, the water passes quickly between the large particles—and so do any natural nutrients and fertilizers you may have added. The advantages of sandy soil are that it contains plenty of air, and roots can grow deep.

Both clay and sandy soil can be improved by adding amendments. With clay soil, the amendment loosens its density, making it easier to work and opening it up so air can enter. In the case of sandy soil, the amendment fills the open spaces between sand particles and helps retain water and nutrients. However, amendments will eventually wash away in sandy soil; you'll need to replenish them on a regular basis.

Soil amendments. The best thing you can add to soil is organic matter, the decaying remains of plants and animals. As it decomposes, it releases nutrients that enrich the soil. These nutrients are changed into forms that can be absorbed by tiny microorganisms and bacteria in the soil. What's left at the end of this process is humus, a soft material that binds with either clay or sand particles to improve their texture.

In general, your best course is to add only organic amendments unless a soil expert tests your soil and specifically recommends doing otherwise. Sometimes, adding an inorganic amendment can

make a problem worse. For example, adding sand to clay makes it even more cementlike and chokes off root growth.

One of the best soil amendments is compost. Other amendment possibilities include various custom-made mixtures, sold bagged or in bulk at garden centers, and products found at suppliers specializing in organic products. Well-aged sawdust and manure are also popular choices.

To add an amendment, spread a layer evenly over the soil and mix it in thoroughly, using a spade or a rotary tiller, to a depth of at least 9 inches.

- If your soil is nearly all clay or sand, the finished mix should contain about half amendment and half soil. For a half-and-half mix, you'll need to spread about 4–5 inches of amendment over the top of the soil.

- If your soil is loam, or if it's been regularly amended in the past, the finished new mix should contain one-quarter amendment and three-quarters soil. For this mix, spread about 2–3 inches over the top of the soil.

Water basics. Many times gardeners find yellow or mottled leaves and assume they're the result of a pest or a disease. While that may be the case, these symptoms can also be caused by too much or too little water.

Except for a few shallow-rooted plants, most plants will root as deep and as wide as nutrients, air, and water permit. With near-perfect conditions, many roots can reach much deeper than is commonly believed. For example, even lawn grass, thought by many to be shallow rooted, can reach down 10–24 inches in the best of conditions.

Most plant problems associated with improper watering are a result of watering too frequently and applying only a little at a time. This pattern causes roots to crowd together near the surface and makes plants more susceptible to stresses associated with dryness or changes in soil temperature.

A number of symptoms can alert you to inadequate water. Most leaves show a dullness, a loss of reflective quality, or inward-rolling edges. Some will wilt. (Some plants, such as tomatoes, will wilt in the heat of a hot day. Instead of immediately watering, wait till evening and check to see whether they have recovered from the wilt. If they haven't, give them water.) A plant may interpret lack of water as the beginning of a drought cycle and, to protect itself,

WATERING GUIDELINES

While it's next to impossible to provide any absolute rules about how often to water, there are some guidelines for *how much* to water at any one time.

- Lawns should be watered to a depth of 6–8 inches at each watering, to encourage deep root growth. (An inch of rainfall usually will penetrate about 12 inches in sandy soil, 7 inches in loam, and 4–5 inches in clay.) Since you'll be applying water through some type of sprinkler, remember that it won't cover the area as evenly as rainfall. You can check its coverage pattern by placing cans, all of the same size, in various areas and checking the water levels in each one.

- Planting beds should be watered to a depth of 2–3 feet. If you have a planting bed that's 4 feet by 5 feet, and if you're using a sprinkler, the time needed to wet it to 2 feet is 30 minutes for clay soil, 20 minutes for loam, and 10 minutes for sand.

- Trees should be watered to a depth of approximately 6 feet. First, create a watering basin—or ridge of soil 4–6 inches high—that's the diameter of the tree canopy. Then, for clay soil, fill the basin, let it drain, and repeat the process three more times. For loam soil, fill the basin twice. For sandy soil, fill the basin once. If it drains so fast that the basin doesn't fill, leave the hose on full strength for 10 to 15 minutes.

This information is based on a hose delivering water at 2–3 gallons per minute (gpm), which is moderate strength. (Full strength is usually 5–10 gpm.) You can check delivery rates by timing water filling a marked container, such as a watering can.

The tree canopy of this young 'Nagami' kumquat tree is narrow and so, too, is its watering basin.

The Science of Lawn Watering

To determine how evenly water is distributed over a lawn, set out same-size containers in a grid as shown. Turn on your irrigation system for about 15 minutes and then measure the water in each container. More than a ¼-inch difference between the levels in the containers indicates that you need to adjust your sprinkling system.

begin to shed leaves. This shedding usually takes place near the base of the plant or the base of individual limbs. A lawn in need of water doesn't spring back when you walk on it, and it also loses its luster, taking on a blue-green cast.

Too much water is also a problem. This difficulty is apt to occur when the soil is very claylike or the plant is in a container. It can also happen if you heavily amend the soil just around the plant when you transplant it. This amended area is like a bathtub, since the water doesn't readily drain into the surrounding soil. Too much water can prevent air from reaching roots, setting up a condition in which the plant rots, the victim of a variety of molds and bacteria that exist in the soil. Some leaves on overwatered plants turn yellow or a pale green and then fall off. The plant grows poorly, and thin stems may droop.

The optimum for most plants is a pattern of watering deeply and then allowing the soil to dry out slightly before watering again (unless directions for a specific plant tell you otherwise).

It's also good to get into the habit of measuring water depth and soil dryness on a regular basis. You can buy a water probe or improvise one with a heavy-duty plant stake: simply push the stake into the soil as far as you can; it will go down easily only as far as the soil is wet. Ideally, the soil will be wet to about 18 inches deep a day or so after watering. As soil dries, you can use a pointed trowel to monitor water depth. Dig the trowel straight down into the soil, sinking it all the way up to its handle. Wiggle it around a bit and check to see whether only the top inch or so is dry, or if dry areas go much deeper. When the top 3–5 inches of soil are completely dry, it's usually time to water again.

Because so many areas of the West receive little rainfall and have extended warm seasons, a drip irrigation system is a highly recommended tool for maintaining a healthy garden. By controlling the amount and frequency of watering through programmable settings, such a system can minimize watering guesswork. New systems let you combine drip emitters, soaker tubing, and miniature sprayers and sprinklers. These systems have several advantages, one of which is slow application with little runoff or evaporation.

Drip Irrigation System

A narrow bed of lettuce nestled between house and path is watered by miniature sprayers.

Fertilizer basics. In addition to water, air, and soil, plants need 13 different nutrients in order to thrive. Lacking them, plants not only falter but also become more susceptible to pests and diseases. The three nutrients most vital to plants—nitrogen (N), phosphorus (P), and potassium (K)—are called macronutrients; the remaining ones are called micronutrients.

Because many parts of the West are deficient in both decomposing plant material and rainfall—two primary sources of nitrogen—nitrogen is often lacking in the soil. Without sufficient nitrogen, plant leaves yellow, from their tips toward the stem and from the bottom of the plant upward. The growth of the plant is also stunted by nitrogen deficiency.

Phosphorus and potassium are needed to maintain healthy root systems and plant structure. They also can affect flower production.

READING A FERTILIZER LABEL

The three major nutrients—nitrogen (N), phosphorus (P), and potassium (K)—are always listed on a fertilizer label in a standard format. Nitrogen is listed first, followed by phosphorus and then potassium. The numbers listed on the label stand for the percentage of each element: a formula of 20-6-12 means the product contains 20 percent nitrogen, 6 percent phosphorus, and 12 percent potassium. Any fertilizer that contains some percentage of each of these three nutrients is called a complete fertilizer.

If you see a formula on a label listed as 21-0-0, you know that it's a single-purpose fertilizer—in this case, containing 21 percent nitrogen only. Plants that require a great deal of nitrogen are commonly called heavy feeders; sometimes nitrogen is all that is needed to get them through their growing season.

A product listed as 3-20-20, with higher amounts of phosphorus and potassium and almost no nitrogen, is marked as a "blossom booster" and recommended to improve flowering, bud set, and bud count for container-grown flowers.

Sometimes a fertilizer will also include some of the micronutrients, such as sulfur, boron, copper, iron, manganese, and zinc. These will be listed in the guaranteed analysis on the label. While they're classified as micronutrients because they're needed in only small amounts, some gardeners believe a balanced NPK formula that includes them provides the best type of fertilizer for general garden use.

To replace nutrients that have been depleted from the soil, gardeners usually add fertilizers. While nitrogen easily works its way to deeper soil levels where it can easily be absorbed by roots, phosphorus and potassium tend to stay closer to the surface. If you have got the chance—perhaps when you're digging up a bed or replacing plants—add phosphorus and potassium to deeper soil levels. (Make sure you thoroughly work the phosphorus and potassium into the soil; you don't want the plant roots to sit on a handful of pure fertilizer.)

Organic and inorganic fertilizers. Fertilizers may be from organic or inorganic sources. Organic fertilizer sources are often natural by-products recycled from other sources. They include compost, manure, bat guano, blood meal, bonemeal, cottonseed meal, alfalfa meal, kelp meal, fish meal, hoof and horn meal, and oak leaf mold. They are available in dry or powdered form and are worked into the top soil layer. Before using any of them, be sure to find out which nutrients they contain and the nutrient percentage per pound. Percentages of the three main nutrients are always listed in the same order: 5-10-10 means 5 percent nitrogen, 10 percent phosphorus, and 10 percent potassium. Many organic fertilizers contain only one of these three elements, so you're most likely to see numerical listings reflecting that composition. For example, bat guano may be 13-0-0.

Inorganic fertilizers, including products that combine fertilizer with an herbicide, are available in various forms. Liquids are sold concentrated or mixed with water and applied with a hose attachment or watering can. Dry formulas are worked into the top soil layer or sometimes just spread evenly on the surface (mostly for lawn turf). If your gardening time is limited, you may want to consider the dry timed-release fertilizers that make nutrients available slowly throughout a growing season.

As a plant absorbs nutrients through its roots, it can't tell the difference between an organic and an inorganic fertilizer. However, there are other differences between these two types that may make one preferable to the other.

Many organic fertilizers also have some soil-amending capabilities. Their nutrients tend to be slow-releasing, and they're stored in the soil until needed by a plant. They have low nutrient grade levels (5-5-5, for example), so they are less likely to burn or otherwise harm a plant if you make a mistake in measuring a dosage. However, because they are slower acting, it will take longer for them to be effective.

One way to recognize inorganic fertilizers is by their higher nutrient grade levels (20-20-20, for example). Some are formulated to be fast acting—meaning that their nutrients are immediately available to plants. Their fast-acting capabilities can be useful if a plant is stressed due to pest infestation and has lost leaves and vigor. Generally, however, the nutrient excess is at best wasteful and detrimental to microscopic organisms that live in the soil, and may be harmful to the environment—nitrogen, for example, is a frequent contaminator of groundwater. Slow-release inorganic fertilizers avoid this problem.

In all cases, follow the directions on the label carefully when applying fertilizers, especially those that are combination products. You can kill plants if you apply more than the recommended amount.

A word about iron. Even if iron is present, plants may not be able to absorb it from alkaline soil. This is most often due to the presence of another substance, usually lime, which prevents utilization of the iron. You can tell that a plant lacks iron if its leaves are yellow but the veins and stems have remained green. If this is the case with one of your plants, treat it with a chelated iron product, available where fertilizers are sold. If the problem is severe, spraying a chelated iron solution directly onto leaves is better than adding it to the soil.

Mulch. There's probably no single weed-prevention technique better than applying a thick mulch over all exposed areas in your garden. It smothers emerging weed seeds as they germinate and makes it easier to pull out those that persevere through the mulch layer. If a plant is susceptible to a soilborne disease, mulching around its base will keep disease-bearing soil from splashing up onto leaves during rain or watering.

In addition to weed and disease prevention, mulch serves many other useful purposes. It keeps the soil's surface temperature down—especially important in areas of the West with long, hot summers, when roots near the surface will wither and die in the heat. It also helps keep the top of the soil from crusting over and taking on cementlike characteristics, particularly a problem if the soil is clayey. If the soil surface crusts over, it's harder for air needed by the plant to penetrate the surface, and irrigation water may just run off.

In colder-winter areas, mulch can also help some plants survive. For example, a thick mulch may keep soil from freezing (when soil is frozen, its water isn't available to plants).

Finally, mulch makes a garden look tidy and more attractive. If you've gone on any local garden tours, you'll notice that the beds are often covered with a fresh layer of thick mulch—it unites the garden visually and gives it a more professional look.

Some of the materials described as amendments (see page 36), such as ground bark, sawdust, compost, and soil conditioners, also work well as mulches. Bark chips of various sizes are frequently used in the West, as is straw, especially in vegetable gardens. Other mulches are available through organic gardening suppliers. A popular one is cocoa bean hulls. While expensive for large areas, it is very attractive for small beds. It gives off a faint chocolate fragrance as a bonus.

If you're using a mulch made from wood products—such as bark chips, wood chips, or fresh sawdust—you need to add nitrogen to the soil as you lay down the mulch. These products are low in nitrogen and will rob existing nitrogen from the soil as they decay. Add ½ pound of nitrogen to each 15 pounds of wood product. To determine nitrogen weight, multiply the percentage of nitrogen listed on the product's label by the product's weight.

Mulch is applied in different thicknesses, depending on its type. In all cases, take care to avoid mounding any mulch up around a plant's trunk, because the trunk could draw moisture from the mulch and rot.

If you use organic mulch, add 1–6 inches each season (1 inch is the minimum for getting any benefit). A standard amount is 2–3 inches. In some circumstances, 6 inches may be a good choice—for example, in a warm-climate vegetable garden. One other note: if you're vegetable gardening in a cool area, you may want to start the season with a clear plastic mulch that will help warm the soil. As the season progresses, you can remove the plastic and replace it with an organic mulch to preserve water and keep the soil cool during any hot spells.

For purposes of pest and disease prevention, it's a good idea to dispose of garden mulch as you go about your fall cleanup tasks. If the mulch is compost or some other organic material, work it into

Straw in the Pumpkin Patch

A thick mulch of straw covers the pumpkin patch. It helps keep the soil surface from drying out and at the same time smothers weeds. An added bonus: the straw keeps the pumpkin bottom dry and clean.

the ground. Otherwise, remove it. If you live in a cold-winter area, wait until spring to apply mulch again. If your area is mild and rainy, apply new mulch after the garden has been thoroughly cleaned and all old and diseased leaves, stems, or plants have been removed. In this situation, an application of fresh mulch before the winter rains will help keep your garden free of any weeds that grow in winter and early spring.

Compost. Compost is the best all-around soil amendment that can be found. It's simple to make compost from organic material in your own garden, although it does take time and space. If you don't have the room to make your own, check to see whether any public agency makes compost available. Many cities (or other refuse-collection units) now collect gardening and yard waste. They either compost it for local residents or sell it to commercial businesses that compost it and sell it to the public. (Compost also makes an excellent mulch. If you use it as mulch, work it into the ground at the end of the growing season.)

A simple, albeit somewhat inefficient, way to make compost is to pile up garden debris, mix it with vegetable and fruit scraps from the kitchen, and let it sit. After about six months, depending on temperature, moisture, and size of materials, the compost will have broken down enough to be used. If you use this method, don't add any diseased leaves or weed seeds to the compost because the temperature generated during decomposition won't be high enough to kill bacteria or weed seeds.

Compost will decompose more rapidly if it's confined in a container that has holes in it to allow air circulation, and if it is turned frequently. The material in the middle is the hottest and decomposes most rapidly; it's hot enough to kill many disease organisms and weed seeds. However, many prudent gardeners, not wanting to take chances, consign diseased plant parts and weeds to the garbage instead of to the compost heap.

Whatever composting method you use, never add diseased rose leaves and stems to compost. The bacterial diseases found on them aren't always killed during the composting process, so you would risk re-introducing the diseases to your garden when you spread out the compost.

A variety of prefabricated compost-bin systems are available for purchase. Some local governments sell them to residents at cost. Check with your recycling center or cooperative extension office to see if such a program exists in your area.

Worm composting is growing in popularity with all gardeners, particularly among those with small gardens such as container gardens on decks or patios. In worm composting, clean and odorless red worms live in a small wooden box. They consume newspaper and kitchen scraps, turning them into rich compost in just a few weeks.

Principles of crop rotation. Although it's not practical for permanent plantings, crop rotation can help prevent the recurrence of certain diseases and pest infestations in vegetable and annual flower gardens. Simply put, rotation means you don't grow the same plant in the same place year after year. When you plant in a new location, you interrupt the life cycle of a pest or disease. For instance, onion maggots in the soil will die out if they don't have onions to eat.

By rotating plants annually, you're also less likely to deplete all nutrients of a certain type.

While it's a good idea to rotate all the plants in your vegetable garden, it's especially important to rotate plantings of any member of the tomato family *(Solanaceae)* — tomato, potato, pepper, and eggplant. These plants are prone to soilborne diseases that prosper when host plants are planted in the same soil year after year.

A buckwheat cover crop

A good way to start a rotation plan is to learn the family names for all the vegetables you plan to grow. Then create a rotation plan that locates same-family members in different spots each season. Every fourth rotation, include a plant from the pea family *(Fabaceae)*, such as beans or peas, which will build soil nutrients back up.

You may want to set aside one crop rotation area for green manure. "Green manure" refers to a crop grown for the sole purpose of tilling it into the bed as a soil improvement. Plants most commonly used include clover, fava beans, and buckwheat. If the growing season in your area is long, you may be able to grow a green manure crop early in the season and plant a different vegetable in that area later. When you plant a green manure crop, work it into the soil when the plants have a high nutrient content—that is, when they're still young and green.

COMPOST BINS
Leave debris in a simple bin (right) and it will decompose slowly over time. A commercial bin (far right) that heats debris speeds up the composting process.

"SAME PLACE NEXT YEAR?" NOT IN THE VEGETABLE GARDEN

Year 1

Year 3

Year 2

Year 4

In this crop rotation scheme, each of the plant types moves on a four-year schedule, making it less likely for a plant to pick up a soilborne disease from a previous year. The climbing peas, members of the legume family, actually put nutrients back into the soil as they rotate.

You may also want to devote your entire vegetable or annual flower garden area to a green manure crop from time to time so that the overall soil quality is improved.

Crop rotation works best in medium to large gardens. In the small garden, rotating a crop only a few feet isn't enough to keep hungry pests from finding it the next season. If you can't rotate crops, make sure you add soil amendments and fertilizers each planting season. If pests are an issue, skip a problem vegetable for a season or two, or grow it away from the vegetable garden entirely, perhaps among the ornamentals.

THE RIGHT PLANT FOR THE RIGHT LOCATION

How do you know which plants are best suited to your garden? While it seems too simple to be useful, one of the best ways to find out is by taking a drive or a stroll through nearby neighborhoods and towns and looking for plants you like. Take a picture or knock on the door to ask for plant names. Or visit a local public garden. Find one of the gardeners, ask questions, and jot down the names of the plants that catch your eye.

Another tip is to check gardening calendars in local newspapers. Each spring, organizations in many communities sponsor local garden tours—usually self-guided. While some take you to large estates that are beyond most people's means, many feature neighborhood gardens not that different from yours in size, location, and budget. Even though the main purpose of going on such a tour is to identify healthy and attractive plants, you may also get ideas about solving problems. For example, you might see how someone else has handled a dark corner, a steep slope, or a poorly draining, marshy area.

You can also find ideas about plants that thrive in Sunset's 24 western garden zones by referring to the "Problem Solving by Plant Type" chapter of this book. It lists plants of every kind—from trees to ground covers, and from perennials to berries—that grow well in the western zones.

Local nurseries are also good sources of information as to whether a plant is well suited for your garden. Carefully read labels and confer with a nursery specialist. Nursery employees will tell you that most customer discussion is about whether a chosen plant will live in the location they have in mind. Determining if the plant takes sun or needs shade causes the greatest confusion. Even if the label clearly says "Plant in a sunny location," the definition of "sunny" can vary widely within zones. A particular plant may need full sun in your garden, but in a warmer zone 15 miles away it may be able to tolerate only morning sun.

Likewise, when you're planning a vegetable garden, everything in the catalogs looks tempting. But think about whether you have enough warmth and sun to grow a watermelon, or enough cool and moist air to ripen an artichoke.

Because gardeners in many parts of the West have the option of growing plants of almost any type, it can be tempting to try everything—from plants that naturally occur in the highlands of China to others native to the tropics of Mexico. To make sure that what you're buying will work in your own backyard, get into the habit of keeping a copy of the *Sunset Western Garden Book* on hand and looking up the plant before filling out that order form. Take the book with you on shopping trips to local nurseries. In addition to giving you several paragraphs of descriptive information and growing tips, each entry clearly states in which of the 24 zones the plant will grow, whether the plant requires shade or sun, and approximately how much water it needs. If the plant has special growing requirements, such as highly acid soil or excellent drainage, these will be clearly identified.

For Success with a Plant, Give It What It Needs

The right location is a site that satisfies the plant's requirements. Failure to attend to the water requirements of these beans has stunted them and left them susceptible to a spider mite infestation (right). Compare them to their well-watered counterparts (far right). Rhododendrons are shade-loving shrubs (below). The one directly below, planted in a sunny location, has suffered sunscald. Sheltered from the direct sun, another rhododendron thrives (below, right).

Plant requirements. The following checklist will help you determine whether a plant is likely to thrive in your garden. It also includes a few tips on caring for plants that are marginal in your area but can thrive with a little extra effort.

- Minimum temperature ranges. The *Sunset Western Garden Book* takes temperature requirements into account in the zones it lists for each plant. Plant labels may also indicate a minimum temperature range. If you're choosing a plant that is just within the minimum, have on hand supplies (such as sprays and plastic sheeting) to protect it during a freeze. If your area is a great deal colder than the minimum, plan to protect the plant with physical barriers during the coldest months or to dig it up and move it into a protected area each winter.

- Sun requirements. Key phrases to look for are "full sun" and "all day sun," or "morning sun" and "filtered sun," but elevation, latitude, and general climate conditions need to be considered as well. Full sun may be too hot for many plants in areas near Phoenix, while morning sun may not be enough in the mountains and short growing season of Wyoming.

- Shade requirements. Most plants that need shade also need moist soil. If your shady area is dry, make sure the shade plant you're considering will thrive with only a little water.

- Soil type. In general, plants prefer soil that is slightly acid to neutral, and somewhere between claylike and sandy in composition. Some plants must have soil that is well drained, and if this is the case you'll find such a requirement noted on its label or in a reference book. If the soil in your garden is claylike, you'll need to amend it before choosing a plant that requires well-drained soil. Other plants, especially the popular azaleas and camellias, prefer acid soil. You can buy special-formula fertiliz-

ers to acidify the soil before planting an acid-loving plant. For more information on soil acidity and alkalinity, see "What Is Soil pH and Why Is It Important?" on page 36.

- Water needs. Some areas of the West receive a great deal of rainfall; many plants thrive in these areas with little or no extra water. Other, major areas of the West receive little rainfall and have suffered severe droughts over the past two decades, causing gardeners to pay more attention to the water needs of plants. Wherever you are, it's best to stick to one kind of gardening, in watering terms. If most of your garden is made up of plants with minimal water requirements, don't succumb to a new one with high water requirements. It is not likely to get enough water and will probably languish. For more information on meeting water needs, see "Watering Guidelines" on page 37.

BUY RESISTANT PLANTS

Another way to prevent problems is to buy plants that have proved resistant to certain pests and diseases. In some cases finding resistant ones is a matter of trial and error. Zinnias are notorious for getting mildew in some gardens and not in others, and the reason is often that one garden has more mildew spores flying around in it than another. If a particular annual flower becomes infected year after year, eliminate it from your garden plan. Gardeners often borrow ideas from each other—look for healthy plants in other people's gardens and ask what they are.

Roses are one of the most popular flowers, and many gardens include at least one or two rose bushes. Yet they can be among the most pest- and disease-prone of any plant on earth. The best tactic is to buy roses that are less vulnerable to disease. Most local chapters of rose societies maintain lists of varieties best suited for local climates.

In general, a good choice is one of the many old garden roses or modern shrub roses—these have good resistance to mildew, rust, and black spot.

If you want to add a tree to your garden, find out if your choice is disease resistant in your area. Nurturing an ornamental shade tree to maturity only to lose it to a disease is devastating to the gardener and to the garden. For instance, the ornamental pear tree is a favorite in many parts of the West. It is a mass of white blossoms in the spring and sports brightly colored foliage in the fall. But it's susceptible to fireblight. If you wish to include an ornamental pear in your garden, check with your local cooperative extension agent to determine if fireblight-resistant varieties are available. In general, the extension offices provide a wealth of information, and the agents are experts on local conditions.

Certain vegetable varieties are more resistant to disease than others. Whether you're buying seeds or transplants, choose a named variety and look for the abbreviations after the variety name that signify its resistant qualities. For example, "Supersweet 100 VF" is a cherry tomato that's resistant to both verticillium wilt (V) and fusarium wilt (F). "Roma VFN" is a form of the popular Italian cooking tomato that's resistant to verticillium wilt, fusarium wilt, and nematodes.

Note: Heirloom vegetables are making a comeback in American gardens, and while gardeners are finding these special plants have superior flavor, shape, color, and other endearing attributes, they may also be more susceptible to disease than are modern variations bred for disease resistance.

IDENTIFYING DISEASE-RESISTANT PLANTS

The following abbreviations are used to indicate the diseases to which certain plants are resistant. Look for these abbreviations on seed packages, and in descriptions of plants in seed and plant catalogs, as well as on nursery labels.

A	Alternaria
ALS	Angular leaf spot
AN	Anthracnose
B	Bolting
BR	Black rot
BS	Black speck
BSR	Bacterial soft rot
BW	Bacterial wilt
C	Cercospora
CBM	Common bean mosaic virus
CMV	Cucumber mosaic virus
DM	Downy mildew
F	Fusarium wilt
H	Heat
HS	Hollow stem
LB	Late blight
LMV	Lettuce mosaic virus
M	Mosaic virus
N	Root knot nematode
PM	Powdery mildew
PVY	Potato virus Y
R	Rust
S	Scab
SCLB	Southern corn leaf blight
SG	Smog
ST	Smut
SW	Stewart's wilt
TP	Tip burn
TMV	Tobacco mosaic virus
V	Verticillium wilt

PLANTING AT THE RIGHT TIME

When you finally find a special plant that you've looked everywhere for, it's certainly tempting to acquire it—even if you're in the middle of a four-month heat wave. But it is going to need extra-special care to survive in the ground if you plant it during the warmest months. It will be putting out root growth slowly, and you'll need to water it as if it were still in a container—sometimes twice a day during extreme heat. If you don't keep up with the watering, so that the plant continually wilts during the course of the hot spell, it will be more susceptible to pest infestation and disease attacks.

Likewise, it's tempting to buy the first annuals of the year just as soon as they come into the nursery. But if you plant earlier than is advised, you'll need to protect the transplants from frost damage and cold soil. Even if you are successful and the cold doesn't kill them outright, they will be more stressed and therefore susceptible to molds and other soil-borne diseases.

These examples remind us that in the garden there really is a season for almost everything. When you take on a plant outside its season, you're more likely to have difficulties.

PROTECTING YOUR PLANTS

Once in place, plants are vulnerable to damage from humans—who may accidentally injure them or just provide inadequate care—and from animals.

Avoiding human damage. Plants can be damaged as you work in the garden, making them more susceptible to pests and disease infestations.

Lawns. Lawns can require the greatest amounts of fertilizers and pesticides of any plant type in the yard. Keeping your lawn healthy will mean that you can reduce the need for heavy and frequent applications of these products.

Mowing a lawn too often and/or keeping it too short are the most common mistakes in lawn care. Grass that has been mowed too short can't produce sufficient nutrients to sustain root growth, and the lawn becomes more susceptible to disease or weed infestation. Only the top third of the grass blades should be removed during mowing, and it is this factor, not the calendar, that should drive the schedule for mowing (see page 44).

Mowing grass at any time shocks the grass plant to some extent, but it's particularly vulnerable under drought conditions, in summer heat, or when it's growing slowly due to cold. Under those conditions, take extra care to make sure that you don't mow too often or too low.

Don't rake up grass clippings. They're about 95 percent water, and when left on the lawn they rapidly decompose, returning useful organic matter and nutrients to the soil.

Pest Resistance Makes a Difference

Many fuchsias die from gall mite infestation (above, right). A few gall-mite–resistant hybrids, such as 'Campo Thilco' (above, left), are now available in nurseries.

CORRECT MOWING HEIGHT

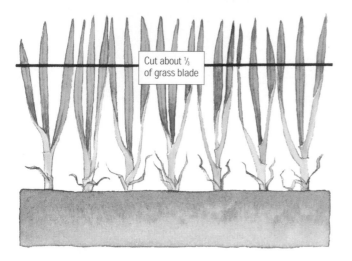

Cut about ⅓ of grass blade

If you have a lawn care service, it's especially important to require that it follow these guidelines. Make sure the mower is set high enough. You'll also want the service to agree to a flexible schedule that takes seasonal growth variations into account. And finally, ask that clippings be left on the lawn so they can decompose.

Trees. Lawn mowers and weed whips damage tree bark, making it easier for certain pests and diseases to penetrate into a tree's interior. When working with these tools near trees, take care to keep a proper distance. Trees can also be damaged if improperly pruned. Not only do such cuts make it easier for pests and diseases to enter but they can also compromise the structural integrity of the tree.

Removing and replacing a damaged tree is costly, and its loss also changes the environment of the surrounding garden area—plants under or near the tree have come to rely on it for shelter from wind and sun. If there's a large tree in your garden that needs attention, or if you aren't comfortable with your pruning skills, enlist the help of a certified arborist to care for it.

Avoiding animal damage. Sometimes the best—or only—way to keep animals and birds out of the garden is to construct barriers of various types.

Ground-level fences, if they're constructed properly, will keep some animals away. In the case of deer, a fence may need to be as high as 7–9 feet. If one fence doesn't work, try building a second fence 4–5 feet from the first. Or add a horizontal extension. Protect young and tender trees from top to bottom with wire cages. Some people have had luck with automatic systems that turn on lights and/or spray water when the deer trip an alarm device. Others report success with encircling the garden with commercially available repellents that contain, among various ingredients, the urine of deer predators.

Gophers can be as difficult to keep out of the garden as deer. They damage plants by eating both roots and tops. Because gophers live in the ground, the only way to eliminate them is to place traps in their major tunnels. If that isn't possible, you can protect individual plants by lining a planting hole with aviary wire, or by constructing raised beds that are completely lined with the wire.

If rabbits are getting into your vegetables, one way you can keep them out is by installing cages over low-growing beds. However, you need to extend the cages down into the ground about 6 inches. Even then, be sure to check regularly to make sure that a rabbit hasn't tunneled under the wire.

Birds eat harmful insects, and for this reason, along with the decline of the songbird population in the West, you should protect the birds in your garden and not begrudge them food and shelter. On the other hand, at certain times you do want to protect fruit and vegetable crops from them. To protect fruit trees, enclose each tree with broad-mesh netting 2 or 3 weeks before the fruit matures. To protect beds of just-planted seeds and tender seedlings, spread

Temporary and Permanent Protection

For temporary protection from birds, cover persimmon trees with netting before the fruits ripen (below, left). Permanently protect plant roots from gopher damage by lining the sides and bottom of a raised bed with aviary wire (below).

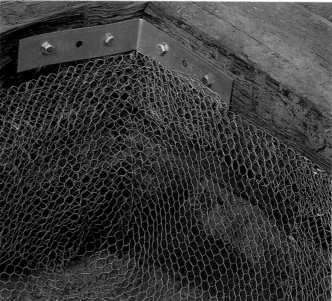

ATTRACTING BENEFICIAL INSECTS

The following plants will draw beneficial insects to your garden and hold down populations of undesirable insects.

Annuals

Aegopodium podagraria. Bishop's weed. Low-growing, 6-inch-tall plant similar to Queen Anne's lace; blooms April to October. Attracts: parasitoid wasps, pirate bugs, syrphid flies.

Agrostemma. Corn cockle. Wispy, 2–3-foot plants with pink cuplike flowers; blooms November through April where winters are mild, May to August elsewhere. Attracts: ladybugs, parasitoid wasps.

Coriandrum sativum. Coriander. Small white flowers on fine-textured, 12–15-inch plant; blooms May and June. Attracts: parasitoid wasps, pirate bugs.

Cosmos bipinnatus. Cosmos. White works best; 1–4-foot fernlike foliage; blooms April to November. Attracts: insidious flower bugs, lacewings, ladybugs.

Layia platyglossa. Tidytips. Yellow-and-white flowers on plants 5–16-inches tall; blooms March to August. Attracts: parasitoid wasps, pirate bugs.

Lobularia maritima. Sweet alyssum. Tiny, white to purple flowers on 6–8-inch plants; blooms all year in mild-winter areas. Attracts: lacewings, parasitoid wasps, pirate bugs.

Nemophila menziesii. Baby blue eyes. Blue flowers on plants 6–10 inches tall; blooms March to May. Attracts: parasitoid wasps, pirate bugs.

Perennials

Achillea. Yarrow. Pink, yellow, red, lavender, and white flowers on plants ranging from a few inches to 3 feet tall; blooms April to September. Attracts: ladybugs, damsel bugs, big-eyed bugs, parasitoid wasps.

Coreopsis sp. Coreopsis. Yellow, orange, and maroon flowers on 1–3-foot plants; blooms May to September. Attracts: lacewings, ladybugs, parasitoid wasps.

Eriogonum. Buckwheat. White, yellow, pink, and rose flowers on 1–4-foot plants; blooms May to October or later. Attracts: pirate bugs.

Foeniculum vulgare. Common fennel. Soft, fernlike foliage and yellow, flat flower clusters on 3–5-foot plants; blooms April to November. Attracts: lacewings, ladybugs, paper wasps, soldier bugs.

Lychnis coronaria. Crown-pink. Soft, gray foliage on 2-foot plants; magenta, pink, and white flowers; blooms April to August. Attracts: parasitoid wasps.

Ruta graveolens. Rue. Blue-gray foliage and small yellow flowers on 2–3-foot plants; blooms in early summer. Attracts: mud wasps, parasitoid wasps, potter wasps.

Tanacetum vulgare. Tansy. Yellow flowers and fernlike foliage on 2–3-foot plants; blooms June and July. Attracts: lacewings, ladybugs, parasitoid wasps, pirate bugs.

Daisy and pink family members attract beneficials to this flower bed.

chicken wire or floating row covers over them for 4 to 6 weeks, or until the stems become sturdy and leaves and stems are less succulent. You can also construct portable row protectors using a hoop or a triangle made with scrap lumber for a frame, covered with cheesecloth or chicken wire. If you use cheesecloth or similar fabric that lets in light, you'll be able to repel certain insects as well. Gardeners in warm-climate zones should remove the covers as the weather turns warm. Even covers made from very lightweight and porous material will begin to trap heat as the temperature rises.

Squirrels can be major pests in the urban garden, especially if you're putting out food for birds. There are bird feeder designs that work fairly well to keep out all but the most persistent squirrels. If squirrels are burying nuts in your container plants—a favorite

storage space—try using small red-lava rock as a mulch. Its coarse surface acts as a deterrent.

Using plants to combat problems. "Companion planting" is a concept that calls for planting two kinds of plants in a bed to discourage insects from attacking one of the two. The most common example, and the one for which there is scientific evidence proving its effectiveness, is planting marigolds in the vegetable garden. Certain soil-living nematodes attack the roots of popular vegetables, including carrots, cucumbers, melons, and tomatoes. Marigold roots—especially the French dwarf varieties such as 'Tangerine', 'Queen Sophia', 'Happy Days', and 'Goldie'—secrete a substance that kills the nematodes. To be effective, though, the marigolds must be planted in thick rows *throughout* the bed. It isn't enough to just line its exterior edge. One problem with this method is that by the time you plant enough marigolds to kill the nematodes, there often isn't much space left for the vegetables. There have been some reports that the marigold toxins may harm other plants. You may

Marigold Allies: Myth or Reality?

Some people think marigolds help keep vegetable gardens healthy. Success has been documented only with French dwarf marigolds such as 'Queen Sophia' (far left) and 'Happy Days' (left). Planting them may be more trouble than it's worth.

want to experiment with a small bed of marigolds interplanted with a test vegetable.

You can also protect your garden by including flowering plants to attract beneficial insects, which eat other insects that wreak havoc in the garden. Beneficials need shelter and some pollen and nectar in addition to their insect diet. The kind of plants they prefer are those with small and/or shallow flowers (see page 45). Among their favorites are some of the easiest plants to grow, including cosmos *(Cosmos bipinnatus)* and sweet alyssum *(Lobularia maritima)*. As a general rule, choose flowering plants from the carrot *(Apiaceae)*, daisy *(Asteraceae)*, and pink *(Caryophyllaceae)* families to attract beneficials.

CREATING HABITATS

For years, the garden has been envisioned as a landscape that includes wide expanses of lawn, closely trimmed shrubs, ornamental trees, and a plot in the rear for annual vegetable and flower beds. While many gardens still follow this model, it has probably been most often challenged in the West. For example, the Sonoran Desert areas of the Southwest, with their hot weather and particular soil types, caused gardeners to rethink garden ideals based on eastern United States or European models. And even in areas of the West where traditional models worked most of the time, recent drought years have caused many to reconsider how to best develop a garden in this region.

INCLUDING NATIVES IN YOUR GARDEN

The western landscape has contributed hundreds of trees, shrubs, flowers, and bulbs to the gardening world. Lewis and Clark and other early explorers described the varied flora of this region. Subsequent collectors, such as David Douglas, took many seeds and cuttings back to England for conservatory collections. Yet in our own gardens, we often eschew natives in favor of plants from either Europe or the eastern United States.

Because they're at home, many native plants are less susceptible to disease and pests. Natives from the acid and somewhat sandy soils of the Pacific Northwest thrive in home gardens that share that soil type and climate. Natives from warmer-climate areas grow, flower, and seed from late fall to early summer—times when most of the rain falls in those areas. They're least bothered by pests and diseases and, once established, require little extra summer water.

Plant sales at local botanic gardens, college horticultural programs, and native plant societies are excellent sources for native plants. Because of their recent rise in popularity, more are being grown commercially throughout the West and are becoming available in local retail nurseries as well.

These attractive, problem-free gardens in Arizona (above, right), California (below, right), and Idaho (below) are composed entirely of native plants.

Homes for Your Fine Feathered Friends

The chickadee house (top) and wren house (right) were built to suit the birds' preferences. The wren house has a 1⅛-inch entry hole, just the right size, and a short chain to minimize swinging. The chickadee house mimics the birds' favored hollow-conifer nesting location. A western bluebird (bottom) feeds an insect to one of its young in a simple yet practical birdhouse.

Throughout western gardens, the amount of lawn is decreasing, and gardeners are using land to grow what they like—you'll even see vegetable gardens in the front yard. In general, a more relaxed and natural style is evolving that features plants that thrive in local climates.

An extension of this approach is the notion of the habitat. Simply put, a habitat is an area that includes food, shelter, and water for the creatures that live in it. Whether you garden on a multi-acre parcel or on an apartment deck, including these three elements is essential to attracting beneficial birds, animals, insects, spiders, and their relatives and approximating the type of balance found in nature. You might follow this approach because it keeps your own garden free of many pests and diseases. Or you might do so because you're concerned about declining populations of birds and other creatures once so abundant throughout the West and, in fact, the entire United States.

Shelter in the garden habitat takes several forms. Dense trees and shrubs provide a safe abode for birds. Among these plants, birds can escape predators, find protection from wind and rain, and have a safe place to construct nests. (Make sure your garden includes some trees and shrubs that have leaves year-round.) Shelter may also be an overturned pot that provides a home for a toad. Or it may mean a pile of leaves for overwintering caterpillars, ensuring butterflies next year.

Diverse plantings that offer a wide variety of nectar and seed sources provide food for birds and beneficial creatures that eat pests. And although some beneficials will be eaten by larger predators, in time a balance evolves that keeps your garden healthy. In mild areas of the West, gardeners include flowering plants for hummingbirds all year. In colder areas, suet and seeds are set out for wintering birds.

Plants that support local habitats aren't always easily found. Large shrubs for background planting and some flowering plants can be purchased at local native plant sales, but smaller and less showy plants and native grasses can be harder to locate. Some specialty growers are propagating a variety of trees, shrubs, and grasses for major restoration projects—some as dramatic as the Glacier Point area of Yosemite National Park, others as mundane as plants near new freeway interchanges. Seeds and plants of this type are now finding their way into specialty mail-order catalogs and retail nurseries that feature local natives. You can also check with local chapters of the Audubon Society and ecology centers to find sources for seeds and plants. You may be able to find the very plants that were in the ground before your subdivision or town was built.

Water in the garden can be as simple as a pond in a half wine barrel or a saucer in a corner for insects. Birds are attracted to running water, such as that provided by fountains. They don't have to be elaborate; try wild-bird supply stores for a variety of simple types.

BE PATIENT

Gardening is popular for many reasons. One is its offer of peaceful, focused, uncluttered solitude. Get in the habit of spending a few minutes in your garden each day with no set purpose except to enjoy it and check its progress.

If you see a few harmful insects or some leaves with holes in them, make a mental note to check another day. Many times, if you leave matters alone, a predator will come along and eat the problem insects.

It may take a while to establish a natural balance, but if you're willing to keep a close eye on matters and take preventive steps, there's a good chance your garden will rarely need pesticides to keep it healthy.

STRIKING A BALANCE

Even with the best planning, insect infestations, diseases, and weeds will find their way into your garden. Here's an overview of recommended methods for managing them. The commonsense approach starts with practices that pose no threat to you or the environment, then moves on to the judicious use of pesticides. The information that follows includes advice on safety and explanations of the wording on pesticide labels, as well as guidelines for choosing between pesticide types and for applying them according to label directions.

FIRST LINE OF DEFENSE

Gardeners have been devising ways to manage pests, diseases, and weeds for as long as there have been gardens. Practices throughout the centuries have emphasized the same principles we follow today: keep plants healthy through the use of fertilizers and mulch, weed frequently, and keep pests away from plants by using barriers. The interior courtyard garden in medieval cloisters was a serene and pleasant setting, but it was also practical—it kept rabbits and deer out of the valuable medicinal herbs that were grown by monks.

Deerproof Cloister

This modern-day interpretation of the classic Spanish home with an interior courtyard serves a practical purpose: it protects the owners' rose collection from the hungry deer that roam nearby.

From early times, gardeners and farmers observed nature and saw that certain insects and other predators controlled pests. They also devised ways to encourage these allies to keep crops healthy. As far back as A.D. 300, for instance, the Chinese established colonies of predatory ants in citrus orchards to control caterpillars and tree-boring insects.

Today, western gardeners benefit from the wisdom of gardening practices developed throughout the centuries, as well as from scientific breakthroughs from modern laboratories. Taken together, these sources provide methods for managing many problems without the need for pesticides.

It's a jungle out there. Your garden is filled with natural predators—in fact, just about everything seems to be busy eating something else. The trick is to find those creatures that eat the pests that eat your plants. Make them your partners, and you'll be able to eliminate many problems. Shrews eat several times their body weight each day as they scurry through the garden. Spiders trap insects in their webs and attack them on the ground, and millions of tiny wasps spend each day busily laying eggs inside the bodies of unsuspecting caterpillars and aphids, killing them in the process.

You should be encouraging these unpaid and unsung partners in the battle to maintain a healthy equilibrium in your garden, and you can do so in a variety of ways. One of the tenets of Integrated Pest Management (IPM), the commonsense approach to pest management, is to use pesticides rarely and as a last resort. Although there

GLOSSARY

Beneficial. Any creature that helps control pests that cause damage to garden plants or agricultural crops is a beneficial. The list includes lizards, snakes, birds, bats, spiders, insects, and many others.

Biological control. A living organism—most commonly an insect, but sometimes a bacterium—introduced into the garden or farm as a method to control unwanted creatures. For example, trichogramma wasps are introduced to lay eggs inside corn earworm eggs and kill those pests before they can hatch. Many biological-control insects may occur naturally in the environment; when used as a control, they're most often introduced in large numbers as a temporary measure to manage a pest infestation.

Parasitoid. Organisms that live on or inside a pest, feeding on a single host for sustenance and causing it to die. Sometimes parasitoids are called parasites, which isn't accurate: A parasite coexists with its host, and while it may weaken and eventually kill it, both thrive for an indeterminate time. A parasitoid, on the other hand, kills its host almost immediately and consumes the corpse while maturing. Most parasitoid insects are dependent on a specific type of pest, are very tiny, and are rarely noticed by humans.

Pest. Any organism that causes specific damage to a garden or a food crop. This includes mammals, insects, and birds, as well as diseases like bacteria, fungi, and viruses. It also includes weeds. Sometimes a creature may be labeled as both beneficial and pest. Birds, for example, are valued for their overall importance to the environment as well as their consumption of unwanted insects and their service as pollinators. Yet they can become pests if they eat fruit or vegetable crops.

Pheromone. A chemical naturally existing within insects (and other creatures) that regulates behavior. Some pheromones signal insects to the location of a food source; others are important in the mating process, attracting males to receptive females. Scientists have duplicated certain pheromones in the laboratory, and these have become key elements in an Integrated Pest Management approach to pest control. Pheromones are added to boxes or other devices that draw pests away from a fruit or vegetable crop to traps, where they die. In addition, pheromones play an important role in monitoring: experts can count the number of pests attracted to a pheromone source in a given time period to help determine the severity of an infestation and the timing of introducing control procedures.

Predator. A creature that feeds on other animals as at least part of its regular diet. The category includes a wide variety of creatures, such as snakes, birds, bats, and many insects. In the context of pest management, "predator" is most often a positive term, referring to a creature that eats or kills a pest we want to eliminate or reduce. The term may bring to mind a large creature, like an eagle or mountain lion, but it may also be a small insect, such as a predatory wasp. In the case of creatures that prey on insects, the terms "predator" and "beneficial" are both used.

---

are many good reasons for not using pesticides indiscriminately, one of the best is to prevent killing the very allies that help keep your garden healthy. So don't use a pesticide unless there's no other recourse, and when you do use one, confine its application to only the infested plant. Curb the impulse to spray large sections of the garden "just for good measure."

Natural predators won't come to your garden if it doesn't provide food, shelter, and water. The small wasps that lay their eggs in caterpillars feed from flower nectar. Because they're so small, they prefer plants with tiny flowers, such as fennel or the widely used herb coriander. The popular perennial yarrow, with its many tiny flowers clustered across a wide, flat surface, is another flowering plant that feeds many tiny insects. Grow such plants, and insect allies will be likely to stop at your garden and, once there, repay your hospitality by laying their eggs in the pests you want to reduce. Good choices are plants from the daisy family (*Asteraceae*) and the carrot family (*Apiaceae*). If you aren't sure which plants are included in these families, a good general rule is to look for plants with tiny flowers, or ones whose flowers are flat. Some mailorder suppliers package seeds specifically to appeal to the tiny beneficials.

The jungle analogy isn't a bad one, for in a jungle, plants are lush and thick and grow at many heights. Such a setting provides an excellent habitat for the natural predators you want to attract. If your garden is mostly flat, with just a few clipped bushes here and there, it isn't going to become a home for natural predators.

Masses of hibernating ladybugs rest on a mountain pine.

Some of the larger creatures that can help manage pests include bats, birds, lizards, frogs, snakes, and toads—recognizable, if rarely seen, allies. It's harder to recognize many of the insects and their cousins because they are small and rapidly fly or run away. One gardener, hoping for parasitoid wasps to help manage the whitefly population, was sure she had none. She went so far as to have an expert examine her garden, and sure enough, the expert found healthy colonies of the tiny wasps. The gardener thought she was looking for something as large as a bumblebee.

In the case of beetles, weevils, and true bugs, it's not always easy to tell the beneficials from the harmfuls. Check the "Encyclopedia of Damaging and Beneficial Creatures" (see page 148) for help in distinguishing the creatures you want to attract.

Ladybugs. Stand in a checkout line in almost any garden or nursery center in the West on a spring day, and you'll see packages of ladybugs for sale (we commonly call these insects ladybugs, but as members of the beetle order, they are also called ladybird beetles). Since ladybugs consume many unwanted pests, it seems to make sense to buy a package or two and release them in your garden, but some ecologists suggest you reconsider. They note that we don't know the long-term effects of removing them from their natural habitat during the winter dormant stage (in California, for example, they come from the Sierra Nevada range). Also, the multicolored Asian ladybug is now being sold commercially, and we don't know the effect it will have on our native ladybug populations.

THE COOPERATIVE EXTENSION SERVICE

Cooperative extension offices have been helping gardeners and farmers throughout the country since 1914. That was the year Congress passed the Smith-Lever Act, an agreement by which colleges and universities would receive funding and resources in exchange for creating programs for local residents in the areas of horticulture, nutrition, and natural- and human-resource development programs.

You may have benefited from the cooperative extension service without having any direct contact with it; its 59 agricultural research stations have led to improved food-crop production throughout the United States, and today its agents and scientists are among the leaders in Integrated Pest Management (IPM) approaches to healthier farms and gardens.

Gardeners and farmers have come to depend on written brochures and in-person information provided by extension agents at the county level, knowing them to be sources of objective and straightforward information. While each office takes advantage of the collective national knowledge and research, it primarily focuses on the local area and provides information geared to regions that are state- and county-wide in size. All offices can offer advice on a host of topics familiar to gardeners in any location: lawn care, mulches, backyard composting, and so forth. But in addition, they provide specialized materials. If you're in New Mexico, for example, you can receive pamphlets such as "Fertilizer Guide for New Mexico," "Growing Chiles in New Mexico," "Nutritional Analysis of New Mexico Blue Corn," "Poinsettias: Year after Year," and "Growing Pistachios in New Mexico."

If you need help identifying a pest, disease, or weed, your local cooperative extension office is a place to seek it. It is the primary public-service outreach system of the state university or college and bases its information and advice on the latest knowledge and research from these schools. The agents can tell you about the natural beneficials in your area and whether any special beneficials have been introduced to help manage local problems. They are experts in disease-resistant plants for local areas and are also knowledgeable about local soil conditions and good choices for mulches and amendments.

In 1972, a busy cooperative extension agent in Snohomish County, Washington, hard-pressed to keep up with the demands on his time from the many urban "farmers" in his jurisdiction, came up with the idea of trained volunteer assistants. From this modest beginning, the Master Gardener program was born. Today, the Master Gardeners number more than 60,000 individuals throughout the country. They receive training in botany, soil science, plant propagation, Integrated Pest Management, pesticide and herbicide use, vegetable and ornamental gardening, plant and weed identification, composting, pruning, and water conservation. Once trained, they repay their education by staffing telephone hot lines and by answering questions in person at garden shows and other events. The Master Gardeners also plant demonstration gardens and participate in special programs designed to bring gardening to all parts of the population.

You can find your local cooperative extension office in the "Resource Directory" (see page 304) or in the county government listings of your phone book.

Most often ladybugs won't stay in your garden—they're just as likely to fly into one of your neighbors' and eat their whiteflies, scales, mealybugs, or potato beetles. You may be able to entice ladybugs to remain, however, if your garden provides a suitable habitat for them, with lush and varied plantings and a water source. If you release them in the evening, they may be more likely to acclimate during their nonflying hours. But even with such measures, few stay. Most often the reason is that they aren't at a metabolic stage where they're ready to feed and lay eggs. (A few specialty mail-order suppliers precondition ladybugs and ship them when they are more likely to remain where they're released.)

It may be that the best way to have ladybugs in your garden is to provide a habitat that will attract and sustain them naturally. If you do choose to purchase ladybugs, monitor them carefully after release. If none remain, this may be a purchase you don't want to repeat in the future.

The ethereal lacewing. With transparent wings as long as its body, the lacewing is one of the more beautiful insects in the garden. (Some believe that the folkloric fairy is modeled after a lacewing.) Adults of the larger types are about ½ inch in length and a delicate green all over—they're sometimes hard to see when motionless on a plant stem or leaf. The smaller ones have the same structure but are brown. Adult lacewings feed on plant nectar and pollen. It's while they're in their larval stage that they consume many garden pests, such as aphids, mealybugs, scale, leafhopper nymphs, whiteflies, small caterpillars, and spider mites, to name a few. The larva looks something like a miniature alligator, with pincerlike mouth parts that suck the fluids from insects and their eggs.

Spreading lacewing eggs by hand

Purchased lacewings are most often shipped as eggs, which you distribute on plants. The eggs soon enter the active larval stage and become adults in about one to three weeks. The commercially available lacewings are often used in the controlled environment of a greenhouse; if released in large numbers and on a staggered basis, they can eliminate a pest infestation that could otherwise ruin an entire crop. For the home garden, you might consider buying smaller numbers, such as 1,000 eggs per 900 square feet. To have natural numbers of lacewings on an ongoing basis, make sure that your garden contains flowering plants (of the types described on pages 45 and 49). The adults will feed in your garden, lay their eggs, and begin the natural process over again.

The lacewing's popularity is growing. However, as with all introduced beneficials, it's a good idea to check with your local cooperative extension office or with some other knowledgeable local source to determine whether lacewings are a good choice for your climate and overall environmental situation. It could be that lacewings might reduce the populations of other natural predators in your garden, for instance.

Beneficial Nematodes: Your Partners in Lawn Care

It's easy to apply beneficial nematodes with a watering can (far left). This lawn (left) is treated with nematode applications during the active growing season as part of its routine maintenance program.

Parasitic nematodes. Learning the differences between beneficial predators and pests is sometimes a confusing task. For example, there are both beneficial and destructive types of nematodes. Both are so small that you can barely see them without a magnifying lens of some sort. About the only difference between the two is what they eat. Beneficial nematodes kill a wide variety of pests that live in the ground or bore into plant trunks and stems. Destructive nematodes kill plants by eating their roots.

The beneficial nematodes are easy to add to the garden and have many excellent attributes that help you manage pest problems. They kill large numbers of pests that spend all or part of their lives in the soil. They've been especially helpful in controlling the larval form of root weevils that are particularly troublesome in western Washington and Oregon, causing problems with azaleas, rhododendrons, roses, viburnums, and strawberries. Other insect pests that can be controlled by nematodes include cutworms, cabbage root maggots, lawn grubs, turf webworms, peach tree borers, iris borers, and flea beetle larvae.

Mail-order suppliers and many garden centers sell beneficial nematodes in a juvenile, dormant state. You can apply them in several ways. One is to mix them with a soil extender, such as vermiculite, and work them either into the top few inches of soil or, if you are adding a new plant to the landscape, right at the root level. You can also soak them in water and apply with a watering can or hose sprayer—an especially valuable technique when introducing them into lawn that's infected with lawn grubs. And finally, you can make a concentrated tea by mixing them with a little water and applying the liquid directly, using a syringe, into cornstalks, squash stems, or other infested plants.

If you're applying nematodes to a lawn or other exposed soil area, make sure you have thoroughly mixed them with water or a soil extender before you use them. Apply nematodes in the late afternoon, as they are sensitive to sunlight and heat. Make sure the soil has been well watered first, and keep the treated areas moist for several weeks after application. The nematodes will remain active for an extended period of time. Some gardeners repeat nematode applications several times during a season, depending on the severity of a problem. Nematodes also can be used in the vegetable garden to manage various pests that feed on squash, carrots, and other edible crops.

As with all introduced beneficials, nematodes may upset the natural balance of predators in the garden. While nematodes eradicate

a wide variety of pests, they shouldn't be seen as a replacement for the good gardening techniques described on pages 34–47. Remember, too, that if you later treat your garden with a pesticide, it will kill the nematodes.

Parasitoid wasps. The parasitoid wasps that play a beneficial role are so small that you probably don't know if any are living in your garden or not. But if your garden is healthy and diverse, chances are that some of these tiny wasps are in residence. There are about 30 different types of parasitoid wasps that occur naturally in zones throughout the West, all of them beneficial. None of them sting humans.

One of these wasps, the *Encarsia formosa,* has been widely used to combat whiteflies. It has been highly successful in the greenhouse environment, where it can be contained and monitored. Public agencies have also introduced wasps throughout various western states to help manage the whitefly problem outside the greenhouse.

In one Northern California area several years ago, when whitefly infestation was especially severe, local nurseries posted temporary signs stating "Don't spray insecticides near whiteflies—beneficial wasps have been released by the county." In Southern California,

Airborne Pest Control

Tiny parasitoid wasps (right) lay their eggs on or inside various insects. As they hatch and mature, the young wasps consume their hosts (left). Since the host insects are often garden pests, parasitoid wasps are the gardener's valuable allies in pest management.

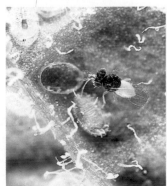

where a particularly destructive form of giant whitefly has been infesting avocados, bananas, citrus, and palms, a specific form of parasitoid wasp, collected from another locale, was released to control this pest.

Another type of beneficial parasitoid wasp is *Trichogramma*, several different species of which are sold commercially to control pests. One kind is aimed at general garden use *(T. pretiosum)*, and others *(T. platneri* or *T. minutum)* are specifically for tree crops on the West Coast.

The parasitoid wasps help manage pest populations by laying their own eggs inside the eggs or the metamorphosing form of the pests. As the wasps develop, they consume their host. For example, *T. pretiosum* lays its eggs inside the eggs of various butterflies and moths. When the eggs hatch, adult wasps emerge rather than caterpillars.

You may decide to purchase parasitoid wasps for your own garden. They are most often shipped in previously parasitized hosts, ready to hatch when you place them in the garden. Once hatched, they'll seek hosts in which they can lay eggs. Because the timing is critical, purchase them only when the pest you are targeting is getting ready to lay eggs.

And as with other beneficials, don't spray with any pesticides after the wasps are released, or they will be killed. As adults, they feed on nectar and pollen, so in addition it's important to grow small-blossomed flowers in the garden. Not only will these flowering plants sustain your wasps, but they'll also attract wasps that exist naturally in your area or that have been introduced into it by governmental agencies.

You'll find that suppliers offer many beneficial creatures to help you manage garden pests. No matter which one you buy, determine in advance whether you want to buy a few beneficials to "seed" your garden so they'll become part of the regular population, or whether you need a large number to manage a problem that is already out of control. If your intent is to help the beneficial find a place in your garden, make sure it has appropriate food to eat at all stages of life (such as flowering plants for adults and, for other stages, creatures that can be parasitized or eaten). Even with your best attempts, the beneficials may not last. When their food or host supply runs low, they tend to move on or die out.

Beneficials are an important element in managing the pests in your garden. With luck, you'll find that many live there naturally. At other times, purchasing them as pest control allies can reduce the need for pesticide.

Clean up and hand-pick. It's surprising how a little time and some simple cleanup chores reduce many problems to a point where they cause little damage.

Buy a hose nozzle that can be set to a sharp stream. Using that setting, blast aphids, mealybugs, lace bugs, spittlebugs, and other insects off plant surfaces. Once on the ground they either die or are consumed by predators. The key to success with this method is to do it on a regular basis and to thoroughly reach all surfaces, both tops and undersides. Water helps keep late-summer spider mites under control as well. These mites like dusty leaves and low humidity. The water blasts dust from plant leaves and helps raise humidity in the immediate area. You'll need to use this method daily to keep spider mites under control at the height of their season.

If you have an aphid and ant problem, the water treatment also helps by removing honeydew secretions on leaves, which often attract sooty molds. Mildew is carried by spores to newly emerging plant leaves. While you're using water to rid plants of insects, aim it at mildew-prone plants to wash off spores in the process.

Another tip from veteran gardeners is to regularly pick off diseased flowers and leaves and clean them up from the ground below the plant. Some diseases are more prevalent at the time of bloom, such as camellia blight. Others become more of a problem in late summer. One such problem is rust, which infects plants such as

Start with Simple Steps

Since camellia petal blight, shown at right, is more prevalent during blooming season, the best defense is to pick up all dropped petals and blossoms from the ground immediately. Sooty mold, like that found on this Carolina jessamine *(Gelsemium sempervirens)* on the far right, can be minimized by cleansing the vine with a strong burst of water. The jet also removes the thrips, seen here, or aphids that often accompany the mold.

Temporary Measures For Temporary Problems

Temporary netting protects a vegetable garden from birds during a crucial stage (left). Flying insects are attracted to the yellow color of the cardboard, which is covered with a sticky material, trapping pests and keeping them off the tomato plants (center). Plastic cartons keep cutworms from reaching vegetable seedlings after transplanting (right).

hollyhocks and squash. Regularly pick off the rust-infected leaves to keep the disease under control. Do this and you'll stop the rust from infesting a whole plant, as well as neighboring plants.

Large predators such as tomato hornworms and snails can be picked from plants. Use gloves or tongs, and drop the pests into a container of water combined with a few drops of dishwashing detergent. Throw them in the trash after they've died. Hand-pick these types of predators on a daily basis when they're at their most prolific, and you'll be surprised to find that you can significantly reduce their numbers.

Barriers. If you have recurring problems with deer, rabbits, gophers, and the like, you'll want to construct permanent barriers, such as fences, before the growing season begins. But other barriers can be put up at a moment's notice, just as soon as you find a pest causing a problem.

Copper banding around vegetable or flower beds is an effective way to keep snails and slugs from crawling into the bed and eating the plants (when the creature makes contact with the copper, a slight electrical discharge takes place, effectively "shocking" the snail or slug, which then hastily retreats). To be effective, the copper band must be at least 3 inches high. Make sure, too, that no plant leaves hang over the edge of the banding, making a bridge to the bed. While copper banding may initially be more expensive than other methods, it can be used again each season, proving cost-effective in the long run.

Some gardeners use diatomaceous earth to make a barrier around the edges of beds. This product is made up of skeletal remains of diatoms, single-celled marine algae. When soft-bodied insects travel through it, the sharp skeletal remains lacerate their bodies, causing the insects to dehydrate and eventually die. If you're going to use this product, you must surround the entire bed with a 3–4-inch strip. Be aware, too, that it won't keep insects from passing over if it's wet, nor will it hinder insects with hard-shelled bodies. It doesn't discriminate, either, and may kill beneficial insects as well as pests. One cautionary note: don't use the product form that's intended for swimming pools; it consists of smooth-edged particles and can be harmful to humans and animals. Instead, buy only the form that's clearly labeled for agricultural and garden use.

To prevent crawling pests from invading vines and fruit and shade trees, you can encircle plant trunks with sticky barriers. These paper or cardboard strips are coated with materials like cas-

tor oil, natural gum resins, and vegetable wax. Insects such as cankerworms, gypsy moth caterpillars, climbing cutworms, and ants cannot make it across the sticky surface.

You can buy the same product in a spray form. Use it to coat yellow cardboard squares and hang them from tree or shrub branches. Because they also trap and kill beneficial flying predators, don't use them indiscriminately, but instead place them next to an infested plant. This material is very sticky; employ it with care if children or pets are in the vicinity and likely to bump into it. Use mineral spirits or cleaning solvent to remove it.

Collars made from paper cups and juice cartons can serve as barriers to protect newly transplanted seedlings. You can also wrap mesh cylinders around young tree trunks to deter gnawing animals, drape mesh over berry vines and fruiting trees, or place row covers over vegetables to keep out birds and other flying creatures.

Ways to knock out weeds. There's just no easy way around it: you must keep weeds under control, or they're likely to take over your garden. Once weeds are established, even herbicides may not solve the problem. Whether you're battling dandelions in the Pacific Northwest or oxalis in California, weeds are the bane of a gardener's existence.

If you're putting in a new lawn or a new garden bed, consider killing weed seeds before they even germinate. Through a process called soil solarization, you can significantly reduce weed problems. Not only will this process kill weed seeds, it will also kill various disease organisms that originate in the soil and later infect

Tip: While solarization is an effective way to kill many weeds and some bacteria and fungi, it isn't always possible to use this method in all affected beds. In some cases, such as the Texas root rot that's a problem in the semiarid and arid Southwest, solarization won't kill the rot. Instead, try adding a rich compost mixture to the soil. The material in the compost decomposes rapidly and can crowd out the fungus.

plants. These include bacteria that cause molds, the spores that cause rust, and fungi that cause problems such as fusarium and verticillium wilt. Soil solarization works if you have a four- to eight-week stretch of warm weather during a dry season. You simply cover the soil with clear plastic sheeting. The plastic radiates heat,

SOLARIZING SOIL TO KILL WEEDS AND DISEASES

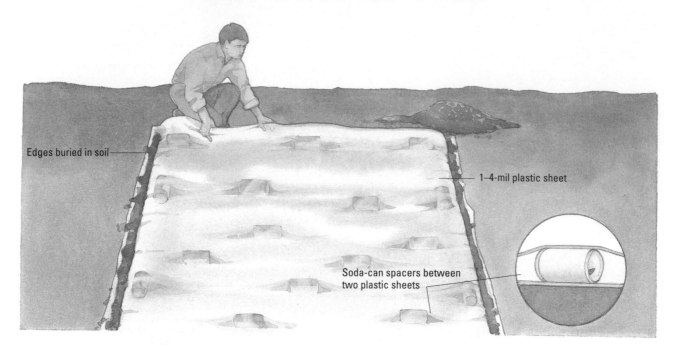

Edges buried in soil

1–4-mil plastic sheet

Soda-can spacers between two plastic sheets

raising the temperature enough to kill most weeds (unfortunately, Bermuda grass and red clover usually survive this process). Earthworms aren't harmed; they simply tunnel deeper into the soil.

Here's how to solarize soil.

- Pick an area that's at least 2 feet wide (it's hard to retain the heat in a bed narrower than this). Clean the bed of all weeds and rocks; if you plan to include an irrigation system, install it now. Thoroughly wet the soil to a depth of 8–12 inches.
- Buy enough 1–4-mil clear plastic to cover the bed twice. Place the first layer of plastic on the ground. Place the second layer over the first, raising it a few inches by placing bricks or cans between the layers. Leave enough plastic around the edges so you can bury it a couple of inches in the soil.
- Wait four to eight weeks before removing the plastic—and now you're ready to plant.

You probably can't dig up everything in your garden and solarize all the soil. Other areas still require traditional methods such as hoeing and digging out young weeds before they become established. It's especially critical to remove them before they flower and disperse more seeds into your garden.

Mulching areas between plants makes it harder for many weeds to grow after germination. Those few that do work their way through the mulch can usually be pulled out more easily than those that grow in unmulched areas. To help keep weeds from growing through a mulch, first lay down sheets of landscape fabric—its meshlike quality lets the soil breath and water penetrate, but few weeds can grow through it.

In some areas it seems that nothing other than an herbicide will dislodge weeds. Some grow between concrete paving and brick paths or come up throughout a gravel driveway. In other situations, a garden or orchard may simply be too large for hand-weeding. In cases such as these, two methods using heat can help you eradicate weeds without using an herbicide.

When heated to a high enough temperature, weeds rapidly dehydrate and die because the water in the cells boils, rupturing the cell membranes and escaping. You can make this happen by pouring boiling water on the weeds—a method you may find effective in getting rid of weeds in walks and pathways that are close to your house. Simply boil water in a teakettle and slowly pour it over each weed for a few seconds.

A more efficient method, and one that can be used over a wide area, is to use a flamer, available from farm and garden suppliers. This tool is a handheld rod with a propane-generated flame at the end; it is similar to devices sold to defrost frozen water pipes. You don't actually burn the weed but heat it. Two seconds of flame are enough to boil the liquid inside the weed.

Hot Ideas for Killing Weeds

Boiling-hot water from a tea kettle kills weeds growing through cracks and pavers (left). A propane-powered flamer doesn't burn weeds; it heats them until their cells burst (right). Take care in using a flamer in dry, fire-prone areas.

Traps. You can choose from a variety of traps, ranging from small cardboard boxes that attract tiny insects to larger devices that trap small mammals or trap and kill them.

You can attract insects to a trap by coating it with a substance called a *pheromone*. Pheromones are secreted chemicals that help regulate behavior of insects and other creatures. Insect traps most frequently contain sex pheromones that attract male insects. Once inside the trap, they are captured by a sticky material or a funnel opening that prevents their escape. Since pheromones are insect specific, they will be successful only with the particular insect causing the problem. The most common traps are those for black cutworms, cabbage loopers, codling moths, corn earworms, and peach tree borers. Such traps can be quite effective in agricultural settings and orchards, where a large number can be placed throughout the acreage. In the home garden, an individual trap or two will probably draw insects to your garden from all over the area, and not all will find their way into the trap. You're more likely to be successful if you coordinate your efforts with neighbors.

Traps that capture and kill gophers and moles are available from farm supply and garden sources. If you want to eliminate a small colony, such traps are the only practical method for doing so. If you live in a rural area, it probably isn't feasible to eliminate all gophers or moles. Instead you can line the bottoms and sides of garden beds with chicken wire to prevent gophers from burrowing into them.

Traps that capture other live animals, such as squirrels, should be used only if they are legal in your area. Finding locations where such animals can safely be released is an increasing problem; animal control agencies can advise you as to whether this practice is safe and legal.

Your kitchen as ally. Baking soda, soy sauce, crushed garlic, cinnamon oil, and other substances from the kitchen can attract pests to their death or keep them from landing on plants and eating tender leaves.

Three of the most troublesome pests in the western garden zones—the snail, the slug, and the earwig—can be attracted to food traps that capture or drown them. One type of trap contains a liquid that appeals to the snail or slug. Use a pie plate or saucer from a clay pot and sink it slightly below ground level, so that the mollusks can easily walk into the trap and drown. Gardeners share many recipes for what to fill the trap with; in most, yeast is an ingredient. Stale beer has been used by many.

Trapping snails and earwigs

Others mix yeast and water, along with various sweeteners such as molasses. These traps work very well for some; others report that they have had less success.

On the other hand, traps laced with soy sauce, beer, or vegetable oil have uniformly been reported as excellent lures for earwigs. Here's how to make an earwig trap: poke holes near the rim of an empty cottage-cheese container, add one of the recommended liquids, put the lid back on the container, and sink it into the ground so that the holes in the carton are at ground level. Remove the container when there are more drowned earwigs than there is liquid and toss it in the garbage.

Some gardeners say they can trap snails, slugs, and earwigs without help from the kitchen. Try putting out overturned clay pots at night and look for snails and slugs in them each morning. Or wrap moistened rolled newspapers with rubber bands and leave them out overnight. Dispose of the earwig-filled papers in sealed plastic bags daily.

You may want to experiment with sprays made from combinations of onions, garlic, hot peppers, or other strong foods. These are usually steeped in a little vegetable oil, then mixed with a small amount of dishwashing soap and diluted with water. If you experiment with these combinations, remember that too strong a mixture of soap can harm plant leaves. Any oil, including vegetable oil, can scorch a leaf in hot weather.

In general you don't want to add more than 2 teaspoons of soap, or 2 teaspoons of oil, per gallon of liquid to any recipe you devise. Such sprays may kill soft-bodied insects on contact, or coat the leaves with a scent that repels the insect from it. (Remember, though, that with any spray, you may be killing beneficial insects as well as pests. Just as with commercial insecticides, spray only the affected plant and only enough to reduce the number of pests to a manageable level.)

All plants contain natural toxins that repel certain pests. Knowing this, some gardeners have had success with concentrated sprays made from healthy plant leaves. Try mixing a bowlful with a little water in a blender or food processor, and strain. Add enough water so the mixture can be sprayed, and apply to the plants you want to protect. Most often this works best if you're spraying the same plant that your mixture came from, or closely related plants. (Designate a blender or food processor exclusively for garden use; don't use the same one that's used for food preparation.)

For all such recipes, check with your local cooperative extension office—the agents are likely to know of recipe combinations that have been found effective in your particular zone.

On plants susceptible to mildew, spraying leaves with plain water can wash off mildew spores before they attach to newly developing leaves. A baking-soda-and-water mixture sometimes improves a plant's ability to resist infestation from mildew spores. Add 2 teaspoons of baking soda to 1 gallon of water and spray plants in the morning. Some rose gardeners report this is as effective as a commercial fungicide in keeping mildew on roses under control.

Sometimes none of these methods works and you decide to buy a commercial product to help manage a problem. The following section discusses why such products are regulated by governmental agencies and how to use them properly.

STRAIGHT TALK ON PESTICIDE SAFETY

Buying a pesticide can be a confusing experience. An array of these products lines the shelves at garden-supply and hardware stores. They all carry labels with directions in fine print, a variety of precautionary statements about hazards, and bold announcements that you will be a lawbreaker if you don't read all the directions and follow them correctly. Even relatively simple products, like insecticidal soaps, are covered by such labels and directions. Learning pesticide basics and understanding label content will help you choose an appropriate pesticide if a problem warrants the use of one.

Read the label! You must read a pesticide label thoroughly and use the product only as described on its label. This is common sense. It's also the law. If you don't mix and apply a pesticide exactly as directed, you may cause serious injury to yourself and others, or cause irreparable harm to the environment or creatures in it. Here are some tips to help you make sense of the scientific terms and small print found on pesticide labels.

Probably the most baffling thing you face in reading a label is figuring out its name. This is because each product carries several names. Some are regulated by scientific bodies, while others are trademarked by a manufacturer. What they have in common is that they are usually difficult to read or pronounce! Get in the habit of looking for a pesticide's *common name*. You'll find it included in the list of active ingredients (a part of the label that by law always appears on the front of a product). This common name is usually followed by the pesticide's chemical name. And while the chemical name may be required by law, it isn't something that you as a consumer need pay attention to. (Some naturally occurring pesticides, like pyrethrin, do not have a chemical name, so you'll find only the common names on the label.)

Here's an example. A pesticide offered by several manufacturers is acephate, one of several pesticides that kill insects. The chemical name for acephate is O,S-dimethyl acetylphosphor-amidothioate. Look on the active ingredients list, and you'll find it listed like this: "Acephate (O,S-dimethyl acetylphosphor-amidothioate)."

Sometimes the pesticide's trade name contains the common name; sometimes it doesn't. You may find a product named, in bold type and bright colors, "Such-and-so's acephate." Or it may have another name altogether, and the only way you know it's acephate is by reading the active ingredient list.

When you purchase a particular pesticide, frequently it's because you received some advice to do so—from the encyclopedia sections of this book, a cooperative extension agent, or another professional. Usually sources will recommend a pesticide by its common name; sometimes they'll mention a brand name as well: "Try a product containing acephate, like such-and-so." Be a smart consumer: always ask if what's being recommended is a common or a brand name, and make sure you always get a common name. This will help you comparison-shop for price, size, formulation,

READING A PESTICIDE LABEL

Precautionary statements: This section may start with the headline "Precautionary statements" or with a repeat of the *signal word* found on the front of the label. Information is customized for product type and its associated toxicity-level category. It tells you of known hazards to humans and domestic animals and to the environment.

First aid instructions: Indicates the immediate action required if the product is ingested or inhaled or comes into contact with the skin or eyes.

Directions for use: Indicates how much of the product to use, and how to mix and apply it.

Plants: Lists the plants that can safely be treated by the pesticide. If it can be used on food crops, also tells you how many days before harvest the product can be applied.

Note to physicians: Specifies the action a physician should take in the event the product is ingested or inhaled or comes into contact with the skin or eyes.

Controls: Lists the pests that the product is formulated to control.

Product name: Provides the pesticide's brand name, may include manufacturer's trade name, often includes marketing information that positions the product against its competitors and attracts the eye of potential buyer. Sometimes the pesticide's official common name is included as part of the brand name, especially if that name has become familiar to the public.

Active ingredients: Lists the common name of the pesticide. Learn to identify pesticides by their common names and look here first to find out exactly what is in the pesticide before purchasing it. The chemical name of the pesticide may also be included in this section.

Signal word: Look for words such as *Caution, Warning, Danger,* or *Poison.* These words signal the toxicity-level category associated with the pesticide. Additional information will be found on the back of the container, under the section called Precautionary statements.

Storage & disposal: Specifies how to safely store and dispose of the product.

Product code identification: Provides the number assigned to the product by the manufacturer and the Environmental Protection Agency (EPA) to identify it; use the number when contacting the manufacturer or EPA about the pesticide.

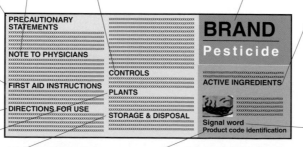

GLOSSARY

Chemical name. The chemical (or chemicals) included in each pesticide is named on its label. Chemical names are usually complex, multi-syllable words. The complexity of chemical names is one factor that makes pesticide label reading difficult. While chemical names are important to scientific and regulatory agencies, gardeners should look for a pesticide's common name for ease in recognizing it.

Common name. The common name of a pesticide is determined by a scientific body, and once designated it is required by law to be included on pesticide labels. Gardeners should ask for pesticide information and recommendations by common rather than trade name; since the chemical represented by a common name will be included in a number of products, having information on all of them will broaden the choice. The common names of pesticides are listed in the active ingredients lists on pesticide labels.

LD50. This term refers to the lethal dose (LD) of a chemical (measured in milligrams per kilogram of body weight [mg/kg]) that kills 50 percent of animals (50) that ingest it in a test situation. In relation to pesticides, the smaller the LD50 rating, the more toxic the pesticide, and vice versa. A pesticide product's LD50 rating is one key factor determining which signal word—*Caution, Warning, Danger,* or *Poison*—is applied to a pesticide. (There are additional LD tests and ratings that refer to toxicity when a pesticide is inhaled, comes in contact with the skin, or comes in contact with the eyes.)

Signal word. By law, the public must be informed of the toxicity levels associated with use of a particular pesticide. This information is conveyed by signal words on pesticide labels. The two signal words most frequently encountered by the general public are *Caution* and *Warning*—they will always be found on the front of the pesticide label. In general, pesticides labeled with the signal word *Caution* are less likely to be dangerous than those labeled *Warning*. A third signal word, *Danger,* refers primarily to products available to trained professionals, who apply them in controlled situations following precise regulations and directions. A fourth signal word, *Poison*—sometimes accompanied by a skull, or a skull and crossbones—indicates the greatest danger. There is a set of regulatory directions and laws specifically for poisons. Only a few of the pesticides that carry the *Poison* signal word are available to the public at large, usually products that kill mammal pests such as moles or gophers.

Toxicity category. Pesticides are categorized according to their toxicity. Category I = *Danger/Poison*. This is a highly toxic rating. If a skull and crossbones appears with the signal word, the pesticide is acutely toxic. Category II = *Warning*. This is a moderately toxic rating. Category III or IV = *Caution*. Category III is a slightly toxic rating, and Category IV, a relatively nontoxic rating. Products with a toxicity level lower than Category IV, or none at all, still may carry the *Caution* signal word because it may have some unwanted effects on some people under certain conditions. Insecticidal soap is one example, as it may cause some eye irritation. Another example is sulfur, a chemical used for centuries as a method for combating mildew on plants. Because it can cause an allergic skin reaction in some individuals or irritate the eyes, it also requires the *Caution* signal word on its label.

Trade name. Trade names are determined by manufacturers and are subject to various trademark and other legal requirements. Several trade names may be used to refer to the same pesticide, each registered by a different manufacturer. A trade name is usually boldly displayed on a pesticide label. Sometimes a product's common name is incorporated into a trade name. To the consumer, the greatest confusion lies in the difference between trade names and common names. Because trade names are associated with specific products, they may come and go as a company's product line changes.

and other factors so you can choose the best form of the pesticide for the problem you want to manage.

Here's an example. Imagine that a prized plant in your collection is hopelessly overrun by insect pests and you haven't been able to reduce their numbers through other methods. A professional inspects the plant and recommends a pesticide to you by its brand name rather than its common name. When you go to purchase the pesticide, you find this particular brand is sold in concentrated form and has enough in the container to cover a 20-acre farm. Rather than buy it, check the label for its common name, and then look for other brands with the same common name. The label should also say that it kills the pest infesting your plant. Chances are, you can find an appropriate product available in a 24-fluid-ounce spray bottle—just the right amount to control the pest in your yard, and it's already mixed.

Precautionary statements. Appearing on various areas of pesticide labels, and printed in type of different sizes and shapes, the terms *Caution* and *Warning* may seem to be just part of the manufacturer's standard wording, but in fact each one is defined legally and each has a specific meaning.

Caution and *Warning* are **signal words**—they signal to you the potential dangers involved in the use of a pesticide so labeled. While the two words may seem similar, the assignment of one or the other is the result of exacting tests required by governmental regulating bodies. Many factors are involved in choosing one pesticide over another, but in general those labeled with the *Caution* signal word usually present the least risk to you or the environment.

(The other signal words are *Danger* and *Poison*. Few products available to the general public carry these designations; those that do—for example, products that kill rats and gophers—may contain poisons such as strychnine.)

Signal words always appear on the front of a label. Each is accompanied by a brief description—for example: "WARNING: Causes eye and skin irritation." Often you will be directed to a side or back panel for further precautionary statements.

Risk assessment. Looking for the *Caution* or *Warning* signal words is one aspect of determining the impact of using a particular pesticide. However, there are several other elements that need to be examined before deciding on the use of a particular pesticide or

> **Tip:** Products labeled with the *Caution* signal word usually use verbs such as "may" or "might" in their descriptions. Those with the *Warning* signal word use "will" or "does," or the wording implies a definite effect rather than a possible one.

choosing one over another. The federal Environmental Protection Agency calls this decision-making process risk assessment. It suggests that consumers take five different factors into account. The factors are:

Assessing Pesticide Risk

Before deciding to use a pesticide, consider several factors. Left: Will it settle onto a fish pond? Center: Is there a possibility that it may find its way into streams or rivers? Bottom: Will children working or playing in the garden come into contact with a pesticide that hasn't dissipated?

Human safety. Toxicity categories (see page 57) measure immediate dangers to the person applying the pesticide and others at the site. They do not, however, measure long-term effects of repeated application.

Off-site movement. Pesticides may be carried beyond their initial site of application through air or water and affect other populations. For example, a pesticide may kill fish if it finds its way into streams, rivers, lakes, or ponds.

Soil contamination. Some pesticides have little effect on the soil at the time of application; others may persist for long periods.

Phytotoxicity. Referring to the poisoning of a plant, this assessment considers the trade-off between eliminating a pest and harming a plant.

Effectiveness. Some pesticides solve a problem with one application. They may rank higher in toxicity or other factors than alternate pesticide choices, yet since they are applied only once, they may be the most effective choice.

Mixing pesticides. It's a difficult chore to read on labels the fine print that tells how to mix and apply a pesticide. Experienced gardeners have come up with various ways to make this simpler, and you might try one of their suggestions. Keep a magnifying glass on the pesticide shelf to make it easier to read the label. Or, if you're deciding between two or more products made from the same common ingredients, you can base part of your buying decision on the readability of the label (some labels take the form of small "booklets" attached to the back of a product—this form allows for slightly larger type and better-organized directions). In the long run, what's probably most important is to set aside enough time for the task, so that you can carefully read and understand the directions involved.

Home gardeners make many mistakes in mixing pesticides, usually when they need to mix an amount whose proportions are not written on the label. Directions may say, "Mix 2 fluid ounces of product in 5 gallons of water." If your pesticide applicator holds just 40 ounces of liquid, you need to do some math. The measurements chart (above right) can help you determine the right amount. Once you've ascertained the amount needed for the applicator you're using, write that information on your own label and attach it to the purchased pesticide container.

MEASUREMENTS CHART

Directions on pesticide labels often call for mixing large amounts of a product. While 5-gallon—or even 1-gallon—amounts may be applicable in some situations, home gardeners generally need smaller amounts, for which there are no directions. This chart will help you calculate amounts for various quantities of pesticides.

1 gallon (gal.)	=	16 cups	=	8 pints	=	4 quarts	=	128 fluid ounces (fl. oz.)
1 quart (qt.)	=	4 cups	=	2 pints			=	32 fl. oz.
1 pint (pt.)	=	2 cups					=	16 fl. oz.
1 cup							=	8 fl. oz.
1 tablespoon	=	3 teaspoons					=	½ fl. oz.
1 teaspoon							=	⅙ fl. oz.

Don't, under any circumstances, mix an amount stronger than what's called for on the label. You may be tempted, thinking "If 2 tablespoons per gallon is called for, maybe I can kill those pests faster with a mixture of 4 tablespoons per gallon." Mixing in any way other than what's directed on the label is against the law, and you may cause irreversible harm by doing so. Although there aren't well-documented studies to back them up, officials believe a great deal of environmental damage is caused by home gardeners who measure and use products incorrectly.

Goggles and masks. Do a random survey of gardeners buying pesticides at a local garden center. Ask whether they follow the label directions that tell them how to protect their body when mixing and applying pesticides. You'll most likely get some hemming and haw-

ing, and more than a few admissions that they don't pay that much attention to these directions. Yet the greatest danger to the user is during the mixing and application process.

For most pesticides, you need to wear a buttoned, long-sleeved shirt; a pair of long pants; and closed shoes. Many gardeners keep a set of these with their gardening supplies. Once they've finished mixing and applying the pesticide, they run these clothes through the washer and dryer, separate from other garments, so they're ready for next time. It's always necessary to wear a pair of gloves; they keep any spills or residues (from spray or dust) from reaching your hands. Put a hat on your head as well. If you're using a Category II pesticide (identified by the *Warning* signal word on its label—see page 57), you may be instructed to wear goggles and a

JUST WHAT IS A PESTICIDE?

Have you tried to shop for a product that kills weeds and been told you need a pesticide? "No," you say, "I don't want to kill a pest, I want to kill a weed." Read on. The U.S. Environmental Protection Agency defines a pest as any living organism that causes damage or economic loss, or transmits or produces diseases. Thus, a pest can be an animal, an insect, a weed, or a host of micro-organisms. The entire spectrum of products that prevent, destroy, repel, or mitigate pests is thus called pesticides. Household products, such as mildew removers and pool chemicals account, for a major portion of pesticide sales.

Gardeners most often use four types of pesticides. They are insecticides (for controlling insects), fungicides (for killing fungi), herbicides (for killing weeds), and molluscicides (for killing snails and slugs). Here's a complete listing of the pesticide types, as defined by the EPA.

Biocides. Kill micro-organisms that reside in the soil or elsewhere and cause disease or other problems.

Fumigants. Produce gas or vapor intended to destroy insects, fungi, bacteria, or rodents; used to disinfect interiors of buildings, and soil before planting.

Fungicides. Kill fungi, many of which can infect and cause diseases in plants; examples of disease-causing fungi include rusts, mildews, blights, and molds).

Herbicides. Kill weeds and other plants that grow where they are considered undesirable.

Insecticides. Kill "bugs" and other insects.

Microbials. Micro-organisms that kill, inhibit, or outcompete pests, including insects or other micro-organisms.

Miticides. Kill mites that feed on plants and animals; also called acaricides.

Molluscicides. Kill snails and slugs.

Nematicides. Kill nematodes (microscopic, wormlike organisms that feed on plant roots).

Ovicides. Kill insect and mite eggs.

Repellents. Repel pests, including birds and insects (for example, mosquitoes, fleas, or ticks).

Rodenticides. Control mice and other rodent pests.

The term "pesticide" also includes related substances, such as the following:

Defoliants. Cause leaves or foliage to drop from a plant, usually to facilitate harvest.

Desiccants. Promote drying of living tissues such as plant tops or insects so that they die.

Insect growth regulators. Disrupt the action of natural insect hormones that control molting, maturity from pupal stage to adult, or other life processes.

Plant growth regulators. Substances (excluding fertilizers or other plant nutrients) that alter the expected growth, flowering, or reproduction rate of plants through chemical rather than physical action.

Protect Yourself When Applying Pesticides

Read pesticide labels carefully and follow them exactly. Many direct you to take extreme care that no liquid mists onto your skin or into your eyes, or is breathed into your lungs. This gardener, spraying fruit trees during winter dormancy, is wearing goggles and a breathing mask. Rubber gloves prevent liquid from seeping onto her hands. Long sleeves and a hat make her protection complete.

face mask. Follow all directions indicating the type of goggles or mask required. The proper protective gear is the only way to prevent the pesticide from reaching your eyes or lungs.

TOOLS OF THE TRADE

It makes sense to have proper tools for applying pesticides. If you have several applicators on hand, you'll be prepared to use the right type and right size for each problem as it arises. In addition to applicators, you'll also want to set aside measuring devices, gloves, masks, and goggles, and perhaps a set of clothes and shoes that you use only when applying pesticides.

Liquid pesticide applicators. The commonsense approach to pest control prescribes trying other methods before deciding to intervene with a pesticide. In keeping with that low-intervention guideline, you'll be trying to keep pesticide application to a minimum. One or two small applicators are probably all that you need. If your garden is large and contains, for example, a substantial fruit orchard, you may be applying larger amounts of a product like dormant oil. In these circumstances, having a large-capacity applicator, perhaps the type that fits on your back, is a good idea.

In addition to simple spray bottles, various small-size pressure pump applicators are available at garden centers and supply stores. They commonly range in size from 24 to 40 fluid ounces. Their pump mechanisms allow you to add pressure to the mixture, resulting in a fine spray that evenly coats an infested plant.

Remember to thoroughly clean any spray applicator right after using it. While most can be used with a variety of products, a separate applicator should be used just for applying herbicides. Herbicides are not easily rinsed from an applicator, and lingering traces can contaminate it, so it shouldn't be used with another pesticide for another purpose.

Don't attempt to improvise by using a spray bottle that isn't specially made for applying pesticides. Pesticide applicators are made of heavy-duty materials and come with printed directions that describe how to use them safely.

Increasingly, manufacturers are offering premixed pesticides in small-size applicators. They're more expensive than concentrated forms that you mix yourself, but they do eliminate the need to measure and mix (the part of the process where mistakes are easily made and dangerous spills take place). Premixed pesticides are available in 24-fluid-ounce applicators and under, making them a good choice for the small garden.

One product gaining popularity is the premixed herbicide, sold in containers that allow you to pressurize the contents and spray with an included wand. This can be a good tool for getting rid of solitary weeds in locations where they can't easily be pulled—especially if it keeps the original pesky weed from spreading to other areas and becoming a greater problem, perhaps suffocating vegetables or ornamentals. (With concentrated herbicides, it isn't worth it to get out the applicator, determine just how small a batch can be mixed, spray one weed, and then take the steps to safely dispose of the leftover herbicide.)

Until recently, the larger-capacity pressurized spray tanks were made of metal and were cumbersome and heavy. Newer plastic models weigh less and are easier to handle. Most hold 1–2 gallons of product. They, too, must be carefully rinsed after use. Because you need one hand to carry and position this type of tank, you may want to consider a backpack type that leaves both hands free. They are much easier to use and are very efficient, especially if you're spraying a large area. Home orchard gardeners often use these for dormant-season oil spraying.

Whether you're spraying one plant or an orchard, you must follow directions for wearing protective clothing and other devices (see page 59).

In all cases, when you spray, keep other people and pets away, cover fish ponds and water sources, and remove any items that people will use later (such as toys, utensils, or garden tools).

Pesticide dusters. Applying pesticides in dust form requires particularly strict adherence to label directions. Dust, more than any other pesticide form, finds its way into your lungs and onto your skin. While a few products, such as pure sulfur, rarely are associated with severe problems, many other dust-formulated pesticides carry Category II toxicity status and the *Warning* signal word on their label. That means you must wear goggles, a face mask, long-sleeves and pants, closed shoes, a hat, and gloves to cover every exposed body part. Dust applicators look a lot like the cartoon images you've seen—they consist of a small tank with a long nozzle that emits a fine dust spray as you turn a crank.

Scientists are concerned about the dangers associated with using dry pesticides; it's a good idea to avoid them if possible. If a dust form of a pesticide is recommended, check to see whether it's available in a liquid form, or if there's an alternative liquid pesticide that may manage the problem. If you do use the dust form, follow all precautions, and spray plants lightly with water first (pesticide dusts adhere better when the plant material is slightly wet).

Granule-spreading applicators. Pesticides applied to lawns are most often formulated as granules. You can spread them with a handheld applicator (turning a crank to distribute the pesticide as you walk), or use a broadcast spreader that applies a row of pesticide as you push a ground-level cart. Lawn pesticides are often combined with fertilizers (products with names that contain both the words "feed" and "weed" in their names and descriptions). While a fertilizer alone can be applied without wearing protective clothing and devices, many labels recommend wearing a mask so as not to inhale any fine powder associated with the granules. If a product also contains a pesticide, such as an herbicide for killing weeds, you must follow its recommended use directions exactly.

The biggest difficulty in using any of the granule-spreading applicators to apply pesticides to lawns is making sure you cover the area equally. With handheld devices, turn the crank at the same speed and walk at an even pace. The broadcast-spreader carts let you adjust settings to distribute material evenly. But even with these, keep to a uniform pace and make sure you don't leave gaps as you pace off "rows." Uneven application means the product may not reach all intended surfaces or may be deposited too heavily on others, causing the lawn to "burn" and die.

Storing pesticides and supplies. The only way to keep children away from pesticides is to store the pesticides under lock and key. Many people set up such locked storage in the garage or a gardening shed. Here are other items to store with or near them.

- Pesticide applicators of various sizes.
- Utensils for measuring teaspoons, tablespoons, liquid fluid ounces, cups, and various in-between sizes. Mark such utensils with a skull and crossbones so they won't find their way back into the kitchen.
- A blender used only for homemade repellent mixtures.
- A measurement conversion chart (like the one on page 59).
- A magnifying glass to aid in reading small print on pesticide containers.
- Eye goggles.
- Face and nose mask with replacement filters.
- Waterproof gloves.
- If there's room, store a hat, a long-sleeved shirt, long pants, and closed shoes that you use only for applying pesticides.

Mixing pesticides. Probably the most dangerous aspect of using a liquid pesticide that must be diluted is the actual measuring and mixing process. The concentrated liquid is much stronger than its diluted counterpart. You must take special care not to spill any on your hands or body. Also beware of accidentally knocking over a bottle of concentrated pesticide and spilling it where it will soak into the soil or flow into a street drain. Set aside a countertop near

A Gardener's Tools

Suppliers are making it easier for you to apply just the right amount of pesticide: large applicators made of lightweight but durable plastic are easier to carry, small applicators are handy for mixing and applying small amounts, and premixed solutions are simplest of all. To ensure accuracy, keep a set of measuring spoons with your applicators. Use them only for pesticides; don't mix them with your kitchen utensils.

No Dumping, Please!

Many urban storm drains empty into water sources populated by fish and other living creatures. Here, a savvy city cautions its citizens to refrain from dumping pesticides down the drain. Call your local water agency to find out how to safely dispose of pesticides in your area. Another precaution you can take: make sure no water runs into a drain from a just-fertilized lawn. Fertilizers rich in nitrogen are water contaminants.

your pesticide cabinet or shelf where you can safely measure pesticides. If that isn't possible and you have to do the mixing in the garden, make sure you use a stable, flat surface.

Safe disposal of pesticides. When you mix a liquid pesticide into an applicator spray bottle or tank, you need to use up the mixture right away. You must not leave it stored inside the bottle or tank. (Doing so is a violation of federal law; it may also corrode the container and clog the applicator nozzle.) Since a commonsense approach to pest management suggests spraying only an infected plant or a small area, you may find yourself with leftover pesticide, even when you mix just a small batch. Unfortunately, some gardeners pour the extra mixture down a sink or a storm drain. This can have devastating effects on the environment. *Don't ever pour a pesticide—either diluted or full strength—onto the ground or into a drain of any type (including the kitchen sink!).* And if you "use it up" by spraying it throughout the garden, you're likely to kill a great number of beneficial insects and upset the entire balance you've worked so hard to achieve.

Instead, call your local recycling center, garbage company, or water agency and find out where you can drop off pesticides. It may be the same place where you can take paint, car oil, and the like. These centers accept both undiluted pesticides in their original containers and diluted solutions that you've mixed. For diluted mixtures, carefully pour the leftover portion into a glass or plastic container with a secure lid. Write the product name (common name and brand name) and its dilution ratio on the container. A pesticide

in powder or granular form (such as the type applied to a lawn using a spreader) should be emptied into a heavy-duty garbage bag, sealed, and labeled.

Most pesticides have a shelf life of about two years, losing a certain percentage of potency after their shelf life expires. If there's ever any question whether the product is toxic enough to perform according to its directions, dispose of it and its container at the type of center mentioned above. (Although some toxicity is lost after a while, don't ever throw old pesticides into the trash.)

ESCALATE THE ATTACK

The "first line of defense" outlined on pages 48–56 is designed to manage problems without using pesticides. Pesticides are not the first choice because they upset the balance of beneficial insects in your garden, they aren't always effective, and they require strict adherence to procedures aimed at avoiding harm to yourself, other people, all sorts of creatures, and the environment.

Yet most gardeners sometimes feel it's appropriate to escalate the attack, so to speak. And you may be surprised, after reading directions for proper use, to find that some products have less impact on you or the environment than you imagined. Discussion of such products and their uses follows. They vary widely, from detergent-based soaps and biological controls for a specific insect to a low-toxicity pesticide derived from a flower. What they have in common is little risk—when properly used—and an ability to help manage a problem where other methods failed.

GLOSSARY

Broad-spectrum pesticide. A pesticide that kills a wide range of pest species, as opposed to one that kills a single or limited number.

Inorganic pesticide. A pesticide containing no carbon. Some inorganic pesticides, such as sulfur, are very low risk, and have been used for thousands of years to prevent and control certain plant diseases. Other inorganic pesticides containing heavy metals—lead, mercury, and tin—have been banned due to their high toxicity levels.

Organic pesticide. A pesticide containing carbon. Organic pesticides range from products derived from plant parts, such as pyrethrum (a relatively low-risk product) to organochlorines like DDT, which—due to its many dangers—has been banned.

Postemergence herbicide. An herbicide that attacks weeds beyond the seedling stage. These products make up the majority of herbicides. Some are selective—that is, they kill only a certain type of plant. Others are nonselective, and will kill any grasslike plant.

Pre-emergence herbicide. An herbicide that works by inhibiting the growth of germinating weed seeds and very young seedlings. To be effective, it needs to be applied in advance of germination.

Systemic insecticide. An insecticide that's capable of being absorbed by plants into the plant sap, or by animals into the bloodstream, without undue harm to the plant or animal; it poisons insects feeding on the plant juice or animal blood. A systemic insecticide can be applied to the soil, where it enters the roots of the plant, travels to the leaves, and kills insects feeding on the leaves.

Pesticides discussed in this section carry a *Caution* signal word on their labels, indicating a low toxicity level. Such rankings mean that, as a minimum, these pesticides may cause some minor skin or eye irritation or an allergic reaction in people using them, or may have harmful effects on other mammals, cold-blooded invertebrates (such as fish), or the environment if the directions on the label are not followed precisely.

Insecticidal soaps. Insecticidal soaps pose little risk to you, domestic animals, or the environment. They carry the *Caution* signal word on their label because they may irritate the eyes, can be harmful if swallowed, and can injure certain sensitive plants. You must take care to avoid spilling an insecticidal soap, either diluted or concentrated, into lakes, streams, and ponds, because it can kill fish. And you must make sure it doesn't contaminate feed or food.

Commercially sold insecticidal soaps are mild poisons made from the salts found in plants and animals. They kill by penetrating the cell membranes of soft-bodied pests such as aphids, whiteflies, spider mites, and others. They may also kill soft-bodied, flightless larvae of beneficial insects you want to support. This is one reason for not spraying them indiscriminately on large areas of the garden. Soaps aren't successful against pests with tough body coverings, nor are they effective on fast-moving insects that can evade the spray. Insecticidal soap works best if sprayed rapidly on all parts of an infected plant or a small group of plants (to better "catch" insects that start to fly away).

Insecticidal soap kills on contact; it has no effect once it has dried on a plant surface. Some plants are soap sensitive, so test it on a small part of the plant first, or wash it off after 30 minutes.

Note: Insecticidal soap is sometimes combined with an additional pesticide. The basic active ingredient of insecticidal soap is potassium salts of fatty acids. If a second pesticide has been included, you'll find its name in the active-ingredient section of the product label, along with additional precautionary statements and directions. After reading its precautionary statements about risk to you or the environment, you may decide to reject a dual or multipart product and instead get one that is only an insecticidal soap.

While most gardeners use insecticidal soaps as insect killers, the soaps can also be effective weed killers. A special formula of insecticidal soap is sold commercially as a weed killer. It has a higher percentage of potassium salts of fatty acids in it than the type sold as an insecticide (it's higher so that it will kill plant tissue). Don't use the insecticidal soap formulated as a weed killer to kill insects, as it will also kill plants that happen to be in the vicinity. The

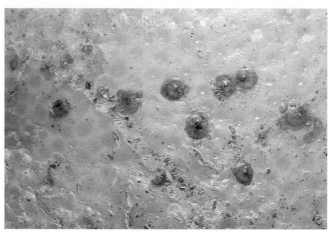

Versatile Oils Manage Many Problems

Commercial orange growers may have to contend with infestations of red scale (shown here on an orange, greatly magnified). Spraying groves with a lightweight oil can minimize such infestations. This use is one of the beneficial roles that oils can play in helping gardeners—both commercial and residential—control a wide variety of pest problems.

weed-killer formula works best on young, succulent weeds; it isn't as effective on older, woody weeds.

Oils. Similar to the insecticidal soaps, oils present few risks to you. They're most often made from either petroleum or paraffinic oil. You'll find the *Caution* signal word on oil labels because they may irritate the eyes, are harmful if swallowed, may cause allergic reactions on the skin, and also may cause some injury if liquid is inhaled and enters the lungs. The oils will kill fish, so take extreme care to avoid letting them get into ponds, streams, or lakes.

The oils have two functions. They kill certain insects, their larvae, and their eggs by smothering them. They also coat limbs and trunks, preventing a disease or a spore from taking hold and infecting the plant.

Both heavier and lighter oils are used to manage pests and diseases. The heavier oils, often called dormant oils, are usually petroleum based. Because they're heavier, they have greater ability to smother insects and coat plants. They are applied in the dormant (and usually colder) season, when there is little extremely warm sunshine to reflect the oil and burn the plant surface. The lighter oils—usually called year-round, extra-fine, or summer oils—are generally paraffin based. While they are lighter and less likely to burn a plant than winter oil, they do interfere with a plant's transpiration and respiration because they coat its leaves. You may want to first spray just a branch or two and observe it for a period of days for any adverse symptoms, such as wilting, before spraying the entire plant.

Match the Treatment to the Target

Insecticidal soaps are useful on soft-bodied pests, such as these aphids busily engaged in sucking juices from a rosebud (far left). The soaps easily penetrate the unprotected body, causing cell membranes to burst. On the other hand, insecticidal soaps aren't effective against hard-bodied insects, such as this western striped cucumber beetle (left).

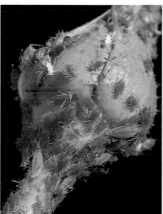

Be Careful with Dormant-Season and Summer-Oil Sprays

Many gardeners are aware of the dangers to fish from soaps and pesticides. But they often don't realize that oil sprays, such as those used on trees during the winter dormant season or in summer to prevent mildews, will also kill fish.

If for some reason you determine a pesticide is also required, read its label carefully to find out whether it can be used if an oil is present. Many pesticides should not be applied to a plant that has first been sprayed with an oil.

If you're using an oil in the winter to prevent disease, read the label directions to determine how many applications are required and how far apart they should be. (A rainstorm right after application destroys its effectiveness.) While winter dormant-oil applications can minimize a full-blown infestation of some types of pests the following spring and summer, remember that they may also kill overwintering eggs of beneficial insects and butterflies. Your decision on how much of your garden to spray during the winter should depend on the severity of a prior year's problems, rather than on an arbitrary general rule.

Because the oils are dual purpose (killing insects and coating plant parts to prevent disease), informal descriptions on their labels vary from "dormant-oil sprays" to "pesticidal oil" and other wordings. Be sure to read the official ingredient listing on the label to make sure you're buying only an oil. Some products use wording on labels that may be confusing. For example, a product identified as a "dormant spray" may, in fact, not be a dormant-oil spray but simply one of a host of products that are applied during the dormant season. It may well be a stronger pesticide, a fungicide, or some combination of oil and other pesticides.

Making your own oils and sprays. You can make an insecticidal soap spray by combining 2 tablespoons of dishwashing detergent in a gallon of water. (To minimize any unwanted effects, use a detergent that's color-free and scent-free.) Always wash this formula off the plant 30 minutes after using; otherwise there is increased danger of plant damage.

A U.S. Department of Agriculture (USDA) formula combining an oil and a soap has also been found effective for controlling the kind of insects affected by insecticidal soaps and commercial oil spray. Mix 1 cup of oil (peanut, safflower, corn, soybean, or sunflower) with 1 tablespoon of liquid dishwashing detergent. To make the spray, use 1½ teaspoons of the oil-detergent mixture for each cup of water. Coat all plant surfaces thoroughly; if necessary, repeat the application in seven to ten days. Note: This spray may burn cauliflower, red cabbage, and squash leaves. (Again, for safest use, choose a detergent that's free of perfumes and dyes, or wash the mixture off the plant after 30 minutes. Most insects will be killed right away, so washing it off after a short period won't minimize its effectiveness.)

Even with homemade oils and sprays you need to take care using them: they can kill fish. You don't want treasured goldfish or koi killed because homemade soap-and-oil products found their way into the pond.

Sulfur. Sulfur has been used for centuries to control disease in the garden, as well as infection in humans. As a garden product, it's effective in preventing powdery mildew, rust, and black spot from infecting a variety of flowers, fruits, and vegetables. It contains the signal word *Caution* on its label because some people are allergic to sulfur, and care should be taken to keep it from touching the skin. It is also harmful if swallowed and can cause eye irritation.

Originally available only as a product that was dusted onto leaves, sulfur is now also available in liquid form for ease in coating

Sulfur: Tried and True

No wonder sulfur has been used for centuries to prevent plant disease: these before-and-after photographs show the difference it can make. The gardener treated this scab-infested apple tree with sulfur and also cleaned up all diseased debris underneath, amended the soil, and mulched the tree during the growing season. One year later a bountiful apple crop was harvested.

all plant surfaces. Sulfur is one of the products, though, that can't be combined with an oil spray. If oil has previously been sprayed on a plant, wait at least four weeks before applying sulfur.

Sulfur is most effective when used at the first hint of infection; once a disease has infected a leaf, no product will get rid of it. Many use sulfur in the vegetable garden to keep mildew outbreaks from taking over plants like peas and beans. It's also a popular choice with rose growers because powdery mildew, rust, and black spot are such common rose problems. On the other hand, it can be toxic to some plants, including cucumber, raspberry, and apricot. (If you have sensitive plants, you might spray with just water, or baking-soda-and-water sprays to keep mildew under control.)

Just as with dormant-oil sprays, take care to read the ingredients list on a sulfur label. A label might advertise "Sulfur plus such-and-so—nature's remedy," but the other ingredients may have higher toxicity levels than the sulfur.

Bacteria-based pesticides. While insecticidal soaps, dormant and summer oils, and sulfur are three mainstays of many a gardener, other pesticides also manage pests and diseases with low impact on the user and the environment.

Bacillus thuringiensis, called BT, is a pathogen that paralyzes and destroys the stomach cells of the insects that consume it. While it presents few risks to humans, products made from the BT pathogen carry the *Caution* signal word on their label: BT may cause skin and eye irritation or an allergic skin reaction.

BT's major use has been to kill leaf-eating caterpillars such as bagworms, budworms, cabbage loopers, cankerworms, fall webworms, gypsy moth caterpillars, hornworms, imported cabbageworms, and tent caterpillars. BT is either sprayed or dusted on plants that caterpillars eat. Once they've ingested a BT-coated leaf, the poison enters their system and causes them to stop feeding; they die within several days. Because BT is inactivated by heat and light, applications should be scheduled in the afternoon or evening or on an overcast day. It's also important to time BT application during the stage when the caterpillars are just beginning to feed. At a more mature stage, they're able to go without food for several days and may pass up eating leaves coated with BT.

BT has many advantages. It kills the caterpillar form of many insects that are detrimental to food crops and ornamental plants. It does so with little danger to humans, other insects and creatures, and the environment. However, because it kills all caterpillar types, it will also kill butterflies, including those on endangered species lists. You'll need to weigh the advantages of BT against its harm to butterflies. Some gardeners grow extra or different plants just to feed butterfly caterpillars, taking care not to spray BT on those plants.

New strains of BT have been developed to control other insect pests. *B. t.* San Diego is toxic to certain beetles, such as the young Colorado potato beetle larvae, and to elm leaf beetle larvae and adults. Strains lethal to other beetles are expected to be available in the future. *B. t. israeliensis*, which is fatal to mosquitoes, is most often used in community-wide abatement programs rather than in the home garden.

You may not find BT products in local garden centers and supply stores. It's most often available through mail-order suppliers and organic gardening retail sources. BT is especially effective in the vegetable garden, where it can be used on all food crops up to harvest. (A similar product is milky spore disease. It's been effective in managing Japanese beetle problems. Fortunately, Japanese beetles are rarely found west of the Rockies, so this product is not one many western gardeners need.)

Protecting Petunias

Use *Bacillus thuringiensis* (BT) to control geranium budworms that devour petunia blossoms (top). The first symptom may be an absence of new blooms (lower left). After being sprayed with BT, the petunia bed returns to good health (lower right). Tip: for best results, spray at the first sign of infestation.

Timing Is Everything

BT is most effective on newly hatched caterpillars. If you see eggs like those of the cabbage white (left), keep a close watch on them and spray the plant leaves just as the caterpillars begin to emerge (right).

OLD MEETS NEW IN PEST CONTROL —THE NEEM TREE

The neem tree (*Azadirachta indica*) has added to the quality of human life for hundreds of years. But only recently have products derived from it started finding their way into the arsenal that western gardeners use to combat garden pests and diseases.

With a wide canopy, height up to 60 feet, and a trunk girth up to 6 feet, the neem tree shelters all below from the hot sun in its tropical and subtropical places of origin. It's found in Southeast Asia, Africa, and similar tropical areas, but in India use of the neem tree has been documented for hundreds of years. The people of India used its twigs as toothbrushes, helping to fight bacterial infections and periodontal disease. They crushed its leaves and rubbed them on wounds to improve healing. Leaves and twigs stored among food grains reduced pest populations in granaries. In India—as well as in other countries where it grows—farmers found they could crush and steep the leaves, mix them with water, and apply the liquid as a pesticide to protect crops.

The rest of the world didn't notice the neem tree's potential until the 1920s. At that time, a severe locust infestation swept through a portion of India where many neem trees grew. Foliage was stripped from every living plant in the area—except the neem tree.

Since then, much has been learned about this tree, and products derived from it are helping to fight garden pests and diseases. While it is classed as a pesticide and care must be taken to follow its use directions exactly as stated by law, many gardeners are finding it has fewer harmful side effects than other products.

Neem tree

Neem contains a number of active components. The main one, named azadirachtin, works as a pesticide in two ways. First, sprayed on leaves, it repels many insects from landing. Second, it upsets regulatory mechanisms in insects that eat leaves sprayed with it. The insects stop eating, they don't metamorphose to their next stage, and they don't reproduce. In most cases, this means death within just a few days. A wide variety of insects is affected, including aphids, beetles, mealybugs, spider mites, root knot nematodes, caterpillars, locusts, whiteflies, and termites. Like similar insecticides that kill through ingestion of leaf material, neem doesn't harm the adult form of some beneficial insects—such as ladybugs, lacewings, and predatory beetles—because they eat pollen and nectar, not leaves.

Other components, perhaps the same ones documented as healing bacterial infections, are probably forms of sulfur. And some gardeners have reported that neem products also help stop the spread of mildew and rust (problems that are often controlled by sulfur sprays).

In choosing any pesticide, you need to look at a variety of factors to decide which of the products available is most appropriate for your situation. Those factors include both its effectiveness and its potential harm to you and the environment. Thus far, neem oil products seem to be as effective as products that have greater potential harm as a result of their toxicity levels, the time before they break down in the soil, and off-site movement after application, such as runoff into nearby lakes, streams, or ponds. Just as the past decade saw a number of pesticides based on pyrethrum (which is made from the flowers of the pyrethrum daisy), you'll most likely soon be seeing more products on garden center shelves that are derived from the neem tree.

Neem oil. Neem oil products also carry the *Caution* signal word; they may cause skin or eye irritation, allergic reaction, or some injury if inhaled into the lungs. Take care that neem oil products are not released into ponds, lakes, and streams. They may also harm bees, so don't spray them onto blossoms that bees feed from. (The bee population throughout the country is in serious decline, so it's important not to use any pesticide that may cause additional damage to these pollinators.)

A product of the neem tree (see above), neem oil (its principal active ingredient is known as azadirachtin) kills soft-bodied insects of the same type that may be killed by an insecticidal soap. In some instances it has also been reported effective in preventing diseases such as mildew, fungus, and rust. Neem oil is an alternative to insecticidal soaps, dormant-oil sprays, and sulfurs and may help manage a pest or disease if other means aren't effective. Neem oil products are often sold under generic-sounding labels, such as "insect and disease killer."

Pyrethrum. Pyrethrum products, made from parts of a daisy-like member of the chrysanthemum family, are perhaps the most widely known of the pesticides derived from nature. Pyrethrum, a dust made from the daisy petals, was the first pesticide extracted from this plant. Later, a more potent one named pyrethrin was extracted from the daisy seeds.

One advantage of pyrethrum products is that they rapidly disintegrate, meaning there is little lasting effect on the environment. However, during application you must take the same care that's mandated for any pesticide with the *Caution* signal word on its label. Pyrethrin, like others with this designation, may irritate the skin and eyes. Although its toxicity is much lower than that of many other pesticides, too many people are lulled into complacency about it because it is derived from flowers. This mistaken impression of harmlessness is furthered by marketing language that uses phrases like "made from flowers," "a botanical pesticide," and "the flower insecticide." Synthetic pyrethrins, called pyrethroids, have

Bees and Pyrethrum

Pesticides containing only pyrethrum dissipate in a few hours. If bees are drinking nectar from plants you want to treat, apply these pesticides in the late afternoon, after the bees have stopped feeding for the day. By the time they return the next day, the pesticide will be gone. Avoid using pesticides containing pyrethrins and pyrethroids where bees are present.

higher toxicity ratings than those made only from the plant, and they persist longer.

In addition, piperonyl butoxide is often added to pyrethrin to make it kill insects more quickly and effectively. Its long-term effects on the environment are not yet known. In many instances the pyrethrin only stuns the pest temporarily, and it is the piperonyl butoxide that actually kills the insect.

The bottom line is that you need to take as much care when mixing and applying a pesticide derived from pyrethrin or pyrethroids as you would with any other pesticide. And while these products can assist in managing insect problems in the ornamental and the vegetable garden, they can also kill beneficial insects and fish and cause harm to the person who applies them without proper precautions.

Pyrethrins find their way into many products. One database listed more than 3,500 different registered products that included pyrethrins. Some are marketed to kill insect pests on roses, others to control pests on garden vegetables, and still others to control insects that prey on ornamental flowers and shrubs—seemingly quite different products. Yet a careful reading of the label shows that each is made with pyrethrin. It is also included in many "bug" spray products and in shampoos and related products that control fleas on pets.

Pyrethrins kill insects on direct contact and are most effective on those with soft bodies. Some insect types have developed a resis-

tance to pyrethrin-based products and, in all cases, insects that can fly rapidly often escape before the spray reaches them.

Combination products. Other plant-based pesticides are available either as single-ingredient pesticides or as part of a combination product. Some combinations include an additional ingredient to help "ensure the kill"—whereas a pyrethrin by itself may only stun an insect, it becomes a more powerful pesticide when boosted by a second. Rotenone, derived from plant roots of several tropical legumes, is one such additive. (It may also be sold alone.) Even though it's botanically based, rotenone is more toxic to vertebrates than either malathion or carbaryl—chemical pesticides that carry the *Warning* signal word on their labels. It's also extremely deadly to fish. Rotenone is sometimes combined with sulfur and marketed as an "organic" vegetable dust that prevents both disease and insect damage. While sulfur alone is an effective disease preventive with low toxicity levels, the addition of rotenone raises its toxicity level, and the label carries stringent warnings about its uses.

Finally, make sure you read the ingredients on the label; don't rely on marketing phrases to help you understand what's in a pesticide. Even though low-toxicity products may prove to be of little danger to you or the environment, you must follow all stated precautions when using them. And when buying a combination product, read its label carefully; several of the ingredients may be "organic" or "natural," but one may carry greater risks than another.

BRINGING IN THE BIG GUNS

There may be occasions that warrant using pesticides stronger than those described above. Perhaps you move to a new home and find the garden overrun with snails and the lawn full of dandelions. You decide to put out snail bait for a couple of nights to get the population under control. Once you've eliminated the first hundred or so, you can then hand-pick the rest. It may be difficult to remove each dandelion by hand, so you decide to apply a small amount of a weed killer to get rid of the dandelions without killing what's left of the lawn. When most of the weeds are dead, you'll reseed, fertilize, and water, bringing the lawn back to health.

Acres of Dandelions

Could you hand-weed a patch of dandelions this size? With this much acreage, you might decide that an herbicide is the most practical way to get the weed problem under control. Later, hand-weeding isolated dandelions may be the best method for maintaining a weed-free garden.

In such a situation, once you've made the decision to use a pesticide, it's daunting to stand in front of those shelves at a nursery or garden supply center. While the products are generally arranged by type—insecticides, herbicides, and fungicides—it isn't easy to make sense of them. The array of advertising words and phrases sometimes makes it hard to read the labels, much less to compare products. Here's some advice:

- Once you've found the appropriate section, check to see whether the product carries a *Caution, Warning,* or *Danger* signal word on its label. While many factors are involved in determining the overall risk assessment of a particular product, those with a *Caution* signal word (little or no short-term human toxicity) are least likely to cause damage to you or the environment. You can, for example, find two different products that kill ants. One carries a *Caution* signal word and the second a *Warning* signal word. In most situations, it makes more sense to buy the one designated *Caution*.

- Compare products by reading pesticide common names on the product ingredient list. Some products advertise the common name prominently on the label, and others don't. If you look only at the bold type, you may miss a similar product that's less expensive or better suited to your purpose (such as a smaller, premixed version).

- Your best choice is a product that contains only one pesticide type. Products that promise to solve several problems may upset the balance in your garden unnecessarily. For example, a product may contain both a fungicide (to kill disease organisms) and an insecticide (to kill insects). If you're in a hurry when shopping for a problem solver, you may not realize you've purchased a combination product. And if you do need to solve two problems, you'll want to be the one making the choice of how to go about it, rather than having the decision made for you by a product manufacturer who doesn't know the complete situation in your garden.

- Look for single-purpose, rather than broad-spectrum, insecticides. A broad-spectrum insecticide is formulated to kill many different types of insects. Most often, you're buying an insecticide because of a problem caused by one insect, not many. The broad-spectrum insecticide is more likely to kill every living insect in its range, destroying the balance in your garden and robbing it of many beneficial creatures. Most insecticides kill several insects of a type, such as caterpillars. Use the "Encyclopedia of Damaging and Beneficial Creatures" (page 148) to become familiar with the types of insect pests. Then you'll be able to tell if an insecticide is single-purpose (killing just one type) or broad-spectrum (killing more than one type). Of course, a more general way to make this determination is to count up the number of insects the pesticide kills. Shorter lists are more likely to be found on single-purpose pesticides.

- Use systemic pesticides with care. A systemic pesticide is absorbed by roots or foliage and incorporated into a plant's living tissue, rather than being deposited on its surface. Thus it won't be washed off by rain nor will it dissipate into the air, as do pesticides that you spray or dust onto plants. Insects die when they eat plant parts that have absorbed the pesticide. Systemic pesticides now on the market kill a wide range of insects and related creatures, including beneficials like honeybees drinking nectar from a treated plant's flowers. However, new products are coming to market that are selective—they kill only a particular insect, notably the aphid.

- If you'll be using a pesticide on a food crop (such as a vegetable garden, berry vines, fruit trees, and the like), read the precautionary statements on the product label to find out (a) if it can be

Persistent Weeds

The stout taproots of some weeds, such as the sowthistle *(Sonchus oleraceus),* make the plants, once established, very hard to remove by hand. If you don't pull these weeds when they are small, you may have to turn to a chemical treatment. The herbicide glyphosate kills the weed, taproot and all, as these before-and-after photographs show.

used on a food crop and (b) how close to harvest it can be applied. Note: Never use a systemic pesticide on a food crop. Even if its active period has passed, pesticide components remain in plant cells.

Killing weeds. Weeds run the gamut from the small English daisy that threads its way into the lawns of the Pacific Northwest to stands of blackberry that cover Northwest properties in mounds over 6 feet tall. Using an herbicide to eradicate a weed problem can be tricky: while you want to kill the weed, you don't want to kill valuable plants as well. Because it's sometimes difficult to spray only the weed, products called pre-emergence herbicides have been developed. They work by inhibiting growth of germinating weed seeds and very young seedlings. You apply them to the soil early in the season before a weed seed germinates. This type of intervention may be the only way, short of removing an entire lawn and starting over, that you can get rid of tenacious weeds like English daisy. Often, you'll find pre-emergence herbicides combined with lawn fertilizers meant to be used in the spring.

There are several pre-emergence herbicides on the market. Common names of some that have proved effective on a range of broad-leafed and/or grasslike plants include DCPA, EPTC, oryzalin, and trifluralin. Read labels to find out what types of weeds the herbicide controls best and, perhaps more important, whether it can be used on a lawn, around ornamentals, or both.

Postemergence herbicides are the various weed sprays that kill plants that have already sprouted. These include products effective on the occasional weed found in the garden as well as on those that have taken over large tracts of land. Two terms important to any discussion about herbicides are "selective" and "nonselective." A selective herbicide kills only a certain type of weed. Two commonly used selective herbicides that mostly kill grasses are fluazifop-butyl and sethoxydim. The most commonly used nonselective herbicide is glyphosate. A recently introduced nonselective product, glufosinate-ammonium, is proving effective against weeds such as dichondra that glyphosate doesn't kill.

Herbicides kill in two ways. Contact herbicides kill merely by reaching the plant's surface. Translocated herbicides are absorbed into the plant, where they interfere with metabolism, causing the plant to die. A commonly used translocated herbicide is triclopyr, effective on hard-to-kill weeds like blackberry and poison oak.

Preventing and curing disease. Diseases are perhaps the most complex garden problems. Many live in the soil and take hold only if a plant is stressed. This is the case for many molds and fungi that attack an overwatered plant (the water blocks out air, and the lack of air helps the disease take hold). Other ailments lie dormant for years and become a problem only when a plant susceptible to the disease is planted in the area. In this situation, about the only thing you can do is move the plant to another location. In many instances, the only solution is to buy disease-resistant varieties (as is the case with fireblight) and keep your plants healthy so they don't become vulnerable to a disease.

Pesticides effective as disease preventers or controllers are called fungicides. Some products only prevent diseases; others can both prevent and control them. The oldest and most common preventer is simple sulfur (see page 64), which has low risk factors associated with its use. It prevents mildew, black spot, and rust.

Other preventive fungicides include copper compounds that resist peach leaf curl, and lime sulfur (calcium polysulfide), which has proved effective against peach leaf curl as well as powdery mildew and various leaf spot diseases. Products with the common

When Help Is Needed

Sometimes a problem is almost impossible to control without help. Walnut blight, which appears on one of these walnuts, is such a disease—it can't be effectively managed without seasonal application of a fungicide.

name chlorothalonil prevent diseases on lawns, fruits, vegetables, and ornamentals.

Some fungicides are systemics, working inside the plant to prevent or eradicate disease. Triforine belongs to this group; it prevents and eradicates powdery mildew, rust, black spot, and a variety of other diseases. While the systemic fungicides are effective in managing diseases in some instances, gardeners must follow all mixing and application directions exactly. Most of the systemics carry the *Warning* or *Danger* signal word on their labels and require that goggles or face masks be used during application.

New research includes the notion of antagonism or competition as a means of preventing some plant diseases. Simply put, this involves the release of organisms that will occupy space on the plant surface before the pest organism (such as powdery mildew) arrives. These products, called biofungicides, are currently available only in agriculture, where they have been used successfully on crops such as grapes. Biofungicides minimize disruption to the ecosystem and pose fewer risks to humans. In the future, they may be available for the home gardener as well.

Using insecticides to kill pests. Most often, if you're standing in front of the pesticide shelves at your local garden center, you're there looking for an insecticide. While you may prevent and manage many diseases and weed problems using the Integrated Pest Management practices discussed in this book, it's sometimes difficult to manage insects using IPM all the time.

Several insecticides that work efficiently and with few side effects have been described above, including insecticidal soaps, dormant oils, certain biological controls, and some derived from plants, such as the pyrethrum daisy and the neem tree. This section talks about other insecticides that you might choose to use in some

Finding Appropriate Solutions

Sometimes the only practical way to get rid of a potentially dangerous pest is with a pesticide. This yellow jacket nest (below) is in a family garden where children and pets play. The mud dauber nest (right) is just above an outdoor eating area. A professional could move the mud dauber nest or use pesticides to kill both kinds of pests.

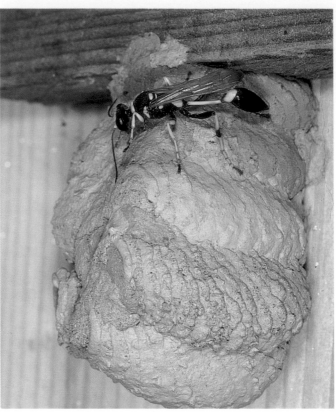

situations. These insecticides carry somewhat higher risk factors, but part of what you do, in deciding to use any product, is make a risk assessment. If you have a few hornworms on one or two tomatoes, you pick them off by hand, deciding that the problem doesn't merit the risk of using an insecticide on a tomato. On the other hand, if there are several hornet nests in your backyard, you may decide that an insecticide containing propoxur presents the lowest risk for everyone. One application, using the proper precautions, makes your yard safe once again for you and your children.

It's not easy to figure out which of the higher-risk pesticides to buy. Here's an example of how difficult it can be. The insecticide chlorpyrifos is the only active ingredient in seven different products that are found on the shelf of a large garden-supply center. The product names and label descriptions differ dramatically: the products are variously described as a fruit tree borer spray, a leaf miner spray, an insect and termite killer, an outdoor flea and tick killer, a lawn-insect killer, an indoor/outdoor insect killer, and an insect killer for lawns, fruits, and nuts. If you had such an array of problems and were considering an insecticide to solve them, you might wonder if you need to buy all seven of these products.

First, look closely at the percentage of active ingredient in each product. A product with a higher proportion of the active ingredient (chlorpyrifos in this example) is needed to control some pests. But it may be too high a level to safely use in other areas—inside the home, for instance, or on fruit or vegetable crops. This difference in the amount of active ingredient needed is one reason there is such a large number of products.

Second, read the fine print on the back of the label to find out just which pests it does control. If the label doesn't contain direc-

tions for the pest you want to control, you can't use it. (Some manufacturers decide not to test and market their product for all pests that the active ingredient may control.) This is the law, as well as common sense.

While the front of the label gives general information, such as "Lawn, Fruit, and Nut Spray," the detailed information on the back of the label lets you see if the product applies to the plant and pest in your garden. Through label reading and smart shopping, you may be able to reduce the number of products stored in your pesticide cabinet. After reading the directions on the seven different chlorpyrifos-based products, you might find that three of them are acceptable for controlling the range of pests that are a problem in your garden.

Even the word "plus" appearing as part of a trade name should give you pause. In one case, "plus" may refer to a wetting agent that makes the product easier to apply. In another product, the word may mean that a second pesticide is included, and one significant enough to change the product's signal-word label from *Caution* to *Warning*. Bottom line: you've got to read labels carefully before buying an insecticide.

One major point always to check for is whether the product can be used around plants that will be eaten and, if so, how long before harvest. For example, two products might say "safe for use on vegetables," but one may indicate it can be used weekly and up to three days before harvest. Another may be used once during the growing season and only up to 30 days before harvest. If you have a major pest problem in your vegetable garden, you don't want to go home with a product to treat that problem and then find out it can't be used on anything edible.

SUMMING UP THE COMMONSENSE APPROACH

This chapter illustrates what is meant by a commonsense approach to managing problems in the garden. It reminds you that good, basic gardening techniques—similar to those used for thousands of years—go a long way toward preventing problems. Remember such things as learning about the soil and climate in your area and doing what you can to improve the soil, and growing plants that make sense: the right plant for the right location.

If you do find a problem or two, chances are you can manage it with simple techniques. You might protect a bed of lettuce from rabbits with a wire cage, or speed the demise of earwigs by luring them to a trap laced with soy sauce. You'll also find that local resources such as the cooperative extension office, working with other agricultural professionals, are helping you by releasing beneficial insects into your neighborhood.

When you do need help to manage a problem, time-honored solutions such as sulfur, oil, and soaps are still useful allies. They've been augmented by innovations like the propane-powered flamers that kill weeds by heating them to a high temperature, and by biological controls like BT that kill only caterpillars and do so without harming you or the ecosystem.

One of the tenets of Integrated Pest Management is that it doesn't preclude your employing pesticides if they're used judiciously as part of an overall management program. If you do decide to use a pesticide, read labels carefully, mix products correctly, and take care in applying them so you don't endanger yourself, others, or the environment.

Next, use the troubleshooting and encyclopedia chapters of this book to identify exactly the pest—be it a weed, a disease, an insect, or other creature—you need to manage, and to learn about recommended solutions.

Finally, while everyone leads busy lives these days, make sure you include some time to stop and smell the flowers—and keep an eye out for pests while you're at it.

Common Sense Leads to Success

This Santa Fe, New Mexico, yard, with its panorama of blue salvia and gray-green iris leaves, epitomizes the healthy garden that can result from prevention, patience, and appropriate pest intervention.

Problem Solving
BY PLANT TYPE

*P*lant categories are based on growth habits and on the roles the plants play in the garden. Some groups are strictly ornamental, others provide structure within the landscape as well as shade, and many supply us with food. Plants within each group also tend to have similar problems. One way to understand an ailing plant, then, in addition to reviewing its life cycle, growth habits, and performance in your climate, is to consider the problems common to its type.

This chapter will help you learn to identify plant problems by highlighting those typical of five groups of plants: trees, shrubs, vines, and ground covers; lawns; annuals, perennials, and bulbs; fruits, nuts, and berries; and vegetables and herbs. Read the introductory material in each section to begin a diagnosis; then compare your plant's condition to the typical problems in each group to zero in on the pest, disease, weed, or cultural difficulty. Finally, turn to the relevant encyclopedia in this book for a full discussion of problem prevention and management.

THE ORIGINS OF PLANT PROBLEMS

You can prevent a host of garden problems before your plants are even in the ground. By selecting plants that fit your site, you'll eliminate difficulties associated with climate incompatibility as well as the hazards introduced by pruning plants that outgrow their space. Careful selection means matching sun-loving plants with sunny sites and shade lovers with dimmer light, and choosing tough performers for low-maintenance landscapes and slow-growing plants for narrow nooks. Avoiding plants that are subject to existing problems in your area also keeps trouble at bay.

At buying time you can waylay potential problems by inspecting plants for disease-free foliage and roots that are not broken or wrapped around the soil inside their container. Before setting out any plant, determine its watering needs and plan how you'll meet them. Overwatering and underwatering alone cause numerous garden troubles. To fully prepare for new garden plants, review pages 34–47 and the checklists that follow.

GETTING A STRONG START

Once you have the right plant for the right place, start it off right. A solid beginning will carry a plant through tough times and give it resources for withstanding stress from weather conditions, as well as from pests, diseases, and weeds.

- Begin with adequate site preparation. Adjust the soil pH to make it compatible with your plant's needs (see page 36). A pH that's too low or too high prevents a plant from absorbing adequate levels of mineral nutrients and impedes performance. Add ample organic matter to improve sand or clay and to support microbial life in the soil. If your soil is heavy, provide good drainage or build raised beds.
- Set out plants at the time of the year when they'll best adapt to their new environment. For lawns, fruit trees, and most ornamentals, that means spring or fall. Plant vegetables according to your local frost timetable.
- Use sound planting techniques appropriate for each type of plant. Trees and shrubs develop extensive root systems and should be planted in unamended soil with organic material spread over the surface as mulch. Herbaceous plants need amendments dug in to nurture their shallow roots. All plants need to have their roots spread out; small root balls on annuals in cell-packs may need to be cut to encourage lateral growth. Set plants in the ground so their crowns aren't too deep and their roots aren't too exposed.

GETTING PLANTS ESTABLISHED

Plants need a settling-in period to establish themselves firmly in their new home. Roots take time to develop the countless tiny root hairs that absorb water and nutrients. As they grow, roots develop depth, girth, and branchlets to anchor the plant and collect food reserves for the expanding top growth. Until its roots are well established, every new plant will need particular attention.

- Watch for sudden hot or cold spells that require extra watering, shade protection, or insulation.
- Pinch plants that need to develop branching for maximum foliage and flowers. Stake those that develop fast vertical growth and can't stand alone.
- Check your watering techniques. A water jet or sprinkler can erode soil and dangerously expose roots. Watch also for burrowing rodents, rabbits, and deer that push or pull new plants out of the ground, leaving roots to dry out.

Representative plant types (clockwise from top left): Weeping willow–leafed pear, Pyrus salicifolia *'Pendula'; native Pacific Coast iris; a well-managed lawn; 'Flame Seedless' grapes.*

PREVENTIVE MAINTENANCE

While some plants seem to take care of themselves for years on end, most require ongoing maintenance. Inspecting plants regularly and following sound cultural practices will help prevent pests, diseases, and weeds from establishing a foothold in your garden.

- Renew organic mulches annually to conserve moisture, control weeds, feed beneficial soil microbes, protect plant roots, and prevent erosion.
- Adjust water and nutrient supplies to suit different stages of a plant's development and the season of the year. Prune only when necessary, thinning ornamental trees and shrubs rather than "topping," or cutting off branch ends.
- Don't underestimate the importance of a clean garden. In the fall, remove weeds and debris where pests overwinter. Control dust and ants year-round to deter insects.
- Take steps to prevent chronic problems. Remove plants susceptible to troubles such as powdery mildew and replace them with resistant varieties; replant on mounds to improve drainage and prevent crown and root rots. Relocate struggling plants to a more favorable site—or simply get rid of them.

PLANTING WITHIN YOUR ZONE

You'll have greatest success with your garden and avoid disappointment with poor performance when you choose plants that thrive in your climate zone. Alternatively, you have to decide how much time and effort you want to spend providing unnatural conditions vital for unsuitable specimens that you want to grow. Availability of water, temperature ranges, and other climate limitations may themselves make the decisions for you. Many plants will survive out of their native climate, but most will not thrive. Certainly palm trees can't endure the cold winters of northern latitudes, but if you make the effort, camellias can be protected or overwintered indoors for outdoor summer enjoyment in most of the western zones. Tomatoes can be coddled in short, cool summers, but showcase beefsteak varieties simply won't do well in dry western climates.

Matching the Plant to the Zone

Arctostaphylos uva-ursi, a native western manzanita commonly called bearberry or kinnikinnick, tolerates winter cold, summer heat, and moist garden conditions better than most other *Arctostaphylos* species. These qualities make it a good evergreen ground cover in Zones 1–9 and 14–24.

- Be aware that microclimates exist. Even though apricots thrive within one region of your zone, they may succumb to blight in another. Peonies may receive sufficient winter chill on a valley floor in mild climates but not on the hillside above.
- Consider devoting a part of your garden to plants native to your zone. Natives may still have problems, but they have a history of success in your area and require little attention once they are established.
- Ask yourself a few questions: What do you expect from your plants? What's the climate compatibility of new plants you're adding to your garden? How much trouble can you tolerate? How long can you persevere in providing unnatural conditions?

RECOGNIZING TROUBLE

Problems inevitably appear in every garden. Most are easily handled, but some will raise questions. Before jumping into a diagnostic process, be sure that symptoms you associate with pests and diseases aren't just part of the natural activity of a plant. Yellowed and dropping foliage on a redwood tree in midsummer may look like trouble, but it's actually an annual process of leaf drop and renewal that all evergreen trees experience, some more frequently than others. Many bark and foliage features may look abnormal if you aren't familiar with habits of the species. Woody stems and twigs, for instance, develop bumpy lenticels—structures that allow gaseous exchanges between the interior and exterior of the plant—that can look like scale insects. Some varieties of perennials and shrubs have unique yellowish or mottled foliage that is normal, not the result of a nutrient deficiency.

KNOW YOUR PLANTS

In tracking down the cause of trouble, try to identify your plant's genus, species, and variety. Know what's normal for the species and the kinds of problems it's likely to develop. Pests and diseases often attack specific plants, so if you know the identity of the plant in question, you may be able to rule out—or in—a number of possible culprits.

Many pests and diseases are attracted to plants at certain times of the year at specific temperature and moisture levels. Their garden invasions are quite regular and can even be predicted. By recognizing the habits of creatures that are normally attracted to plants in your garden, you can take preventive steps in anticipation of their arrival. For instance, cole crops attract cabbage moths, but row covers keep the moths out of beds and prevent destruction by their ravenous larvae. Pheromone traps waylay other insects at predictable mating times. When you know your plants, you also know how much insect and disease damage they can tolerate without application of controls.

MEET FRIENDLY HELPERS

Don't be alarmed by every crawling or flying garden intruder. Many are beneficial insects or organisms that are part of the ecosystem of the garden and protect it in many subtle ways. Learn to recognize beneficial creatures and let them play out their natural roles before you mistakenly take steps to eliminate them. Beneficials play a key role in pest management, solving many thorny problems on their own as well as eliminating the necessity of applying additional controls (see pages 48 and 49 and the "Encyclopedia of Damaging and Beneficial Creatures," page 148, which contains entries on a number of beneficials).

DIAGNOSING PLANT PROBLEMS

Many garden problems show up early. When, in addition, an offending insect or organism is present, diagnosis and management are fairly easy. Sometimes, though, garden problems progress until a plant's leaves are looking dull or even dropping. By this stage, the disease organism or the pest may be long gone, and any search for it will be futile. Looking for signs that it left behind is often your only recourse. While you're examining a plant, however, keep in mind that its difficulties aren't necessarily traceable to the predations of some insect or infection. Many problem sources are cultural—that is, they arise from the care plants are given; others are chemical, caused by a nutrient imbalance; and still others are environmental or physical, arising either from weather changes or from breakage.

LOOKING FOR SYMPTOMS AND SIGNS

Symptoms are those changes in the appearance of a plant caused by the offending pest, disease, or cultural or physical factor that has intruded on normal growth and activity. Symptoms tell you that something has happened to the plant. Discoloration, distorted leaves and shoots, leaf drop, dying stems and branches, oozing cankers, or bulging galls are all departures from normal plant growth and development.

When you see such changes, it's time to look for causal signs. You may be able to spot the offending organism or find clues. Every insect or pest has a specific means of attacking a plant, and it leaves behind evidence of its presence. Typical signs are ragged or chewed leaves, sticky secretions, drops or specks of excrement, webs, mushrooms, and eggs.

Note all the symptoms and signs you can find. It helps to have as much information as possible to isolate disease problems and to distinguish between damage from organisms and that from chemical or physical causes. The growing conditions themselves may even be the source of the problem. Diligent

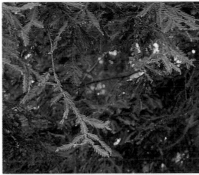

Normal or Not?

From top: What looks like an insect or disease problem may be part of a natural process, such as the annual summer leaf drop on redwood. The bumps on this deodar cedar may look like scale insects but are actually lenticels, which allow the tree to "breathe." Typical insect damage is somewhat easier to identify: weevils notch leaf edges, as on this peony foliage, and thrips leave brown edges on rose petals.

sleuthing will help you narrow the field so you can focus on the most likely suspects.

FINDING TROUBLE SPOTS

Give your plants a thorough inspection to locate the real source of trouble. What appears to be the problem may in reality be a symptom. For example, wilted leaves may not be a foliage problem but an indicator of root rot. Take a step-by-step approach to cover all plant parts, eliminate trouble-free areas, and zero in on the real source of the damage.

Leaves. Start with the most obvious part of the plant, the foliage. Examine both the tops and undersides. Many pests feed or lay their eggs on the soft underside of leaves, where the intruders are shaded and can go unnoticed. Look for twisted, curled, or otherwise distorted areas, especially at branch tips and side shoots. Holes, spots, and chewed edges are obvious signs. Feel the leaves for stickiness, bumps, or depressions. Notice zones or patterns of discoloration, reduction in size, or change in vigor. Look for powdery coatings, webbing, and specks or globs of insect excrement. Use a magnifying lens for a close-up look at tiny creatures.

Flowers and fruit. If flowers or fruit are present, inspect them for entry holes that signal infestation or other damage, such as discoloration, spotting, or malformations. If there are no flowers or fruit, should there be?

Stems. Look carefully at the branches and stems or trunk of the plant, searching for wounds, holes, dieback, or oozing liquid. Feel the surface for sunken spots. Note the locations of wounds—are they close to the ground, higher up, or near branch tips? Look at the junctures of branches and stems and at petioles, where leaves are attached to the stems, checking for colonies of insects.

Crown. Check the crown (where the stem separates from the roots) for injury or bumpy growths. Break off loose or damp bark to locate the source of moisture or the extent of damage. Notice any sunken areas or discoloration (healthy underlying tissue is white or pale green).

Roots and soil. Don't ignore the soil in the root zone or the roots themselves. The soil should be moist, but never soggy, no less than 2 inches beneath the surface in an area at least as wide as the drip line of the plant—the soil area under a plant that extends to the outermost branches. Look at large sections of root as well as fibrous ends for rot, infestation, chewed-off areas, or nodules. Healthy roots are usually white and relatively odor-free, whereas damaged roots are discolored and may have an unpleasant smell.

Problem Solving for
TREES, SHRUBS, VINES, AND GROUND COVERS

In their juvenile phase, many eucalyptus species form round, bluish leaves.

Trees, shrubs, vines, and ground covers are the most familiar and valuable plants in the landscape. Throughout the seasons, they bring beauty and utility to western gardens. Each year they grow taller and more robust, filling in the garden framework, defining boundaries, and blanketing the soil. Keeping them pest- and disease-free will prolong their lives, ensuring both your pleasure in them and their contribution to your garden.

DEFINING THESE PLANT TYPES

Trees and shrubs have more similarities than differences, but each has distinctive characteristics. Generally, trees have a single trunk, while shrubs develop several stems that multiply at the base over many years. Trees have a greater potential for vertical growth, many in the West reaching heights that defy most imaginations. Shrubs rarely exceed 15 or 20 feet. To confuse the distinction, though, shrubs can be trained to grow on a single stem, while some trees naturally develop two or more trunks, and many can be trained to do so. However, these multiple trunks, unlike those of shrubs, assume roughly equal proportions. Shrubs and trees both grow branches from the ground up. On trees, the lower branches are generally pruned away for attractiveness and convenience and to maximize views.

Trees and shrubs are further defined as evergreen or deciduous. Deciduous plants typically drop all their leaves at one time, just before their annual dormancy, the period during which they rest from active growth and protect themselves from excess heat, cold, or drought. Evergreens replace their foliage slowly over one to several years and so appear green continuously. Most evergreens do experience periods of dormancy, but not as obviously as deciduous plants do.

Vines are actually flexible shrubs that require support and continue to grow in height. Because their nature is to climb, vines have various clinging and twining devices to lift them above lower-growing plants and spread their foliage vertically. For instance, trumpet vine has aerial roots, which serve to anchor it. Some vines are grown horizontally as a sprawling mass, rooting as they grow and creating a ground cover.

A ground cover is any planting in mass that protects the soil and creates a uniform appearance. (Lawn grasses, however, are in a category by themselves.) Two kinds of perennial plants are typically used as ground covers: low woody shrubs with trailing branches and low-growing herbaceous plants. Some ground covers are evergreen; others die to the ground each winter, sprouting new growth in the spring.

LIFE STAGES AND GROWTH HABITS

Trees, shrubs, vines, and ground covers, like other plants, begin their life cycles in a juvenile phase during which they become established and start producing foliage. A few species, such as eucalyptus, develop specialized leaves during this early period. When their genetic timetable gives the signal to mature, these plants flower, fruit, and produce seed. The juvenile period varies from species to species; hence, we wait longer for wisterias and magnolias to flower than we do for azaleas. Nurseries try to supply home gardeners with early-maturing varieties, which have been developed through grafting, budding, or cuttings.

The mature phase of all perennial plants lasts at least two years, although most live far longer, and under ideal conditions they can

Suitable Sites

Low-growing *Ceanothus maritimus* 'Frosty Dawn' (right) is an excellent ground cover in cool-summer and coastal regions, but it suffers where summers are hot. Choose taller, multi-stemmed shrubs such as *Cornus alba* 'Sibirica' (center right) for large-scale ground covers, screens, or architectural effects. Support heavy, rampant vines like this blueberry climber, or porcelain berry *(Ampelopsis brevipedunculata)* (far right), with a sturdy arbor or a concrete wall.

INTERIOR OF A WOODY STEM

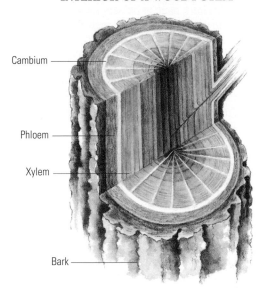

Cambium

Phloem

Xylem

Bark

grow to great age. There are a number of woody plants, such as some pines and rockrose *(Cistus)*, that tend to be short-lived. Many hardy perennial ground covers and some tender shrubs, such as St. Johnswort *(Hypericum)* and buddleia, achieve multiple years of growth by dying to the ground in cold weather and regrowing the following spring.

When you acquire a plant, it helps to know how long it is expected to live, so that you can anticipate declining performance as it approaches the end of its life span. Many plants become stressed in advanced age and are prey to pests and diseases. Cultural conditions also determine whether a plant will be long- or short-lived. Long-lived trees such as oaks deserve special locations and care that will not undermine the specialized techniques they have developed to survive. Giant sequoias, for instance, naturally grow widely separated at high elevations, yet in home landscapes you may see them enduring high temperatures in closely planted rows or crowded front yards. As a result, they are inevitably prey to branch dieback, a disease that shortens their life span.

Some trees and shrubs perpetuate their existence by developing extensive underground stem and root systems that spread widely and send up colonies, all part of a single plant. Aspens and aralias can spread over vast areas, with older stems or trunks dying and newer ones carrying on to give the trees or shrubs a very long life.

Permanence is the outstanding characteristic of plants in this group. They have developed habits of growth and renewal that give them strength and resilience in the climates to which they have adapted. For example, deciduous trees generally drop their leaves in the fall and become dormant during the long, cold winter. But California buckeyes are summer-deciduous, dropping their leaves in midsummer or July and becoming dormant during the hot, dry summer. Some vines, lacking support, manage to climb by twisting around themselves or around other plants. Understanding how plants grow and adapt will help you recognize their strengths and their vulnerabilities.

ROOTS

Trees and shrubs develop complex root systems that often interlock with neighboring plants in their communities. Healthy roots allow lush top growth and also provide resources to survive dormancy and stress. It used to be thought that roots penetrated deep into the soil, mirroring the aboveground shape of the tree or shrub. Research has shown, however, that most roots are shallow, with as much as 80 percent of their growth in the top 2 feet of soil where they can access water and oxygen. And roots rarely limit themselves to the area within the drip line, but they spread well beyond in ever-expanding irregular patterns. Feeder roots are typically just below the soil and far from their stems.

Many ground covers are prized for their habits of low-spreading growth by underground rhizomes or creeping roots. Some of the densest ones root as they spread, blocking out all competition below their mounding or matlike shapes.

STEMS

Buds that form at the tips of stems direct the growth of trees, shrubs, vines, and ground covers. When shoots are damaged or removed through pruning or breakage, new growth begins in buds farther down the stem. Take care when pruning to follow the plant's natural growth habit, or its shape will be distorted. Some shrubs, such as mock orange *(Philadelphus)*, rose, and weigela, need to have their older stems removed each year to ensure vigorous growth and flowering. On other plants, it's necessary to remove stems that form suckers from the crown and root areas, but you can use them to propagate new plants.

Inside the stem, the cambium layer produces new vascular tissue each year to carry water and food throughout the plant. This yearly tissue growth—the wood of the stem or trunk—adds to the plant's girth. If the stem tissue is damaged, this flow is interrupted and growth slows. Plants recover quickly from minor injuries; recovery from large bark fractures is slower, and wounds may not heal before pests and diseases exploit them.

LEAVES

The essential function of leaves is to manufacture sugars to feed the plant. In the process of photosynthesis, leaves use the energy of sunlight to transform water and carbon dioxide into food, releasing oxygen into the atmosphere as a by-product. A plant that is subjected to excessive pruning or that loses its leaves to environmental stress, pests, or disease has its ability to produce food diminished. Plants protect themselves against this hazard with a dormant bud at each leaf axil that is capable of producing a new leaf or even a new branch if necessary.

Leaves develop a thick protective coating on their upper surface; the softer tissue underneath is more vulnerable to insect attack. Insects are most strongly drawn to succulent growth in spring, but if a plant is heavily fertilized by water-soluble nitrogen during any season, insects will be attracted to the lush new growth. In cold-winter areas, fertilizing in late summer or early fall will produce tender new leaves that will be vulnerable to both insects and early frost.

FLOWERS

Flowers are the reproductive organs of plants. They produce fruiting structures and seeds, but to gardeners their reproductive function is beside the point, which is the beauty of the blooms. Many flowering species, such as clematis, are grown for their ornamental seed heads, and others, such as cotoneaster, for their colorful fruits. Some species produce male and female flowers on separate plants that are notably different. The male silktassel *(Garrya)* shrub, with its long, decorative catkins, for example, is more ornamental than the female. In other species, flowers on the male plants are insignificant and only the female produces showy blooms. Sexual differentiation has other effects: the male ginkgo is the preferred landscape plant, since fruits of the female have an unpleasant odor.

After flowering, the plant directs its energy to seed production. When plants are under great stress, they may flower profusely as they try to set seed for the next generation. To promote repeated flowering on shrubs and vines such as spiraea, or to induce the plant to produce foliage after flowering as on mountain laurel (*Kalmia*), it helps to trim off seed heads. Clipping spent blooms off plants like rhododendron and Catalina ironwood (*Lyonothamnus*) improves their appearance; but as their height increases, trimming becomes difficult and you are left with the problem of old brown clusters. In some cases—mimosa or silk tree (*Albizia*), for instance—dazzling floral displays leave a litter of spent blossoms and pods beneath the tree.

PREVENTING PROBLEMS WITH TREES, SHRUBS, VINES, AND GROUND COVERS

The surest way to avoid problems in permanent landscapes is to plant the right plant in the right place. Once plants are well established, with their growing conditions met, preventive maintenance is the next most critical factor in keeping them healthy. For general guidance on problem-preventing techniques, see pages 34–47.

PLANTING AND STAKING

Trees, shrubs, and large vines should be planted directly into native soil. Don't add soil amendments, or the plant roots will confine themselves to the amended zone and won't expand into the surrounding soil. This will retard growth. In severe cases, plants may become dwarfed.

Instead, loosen the ground in a 2–3-foot area around the planting hole. If the roots are wrapped around the soil inside the container, be sure to straighten them out, or cut the root ball. Circled roots can actually strangle the plant. Set the root ball on firm or undisturbed soil inside the hole, with the roots spread out. The crown area should be in a slight mound above soil level after backfilling. Protect the soil over the root zone by covering it with organic mulch (keep it away from the trunk). Paint exposed trunks with diluted interior white latex paint to prevent sunscald.

Always remove the nursery stake at planting time. Unstaked trees develop stronger trunks than staked trees, so add support stakes only if the tree will not stand alone or if the root ball needs to be anchored. Set two or three sturdy stakes with soft and flexible ties 12 inches from the trunk and perpendicular to the prevailing winds. Remove support stakes within 6 to 12 months. Support vines as appropriate to their growth habits, adjusting ties as the vines grow to prevent damage to expanding stems.

TRIMMING

Many flowering shrubs, vines, and ground covers require annual trimming to correct their shape and promote blossoming. Trimming at the wrong time of year, however, risks removing blossoms. The key is to know when the plant sets flowering buds: on last year's growth after flowering, or on the current season's growth after dormancy. Rhododendrons and azaleas set buds shortly after they bloom and hold the buds over winter. Routinely trimming an azalea during the winter, then, means losing spring flowers. A good way to tell the right time of year to trim a plant is by its flowering time. Most species flowering in early spring bloom on old wood; later-blooming species such as buddleia and rose bloom on growth produced during the current season.

PRUNING

Well-placed plants need pruning only to remove damaged or dead wood, to keep the desired shape, and to maintain vigor. Pruning should always be thinning (removing a whole branch down to its joint with the trunk), never topping (chopping off the ends of branches)—to remove branches for air circulation, reduce wind resistance, or allow light penetration. Try to spread the removal of large branches over a period of several years. Leave short, lower branches intact along the trunk of a young tree for several years. On shrubs, vines, and ground covers, cut back stems as needed over two to three years to encourage strong new growth from the base and to improve shape, foliage production, or flowering. To avoid masses of tangled stems, prune fast-growing vines regularly. All

PLANTING A TREE OR SHRUB

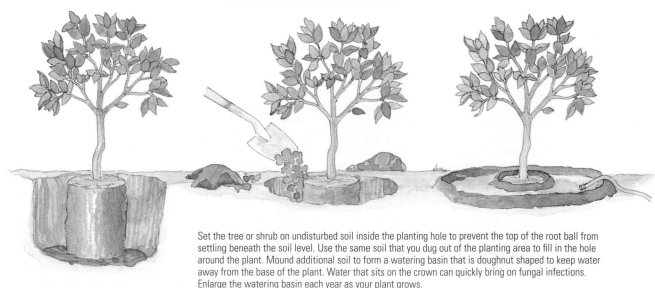

Set the tree or shrub on undisturbed soil inside the planting hole to prevent the top of the root ball from settling beneath the soil level. Use the same soil that you dug out of the planting area to fill in the hole around the plant. Mound additional soil to form a watering basin that is doughnut shaped to keep water away from the base of the plant. Water that sits on the crown can quickly bring on fungal infections. Enlarge the watering basin each year as your plant grows.

THINNING AND HEADING BACK

To thin a shrub or tree, remove a stem or branch at its base (left). When heading back (right), cut shoots to a bud; cut an older branch to a twig, which will become the new growing tip. Heading, or topping, can ruin the shape of a tree, but it will encourage a young shrub to grow more compactly.

other reasons for pruning should be questioned. Most pruning stimulates growth and may cause unnatural shapes. On many young trees, including Atlas cedar and liquidambar, the central trunk or "leader" should never be shortened, or the tree will be deformed.

WATERING AND FERTILIZING

In many western zones where rainfall is scant or is concentrated in one season, supplemental deep watering is crucial for maintaining healthy root systems. Infrequent deep waterings are much preferred to briefer shallow applications. Test for soil moisture near the drip line with a long metal rod. If it easily penetrates the soil to a depth of 18 inches, you have applied enough water. Remember that as your trees and shrubs grow and their root systems expand, they need water farther away from the main trunk or stem.

At planting time, use only a slow-release fertilizer in the bottom of the planting hole to supply phosphorous and potassium to developing roots. Then, before the onset of the growing season, water-in nitrogen fertilizer for all shrubs and trees more than two years old. When your plants reach their optimum size, fertilize only if their foliage indicates that they need nutrients or if the plants seem to lack vigor. Too much succulent growth on mature plants may invite a pest or disease problem.

PLANTING GROUND COVERS

Shallow-rooted ground covers benefit from organic amendments tilled into their entire growing area at planting time and spread over the surface as mulch after plants are in the ground. As they age and drop foliage under their dense covers, ground covers continuously provide themselves with organic matter for a constant, though low, nutrient supply. Supplement this with slow-release fertilizers applied annually.

To thoroughly cover an area, plant ground covers in a hexagonal grid, placing clumping forms closer together than spreaders. You should have coverage in one year for most plants and in two years for slow growers. Plants set too close together compete for water and nutrients in the root zone; spaced too widely, they may be crowded out by weeds. In cold-winter zones, set out plants at least six weeks before the first frost date. Use a knife to cut blocks of ivy or other low ground covers grown in flats, and plant them as individual plugs. Keep the root zone moist and weeds in check while plants get established. Encourage fast horizontal growth by pegging down long runners and cutting back vertical stems on mounding forms.

GROOMING GROUND COVERS

Semiannual inspections and grooming are helpful, even for low-maintenance ground covers, to keep them in prime condition. Look for overcrowding that cuts down on air circulation and promotes disease. Every year or two at the start of the growing season, mow or shear creeping spreaders such as ivy, winter creeper, and St. Johnswort; thin crowded beds of daylilies and clumping plants. On small shrubs used as ground covers, cut out dead and crowded branches to the main stem; cut back shoots to increase density. Trim off frost damage on new growth and look for discoloration or stunting from nutrient deficiencies.

COMMON PROBLEMS OF TREES, SHRUBS, VINES, AND GROUND COVERS

Many trees, shrubs, vines, and ground covers can survive in all climate zones in the West. However, for the fewest problems, grow plants only in those zones where they thrive. Climate factors are critical, since landscape plants are often chosen for long-term function as well as enjoyment. In cold interior and warm coastal zones, gardeners depend on trees, shrubs, and vines for windbreaks, property boundaries, and patio enclosures, but different species suit each zone. In northern latitudes and high elevations, trees must be able to bear up under ice storms and short growing seasons; in warm-winter climates, they must be able to forgo winter chilling and sustain constant growth; in coastal gardens, they must be able to withstand strong winds and salty air. There are many plants suited to the conditions of all western climates, but it's important to choose the ones that will tend to have the fewest problems.

Besides avoiding conditions in your local area that you know will induce stress and favor pests and diseases, it is helpful to be aware of other potential problems not related to climate and to know their causes and methods of prevention.

NEGLECT

Neglect is perhaps the greatest problem afflicting long-lived landscape plants. Plants may be taken for granted for years, until they begin to decline, at which point it may be too late to help them with improved care. Sometimes the best option is to replace the plant with a species that is easier to maintain or more disease-resistant, especially if the plant has become hazardous. Shrubs, ground covers, and vines may recover through rejuvenation, corrective pruning, dividing, and fertilizing. Check for interference from neighboring shrubs and trees, for competition from weeds or other plants in the root zone, for lack of sun or shade during years of growth, and for damage from hostile weather. Don't overlook the possibility of damage from the effects of pets, wildlife, smog, or ozone. For greater long-term success, select new plants that are resistant to problems that have shown up in your garden.

ROOT AND CROWN PROBLEMS

Excavation and trenching during construction projects may damage roots, and frequently sever and kill them—and, in short order, the plant itself. If the surface level of the soil is lowered by grading, large portions of surface-feeding roots may be destroyed; if fill is added over the existing soil, the roots can suffocate. Burying the crown too deeply can cause death from fungal growths. Overhead irrigation may hit the trunks of trees and shrubs, causing crown rot where moisture settles at soil level.

Shallow rooting is normal for some species, such as rhododendron and white alder. In other species, however, a lack of water at lower soil depths, compacted soil, or hardpan layers will prevent the deep root growth that the plants need. Another problem arises when roots lift driveways and sidewalks or invade other plantings. Severing such roots seriously weakens a plant's health and stability. In lawns, shallow rooting results from competition for limited water. All plants, especially shallow-rooted ones in lawns, should be allowed an open area at least 3–4 feet in circumference and covered with 2–3 inches of mulch. Provide larger spaces for water-sensitive trees. Keep mulch 6 inches away from the trunk or stems to prevent crown rot.

Many root problems are caused by fungi that become active in waterlogged soil after heavy rains or overwatering. Root fungal infections usually manifest themselves at the ends of conducting tissue—that is, as tip and branch dieback, which has the potential of killing entire plants. Pests, such as root knot nematodes, may stunt the growth of woody landscape plants. Poor soils can be a cause of slow growth because they may not contain beneficial mycorrhizae—microscopic organisms that grow on root tips and aid in nutrient uptake.

FOLIAGE AND STEM PROBLEMS

Trees and shrubs lose their leaves during normal dormancy. They also drop foliage when stressed from insect or disease damage, or when certain environmental conditions such as drought or a sudden cold snap bring untimely dormancy. Such defoliation is potentially serious, but loss of leaves in itself does not signal the death of a tree. Certainly, leafless dormant trees are merely resting.

Minor foliage and stem damage is common on all types of plants. On an ornamental plant, chewed leaf parts, webbing, discoloration, leaf spots, rusts, and mildews create an unattractive appearance but are not serious. Repetitive minor damage is a problem, however, when plants do not recover from stress. More serious injury from beetles, borers, or fungal and bacterial diseases such as fireblight and wilts can be fatal.

TIP

Fence off trees near construction sites early in the planning stage or prior to excavation. Prohibit any earth movement at least 10 feet beyond the drip line around the tree. Protecting tree roots prevents loss of feeder roots, reduces stress and susceptibility to pests, and prolongs a tree's life.

Foliage damage on conifers is not always obvious in early stages. Carefully inspect these trees and shrubs to detect insect and disease problems before they get out of hand. Heavy and repeated infestations can be serious, causing branch dieback or loss of the entire plant.

WOUNDED BARK

Oozing sap is generally a sign of damaged bark, although it can also be caused by cankers or borers. Or it can be a natural occurrence if no other symptoms are present. Damaged bark opens trees, shrubs, and vines to attack by insects and disease organisms. Common causes are improper pruning, staking, and tying. Damage from vehicles, string trimmers, and lawn mowers can be even more severe. Bark damage also results from weather conditions, such as freezing or lightning strikes. Sunburn is common on young trees before they develop a protective canopy, or when pruning removes the foliage and exposes interior branches.

Damaged bark can also be caused by animals. Wildlife pests—and even household pets—can seriously injure woody plants by rubbing and chewing on trunks and feeding on tender bark near the soil line, sometimes girdling the plant and killing it.

WILTING

Drought and, paradoxically, overwatering (or waterlogged soil after heavy rains) are the most common causes of wilting. Wilting may also be triggered by stress from high winds or intense sun, or by diseases that invade water-conducting vessels through the roots and move to stems and leaves. Once wilting occurs, it may be too late to save the plant. Some species, such as spruce, don't show stress by wilting and can die from drought with little or no warning.

UNUSUAL GROWTHS

Mushrooms and conks (fungal fruiting bodies) on bark or around the base of a tree indicate a hazardous condition from decay inside. Other, less threatening growths are seen more frequently. Parasitic mistletoe, although desirable as holiday decor, extracts moisture and nutrients from its host, causing overall stunting and endangering branches at the point of attachment. Mosses and lichens that green up during rainy seasons are unattractive in some settings but are basically harmless. Galls, or abnormal swellings, are usually caused by insect or mite secretions and in themselves have no known ill effects.

An awareness of the problems that may threaten your trees, shrubs, vines, or ground covers will enable you to create conditions that prevent their occurrence or to spot trouble early enough to prevent major damage. By knowing how these plants grow and flourish, you can nurture them to continued health and long life.

Staking a Tree

Wire will damage the trunk and may kill the tree, even when cushioned by lengths of hose. Instead, use two stakes and broad, flexible ties.

THE MOST COMMON SPECIES AND THE MOST COMMON PROBLEMS

These listings tell you the botanical and common name of the plant and the western zones where it thrives. One of the common problems afflicting the plant in the West is featured, and, where available, resistant varieties are listed.

SYMBOLS: ✿ TREES ⚘ SHRUBS ⚘ VINES ♛ GROUND COVERS

ABIES

✿ FIR

⚖ ZONES: VARY BY SPECIES

CYTOSPORA CANKER

Color change in needles is usually the first noticeable sign of a problem. Needles affected by canker turn red and brown, then tan. The infected areas on stems or branches are usually sunken oval lesions that may ooze liquid or be dotted with small protrusions from the fungus. Entire branches may redden and die. The tree may block the spread of the canker by surrounding it with callus tissue, or the canker may girdle and kill the tree.

Other plant problems. COMMON PESTS: aphids, budworms, moths, scales, spider mites. COMMON DISEASES: crown and collar rot, needle cast, needle and twig blight, rust. OTHER: dwarf mistletoe.

Notes: Firs show some tolerance for dry lowland conditions, but they thrive at upper elevations. Most need ample water, room to grow, and shade protection in hot, dry climates. Some firs that naturally grow in pendulous or contorted shapes are considered specialty trees rather than deformed specimens.

ACACIA

✿ ACACIA

⚖ ZONES: 8, 9, 12–24; VARY BY SPECIES

ACACIA PSYLLIDS

Tiny green or brown insects appear on tender growing tips, generally in spring. They suck sap from the undersides of leaves, causing shoots and leaves to turn yellow or brown, wilt or curl up, and die. Pellets of honeydew secretions and black sooty mold may be visible. Commonly called plant lice, psyllids are less than ⅛ inch long and resemble miniature cicadas. They may be accompanied by beneficial beetles and bugs that prey on them.

Other plant problems. COMMON PESTS: caterpillars, leafhoppers, sapsuckers, scales. COMMON DISEASES: root and crown rot. OTHER: chlorosis, frost damage, invasive roots, wind damage from poorly anchored trees.

Resistant varieties. Several acacia species are resistant to acacia psyllids, including *A. craspedocarpa*, pearl acacia (*A. podalyriifolia*), kangaroo thorn (*A. armata*), and *A. dealbata*. Plant blackwood acacia (*A. melanoxylon*), which is not resistant, away from patios and walkways to avoid problems from litter, suckering, and shallow roots.

ACER

✿ MAPLE

⚖ ZONES: VARY BY SPECIES

VERTICILLIUM WILT

Verticillium wilt starts with yellowing of leaf margins, then of entire leaves. Wilting and browning follow, confined mostly to one side of the plant. The progression is usually upward or outward from the base of the plant or on an affected branch to the tips. Dead leaves may fall or remain on branches. Tissue just under the bark is discolored, frequently streaked dark brown, green, or black from the invading fungus. Verticillium wilt often strikes when the tree is stressed from a shortage of water. In severe cases, the tree will die.

Other plant problems. COMMON PESTS: aphids, beetles, borers, caterpillars, leafhoppers, mealybugs, sapsuckers, scales, spider mites, whiteflies. COMMON DISEASES: anthracnose, canker, powdery mildew, slime flux. OTHER: chlorosis, leaf scorch.

Notes: Maple species most affected by verticillium wilt are silver maple (A. saccharinum), Norway maple (A. platanoides), sugar maple (A. saccharum), and red maple (A. rubrum). Leaf scorch is common on newly planted trees in lawns and in planter boxes if

they're not getting enough water. As they grow, maples must have ready access to water to support their large canopies.

AJUGA reptans

♛ AJUGA, CARPET BUGLE

⚖ ZONES: ALL

CROWN AND ROOT ROT

Green, variegated, and bronze-leafed varieties planted in heavy, soggy soil exhibit poor growth, wilting, yellowing, and leaf drop from fungi. Symptoms usually appear in spring after crowns have been damaged and roots are dead. Fungal strands and fruiting bodies may be visible among rotting roots. Rots develop among crowded plants with poor air circulation. Removing old leaves in late fall and dividing plantings every few years keeps plants healthy and improves air movement. Make divisions in the fall and replant in amended, well-drained soil.

Other plant problems. COMMON PESTS: aphids, nematodes. COMMON DISEASES: powdery mildew. OTHER: leaf yellowing and scorch from excessive heat, sun, or humidity.

Notes: Ajuga leaves grow larger and plants grow taller in partial shade; shaded plants may need more frequent division. To renew tidy appearance of plants with dead flower stalks, mow after flowering. Fill in bare patches with divisions.

ALNUS

✿ ALDER

⚖ ZONES: VARY BY SPECIES

LACE BUGS

In summer, leaves appear bleached, mottled, or blotchy, with yellow flecks or stippling, due to adult bugs and nymphs sucking plant juices. In severe cases, distortion follows. Bugs feed on the undersides of leaves, where they often deposit dark spots of excrement. Damage from lace bugs is similar to that from mites or thrips; however, mites do not leave signs of excrement, and lace bugs are about ⅛ inch long, while individual thrips can only be seen with a magnifying glass.

Other plant problems. COMMON PESTS: aphids, borers, flea beetles, gall midges, leaf miners, psyllids, scales, tent caterpillars. COMMON DISEASES: cankers, leaf rust. OTHER: shallow, invasive roots.

Notes: Red alder (A. oregona) is subject to infestations of tent caterpillars in the Northwest. Throughout the West, severe scale infestations can cause loss of vigor and dieback. Most alders are fast growing and thrive only in ample moisture—along stream beds, for example, where they seed themselves prolifically.

ARBUTUS

✿ MADRONE

❧ ZONES: 3–7, 14–19

MADRONE SHIELD BEARERS

In the fall, leaves develop crooked tunnels and brown, dead patches from larvae mining inside (see leaf miners). In winter, larvae cut holes in the foliage, as though with a paper punch, before they drop to the ground or move to the bark to pupate. The potential problem cannot be seen, because the eggs are hidden in the leaves. Heavy infestations result in numerous holes, but trees tolerate moderate damage with no effect other than disfigurement.

Other plant problems. COMMON PESTS: aphids, borers, psyllids, scales, tent caterpillars, whiteflies. COMMON DISEASES: canker and dieback, leaf spot, root rot. OTHER: difficulty in transplanting.

Notes: Transplanting a madrone from a large nursery can into the garden is often unsuccessful. Instead, set out young plants from tubes or small containers before roots are well developed. Where trees are subjected to excess moisture, their growth may slow when problems arise. Give madrones infrequent and deep waterings, fast drainage, and acid soil. Healthy trees are not bothered by most insects and diseases.

ARCTOSTAPHYLOS

❧ MANZANITA, BEARBERRY

❧ ZONES: VARY BY SPECIES

MANZANITA LEAF GALL APHIDS

Fleshy, bulbous red galls appear along leaf edges, disfiguring the foliage and retarding plant growth. These galls are enclosing aphids feeding on leaves. They appear on new growth, more commonly on plants that have been sheared and irrigated in a landscape situation rather than on manzanitas in the wild. Other than disfiguring foliage, the galls have minimal impact on plants.

Other plant problems. COMMON PESTS: borers, mealybugs, other aphids, psyllids, scales, tent caterpillars, whiteflies. COMMON DISEASES: fungal cankers, root rot.

Notes: Other types of aphids and some scales also feed on manzanita and cause dieback of shoots but do not threaten plants. The greatest damage is from fungal diseases that thrive in excess water in warm, heavy soils. Loose, well-drained soils are crucial for success with manzanitas. Many named varieties have been developed to withstand summer irrigation and fertilizing. A. 'Austin Hill', A. bakeri 'Louis Edmunds', A. densiflora 'Howard McMinn', and A. uva-ursi 'Radiant' accept garden conditions more readily than do other varieties.

AUCUBA

❧ JAPANESE AUCUBA

❧ ZONES: 4–24

BLACKENED FOLIAGE

Aucuba leaves blacken and look charred when they are exposed to direct sunlight or strong reflected light for long periods. No pest or disease is involved in this cultural disorder, and all green-leafed and variegated varieties are affected. Charring can be avoided by planting in areas with only limited, filtered morning sun. Aucuba can tolerate and thrive in even dense shade and the low light intensities inside entryways and under trees, and they compete successfully with tree roots.

Other plant problems. COMMON PESTS: aphids, mealybugs, scales, spider mites. COMMON DISEASES: leaf spot. OTHER: legginess.

Notes: Black sooty mold that grows on honeydew from aphids, mealybugs, and scales appears similar to sun-damaged foliage, but it can be scraped off leaves whereas charring permeates the leaf tissue. Aphid infestations may reduce vigor and slow growth; heavy scale infestations cause decline and dieback. Promote fuller growth by pruning the oldest stems to the ground every few years.

BACCHARIS

❧ BACCHARIS

❧ ZONES: VARY BY SPECIES

BLACK SCALES

Large populations of black scales hatch from eggs in late spring and feed on leaves. Nymphs are brown with a ridge on their back; adults are black and larger. Crawlers emerge from scales and relocate along twigs, where they develop a protective covering. During feeding, sticky honeydew accumulates on leaves and twigs; black sooty mold may be present. Plants perform poorly under heavy infestations.

Other plant problems. COMMON PESTS: borers, gall-forming insects, lace bugs, leaf beetles, loopers, mites. COMMON DISEASES: root rot. OTHER: exposed twiggy stems and woody branches, cottony seeds on female plants.

Notes: Exposed bare stems appear to be dead though they support foliage at their tips. Improve appearance and maintain compactness by shearing plants or pruning hard in late winter or early spring before growth begins. Remove bare, arching branches to stimulate growth of new replacement stems. Baccharis 'Centennial' (zones 10–13) is tolerant of desert heat and resists root rot caused by soilborne fungi.

BETULA

✿ BIRCH

❧ ZONES: VARY BY SPECIES

BRONZE BIRCH BORERS

Drought stress and high soil temperatures precede attacks by bronze birch borers, which are indicated by wet spots and dark stains on bumpy, ridged surfaces on the bark. Look for tiny D-shaped holes in bark in branch crotches where borers enter to feed on cambium tissue. Girdling from borer activity causes branches and limbs to die back, starting at the tips and eventually reaching the main stems.

Other plant problems. COMMON PESTS: aphids, caterpillars, lace bugs, leafhoppers, leaf miners, sapsuckers, scales. COMMON DISEASES: canker, rust, slime flux, sooty mold, witches' broom. OTHER: drought stress.

Resistant varieties. Birches resistant to borer attacks include monarch birch (*B. maximowicziana*), Zones 3–9, 14–24; paper birch (*B. papyrifera*), Zones 1–6; whitebarked Himalayan birch (*B. jaquemontii*), Zones 3–11, 14–17; *B. platyphylla* 'Whitespire', Zones 1–11, 14–24; and heritage birch (*B. nigra* 'Heritage'), all zones. River birch (*B. nigra*) is the most trouble-free species. All birch species perform best in their native regions. Mulches help to moderate soil temperatures.

BUXUS

🌿 BOXWOOD

✂ ZONES: VARY BY SPECIES

ROOT KNOT NEMATODES

Stunted growth and yellowing, wilted foliage in hot weather are symptoms of root knot nematodes. Upon checking roots, you will see hardened galls or swellings attached to roots and not easily dislodged. Secondary problems such as crown gall, bacterial wilt, and root rot may follow as a result of the plant's weakened condition. In severe cases, plants die.

Other plant problems. COMMON PESTS: mealybugs, psyllids, scales, spider mites, webworms. COMMON DISEASES: blight, canker; crown and collar rot, leaf spot. OTHER: summer and winter leafburn.

Notes: Boxwood is easy to ignore since it has few problems, but it is likely to suffer nutrient deficiencies without annual fertilizing. Hosing down plants every few weeks in summer keeps them dust-free and less susceptible to spider mites. Good drainage is essential for preventing rots from soilborne fungi. Weakened plants are more likely to suffer rot damage than vigorous ones. Pale foliage may indicate poor drainage. Buxus microphylla and its varieties are more resistant to nematodes and more disease-resistant in general than B. sempervirens.

CAMELLIA

🌿 CAMELLIA

✂ ZONES: 4–9, 12, 14–24

CAMELLIA PETAL BLIGHT

Perfectly formed flowers can be ruined by camellia petal blight. The petals turn tan or brown at the edges, then toward the center of the blossoms. As flowers continue to rot, they drop to the ground and the fungus reinfects the soil, where it breeds. White and pale pink blossoms are the most susceptible. All the blossoms may be affected, and once the blight begins, there is no treatment until the bloom season has ended.

Other plant problems. COMMON PESTS: aphids, leaf galls, scales. COMMON DISEASES: collar, foot, and crown rot; sooty mold. OTHER: bud drop; chlorosis; leafburn from salt, sun, or wind; leaf drop from overfertilizing; petal burn from sun and wind.

Notes: Don't confuse normal bud drop with camellia petal blight. Camellias normally set more buds than they can open, some varieties more than others. Dense growth may interfere with blossoming as well. Prune to thin as needed and to renew flowering wood if blossoming is light.

CAMPSIS

🌿 TRUMPET VINE

✂ ZONES: VARY BY SPECIES

BUD DROP

Plants laden with developing buds may lose them from premature bud drop. Causes include late frosts and soil that is too rich or poorly drained. Bud drop can also result from overwatering, underwatering, or low humidity, especially during summer. The problem may actually date back to the previous growth season, when buds were forming prior to dormancy.

Other plant problems. COMMON PESTS: aphids, scales, spider mites, whiteflies. COMMON DISEASES: blight, leaf spot, powdery mildew. OTHER: leafburn, loss of flowering wood, rampant growth, suckering roots.

Notes: Flowers appear on wood produced in the current season. Pruning during the spring and summer to restrain growth effectively removes all chance of blossoming. Prune in early spring before growth begins, by heading back and by thinning stems. Periodic hard pruning during dormancy keeps the vine in bounds and renews weak branches. Unpruned vines may become too heavy to be self-clinging and may tumble.

CEANOTHUS

🌿 CEANOTHUS

✂ ZONES: 1–9, 14–24

PACIFIC FLATHEADED BORERS

Wet spots on branches or branch dieback is usually the first indication of the Pacific flatheaded borer. Subsequent symptoms are cracked bark and then death of entire branches. Severely stressed plants are likely to be lost from borer activity. Since borers are attracted to diseased, stressed, or injured plants, shrubs may exhibit decline before they are infested. Evaluate site, soil, and moisture requirements for your species to find the reasons for lack of vigor.

Other plant problems. COMMON PESTS: aphids, gall moths, mealybugs, psyllids, tent caterpillars, whiteflies. COMMON DISEASES: canker, root rot. OTHER: short life span.

Notes: Ceanothus tend to be short-lived in garden situations. They are prone to oak root fungus and other root rots from summer moisture. Some ceanothus species, including C. gloriosus, C. gloriosus exaltatus, C. impressus, C. rigidus, and C. prostratus, are resistant to infestation by the stem gall moth.

CHAMAECYPARIS

🌲 FALSE CYPRESS

✂ ZONES: VARY BY SPECIES

CEDAR AND CYPRESS BARK BEETLES

Dead shoots hanging on branch tips like tan-colored flags are signs of cedar and cypress bark beetles. Stressed, unhealthy trees attract the female beetles, which bore into the trunk and large limbs. Inside, boring continues between the bark and the wood, interrupting the flow of nutrients and water and causing damage to twigs and shoots. Pitch and granular excrement resembling sawdust may flow out of holes in the wood. Healthy trees can withstand minor damage, but the beetles will continue to feed on weak trees, often girdling their trunks and killing them.

Other plant problems. COMMON PESTS: aphids, cypress tip miners, mealybugs, mites, sawflies, scales. COMMON DISEASES: blight, canker, root rot, rust, witches' broom.

Notes: Vigorous trees are rarely attacked by borers. Stress from over- or underwatering, root rot or other diseases, injury, or insects weakens the tree and attracts these destructive insects. Different Chamaecyparis species have different cultural requirements that must be satisfied for strong growth.

CLEMATIS

🌿 CLEMATIS

✂ ZONES: ALL; BEST IN 1–6, 15–17

FUNGAL STEM ROT

Without warning, clematis vines in full bud may begin to wilt, then turn brown and die. A fungus that enters the stem quickly kills all aboveground growth. The roots are unaffected and will produce new shoots after the vine is cut to the ground. Growth and blossoming are slowed, but the vine is rarely killed by the fungus. The stress of losing foliage may trigger dormancy, causing roots to become inactive for the rest of the growing season or longer. Leave roots in place for 1 to 3 years since these are tough survivors and may eventually resume growth.

Other plant problems. COMMON PESTS: birds, earwigs, rodents, slugs, snails. COMMON DISEASES: fungal wilt, leaf spot, powdery mildew. OTHER: frost damage, retarded growth from exposed roots.

Resistant varieties. Large-flowered hybrids are more affected by clematis fungal wilt than the smaller-flowered hybrids. All clematis are subject to powdery mildew, which coats leaves; in severe cases, it causes distorted growth and unopened buds.

CORNUS

🌳 DOGWOOD

✂ ZONES: VARY BY SPECIES

CICADAS

In late spring or early summer, cicadas periodically show up to feed on trees, and dogwoods are one of their favorites. The immature cicadas suck sap from tree roots, which may reduce flowering and slow growth. The adults suck sap and cut slits in twigs to lay eggs. Twig feeding is less injurious to trees than the damage from cutting, which usually kills small stems. You can recognize cicadas from their sound more than by sight: their dark bodies and transparent wings are difficult to see on brown stems.

Other plant problems. COMMON PESTS: aphids, borers, leaf miners, scales, whiteflies. COMMON DISEASES: anthracnose, canker, crown and collar rot, flower and leaf blight, leaf spot, powdery mildew, twig blight. OTHER: sunburn.

Resistant varieties. *Cornus kousa* is a beautiful and disease-resistant species, especially suitable for the Pacific Northwest, where diseases are common among dogwoods. Many varieties are available. Resistant trees are less vulnerable to attack from pests, especially borers, which shorten their lives.

COTONEASTER

🌿 COTONEASTER

✂ ZONES: VARY BY SPECIES

OAK ROOT FUNGUS

Oak root fungus affects the roots of many plants other than oaks. The visible symptoms of its presence on cotoneaster are dull or yellowed leaves, an overall decline in performance, or wilting foliage. Branches or entire plants may suddenly die. To verify the presence of this fungus, examine the roots, checking for fan-shaped fungal tissue just under the outer root covering. Plants become infected only when they are planted in soil where the fungus is already present.

Other plant problems. COMMON PESTS: aphids, borers, lace bugs, scales, spider mites, webworms. COMMON DISEASES: fireblight, leaf spot, root rot. OTHER: overwatering, leggy growth.

Notes: In some climate zones, toadstools form at the base of infected plants. Since toadstools from other fungi also grow at the soil line on many plants, examining roots is a better method of identifying oak root fungus. All cotoneasters are susceptible, but many other woody and herbaceous plants are resistant. The appearance of established, healthy cotoneasters is improved by pruning out the oldest wood each year.

CRATAEGUS

🌳 HAWTHORN

✂ ZONES: 1–12; 14–17

BUFFALO TREEHOPPERS

Damage from buffalo treehoppers is threefold. Minor damage occurs from these insects' sucking plant juices and depositing honeydew secretions on leaves and twigs. The sugary honeydew then sustains the growth of mold, which covers foliage with sooty black residues. The greatest damage occurs on branches or twigs where treehoppers slit into tender wood to lay their eggs. Ruptures in the tissue of young trees interfere with growth, although older, established trees tolerate some damaged wood and frequent dieback of branch tips.

Other plant problems. COMMON PESTS: aphids, leaf rollers, mites, moths, sawflies, scales. COMMON DISEASES: fireblight, leaf and stem blight, leaf spot, rusts. OTHER: thorns.

Notes: Most hawthorns, as their name suggests, bear thorns. On cockspur hawthorn (C. crus-galli) and Washington hawthorn (C. phaenopyrum), thorns may grow up to 3 inches in length. The thorns can be dangerous when the tree is planted near walkways and play areas, so site these trees carefully. Frequent trimming of branches can leave hawthorn susceptible to infection.

CUPRESSUS

🌲 CYPRESS

✂ ZONES: VARY BY SPECIES

CYPRESS TIP MINERS

A common late fall and winter pest on cypress trees, the cypress tip miner causes tips of foliage to turn yellow or brown until the following spring and summer, when needles green up again. The damage is done as larvae hatch from eggs laid in branch tips and feed on the tender foliage. They spin silken cocoons between twiggy growing tips to complete their entire life cycle in the tree.

Other plant problems. COMMON PESTS: aphids, bark beetles, mealybugs, mites, sawflies, scales. COMMON DISEASES: canker, rust, scab. OTHER: overwatering or underwatering, depending on species.

Notes: The cypress tip miner invades other members of the cypress family. Damage can be serious on junipers and arborvitae; see Juniperus for resistant varieties. Cypress infected with the incurable cypress canker fungus should be removed to prevent its spreading to other trees.

EUONYMUS

🌿 EUONYMUS

☘ ZONES: VARY BY SPECIES

EUONYMUS SCALES

These scales cause yellow or brown spots on euonymus leaves. The male insects are fuzzy, white, and oblong, while female scales are brownish black and convex; both types have yellowish areas at the ends. You can find them throughout the growing season on foliage and on tougher stems. In spring, young orange crawlers emerge from overwintering scales and begin feeding.

Other plant problems. COMMON PESTS: borers, nematodes, spider mites, thrips, weevils. COMMON DISEASES: anthracnose, powdery mildew, crown gall.

Resistant varieties. *Euonymus japonica* is plagued by euonymus scales and by other problems more than are other *Euonymus* species. It is not affected by powdery mildew, in Zones 4–6. In other zones, plants succumb to mildew less when they are planted in full sun with good air circulation. In areas where euonymus scale is severe, *E. japonica* should be replaced with another species.

FRAXINUS

❀ ASH

☘ ZONES: VARY BY SPECIES

TENT CATERPILLARS

In spring, tent caterpillars feed on leaves, often to the point of defoliating the tree. Twigs and branch forks become covered with silken webs. Trees are rarely severely damaged unless defoliation is repetitive on young or otherwise stressed trees. In such cases, branches will die back or the entire tree may die. Infestations can recur during a season, and caterpillars may also feed on nearby trees. Only deciduous trees are affected.

Other plant problems. COMMON PESTS: aphids, borers, carpenterworms, lace bugs, leaf miners, sawflies, scales, whiteflies. COMMON DISEASES: anthracnose, cankers, leaf spot, root rot, rust, verticillium wilt. OTHER: litter from winged seeds.

Notes: Leaf edges on white ash (F. americana) burn in hot, windy sites. This species suffers from a general decline that causes dieback. Try to avoid purchasing both male and female trees. When female trees are pollinated, they produce a heavy crop of winged seeds that result in litter and nuisance seedlings.

FUCHSIA

🌿 FUCHSIA

☘ ZONES: VARY BY SPECIES

FUCHSIA GALL MITES

Distorted leaves and shoots are the result of fuchsia gall mite infestation, a serious condition since the 1980s. Damage varies from plant to plant, sometimes appearing as thickened leaves and irregularly shaped galls. In warm-climate zones, damage continues all year on foliage and moves to flowers during the bloom period. The problem is mostly aesthetic, since affected growing tips are clearly visible. Mite populations are fewer on healthy and dust-free plants.

Other plant problems. COMMON PESTS: aphids, mealybugs, whiteflies. COMMON DISEASES: rust, verticillium wilt. OTHER: drought stress, frost damage, legginess, nutrient deficiencies, sunburn.

Resistant varieties. Varieties resistant to fuchsia gall mites include 'Baby Chang', 'Carnival', 'Chance Encounter', 'Cinnabarina', 'Isis', 'Mendocino Mini', 'Miniature Jewels', 'Mrs. Victor Reiter', 'Ocean Mist', 'Space Shuttle', and 'Trumpeter'. Many of the species fuchsias are also resistant. When growing fuchsia in containers, avoid leafburn by adjusting location with seasonal changes in the angle of the sun. Container plants need heavy annual pruning in spring to stimulate new growth and blooms.

GLEDITSIA

❀ HONEY LOCUST

☘ ZONES: 1–16, 18–20

POD GALL MIDGES

Honey locust trees with large populations of pod gall midges become nearly or completely defoliated by midsummer and begin an early dormancy, remaining leafless until the following spring. Although they appear to be dead, trees are rarely killed by the insects or by loss of foliage, but the condition is a nuisance since the tree is usually planted for either its shade or the delicate color and pattern of the foliage. Before leaves drop, the tips develop swollen red or brown galls that contain tiny larvae of the small flying insects. Several generations a year continue feeding on honey locusts.

Other plant problems. COMMON PESTS: borers, mimosa webworms, spider mites, whiteflies. COMMON DISEASES: cankers, leaf spot, root rot, witches' broom. OTHER: wind breakage.

Notes: Select a variety of honey locust for light or dense shade and for the shape that suits your landscape. Don't choose a fast grower that would need cutting back, as pruning cuts may provide an inroad for diseases. Many of these trees are destroyed by cankers.

HEBE

🌿 HEBE

☘ ZONES: 14–24

FUSARIUM WILT

Hebes are particularly susceptible to fusarium wilt. Some leaves develop brown patches, usually starting on lower parts of the shrub and on one side only. Older leaves turn yellow and drop. If the disease does not progress, stunting results. More commonly, the entire plant wilts and dies. Infection begins in the roots from soilborne fungi and invades the vascular, or conducting, tissues of the stems. Discoloration of stem wood is a good indicator of the disease.

Other plant problems. COMMON PESTS: aphids, scales. COMMON DISEASES: leaf spot, root rot, verticillium wilt. OTHER: frost and heat damage.

Notes: If one hebe shrub is killed by fusarium wilt, do not plant another in the same location since the fungus lives in the soil. Install a new hebe in another location and plant a different species in the problem area—the specific fusarium fungus that killed the hebe will not affect a different plant species.

HEDERA

❧ IVY

🌿 ZONES: VARY BY SPECIES

EDEMA

When excess water collects in the conducting vessels in ivy leaves, small blisterlike swellings appear. Water rising from the roots exerts pressure against leaf tissue and causes the swellings to break. Broken cellulose tissue loses its normal green color, and the result is a series of tan or brown spots surrounded by corky tissue on the undersides of leaves. Some leaves will yellow and drop; others remain intact unless removed or until they drop from age. Edema is an abiotic disorder—that is, its cause is not a plant, insect, or disease. It occurs most often on cool evenings when the soil is saturated and relative humidity is high.

Other plant problems. COMMON PESTS: aphids, rodents, scales, slugs, snails. COMMON DISEASES: root rot. OTHER: invasive growth, sunburn.

Notes: Ivy develops its familiar foliage and creeping growth habit during a juvenile phase of development. When plants mature after many years, the leaves lose their lobes, stems tend to grow more upright than horizontal, and fruits develop. When the vines are no longer a suitable ground cover, they need to be replaced.

HIBISCUS

🌿 HIBISCUS

🌿 ZONES: VARY BY SPECIES

RINGSPOT VIRUS

In some plants, such as *Nandina,* variegated foliage is a desirable trait. However, color patterns that are not normal to a species are typical results of a viral infection. Yellow to brown ring patterns on otherwise healthy hibiscus leaves are probably caused by ringspot virus. Plant growth may be slowed from loss of chlorophyll in the foliage, but plants tend to remain healthy. In some cases, the affected areas drop out of the leaf.

Other plant problems. COMMON PESTS: aphids, beetles, mealybugs, scales, whiteflies. COMMON DISEASES: root rot. OTHER: frost and wind damage, sunburn.

Notes: To avoid early frost damage to tender shoots, stop fertilizing hibiscus in mid- to late summer. This allows growth to slow prior to cold weather and dormancy. Fertilizing in late fall does not stimulate growth until the ground is warm in spring.

HYDRANGEA

🌿 HYDRANGEA

🌿 ZONES: VARY BY SPECIES

FROST DAMAGE

Most hydrangeas do well in Zones 1–21, except bigleaf hydrangea (*H. macrophylla*), which performs best in Zones 2–9 and 14–24. Even though these plants demonstrate great cold tolerance, they can lose blossoms in cold temperatures. If oakleaf hydrangea (*H. quercifolia*), for instance, is subjected to temperatures below 0°F, it will not flower during the current year. The same is true of bigleaf hydrangea: its terminal flower buds are formed the previous summer, and if damaged by late spring frosts they will not produce blossoms.

Other plant problems. COMMON PESTS: aphids, scales, slugs, snails. COMMON DISEASES: bacterial wilt, leaf spot, powdery mildew, root rot, rust. OTHER: faded flowers, loss of flowering wood.

Notes: Careful siting is important to keep water-hungry hydrangeas away from competing roots and to provide enough shade so that blossoms will not fade. Rejuvenate flowering wood by removing two or three of the oldest stems each year.

HYPERICUM

🌿 HYPERICUM, ST. JOHNSWORT

🌿 ZONES: 4–24

RUST

Orange-colored rust pustules accumulate on the undersides of leaves, causing the upper surfaces to appear spotted. If this fungal infection is severe, leaves may drop. Growth is likely to slow until the plant regains its vigor and replaces the lost foliage. Healthy plants survive rust infections with little damage, but severe cases can cause foliage to shrivel. Removing leaves improves appearance and destroys the fungal spores.

Other plant problems. COMMON PESTS: beetles, scales, thrips. COMMON DISEASES: root rot, wilt. OTHER: leaf scorch, stress from excess heat and drought.

Notes: Most hypericums are tolerant of heat and drought, but some are easily stressed in summer from lack of water. When you observe dull and drooping foliage, plants should be watered. If rust is a problem, avoid overhead watering, or water early in the day so that the sun can dry the foliage.

ILEX

🌿 HOLLY

🌿 ZONES: VARY BY SPECIES

NEEDS A POLLENIZER

Holly shrubs and trees are grown for their foliage and their brilliant displays of berries. Among the numerous holly species, berry color varies from red, orange, and yellow to black. The berries form after flowering, and they are prized for fall and winter displays. Plants are dioecious—that is, they bear male and female flowers on separate plants. There are a few exceptions, but generally two plants—one a pollenizer—are needed for berries to be produced. Failure of a plant to produce berries means that either the plant is a male or it is an unpollinated female. One male pollenizer is sufficient for about ten female plants.

Other plant problems. COMMON PESTS: beetles, moths, leaf miners, nematodes, scales, spider mites, whiteflies. COMMON DISEASES: anthracnose; canker and dieback; collar, root and crown rot; leaf spots; powdery mildew. OTHER: leaf scorch.

Resistant varieties. Among the more disease-resistant species of holly are *I. attenuata, I. cornuta, I. crenata, I. latifolia, I. meserveae,* and *I. vomitoria.*

JUNIPERUS

🌿 JUNIPER

✂ ZONES: ALL

ROOT ROT

Planted in lawns where compacted soil and poor drainage constantly create moisture, junipers frequently suffer from root rot. Some fungal strains are active in warm, moist conditions while others flourish in cool, moist weather. Fungal activity deteriorates feeder rootlets, larger anchoring roots, and crowns. As the roots are killed, twigs and branches die back. If conditions do not improve, entire plants are lost. Junipers can thrive on little or no supplemental watering in summer and should be kept as dry as possible to prevent rot.

Other plant problems. COMMON PESTS: aphids, beetles, borers, needle miners, scales, spider mites. COMMON DISEASES: juniper twig blight, oak root fungus, rusts. OTHER: legginess in shade, sunburn.

Notes: Junipers are subject to damage from the cypress tip miners. The following varieties are resistant: J. chinensis sargentii *'Glauca',* J. c. *'Kaizuka', and* J. scopulorum *'Erecta Glauca'.*

LAGERSTROEMIA indica

🌸 CRAPE MYRTLE

✂ ZONES: ALL

POWDERY MILDEW

In Zones 15–17 and 22–24, powdery mildew is a serious problem of crape myrtle. This fungal disease is characterized by the white, powdery material that forms on leaves and stems. Affected areas are often distorted from the penetration of the fungus into the plant tissue. Fungal growth begins in dry, humid, or foggy conditions and in the absence of rain. When these conditions abate, the tree is left with stunted leaves that detract from the brilliance of the floral display.

Other plant problems. COMMON PESTS: aphids, scales. COMMON DISEASES: black spot, leaf spot, root rot, sooty mold. OTHER: chlorosis, leafburn.

Resistant varieties. Crape myrtle performs best in Zones 7–10, 12–14, and 18–21. Japanese crape myrtle, *L. fauriei*, and the Indian-tribe hybrids are the most resistant to powdery mildew. Resistant varieties include 'Catawba', 'Cherokee', 'Hopi', 'Osage', 'Pecos', 'Seminole', 'Zuni', and others.

LONICERA

🦋 HONEYSUCKLE

✂ ZONES: VARY BY SPECIES

SOOTY MOLD

Honeysuckle vines can become host to a flaky black sooty mold. This fungal growth appears mainly on the upper surface of leaves where sugary sap—called honeydew—accumulates. The sap, a perfect medium for the growth of sooty mold, is excess liquid that drips from aphids, mealybugs, scales, whiteflies, and other sucking insects as they feed. Hosing down vines with strong streams of water clears them of attacking insects as well as cleaning off the sooty mold. The problem is more of a nuisance than a threat to the health of the vine.

Other plant problems. COMMON PESTS: aphids, caterpillars, flea beetles, mealybugs, mites, scales, whiteflies. COMMON DISEASES: crown gall, leaf spot, powdery mildew, root rot, witches' broom. OTHER: rampant growth.

Notes: Certain aphids feeding on honeysuckle inject toxic saliva into stems, causing a rush of distorted new growth called witches' broom (see Syringa, *pages 94, 240). These growths can be pruned off or left to die back in winter. The normal rampant growth of honeysuckle stems can be cut to the ground as needed to control growth.*

MAGNOLIA

🌸 MAGNOLIA

✂ ZONES: VARY BY SPECIES

SLIME FLUX

Established magnolia trees sometimes experience a condition called wetwood or slime flux. A bacterial infection causes foul-smelling fluid to ooze from inside the wood through injured areas of bark, leaving discolored and water-soaked areas on the trunk or branches.

As the fluid dries, it leaves a gray film on the tree. If fluid and gases do not drain completely through holes in the bark and instead accumulate inside the tree, the disease may cause foliage to wilt and some branches to die back.

Other plant problems. COMMON PESTS: loopers, mealybugs, sapsuckers, scales, thrips. COMMON DISEASES: canker and dieback, leaf blight, leaf spot, mildew, verticillium wilt. OTHER: frost damage, leaf drop, limb breakage.

Notes: Leaf drop from evergreen magnolias can be bothersome when large, leathery leaves fall daily onto neat, manicured lawns. Though only a few leaves fall each day from mature trees, some litter is constant year-round. The blossoms of magnolia varieties that flower in late winter or very early spring are subject to frost damage.

MALUS

🌸 CRABAPPLE

✂ ZONES: 1–21

APPLE SCAB

Apple scab is a troublesome disease that can defoliate susceptible crabapple varieties, most often in late spring or early summer. Overwintering fungal spores are splashed onto crabapple foliage by rains or irrigation during warm, humid weather. When temperatures rise and humidity falls, the problem dissipates. Scab begins as round, raised, green or black spots on leaves; the spots sometimes turn red or yellow. Fruit may also be damaged by sunken spots and it, too, may drop.

Other plant problems. COMMON PESTS: aphids, borers, scales, spider mites, tent caterpillars, whiteflies. COMMON DISEASES: cedar-apple rust, fireblight, leaf spot, powdery mildew. OTHER: suckering growth.

Resistant varieties. Many crabapple varieties are highly susceptible to diseases. Select carefully to avoid serious problems. New crabapple varieties carrying improved resistance to scab, rust, and powdery mildew include 'Adams', 'Autumn Glory', 'Beauty', 'Molten Lava', 'Prairifire', and 'Robinson'.

MORUS alba

❀ MULBERRY

✄ ZONES: ALL

FALL WEBWORMS

Mulberry leaves are a target of the fall webworm, which feeds on deciduous trees and shrubs. The worms chew foliage inside silken tents, or webs, spun around the outer extremities of the tree; in dry weather they sometimes venture out of their webs. Feeding begins in midsummer and continues in most cases until fall. Worms are capable of covering an entire canopy with webbing and completely defoliating a tree.

Other plant problems. COMMON PESTS: mites, nematodes, scales, whiteflies. COMMON DISEASES: bacterial canker, leaf spot, powdery mildew, slime flux. OTHER: breakage, litter, pollen, shallow roots.

Notes: Birds are attracted to mulberries, and in summer the fruit stains patios and anything else under the tree. Fruitless forms do not have the litter problem. Lower branches on fruitless trees are wide spreading and should always be cut back to the trunk. Pruning is not necessary if you plant trees where they have room to spread. If trees become infected with bacterial canker, remove diseased branches immediately.

NANDINA

🌿 DOMESTIC BAMBOO, HEAVENLY BAMBOO

✄ ZONES: 5–24

VIRUS INFECTION

Nandina is treated with a virus to give foliage a mottled, multicolored look. Colors range from pale cream to deep red tones and are most highly developed on plants in full sun. Foliage on some plants becomes crinkled and slightly twisted, and the color patches are broken and irregular. This effect is considered an ornamental attribute and not a disease problem as it might be in another species. The virus does not harm plants other than causing slight distortion on the narrow leaves; some varieties react to the virus more than others.

Other plant problems. COMMON PESTS: mealybugs, scales. COMMON DISEASES: none. OTHER: chlorosis, frost damage, litter, sunburn.

Notes: After nandina berries drop, twiggy branchlets turn brown and persist on stems for long periods if not deadheaded. Litter from tiny, shattered flower petals is a problem on patios and walkways. These shrubs thrive in sun or shade, but in either exposure they bend toward open space if planted too close to a solid wall.

NERIUM

🌿 OLEANDER

✄ ZONES: 8–16, 18–24

BACTERIAL CANKER

During wet weather bacterial canker, also called bacterial blight, causes an oozing of foul-smelling material from cankers on stems. All parts of the shrub can be affected; flowers may not open and leaves may develop spots and may wilt and shrivel. Discolored areas develop on stems where the secretions occur; stem tips may die back.

Other plant problems. COMMON PESTS: aphids, mealybugs, scales. COMMON DISEASES: bacterial gall, leaf scorch. OTHER: long-lasting dead flower clusters on double-flowered varieties; poisonous.

Notes: Leafhoppers transmit a blight called leaf scorch, a new disease that is known only in Southern California. It has no known treatment and is fatal to affected plants; pruning away diseased plant parts does not offer any control. Another bacterial strain present wherever oleanders grow causes blackened, deformed flowers, split branches, and warty, gall-like growths. All oleander varieties are extremely poisonous.

PACHYSANDRA

🌿 JAPANESE SPURGE

✄ ZONES: 1–10, 14–21

LEAF AND STEM BLIGHT

Entire plantings of *Pachysandra* can be killed by severe cases of leaf and stem blight. The disease moves easily through the low foliage as spores are spread by wind and water. Problems are worse where the ground cover holds in moisture during warm, wet weather. Leaves turn yellow, tan, or gray, then brown as they shrivel and die. Stem tissue is also infected,

showing blotchy, discolored areas. Removing infected material and increasing air circulation may slow the spread of the fungus.

Other plant problems. COMMON PESTS: nematodes, scales, spider mites. COMMON DISEASES: root rot. OTHER: chlorosis; stress from extreme heat, humidity, or drought.

Resistant varieties. *P. procumbens* (Allegheny spurge) resists leaf and stem blight fungus. Foliage tends to yellow in full sun, but do not confuse this reaction with yellowing from chlorosis, which occurs frequently in alkaline conditions. Japanese spurge performs best in neutral or slightly acid soils.

PALMS

❀ VARIOUS SPECIES

✄ ZONES: VARY BY SPECIES

PINK ROT FUNGUS

Wounds that occur from trimming fronds off tree trunks commonly allow the invasion of pink rot fungus. Cankers develop on trunks or around the base of palms, causing splits and deformed growth. In some cases, masses of pink spores may be visible around stem wounds and dying leaves; trees may be killed. All palms are vulnerable to pink rot.

Other plant problems. COMMON PESTS: borers, leaf skeletonizers, mealybugs, nematodes, sapsuckers, scales, spider mites, thrips. COMMON DISEASES: fusarium wilt, heart rot. OTHER: frost damage, nutrient deficiencies.

Notes: Potted palms often suffer from nutrient deficiencies, especially in hot zones. Container mixes must provide excellent drainage, and palms should be repotted into increasingly larger pots to allow for root expansion and normal growth. They benefit from hosing down to remove sucking insects and dust; in coastal areas, hose off salt accumulations. Palms perform best when planted in full sun in soil amended with organic matter other than manure.

PASSIFLORA

🌿 PASSION VINE

🗓 ZONES: VARY BY SPECIES

CATERPILLARS

Passion vine is a favorite of caterpillars. Various larvae of moths and butterflies enjoy the succulent foliage, although they seem to prefer the nonfruiting to the fruiting species. Vines may assume a tattered look but are rarely damaged, since leaves are quickly replaced. But caterpillars can devour the vines to the point of defoliating the plant. Infestations can recur during a season, and caterpillars may feed on nearby plants as well.

Other plant problems. COMMON PESTS: mealybugs, nematodes, scales, thrips. COMMON DISEASES: collar rot, leaf spot, powdery mildew. OTHER: frost damage.

Notes: In zones where nematodes are prevalent in the soil, passion vines may be at risk—if they survive at all. Success may depend on container culture in sterile soil mixes. In cold zones, passion vines grown in containers can survive winters if protected indoors. Prune out tangled growth in early spring; vines can be cut to the ground.

PICEA

🌲 SPRUCE

🗓 ZONES: 1–6, 14–17

SPRUCE GALL ADELGIDS

The spruce gall adelgid injects a toxic material into tender stem shoots as it feeds at the base of needles. The toxin causes cone-shaped growths, or galls, up to 3 inches wide and varying in color from light green to purple. The galls surround the adelgids until midsummer,

when nymphs emerge to begin a new life cycle. Galls do little to harm the tree, but they are unsightly as they harden and persist on branches for several years. With large adelgid populations feeding on trees, needles turn yellow and drop, and branch tips wilt and die back. Healthy trees are more able to withstand insect populations than stressed trees.

Other plant problems. COMMON PESTS: aphids, borers, budworms, needle miners, sapsuckers, sawflies, scales, spider mites, weevils. COMMON DISEASES: canker and dieback, root rot, rusts. OTHER: drought stress, pollution.

Notes: The shallow rooting system of spruces depends on constant moisture. A few species are more tolerant of dry conditions, but, in general, lack of adequate water can cause nearly instantaneous death.

PINUS

🌲 PINE

🗓 ZONES: VARY BY SPECIES

WESTERN GALL RUST

Pine trees in the West fall prey to western gall rust. In spring when shoots are wet, they are receptive to wind- or animal-borne spores that emanate from existing galls. The galls are round swellings that develop on young shoots and grow slowly over several years, interrupting sap movement through stems and often causing distorted, stunted growth or witches' brooms. In many cases, normal growth continues and galls enlarge as limbs grow. If other fungi or insects invade a gall, the branch itself usually dies. Severely infected large branches weaken the tree and make it hazardous.

Other plant problems. COMMON PESTS: adelgids, aphids, bark beetles, borers, mealybugs, moths, nematodes, sapsuckers, sawflies, scales, spider mites, weevils. COMMON DISEASES: canker, fungal rots, needle cast, pine rusts. OTHER: pollution.

Notes: Pines are host to many pests and diseases. Out of their native environments, they need excellent drainage and infertile soil to withstand infestations. In garden situations, they frequently develop a yellowed appearance on older growth from underwatering, overwatering, or overfertilizing. Stress from poor cultural conditions and age commonly invites cankers and borers.

PLATANUS

🌳 SYCAMORE

🗓 ZONES: VARY BY SPECIES

ANTHRACNOSE

Anthracnose infects leaves, petioles, and tender shoots in spring just after growth begins. Moisture from rain or fog provides favorable conditions for the fungus, which

shrivels new growth and kills tissue along the veins of mature leaves, resulting in large brown blotches. Many leaves fall, and in severe cases the entire tree may become defoliated; foliage regrows as the fungus becomes inactive. Infection may cause twig dieback and cankers on small branches where fungal spores rest until the next year, when the cycle begins again. Powdery mildew causes a similar shriveling of shoot tips, but it does not kill older leaves.

Other plant problems. COMMON PESTS: aphids, borers, lace bugs, leaf skeletonizers, psyllids, scales, spider mites, webworms, whiteflies. COMMON DISEASES: canker, powdery mildew, slime flux. OTHER: ozone pollution.

Resistant varieties. Where anthracnose is a chronic problem, plant resistant varieties of *P. acerifolia.* 'Bloodgood' is resistant but may be affected by pollution. 'Columbia' and 'Liberty' resist both anthracnose and powdery mildew, and 'Yarwood' resists powdery mildew.

PLATYCLADUS orientalis (Thuja orientalis)

🌿 ORIENTAL ARBORVITAE

🗓 ZONES: ALL

CONIFER SAWFLIES

Yellow or green larvae with dark stripes or spots, frequently feeding in pairs or large masses, cause damage to needles. Buds are often destroyed and shoots may die back. Adults cut—or saw—depressions in the needles, in which they lay eggs. You can distinguish sawfly larvae from caterpillars by the "feet" or appendages on each sawfly larval segment. Some species with fewer legs spin webs, then cluster inside to feed on needles.

Other plant problems. COMMON PESTS: aphids, leaf miners, mealybugs, scales, spider mites. COMMON DISEASES: leaf and twig blight, root rot. OTHER: leafburn, winter leaf browning.

Notes: In the Rocky Mountains, arborvitae performs best in partial shade, especially in winter. In all zones, foundation plantings and hedgerows of oriental arborvitae need protection from heat reflected off light-colored walls or paving. Avoid buying large-growing varieties for small spaces: shape and character are ruined by pruning.

POPULUS

❀ POPLAR

✿ ZONES: VARY BY SPECIES

TUSSOCK MOTHS

These moths have hairy larvae with white or light-colored tufts on their upper bodies. The larvae begin feeding on the foliage of the upper canopy in the spring and work their way down. As they feed, they drop tan-colored pellets of excrement. These caterpillars are able to defoliate a tree; however, the damage is not permanent, as new leaves will replace those destroyed. Some moth species produce a second generation of larvae that begin feeding in late summer and fall; leaves destroyed late in the season are not replaced.

Other plant problems. COMMON PESTS: aphids, beetles, caterpillars, lace bugs, leaf miners, scales, treehoppers. COMMON DISEASES: bacterial canker, canker and dieback, crown gall, heart rot, leaf spot, root rot, rusts, slime flux. OTHER: invasive roots, litter, suckering.

Notes: Poplars cause serious problems when their invasive roots lift pavement, invade sewage lines, and send up suckers in lawns. Select a planting site for a poplar carefully, since new trees appear from suckering roots, and you may end up with a grove rather than a single specimen.

PRUNUS

❀ FLOWERING CHERRY

✿ ZONES: VARY BY SPECIES

CROWN ROT

Flowering cherry is sensitive to several fungal rots that survive in the soil and affect lower plant parts, causing decay in the bark and vascular tissue of the rootstock. Trees may die quickly from the fungi or languish for years. Leaves often turn yellow. Branches die back, detracting from the shape and attractiveness of the tree. Lower trunk areas show bare spots or exposed interior wood. If trees survive, trunks are rimmed with callused growths that block off the damaged areas.

Other plant problems. COMMON PESTS: aphids, borers, caterpillars, lace bugs, leafhoppers, nematodes, pear slugs, scales, spider mites, treehoppers. COMMON DISEASES: blight,

canker and dieback, crown gall, peach leaf curl, leaf spot, powdery mildew, shot hole fungus. OTHER: frost damage.

Notes: Flowering cherries depend on excellent health for reliably profuse floral displays. Good drainage is paramount, as are sun, adequate moisture, fertile soil, and good air circulation. Where soils are heavy, plant on raised mounds.

PRUNUS

❀ FLOWERING PLUM

✿ ZONES: 2–22

SHOT HOLE FUNGUS

Fungal growth on leaves of flowering plum and other *Prunus* species creates red, green, yellow, or black spots on leaves. When leaf tissue dies, the spots drop out and leave round holes, as if the leaves had been subjected to a barrage of buckshot. Occasionally the spots enlarge and merge together before dropping, weakening the leaf and causing it to fall. On trunks and branches, the fungal growth develops as expanding circles and does not cause tissue to drop out.

Other plant problems. COMMON PESTS: aphids, borers, caterpillars, scales, slugs, spider mites. COMMON DISEASES: canker, crown gall, leaf spot, root rot. OTHER: suckering stems, weak crotches.

Notes: Most holes in flowering plum foliage are caused by chewing insects rather than fungi. Many caterpillars feed openly on leaves, some rolling or folding them and others feeding under tents or inside tunnels. Trees stressed by drought or other problems may experience slow growth, but healthy trees can withstand foliage attacks by fungi and caterpillars.

PYRACANTHA

❦ FIRETHORN

✿ ZONES: VARY BY SPECIES

WOOLLY APPLE APHIDS

A typical sign of woolly apple aphids is the presence of small clumps of white, cottony material on bark or curled leaves. You may also find swollen, gall-like areas on the bark. The

aphids suck sap from branches, twigs, and leaves, leaving sticky honeydew behind. Problems result more from the bothersome sticky residues than from the actual damage to the plant. Black sooty mold usually develops on leaves and surrounding areas. Greater damage occurs in winter, when aphids burrow into the soil and feed on roots.

Other plant problems. COMMON PESTS: moths, scales, spider mites. COMMON DISEASES: apple scab, fireblight, leaf and twig blight, leaf spot, root rot. OTHER: persistent faded blossom clusters, scraggly growth.

Notes: Pyracantha is related to apple and pear and, like them, is affected by fireblight and scab. 'Apache', 'Mohave', 'Navaho', 'Pueblo', 'Shawnee', 'Teton', and 'Rutgers' varieties show good resistance. During dry weather, hose down plants with a strong water spray to remove faded blossom clusters and dust. Dust may encourage spider mites.

PYRUS

❀ ORNAMENTAL PEAR

✿ ZONES: VARY BY SPECIES

FIREBLIGHT

Ornamental pear trees, like the fruiting species, suffer from fireblight. Affected plants suddenly wilt, then shrivel and blacken at blossoms and shoot tips. Branch ends appear scorched or charred as though by fire and typically develop a shepherd's-crook shape. Severe infections reach farther down the branches and result in dark, sunken cankers. If cankers expand far enough and girdle a limb, it will die.

Other plant problems. COMMON PESTS: aphids, rust mites. COMMON DISEASES: leaf spot. OTHER: frost damage, splitting from narrow-angled branch attachment.

Resistant varieties. *P. calleryana* 'Bradford', 'Capital', and 'Whitehouse' varieties are all resistant to fireblight. Watch for development of fireblight in warm weather, with prolonged humidity from rain, fog, dew, or irrigation. In these conditions, avoid applying high-nitrogen fertilizers to ornamental pears, as the ensuing rapid growth is highly susceptible. Zones at high elevations and east of the Rocky Mountains have a high frequency of fireblight.

QUERCUS

🌿 OAK

ZONES: VARY BY SPECIES

OAK GALL WASPS

Female gall wasps lay eggs in the stem and leaf tissue of oak trees. When the minuscule larvae hatch and begin to feed, they inject a substance into the wood or leaf that stimulates cells to form galls. Galls vary from swellings within twigs to colorful appendages on stems and leaves, from white star shapes or amber bumps to baseball-size globes. Galls are curious phenomena that are poorly understood, but they are apparently protective to wasp larvae and harmless to oak trees.

Other plant problems. COMMON PESTS: aphids, borers, caterpillars, Fuller rose weevils, leaf miners, mealybugs, oakworms, scales, weevils, whiteflies. COMMON DISEASES: anthracnose, crown and root rots, oak root fungus, powdery mildew, slime flux, twig blight, witches' broom. OTHER: chlorosis, mistletoe.

Notes: Tent caterpillars periodically infest oak trees and feed heavily to the point of defoliation. Trees are sometimes forced into dormancy or, more commonly, they develop new leaves. Trees may look "ratty," but they are tough survivors. Oaks that are native to dry summer climates, however, cannot survive constant moisture in warm seasons or the accumulation of moisture from irrigation around their trunk and crown.

RHAPHIOLEPIS indica

🌿 INDIA HAWTHORN

ZONES: 8–10, 12–24; MARGINAL IN 4–7

LEAF SPOT FUNGUS

Leaf spot fungal disease usually appears on older leaves, first as small red or brown dots, often surrounded with a yellow or black halo. The discoloration darkens and enlarges as leaves age. Some leaf spots enlarge to the point of crossing over veins. In severe cases, leaves drop and growth slows, but defoliation rarely kills the plant.

Other plant problems. COMMON PESTS: aphids, flathead borers, weevils. COMMON DISEASES: fireblight. OTHER: frost damage, leafburn, leggy growth.

Notes: India hawthorns that receive overhead watering are especially susceptible to leaf spot fungus, since the fungal spores depend on water on the leaf surface to survive. Good air circulation and a sunny exposure are important for good plant health. 'Enchantress', 'Majestic Beauty', 'Pink Lady', and 'Snow White' resist leaf spot. To prevent leafburn in hot summer zones, protect India hawthorn from reflected heat and provide filtered shade.

RHODODENDRON

🌿 AZALEA

ZONES: 4–6, 15–17; VARY BY SPECIES

CHLOROSIS

Yellowing of new leaves signals chlorosis, an iron deficiency. In mild cases, only the areas between the leaf veins turn yellow, while the veins remain distinctively dark green. The condition results from a decrease in the uptake of iron from the soil. The iron has become unavailable to the plant, due most frequently to a high pH or waterlogged soil.

Other plant problems. COMMON PESTS: aphids, borers, leaf miners, nematodes, scales, spider mites, thrips, weevils. COMMON DISEASES: flower blight, leaf spot, powdery mildew, root and crown rot. OTHER: frost damage, leafburn from dissolved salts and wind.

Notes: Azaleas suffer windburn primarily on new foliage, while they show damage from salt burn on older leaves. Freeze damage and heat stress are both more severe on evergreen varieties of azaleas.

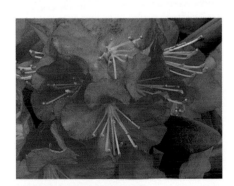

RHODODENDRON

🌿 RHODODENDRON

ZONES: 4–6, 15–17; VARY BY SPECIES

BLACK VINE WEEVILS

From spring through summer, weevil larvae are active below ground, gnawing or completely eating roots, which causes top growth to flag. In severe infestations, leaves drop, causing further decline. The bark is often damaged on stems near the soil where larvae eggs hatch. Night-feeding adult weevils create holes or notches along the edges of leaves and flowers.

Growth may be stunted, and plants may wilt and die. Nearby azaleas may also show evidence of weevil damage.

Other plant problems. COMMON PESTS: borers, lace bugs, nematodes, scales, spider mites, thrips, whiteflies. COMMON DISEASES: flower blight, leaf spot, root and crown rot, rust. OTHER: chlorosis, frost damage, leafburn from dissolved salts in containers or in the soil, windburn.

Resistant varieties. Rhododendron varieties resistant to adult root weevils include 'P. J. Mezzitt', 'Jock', 'Sapphire', 'Rose Elf', 'Cilpimense', 'Lucky Strike', 'Exbury Naomi', and 'Virginia Richards'. The roots are extremely sensitive to both poor drainage and drought. They will rot in excess water and die from exposure if not covered with a mulch.

ROBINIA

🌿 LOCUST

ZONES: ALL

CARPENTER WORMS

Locust trees are favorite feeding grounds of carpenter worms, the larvae of large, gray moths. Carpenter worms burrow for up to four years inside trees, mostly in the heartwood. Vigorous and healthy trees can withstand low populations, but the burrowing causes some trees to become gnarled or to show discoloration on limbs. The burrowing tunnels may ooze liquid or be filled with frass, the sawdustlike excrement of the larvae. If generations persist in a tree, some branches will be lost and the entire tree weakened.

Other plant problems. COMMON PESTS: bark beetles, borers, leaf miner beetles. COMMON DISEASES: heart rot. OTHER: suckering roots, wind damage.

Notes: Leaf miner infestation may cause locust trees to drop their leaves; adults chew the outer leaf parts and the larvae tunnel inside. These trees are fast growing and brittle, making them vulnerable to wind damage. If damage exposes the interior wood, beetles and moisture may invade.

ROSA

🌿 ROSE

🌡 ZONES: ALL

BLACK SPOT

After new growth emerges in spring and the weather warms, fringed black spots, usually with a yellow halo, appear on leaves and stems. Young canes may develop raised, reddish blotches. Constant high humidity fosters fast growth of fungal spores; they do not develop on dry foliage or in very hot weather. Good air circulation and drip irrigation promote good health. Mild infections can be tolerated, but severe cases cause defoliation.

Other plant problems. COMMON PESTS: aphids, beetles, borers, corn earworms, rose curculios, fall webworms, leaf-cutting bees, nematodes, rose chafers, sawflies, scales, spider mites, thrips, whiteflies. COMMON DISEASES: botrytis, canker and dieback, crown gall, downy mildew, oak root fungus, rust, root rot, verticillium wilt. OTHER: frost damage.

Resistant varieties. Disease resistance is sometimes claimed but is actually erratic, since the fungus causing black spot changes constantly. Tea roses, hybrid teas, hybrid perpetuals, Pernetianas, Austrian briers, and polyanthas are most susceptible. Rugosa hybrids, moss roses, and Wichuraianas are somewhat resistant, as are a few named varieties: 'Alexander McKenzie', 'Crimson Glory', 'The Fairy', 'Lafter', and 'Meidiland' shrub roses.

SALIX

🌲 WILLOW

🌡 ZONES: ALL

SAPSUCKERS

You can distinguish random borer damage from sapsucker holes by the more or less even horizontal rows that sapsuckers—a kind of woodpecker—drill into tree trunks. These birds penetrate bark until they reach and feed on conducting tissue carrying sap. Sap may ooze from the holes and provide entry points for disease organisms, especially on less vigorous trees. Healthy trees can withstand limited sapsucker activity, unless drilling girdles the tree.

Other plant problems. COMMON PESTS: aphids, beetles, borers, caterpillars, lace bugs,

moths, sawflies, scales, spider mites. COMMON DISEASES: canker; crown, heart, and root rot; rust; slime flux; twig blight. OTHER: breakage; shallow, invasive roots.

Notes: Locate weeping willows carefully to protect their brittle wood from breakage in high winds and to give them plenty of space to spread. Removing branches for any reason damages their graceful form. Roots compete vigorously; in lawns, cover the root zone with a large circle of shallow mulch.

SEQUOIADENDRON

🌲 GIANT SEQUOIA

🌡 ZONES: ALL

CANKER AND DIEBACK

Giant sequoia growing in lower elevations frequently become weakened from drought stress and therefore are subject to fungal diseases. Canker and dieback are especially common in landscapes in hot-summer zones. Branches anywhere in the tree can be killed by the fungus. Newly affected needles turn reddish brown, with stems often oozing yellow pitch. Eventually the foliage turns pale and drops off, leaving bare branches.

Other plant problems. COMMON PESTS: moths, scale, spider mites. COMMON DISEASES: fungal diseases. OTHER: shallow roots.

Notes: Spruce spider mites feed on giant sequoia throughout two generations a year, causing the most damage in spring, with lighter damage in fall. These sucking mites give needles a bronze or brownish cast. The larvae of the sequoia pitch moth, a borer, carve out small areas of bark that fill with pitch and spill out onto the trunk in small sticky masses or baseball-size globules. Pitch moth damage is more unsightly than it is destructive.

SYRINGA

🌿 LILAC

🌡 ZONES: VARY BY SPECIES

WITCHES' BROOM

Certain toxins that are injected into plant tissues by invading organisms cause a rush of distorted new growth called witches' broom.

The toxins may come from feeding insects, such as aphids; from plant parasites, such as mistletoe; or from disease organisms, such as powdery mildew. The twiggy growths that develop at stem tips are not harmful; they brown and die quickly. Prune them off to improve the appearance of the shrub, making cuts 6–12 inches below the affected area.

Other plant problems. COMMON PESTS: aphids, borers, caterpillars, cucumber beetles, leaf miners, mealybugs, scales, spider mites, whiteflies. COMMON DISEASES: bacterial canker, downy mildew, leaf spot, powdery mildew, ringspot virus, root rot, verticillium wilt. OTHER: legginess.

Notes: Flower loss results from winter pruning. Cut the oldest stems to the ground in winter to renew growth, and cut back stems immediately after flowering to induce bushiness. S. reticulata, tree lilac, is resistant to borers, mildew, and scales.

TAXUS

🌲 YEW

🌡 ZONES: VARY BY SPECIES

WINTER BURN

Yews require protection from winter winds that desiccate leaf tissue. When activity slows in winter and the ground freezes, plants are unable to take up water from the soil to replenish moisture lost in harsh winds. Needles take on a pale cast, then a darker tan appearance along stem tips. Severe winter burn causes some branch dieback, but it can be pruned out after growth begins in the spring.

Other plant problems. COMMON PESTS: mealybugs, nematodes, scales, weevils. COMMON DISEASES: crown and root rot, needle blight, twig blight. OTHER: heat and cold damage, poisonous.

Resistant varieties. Slow-growing and low, *T. cuspidata* 'Nana' (Zones 1–6, 14–17) and shrubby *T. media* 'Tauntonii' (Zones 3–9, 14–24) are somewhat resistant to winter burn. Yews are sensitive to soggy soil and require careful planting that provides good drainage.

THUJA

🌿 ARBORVITAE, WESTERN RED CEDAR
🌡 ZONES: VARY BY SPECIES

NEEDLE AND TWIG BLIGHT

Fungal growths affect *Thuja* species, causing dieback on needles and twiggy branch tips. Fungal spores enter the needles, spread through young shoots, and girdle and kill stems. The tree may appear unattractive, with scattered dead shoots and twigs throughout. Patches of bark may be discolored by oozing resin. In severe cases, fungal damage may spread and girdle the main trunk, causing the death of a tree.

Other plant problems. COMMON PESTS: aphids, bark beetles, leaf miners, scales, spider mites. COMMON DISEASES: canker, heart rot, juniper twig blight. OTHER: heat and drought stress, legginess in shade, needle drop, snow damage, winter burn.

Resistant varieties. *T. occidentalis* 'Emerald' holds its bright green color through winter and demonstrates heat tolerance as well. 'Nigra', 'Techny', 'Wareana', and 'Wintergreen' also hold their color in winter. Globe-shaped and pyramidal forms are easily damaged when heavy snow accumulates on the branches. Wrap heavy twine around shrubs prior to snowfall to support branches and prevent breakage.

TRACHELOSPERMUM

🌿 STAR JASMINE
🌡 ZONES: VARY BY SPECIES

SUNBURN

Though star jasmine thrives in full sun, its leaves burn from intense sunlight. In cooler zones where summer sun is less harsh, planting in full sun should not be a problem. In hotter zones, provide some summer shade to prevent leaf tissue damage and disfigurement. Burns appear as brown areas surrounded by yellow, in the center of the leaves. As leaf tissue dies, the centers fall out. Plants survive unharmed unless damage is extensive. Trimming off trailing branches stimulates new growth.

Other plant problems. COMMON PESTS: mealybugs, scales, spider mites. COMMON DISEASES: black sooty mold. OTHER: chlorosis, frost damage.

Notes: Do not confuse chlorotic yellowing of leaves with sunburn. If star jasmine develops chlorosis, newer leaves will turn yellow from an iron deficiency. The veins will remain green, except in severe cases when entire leaves will change color. Iron sulfates and iron chelates added to the soil will make iron available to plants.

TSUGA

🌿 HEMLOCK
🌡 ZONES: 1–7, 14–17

RUST MITES

The hemlock rust mite causes needles to discolor and drop. These small mites, which can be seen only with a magnifying lens or under a microscope, feed by sucking sap from the undersides of needles. Hot, dry conditions, which are generally unfavorable to hemlocks, support mite populations. If stress from drought and mites continues, it will eventually weaken a tree.

Other plant problems. COMMON PESTS: borers, budworms, leaf miners, loopers, sapsuckers, sawflies, scales, spider mites, weevils. COMMON DISEASES: canker, crown and root rot, slime flux. OTHER: drought, sun, and wind damage.

Notes: Hemlocks suffer when grown out of their native environments. Heat, drought, and wind cause great stress and lead to dieback; quick death results when these conditions are severe.

ULMUS

🌿 ELM
🌡 ZONES: VARY BY SPECIES

ELM LEAF BEETLE

Elms suffer extensive damage from this beetle. The adults feed on leaves, leaving round holes, and the larvae skeletonize leaf surfaces. Foliage destruction continues throughout the growing season as successive generations pupate and hatch. The larvae move from the treetops to the base of the tree, where they form yellow pupae; adults lay yellow eggs on the undersides of leaves. Defoliation weakens trees and makes them vulnerable to bark beetles and Dutch elm disease.

Other plant problems. COMMON PESTS: aphids, beetles, caterpillars, leafhoppers, scales. COMMON DISEASES: anthracnose, Dutch elm disease, mosaic virus, root rot, slime flux. OTHER: litter, shallow and invasive roots, breakage from narrow crotches.

Resistant varieties. European elms *U. glabra*, *U. hollandica*, and *U. minor* are the most susceptible to leaf beetle damage, Siberian and American elms *U. pumila* and *U. americana* are less so. Chinese elm *U. parvifolia* is most resistant. To prevent the spread of Dutch elm disease, avoid pruning trees; bark beetles, which spread the fungal disease, are attracted to fresh pruning wounds.

VIBURNUM

🌿 VIBURNUM
🌡 ZONES: VARY BY SPECIES

SPIDER MITES

Resembling tiny spiders, spider mites spin webs around leaves and suck plant juices from the undersides. They are less a problem in cool, damp weather than in arid conditions. Their feeding makes leaves look pale or bleached, and sometimes flecked or stippled. Foliage is left unattractive and weakened, though damage is not usually severe.

Other plant problems. COMMON PESTS: aphids, beetles, borers, scales, thrips. COMMON DISEASES: anthracnose, crown gall, leaf spot, powdery mildew, root rot, rusts. OTHER: heat, sun, and cold damage; legginess.

Resistant varieties. Do not use sulfur sprays to manage spider mite populations; sulfur damages viburnum foliage. *V. burkwoodii* 'Mohawk' is resistant to powdery mildew and bacterial leaf spot. Aphids cause distortion and damage to new growth on *V. opulus* 'Roseum'; *V. sargentii* and its varieties resist aphid infestations.

Problem Solving for

LAWNS

Lawns have a long tradition as part of American landscaping. In the West, however, their history is fairly short and their presence often controversial. In many western gardens, arid conditions limit the size of lawns, if not their very existence.

Fortunately, dozens of new turf varieties with improved pest and disease resistance and low moisture requirements are making it possible to integrate a lawn, albeit a small one, into dry-climate gardens. Along with new turf varieties, new concepts of what constitutes a lawn are encouraging more and more western gardeners to forgo traditional manicured lawns in favor of tougher, taller grasses and other plants that are less likely to attract pests and diseases and demand less of limited water resources.

WHAT IS A LAWN?

Lawns are the most common type of ground cover, one of the easiest ways to protect stretches of bare ground. Most lawns are mass plantings of turf grasses, but some are composed of small broadleafed plants like dichondra or thyme. They all consist of groups of plants crowded closely together, with their roots in vigorous competition for limited moisture and nutrients.

TURF TYPES

Turf grasses are classified as either warm-season or cool-season. Warm-season grasses thrive in southern zones where hot summers stimulate vigorous growth and cool winters turn them brown and dormant. Cool-season grasses withstand low winter temperatures, growing actively during spring and fall and more slowly in summer. They do best in the North and in western coastal regions.

Grass types are also classified as creeping or clumping. Creeping grasses, such as Kentucky bluegrass, Bermuda grass, and other warm-season grasses, spread by rhizomes or stolons or both. They generally spread and block out weeds faster than clumping types, but their dense growth is more prone to thatch—a spongy layer of stems, roots, and dead grass on top of the soil that can harbor pests and diseases. Clumping grasses such as fescues and perennial ryegrass, which fill in an empty expanse more slowly and spottily, tend not to build up thatch. Cool-season creeping and clumping grass types are often mixed together for a tough lawn.

Most lawns are blends or mixes of two or more different kinds of turf grasses, each with different growth habits. *Blends* are different varieties of the same grass species, whereas a *mixture* is composed of two or more different species. By planting a combination of grasses, you provide your lawn with reserves for fending off pests, diseases, or environmental stresses that affect one grass type but not another.

HOW GRASSES GROW

Most lawn grasses grow from seed into small, narrow-leafed plants that are seldom allowed to reach full maturity. Mowing prevents them from developing flowers and setting seed. When seeds germinate, new grass plants develop either as annuals that will last only one year or as perennials that will continue to grow as long as conditions allow. High-quality lawns are made up only of perennial grasses.

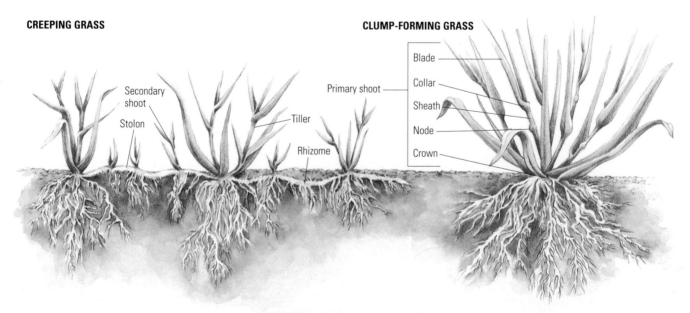

CREEPING GRASS

Secondary shoot

Stolon

Tiller

Rhizome

CLUMP-FORMING GRASS

Blade

Collar

Primary shoot

Sheath

Node

Crown

GROWTH HABITS OF GRASSES

Clump-forming bunchgrasses and creeping spreaders produce primary shoots of sheathed grass blades, or leaves, and secondary side shoots, or tillers. Bunchgrasses form an abundance of tillers close to the primary shoots in slow-growing, expanding clumps. Creeping grasses develop secondary shoots along horizontal stems, either from underground stems (rhizomes) or from low-lying aboveground stems (stolons).

St. Augustine grass and some varieties of Bermuda and zoysia grass are sterile perennials and do not develop viable seeds. These grasses must be propagated by vegetative means—that is, from plugs, sprigs, or sod. Plugs are small sections of turf raised in cell-packs like petunias or cut from rolls of sod. Sprigs are rooted sections of horizontal stems, stolons, and rhizomes, that you can buy by the bushel or make by tearing apart sod strips.

Turf grasses grow differently than most other plants. Rather than developing buds and shoots from the top of the plant, grasses regenerate from the bottom up, from growing points near the crown just above the soil. The low position of the crown protects modern grasses during mowing, just as it did older parent strains that withstood grazing for centuries.

Grass plants constantly renew themselves in two ways. Above-ground, older leaves wither and die and new ones take their place. Belowground, fibrous root systems also continuously expand, die, and produce new growth. Deep and thick root systems are essential for developing drought tolerance and producing a healthy turf thick with extensive secondary growth.

CLIMATE CONSIDERATIONS

Excessive cold, heat, and drought pose serious problems for lawns in many western regions. In alpine and far northern zones, turf grass will not survive when desiccating winds and lack of insulating snows accompany abnormally low winter temperatures. Lawns also die in winter in moderately cold zones if they are dry for long periods, even during dormancy. Supplemental irrigation before the ground freezes can prevent this type of winterkill. However, lawns can also die in winter from other causes, such as long-lasting coats of ice and fungal diseases under melting snow, and there is no way to prevent these problems. In such cases, expansive turf grass lawns are clearly not the ground cover of choice and should be avoided in favor of native grasses, shrubs, or other ground covers.

In desert and chaparral regions where water is scarce and precious, lawns are a luxury. Many wise gardeners are avoiding them altogether in favor of native xeriscapes, water-conserving plantings that use little or no supplemental irrigation. Small native bunch-grasses or postage-stamp lawns of specialized drought-tolerant varieties are reasonable alternatives that give the suggestion of turf.

Even in the Pacific Northwest and certain mountain regions where rainfall is abundant, lawns need supplemental irrigation during dry periods. In these areas, it's critical to choose new turf types for disease resistance as well as for drought tolerance.

Many gardeners feel it is inappropriate to indulge in lawns that need considerable water. Indeed, water-use restrictions imposed by many communities have resulted in lawns that are small or composed of only native, drought-tolerant grasses instead of traditional thirsty favorites. Some new varieties of buffalo grass, for instance, need summer irrigation only once a month, and deep-rooted tall fescues also have improved tolerance to dry spells.

PROBLEMS COMMON TO LAWNS

The healthiest lawns are made up of grasses that are well suited to their climate and maintained with minimal applications of fertilizers and chemicals. Healthy lawns are lush and green, deep rooted, and aerated with thriving colonies of soil microbes that maintain a balanced ecosystem beneath the surface. These microbes are nurtured by the organic matter that lawns naturally provide to them, and in turn they break it into nutrients that the grasses utilize as they regenerate themselves.

CLIMATE MAP FOR TURF GRASSES

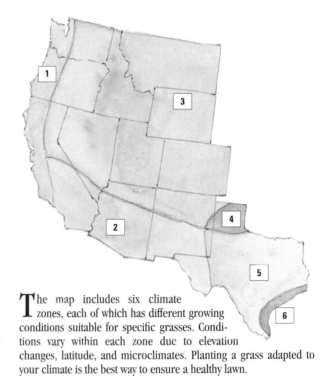

The map includes six climate zones, each of which has different growing conditions suitable for specific grasses. Conditions vary within each zone due to elevation changes, latitude, and microclimates. Planting a grass adapted to your climate is the best way to ensure a healthy lawn.

Zone 1: West and Pacific Northwest
In this region of plentiful rainfall—except for dry summers in the lower regions—seasons have few extremes. Cool-season fescues, Kentucky bluegrass, and perennial ryegrass give year-round green color.

Zone 2: Southwest
In this dry zone with hot summers, plant Bermuda, zoysia, and buffalo grasses anywhere; St. Augustine grass, seashore paspalum, and dichondra in the Far West; and tall fescues in the cooler northern reaches. During dormancy, overseed warm-season grasses with perennial ryegrass.

Zone 3: Mountains and Plains
Temperatures range broadly in this semiarid zone. Plant and irrigate nonnative, cool-season Kentucky and rough-stalk bluegrasses and fescues in the North, warm-season Bermuda grass and zoysia in the South. The most drought-tolerant grasses are varieties of buffalo grass, native blue grama, and crested wheatgrass.

Zone 4: Midcentral
Both warm- and cool-season grasses can be grown here, although temperatures fluctuate widely and can be extreme in both summer and winter. Adapted varieties of Kentucky and rough-stalk blue-grasses, tall fescues, and zoysia perform well. Perennial ryegrass can be planted with cold-tolerant varieties of Bermuda grass.

Zone 5: Central South
Plentiful rainfall in a warm, humid climate suits Bermuda grass, centipede grass, tall fescue, and zoysia. Kentucky bluegrass will grow near the midcentral zone, and St. Augustine grass toward the coast.

Zone 6: Gulf Coast and Hawaii
These semitropical and tropical regions have a year-round growing season that features high rainfall nearly everywhere. Bermuda grass, centipede grass, St. Augustine grass, and zoysia are best. In winter, overseed warm-season grasses, which turn brown, with fine fescues and perennial ryegrass.

PROBLEMS OF LAWNS

PEST PROBLEMS	SIGNS/SYMPTOMS
Armyworms, billbugs, cutworms, chinch bugs, grubs, mole crickets, sod webworms	Brown areas
Billbugs, chinch bugs, leafhoppers, grubs, mites, root nematodes	Yellow or tan areas
Billbugs, grubs, mole crickets	Loose turf
Leafhoppers	Swarms of hopping insects
Moles, gophers, ground squirrels	Dirt mounds
Pets or wildlife	Brown spots from urine
Skunks, raccoons, opossums, armadillos	Ravaged turf from digging for grubs

DISEASE PROBLEMS	SIGNS/SYMPTOMS
Brown patch, red thread, snow mold, sclerotium rot	Brown areas or rings
Anthracnose, dollar spot, fusarium	Yellow or tan areas
Blight, snow mold, summer patch	
Fairy ring	Green or brown rings
Dollar spot, red thread, pythium blight, snow mold	Threads or webbing
Anthracnose, leaf spot, pythium blight, rust, stripe smut	Discolored, spotted or streaked leaf blades
Snow mold	Loose turf
Leaf spot	Thin brown or yellow patches
Anthracnose, pythium blight, snow mold	Water-soaked grass

ENVIRONMENTAL PROBLEMS	SIGNS/SYMPTOMS
Dormant lawn	Tan color in cold winters or hot summers
Shade	Thin growth or bare spots, brown patch, powdery mildew, snow mold, leaf spot, pythium blight, red thread
Salt or fuel burn	Dead patches, contaminated soil
Bare spots	Buried debris
Competing tree roots	Thin areas, water-stressed lawn

Mole damage and sod webworms in lawns

INSECT PESTS

Lawns are home to numerous species of animal life. Most aren't pests at all, but beneficial or benign creatures living in a natural balance. Pests do appear from time to time, often in the absence of natural predators or in the presence of stress or cultural difficulties. A healthy lawn can usually tolerate low insect populations and ward off infestations. Most insect pest problems can be controlled by adjusting management practices or using moderate methods of control. Simply removing thatch can get rid of some offenders, such as armyworms and cutworms. Decreasing nitrogen fertilizers way-lays greenbug (aphid) attacks, and planting resistant varieties can discourage sod webworms.

Diagnosing problems. When looking for insect pests, confine yourself to a limited area and look belowground if you don't find any problem above the soil. Finding a few pests is normal, but large populations may require treatment. Make your closest examination at the perimeter of the problem area, where the damage is invading healthy lawn.

- Test the lawn for sod webworms, cutworms, or other caterpillars in a 1-square-yard area by saturating the soil with $\frac{1}{8}-\frac{1}{4}$ cup of liquid detergent in 1 gallon of water. If more than 5 larvae or cutworms and more than 15 sod webworms come to the surface, apply treatment.
- You can detect grubs—beetle larvae that feed on roots in summer—by the loose turf on the soil surface. Dig into the soil to count the larvae. Your lawn can probably tolerate 5 grubs per square foot, but 20 per square foot should be treated to prevent further damage.
- Billbugs can also destroy a lawn's root system, cutting off turf aboveground. If the turf can be rolled back and you find bugs on the soil and larvae on the roots, pursue treatment.
- Test for tiny chinch bugs by pushing a bottomless can into the soil, then filling it with soapy water. If chinch bugs are present, they will float to the surface. More than 20 bugs in a square-foot area are considered an infestation.

Endophyte protection. Certain varieties of perennial ryegrass and tall fescue are host to microscopic beneficial fungi that kill many kinds of insects. These fungi are called endophytes, indicating the intercellular relationship between the grass tissue and the fungi. Besides repelling insects, endophytic grasses have also shown superior disease resistance, drought tolerance, and endurance.

When you purchase endophytic seed, ask your dealer or nursery staff about its level of resistance and its life expectancy. Each variety and seed lot is different. The protective fungi inside are alive, and the seed must be planted within a specific time frame if it is to produce the desired results.

OTHER ANIMAL PESTS

Many pest problems involve tougher, smarter critters: wildlife and pets. Underground denizens such as pocket gophers and aboveground marauders like skunks are always on the outskirts of lawns in rural areas and many suburban ones. Much of the damage they cause is minor and limited to small spots, but it can look like disease problems and may be tricky to diagnose. Repairs can be annoying and time-consuming.

Aboveground pests. Skunks, raccoons, opossums, and armadillos are usually secondary pests, drawn to lawns with high populations of grubs. Crumpled sections of loose turf and evidence of digging signal their presence. Traps can be effective if the animals are subsequently relocated out of the area; however, this can be

Nighttime Nuisance

Armadillos, nocturnal feeders in the Southwest, will venture into lawns to dig for grubs. In other regions, torn-up turf is usually the work of skunks or raccoons grubbing for larvae.

Diagnosing a specific lawn disease is difficult even for professionals, since various fungal activities are similar. The accompanying charts on disease symptoms and cultural practices will help you pinpoint the nature of the problem and get started dealing with it. You may not need to make a specific identification if you can manage the problem and prevent it from escalating. However, fungal problems are easier to prevent than to cure. Careful cultural practices—or lawn management techniques—suited to the needs of your turf grass prevent diseases from developing and spreading. Changing the lawn environment and waiting for the organism to complete a particular stage of its life cycle may be all you need to do to control a problem.

Resistant varieties. If your lawn is plagued by disease, consider replacing it with a new resistant variety. Many varieties of Kentucky bluegrass, perennial ryegrass, tall fescue, and fine fescue are resistant to several fungal infections. Ask your local cooperative extension agent or nursery consultant for names of new types developed to resist diseases common in your area. Resistance varies from one climate zone to another, so planting blends or mixes of two or more different grasses further ensures high performance. Many new varieties combine drought tolerance with disease resistance, allowing you to cut back on costly and time-consuming maintenance and have a healthier lawn as well.

WEEDS

Dense turf blocks out most weeds, but inevitably some appear. Whether they become a problem depends on your tolerance level. If you enjoy blooming clover and English daisies in your lawn, you may not mind chickweed or a few dandelions. Newly popular alternative lawns include plants other than traditional turf grasses. But if you prefer a uniform traditional lawn, then any weed may sound an alarm. Weekly inspection and quick wielding of a weeding tool will take care of most problems. Neglected turf with up to 50 percent weed growth can be reclaimed, but if you have more weeds, it pays to eradicate everything and put in a new lawn.

Weed sources. In established lawns, weed seeds are constantly blown in by the wind and tracked in by people and pets. New lawns get weeds from two sources: from the soil, when the existing seeds

a less humane solution than it appears, as the relocated animals are at a disadvantage in their totally unfamiliar new home and may not survive. Removing the attraction by lowering the grub population is probably a better tactic.

Pets, especially female dogs, inflict noticeable damage in the form of urine burns. Grass quickly turns yellow, then brown, creating circles of dead turf. Flushing the area with water sometimes keeps roots alive, but dog urine is high in salts, which can be lethal. The solutions are reseeding, patching with sod, or waiting for normal growth to fill in the bare spots—and figuring out a way to keep dogs off the lawn.

Belowground pests. Burrowing pocket gophers, moles, and ground squirrels all push soil mounds onto the lawn, but their habits differ, and so do controls. Gophers leave a telltale crescent- or fan-shaped mound of soil, while moles create shallow tunnels so they can feed on worms and grubs close to the surface. Although you may be tempted to try noisemakers and homemade remedies, trapping is the only management method that really works.

DISEASES

The most common lawn diseases are fungal infections. They can usually be traced to two sources: (1) trying to grow a particular turf grass in an unsuitable climate, or (2) a high-maintenance manicured lawn. Since turf grasses have very specific climatic needs, they are vulnerable to fungal invasions when planted in the wrong place. Lawns that are subject to high-maintenance practices—frequent doses of fertilizer, low mowing, and constant moisture—are weak from shallow rooting and loss of beneficial soil microbes.

Consult herbicide labels to see if they work on narrow-leafed, or grasslike, weeds such as crabgrass (left) or on broad-leafed ones such as mallow (right).

germinate, and from new seed included in a grass-seed package. It is required by law that grass-seed labels reveal the percentage of weeds in the seed. Look for figures close to zero. Don't buy seed containing noxious weeds or crop seeds that will spoil your lawn.

Conditions that encourage weeds. Broad-leafed weeds are the most common, as well as the easiest to see and eradicate. Narrow-leafed weeds, which are undesirable grasses, can go unrecognized, then spread and become harder to manage. Getting rid of weeds before they set seed and proliferate is a key to their control. But control goes hand in hand with managing the overall condition of your lawn: weeds become established in poor growing conditions. Problems to look for when weeds persist are

- overly acidic or alkaline soil
- low fertility
- compacted soil with poor drainage
- shade, thin turf, and excessive moisture
- shallow rooting
- dry soil from shallow watering
- too-low mowing height

Any of these conditions can affect the performance of all the desired plants in your yard, so you can use the presence of weeds to diagnose potential garden problems. See page 109.

Weeds in dormant lawns. Warm-season lawns develop problems during their cool-season dormancy, when weeds face less competition in the root zone. Overplanting with a cool-season grass just prior to dormancy prevents weed infiltration by increasing competition. Fescues or perennial ryegrass are good choices: once the dormant period is over, they will die back due to heat and competition from the now-active warm-season grasses.

UNDERSTANDING CULTURAL PROBLEMS

The most common problems in lawn care arise from inadequate site and soil preparation and incorrect maintenance. Careful planning from the beginning is needed to get the slope and drainage right, establish correct levels of nutrients and amendments, and adjust the pH. Once your lawn is up and growing, its health and performance are completely dependent on the care you give it. Some precision in judging the watering, mowing, and fertilizing needs of your type of turf grass goes a long way toward keeping your lawn problem-free. Misjudging those needs, or neglecting them, results in poor performance, weed infestation, pests, and diseases.

Watering. Different varieties of turf grass have their own specific watering needs, but all of them benefit from deep watering at infrequent intervals. Deep watering, or soaking the soil to a depth of 6–8 inches, promotes a healthy root system that strengthens individual grass plants against stress. If your soil is compacted, you may need to irrigate slowly to prevent runoff. Most lawns will thrive with 1–2 inches of water a week, from either rain or irrigation. By watering on demand rather than on a schedule, you never risk damaging your lawn from excess moisture or drought.

Giving a lawn more water than it needs does more than invite pests and fungal growth. It can also leach away nutrients and pro-

mote excessive and unnecessary growth. Frequent light watering damages lawns, since it encourages shallow rooting and thatch development. Roots that can't find deep moisture tend to grow in the thatch layer and get caught in a cycle of rooting, drying out, and dying. The thicker the thatch, the more it resists water penetration, and the cycle continues.

Fertilizing. Many lawns live their entire lives without any fertilizer other than lawn clippings. Clippings alone left on the lawn after mowing can supply up to one-half its nitrogen requirements. If your lawn needs more, give it timely applications of fertilizer, being careful to apply the correct amount.

For cool-season grasses, apply a slow-release product in the spring and fall just as active growth begins, to provide nutrients over an extended period without promoting sudden, rapid growth. A late fall application after the first frost gives a boost to new growth the following spring. Warm-season grasses do best with light monthly fertilizer applications over several months.

For steady, vigorous growth, use only the minimum amount of fertilizers. Excess creates conditions favorable to pests and diseases; it will also leach away, polluting ground water. Excessive nitrogen, especially in fast-release products, can harm your lawn more than help it by killing soil microbes and upsetting the balance of the soil's ecosystem.

Mowing. Each grass type has specific mowing requirements that suit its growth habit. Maximum and minimum recommended heights vary depending on the season. Mowing at the lowest recommended height helps get growth started in the spring and settle the turf down for dormant periods in the fall and winter. Mowing at maximum heights is best during periods of active growth and stress. Grasses depend on maximum blade surface to capture the sun's energy for photosynthesis and to send food to the roots for developing depth, vigor, and resilience.

Each time you cut your grass, you shock it to some degree. The less blade area you remove, the less the stress and interruption of the food supply. Cutting only one-third of the blade at a single mowing keeps stress to a minimum. Since lawn growth varies, the best mowing practices depend on growth rate and demand, rather than on any schedule. When growth speeds up, you may need to mow every four or five days, but as it slows down, you can decrease your mowing to once every one to three weeks.

Dethatching and aerating. Heavy thatch build-up and compacted soil lead to overall poor performance in lawns. Both conditions block out air (roots and soil microbes need oxygen for respiration and growth), prevent water penetration (the soil needs airways for good drainage) and therefore deep rooting, and encourage problems with diseases and insect pests.

When thatch is excessively thick, you can feel a sponginess underfoot. At a more moderate stage of development, though, thatch is sometimes difficult to recognize. Use a hand trowel or your fingers to pull apart material beneath the turf. Look for a fibrous, corky material with roots growing in it but without the grit of the lower soil layer. To remove thatch, use a dethatching rake for

MAXIMUM AND MINIMUM MOWING HEIGHTS	
Bent grass	¼–1 inch
Bermuda grass	1½–2 inches
Hybrid Bermuda grass	½–¾ inch
Kentucky bluegrass	1½–3 inches
Rough-stalked bluegrass	1½–3 inches
Buffalo grass	2–5 inches
Chewings fescue	1–2½ inches
Creeping red fescue	1½–2½ inches
Hard fescue	1½–2½ inches
Tall fescue	1½–4 inches
Perennial ryegrass	1½–2½ inches
St. Augustine grass	1–3 inches
Zoysia grass	1–2 inches

Dealing with Thatch

Some thatch is normal, as in this bent grass lawn at left. However, a heavy layer of thatch—a buildup of stems, roots, stolons, and rhizomes—blocks water and harbors insects and diseases. Rake out a shallow thatch layer with a curved dethatching rake; tackle layers thicker than ½ inch with a power rake. Use a flail reel or vertical cutter (below) on the toughest jobs.

shallow layers; rent a deeper-cutting flail dethatcher for layers more than 1 inch deep.

Although grasses that spread by stolons and rhizomes tend to build up thatch quickly, you can keep it at low levels by top-dressing your lawn once or twice a year with a ¼-inch layer of organic material such as finely screened compost. This valuable diet feeds the microorganisms that in turn decompose the thatch.

Earthworms aerate loam soil, but in heavy and compacted soil, mechanical treatments may be necessary. For the best treatment, rent a power aerator every year or two. It will lift out plugs or cores and deposit them on the lawn surface. Break up the cores, add a topdressing of fine compost, and rake the surface smooth.

Environmental problems. Though not brought on by gardening practices, environmental problems can usually be corrected by adjustments in management. Shade problems, for instance, develop over time as trees grow dense canopies that block out sun. Thin selectively to allow more light to reach grass and prevent sparse growth. Sparse lawns also are caused by heavy competition from shallow tree roots. When neither lawn nor trees are deep watered, roots are forced to remain in the shallow layers of soil. Tree roots

are able to outcompete turf, and lawns remain thin. Change your watering patterns to correct this situation.

Weather is, of course, impossible to control, but selecting cultivars adapted to conditions typical of your climate zone prevents many problems. Older varieties of bluegrass, such as the once-popular but disease-ridden 'Merion', are poor choices for harsh-climate zones. New cultivars, like snow mold–resistant 'Dormie' for cold areas and summer patch–resistant 'Glade' and 'Nassau' in dry, windy climates, help keep problems to a minimum.

CULTURAL PROBLEMS OF LAWNS

Effective problem solving depends on an accurate interpretation of your lawn's conditions. Once you recognize the effects of your lawn management practices, you will be able to make adjustments and eliminate conditions that promote pests and diseases.

PROBLEMS	RESULTING CONDITIONS
Inadequate soil preparation	Yellow turf from poor drainage; overly acid or alkaline conditions; fairy ring on rotting buried roots or construction lumber
Overwatering	Soggy soil, yellow leaves, rotting roots, shallow rooting; anthracnose, pythium blight, brown patch
Underwatering	Dull surface, footprints show; wilting and thin areas; weeds; shallow rooting, thatch formation; tan spots from uneven sprinkler coverage; patches of newly laid dead sod; fusarium blight (summer patch)
Untimely watering	Lack of water penetration into heavy soil, shallow rooting; lawn tan and stressed between waterings; lawn does not dry out; rust, dollar spot, fusarium blight (summer patch)
Underfertilizing	Slow, sparse growth; yellow cast from nitrogen deficiency or chlorosis; dollar spot, red thread, anthracnose, fairy ring
Overfertilizing	Rapid top growth with deep blue color; shallow rooting; loss of microbial population; fusarium blight (summer patch), brown patch, snow mold
Uneven fertilizing	Brown strips from overlapping spreader application; brown splotches from uneven hand application or spills
Dull mower blades	Uneven blade tops and tan cast to lawn
Low mowing	Tan spots on scalped areas; weak root system; leaf spot
Thatch buildup	Shallow rooting from lack of water penetration; brown patch, dollar spot, sclerotium rot; armyworms, cutworms, mites, billbugs, chinch bugs, sod webworms, grubs
Compacted soil	Weak root system from slow water penetration; lack of air and poor drainage; snow mold, leaf spot, pythium blight, brown patch, billbugs, sod webworms

THE MOST COMMON SPECIES AND THE MOST COMMON PROBLEMS

These listings tell you the botanical and common name of each grass and the western zones where it thrives. One of the common problems afflicting the grass in the West is featured, and, where available, resistant varieties are listed.

AGROSTIS

BENT GRASS

✔ ZONES: ALL

ANTHRACNOSE

Bent grass is particularly susceptible to anthracnose, a fungal infection that strikes during hot weather and is often brought on by overwatering. Irregular, blotchy patches usually less than 1 foot in diameter develop in the turf. Grass blades turn brown, then fade to light tan.

Other plant problems. COMMON PESTS: chinch bugs, cutworms, mole crickets, sod webworms, white grubs. COMMON DISEASES: brown patch, dollar spot, leaf spot, red thread, rust, snow mold, stripe smut, summer patch.

Grass strengths. Excellent surface for putting greens and low, closely mowed lawns.

Grass weaknesses. Bent grass requires the most intense management of any turf grass. Its manicured look is possible only with high doses of fertilizer and special mowing, dethatching, and aerating equipment. Roots are naturally shallow and require frequent watering. In summer heat, bent grass lawns must be monitored closely and watered with precision as the soil begins to dry, as this grass suffers profoundly from both heat stress and overwatering. The heavy maintenance required, along with dense growth of stolons and rhizomes, makes caring for bent grass a constant struggle with environmental conditions, insects, and diseases. Lawn management often involves the application of fungicides as a preventive measure.

Resistant varieties. Colonial bent grass (*A. tenuis*) is less disease prone than creeping bent grass (*A. stolonifera*). 'Penncross' is somewhat disease resistant and wear tolerant.

BUCHLOE dactyloides

BUFFALO GRASS

✔ ZONES: 1–3, 10, 11

DORMANT TURF

During dry summers, unirrigated buffalo grass lawns lose their normal blue-green appearance, turn straw colored, and enter dormancy. Where lawns receive some moisture during the summer, loss of color comes after the first hard frost. Lawns green up again in the spring, when warm, moist weather returns.

Other plant problems. COMMON PESTS: chinch bugs, mealybugs, mites, webworms. COMMON DISEASES: fungal diseases rarely occur.

Grass strengths. Buffalo grass thrives in heavy soil with low moisture content, withstands drought and temperature extremes, and requires little maintenance. Once established, its dense, fine-textured turf blocks out weeds. Nitrogen requirements are low, as are mowing needs—as seldom as twice per season for unirrigated, low-growing varieties.

Grass weaknesses. Seeded buffalo grass is slow to establish in new lawns and subject to weed invasion after seeding. It is more difficult to establish in sandy soil than in clay. Surface runners can invade nearby garden beds. It does not tolerate shade or heavy use. Without irrigation, lawns turn brown and enter a long dormancy in dry summers.

Resistant varieties. 'Tatanka' is adapted to resist diseases in high-humidity zones in the midlatitudes in the Rocky Mountain states and in southern zones in Oregon and Idaho. 'Cody' shows greater heat and drought tolerance in arid zones from Arizona to Montana. 'Bison' resists cold damage and is extremely drought tolerant.

CYNODON

HYBRID BERMUDA GRASS

✔ ZONES: 8, 9, 12–24

BERMUDA GRASS MITES

Mites thrive in warm humid weather and overfertilized lawns with thick thatch layers. They suck sap from blades, stems, and crowns, causing grass to grow in tight rosettes. Grass turns yellow and brown, then dies. Test for mites by shaking grass clumps over dark paper; the light specks that fall out are mites.

Other plant problems. COMMON PESTS: armyworms, billbugs, cutworms, mealybugs, nematodes, sod webworms, white grubs. COMMON DISEASES: brown patch, dollar spot, leaf spot, pythium blight.

Grass strengths. Hybrid Bermuda grass thrives in warm climates in the Southwest and along the coast. Hybrid varieties are greener in winter than common Bermuda grass and have more pest and disease resistance. Roots are deep and provide some drought tolerance. The grass is fine textured and can be mowed low for a smooth, uniform surface.

Grass weaknesses. Hybrid varieties make a high-maintenance turf that requires frequent mowing and thatch removal; they also have high water and fertilizer requirements. Besides their costly maintenance, hybrids are more expensive to plant than common Bermuda grass, since all varieties are sterile and must be planted from sod or sprigs. The grass does not tolerate shade.

Resistant varieties. 'Tifway' resists cold and wear and holds color in winter; 'Tiflawn' resists insects, diseases, and wear; 'Tifgreen' is resistant to cold and some diseases; 'Santa Ana' resists smog damage and holds color in winter; 'Ormond' resists disease; 'Tufcote' resists cold and wear; 'Midway' is resistant to cold and some diseases.

CYNODON dactylon

COMMON BERMUDA GRASS

✔ ZONES: 8, 9, 12–24

BROWN PATCH

Brown patch occurs in warm weather in overfertilized lawns with thick thatch layers. Irregular patches or circles of brown or gray dying grass may begin as water-soaked spots with purplish borders. Affected areas often reach several feet in diameter. Centers sometimes recover, leaving brown rings on the lawn.

Other plant problems. COMMON PESTS: armyworms, billbugs, cutworms, mealybugs, mites, nematodes, sod webworms, white grubs. COMMON DISEASES: dollar spot, leaf spot, pythium blight.

Grass strengths. Bermuda grass thrives in warm climates in the Southwest and along the coast. A very heat- and drought-tolerant turf grass, common Bermuda grass is deep rooted and fast growing. It resists most pests and diseases when well maintained and develops one of the toughest surfaces for heavy wear. It can be overseeded with a cool-season grass for winter color.

Grass weaknesses. Bermuda grass requires frequent mowing. It does not tolerate shade, turns brown while dormant in winter, and develops thick layers of thatch that require frequent maintenance for pest and disease control. Its invasive root system classifies it as a weed in other lawn and garden situations, where it completely takes over and becomes nearly impossible to eradicate.

Resistant varieties. 'U-3' resists cold; 'OKS 91-11' demonstrates cold tolerance.

DICHONDRA micrantha

DICHONDRA

☘ ZONES: 8–10, 12–24

FLEA BEETLES

Adult flea beetles damage small, round dichondra leaves in shot hole patterns. The larvae feed primarily on roots, causing leaves to turn brown, first along the edges, then in the center. Established lawns withstand beetle damage more readily than seedlings, which may be killed in heavy infestations.

Other plant problems. COMMON PESTS: cutworms, nematodes, slugs, snails, spider mites. COMMON DISEASES: brown patch, leaf spot, sclerotium rot.

Grass strengths. Dichondra is a fast-growing perennial with small, broad leaves that behaves very much like turf grass. You can plant it mixed with grass seed or alone for a low, smooth carpet. It needs very little mowing in sunny, high-use areas. Dichondra differs from other ground covers in its ability to withstand the kind of traffic that lawns get. It grows well in heat, sun, and light shade, tolerating both light and heavy soils.

Grass weaknesses. Widespread flea beetle damage reduces large lawns to ratty tracts. If water and fertilizer needs are not met, lawns become stressed and easy targets for other

insects and fungal diseases. Dichondra in light to moderate shade requires frequent mowing and watering. In mixed turf-grass lawns, it can be killed by broadleaf herbicides. When it grows unchecked, dichondra is considered a weed. It reseeds easily and spreads by underground runners, easily invading nearby ground covers, flower beds, and shrub borders.

Notes: Although dichondra is adapted to mild-winter climates in the West and Southwest, it is plagued with problems in lawns. Best use is in small-scale plantings.

FESTUCA arundinacea

TALL FESCUE

☘ ZONES: ALL

WHITE GRUBS

Grubs are larval forms of insects known as June bugs (May beetles) and Japanese beetles. The larvae live in the soil from several months to up to three years before they pupate and emerge as adults. They feed heavily on grass roots, to the point of severing them from grass blades on the surface. If dead grass can be rolled up like sod, grubs are the likely cause of the damage.

Other plant problems. COMMON PESTS: cutworms, leafhoppers, sod webworms. COMMON DISEASES: brown patch, dollar spot, leaf spot, pythium blight, snow mold.

Grass strengths. Tall fescues are the deepest rooted and most heat tolerant of the cool-season grasses. Improved varieties have the added strengths of drought tolerance and disease resistance. In addition, new slow-growing dwarf varieties need only infrequent fertilization and mowing. Excellent varieties are bred for many of the western zones.

Grass weaknesses. Older varieties are coarse and weedy looking. Some grow at faster rates than other grass types in a mixed lawn, especially in very high temperatures. Many varieties have a low tolerance for shade, and none tolerate extremely low temperatures.

Resistant varieties. 'Bonsai', 'Shenandoah', 'SR 8200', 'Phoenix', 'Mesa', 'Titan', and 'Tribute' are fortified with endophytes to resist insect pests. 'Jaguar', 'Mustang', and 'Leprechaun' have good disease resistance.

FESTUCA longifolia

HARD FESCUE

☘ ZONES: ALL

SNOW MOLD

Cool, sunless lawns fall victim to this fungal disorder in winter and spring. Excessively wet sites or lawns under slow-melting snow are commonly affected. They are made more vulnerable by overfertilizing in autumn. Grass may be covered with gray mold or appear reddish brown, then tan. Gray or pink circular patches with pale, threadlike strands are frequently visible in morning light.

Other plant problems. COMMON PESTS: chinch bugs, cutworms, leafhoppers, sod webworms. COMMON DISEASES: brown patch, leaf spot, pythium blight.

Grass strengths. Hard fescue shows excellent shade and drought tolerance in cool-season lawns, especially in northern zones. It is a low-maintenance grass with low fertilization requirements. This species shows the most disease resistance of the fescues and the best green color during periods of cold and drought. It can be left to grow to 12 inches for an unmowed, low-maintenance ground cover that blocks out weeds.

Grass weaknesses. The clumping habit of this slowest-growing fescue leaves open spaces that are slow to fill in if the turf becomes thin or damaged. Semierect tufts are fine textured but tend to mow unevenly and can leave lawns with a tan cast.

Resistant varieties. 'Aurora', 'Reliant', and 'SR 3000' are endophytic varieties. 'Biljart', 'Scaldis', 'Tournament', and 'Waldina' show good disease resistance. Lawns that are well aerated and raked clean of leaves and debris prior to winter snow and rains are less susceptible to snow mold. Snow removal from lawns is also a precaution against this disease.

FESTUCA rubra commutata

CHEWINGS FESCUE

✂ ZONES: ALL

CUTWORMS

Cutworms are the larval form of various night-flying moths. The ravenous larvae feed at night and rest during the day in protective thatch layers. They destroy small sections of lawn at a time by cutting off the blades at the soil level and feeding on crowns. Brown, irregular patches appear in the grass from spring through fall, as several generations are produced throughout the year.

Other plant problems. COMMON PESTS: chinch bugs, leafhoppers, sod webworms, white grubs. COMMON DISEASES: brown patch, dollar spot, leaf spot, red thread, snow mold, pythium blight.

Grass strengths. This fine fescue has excellent shade and drought tolerance. It tolerates poor soil, as well as moderate doses of fertilizers. It mixes well with Kentucky bluegrass, taking over shaded areas as bluegrass diminishes and yielding as bluegrass becomes dominant. Chewings fescue is a good choice for overseeding shaded, dormant Bermuda grass lawns.

Grass weaknesses. This species is more susceptible to fungal diseases than hard fescue, especially in hot, wet weather. Its clumping habit causes it to be slow to recover from wear or root damage. It does not tolerate temperature extremes.

Resistant varieties. Chewings fescue is a good choice for mixed-grass lawns in cool-summer climates, northern latitudes, and the Pacific Northwest. Disease-resistant varieties include 'Shadow', 'Jamestown', and 'Highlight'; 'Jamestown II' contains endophytes.

FESTUCA rubra rubra

CREEPING RED FESCUE

✂ ZONES: ALL

SOD WEBWORMS

Buff-colored moths that fly over the lawn at night are adult forms of these web-spinning caterpillars. The larvae feed on grass blades, causing brown patches to spread across the lawn as succeeding generations are produced.

The larvae build protective tunnels in thatch layers, where they drag grass blades, feed, and eventually pupate.

Other plant problems. COMMON PESTS: chinch bugs, cutworms, leafhoppers, white grubs. COMMON DISEASES: brown patch, dollar spot, leaf spot, powdery mildew, pythium blight, red thread, snow mold.

Grass strengths. The most shade tolerant of the fine fescues and of all good lawn grasses, this creeping grass is widely used as a companion with other turf types. Seedlings are vigorous and valuable in mixes for a fast cover. It is a good choice for overseeding dormant warm-season lawns. New varieties have increased cold and drought tolerance.

Grass weaknesses. Creeping rhizomes are wide spreading but slow to fill in. The grass is subject to fungal diseases in hot, wet weather. It cannot tolerate wet, poorly drained soil.

Resistant varieties. 'Dawson' and 'Ruby' resist powdery mildew; 'Boreal', 'Ensylva', 'Fortress', 'Pennlawn', 'Rainier', and 'Ruby' resist red thread fungus. 'Arctared' and 'Boreal' have extra cold tolerance for northern zones.

LOLIUM multiflorum

ANNUAL RYEGRASS, ITALIAN RYEGRASS

✂ ZONES: ALL

RUST

Annual ryegrass is particularly susceptible to rust fungi. Pustules on individual grass blades give the lawn an overall orangish cast. As pustules break open, rust powder (spores) rubs off and collects on shoes and equipment that move through the lawn, spreading the disease. As the grass is weakened by fungal activity, it turns yellow and thins. Fast-growing annual ryegrass should be mowed frequently to remove as much rust as possible from tall grass blades.

Other plant problems. COMMON PESTS: cutworms, leafhoppers, white grubs. COMMON DISEASES: brown patch, damping off, gray leaf spot, pythium blight, red thread.

Grass strengths. Fast germinating and fast growing, annual ryegrass establishes quickly to make a temporary ground cover.

Grass weaknesses. Annual ryegrass is one of the least desirable lawn grasses due to its coarse texture, shallow rooting, and weedy appearance. Performance is often poor due to its intolerance of shade and temperature extremes and its high water requirements. Its aggressive, clumping growth habit requires frequent mowing and gives it an uneven surface.

Notes: Annual ryegrass continues to be used for overseeding warm-season dormant lawns and as a fast-growing companion for seeded, cool-season grasses. Momentum, habit, and low cost seem to keep it ever present, despite its shortcomings and the obvious superiority of other grasses.

LOLIUM perenne

PERENNIAL RYEGRASS

✂ ZONES: ALL

PYTHIUM BLIGHT

This common grass disease wilts turf in irregular, small, usually shaded patches that gradually increase in size to form large areas. Infected blades turn dark from watery secretions and mat together in greasy-looking spots. (Grease spot is another name for the condition.) Other symptoms include greasy streaks through the lawn and a white, cottony mold on leaf blades. Hot, humid weather, poor drainage, and overfertilization promote the disease.

Other plant problems. COMMON PESTS: cutworms, leafhoppers, sod webworms, white grubs. COMMON DISEASES: brown patch, dollar spot, leaf spot, red thread, rust, snow mold, stripe smut.

Grass strengths. The rapid rate of germination makes perennial ryegrass a valuable component of cool-season grass mixes. As it quickly establishes, it provides a fast cover and protective shade for slower-germinating species. This is the grass of preference for toughness and wearability and for overseeding dormant warm-season lawns. It shows some tolerance of shade and salinity.

Grass weaknesses. Perennial ryegrass does not withstand extremes of high and low temperatures over long periods of time. Its clumping tendency causes stems to flatten under mower blades and, in older grass strains, to tear rather than cut evenly.

Notes: Varieties are bred for specific climate zones. The grass grows best in moderate climates. It is not recommended for extreme northern latitudes or high elevations of the Rocky Mountains and Sierra Nevada, although dormancy does offer protection where winters are not as extreme. Numerous varieties are protected from insects by endophytes; even more offer disease resistance.

POA pratensis

KENTUCKY BLUEGRASS

✹ ZONES: 1–7; MARGINALLY IN 8–11, 14–17

FUSARIUM BLIGHT (SUMMER PATCH)

This disease occurs under hot, dry, windy conditions in water-stressed, overfertilized lawns with heavy thatch layers. Circular spots or crescents from just a few inches to 2 feet in diameter appear in the lawn, often with a healthy center or eye. Grass blades and stems tend to die from the top down. Lawns will recover with improved management practices and reseeding.

Other plant problems. COMMON PESTS: chinch bugs, cutworms, leafhoppers, sod webworms, white grubs. COMMON DISEASES: anthracnose, brown patch, dollar spot, leaf spot, powdery mildew, red thread, rust, snow mold, stripe smut.

Grass strengths. Numerous new varieties invest Kentucky bluegrass with resistance against nearly every lawn disease. Its cold tolerance makes lawns possible in the coldest zones, including those at high elevations. Many varieties tolerate some shade and drought. Bluegrass lawns are able to survive periods of drought in hot summers by going dormant, then resuming growth with the return of rain or irrigation.

Grass weaknesses. Kentucky bluegrass is not recommended for the desert or subtropical conditions of Zones 12, 13, and 18–24; it is marginally successful in dry-summer climate Zones 8–11 and 14–17. Water requirements are high and heat tolerance is moderate to low. Regular fertilizing and dethatching are needed for a high-quality appearance.

Notes: As the standard grass for beautiful cool-season lawns, Kentucky bluegrass has benefited from extensive research. Varieties bred to thrive in specific climate zones are widely available, leaving little reason to plant old and unnamed generic strains.

POA trivialis

ROUGH-STALKED BLUEGRASS

✹ ZONES: 1–11, 14–17

DOLLAR SPOT

Numerous small brown spots about the size of a silver dollar are signs of this fungal infection. New spots usually appear water soaked, then merge and dry to form larger, straw-colored areas. Individual blades look yellow with red tints. The fungus tends to appear in spring and fall when weather patterns bring warm, humid days, cool nights, and mornings with heavy dew. Lawns with well-developed thatch layers and those deficient in nitrogen are most susceptible.

Other plant problems. COMMON PESTS: cutworms, leafhoppers, sod webworms, white grubs. COMMON DISEASES: anthracnose, brown patch, leaf spot, red thread, rust, stripe smut.

Grass strengths. In cool, moist sites with heavy shade, where other grasses have difficulty thriving, rough-stalked bluegrass provides a fine-textured turf.

Grass weaknesses. This bluegrass performs well only in moderate temperatures, shade, and moist soils. Heat, drought, salinity, and alkalinity reduce performance or prevent growth altogether. Turf produced from this stoloniferous grass lacks density; it does not withstand traffic. Weed infiltration is difficult to manage, since many herbicides cause injury to the grass. High watering requirements keep the turf environment moist and encourage fungal diseases.

Notes: Rough-stalked bluegrass is well suited to northern coastal zones, especially those with heavy, fine-textured soils. It is also an option in mountain zones at high elevations in the Southwest where there are shade and ample water for its shallow roots. This grass does best in infertile soil.

STENOTAPHRUM secundatum

ST. AUGUSTINE GRASS

✹ ZONES: 12, 13, 18–24

GRAY LEAF SPOT

Young seedlings are most affected by this leaf spot fungus. Pale spots, sometimes surrounded by red or purple margins, appear on grass blades and stems. Affected plants wither and die, but the entire lawn is not lost, as unaffected plants become resistant. In established lawns, warm, moist conditions, shade, low mowing, and high-nitrogen fertilizers contribute to the disease.

Other plant problems. COMMON PESTS: armyworms, chinch bugs, cutworms, ground pearls, mole crickets, sod webworms, white grubs. COMMON DISEASES: brown patch, downy mildew, pythium blight, rust, St. Augustine grass decline (SAD) virus.

Grass strengths. With supplemental irrigation, St. Augustine grass thrives in warm climates in the Southwest, where it is sometimes called carpetgrass. It is the most shade tolerant of the warm-season grasses. Fast, dense growth blocks out weeds. It tolerates extreme heat and

salinity and a wide range of pH and soil conditions, and it requires infrequent mowing.

Grass weaknesses. Heavy thatch buildup calls for regular dethatching for deep water penetration and pest and disease control. The deep green color fades in cool winter temperatures; texture is coarse. St. Augustine grass is less drought and cold tolerant than Bermuda grass.

Resistant varieties. 'Roselawn' and 'Tamlawn' resist leaf spot; 'Floratam', 'Seville', and 'Raleigh' resist SAD; 'Floralawn' resists insects; 'FX-10' resists drought; 'Raleigh' resists cold. SAD is known to exist only in Texas and Louisiana.

ZOYSIA

ZOYSIA

✹ ZONES: VARY BY SPECIES

CHINCH BUGS

Chinch bugs cause yellow circular patches to appear in lawns during hot, dry weather. Stressed lawns in full sun suffer damage first from red nymphs, then from black and white adults. Dead patches slowly enlarge as insects feed on the edges of yellowing circles. The grass dies from toxins that the bugs secrete as they feed on plant juices.

Other plant problems. COMMON PESTS: armyworms, billbugs, sod webworms, white grubs. COMMON DISEASES: brown patch, dollar spot, leaf spot, rust.

Grass strengths. Deep rooted and extremely heat and drought tolerant, zoysia grasses are adaptable to a wide range of pH and soil conditions, from sand to clay. They are among the first warm-season grasses to green up in spring. Growth is low, even, and attractive.

Grass weaknesses. Zoysias lose their green color during hot summers and severe drought and after the first hard frost. They are slow to establish and to recoup from wear damage and are intolerant of poorly drained soil. Organic material from stolons and rhizomes tends to build up in thick thatch layers.

Resistant varieties. 'Meyer' is tolerant of cold and drought. 'El Toro' and 'Emerald' tolerate some shade. 'De Anza', 'Victoria', and 'Diamond' hold green color during winter.

Problem Solving for

ANNUALS,

PERENNIALS,

AND BULBS

Splashes of color from flowering annuals enliven every garden. With the right conditions, annuals respond with fast, vigorous growth for an exuberant, though usually brief, appearance. Perennials take longer to establish themselves and rarely perform as quickly as annuals. Their first few seasons are usually only a prelude to the beauty of their mature bloom and foliage displays. Bulbs bring something of both types to the garden. All are valued for enriching landscapes with both continuity and change. Their dependable performance rests largely on good cultural care and climate compatibility.

LIFE CYCLES OF ANNUALS AND PERENNIALS

An annual is a plant that completes its life cycle in one year or less. It grows quickly from seed, blooms, sets seed, and dies all in one growing season. Most familiar are summer-blooming annuals such as marigolds and petunias, plants that are too tender to survive frosts or freezing. Biennials such as Canterbury bells are plants that complete their life cycle in two years but are treated as annuals. They are set out in the fall or spring as clumps of foliage that will flower and complete their life cycle within a year after planting.

Perennials are plants that live more than two years. Herbaceous perennials die to the ground each year during dormancy. Some species, such as bergenia, are evergreen and retain much of the same appearance throughout the year. Impatiens, geranium, and other perennials known as "tender" are treated as annuals in all but the warmest climates and are grown as single-season plants. The life spans of nontender perennials vary considerably. Under ideal conditions, anemones and euphorbias, for instance, can live for decades, whereas delphiniums may last only a few years. Supplying perennials with excellent growing conditions encourages a long and healthy life.

YEARLY GROWTH AND BLOOM CYCLES

Annuals begin their brief life cycle as they germinate from seed. Timely planting gives their small, shallow root systems a boost: they grow best when they become established in spring as the soil warms or in fall as it cools down. Some species such as stocks, which are treated as winter annuals, are sensitive to day length—they must be set out while days are longer than nights or they may rush to maturity, stunted and poorly established.

Perennials begin their yearly growth and bloom cycle in spring, when shoots emerge. Spring-blooming species appear early and put on fast growth, while summer and fall bloomers tend to progress more slowly. After seed is produced, the foliage on most perennials dies back as plants prepare for dormancy. A few, such as hellebores, retain their leaves until new growth begins again in spring.

Growth requirements. Annuals rely on constant access to moisture and nutrients for fast growth and abundant bloom. Perennials also need supplemental fertilizers for steady growth, but their capacity to store food over winter means they don't need it as often. Applying slow-release materials is the best way to provide both types with a steady supply of nutrients. Fast-release, water-soluble products stimulate a rush of growth that produces succulent young foliage attractive to pests. An oversupply of nitrogen also inhibits flowering. The best time to apply nitrogen fertilizers is before the normal growth cycle in fall or early spring.

Grooming for growth. Though annual and perennial habits vary from species to species, most require a certain amount of grooming for dense growth and continuous flower production. Removing weak stems in favor of stronger ones on plants like penstemon and false dragonhead *(Physostegia)* improves their performance. Some plants will form a more attractive shape if you pinch back the flowering tips; this will stimulate the development of additional flowering points along stems. Deadheading (removing faded blossoms) diverts the plant's energy away from seed production and back into flowering. Some perennials, such as peonies, do not repeat bloom; these types should nonetheless be deadheaded after flowering, as this will direct the plant's energy into foliage growth for food production and winter storage.

BULBS AND BULB TYPES

Bulbs are a specialized group of perennials that develop a unique organ for storing food. The term "bulb" applies to a number of plants that are not true bulbs—corms, rhizomes, tubers, and tuberous roots (see illustration, page 105). All are lumped into the bulb category since they all hold nutrients in reserve underground. This storage unit contains all of the resources the plant needs to complete its life cycle when the right combination of moisture and soil temperature triggers growth.

GROWTH HABITS OF BULBS

True bulbs, such as lily and tulip, are composed of specialized leaves tightly packed together on a short modified stem and covered with papery scales. Other bulblike structures are also fleshy and are composed mostly of stem sections. All have growing points at the top that develop into new plants each year, with new or enlarged storage units. Single tubers, such as begonia, can last for many years, while daylily tuberous roots multiply their numbers annually. Corms such as gladiolus last just one year. During the annual growth cycle, the old corm shrivels as a new one forms from a bud on top. Rhizomes such as iris are thickened stems with a primary growing point (bud) at one end. Each year, old centers become woody while new sections produce foliage and flowers.

After bloom, bulbs, like other plants, channel their energy into seed production. By removing spent flowers, you can redirect the plant's activity away from seeds into replenishing food supplies in underground storage, essential for next year's growth and bloom. Bulbs perform best when fertilizer is applied annually during this growth period after bloom.

THE FIVE BULB TYPES

True bulb and bulblet. A true bulb is a short underground stem (on a solid basal plate) surrounded by modified fleshy leaves (scales) that protect and store food for use by the embryonic plant. Outer scales are dry and form a papery covering (tunic).

The new bulb (often called an offset) is formed from a lateral bud on the basal plate; the old bulb may die or, like daffodils, come back each year. Bulblets can be separated from the mother bulb and replanted to increase the stock of the original plant. Bulbils are small bulbs that form in the axils of leaves, in flowers, or on stems of certain bulbous plants.

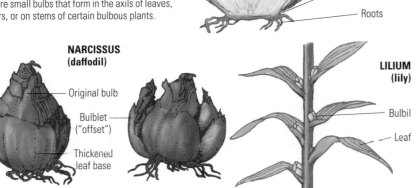

ALLIUM (onion)
- Tunic
- Fleshy leaves (scales)
- Embryonic plant
- Basal plate
- Roots

NARCISSUS (daffodil)
- Original bulb
- Bulblet ("offset")
- Thickened leaf base

LILIUM (lily)
- Bulbil
- Leaf

Corm and cormel. A corm is a swollen, underground stem base—solid tissue (in contrast to bulb scales) but with a basal plate from which roots grow. The growth point is on the top; many corms have tunics that consist of dried bases of the previous season's leaves. An individual corm lasts one year. New corms form from axillary buds on the top of an old corm as it completes its growth cycle. Fingernail-size cormels will take 2 to 3 years to flower; larger corms should bloom the following year.

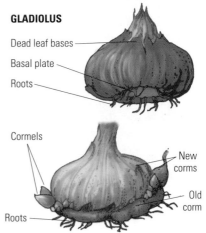

GLADIOLUS
- Dead leaf bases
- Basal plate
- Roots
- Cormels
- New corms
- Old corm
- Roots

Rhizome. A rhizome is a thickened stem that grows partially or entirely beneath the ground. Roots generally grow from the underside; the principal growing point is at the tip, although additional growing points will form along the rhizome's length. To divide, cut into sections that have visible growing points.

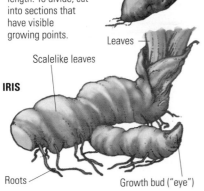

ZANTEDESCHIA (calla)
- Growth bud ("eye")
- Leaves

IRIS
- Scalelike leaves
- Roots
- Growth bud ("eye")

Tuber. A tuber is a swollen, underground stem base, like a corm, but it lacks the corm's distinct organization. There is no basal plate, so roots can grow from all sides; multiple growth points are distributed over the upper surface—each is a scalelike leaf with a growth bud in its axil. An individual tuber can last for many years. Some (*Cyclamen,* for example) continually enlarge, but never produce offsets; others (such as *Caladium)* form protuberances that can be removed and planted separately. Divide tubers by cutting into sections that have growth buds.

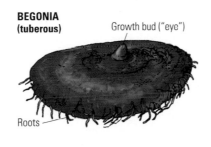

BEGONIA (tuberous)
- Growth bud ("eye")
- Roots

Tuberous roots. Tuberous roots are actual roots (rather than stems) that are specialized to store nutrients. In a full-grown dahlia, daylily, or other tuberous-rooted plant, the roots grow in a cluster, with the swollen tuberous portions radiating out from a central point. Growth buds are at the bases of old stems rather than on the tuberous roots. To divide, cut apart so that each division contains both roots and part of the stem's base with one or more growth buds.

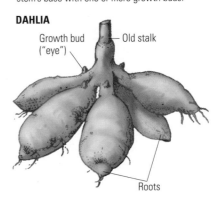

DAHLIA
- Growth bud ("eye")
- Old stalk
- Roots

PREVENTING PROBLEMS WITH ANNUALS, PERENNIALS, AND BULBS

Problems in gardening with annuals, perennials, and bulbs originate from a myriad of sources. Perhaps surprisingly, more problems arise from deficiencies in cultural care than from the presence of pests and diseases. Still, it is always wise to select resistant cultivars for diseases that are common in your area. See page 73 for more details on starting and establishing plants.

GETTING STARTED

The first step to enjoying success with herbaceous ornamentals is to bring healthy plants into your garden. If you raise plants from seed, use a sterile starting mix to avoid damping-off diseases—decays or rots caused by soil-borne fungi that create damage before, during, and after germination. These fungi are present in planting mixes and in unsterilized soil and tend to be activated by conditions that are excessively moist and overly fertile.

Starting from Seed

Use a two-step method to start most annuals and perennials from seed. First, sow seeds in a row or scattered randomly, in a sterile starter mix in flats. When the seedlings develop their second set of true leaves, they're ready for transplanting into individual containers. These chocolate cosmos are hardening off in a well-lighted outdoor area. After one to two weeks, they'll be ready for planting in a garden bed.

Once seedlings are ready for transplant, harden them off: plants that have been protected in a warm, humid, windless environment need to be acclimated slowly to garden conditions. Exposing them for a few hours each day to cooler temperatures and outdoor air allows the cell walls of the outer layers to thicken and harden. You should also wait to plant until the soil has warmed and dried out from winter rains.

Inspect new plants for insects, egg clusters, and foliage diseases. Look over pots of gift plants for Bermuda grass or other weeds that might have come from another garden. When selecting new bulbs, look for large, firm ones; never purchase undersized bulbs or any that are soft or moldy.

The right site. Sun-loving plants must receive at least six hours of bright sunlight each day for heavy bloom. Reflected light helps, but it can also burn foliage and dry out soil. Shade-tolerant species can withstand some morning or filtered sun, but they must be protected from harsh afternoon exposure and sunburn.

Know what the mature size of your plants will be, to avoid overcrowding and excessive root competition with nearby companions. Keep in mind that some plants do not transplant easily; each time they are moved, roots are damaged and growth slows. Taking extra time to lay out a garden plan before planting is best for your plants in the long run.

The right soil. If you add topsoil to your beds, thoroughly mix it in when you add organic matter. To get soils to combine well, add more of the type of soil you already have rather than mixing soil types—for example, add a clay loam to heavy clay soil rather than adding sand. Combining different soil textures can create more problems than it solves, since water will not move readily from one type of soil to another. Poorly mixed soils lead to root rot due to excessive wetness.

Check the pH requirements for your plants and bulbs and amend the soil accordingly. Dig organic matter into the top 8–12 inches and add slow-release, complete fertilizers to meet nutrient needs, allowing more nitrogen for foliage plants. For an extra boost for flowering plants and bulbs, you can mix bonemeal deep into the bottom of the planting hole.

Provide drainage. Good drainage helps prevent root, crown, and stem fungal diseases. Sensitive root systems and dormant bulbs cannot tolerate waterlogged soil, especially in winter. Organic matter added for soil conditioning and nutrient sources will also improve drainage. If your soil is heavy, increase the volume of amendments equal to the tilling depth: 8–12 inches of compost, for instance, tilled in 8–12 inches deep. Dig in amendments thoroughly to avoid pockets that will not absorb water. For the best drainage, plant on mounds.

ONGOING CARE

Few perennials give you the pleasure you expect from them without any care. Some attention to feeding, along with a few maintenance chores, is essential for them to flourish in maturity.

Dividing. Dividing perennials avoids crowding and renews the vigor needed for heavy bloom. Most benefit from dividing every three to five years, although perennials like lamb's ears *(Stachys)* may require yearly division, while bleeding heart *(Dicentra)* may never need it. Divide perennials carefully, taking care to protect the crowns and keep root damage to a minimum. Exposing the root ball and cutting or dividing by hand are less risky than splitting sections in the ground. When you replant the divided sections, renew soil amendments and nutrients in the root zone, especially phosphorus and potassium.

Maintaining. Regular garden inspections while you groom and water plants will help you find seasonal pests and problems in their incipient stages, when they are easy to control. Pick off slugs, snails, caterpillars, and leaves showing signs of fungal leaf spot as soon as they appear. Stake or otherwise support plants that topple under their own weight, to prevent foliage from rotting on moist soil. Get to know the different nutrient and water requirements for each species. Needs vary widely; try to keep plants with similar requirements in the same areas rather than introducing water-hungry lobelia, for example, into a bed of lavender.

Protecting. Clear out and compost weeds and debris so you don't provide breeding grounds for diseases and insects. In cold-winter zones, leave dead stems on perennials to protect their

Good Drainage Is Essential

Clay soils, desirable for their high nutrient content and capacity to hold water in arid regions, must be managed carefully to provide the necessary drainage. Otherwise, summer irrigation and winter rains result in waterlogged soil, and roots will rot. Mound large beds at least 6–12 inches above grade and smaller beds 4–6 inches. The perennials in this well-drained mound planting can bloom for years.

crowns. Only after the ground freezes should you add insulating leaves, straw, or evergreen boughs for defense against alternate freezing and thawing. Remove them as soon as thawing begins in spring, to prevent rot from warmth and moisture caught underneath. Watch for exposed roots that are heaved out of the ground and early growth that needs additional insulation.

BULB CULTURE

Hundreds of bulb species are garden-worthy and easy to grow. However, bulbs have a character of their own and demand special attention to keep them healthy and viable for many years. For their brief show to be worthwhile, planting and care must be precise and tailored to each type.

Planting. Plant spring-flowering bulbs in early to late fall, after the soil has begun to cool; plant fall-flowering bulbs in late summer for the current year, or in late fall to delay bloom until the next year. Set bulbs at the correct depth for each species. A general rule is to set them at a depth below the soil equal to three or four times the largest dimension of the bulb. At planting time, dig a slow-release fertilizer that contains nitrogen, phosphorous, and potassium into the root zone below the bulb, since these nutrients will not move there from the surface. Give bulbs protection from rodents and burrowing animals by planting them in wire baskets.

Maintaining foliage. It is important to leave bulb foliage undisturbed after bloom, until it begins to die. It continues to manufacture food for underground storage, replacing the depleted reserves that produced this year's flowers. Removing foliage reduces the nutrients stored in the bulb for next year's blossoms.

> ### TIP
>
> Guard against broken stems and eliminate the need to stake dahlias and gladioli by planting individual tubers and corms in holes 8–12 inches deep. Cover sprouts and buds with a few inches of soil. As stems grow, continue filling in the planting hole with more soil. The mature stems will be strong and rarely require staking.

Digging and storing. Bulbs need to be lifted for several reasons. Many bulbs, such as paper whites, become crowded quickly; periodic thinning is needed to maintain vigor and flowering. Dahlias and gladioli must be lifted annually for division and protection from low temperatures. Dig carefully so as to avoid cutting into fleshy growth and providing an entry for diseases. Before storing the bulbs, clean off soil and dry them, discarding soft, spongy, damaged ones. Provide a cool, dry storage environment to prevent roots from shriveling and drying. Store each species under the conditions needed to protect the living, but dormant, tissue and buds. Narcissus, for example, can be destroyed at temperatures above 80°F. Tulips and hyacinths must have at least six weeks of temperatures below 50°F. Dahlias retain vigor when stored in dry sand, perlite, or leaves at 40–45°F.

COMMON PROBLEMS OF ANNUALS, PERENNIALS, AND BULBS

Coddling one or two annuals through a bloom season in a difficult climate takes a certain effort over a short term, but it can be richly rewarding. Mismatching perennials and bulbs with environmental conditions, however, can spell disaster. These plants react resolutely to humidity and dryness, excess moisture, day length and length of season, wind and fog, as well as low winter temperatures and high summer nighttime temperatures. Nothing short of magic will prompt a hosta to prosper in coastal sand, or Cleveland sage in the damp Northwest. Poorly adapted plants are problem prone and need constant attention so they do not weaken or succumb to pests. The first question to ask about a languishing herbaceous plant should be: Does it fit this climate zone?

KNOWING THE NATIVES

Many western ornamental favorites are actually native to the Far East—China, Japan, or Korea—and have become popular despite their common need for summer water, which can be unreasonable in the many dry western zones. As dry-zone gardeners have begun thinking about more appropriate plants, they have tended to focus on western natives. However, a word of caution is in order here.

Ornamental Natives

For bright blossoms and low irrigation requirements, substitute native arrowleaf balsamroot, *Balsamorhiza sagittata* (above), for water-hungry sunflowers in all but desert zones. Seaside daisies or beach asters, *Erigeron glaucus* (below, left), bloom for months with minimal summer water in Zones 4–6, 15–17, and 22–24. *Penstemon pinifolius* (above, left) thrives in all western zones and is an excellent choice for rock gardens.

Simply being native does not necessarily qualify a plant as a low-maintenance, low-water–requiring panacea for arid climates. In reality, western natives come from habitats as diverse as riparian meadows and high-elevation deserts. What's needed is not just a western native; the solution is to seek out zone-compatible plants.

If your annuals, perennials, or bulbs are showing any of the following conditions, it is likely they are not suited to your zone.

- Earlier or later flowering than normal
- Shorter or taller height than normal
- Decline in foliage mass
- Reduction in performance
- Weak stems
- Rotting over the winter

DISEASES

Bacterial diseases appear as wilts and blights, spots on foliage, scab and soft rots on bulbs. Fungi cause similar leaf spots and bulb rot and, in addition, rusts, wilts, and mildews on stems and leaves, and rots on flowers, stems, crowns, and roots. A few viruses show up as mottling and unusual variegation on flowers and foliage. They become a serious problem when they cause stunting and disfigurement and when they weaken bulbs.

PESTS

Pests are unpredictable and random problems in the ornamental garden. They appear in various stages of their life cycles, feeding rapidly during brief stays. Keeping plants in vigorous good health, inspecting regularly, and encouraging the presence of natural predators all help keep pest problems to a minimum. The encyclopedia sections of this book provide information on managing any infestation. See page 75 for guidance on diagnosing problems.

Insects. Examine plants at each stage of their growth for insects or their signs. Look at flowers, shoots, foliage, and stems. Aphids and other sucking insects tend to appear in clusters and leave sticky

Yellow-bellied marmot

residues. They may do more damage as a vector, transmitting diseases, than by eating plant parts. Leafhoppers, for instance, spread a yellowing and stunting disease called aster yellows that is caused by a phytoplasma and is easily transmitted to susceptible plants. There is no treatment for aster yellows.

A hand lens is useful in determining the cause of browned edges, silvery or pale streaks, and small spots and stippling—mites and thrips and some beetles are minuscule and difficult to identify. Examine bulbs closely for boring larvae.

Vertebrate pests. Gardeners in rural and suburban areas have experimented with countless measures to protect their plants against rabbits, marmots, pocket gophers, deer, and other vertebrate pests, but exclusion remains the best control. Perhaps better yet is to limit vulnerable gardens and landscapes, insofar as possible, to resistant plants. If you're troubled by rabbits and gophers this may prove difficult, since they will eat so many plants, but the list of deer-resistant plants is long. However, resistance varies from one zone to another, so consult local lists available from your cooperative extension agent.

WEEDS

Weeds are sure to show up even in the tidiest of gardens. While they make an ornamental garden less attractive, their real harm is in the root zone, where they compete for water and nutrients. Many also harbor insects and diseases that can infest the garden. Preventing weeds from germinating at all by using mulches is the best line of defense (see page 39). Before you remove those weeds that do appear, try to identify them (see "Encyclopedia of Weeds," pages 256–303). Certain weeds are good indicators of soil conditions, and their presence may point out a potential problem (see box below).

CULTURAL PROBLEMS

If your problems with annuals, perennials, and bulbs don't go away after you have eliminated pests and diseases, look again at where they are growing. Are they suited to sun or shade? Is the soil well drained? Do your perennials need dividing? Remember that good cultural care and climate compatibility are keys to successful gardening in the West. Look over "Preventing Problems" (pages 105–107) for guidelines on resolving cultural problems.

DEER-RESISTANT PLANTS

Acanthus mollis

Hemerocallis

Kniphofia

Romneya coulteri

Acanthus mollis
Agapanthus
Arabis
Calendula officinalis
Cerastium
Digitalis
Erysimum
Eschscholzia
Euphorbia
Galium odoratum
Helichrysum
Helleborus
Hemerocallis
Herbs
Iris
Kniphofia
Leucojum
Liriope
Lychnis coronaria
Narcissus
Nepeta
Ophiopogon
Ornamental grasses
Osteospermum
Papaver
Phlomis
Plecostachys
Romneya coulteri
Stachys byzantina
Teucrium
Tulipa

WEEDS AS INDICATORS OF SOIL PROBLEMS

If the listed weeds appear in your garden, they indicate the following soil problem:

Chickweed

Acid soil
chickweed
curly dock
moss
plantain
red sorrel
yarrow

Alkaline soil
chicory
shepherd's purse

Infertile soil
black medic
crabgrass
plantain
thistle
yarrow

Compacted soil
annual bluegrass
bindweed
chickweed
goosegrass
plantain
prostrate knotweed
quack grass
thistle
white clover

Poor drainage
barnyard grass
buttercup
crabgrass
curly dock
ground ivy
henbit
nutsedge
plantain

Nutsedge

THE MOST COMMON SPECIES AND THE MOST COMMON PROBLEMS

These listings tell you the botanical and common name of each plant and the western zones where it thrives. One of the common problems afflicting the plant in the West is featured, and, where available, resistant varieties are listed.

SYMBOLS: ✿ ANNUALS ☙ PERENNIALS ♠ BULBS

ALCEA rosea

☙ HOLLYHOCK

✐ ZONES: ALL

RUST

Rust-colored pustules on the undersides of leaves cause leaf surfaces to look yellow and blotchy. Rain, heavy dew, or irrigation can spread rust throughout the foliage. Yellowed leaves eventually fall and leave plants weakened, though flowering may continue. Watch for rust and remove infected leaves immediately to prevent damage and loss of plants.

Other plant problems. COMMON PESTS: beetles, leafhoppers, mealybugs, nematodes, slugs, snails, spider mites, thrips, whiteflies. COMMON DISEASES: anthracnose, root rot.

Notes: Some hollyhock species are biennials, others perennials. Know what type you have before expecting plants to regrow each spring. Most will self-sow. Monthly fertilizer applications encourage rebloom in the fall, if plants are cut back just above the ground after summer flowering. Inspect plants regularly for slugs, snails, and Japanese beetles.

ANTIRRHINUM majus

✿ SNAPDRAGON

✐ ZONES: ALL

FUSARIUM WILT

Fusarium wilt begins in the roots, though the first sign is wilting foliage. Slowly, older leaves turn yellow and develop brown, dead areas. The infection may move up the plant on one side only, or the entire plant may become stunted. The fungus darkens and destroys the insides of stems, causing additional wilting. Plants that continue to deteriorate will eventually die.

Other plant problems. COMMON PESTS: aphids, corn earworms, loopers, nematodes, slugs, snails, spider mites. COMMON DISEASES: aster yellows, botrytis blight, damping off, downy mildew, root and stem rot, rust, verticillium wilt.

Notes: A few snapdragon varieties are rust resistant, including dwarf 'Double Sweetheart', 'Little Darling', and 'Royal Carpet'. Watering early in the day and changing planting locations from one year to the next help to cut down on rust problems. Use a sterile mix when growing snapdragons from seed, since seedlings are very susceptible to damping-off fungus. In cold zones, wait until spring to set out plants; in mild-winter climates, set them out to form buds in early fall before nighttime temperatures drop below 50°F. Once buds have set, flowering will continue through spring and summer.

AQUILEGIA

☙ COLUMBINE

✐ ZONES: ALL

LEAF MINERS

The columbine leaf miner tunnels through narrow leaf interiors. Pick off infected leaves as soon as you notice the characteristic white blotchy markings that show its trail. Cut back stems after bloom and again in the fall; discard stems and leaves or compost them in a hot pile. The larvae hatch inside the leaves where the adults lay eggs. In winter, they pupate in the soil.

Other plant problems. COMMON PESTS: aphids, borers, spider mites, whiteflies. COMMON DISEASES: crown rot, leaf spot, mosaic virus, powdery mildew, rust.

Notes: Columbines do not perform well for long periods. Remove those more than three years old to provide space for younger, more vigorous plants. Leave seed heads for self-sowing unless you want specific colors. Not all species come true from seed; hybridization occurs readily as plants near each other cross-pollinate. Older seeds may require six weeks of cold treatment before they will germinate. Do not permit soil or mulch to become soggy; keep wet mulch a few inches away from crown and stem areas, since columbines are sensitive to crown rot.

ASTER

☙ ASTER

✐ ZONES: ALL

BLACK BLISTER BEETLE

The black blister beetle, or aster beetle, damages asters in summer. It feeds heavily on leaves, to the point of defoliation in severe cases. Beetles are damaging to plants in their adult form only. Larval forms, called grubs, are not garden pests, but they feed underground on grasshopper eggs. They overwinter in the soil as larvae and pupate in the spring.

Other plant problems. COMMON PESTS: aphids, borers, leafhoppers, slugs, snails, spittlebugs, tarnished plant bugs, thrips, whiteflies. COMMON DISEASES: fungal leaf spot, mosaic virus, powdery mildew, root rot, verticillium wilt.

Notes: Hand-picking is an effective method of managing beetles. Wear gloves to protect your hands, since secretions cause painful blisters. Divide clumps of vigorous-growing species of asters annually to keep top growth under control and to prevent invasive roots from spreading widely. Clumps can expand to several feet in diameter.

BEGONIA

☙ BEGONIA

✐ ZONES: 14–24; OR TREATED AS ANNUALS

MEALYBUGS

Mealybugs move slowly over begonia leaves and stems. They cluster on tender growth, usually in stem crotches or leaf axils. The female bugs are recognizable by their protective waxy or mealy coating. Colonies, which congregate mostly on stem tissue, look like cottony mounds. As they feed, mealybugs excrete sticky honeydew, which often develops black sooty mold.

Other plant problems. COMMON PESTS: aphids, slugs, snails, thrips, whiteflies, wireworms. COMMON DISEASES: bacterial leaf spot, botrytis blight, damping off, fungal leaf spot, powdery mildew, root rot.

Notes: Begonias need moist soil for top performance, but water them only when the surface begins to dry out—soggy soil causes them to develop root rot.

CALENDULA officinalis

🌿 CALENDULA, POT MARIGOLD

🌡 ZONES: ALL

MOSAIC VIRUS

Abnormal leaf colors are symptoms of the mosaic virus. Leaves show yellow or pale green blotches or streaking. Affected plants usually become stunted or distorted, and plants produce fewer flowers. The virus may not be a problem unless large beds of plants are disfigured and detract from an ornamental effect.

Other plant problems. COMMON PESTS: aphids, cabbage loopers, corn earworms, cutworms, leafhoppers, spider mites. COMMON DISEASES: fungal leaf spot, powdery mildew, root and stem rot.

Notes: This annual plant behaves much like a perennial in mild climates along the coast, where it blooms nearly year-round. Blossoming is most prolific when faded flower heads are removed. Leaving some seed heads, however, allows reseeding and a continuous supply of new plants. Older ones tend to develop woody stems. Pale yellow flower color may revert to orange in self-sown plants. Calendulas do not do well in excessively moist or fertile soil. In hot, humid zones, flowering stops as temperatures rise. 'Pacific Beauty' is somewhat heat tolerant.

CAMPANULA

🌿 BELLFLOWER

🌡 ZONES: BEST IN 1–9, 14–24

SLUGS AND SNAILS

These common garden pests thrive in moist, shady sites. They often hide under foliage rosettes for protection from drying sunlight. Silvery trails along the ground and on leaves are signs of their presence. Left unchecked, slugs and snails can decimate plants in a short time. Make early morning forays into the garden, especially in damp weather, and hand-pick them to control their populations and to protect plants from looking ragged.

Other plant problems. COMMON PESTS: aphids, thrips. COMMON DISEASES: crown rot, fungal leaf spot, fusarium wilt, root rot, rust.

Notes: Bellflowers in wet soil can be killed by a fungal disease that decays stem and crown tissue. Scottish bluebells (C. rotundifolia), however, thrive in marshy sites and are resistant. A rust fungus (Coleosporium species) that commonly infects pine needles lives alternately on bellflowers. If the rust is a problem in your zone, keep all bellflowers at least 1,000 feet away from susceptible pines. Remove and destroy infected bellflower plants.

CHRYSANTHEMUM

🌿 🌱 CHRYSANTHEMUM

🌡 ZONES: VARY BY SPECIES

CUCUMBER BEETLES

Adult beetles chew large holes in flowers and foliage, leaving them frayed and unattractive. If buds are damaged, they may fail to fully open. Beetle activity does not affect the plant's growth unless foliage is completely stripped; however, flowers are often too damaged to be used in bouquets.

Other plant problems. COMMON PESTS: aphids, borers, corn earworms, cutworms, lace bugs, leaf miners, loopers, slugs, snails, spider mites, tarnished plant bugs, thrips, whiteflies. COMMON DISEASES: aster yellows, bacterial blight, crown gall, fusarium wilt, leaf spot, mosaic virus, powdery mildew, root rot, rust.

Notes: Though chrysanthemums are subject to numerous pests and diseases, healthy plants have relatively few problems. Aphids seem to be universally present; stem borers are often a problem in desert zones. These plants are sensitive to watering: overwatering causes leaves to blacken, yellow, and drop; underwatering results in woody stems and loss of lower leaves. Encourage compactness by cutting back stems several times or pinching throughout the summer, before buds form for fall bloom. Stake tall stems to prevent breakage.

COSMOS

🌿 COSMOS

🌡 ZONES: VARY BY SPECIES

CANKER AND DIEBACK

Fungi in the soil cause cankers—dark, sunken spots—to form on stems and crowns. As the cankers enlarge, the stems collapse. The fungi destroy water-conducting tissue, and the foliage wilts and dies. To reduce the threat of fungal disease, keep plants on the dry side, avoid overcrowding, and plant in beds where there is good air circulation.

Other plant problems. COMMON PESTS: aphids, beetles, borers, leafhoppers, spider mites, thrips. COMMON DISEASES: aster yellows, fusarium wilt, mosaic virus, powdery mildew, root rot, rusts.

Notes: Cosmos perform best in somewhat infertile soil, thriving even in desert zones. Soil that is too rich causes weak stems and increases the need for staking. Seed heads detract from the plants' appearance and should be removed.

DAHLIA

🌿 DAHLIA

🌡 ZONES: ALL

BULB ROT

Fleshy dahlia bulbs (tuberous roots) that are planted in cold, wet soil in spring are easily destroyed by fungal rots. Tubers quickly darken and become mushy before roots develop or shoots appear above the ground. Delay planting until the soil warms and is moist but not wet. Since tubers contain ample food reserves to support early growth, wait to water until the soil begins to dry out.

Other plant problems. COMMON PESTS: aphids, cucumber beetles, borers, earwigs, leafhoppers, leaf miners, slugs, snails, tarnished plant bugs, wireworms. COMMON DISEASES: bacterial soft rot, fusarium wilt, mosaic virus, powdery mildew, ringspot virus, root rot, verticillium wilt.

Notes: If left in the ground over winter in moderate western zones, dahlias may survive the cold but not the wet soil.

DELPHINIUM

🌱 DELPHINIUM

🌡 ZONES: VARY BY SPECIES

CUTWORMS

Night-feeding cutworms destroy delphiniums by chewing off seedlings at ground level, causing them to topple and die. Older plants may show some ragged foliage or chewed holes. These larvae hide in the soil in the daytime. You can keep them away from stems if you push paper cups or collars a few inches into the soil at planting time.

Other plant problems. COMMON PESTS: aphids, leafhoppers, leaf miners, slugs, snails, spider mites, thrips. COMMON DISEASES: bacterial canker, crown rot, fusarium wilt, leaf spot, mosaic virus, powdery mildew, root rot.

Notes: Most delphiniums do best in cool, maritime climates with warm summers. Hot, dry weather reduces performance. Soil requirements are strict: a neutral to slightly alkaline pH (add lime to increase alkalinity if necessary), excellent drainage, and high nutrient levels. Rots are common where drainage is slow; flowering is reduced in poor, infertile soil. Brittle stems must be staked for protection against wind and rain.

DIANTHUS

🌱 CARNATION, PINKS, SWEET WILLIAM

🌡 ZONES: ALL

SPITTLEBUGS

Spittlebugs are difficult to see underneath the dabs of white froth that cover them. The foamy bubbles protect nymphs from sunlight and predators; adults move around like leaf-hoppers, unprotected. Some spittlebugs spend only part of their life cycle on *Dianthus* and other tender garden plants, where they suck plant juices before moving on to host trees or shrubs. Damage is usually inconsequential, but if feeding is heavy, it results in stunting and loss of vigor.

Other plant problems. COMMON PESTS: aphids, cutworms, earwigs, loopers, mealybugs, slugs, snails, spider mites, thrips. COMMON DISEASES: bacterial leaf spot, bacterial wilt, crown rot, damping off, fungal leaf spot, fusarium wilt, powdery mildew, root rot, rust, verticillium wilt.

Notes: Dianthus includes species of tall, tender, disease-prone flowers as well as species that form tough mats capable of surviving extreme drought. Know the type of plant you have, since requirements vary widely. All are sensitive to overwatering, prefer slightly alkaline soil, and require full sun.

DIGITALIS

🌱 FOXGLOVE

🌡 ZONES: ALL

SPIDER MITES

Spider mites thrive in hot, arid conditions. Their pinpoint size is difficult to see without a hand lens, but their damage is obvious. Foliage appears stippled with yellow dots, sometimes fading to bronze. Leaves may drop prematurely and weaken plants enough to reduce flowering. Sometimes large colonies spin webs around leaf edges or shoot tips, enclosing the mites feeding on plant juices inside.

Other plant problems. COMMON PESTS: slugs, snails. COMMON DISEASES: crown rot, fungal leaf spot, fusarium wilt. OTHER: Poisonous.

Notes: Finding the right balance of sun and shade, moisture and dryness is key for keeping foxglove culture simple. Plants reseed prolifically, keeping biennial forms in your garden for years. Flowering will repeat if tall stems are cut back to the side stems after flowering. If fungal leaf spots disfigure the foliage by midsummer, cut plants to the ground. All parts of Digitalis are poisonous.

GLADIOLUS

🌱 GLADIOLUS

🌡 ZONES: ALL

THRIPS

Thrips are the most damaging pest to gladiolus foliage and flowers. They scrape openings in plant tissue to feed on plant juices and lay their eggs inside. These minute cuts cause silvery flecks on foliage and silver or brown blemishes on flowers and buds. Several generations continue to damage plants each year. If thrips infest gladiolus bulbs (corms), they can cause damage during winter storage.

Other plant problems. COMMON PESTS: aphids, beetles, cutworms, spider mites, tarnished plant bugs. COMMON DISEASES: bacterial canker, botrytis blight, fungal leaf spot, mosaic virus, root rot.

Notes: Perfect blooms on strong stems depend on well-drained, humus-rich soil that is not overfertilized. Corms will rot if planted too early in cold, wet soil or if soil is overwatered at any time. New varieties are more disease resistant than older varieties. To prevent winter fungal damage, store corms uncovered in a well-ventilated location.

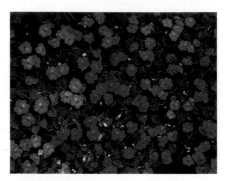

IMPATIENS

🌿 BALSAM, TOUCH-ME-NOT, BUSY LIZZIES

🌡 ZONES: VARY BY SPECIES

ROOT ROT

This fungal disease occurs in hot, humid weather. Plants yellow and wilt, then wither and die. Hardened lumps of fungal masses may be visible on affected plants or on the surrounding soil surface. Root rot often begins at the base of plants, then spreads throughout. A white mold frequently coats stems. Affected plants should be destroyed; set out new plants in a different location.

Other plant problems. COMMON PESTS: aphids, cucumber beetles, mealybugs, nematodes, scales, slugs, snails, spider mites, tarnished plant bugs, weevils. COMMON DISEASES: bacterial and fungal leaf spots, damping off.

Notes: Different Impatiens species tolerate different levels of sun and shade, heat and humidity. All demand adequate moisture, especially during hot and windy conditions. Impatiens wilt to the point of collapse if the soil dries out. Although they recover, leaf drop results in spindly-looking plants. Young plants need regular pinching to develop fullness. Plants may develop leaf spot fungus; pick off and destroy infected leaves.

IRIS

🌿 IRIS

✂ ZONES: VARY BY SPECIES

FUNGAL LEAF SPOT

Leaf spot can destroy stately iris foliage, weaken plants, and reduce flowering potential. The symptoms range from small dots to large elliptical spots with yellow and brown discoloration covering most of a leaf. The fungi thrive in moist conditions but can be controlled with a fungicide to prevent loss of the foliage. In cold-winter climates, cut back and destroy infected foliage in late fall.

Other plant problems. COMMON PESTS: aphids, borers, nematodes, slugs, snails, spider mites, thrips, weevils, whiteflies, wireworms. COMMON DISEASES: bacterial soft rot, botrytis blight, crown rot, root rot, rust, scorch.

Notes: Iris borers, nematodes, bulb whiteflies, and other pests feed underground on rhizomes and weaken plants, opening them to possible infection from bacteria. Bacterial infections also strike rhizomes injured by cultivating tools or cold damage. Whereas fungal infections, which occur most often in overly wet soils, can be treated with fungicides, plants afflicted with bacterial disease must be destroyed.

LATHYRUS

🌿 SWEET PEA

✂ ZONES: VARY BY SPECIES

BACTERIAL CANKER

Water-soaked or greasy spots and streaks are signs of a bacterial infection. The discoloration starts near the ground and moves up the stems as the infection spreads. Spots often ooze liquid as they enlarge. If they spread far enough, they girdle and kill the stems. Leaves and flowers also develop water-soaked spots, turn brown, and die. Infected plants should be pulled out and destroyed. Plant sweet peas in a different location each year.

Other plant problems. COMMON PESTS: aphids, slugs, snails. COMMON DISEASES: anthracnose, collar rot, mosaic virus, nematodes, powdery mildew, root rot.

Resistant varieties. Sweet peas thrive in cool, moist conditions in all zones. Although some strains are heat resistant, high heat kills most. Early-flowering varieties have no heat resistance but can be planted in late summer in Zones 12, 13, 17, and 21–24 for winter bloom. Spring-flowering heat-resistant types can be planted in fall and winter in Zones 7–9 and 12–24. Strains that bloom in summer have some heat resistance except in Zones 7–15 and 18–21.

LILIUM

🌿 LILY

✂ ZONES: ALL

NEMATODES

Nematodes are microscopic worms that are most common in mild-winter climate zones, where they are not killed by hard freezes. Their damage to bulbs causes foliage to yellow and wilt, become stunted, and—in severe infestations—die. Roots become swollen and shallow, with hard nodules that prevent plants from absorbing nutrients.

Other plant problems. COMMON PESTS: aphids, mealybugs, mites, scales, slugs, snails, thrips. COMMON DISEASES: botrytis blight, chlorosis, fusarium wilt, leaf scorch, mosaic virus, root rot, rust.

Notes: Several fungal diseases infect lily bulbs, rotting them in the ground or in storage. Sometimes bulbs form dark, sunken lesions; at other times they develop white, pink, or gray molds. Infected bulbs cause lily foliage to turn yellow, wilt, or become stunted; they should be destroyed. Fungal infections that infect leaves and flowers may spread into bulbs.

NARCISSUS

🌿 DAFFODIL

✂ ZONES: ALL

BULB FLIES

The narcissus bulb fly resembles a tiny yellow and black bumble bee. It lays its eggs at the base of flower stems or on the ground nearby. Grayish white maggots hatch and burrow into bulbs in summer, stripping bulb interiors and leaving them soft, pithy, and vulnerable to bacterial and fungal diseases. Bulbs that are not ruined sprout inferior foliage and are too weakened to flower. Larvae overwinter in bulbs or in the soil. Destroy all infected bulbs.

Other plant problems. COMMON PESTS: aphids, mealybugs, mites, nematodes, slugs, snails, thrips. COMMON DISEASES: botrytis blight, fusarium rot, leaf scorch, leaf spot, mosaic virus.

Notes: When flowers decrease in size and number from overcrowding—usually after three to five years—lift and divide bulbs when foliage yellows and dies back. Separate only those bulbs that come apart easily; replant the bulbs—bulbs held in storage for more than three weeks begin to decline.

NICOTIANA

🌿 FLOWERING TOBACCO

✂ ZONES: ALL

HORNWORMS

These horned green larvae are nearly identical to tomato hornworms, differing only in the color of the horn (black on tomato worms, red on tobacco worms). In midsummer, they emerge from eggs laid on the undersides of leaves. Larvae feed upside down on plants, decimating foliage and stripping stems bare. Worms are the same color as the foliage and are difficult to see—you may not notice them until they eat several leaves. The black, pebbly excrement is easier to spot.

Other plant problems. COMMON PESTS: aphids, beetles, corn earworms, cutworms, slugs, snails, tobacco budworms. COMMON DISEASES: mosaic virus, powdery mildew.

Notes: You will need to stake tall varieties of flowering tobacco. They become top-heavy and will topple and break. All tobacco plants are poisonous if eaten. Keep flowering tobacco plants away from tomato, pepper, and eggplant—they are all in the same family (Solanaceae), *and diseases can be transmitted from one plant type to another.*

PAEONIA

🌿 PEONY

✎ ZONES: 1–11, 14–16

ROSE CHAFERS

Adults attack peonies individually or in swarms. As they chew holes in leaves and flower petals, they drop black excrement onto lower leaves. Rose chafers can destroy foliage completely, leaving only remnants of lacy patterns. Hand-pick insects during the few weeks that they are active. They may be more common in areas with sandy soil, since that is where females prefer to lay eggs.

Other plant problems. COMMON PESTS: scales, thrips. COMMON DISEASES: botrytis blight, crown rot, fusarium wilt, root rot, verticillium wilt.

Notes: Botrytis blight, a fungal disease, causes brown spots on buds and leaves. Plump buds may be treated with a fungicide; wilted buds and stems should be removed. Cut off spotted foliage and destroy all infected plant parts. At planting time, keep manure away from roots to prevent rot; set tubers with eyes no more than 2 inches below the soil. Deep planting and lack of adequate winter chill may prevent flowering. Ants may be seen on or around peonies, but they are not a problem and do not require controls.

PAPAVER

🌿 POPPY

✎ ZONES: VARY BY SPECIES

CORN EARWORMS

These brown, striped larvae of night-flying moths chew irregular holes in buds and foliage or eat them off completely. If damaged buds open at all, the flowers are tattered. Insects are active in spring and summer in cold zones, year-round in mild climates. They feed on other vegetable crops and are also known as tomato fruitworms.

Other plant problems. COMMON PESTS: aphids, leafhoppers, mealybugs, rose chafers, slugs, snails, tarnished plant bugs. COMMON DISEASES: bacterial canker, botrytis blight, curly top virus, downy mildew, leaf spot, powdery mildew, verticillium wilt.

Notes: Downy mildew may affect poppy seedlings or mature plants. Symptoms are pale spots on leaves covered with a white or gray mold. Affected plants with distorted stems may fail to flower. Stems may weaken at the base and die. Destroy affected plants and seeds. To prevent fungal infections, keep plants on the dry side.

PELARGONIUM

🌿 GERANIUM

✎ ZONES: 8, 9, 12–24 (SUMMER ANNUALS IN OTHER ZONES)

GERANIUM BUDWORMS

Also known as tobacco budworms, these greenish, tan, or reddish worms tunnel into buds, destroying them from the inside. They are sometimes seen feeding on opened blossoms. In severe infestations, worms destroy all buds and the plants do not bloom. Problems are common in mild climates; the worms can't survive cold winters.

Other plant problems. COMMON PESTS: aphids, mealybugs, slugs, snails, spider mites, whiteflies. COMMON DISEASES: bacterial blight, botrytis blight, edema, leaf spot, mosaic virus, oak root fungus, root rot, rust, verticillium wilt.

Notes: Whiteflies and aphids attack Lady Washington pelargoniums (P. domesticum); ivy geraniums (P. peltatum) attract spider mites. Pinch tips on all geraniums as they grow to prevent legginess. Stems can be cut back hard if foliage is damaged by frosts or plants are grown in too much shade. New varieties have improved heat tolerance and disease resistance.

PETUNIA hybrida

🌿 PETUNIA

✎ ZONES: ALL

LOOPERS

Loopers—also called inchworms—are small, greenish worms that push themselves forward in a characteristic looping movement. Several generations may appear each year. Loopers feed heavily on foliage, disfiguring mature plants and weakening young ones; they can kill seedlings. Hand-picking effectively reduces populations, though the loopers' green color makes them difficult to spot.

Other plant problems. COMMON PESTS: aphids, armyworms, beetles, corn earworms, cutworms, geranium budworms, hornworms, slugs, snails, spider mites, thrips, whiteflies. COMMON DISEASES: botrytis blight, crown rot, damping off, mosaic virus, powdery mildew, root rot, verticillium wilt.

Notes: Look for holes in buds, evidence of the geranium or tobacco budworm; pick off worm-infested buds and blossoms. Remove leaves and flowers infected with botrytis rot. Multiflora petunias with numerous smaller blooms are more rot resistant than grandifloras with fewer numbers of larger blooms. Grandifloras are also more damaged by heavy rains. In Zones 12 and 13, petunias do not tolerate summer heat; in these zones, plant in fall for early spring color.

PHLOX

🌿 PHLOX

✎ ZONES: VARY BY SPECIES

POWDERY MILDEW

A white or gray feltlike coating on leaves and stems in summer is characteristic of powdery mildew. This disease is common in dry weather, particularly when days are warm and nights are cool; it is less common in areas of high rainfall. Fungal growth penetrates leaves and stems to feed on plant tissue and sometimes causes distortion. Plants may continue to grow and bloom; or they may wither, lose vigor, and die. Do not apply fungicides containing sulfur when temperatures exceed 80°F.

Other plant problems. COMMON PESTS: aphids, leafhoppers, spider mites, wireworms. COMMON DISEASES: damping off, root rot, rust.

Notes: P. paniculata is particularly vulnerable to mildew and to spider mites. P. maculata, P. caroliniana, and their numerous varieties are somewhat resistant to both mildew and mites. When setting out plants, avoid crowding or planting too close to walls. Phlox need good air circulation to discourage disease. Mature plants may require thinning.

SALVIA

🌿 🌸 SAGE

🌡 ZONES: VARY BY SPECIES

VERTICILLIUM WILT

This destructive disease is caused by a fungus that lives in the soil for many years. Infection moves up through the roots into the water-conductive tubes of plants. Plants wilt in the heat of day even though moisture is plentiful. Leaves turn yellow, then brown, and die. A characteristic of this wilt is the progression of leaf damage upward or outward from the base of the plant or of individual stems.

Other plant problems. COMMON PESTS: aphids, borers, leafhoppers, spider mites, whiteflies. COMMON DISEASES: damping off, leaf blight, powdery mildew, root rot.

Notes: Know the cultural preferences and growth habits of your salvias, since the numerous species are widely varied. Some endure ordinary garden conditions and even demand constant moisture or foliage will dry out. Other varieties are highly drought tolerant and adapted to dry conditions and will rot easily in moist soil. Some tend to be spindly if they do not receive regular pinching to develop bushiness.

TAGETES

🌿 MARIGOLD

🌡 ZONES: VARY BY SPECIES

TARNISHED PLANT BUG

This mottled brown bug with a shield-shaped body sucks sap from flower buds and plant stems. The bugs inject a toxic substance as they feed, causing blackened shoots and deformed plant parts. Several generations are produced each year from midspring through late summer; both adults and nymphs feed on plants. Bugs overwinter in nearby weeds and garden debris.

Other plant problems. COMMON PESTS: aphids, beetles, corn earworms, cutworms, geranium budworms, hornworms, slugs, snails, spider mites, thrips, whiteflies. COMMON DISEASES: botrytis blight, crown gall, damping off, fusarium wilt, leaf spot, mosaic virus, root rot, stem rot.

Notes: Constant deadheading will give you blooms throughout the summer. Urban smog

may damage seedlings, but plants usually recover as they mature. Several marigold varieties thrive in all climate zones. Flowering in desert climates is best in fall. Perennial *T. lemmonii is suited to Zones 8–10 and 12–24; T. lucida does well in Zones 8, 9, and 12–24 but is usually grown as an annual. Marigolds deter nematodes in vegetable gardens, but only if they are planted in large numbers throughout the vegetable bed.*

TULIPA

🌷 TULIP

🌡 ZONES: ALL

BOTRYTIS BLIGHT

Wet conditions promote botrytis fungal growths on leaves, flowers, and bulbs. If flower buds fail to open, inspect bulbs for discolored, sunken areas and small, hardened, pebbly growths. On flowers and leaves, you will see yellow or reddish brown areas with small dots in the center. As spots enlarge, they become covered with gray mold. Foliage often becomes distorted and dies. Destroy all infected bulbs, stems, and flowers.

Other plant problems. COMMON PESTS: aphids, beetles, flea beetles, mealybugs, tarnished plant bugs, thrips, whiteflies, wireworms. COMMON DISEASES: anthracnose, bulb rot, fusarium wilt, mosaic virus, powdery mildew, root rot.

Notes: Bud blast—a problem caused by poor growing conditions, insects, or diseases—prevents buds on tulips and other bulbs from flowering normally. Buds form but become distorted and discolored and fail to open. With tulips, the problem is often due to inadequate chilling. In warm-climate zones, chill bulbs for several weeks in the refrigerator, or plant more heat-tolerant strains.

VIOLA

🌸 VIOLA, VIOLET, PANSY

🌡 ZONES: VARY BY SPECIES

WIREWORMS

Pansies and violas are susceptible to damage from wireworms, especially when they are planted over spring-blooming bulbs. In cool, moist weather in spring and fall, the shiny, seg-

mented, reddish brown worms migrate close to the soil surface to feed on roots. The plants wilt and die as roots are destroyed. In warmer months, the worms remain deeper in the ground and bore into bulbs and deeper roots.

Other plant problems. COMMON PESTS: aphids, cutworms, flea beetles, mealybugs, nematodes, slugs, snails, spider mites. COMMON DISEASES: downy mildew, powdery mildew, root and stem rot.

Notes: F_1 and F_2 hybrids such as the 'Universal' strain are the most heat-resistant pansies, though even they may not be able to perform past midsummer before they succumb to heat. Johnny-jump-ups (V. tricolor) are somewhat more tolerant of heat, but all violas do best in cool seasons, and they are able to withstand light frosts. New varieties have the greatest heat and cold tolerance.

ZINNIA

🌿 ZINNIA

🌡 ZONES: ALL

DAMPING OFF

Plants grown from seed are susceptible to damping-off fungal infections. The fungi are present in nearly all soils and can kill seedlings as they germinate or after they emerge above the soil. Seedlings in cold, wet, poorly drained soils with a high nitrogen content are at greatest risk. You can guard against damping off by using a sterile germinating mix or by solarizing soil (see page 54). It also helps to withhold nitrogen fertilizers until seedlings have a well-developed root system.

Other plant problems. COMMON PESTS: aphids, beetles, earwigs, leaf rollers, spider mites, tarnished plant bugs. COMMON DISEASES: botrytis blight, canker and dieback, leaf blight, leaf spot, mosaic virus, powdery mildew, root rot.

Notes: Zinnias do not gain from early planting; they will languish until the weather is hot. Powdery mildew is a problem mostly in late summer and fall in foggy climates or on plants that are given overhead irrigation. Heavy dew and shade also promote mildew. The Pulcino and Pinwheel strains offer some resistance.

Problem Solving for
FRUITS, NUTS, AND BERRIES

Few things are more satisfying for gardeners than harvesting fresh, ripe fruit. A succulent peach, a bowl of raspberries, fresh cracked almonds—these make the months or years of waiting for a crop worthwhile. Perfect fruits, nuts, and berries don't just happen, as most gardeners know. They are often plagued by pest and disease problems and thwarted by turns in the weather. The key to growing successful crops is finding the right varieties for your climate.

CLASSIFYING FRUITS, NUTS, AND BERRIES

Fruits are grouped here for convenience according to their botanical structure or growth habit. Nuts and many fruits are tree crops; small fruits grow on shrubs, vines, and canes. Strawberries are unique, low-growing fruits of a perennial herb and are categorized separately. Most fruits also fall into subcategories.

TREE FRUITS

Four types of tree fruits (including nuts, which are actually fruits) are commonly grown in the West.

- Pomes—apples, pears, quince, and loquats—are those with a center core holding the seeds.
- Stone fruits—plums, prunes, peaches, nectarines, apricots, and cherries—contain a single seed or stone.
- Citrus fruits include oranges, lemons, grapefruit, limes, as well as less familiar hybrids such as tangors and limequats. Their juice-filled cells do not always produce seeds.
- Nuts are themselves seeds and true fruits. As nuts ripen, the outer leathery hull splits open to reveal their hard shell.

SMALL FRUITS

The small fruits are mostly shrubs or vines. Nearly all individual plants are large and vigorous and produce abundantly, but the fruits they bear are small in size.

- Cane berries, or bramble fruits, grow on renewable upright or trailing stems (canes). These include raspberries, blackberries, and several hybrids such as boysenberries and olallieberries.
- Grapes, which have more of a vining habit, also produce canes. Grape canes are the mature shoots, which must be pruned selectively and trained for fruit production.
- Bush berries—blueberries, currants, and gooseberries—are food crops but are also grown as ornamental shrubs.

CLIMATE COMPATIBILITY

Growing fruits, nuts, and berries in the West begins with accepting the limits of your climate. These crops yield top performance and produce a reliable crop only in specific zones. Since many trees take years before they reach productivity, it is helpful to know at planting time whether your tree of choice will ever produce. Your county cooperative extension agent (see page 50) can be of great help in pointing out the limitations of your climate and suggesting varieties that have a history of success.

HARDINESS AND SEASONAL REQUIREMENTS

In cold-winter zones, select fruits and nuts for their hardiness. Gardeners in cold zones can grow crops suited to warm climates if the plants are hardy enough. Many—but not all—species thrive in cold climates; in fact, with the exception of tropical fruits, most require a certain amount of winter chill.

But winter is only half of the climate equation. Besides requiring cold, most fruits and nuts will form and mature only when provided summer heat and humidity, exposure to sun, and a long growing season. Blueberries are an exception, thriving best in the Pacific Northwest, and strawberries are another, with varieties suited to every western zone.

Tree crops. Apples, pears, sour cherries, and some plums are among the hardiest fruits. Apples and Asian pears can be grown in every western climate, although only a few apple varieties are adapted to warm zones. European and hybrid pears are good choices for western climates, except for the highest elevations and hottest deserts. Sweet cherries are limited to zones with long winters and hot summers; sour cherries can tolerate milder winters.

Growing Cane Berries

Trailing cane berries need support. Trellising is the best way to handle the lateral growth; use wires or train the long canes over a fence. After harvest, cut to the ground all canes that bore fruit. Prune new growth to 6 feet and tie it to the trellis. Be sure to choose a variety developed for your zone.

Lemons Year-Round

Enjoy 'Meyer' lemons in any zone by planting a tree in a container for wintering indoors. Planted in the ground, this small tree can reach 12–15 feet, a size it rarely achieves in a container. Choose dwarf rootstock to keep it under 6 feet. 'Improved Meyer' is a virus-free selection; this variety is also rounder, more thin skinned, and less acidic than standard commercial lemons. Even young plants will produce fruit.

European plums are adapted to longer, colder winters than Japanese plums, which bloom early and are damaged by late frosts. Neither can be grown in low deserts.

Peaches and nectarines have strict climate requirements. They are less cold tolerant than apples, yet they will not survive in zones with warm winters or cool summers. Apricots can be grown throughout the West where there is adequate winter chill, little or no likelihood of late frosts to damage fruit, and low enough humidity to avoid fungal problems. They will not endure summer heat in low deserts. Of the citrus crops, kumquats, 'Meyer' lemons, and Satsuma oranges tolerate the most cold—they're hardy to 15–20°F. (See the pages that follow for the specific zone identification of most crops.)

Cane and bush berries. Raspberries perform best in cold-winter zones where summers remain cool. As soon as weather turns hot—either dry or humid—plants and berries suffer. Numerous varieties of blackberries, which tolerate warmer climates, have been bred for specific western zones. Blueberries thrive in cool, moist conditions, but they can be coddled in zones where winters are cold and summers are not too hot.

Grapes. European grapes do best in mild-winter zones of the West; many are wine grapes with a high heat requirement and a cold tolerance to about 5°F. Popular table varieties such as 'Flame', 'Thompson Seedless', and 'Black Monukka' are also European types; their zone requirements vary by variety. American grapes grow best in cold-winter zones with moderately hot summers.

Nuts. Macadamia nuts, the least-hardy nut crop grown in the West, can survive light frosts only; they need a long growing season to mature. Almonds withstand greater cold, but they bloom early and are at risk where long winters damage blossoms or developing nuts. Pistachios take freezing temperatures and require a longer chill than almonds. They also need higher summer temperatures for a crop to develop.

Though they can be grown in most western climates as an ornamental tree, pecans demand long, hot summers for nuts to mature. Chestnuts and filberts both withstand long, cold winters and higher elevations, though filberts blossom early and may be damaged by spring frosts. Neither produces a reliable crop in hot, dry climates that lack sufficient winter cold. Walnuts can be grown throughout the West; you can find a variety developed for any zone's growing season.

Hardy European Grapes

'Black Monukka' (left) is one of the hardiest European varieties, suitable for Zones 3, 7–9, and 11–21. 'Flame Seedless' (far left), an early-ripening variety, is best in Zones 6–9 and 12–21. Although these grapes require less heat than the popular 'Thompson Seedless', in cooler zones they'll do well when planted in a hot spot in your garden.

THE CHILLING FACTOR

Without adequate winter chill, fruits and nuts may fail to bloom, or they may decline in health and vigor to the point of dying. The amount of cold required—the chilling factor—is a specific number of hours accumulated during dormancy. In zones where winter temperatures regularly fall below 45°F, chilling is not a problem, but it can be where winter temperatures regularly rise above 60°F. Along the Pacific Coast and into the Southwest are areas that receive too little winter chill for some fruits to reliably produce a crop every year. In cold zones, choose varieties with long chilling requirements. They will stay dormant until warm weather begins. Trees with low chilling requirements begin growth early and suffer freeze damage as winter lingers. The accompanying chart shows the range of necessary chill for different species.

MICROCLIMATES

If you live in a climate that is only marginally suitable for a fruit or nut variety that you want to grow, try to find a suitable microclimate in your garden. Conditions in a microclimate differ from those in a climate zone due to trapped heat or cold, blocked wind, or other factors such as the presence of a pond or lake. You may find a low spot that collects enough cold air at night and warmth from sun during the day to support apples or cherries that would not get the right conditions on a slope or hilltop. The north side of a building or a south-facing wall could provide an environment for bush berries if other conditions are favorable.

CHILLING REQUIREMENTS

Each fruit and nut variety has its own specific chilling requirement. Those that require the fewest hours of winter cold are best for the warmest zones.

Almond	200–500 hours
Apple	400–1,200 hours
Apricot	600–1,000 hours
Asian pear	400–750 hours
Blackberry	200–700 hours
Blueberry	700–1,200 hours
Cherry	800–1,200 hours
Chestnut	400–750 hours
European pear	600–1,500 hours
European plum	700–1,100 hours
Filbert	800–1,600 hours
Grape	100–500 hours
Japanese plum	400–1,000 hours
Peach, nectarine	350–1,200 hours
Pecan	600–900 hours
Raspberry	800–1,700 hours
Walnut	500–1,500 hours

PREVENTING PROBLEMS

It pays to take time when purchasing fruit, nut, and berry varieties to find out if they are adapted to your climate. Many garden centers sell plants that have a wide appeal, but they may not be the best choice for your zone. Once you have the right plants, plan a maintenance program for each species. When plants are part of a cultural system conducive to production, they tend to be problem-free.

SELECTING FOR SIZE AND RESISTANCE

All commercially available fruit trees and many nut trees are budded or grafted onto a rootstock—the lower part of the plant that furnishes the root system. Selecting the right rootstock is in itself a deterrent to pest and disease problems. Rootstock is naturally suited to specific climates; if you plant in zones where it is adapted, it will have few problems. It is worthwhile to spend as much time selecting rootstock as selecting a fruit or nut variety.

Rootstocks for apples, for example, offer choices in terms of the size of the mature tree and the pests it resists. Some rootstocks are more resistant to rot, nematodes, and the woolly apple aphid than others. Dwarfing stocks have shallow and narrow-spreading root systems that limit the size of the mature canopy. Choose a rootstock that will produce a tree of a size that you can handle and one resistant to the pests and diseases most common in your area.

When selecting small fruits, your options are somewhat different. You can choose a species for its disease resistance and for its

GROWING STRAWBERRIES

Strawberries—unlike other berries—can be grown in every climate, from the coldest-winter zones to year-round mild climates. They are light sensitive, so different varieties are classified as either short-day or day-neutral. Short-day varieties produce in fall, winter, and spring. Day-neutral types are everbearing except in high temperatures.

Growing Points for Healthy Berries

- Select a sunny site protected from frosts.
- Amend soil with liberal amounts of organic matter.
- Keep the base of plants at soil level to avoid burying the crown.
- On everbearing varieties, remove blossoms for several months after planting. On other varieties, remove blossoms for the first year.
- Mulch with straw in winter to protect the plants from alternate periods of freezing and thawing. Remove straw as new growth begins in spring.
- Replant every three years to maintain vigorous production.

Vertical Gardening

Many yards have limited room for gardening. But you can enjoy an apple orchard—even in the narrow space between a walkway and a house or garage—if you espalier young trees that have been grafted on a dwarfing rootstock. This 'Spartan' apple is being trained on a south-facing wall.

Planting. If you have heavy soil that is slow to drain, plant all fruits, nuts, and berries on raised mounds. Planting high in any soil allows moisture to drain away from the crown area, keeping it dry and less susceptible to fungal rots. Set plants with the graft union about 2 inches above soil level, taking care never to bury the graft. You will lose the dwarfing advantage of the rootstock if the grafted stem begins to root and take over.

Don't add any amendments to a planting hole for fruit and nut trees. Amendments encourage roots to stay in the root ball rather than move quickly into the surrounding soil. Instead, spread an organic mulch over the soil surface.

When you plant small fruits, however, go ahead and add amendments. The root systems of these plants are generally restricted to shallow depths. But be sure to amend a large area into which the roots will grow, not just the planting hole. Set out plants carefully to prevent crowns from settling into loose soil. Cane berries die quickly from being planted too low.

Training. During the first few years that it takes for fruit trees to mature, you need to train their branching structure by pruning to develop sturdy branches that will be able to support a heavy load of fruit over a number of years. If you train branches to develop low to the ground, you will make harvesting easy.

The growth habits of each fruit group are different, so you will need to familiarize yourself with various training techniques (see "How Plants Bear Fruit," page 121). If you shape their structure

growth habits. You might have space for upright raspberry canes, but not for vigorous, trailing boysenberries. It's a common problem to underestimate the size of mature vines and shrubs and crowd too many plants into too small a space. When plants are overcrowded, you will end up with smaller fruits, fungal diseases from poor air circulation, and a tangled mass of growth. Allow plenty of room for each plant; you can always add more later as space allows.

ESTABLISHING PLANTS

Get your plants off to a good start in deep, well-drained soil with access to even moisture. Test the soil for pH and make adjustments as needed or choose varieties that are suited to existing conditions. Don't add fertilizers at planting time; they can burn roots. Wait until the second spring or summer to fertilize. Bare-root plants have enough stored food to survive the first year. (See "Life Stages and Growth Habits" on page 76 for more information on establishing fruit trees and shrubs.)

Training a Fruit Tree

Taking the time to train a young fruit tree pays off at harvest time—the fruit is easy to reach. To train a young tree, cut back the trunk to 2 feet above the ground when you plant it. This will cause branching to begin even lower. The second year, choose three or four main scaffold branches that form a vase shape, keeping the center of the tree open.

Summer Pruning to Control Size

Fruit trees like this 'Mutsu' apple planted on dwarfing rootstock can be kept at a convenient 8-foot height with summer pruning. Between June and August, trim back pencil-thin side branches (far left). The improved air circulation that results (left) also enhances disease resistance.

while they are young, after your trees start to bear you can prune to encourage new fruiting wood and to control the size of your crop. Your trees will then consistently produce large crops.

MAINTAINING AND PROTECTING PLANTS

As your fruit and nut trees and berry vines mature, be sure to increase the amount of water you give them in irrigated systems. Your trees will stay healthier if they have constant access to moisture. Dry conditions stress plants and leave them vulnerable to borers and other problems.

Get to know the cultural needs of each fruit and nut crop, including rates of growth and stages of development. It helps to follow a calendar of operations for applying fertilizers and spraying, and a pest and disease timetable to remind you when to look for signs of early infestations. Become familiar with seasonal risks by making regular inspections.

- Recognize changes in dormant buds. Apply sprays before buds swell or as they open, depending on the pest or disease you are dealing with. The dormant period is the only time that you can control some problems, such as peach leaf curl.
- Check developing fruit and thin as needed after normal fruit drop occurs. Set out traps and netting to exclude pests.
- Prune in summer to limit growth and to keep trees at a manageable size. Prune in winter to renew fruiting wood and to stimulate vigorous growth. Remove suckers that grow from the rootstock as soon as they appear.
- Clean up in autumn to prevent pests and diseases from breeding and overwintering in debris.

COMMON PROBLEMS OF FRUITS, NUTS, AND BERRIES

One of the biggest problems facing home gardeners is evaluating pest and disease threats to food crops. Many problems are temporary, have a low impact, and don't need to be controlled. Commercial growers are pressured by market demands to produce spotless produce in quantity, but in your home garden you can tolerate blemishes and interference from pests and still reap so much that you may have to give away the surplus.

COMMON DISEASE PROBLEMS

Diseases such as wilts and rots, usually arise from soil conditions, poor drainage and mistakes made at planting time. Problems with bacterial canker (gummosis) and dieback often arise from environmental stress—and stress for fruits, nuts, and berries can usually be traced to a climate problem. You may find out that other species are better adapted to your zone.

Diseases affecting crops themselves are often related to weather, although some, like apple scab and brown rot, may strike regularly. You can avoid some disease problems simply by pruning at the right time of the year. Peaches, for instance, should be pruned in late spring to prevent a fungal disease from invading pruning wounds. Apricots should be pruned in late summer or fall to prevent *Eutypa* fungus and dieback.

INSECT AND PEST PROBLEMS

A few pest problems—such as borers—can escalate to threaten the life of a plant. Others, such as codling moth, can destroy a crop. Once you have an insect infestation, it may be too late to do anything about it. For many pests, such as scales, peach twig borers, and aphid and mite eggs, your only opportunity for significant control is during dormancy. However, setting out pheromone traps or netting at the appropriate time, setting traps for wildlife, replanting in gopher-proof hardware cloth, raising deer fences to 12 feet—these kinds of practices can solve many problems as they arise, or even prevent them altogether.

Keeping the Soil Cool

Fruit trees, like ornamental trees, do best when the soil over their root zones is covered with a light mulch. Mow grassy pathways or plant them with clover.

WEED COMPETITION

Try to root out weeds while they're young. The bigger and tougher their roots get, the harder they are to manage and the more they compete for water and nutrients. Young trees and plants do better without competition. As plants mature, weeds are less of a hindrance, but their root competition will cut fruit production. If weeds harbor insect pests or hold moisture and promote fungal diseases, they become a serious concern.

Planting cover crops and cultivating them into the ground before they mature can help to control weeds. If kept away from the crowns of plants, a cover crop can be left in place as a competitor to slow down fast tree growth, as long as you supply adequate nutrients.

POLLINATION AND FRUIT SET

Lack of pollination and fruit set is a serious problem for fruit and nut crops. Some trees are self-fruitful and produce their own pollen. Many apples, cherries, plums, pears, and nuts depend on pollen from a second tree. Planting two varieties guarantees a superior rate of pollination and fruit set for all trees, whether they require a pollenizer or not. You don't need to plant pollenizers right next to each other, but they should be no more than 100 feet apart. Both varieties must bloom at the same time.

> ### TIP
>
> You can take a shortcut in providing a pollenizer for trees that are not self-fruitful. Get branches in bloom from the pollinating-tree variety and set them out in buckets under your tree. Bees and insects visit the branches and carry pollen to your blossoms, eliminating the need for a second tree.

Early or late blossoming, absence of insect pollinators, and rain interfere with pollination. Late frosts, rain, and lack of adequate chill can cause fruit drop and loss of part or all of a crop. Some tree crops tend toward biennial bearing—heavy one year and light, or nonexistent, the next. If you thin fruit each year, prune in summer, and try to keep your trees stress-free, the size of crops should even out year to year.

If you are disappointed that your young trees are taking too long to produce fruit, it may be that they are simply not yet mature enough. Some trees bear crops at a young age; others take longer to reach maturity. It is not unusual for some apples, pears, and sweet cherries to take five to eight years before they bear. (See "Life Stages and Growth Habits" earlier in this chapter on page 76.)

Before you remove a tree that has not set a sizable fruit or nut crop, consider whether additional factors may be at work. If any of the following conditions are affecting the tree and if it is otherwise in good health, give it another year.

- Excessive nitrogen fertilizer
- Deficiency of a micronutrient such as boron, zinc, or manganese
- Shade and competition among closely planted trees
- Incompatible varieties for successful pollination
- Wind and cold at blossom time

HOW PLANTS BEAR FRUIT

Before you begin pruning, look over the tree and find the fruiting wood and spurs. Once you see where the fruit grows, you know which branches to trim. Careless pruning promotes growth and reduces fruiting; artful pruning creates a balance between the two.

- Apples, pears, and cherries bear fruit on spurs that have a ten-year life span or longer. Prune to encourage low branching and some renewal wood.

- Peaches and nectarines bear only on wood that grew the previous season; fruiting wood must be renewed annually by removing up to two-thirds of the previous year's growth.

- Both Japanese and European plums bear on spurs that live six to eight years. Japanese plums also produce fruit on wood that grew the last season; however, these branches may be removed in pruning away rampant growth.

- Apricots bear most fruit on spurs that were formed the previous year. These spurs remain fruitful about three years; prune to develop replacement spurs.

- Almonds bear on spurs that produce for about five years; they require little pruning, although stimulating renewal wood annually produces consistent, heavy crops.

- Walnuts and pecans bear nuts terminally on spurs on older varieties, laterally on shoots on newer varieties. Young trees require heavier pruning than mature trees.

- Grapes are pruned according to the variety. Most American grapes and a few European varieties are cane-pruned, with one-year-old canes retaining 10 to 12 buds, whereas European types are spur-pruned, with canes cut back to 2 or 3 buds.

- Cane berries grow on perennial roots with biennial canes that produce vegetative growth the first year and bear fruit the second. Tip-prune blackberry canes as they are trellised to force lateral growth where fruit is produced. Prune out the weakest canes before fruiting and remove old canes after fruiting. Raspberries need pruning only on everbearing types: cut canes to 3–4 feet at the end of the first season for fruit on laterals the next spring.

This mature black walnut no longer requires pruning.

THE MOST COMMON SPECIES AND THE MOST COMMON PROBLEMS

These listings tell you the botanical and common name of each plant and the western zones where it thrives. One of the common problems afflicting the plant in the West is featured, and, where available, resistant varieties are listed.

SYMBOLS: 🍎 FRUITS 🌰 NUTS 🫐 BERRIES

ALMOND

🌰 *PRUNUS DULCIS*

✂ ZONES: 8–10, 12–16, 19–21

NAVEL ORANGE WORMS

The navel orange worm is a pale gray caterpillar that tunnels inside almond shells as soon as hulls begin to open. Worms destroy nuts with their feeding and their messy excrement. They sometimes spin a fine white webbing inside shells. Adult moths lay eggs on "mummies"—last year's shriveled shells—left hanging in trees and also on the hulls of ripening nuts.

Other plant problems. COMMON PESTS: birds, borers, leafrollers, oriental fruit moths, scales, spider mites, squirrels. COMMON DISEASES: bacterial canker, brown rot, crown gall, crown rot, dieback, gray mold, leaf spot, oak root fungus, root rot, shot hole fungus, verticillium wilt. OTHER: frost damage, poor pollination.

Resistant varieties. Varieties resistant to verticillium wilt are available.

Notes: Almonds are not self-fertile and require a second variety as a pollinator; both must bloom at the same time. 'Hall', 'Mission', and 'Thompson' are late-blooming varieties and are less subject to frost damage.

APPLE

🍎 *MALUS SYLVESTRIS, M. DOMESTICA*

✂ ZONES: ALL

CODLING MOTHS

Codling moth is one of the most serious apple pests. Several generations of brown moths lay eggs on leaves and fruit in summer. Eggs hatch and produce larvae—the classic worms in the apple—that burrow into apple cores, leaving small blemishes on the outer surface and masses of brown frass, or excrement, within. Apples often drop prematurely.

Other plant problems. COMMON PESTS: aphids, apple maggots, birds, borers, leaf rollers, scales, spider mites, squirrels, western tussock moths. COMMON DISEASES: anthracnose, canker, crown gall, fireblight, powdery mildew, rust, scab. OTHER: breakage, lack of adequate winter chill, russeting, sunburn.

Resistant varieties. 'Delicious', 'Empire', 'Golden Delicious', 'Liberty', 'Stayman', and 'Winesap' are resistant to fireblight. 'Liberty', 'Priscilla', 'Sir Prize', and 'Prima' resist scab.

Notes: Among the varieties with low chilling requirements suitable for warm climates are 'Anna' (100 hours), 'Dorset Golden' (100 hours), and 'Fuji' (300 hours).

APRICOT

🍎 *PRUNUS ARMENIACA*

✂ ZONES: VARY BY VARIETY

BROWN ROT

At blossom time, brown rot causes gummy liquid to ooze from the base of flowers and along twigs, causing shoots to die back. When fruit develops, the rot begins as small, pale to dark brown blemishes over the surface. Spots spread rapidly, and the fungus moves to the nearby twigs. The fungus remains on infected twigs and on hardened, rotted fruits called mummies that hang on the tree over winter.

Other plant problems. COMMON PESTS: aphids, beetles, borers, caterpillars, codling moths, earwigs, leaf rollers, scales, spider mites, stinkbugs. COMMON DISEASES: bacterial canker, canker and dieback, crown rot, gray mold, oak root fungus, powdery mildew, root rot, shot hole fungus. OTHER: frost damage.

Resistant varieties. 'Harcot', 'Harglow', and 'Tilton' show some resistance to brown rot and other diseases. 'Moongold', 'Goldrich', 'Sun-Glow', and 'Sungold' are the most cold resistant. 'Puget Gold' also shows disease resistance.

BLACKBERRY

🫐 *RUBUS*, VARIOUS SPECIES

✂ ZONES: VARY BY VARIETY

RED-BERRY MITES

As berries ripen, mites cause individual drupelets (fleshy sections of each berry) to turn red and harden. Part—or sometimes all—of a berry continues to develop abnormally and tastes sour. 'Himalaya' and 'Evergreen' varieties are the most susceptible.

Other plant problems. COMMON PESTS: aphids, borers, cutworms, leaf rollers, raspberry cane borers, raspberry sawflies, scales, spider mites, thrips. COMMON DISEASES: crown gall, downy mildew, leaf and cane spot, root rot, rust, verticillium wilt, viral infections. OTHER: frost damage, rampant growth.

Resistant varieties. Ollallieberries need less winter chilling and can be grown in warm-winter climates; they are resistant to verticillium wilt.

Notes: You can protect trailing blackberries against winter damage in the coldest zones by leaving canes on the ground and covering them with soil, snow, or straw mulch. To limit rampant growth, lift up canes before lateral growth begins in spring. Pull out suckers as they appear.

BLUEBERRY

🫐 *VACCINUM*, VARIOUS SPECIES

✂ ZONES: 4–6, 17; WITH CARE 2, 3, 7–9, 14–16

BIRDS

Starlings, robins, blue jays, bluebirds, and other species feed on blueberries. Birds begin robbing berries before they ripen and often continue until bushes are completely stripped. Nylon mesh will protect berries if it is secured firmly at ground level to prevent birds from finding entries.

Other plant problems. COMMON PESTS: aphids, black vine weevils, orange tortrix, scales, thrips. COMMON DISEASES: gray mold, root rot. OTHER: chlorosis, drought.

Resistant varieties. Dwarf varieties 'North-blue', 'North Country', and 'Northsky' are all extremely hardy.

Notes: Blueberries require acid soil. If pH is above 5.0, they are likely to develop chlorosis. They must also have constant moisture, but their roots will rot in soils that are too wet. Prune after the third year to renew fruiting wood, prevent spindly growth, and encourage strong stems. Fruiting occurs on one-year-old wood.

CARYA illinoensis

 PECAN

 ZONES: 8–10, 12–14, 18–20

CROWN GALL

Crown gall infects fruit and nut trees in nurseries, but galls may not be visible when you purchase plants. They look like woody tumors or bumpy warts growing near the base of plants or along the roots, and sometimes on branches. Bacteria that cause the galls enter the plant through cuts or wounds from planting or pruning. If galls grow quickly on young plants, they can girdle the roots and kill them. Mature plants can tolerate galls.

Other plant problems. COMMON PESTS: aphids, borers, caterpillars, scales. COMMON DISEASES: leaf spot, scab, verticillium wilt. OTHER: pecan rosette.

Resistant varieties. 'Cherokee', 'Cheyenne', 'Choctaw', 'Mohawk', and 'Wichita' are heat resistant and thrive in desert zones. Pecans are resistant to oak root fungus.

Notes: You can expect a nut crop from pecan trees in the zones listed. In Zones 4–7, 15, 16, or 21–23, crops are unreliable, but Carya makes an excellent ornamental shade tree.

CHERRY

 PRUNUS, VARIOUS SPECIES

 ZONES: VARY BY TYPE

BACTERIAL CANKER

This disease—also called gummosis—causes serious damage to young cherry trees. The usual signs are cankers, which are dark sunken spots on the bark, trunk, or branches with amber-colored gummy masses oozing out. The disease is more common in warm zones where the trees have a shorter period of dormancy.

Other plant problems. COMMON PESTS: aphids, apple maggots, birds, borers, caterpillars, scales, spider mites, stinkbugs. COMMON DISEASES: brown rot, buckskin disease, canker and dieback, crown rot, gray mold, leaf spot, oak root fungus, powdery mildew, root rot. OTHER: cracked fruit, genetic deformities.

Resistant varieties. Sweet cherries 'Angela' and 'Chinook' resist buckskin disease; 'Jubilee', 'Larian', 'Rainier', 'Sam', 'Stella', and 'Van' resist cracking. Sour 'Montmorency' resists cracking and diseases.

Notes: Birds cause serious damage to cherry crops as they peck at fruits, exposing them to brown rot and botrytis diseases. If you notice branches with deformed leaves and fruit on 'Bing' and 'Black Tartarian' sweet cherries, cut them out; genetic deformities occur sporadically on these varieties. Both sweet and sour cherries may crack from late rains.

CITRUS

 VARIOUS GENERA AND SPECIES

 ZONES: 8, 9, 12–24

LEAF ROLLERS

Several different types of leaf-roller caterpillars feed on leaves, shoots, and fruit. Larvae roll themselves up inside leaves, sometimes spinning a web to join fruit and leaves together. Other pests and fungal rots later enter the holes that leaf rollers chew in fruit.

Other plant problems. COMMON PESTS: ants, aphids, mealybugs, mites, scales, slugs, snails, thrips. COMMON DISEASES: bacterial canker, brown rot, root rot. OTHER: frost damage, nitrogen deficiency, sunburn.

Resistant varieties. 'Lisbon' is similar to 'Eureka', but is better adapted to high heat. 'Mediterranean' and Satsuma mandarins are cold-hardy; Satsuma is somewhat more cold tolerant and requires less heat to ripen.

Notes: Citrus crops require climates with long growing seasons—mild winters to prevent freezing and summer heat to produce sweetness. Grapefruit can take up to 18 months to ripen after bloom. If you live in a climate zone where citrus is only marginally successful, look around your garden for a suitable microclimate. Try 'Valencia' oranges, which can hang on the tree for months, increasing in sweetness.

GRAPES

 VITIS VINIFERA

 ZONES: VARY BY VARIETY

WESTERN GRAPELEAF SKELETONIZERS

This yellow and blue caterpillar has spiny black tufts on its back. It feeds first on the undersides of foliage but eventually consumes the entire leaf, leaving only the vein "skeleton." Damage begins in early summer and continues through three generations each year.

Other plant problems. COMMON PESTS: birds, leafhoppers, leaf rollers, mealybugs, nematodes, phylloxera, scales, spider mites, whiteflies. COMMON DISEASES: anthracnose, crown gall, dieback, downy mildew, gray mold, oak root fungus, powdery mildew, root rot, verticillium wilt. OTHER: frost damage, rampant growth.

Resistant varieties: Most American varieties are immune to powdery mildew. 'Black Spanish' offers additional disease resistance. 'Black Monukka' and 'Pearl of Csaba' are the most cold-hardy of the European varieties.

Notes: Control leafhoppers, mealybugs, and whiteflies to prevent sticky honeydew from collecting in grape clusters.

PEACH AND NECTARINE

 PRUNUS PERSICA

 ZONES: VARY BY VARIETY

PEACH LEAF CURL

Leaf curl is a common problem on peaches and nectarines during cool, rainy springs. Repeated cases weaken trees, slow growth, and reduce fruiting. Leaves turn red, look bumpy, then curl and twist. The disease can only be controlled by repeated spray applications during the dormant season; once it appears in the spring, nothing can be done. New leaves will replace damaged ones that drop.

Other plant problems. COMMON PESTS: aphids, borers, leaf rollers, scales, spider mites, stinkbugs. COMMON DISEASES: bacterial canker, brown rot, canker and dieback, crown gall, crown rot, oak root fungus, powdery mildew, root rot, shot hole fungus. OTHER: heavy bearing.

Resistant varieties. 'Q1-8' is a new white-fleshed variety resistant to leaf curl; 'Frost' is a resistant yellow freestone. 'Indian Free', a yellow freestone, shows some resistance. Other varieties resist brown rot, bacterial canker, and bacterial leaf spot. Choose disease-resistant peaches that have been developed to tolerate the heat and cold of your zone.

Notes: Peach and nectarine trees are often damaged by shot hole fungus (also called peach blight), a leaf spot disease that injures developing buds and twigs.

PEAR

🌿 *PYRUS COMMUNIS*

🌡 ZONES: 1–11, 14–18

PEAR PSYLLIDS

These aphidlike insects are the most damaging insect pest on pears. They produce several generations each year, scarring fruit and causing leaves to yellow and drop early. Honeydew collects under leaves and on fruit, often with black sooty mold. The psyllid transmits pear decline, a disease that turns leaves purple and causes trees to decline in vigor.

Other plant problems. COMMON PESTS: aphids, apple maggots, borers, caterpillars, codling moths, leaf rollers, mealybugs, pear rust mites, sawflies, scales. COMMON DISEASES: bacterial blast and canker, crown gall, dieback, fireblight, leaf spot, rust, scab.

Resistant varieties. Pears are resistant to oak root fungus and take damp, heavy soil better than most fruit trees. 'Fan Stil', 'Flordahome', 'Kieffer', 'Hood', 'Magness', 'Monterrey', 'Moonglow', 'Seckel', and 'Winter Nelis' are all resistant to fireblight; 'Comice' shows some resistance.

Notes: Fireblight is a serious disease of pears. Overfertilized trees and tender young shoots are easily damaged; entire branches may die back quickly. The disease is easily transmitted; take care to sterilize pruning equipment when cutting back damaged stems.

PLUM

🌿 *PRUNUS DOMESTICA*

🌡 ZONES: VARY BY VARIETY

PEACH TWIG BORERS

As these caterpillars emerge from their cocoons in spring, they bore into growing tips of twigs and kill developing shoots. Their damage is most serious on young trees, since branches are prevented from growing normally. A second generation feeds around the stems of ripening fruit in summer.

Other plant problems. COMMON PESTS: aphids, apple maggots, birds, bud moths, codling moths, leaf rollers, mites, orange tortrix, squirrels. COMMON DISEASES: bacterial canker, brown rot, canker and dieback, crown rot, gray mold, powdery mildew, root rot. OTHER: breakage, excessive growth, heavy bearing.

Resistant varieties. Certain hybrids—'Compass', 'Pipestone', 'Sapa', 'Sapalta', and 'Waneta'—are suitable for zones with exceptionally cold winters.

Notes: Japanese plums set enormous quantities of fruit and must be thinned heavily. Space fruits about every 6 inches along branches. Control rampant and excessive

growth with summer pruning. Try to avoid creating V-shaped crotches; they are weak and the tree is likely to split.

RASPBERRY

🌿 *RUBUS*, VARIOUS SPECIES

🌡 ZONES: BEST IN 4–6, 15–17

CANE BORERS

In spring, adult beetles puncture berry canes to lay their eggs near the growing tips. The punctures girdle the canes, causing shoots to wilt and die. After the eggs hatch, the larvae remain in the canes for up to two years, feeding as they bore toward the base. The infected parts should be cut off and destroyed.

Other plant problems. COMMON PESTS: aphids, crown borers, cutworms, leaf rollers, raspberry sawflies, red-berry mites, scales, spider mites. COMMON DISEASES: anthracnose, crown gall, dwarf virus, powdery mildew, root rot, verticillium wilt. OTHER: spring dieback, suckering growth.

Resistant varieties. 'Southland' and 'Willamette' are disease resistant. 'Chilliwack', 'Haida', 'Newburgh', 'Summit', and 'Sumner' are resistant to root rot.

Notes: Several viral diseases affect raspberries, causing weak, lanky canes, crumbling berries, and poor productivity; 'Fall Gold' is very susceptible. Affected plants should be removed and destroyed. Dieback in spring may begin with wilting canes and dying shoots; it can follow winter-freeze injury, drought, insufficient chilling, or delayed leafing-out.

STRAWBERRY

🌿 *FRAGARIA*, VARIOUS SPECIES

🌡 ZONES: ALL

GRAY MOLD

Also known as botrytis, gray mold is a serious strawberry disease that rots berries during cool, wet weather. Brown blotches may appear first; they then become covered with gray or white furry growths. The mold grows on injured or weak spots on fruit and on dying leaves and stems.

Other plant problems. COMMON PESTS: aphids, birds, cutworms, cyclamen mites, rose

chafers, slugs, snails, spider mites, strawberry crown moths, weevils. COMMON DISEASES: bacterial leaf spot, powdery mildew, red stele root rot, verticillium wilt, yellows. OTHER: salt injury, tip burn.

Resistant varieties: 'Shuksan' is resistant to gray mold. 'Benton', 'Hood', 'Puget Beauty', and 'Tillikum' are mildew resistant. 'Brighton' and 'Hecker' resist verticillium wilt. 'Olympus', 'Puget Beauty', 'Quinault', 'Selva', 'Totem', and 'Tristar' resist red stele root rot.

Notes: A plastic mulch barrier prevents gray mold by keeping berries off the soil and away from fungal spores. Manure fertilizers and soils high in salts can burn strawberry leaves and cause poor root development.

WALNUT

🌿 *JUGLANS*, VARIOUS SPECIES

🌡 ZONES: VARY BY SPECIES

WALNUT HUSK FLIES

Numerous tiny larvae of this fly hatch from eggs laid in hulls. The maggots first cause black spots on the outside of the green hulls; then the spots spread and become mushy. The soft, rotted hulls are difficult to remove from around the shell. Shells and nuts are not seriously damaged, but they may be stained and somewhat disfigured.

Other plant problems. COMMON PESTS: aphids, caterpillars, codling moths, leaf rollers, navel orange worms, scales, spider mites, squirrels. COMMON DISEASES: blight, canker, crown rot, oak root fungus, root rot.

Resistant varieties. 'Payne', 'Ashley', 'Placentia', and 'Erhardt' resist husk fly damage. 'Ambassador' resists blight and codling moths; 'Carmelo' and 'Chandler' show some resistance. California black walnut (*Juglans hindsii*) and Southern California black walnut (*J. californica*) are resistant to oak root fungus.

Notes: Walnut varieties are zone specific. Grow only those adapted to your zone. 'Drummond', 'Payne', and 'Placentia' are suited for the warmest zones. Plant trees where leaf drop and honeydew from aphids do not create a litter problem.

Problem Solving for
VEGETABLES
AND HERBS

Considered a fruit but grown with vegetables, golden Siberian water-melon is in the cucurbit family, along with winter butternut squash.

Whether you have planted vegetables and herbs for your family's dinner or for the simple joy of watching your garden grow, bountiful crops bring great satisfaction. Garden woes—weeds, pests, growing problems, and bad weather—disturb that pleasure. You may not be able to do much about the weather, but if you take a few precautions, you can avoid or easily manage most other garden problems and enjoy plenty of good-tasting, healthful produce and aromatic, practical herbs.

VEGETABLE GROUPS

Vegetables are usually divided into groups according to family, such as the tomato family, or according to growth habit, such as leafy greens or root crops. It helps to think of vegetables as part of a group since the same problems usually affect the entire lot, and the culture (the soil type and the use of water and fertilizer) is generally the same. If you find squash bugs, for instance, in your pumpkins, you will know to look for them among the melons as well.

Being familiar with the vegetable groups also makes it easier to rotate crops effectively. Tomatoes are highly susceptible to wilt diseases and do best when rotated each year, but they should not be replaced by another family member, such as peppers, since the entire *Solanaceae* group can be infected by the same fungus (see "Vegetable Groups," below).

SEASONAL CATEGORIES

Vegetables are also divided into warm-season and cool-season categories, depending on the time of year and environmental factors that are best for their growth. Besides air temperatures, vegetables

react to soil temperatures and day length, thriving and maturing only when climate conditions are right.

Warm-season. Warm-season vegetables are the crops that grow in summer. They need warm soil and air and long days of high temperatures to set fruit and mature. They don't tolerate cold and frost. Peppers, for instance, must have warm temperatures both day and night. Muskmelons require 2½–4 months of warm weather and often have difficulty maturing even then if either soil or air temperatures drop significantly. In zones with short or cool summers, warm-season crops like melons benefit from special management, such as covering the soil with plastic to raise temperatures a few degrees in and just above the soil.

VEGETABLE GROUPS

Purple broccoli

Cole crops, or brassicas (*Brassicaceae*)
broccoli
brussels sprouts
cabbage
cauliflower
kale
kohlrabi
rutabaga

Cucurbits (*Cucurbitaceae*)
cucumber
gourd
muskmelon
pumpkin
squash
watermelon

Leafy greens
chard
endive
lettuce
spinach

Legumes
bean
pea

Onion group
garlic
leek
onion

Root crops
beet
carrot
parsnip
radish
turnip

Tomato family (*Solanaceae*)
eggplant
pepper
potato
tomato

Seasonal Gardens

Even before the soil warms up in spring, you can have a productive garden (top). When the lettuce, onion, Chinese cabbage, broccoli, and other cool-season crops mature, it will be time to plant beans and set out pepper, tomato, cucurbits, and other warm-season crops (bottom). In most western zones there is still time in early fall for another round of cool-season vegetables before frost.

Asparagus, artichoke, and rhubarb are long-lived perennial plants, though not in all western zones. Artichoke thrives only in Zones 8 and 9 and 14–24; rhubarb is best in Zones 1–11. Asparagus lives for decades in the same bed; rhubarb may need dividing after five or six years.

PREVENTING PROBLEMS WITH VEGETABLES

A few gardeners with green thumbs seem to throw out a handful of seeds and reap a cornucopia of produce. Most gardeners, though, need to work at fertilizing and weeding to keep plants growing vigorously. Well-cultivated vegetables, like other garden plants, are healthier and more problem-free than are stressed plants. Adequate moisture and well-tilled soil are basic, but remember, too, that stresses come from climate incompatibility. Vegetables developed for your zone, those bred for insect and disease resistance, and crops planted at the right time of year will have fewer problems.

BUILDING SOIL

If you think of building the soil as a step in growing a garden, you will be on your way to success. Loose, moist, well-aerated soil with large amounts of well-decomposed organic matter is essential for growing great vegetables.

- Choose a sunny site where the soil will warm fast in spring. Try to avoid areas infiltrated by roots of trees and shrubs. With too much competition, the soil will dry out fast, nutrients will be used up, and the vegetables will fall short of your expectations.
- Amend clay and sandy soils with 2–3 inches of organic matter dug in thoroughly, 8–10 inches deep. Compost is one of the best amendments you can use. It opens up clay soil by wedging its way between microscopic clay particles, and it fills in pores between grains of sandy soil so that water does not drain away so quickly.
- Build narrow beds and paths to keep from walking on planted areas. Raised beds have the advantage of fast drainage and better air circulation, important if your soil is heavy. They also warm up faster in spring and have more surface area to take in oxygen. Prepare your beds in fall, if you can, for spring planting. In spring, work in more organic matter and smooth the surface before seeds or plants go in.

SOWING AND TRANSPLANTING

Plan to start seeds or set out transplants around your last frost date in spring or before your first frost date in fall; warm-season crops need to mature in summer heat, while cool-season crops need to avoid summer heat. If you don't know your last frost date, you can find it out from your county cooperative extension agent. Planting dates vary from zone to zone. Allow enough time after planting for crops to mature, but schedule carefully to avoid killing frosts as

Cool-season. Cool-season vegetables grow best when temperatures are 10–15°F below those needed by warm-season crops. These vegetables thrive in early spring and fall, maturing before or after the hottest summer days. Cole crops, leafy greens, peas, and most root crops are cool-season vegetables. Many are able to endure some frost. If you live in a mild-winter zone where frosts are light and infrequent, snows are rare, and the ground does not freeze, you can grow many cool-season vegetables all winter.

ANNUAL AND PERENNIAL VEGETABLES

Nearly all vegetables are annual plants that sprout, produce foliage, flower, and fruit, and go to seed all in one year. Since leafy greens are usually harvested in their vegetative stage, they rarely complete their life cycle in most gardens. Many—cucumbers, peppers, tomatoes—reach the fruit stage; some, such as peas and beans, are the seeds themselves.

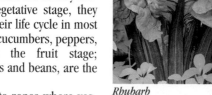

Rhubarb

In warm-climate zones where vegetable plants are not threatened by cold weather, some annual plants continue to produce longer than a year if nutrients are supplied to keep them going. Pepper, tomato, and eggplant can live for years.

Gardening in Raised Beds

Raised beds are the ideal solution to garden soils that are poor and slow to drain, but they have other advantages too. Quick to warm up in spring and easy to tend, they give your garden a well-organized look. Line the bottom of the beds with ¼-inch galvanized hardware cloth if burrowing rodents are a problem.

Thinning. It may seem a waste to go along and thin out healthy seedlings. But that's exactly what you need to do to get the proper spacing that produces large, well-formed vegetables. Root vegetables and leafy greens especially need lots of room to spread their roots. Thin several times before you reach the recommended spacing; allow seedlings to grow a little between thinnings so you can select the strongest ones to mature.

Hardening off. Be sure to introduce your transplants gradually to outside sun and air. You'll risk losing them if they're rushed from the greenhouse or indoors to the garden. They need to slowly harden off—to thicken leaf and stem tissue—for a week or so. Set plants out in the day and protect them at night if there is a chance of frost. If you set seedlings directly into garden beds straight from the hothouse, you risk losing them to sunburn, cold, and wind exposure. Don't be too gentle when you do set out transplants; push the roots firmly into contact with moist soil, then water and mulch.

WATERING

Strive for a balance in watering. Overwatering is usually worse than underwatering since roots rot in soggy conditions, but underwatering stresses and weakens plants. If you subject your crops to alternate periods of wilting and recovery, you will be disappointed with the results. Most vegetables have critical growth periods when they can suffer irreversible damage from drought. Cucumbers and lettuce become bitter; root vegetables become woody or hot.

- In dry-summer zones, set up an irrigation system that will give plants constant access to moisture.
- Cover soil with a layer of organic mulch to conserve moisture and prevent the surface from crusting over. A hard surface excludes air and causes runoff.

FERTILIZING

Nearly all crops benefit from supplemental fertilizers to prevent nutrient deficiencies. Your vegetables will respond best when you fertilize with the right amounts at the right time. It is important to

well. If you find a suitable microclimate, or protect plants from frosts, you can cheat a little, escape cold damage, and eke out a longer growing season. (See page 118 on microclimates.)

Seeding. Follow planting instructions on seed packets carefully. Look for directions on planting depth, soil temperature, and light or darkness for germinating seeds. Lettuce, for instance, must have light to germinate. If you plant directly into the soil, use a soil thermometer to be sure that the soil isn't too cold and won't rot seeds. Many gardeners germinate seeds indoors where they are able to control the temperature. However, this can result in lanky seedlings, due to inadequate light after germination. If this is a consistent problem, you may want to delay starting seeds so that the seedlings have less time indoors.

Damping-off fungi that break down organic matter in the soil also attack seeds and seedlings. If you have tilled under old crops, check your soil to be sure that all of the debris has decomposed before you sow seed. If you have trouble starting seeds in your outdoor beds, you may find it necessary to resort to seeding in sterile mixes in containers.

Sowing in Garden Beds

Thin seedlings to the spacing recommended on your seed packets. Some vegetables, like broccoli and cabbage, need up to 18 inches between plants. To thin, pinch seedlings just above the soil surface to minimize disturbing delicate roots tangled beneath the surface. A soil thermometer can tell you whether the soil is warm enough to plant in early spring or cool enough in late summer.

follow directions on commercial products so that you don't over-fertilize and burn roots.

■ Slow-release organic products are the safest; they supply a steady stream of nutrients. Always water-in soluble and liquid fertilizers; they have the greatest potential for burning roots.

■ Wait to fertilize in spring until the soil is warm enough for beneficial microorganisms to break down materials into forms that plants can absorb.

■ For a springtime boost to soil fertility, turn under bell beans, rye, or other cover crops before they flower.

■ Avoid high-nitrogen fertilizers, which encourage lush foliage at the expense of fruit production and attract insects to the tender new growth.

CROP ROTATION

If you divide your garden into sections and rotate crops by planting them in a different area each year, you will prevent a buildup of various insects and disease organisms. Tomato, pepper, eggplant, and other members of the *Solanaceae* family should be moved each year to avoid wilt diseases. Don't replace them, however, with cucurbits; they are susceptible to many of the same problems.

Plants susceptible to nematode damage should also be rotated. These include cole crops, beets, and spinach. Rotate in some of the bean and tomato varieties that are nematode resistant. If you have the space, it helps to leave a section unplanted except for a cover crop such as wheat or barley that helps reduce nematodes.

Corn, cole crops, and pepper plants are heavy feeders and deplete the soil of many nutrients. Replace these crops with legumes or root vegetables that feed more lightly and let the soil recover. Some gardeners like to rotate in plants from their flower garden, lay sheet compost over a bed, or simply mulch heavily during a warm season and wait one or two seasons to plant. You may want to try planting only cool-season crops in a few beds to give the soil some rest.

POTATOES

Potatoes are usually thought of as a root crop, but they're actually a member of the tomato family. Give potatoes plenty of space to develop and plant them before the weather gets hot.

■ Purchase certified disease-free seed potatoes, early- or late-maturing varieties that are suited to your climate zone.

■ Expose seed potatoes to warm, humid air for two or three days at 50–70°F until cut sides are callused over.

■ Plant small potatoes with at least one eye in each section for the best yield. Wait until the soil warms. Ideal temperatures range from 55–70°F.

■ Amend soil to provide good drainage and aeration; use only fully decomposed organic matter to avoid diseases. Plant on hills to allow maximum oxygen to reach developing roots and tubers.

■ Provide consistent moisture, or water infrequently but deeply, since 90 percent of the growth is in the top 12–15 inches of soil.

■ Cover stems with thick layers of straw, hay, or dead leaves when growing potatoes aboveground. Sunlight produces solanine, a toxic green substance that makes potatoes inedible.

PESTS AND DISEASES

Pest problems can't be avoided entirely even in the healthiest gardens. Many insects and pathogens are airborne and ever-present, but they don't become active unless conditions invite them. If your garden is well nourished and stress-free, you will have few pest intruders. Detection, traps, and barriers are the best protection you can provide besides healthy plants. Hand-picking, biological controls, and hosing off plants are also effective deterrents.

Design for Crop Rotation

Whether you garden by the acre or in a corner of your backyard, keep a record of what's planted in each plot and devise a system of crop rotation. In moderate-size gardens like the carefully designed one pictured here, rotate crops from one section to the other. In small gardens, change the location of the beds every two or three years.

Insects. Resident insects are a problem in soils in some zones. Wireworms show up in freshly turned sod; symphylans are troubling in parts of the Northwest. Both feed on organic debris as well as developing roots. Extra-rich soil, crop rotation, and dry gardening reduce these problems but cannot completely prevent them. If you live in a zone where nematodes are a problem, you may want to solarize your soil (see page 54).

You can prevent most insect problems from becoming serious if you make regular garden inspections. Watch seedlings for cutworm damage if you haven't set out protective collars. Keep an eye out for white cabbage butterflies, then look for the green larvae and hand-pick when they appear. Hand-pick Mexican bean beetles and cucumber beetles before they seriously damage foliage.

Your garden will inevitably host butterfly and moth larvae—they're normal to some extent. You may want to plant some of their favorite feeding plants to lure them away from the vegetables. (See the "Encyclopedia of Damaging and Beneficial Creatures" for the larvae that can be pests, and the plants that they eat.)

Disease resistance. If you have favorite, older vegetable varieties that are disease-prone, it may be time to try new, resistant ones. Some heirloom vegetables are fairly disease free, but not necessarily in every garden. New varieties are bred to resist specific diseases and to thrive in specific zones. You can find resistance to bacterial and viral diseases, powdery and downy mildews, anthracnose, fusarium and verticillium wilts, scab, rots, and blights. It helps to choose seeds from a company that has developed varieties that are resistant to problems in your climate zone.

As soon as you notice diseases among your vegetables, pull out the affected plants and destroy them. Leaving plants in place means that the disease will spread to other plants and throughout the soil.

WEEDS

Weeds compete with vegetables for light, moisture, space, and nutrients. The competition weakens crops and makes them more susceptible to insect damage. Weed patches also harbor pests, such as armyworms and cutworms, slugs and snails, thrips, and various beetles—all of which will damage vegetables. If you work out a weed management program, you will protect your crops as well as save the time and energy required for pulling and hoeing. Thick layers of mulch and soil solarization are effective ways to keep down weeds.

ENVIRONMENTAL PROBLEMS

Your garden may be flourishing when sudden changes in the weather disturb your crops. Try to recognize the effects of weather. A change in foliage color may just be a temporary reaction to cold, wet soil rather than chlorosis and nutrient deficiency. Some weather changes, however, have irreversible effects. A heat wave will bring an early end to peas or cause lettuce to bolt. A heavy rain could lead to a growth spurt and cause cabbage heads to crack. A late spring frost may mean replanting a crop; in fall, it may signal the end of peppers and tomatoes.

HERB GROUPS

Herbs are a catchall group of plants with a long and fascinating history. They include plants for culinary and medicinal use as well as for fragrance and cosmetics, dyes and insect repellents, rituals and decor. Herbs are grouped according to their use more than their garden culture, but several distinctions are worth noting that will help you solve problems in your herb garden.

ANNUAL AND PERENNIAL HERBS

The annual herbs—basil, borage, coriander, dill, summer savory, and others—are much like annual vegetables. They put forth a burst of growth, bloom, and seed production in summer gardens. Borage and dill seem to thrive with little water, while summer savory, coriander, and others are more water dependent.

Many perennial herbs can be grown in every western climate. Some, like scented geraniums and lemon verbena *(Aloysia),* survive only in the warmest zones, but they can be treated as annuals or overwintered inside for use in the summer garden. Lemon balm *(Melissa)* and lovage *(Levisticum),* chicory and chamomile *(Chamaemelum),* and dozens of other perennials grow well year after year in all zones.

Though quite a few herbs are classified as perennials, you will need to keep an eye on them during winter to help them survive. Many varieties of lavender, for instance, are fairly tender and just will not survive freezing temperatures. Give a little extra protection to hardier varieties like germander *(Teucrium)* and horehound *(Marrubium)* that need dry, well-drained soils. They can withstand the low temperatures of all zones, but their roots will rot if they sit in soggy soil waiting for spring.

HERBS IN DRY SITES

A large group of herbs is native to Mediterranean climates with dry, infertile soils. Aloe and agrimony *(Agrimonia),* thyme and oregano, wormwood *(Artemisia)* and yarrow *(Achillea)* need to be treated separately from average garden herbs that rely on moist and nutrient-rich loam. The Mediterranean herbs fill an important niche in garden culture since you can use them in tough spots where most other plants would fail. Many are extremely drought tolerant and can survive without supplemental irrigation in western zones where there is little or no summer rainfall.

IMPROVING CORN YIELDS

Corn depends on a certain amount of summer heat before it will tassel and form kernels. When you buy seed, look for the varieties labeled "early" for planting in zones with short, cool summers; buy "late" varieties for successive plantings where high heat continues for several months. Frost any time during the growing season will damage the crop.

Pollination. Corn is wind pollinated. If rows are long and few, it is likely that some of the ears will not be pollinated. Plant corn in blocks of short rows rather than one or two long, narrow ones. Limit the number of plants in each block to no more than three per 3 linear feet in each direction. Space rows 3 feet apart. If you plant thickly, be sure to thin the seedlings for the correct spacing. Suckers, however, can be left intact since they actually improve yields. Extended rainy periods, damage from worm pests, and overcrowding also prevent complete pollination.

Earworms. Guard against the damaging corn earworm by applying mineral oil to corn silks with a medicine dropper. Three days after silks appear, put 20 drops on the base of silks on each ear. Repeat every three days until silks turn brown.

Sweetness. Hybrid supersweet varieties of corn cross-pollinate with ease. They should be spaced at least 40 feet apart, planted at intervals of three to four weeks, or separated by wind-deflecting barriers. Otherwise extra-sweet varieties planted with standard types will lose their sweetness.

Attracting Beneficials

Heliopsis and phlox brighten this summer garden while fennel **(Foeniculum)** and yarrow **(Achillea)** invite beneficial insects. **Nasturtium, marigold, angelica, and goldenrod (Solidago)** also attract ladybugs, wasps, and other helpful predators.

HERBS IN SUN AND SHADE

Another distinction is between sun-loving and shade-loving herbs. Nearly all culinary herbs must have full sun to thrive, but a few, such as agrimony *(Agrimonia),* angelica *(Angelica),* ginger *(Zingiber),* and wintergreen *(Gaultheria),* prefer shade. Chervil *(Anthriscus)* needs semishade and cool seasons since it fades in hot weather, and its relative, sweet cicely *(Myrrhis),* enjoys a bit of shade in the heat of summer. Many others, including lemon balm *(Melissa),* mint *(Mentha),* and parsley, can also be grown in part shade.

PREVENTING PROBLEMS WITH HERBS

Ultimately, gardening with herbs is no different from raising vegetables or ornamental flowers. If you know the needs of the herb and have the climate to grow it, you are on your way to developing a problem-free herb garden.

HERB BEDS

If you prepare well-drained soil for your herbs well ahead of planting time, you should have good luck with all of them. Despite the differing preferences among them, excellent drainage is basic to nearly all. Compost is one of the best amendments you can use for loosening soil. Besides providing good drainage, it slowly releases small amounts of nutrients over a period of time. Most herbs can't handle much fertility, so compost is just right. Be sure that it is well decomposed and turned into the soil a time or two before planting, to destroy any germinating weeds.

CULTURAL PROBLEMS

There are several steps you can take in herb culture to avoid some common problems.

- Try to have a weed-free planting bed, especially for those herbs with tiny seeds. As they sprout, they'll get lost if weeds are competing alongside.

- You'll want clean foliage on most herbs. To keep soil from splashing up, cover the soil with a mulch. Use a light, fine material around seedlings and low-growing, matlike herbs; use thicker layers of coarser materials around larger, shrubby herbs.
- Herbs are beautiful mixed in with vegetable crops, but select companions carefully so that you are not planting a Mediterranean herb that wants dry, infertile soil into a rich, moist bed.
- If conditions are too rich, herbs are likely to develop weak stems and topple. Some naturally get top-heavy and need staking. Tie stems to some kind of support and keep them off the ground to prevent rot and damaged foliage. If you tie a clump together with twine and support it with a stake, make the tie loose so there is good air circulation.

PESTS AND DISEASES

Herbs are rarely bothered by serious pest and disease problems. Numerous herbs such as basil and lavender contain aromatic oils in glands in leaves, stems, or roots that naturally repel insects and disease organisms. These have few pests. But not all herbs are invulnerable. Seedlings are subject to the same damping-off problems as vegetables. Foliage on tender herbs can be attacked by aphids and whiteflies; slugs and snails seem to enjoy many of them. Fennel *(Foeniculum),* parsley, and dill are feeding plants for the anise swallowtail butterfly.

As you make regular inspections, you can pick off bothersome insects or use water or soap sprays as appropriate. Remember that residues left on leaves may be ruinous for culinary or medicinal use and may alter aromatic quality or color for ornamental use. If you find rust disease, botrytis rots on flowers or leaves, leaf spots, or powdery mildew, it is a good idea to remove these plants and reevaluate the cultural conditions where they are growing. Another location and different conditions may suit them better.

Lavender cotton

Comfrey

AVOIDING ROOT ROT

Root rot from wet soil is one of the most common disease problems. When herbs such as thyme and lavender cotton *(Santolina)* that require dry, sundrenched, and well-drained soil are planted in heavy, moist conditions, they succumb to rot diseases. Herbs like echinacea *(Echinacea),* which can take normal garden conditions, will rot in cold, wet soil. Others, such as chicory and safflower *(Carthamus),* do better in poor soils and will rot in moist, humus-rich sites.

INVASIVENESS

Some herbs create problems in themselves. Various mints and violets, for instance, will take over a damp site and become aggressive nuisances. Once comfrey *(Symphytum)* establishes itself, it may be set for a lifetime. Mullein *(Verbascum)* and fennel self-sow to the point of invasion. And sweet woodruff *(Galium)* will take over as a ground cover by traveling on its underground stems. All of these vigorous growers can be corralled, but it does take some effort. Be sure you want them permanently before you move them from pots into the ground.

THE MOST COMMON SPECIES AND THE MOST COMMON PROBLEMS

These listings tell you the botanical and common name of the plant and the western zones where it thrives. One of the common problems afflicting the plant in the West is featured, and, where available, resistant varieties are listed.

SYMBOLS: ✐ VEGETABLES ✿ HERBS

ALOE vera
✿ MEDICINAL ALOE

✐ ZONES: 8, 9, 12–24

MEALYBUGS

Mealybugs cluster inside leaves and against stems, covering themselves with dense powdery or cottony coatings. They feed in colonies, causing damage by sucking juices from leaves. As they feed, mealybugs excrete honeydew, which often attracts ants and promotes black sooty mold.

Other plant problems. COMMON PESTS: scales, thrips. COMMON DISEASES: root rot. OTHER: frost damage, sunburn.

Notes: Medicinal aloe does best outdoors in Zones 12 and 13. It withstands severe drought, surviving without irrigation. In other zones listed, provide some afternoon shade to relieve summer heat and avoid sunburn and shriveled leaves. Leaves will stay greener and plumper if you give aloe some water every other week or so. Where soil is not well drained, aloe may not survive ordinary, moist garden conditions. Its roots are very sensitive to wet soil; it can die from root rot during winter rains.

ALOYSIA triphylla
✿ LEMON VERBENA

✐ ZONES: 9, 10, 12–24

SPIDER MITES

Spider mites, which thrive in dry, dusty conditions, weaken plants by sucking plant juices. Affected foliage appears pinpricked or stippled with yellow dots and sometimes develops a bronzy sheen. The leaves may drop prematurely, weakening plants enough to reduce flowering. Sometimes, large colonies spin webs around leaf edges or shoot tips, enclosing the microscopic mites as they feed.

Other plant problems. COMMON PESTS: thrips, whiteflies. COMMON DISEASES: anthracnose, leaf spot, powdery mildew, root rot. OTHER: frost damage.

Notes: Hose off plants periodically with a strong jet of water to keep foliage clean and to discourage spider mites. In spring, wait to cut back woody, leggy stems until after your last frost date; new growth is easily damaged by cold and frost. Don't worry about cutting shrubs back hard—they can take severe pruning and in fact need it for an attractive bushy appearance. In colder zones, plant lemon verbena against a sunny, south-facing wall; it is more likely to survive through winter in such a location.

ANETHUM graveolens
✿ DILL

✐ ZONES: ALL

PARSLEYWORMS

It is startling to find these 2-inch larvae, bright green with yellow and black stripes, feeding on dill. With two orange horns protruding, they look like formidable pests. If you can spare some dill, anise, or parsley leaves and leave these caterpillars to feed, however, they will eventually turn into beautiful yellow and black swallowtail butterflies.

Other plant problems. COMMON PESTS: aphids. COMMON DISEASES: mosaic virus. OTHER: invasiveness from self-sowing.

Notes: Dill is an annual herb that self-sows readily and eventually appears throughout the garden after a few years. Thin seedlings to allow 1–2 feet between plants. If it is left overcrowded, root competition will stunt dill, and you will not get large seed heads. To prevent mosaic virus from discoloring the foliage, don't smoke in the garden, and wash your hands after handling tobacco, which harbors the virus.

ARTEMISIA dracunculus
✿ FRENCH OR TRUE TARRAGON

✐ ZONES: ALL

ROOT ROT

In winter, tarragon dies to the ground and needs protection against winter cold and root rot. A thick mulch after the ground freezes will protect it from cold, but the mulch must be removed in spring to allow the soil to dry out—any moisture trapped inside will hasten root rot. In summer, heavy, wet conditions will also cause rot. Light, dry soils and raised beds are the best planting sites.

Other plant problems. COMMON PESTS: none. COMMON DISEASES: powdery mildew. OTHER: frost damage.

Notes: For true French culinary tarragon, you must acquire plants propagated from cuttings. Plants grown from seed are not true to type but are usually Russian tarragon, Artemisia dracunculus sativa, which has a bitter flavor. French tarragon does not set seed. To keep plants vigorous, divide and replant established clumps every two or three years.

TIP

Take some time to lay out an orderly design before you begin planting your herb garden. Cluster culinary herbs together for easy access; keep herbs with low water requirements together for easy care. For a typical quantity of herbs, allow a minimum of 2–3 square feet for culinary herbs, such as basil and cilantro, that need frequent replanting; at least 1 square foot for small herbs, such as chives and parsley; and 3–4 square feet for shrubby forms, such as lemon verbena and artemisia. If you plant all your herbs together, your herb bed can be part of a crop rotation plan for your vegetable garden.

ASPARAGUS

➤ *ASPARAGUS OFFICINALIS*

✎ ZONES: ALL

ASPARAGUS BEETLES

Blue-black, yellow-spotted adults and olive-green larvae chew on tender asparagus spears, leaving them scarred with brown blemishes, although still edible. When the beetles' black eggs appear on the asparagus, cut the spears and wash off the eggs. Hand-pick larvae and beetles and destroy them.

Other plant problems. COMMON PESTS: aphids, slugs, snails, spider mites. COMMON DISEASES: asparagus rust, crown rot, fusarium rot, fusarium wilt. OTHER: frost damage, spindly growth.

Resistant varieties. 'Jersey King' has some resistance to fusarium wilt and asparagus rust.

Notes: Asparagus plants that have been stressed from pests, drought, weed competition, lack of nutrients, or overharvesting produce spindly growth—or none at all—the following year. Allow plants to recover by leaving all spears in the ground, skipping harvesting for at least one year. Keep beds weed-free; fertilize and mulch to improve production. Always allow ferny foliage to develop; it manufactures food that is stored in the roots to produce spring growth.

BEAN

➤ *PHASEOLUS*, VARIOUS SPECIES

✎ ZONES: ALL

MEXICAN BEAN BEETLES

These copper-colored beetles resemble beneficial ladybugs in size and shape. Their small, yellow larvae are legless and feed with adults on the undersides of leaves. Beetles feed on all types of bean foliage, chewing lacy patterns and heavily damaging some plants. They may also eat the stems and bean pods.

Other plant problems. COMMON PESTS: aphids, corn earworms, cucumber beetles, earwigs, leafhoppers, nematodes, spider mites, thrips, weevils, whiteflies. COMMON DISEASES: anthracnose, bacterial canker, curly top virus, damping off, downy mildew, fusarium wilt, mosaic virus, powdery mildew, rust. OTHER: heat and drought damage, smog damage.

Resistant varieties. Treated seed helps prevent damping off. Many varieties offer resistance to anthracnose, bacterial canker, downy mildew, mosaic virus, powdery mildew, and rust.

Notes: Don't cultivate the soil around beans when plants are wet, to avoid spreading diseases. Untreated seed may rot if planted in cold soil (below 60°F). If you suspect a nutrient deficiency, check soil pH; beans prefer a mildly acidic soil with a pH of 5.5–6.5.

BEET

➤ *BETA VULGARIS*

✎ ZONES: ALL

CURLY TOP VIRUS

You will recognize this virus by the upward-curling leaves on beets. Veins turn purple or bronze, and the leaves get thick and leathery or brittle. The disease is spread by the beet leafhopper and cannot be easily controlled.

Other plant problems. COMMON PESTS: aphids, armyworms, cabbage loopers, earwigs, flea beetles, gophers, leaf miners, mice, moles, nematodes, webworms, wireworms. COMMON DISEASES: downy mildew, fungal leaf spot, root rot, scab, verticillium wilt. OTHER: bolting.

Resistant varieties. Treated seed helps prevent damping off on cold soil. There are a few varieties that resist downy mildew, leaf spot, root rot, and bolting.

Notes: Beets are a cool-season crop; they become tough and woody when planted in summer. For a fall crop, sow seed ten weeks before your first hard frost. Prepare a bed of fine soil 10–12 inches deep to produce well-formed beets. Keep the pH in the neutral zone and not below 6.0. Sow seed thickly for good sprouting, then thin heavily.

BROCCOLI

➤ *BRASSICA OLERACEA*, BOTRYTIS GROUP, ITALICA GROUP

✎ ZONES: ALL

CLUB ROOT

This fungus causes misshapen roots with swellings or knots on broccoli and other cole crops. Leaves turn yellow and wilt during the day; growth slows, and plants die. Since the fungus can live for several years in the soil, rotate crops, replacing cole crops with those that are not affected.

Other plant problems. COMMON PESTS: aphids, cabbage loopers, cabbageworms, cutworms, harlequin bugs, nematodes, slugs, snails. COMMON DISEASES: bacterial leaf spot, black rot, downy mildew. OTHER: bolting, frost damage, heat stress.

Resistant varieties. Look for varieties resistant to bacterial leaf spot, black rot, and downy mildew.

Notes: Follow spacing instructions carefully for broccoli, leaving 12–24 inches between plants—most varieties will not put out large heads if they are crowded. Small heads also result from slow germination in garden beds; you will be likely to have more success in all zones if you sow seed indoors and then set out transplants.

BRUSSELS SPROUTS

➤ *BRASSICA OLERACEA*, GEMMIFERA GROUP

✎ ZONES: ALL

CABBAGEWORMS

Imported cabbageworms are velvety, light-green caterpillars similar to cabbage loopers (see Celery, opposite; also page 162), but plumper and without the looping movement. Cabbageworms eat large, irregular holes in leaves and tunnel into sprouts. Worms are the same color as the plant and are hard to spot. Look for granules of dark green excrement, which show up on the leaves.

Other plant problems. COMMON PESTS: aphids, cabbage loopers, cutworms, harlequin bugs, nematodes, root maggots, wireworms. COMMON DISEASES: bacterial soft rot (black leg), black rot, club root, downy mildew, fusarium wilt, verticillium wilt. OTHER: frost damage, heat stress.

Resistant varieties. Treated seed resists bacterial soft rot and black rot.

Notes: In zones with long, hot, dry summers, you may not always get a reliable crop, since brussels sprouts require a long, cool growing season. The sprouts will be sweeter if you harvest them after a frost; however, timing is critical so they don't suffer frost damage.

CABBAGE

- *BRASSICA OLERACEA, CAPITATA GROUP*
- ZONES: ALL

SPLIT HEADS

Cabbage heads split or crack when watered heavily after the soil has dried out. Water regularly to avoid dry soil. When heads are nearly mature, give them a quarter-turn twist to break a few roots and cut down on splitting.

Other plant problems. COMMON PESTS: aphids, cabbage loopers, cabbageworms, cutworms, earwigs, flea beetles, harlequin bugs, root maggots. COMMON DISEASES: aster yellows, club root, downy mildew, fusarium wilt, verticillium wilt. OTHER: frost damage, heat stress, tip burn.

Resistant varieties. Treated seed resists bacterial soft rot (black leg) and black rot. Some varieties resist bolting, heat, and splitting. Many varieties resist aster yellows and thrips.

Notes: If young plants are stressed by cold, soggy soil, slow germination, or excessive fertilization, heads may bolt or lose their round, firm shape. Late-maturing varieties are best for storing. Rotate cabbage, and all cole crops, annually.

CARROT

- *DAUCUS CAROTA, D. SATIVUS*
- ZONES: ALL

CARROT RUST FLIES

Carrot rust flies lay their eggs in young, leafy tops or in the soil. Damage is done by the firm white larvae, which usually burrow into carrots and reduce them to mush, although some-

times the problem is minor and limited to brown tracks carved on the outside. Exclude flies with row covers until plants are 6–8 inches tall.

Other plant problems. COMMON PESTS: carrot weevils, nematodes, parsleyworms (larvae of the swallowtail butterfly), root maggots. COMMON DISEASES: aster yellows, bacterial soft rot, downy mildew, leaf blight, powdery mildew, scab. OTHER: bolting, cracking, splitting.

Resistant varieties. Some varieties are resistant to leaf blight, powdery mildew, bolting, cracking, and splitting. 'Flyaway' resists carrot rust flies.

Notes: If your carrots develop split roots, cut back on nitrogen fertilizer or manure and keep the soil evenly moist to prevent alternate periods of wet and dry soil. You can prevent soil from crusting over seeds and get improved germination if you cover seeds with a fine layer of peat moss, vermiculite, or sawdust, then keep the surface moist until carrots sprout. Thin to prevent overcrowding. In mild-winter zones, you can grow carrots year-round.

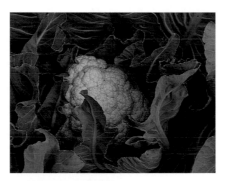

CAULIFLOWER

- *BRASSICA OLERACEA, BOTRYTIS GROUP*
- ZONES: ALL

HARLEQUIN BUGS

Harlequin bugs are shield-shaped, shiny black stinkbugs with orange-red markings. They feed on cauliflower foliage and other cole crops, leaving pale yellow or white blotches as they suck juices. Heavily damaged plants may wilt and die.

Other plant problems. COMMON PESTS: aphids, cabbage loopers, cabbageworms, cutworms, earwigs, flea beetles, nematodes, root maggots. COMMON DISEASES: aster yellows, bacterial soft rot (black leg), black rot, club root, damping off, downy mildew, fusarium wilt. OTHER: boron deficiency, frost damage, heat stress.

Resistant varieties. Some varieties are resistant to black rot and heat stress.

Notes: Keep cauliflower plants growing steadily to prevent bolting or undersized heads. Space plants 24 inches apart to avoid stress from overcrowding. Select your spring planting dates carefully so that heads will

mature before hot weather in summer. In cold zones, plant in spring and midsummer; in warm zones, plant again in fall or winter.

CELERY

- *APIUM GRAVEOLENS, A. DULCE*
- ZONES: ALL

CABBAGE LOOPERS

Cabbage loopers are small, greenish worms that push themselves forward in a characteristic movement that causes their center section to round upward in a loop. Several generations may appear each year. Loopers feed heavily on leaves and stems, disfiguring mature plants and weakening young ones; they can kill seedlings.

Other plant problems. COMMON PESTS: carrot rust flies, carrot weevils, nematodes, parsleyworms (larvae of the swallowtail butterfly), slugs, snails. COMMON DISEASES: aster yellows, bacterial soft rot, downy mildew, fusarium wilt, late blight, leaf and stem blight, mosaic virus. OTHER: bolting, overcrowding.

Resistant varieties. A few varieties are somewhat resistant to fusarium and yellows.

Notes: Rotate celery crops to avoid leaf blight and fusarium diseases. To avoid bolting, wait to transplant until nighttime temperatures are steadily above 55°F. For firm, full celery bunches, fertilize every 2–3 weeks and keep the soil evenly moist.

CORN

- *ZEA MAYS*
- ZONES: ALL

CORN EARWORMS

Also known as the tomato fruitworm and the cotton bollworm, this caterpillar changes its appearance as it grows. Young worms are tiny and white with black heads; older ones are longer and green to black with lengthwise stripes. Worms feed on developing corn silks, sometimes preventing complete pollination, and on kernels near the tips of ears.

Other plant problems. COMMON PESTS: armyworms, chinch bugs, cucumber beetles, European corn borers, flea beetles, Japanese beetles, raccoons, seedcorn maggots. COMMON DISEASES: bacterial wilt, corn smut, leaf and stem blight.

Resistant varieties. Treated seed prevents fungal rots before germination. Many varieties are bred to germinate in cold soil.

Notes: For best success in germinating corn, wait to plant until the soil temperature is 65°F. You can prevent most diseases by rotating your crops at least every three years and cleaning up and composting corn debris in the fall. Plant corn in blocks, and thin stalks to 12 inches apart for good pollination.

CUCUMBER

🌱 *CUCUMIS SATIVUS*

🌿 ZONES: ALL

CUCUMBER BEETLES

These yellowish green beetles with black spots or stripes chew holes in flowers and leaves and damage developing shoots. They also spread bacterial wilt and a mosaic virus. Larvae of the western striped cucumber beetle damage cucurbits by feeding on roots.

Other plant problems. COMMON PESTS: borers, leafhoppers, nematodes, spider mites, squash bugs. COMMON DISEASES: anthracnose, bacterial leaf spot, bacterial wilt, downy mildew, fusarium wilt, powdery mildew, scab. OTHER: poor fruit set.

Resistant varieties. Cucumbers have been bred to resist anthracnose, leaf spot, downy mildew, mosaic virus, powdery mildew, scab, and other diseases.

Notes: Cucumbers will not survive frosts. Seeds germinate best when the soil warms to 70°F; blossoms may drop if nighttime temperatures are cool. You can use black plastic mulch and floating row covers to provide extra warmth.

ECHINACEA angustifolia

🌿 ECHINACEA

🌿 ZONES: ALL

CROWN ROT

This wildflower, which is native to the central North American continent, is found in fairly dry prairie habitats. In the garden, it prefers some moisture, but it will die from rot in constantly wet soils; it cannot tolerate cold, soggy soil in winter. Plant on raised mounds to provide good drainage. Keep mulch several inches away from crowns to prevent rot.

Other plant problems. COMMON PESTS: aphids, beetles. COMMON DISEASES: leaf spot. OTHER: drought stress.

Notes: Space echinacea plants 1½–2 feet apart and mulch to prevent weed competition. Wait to harvest roots until frosts have killed the foliage. Trim crowns, leaving some root intact; replant. Let plants grow for a few years before harvesting again. You will get continuous summer flowering if you clip off dead flower heads.

EGGPLANT

🌱 *SOLANUM MELONGENA*

🌿 ZONES: ALL

POOR FRUIT SET

Eggplant requires full sun and warm days and nights to set fruit. When fruit does not set, try laying down a black plastic mulch to warm the soil. Eggplant is self-fruitful; if pollination is poor, you can assist by tapping the flowers during warm afternoons.

Other plant problems. COMMON PESTS: aphids, Colorado potato beetles, corn earworms, cucumber beetles, flea beetles, leaf rollers, nematodes, spittlebugs, tomato hornworms, weevils, whiteflies. COMMON DISEASES: curly top virus, mosaic virus, verticillium wilt. OTHER: cold and heat stress.

Resistant varieties. Varieties are available that will set fruit in cool weather or under heat stress. Most varieties are disease resistant, some to mosaic virus.

Notes: Rotate eggplants each year, but do not plant them in a bed where tomatoes or potatoes were just grown.

GARLIC

🌱 *ALLIUM SATIVUM*

🌿 ZONES: ALL

SMUT

The smut fungus causes black spots and streaks on leaves and between individual garlic cloves. After the garlic is harvested, the spots generally release a black powder. Smut is more common in northern zones when summer weather is cool. Remove and destroy all smut-infected plants and don't replant garlic or other onion-family plants in the same bed for several years.

Other plant problems. COMMON PESTS: aphids, nematodes, root maggots, thrips. COMMON DISEASES: downy mildew, fusarium rot, pink root, white rot. OTHER: bolting, cold damage.

Resistant varieties. Varieties are available that are resistant to cold stress and diseases.

Notes: Garlic can be planted in the spring or fall, but fall is best in zones where the ground freezes—there will be some root growth for four to six weeks before a hard freeze. Mulch after freezing to prevent bulbs from being forced out of the ground by alternate freezing and thawing.

LAVANDULA

🌿 LAVENDER

🌿 ZONES: VARY BY SPECIES

ORANGE TORTRIX

This green or orange caterpillar spins protective webs around lavender leaves and feeds inside. To control it, pick off damaged foliage and worms; look for cream-colored eggs on the upper surface of leaves. This caterpillar also feeds on grapefruit trees, rolling itself inside their leaves.

Other plant problems. COMMON PESTS: nematodes. COMMON DISEASES: leaf spot, root rot. OTHER: breakage, frost damage.

Notes: In zones where lavender survives as a perennial, cut back stems to about 6 inches in late fall, after flowering has finished. If you wait until spring to cut back the stems, plants are apt to break and split from winter wind or rain damage. Plant in loose, fast-draining soil to avoid rot diseases. Do not fertilize; rich soil causes weak stems and poorly formed shrubs. Take cuttings to propagate shrubs since seeds can be difficult to germinate and strains do not reliably produce true to the variety.

LETTUCE

🌿 *LACTUCA SATIVA*

🌡 ZONES: SUMMER 1–7, 10, 11; COOL-SEASON 8, 9, 12–24

BACTERIAL SOFT ROT

This bacterial rot affects both healthy plants and those damaged by insects or physical injury. Mushy spots develop inside the lettuce while the outsides seem fine. The infected area usually has a foul smell. Cut and destroy damaged heads to prevent the bacteria from spreading; thin plants to prevent overcrowding. Tip burn causes a similar brown rotting on leaf edges, but the heads don't become mushy.

Other plant problems. COMMON PESTS: aphids, armyworms, birds, cabbage loopers, corn carworms, cutworms, nematodes, slugs, snails, tobacco budworms. COMMON DISEASES: bacterial leaf spot, damping off, downy mildew, gray mold, mosaic virus, powdery mildew. OTHER: frost damage, heat stress, smog damage, tip burn.

Resistant varieties. Some varieties resist bolting, downy mildew, mosaic virus, and tip burn.

Notes: Cutworms cut off young plants at the soil level at night; armyworms and corn earworms feed on crowns inside developing leaves. Loopers chew holes in leaves and tunnel into mature heads.

MELON

🌿 *CUCUMIS MELO*

🌡 ZONES: ALL

SQUASH BUGS

Squash bugs are pests on all cucurbits. Both adults and nymphs feed mostly at night, sucking juices from stems and the undersides of leaves. This causes leaves to turn yellow and then brown; the vines wilt. Heavily damaged leaves and stems turn completely black. Bugs often hide under dead leaves and in undecomposed organic matter in the soil.

Other plant problems. COMMON PESTS: aphids, birds, cucumber beetles, leafhoppers, nematodes, spider mites, whiteflies, wireworms. COMMON DISEASES: bacterial leaf spot, bacterial wilt, downy mildew, fusarium wilt, powdery mildew, verticillium wilt. OTHER: acid soil.

Resistant varieties. Look for varieties resistant to fusarium wilt and powdery mildew.

Notes: Ribbed muskmelons with netted skin are the most widely adapted to western climate zones. They prefer sandy, nearly neutral or slightly alkaline soil and warm weather. In zones with short growing seasons, use row covers or plastic mulch to raise temperatures around the plants.

MENTHA

🌿 MINT

🌡 ZONES: VARY BY SPECIES

SLUGS AND SNAILS

Slugs and snails hide in and under thick mint clumps. At night and in early morning hours, they come out to feed, leaving silvery trails as they move through the plants. They are more of a problem in cooler, moist zones along the coast. Hand-pick or set out bait to control.

Other plant problems. COMMON PESTS: aphids, borers, cutworms, flea beetles, nematodes, loopers, spider mites, weevils. COMMON DISEASES: anthracnose, rust, verticillium wilt. OTHER: woody growth.

Resistant varieties. Some species and varieties are more resistant than others.

Notes: Mint is one of the most invasive herbs. It spreads fast by underground stems and is difficult to eradicate once it gets away from you. Sink plastic barriers into the ground 10 inches deep or more to limit its rampant growth. It grows especially vigorously in moist spots but needs protection from full sun in zones with hot summers. Pinch back stems to prevent legginess. Cut plants to the ground in late fall to prevent pests from overwintering in debris.

MONARDA didyma

🌿 BEE BALM, BERGAMOT

🌡 ZONES: ALL

POWDERY MILDEW

Powdery mildew is a white or gray, feltlike coating on leaves and stems. You'll see it most often in dry conditions when days are warm and nights cool. Plants in shade are commonly affected. The mildew fungus grows into leaves and stems to feed on plant tissue; it sometimes causes leaves to pucker and curl. Plants may continue to grow and bloom; or they may wither, lose vigor, and die.

Other plant problems. COMMON PESTS: borers. COMMON DISEASES: crown rot, leaf spot. OTHER: drought stress, invasiveness.

Resistant varieties. *M. fistulosa*, *M. pringlei*, and *M. punctata* are less susceptible to powdery mildew than *M. didyma*.

Notes: Bee balm clumps enlarge as stems grow up from underground rhizomes. If you thin these stands so plants are not overcrowded and keep the soil moist, powdery mildew is less of a problem. Give them 18–24 inches of space; divide every three years to renew plants or when the centers begin to die out.

ONION

🌿 *ALLIUM CEPA*

🌡 ZONES: ALL

BOLTING

Bolting depends on temperature, variety, and the size of the plant. Most varieties bolt between 40°F and 45°F. In spring-seeded onions, long periods of cool weather cause bolting. Onions planted from seed in fall will bolt if they begin to grow quickly, then are forced by cool weather to suddenly slow down. Larger plants and sets usually bolt faster than smaller ones. Sets ½ inch or more and plants ¼ inch or more in diameter are more likely to bolt. You can reduce bolting in sets by storing them at 30–32°F.

Other plant problems. COMMON PESTS: onion maggots, thrips. COMMON DISEASES: downy mildew, fusarium rot, fusarium wilt, mosaic virus, pink root, purple blotch, smut. OTHER: infertile soil, weeds.

Resistant varieties. Many varieties resist pink root and fusarium. 'Stockton Yellow Globe' and 'Italian Red' resist bolting.

Notes: For success with onions in your zone, choose early or late varieties adapted for northerly or southerly latitudes and day length, and plant on the recommended dates. Keep all weeds out of onions; they are an onion's worst enemy.

ORIGANUM vulgare

🌿 OREGANO

🌡 ZONES: ALL

APHIDS

These pear-shaped, soft-bodied insects range in color from orange to green to black. They suck juices from plants, scarring leaves and causing foliage to pucker. Sticky honeydew drips as they feed. The black coating that develops on the foliage is a sooty mold that grows on the honeydew.

Other plant problems. COMMON PESTS: leaf miners, spider mites. COMMON DISEASES: root rot. OTHER: poor germination.

Notes: Oregano, like most other Mediterranean herbs, grows best in dry, average soils. Adding excess nitrogen fertilizer causes lanky growth and tender shoots, which attract aphids. If you add too much compost or other organic soil amendments, the soil may hold too much moisture and rot the roots, especially during cold weather. For best germination, keep the seedbed moist, but leave the tiny seeds uncovered on top of the soil.

PARSLEY

🌿 PETROSELINUM CRISPUM

🌡 ZONES: ALL

POOR GERMINATION

Parsley seeds take a minimum of 14–21 days to sprout, but it often takes longer—sometimes weeks—before sprouts appear. If the seedbed is not kept moist the entire time, seeds will dry out and die. Their tiny size makes parsley seeds difficult to handle; sow them only ¼ inch deep. To improve germination, soak them in warm water for 24 hours or freeze moistened seeds overnight before planting.

Other plant problems. COMMON PESTS: carrot rust flies, nematodes, parsleyworms. COMMON DISEASES: crown rot, mosaic virus. OTHER: leaf discoloration.

Resistant varieties. Some varieties resist loss of leaf color.

Notes: Plant parsley in April in Zones 1–7; December–May in Zones 8–11 and 14–24; September–October in Zones 12 and 13. To

keep seeds moist before germination, cover with vermiculite, sawdust, or other organic material that holds moisture well. Plant when the soil temperature is 50°F to 75°F.

PEA

🌱 PISUM SATIVUM

🌡 ZONES: ALL

FUSARIUM WILT

Lower leaves turn yellow first, often on one side only. Eventually, entire plants become stunted, wilt, and die. If you cut open the lower part of a stem on an infected plant, it will be reddish orange inside. The fungus destroys the water-conducting vessels in the stems.

Other plant problems. COMMON PESTS: aphids, armyworms, birds, cucumber beetles, corn earworms, earwigs, leaf miners, nematodes, spider mites, thrips. COMMON DISEASES: downy mildew, mosaic virus, powdery mildew, root rot, viral wilts. OTHER: heat damage.

Resistant varieties. Numerous varieties resist viral diseases, powdery mildew, fusarium, and root rot.

Notes: Pull out and destroy plants infected with fusarium wilt. Be sure to rotate crops annually to prevent a buildup of the fungus. Don't plant other crops susceptible to fusarium in infected beds, since the fungus lives in the soil for several years. Peas must be planted as a cool-weather crop.

PEPPER

🌱 CAPSICUM, VARIOUS SPECIES

🌡 ZONES: ALL

BLOSSOM-END ROT

Like tomatoes, peppers develop blossom-end rot when the soil is alternately wet and dry. Peppers develop a brownish black, soft rot on the bottom where the blossom was attached. If you add compost and calcium fertilizer to the soil before planting and keep the soil evenly moist as plants grow, you should have less rot.

Other plant problems. COMMON PESTS: aphids, Colorado potato beetles, corn earworms, cutworms, flea beetles, nematodes, pepper maggots, pepper weevils, spittlebugs,

tomato hornworms, whiteflies. COMMON DISEASES: bacterial leaf spot, bacterial soft rot (black leg), fusarium wilt, mosaic virus, powdery mildew, verticillium wilt, viral wilts. OTHER: poor fruit set.

Resistant varieties. Many varieties resist viral and bacterial diseases.

Notes: Peppers are a warm-season crop that will fruit only when nighttime temperatures stay warm. They do best when seed is started indoors and plants are set out into warm soil. Be sure roots are well developed before transplanting. Use row covers or plastic mulch to raise garden temperature a few degrees if you live in a cool zone.

POTATO

🌱 SOLANUM TUBEROSUM

🌡 ZONES: ALL

LATE BLIGHT

Blight begins in late summer with water-soaked spots on leaves. The spots grow pale, and the leaves shrivel and die. In high humidity, the spots may have a gray or white mold. The potato tubers develop brown spots and rot, giving off a foul odor. Destroy all infected foliage and potatoes.

Other plant problems. COMMON PESTS: aphids, cabbage loopers, Colorado potato beetles, cucumber beetles, earwigs, flea beetles, leafhoppers, nematodes, potato tuber worms, tomato hornworms, wireworms. COMMON DISEASES: aster yellows, bacterial soft rot (black leg), pink root, powdery mildew, root rot, scab, verticillium wilt, viral diseases. OTHER: frost damage, heat stress.

Resistant varieties. Different varieties show resistance to early and late blight, heat, scab, verticillium wilt, and viral diseases.

Notes: Choose early-maturing, midseason, or late-maturing varieties adapted to the length of the growing season in your zone. Potatoes planted in warm soil show stronger growth and more disease resistance. The soil should be moist at planting time, but to avoid disease problems, wait until plants are up and well established before you begin regular watering. Moisten the soil lightly if it begins to dry out.

SPINACH

🌱 *SPINACIA OLERACEA*
⚠ ZONES: ALL

LEAF MINERS

Leaf miners are larvae that tunnel inside leaves and give them a blotchy appearance. Pick off and destroy infected leaves. You can keep adult flies away from plants by covering them with screening, row covers, or cold caps and keeping the surrounding areas weed-free.

Other plant problems. COMMON PESTS: aphids, cabbage loopers, cucumber beetles, nematodes. COMMON DISEASES: aster yellows, blight, curly top virus, damping off, fusarium wilt, mosaic virus, verticillium wilt. OTHER: bolting.

Resistant varieties. Select varieties to resist bolting, viral blights, and downy mildew.

RADISH

🌱 *RAPHANUS SATIVUS*
⚠ ZONES: ALL

CABBAGE ROOT MAGGOTS

Cabbage maggots cause only minor damage to the outsides of radishes, but if they tunnel inside, the radishes are ruined by holes and brown streaks. The maggots feed mostly on roots, but they also chew stems, causing foliage to wilt and turn yellow. If the roots are seriously damaged, the plants will die.

Other plant problems. COMMON PESTS: flea beetles, harlequin bugs, leafhoppers, nematodes, root maggots, wireworms. COMMON DISEASES: black rot, damping off, downy mildew, fusarium wilt, mosaic virus, scab, verticillium wilt. OTHER: heat stress, pithiness.

Resistant varieties. Many varieties resist bolting and pithiness; some resist fusarium and club root.

Notes: For crisp, mild radishes, plant in fertile soil and keep the bed moist until harvest. Thin to reduce root competition. Harvest radishes as soon as they are ready; leaving them in the ground makes them pithy and hollow inside. In cold-winter climates, sow radishes in spring and fall. In mild-winter zones, sow again in winter.

TOMATO

🌱 *LYCOPERSICON ESCULENTUM*
⚠ ZONES: ALL

EARLY BLIGHT

Early varieties are most susceptible to early blight, especially in moist weather after plants begin to fruit. The first signs are brown areas on leaves, surrounded by a yellow ring. Leaves eventually are killed. Clean up infected foliage and rotate crops each year.

Other plant problems. COMMON PESTS: Colorado potato beetles, corn earworms, flea beetles, fruitworms, nematodes, tomato hornworms, whiteflies. COMMON DISEASES: aster yellows, curly top virus, damping off, fusarium wilt, leaf and stem blight, mosaic virus, powdery mildew, verticillium wilt. OTHER: blossom-end rot, cracked fruit, poor fruit set.

Resistant varieties. Numerous varieties resist verticillium and fusarium wilts, nematodes, tobacco mosaic virus, and cracking.

Notes: Choose early, midseason, and late varieties to suit the length of the growing season in your zone. Plant as early as February or early March in Zones 12 and 13; April, May, or early June in Zones 7–9 and 14–24; and May or early June in Zones 1–6, 10, and 11. Water deeply, since plants are deep rooted. Alternate periods of wet and dry cause cracking and blossom-end rot.

SQUASH

🌱 *CUCURBITA, VARIOUS SPECIES*
⚠ ZONES: ALL

SQUASH VINE BORERS

In early summer, these white caterpillars with dark heads bore into the base of stems. Plants wilt suddenly and die. If you look near the base of stems and on the ground, you can find greenish, sawdusty excrement piled up. You can limit the damage to plants by locating the entry point, slitting open the stem, and killing the borer.

Other plant problems. COMMON PESTS: aphids, cucumber beetles, leafhoppers, nematodes, spider mites, squash bugs. COMMON DISEASES: bacterial leaf spot, curly top virus, downy mildew, powdery mildew. OTHER: frost damage, incomplete pollination, poor fruit set.

Resistant varieties. Virus-resistant varieties are available.

Notes: Bad weather and a shortage of pollinating insects may cause poor fruit set. If this is a problem, try transferring pollen by hand from male to female flowers. You can recognize male flowers by the enlarged bulge just behind the blossom. It is common for the first few blossoms or fruits to shrivel and drop since these are male flowers and will not produce mature squash.

TURNIP

🌱 *BRASSICA RAPA, RAPIFERA GROUP*
⚠ ZONES: ALL

WIREWORMS

These reddish brown, hard worms feed on turnips underground. They are most likely to be troublesome in poorly drained soil and in new garden beds made from breaking up sod. Till soil and mix in compost to improve drainage; too much organic matter, however, actually encourages wireworms. Rotating crops helps prevent damage.

Other plant problems. COMMON PESTS: cabbage loopers, caterpillars, flea beetles, harlequin bugs, nematodes, root maggots, weevils. COMMON DISEASES: club root, fusarium wilt, scab, viral diseases. OTHER: frost damage.

Resistant varieties. Some varieties resist bolting, root maggots, and viral diseases.

Notes: In cold-winter zones, plant turnips in spring for summer harvest, or plant in late summer for a fall harvest. In mild-winter zones, plant from September to March. Choose specific varieties bred for turnip greens, small roots, or winter storage. Set up floating row covers immediately after seeding to keep turnips free of insects.

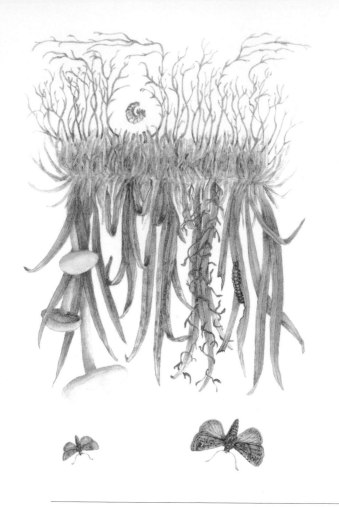

SYMPTOMS AND CAUSES
at a Glance

I n this chapter, you'll find a quick reference guide to possible causes of plant problems, organized by plant part (such as leaves or fruit). The guide lists visible evidence of damage—yellowing, brown patches, holes in bark, shriveled blossoms—and the pests, diseases, and cultural conditions that could be causing it. Armed with this information, you can go right to the encyclopedia entries to identify the culprit and find appropriate techniques for managing the problem.

It's not easy to diagnose the cause—or causes—of a plant's faltering performance. To start, you need to note the signs and symptoms of a problem. Using the guide that follows, you may be able to finger the culprit quickly. Or you may need to investigate further, perhaps requesting the help of the staff at a local nursery or your cooperative extension agent. In either case, you'll find it easier if you do a thorough, systematic check for damage.

To make your examination, obtain a hand lens or an inexpensive magnifying glass. Writing down your observations or drawing pictures will help you keep track of the information you gather, as well as allow you to explain the problem to a consultant clearly and completely. You'll also have a record that you can consult in future years.

STEP-BY-STEP DAMAGE ANALYSIS

Here are four easy steps to analyzing the symptoms and causes in your garden.

1. Identify the plant. Is it deciduous or evergreen? What should it look like at this time of year? Don't mistake a normal stage such as seasonal leaf or winter dieback for a plant problem. Read the appropriate section of "Problem Solving by Plant Type" (pages 72–137) to learn more about this kind of plant, its growth habits and life cycle, and the kinds of problems it's likely to develop.

2. Identify the part or parts of the plant that are affected. Scrape away some of the dirt surrounding the plant and try to determine whether the roots look normal. If a number of plants are affected, dig up one of them to examine it more closely. On leaves, is the problem on the upper surface, the lower, or both? Is it on lower, older leaves, on younger, newer leaves, or both? On one branch or on many of the branches? Is it a general branch problem, or is the damage starting at the ends of branches and progressing back toward the trunk? If there are leaf spots, what color, size, and shape are they? Are leaves distorted? Is there any webbing? If areas on the leaves are yellowing or browning, are they in the center, on the tip, or the edges? Are the veins the same color as the leaf? Do you see anything that looks like fungus on the leaf? If so, what color is it? Is there damage on the stems? If you cut a stem, do you see anything, such as discoloration, inside? Is there any unusual external ooze on the plant? Any odd-appearing growths, such as galls or mushrooms? What do you find when you cut open a damaged fruit or vegetable—is the damage more on the outside or in the interior?

3. Identify any diseases or cultural problems affecting the plant. Might it be suffering from air pollution or frost damage? When uniform damage (affecting all the plants, of various types) and nonuniform patterns (involving only one kind of plant). When various plant types are involved, they may be suffering from a cultural problem rather than a disease. When only one type of plant is damaged, a pest or disease may be the cause. To identify diseases and cultural problems that affect plants, consult the "Encyclopedia of Plant Diseases and Cultural Problems," page 208.

4. Identify any pests attacking the plant. Look for insect damage or the insects themselves. If you find pests, try to identify them using the photographs in the "Encyclopedia of Damaging and Beneficial Creatures," page 148. If you need to ask someone else's help in identifying a pest and you can't capture it, draw a sketch, noting size, colors, and markings.

Correct diagnosis is important for accurate, effective problem prevention and management. Once you know the identity of the culprit, you can start solving your garden problems.

Gardeners know much can go wrong. Clockwise from top left, a rose can suffer (clockwise from top) aphids, black spot, rust, downy mildew, spider mites, scale, leaf-cutting bees, and rose mosaic virus. The apple is prey to powdery mildew, anthracnose, leaf rollers, fireblight, codling moths, apple scab, and cedar-apple rust. Lawns host fairy ring, cutworm grubs, rust, red thread, and thatch. A tomato is susceptible to blossom-end rot, late blight, fusarium wilt, root nematodes, bacterial canker, and tomato hornworms.

ROOTS, STEMS

ROOTS

MAJOR SYMPTOMS	POSSIBLE CAUSES
Blackened roots	DISEASES: fusarium wilt, root rots CULTURAL PROBLEMS: excessive watering
Irregular swelling	PESTS: borers, grape phylloxera, root knot nematodes DISEASES: club root, crown gall, oak root fungus
Rotting off	DISEASES: verticillium wilt CULTURAL PROBLEMS: excessive watering
White fungus	DISEASES: oak root fungus

STEMS

MAJOR SYMPTOMS	POSSIBLE CAUSES
Black patches	DISEASES: fusarium wilt
Blackening	CULTURAL PROBLEMS: cold
Brittleness, dieback	PESTS: borers DISEASES: bacterial wilt
Cankers with golden ooze	DISEASES: bacterial canker
Cottony growth	DISEASES: fusarium wilt
Discolored or dead patches	DISEASES: gray mold
Dry, brown patches	CULTURAL PROBLEMS: cold
Excrement around holes	PESTS: squash vine borers
Gnawed stem bases	PESTS: cutworms
Honeydew, sooty mold	PESTS: scales
Longitudinal brown stripes	DISEASES: verticillium wilt
Mildew	DISEASES: fusarium wilt
Ooze	DISEASES: bacterial wilt
Small cankers	DISEASES: cytospora canker
Splitting	CULTURAL PROBLEMS: cold
Swellings	DISEASES: crown gall
White froth	PESTS: spittlebugs
Wilting	PESTS: nematodes, squash vine borers

TREE BARK, BRANCHES

MAJOR SYMPTOMS	POSSIBLE CAUSES
Broomlike growth	DISEASES: witches' broom
Cankers	DISEASES: bacterial canker, cytospora canker, fireblight

Galls	PESTS: gall midges, gall wasps, spruce gall adelgids DISEASES: cedar-apple rust, crown gall
Ooze	PESTS: borers DISEASES: bacterial canker, cytospora canker, fireblight, slime flux
Sawdust	PESTS: borers

MAJOR SYMPTOMS	POSSIBLE CAUSES

TREE BARK

Abnormally colored bark	DISEASES: crown and collar rot, fireblight CULTURAL PROBLEMS: sunscald
Chewed bark	PESTS: gophers, rabbits, squirrels, voles
Damaged tree base	CULTURAL PROBLEMS: mechanical injury (lawn mower, weed trimmer)
Holes	PESTS: bark beetles, borers DISEASES: Dutch elm disease
Mushrooms on tree crown	DISEASES: oak root fungus
Small brown or gray bumps	PESTS: scales, in particular oyster shell scale
Splitting bark	CULTURAL PROBLEMS: cold, lightning, sunscald
White growth on tree base	DISEASES: oak root fungus

MAJOR SYMPTOMS	POSSIBLE CAUSES

BRANCHES

Dead branches and twigs	PESTS: scales, weevils DISEASES: anthracnose CULTURAL PROBLEMS: lightning, physical injury (construction damage)
Deformed twigs	DISEASES: brown rot of stone fruit, fireblight, peach leaf curl
Limb breakage	DISEASES: cytospora canker, heart rot CULTURAL PROBLEMS: lightning, wind, winter snow load (see cold, winter injury)

LEAVES

MAJOR SYMPTOMS	POSSIBLE CAUSES

DISCOLORED OR WILTED LEAVES

Black or brown spots on leaves	DISEASES: anthracnose, bacterial leaf spot, black spot, cherry leaf spot, early blight, fusarium wilt, septoria leaf spot, strawberry leaf spot
Black or scorched leaves	PESTS: rose midges, squash bugs DISEASES: anthracnose, bacterial leaf spot, fireblight, peach leaf curl, viruses CULTURAL PROBLEMS: frost (see cold, winter injury), leaf scorch
Bleached leaves	CULTURAL PROBLEMS: excessive sunlight
Brown blotches on leaves	PESTS: lace bugs, leaf miners, nematodes, thrips DISEASES: anthracnose, downy mildew (upper surface), purple blotch CULTURAL PROBLEMS: sunscald
Brown leaves	DISEASES: shot hole CULTURAL PROBLEMS: cold, leaf scorch, mechanical injury
Brown tips and edges of leaves	PESTS: leafhoppers DISEASES: aster yellows, late blight CULTURAL PROBLEMS: leaf scorch, salt damage
Discolored leaves with small bumps	PESTS: scales
Dried or withered leaves	PESTS: spider mites DISEASES: downy mildew CULTURAL PROBLEMS: salt damage

MAJOR SYMPTOMS	POSSIBLE CAUSES
Fringed black or brown spots with yellow halos on leaves	DISEASES: black spot, septoria leaf spot
Gray areas on leaves	PESTS: thrips DISEASES: apple scab, late blight
Leaf drop	PESTS: blister mites DISEASES: anthracnose, apple scab, black spot, cherry leaf spot, Dutch elm disease, oak root fungus, slime flux
Mottled leaves	PESTS: leafhoppers, spider mites DISEASES: ringspot viruses, rose mosaic virus, verticillium wilt CULTURAL PROBLEMS: air pollution
Needle discoloration	DISEASES: cedar-apple rust, juniper twig blight, needle cast, Pacific Coast pear rust CULTURAL PROBLEMS: air pollution, inadequate watering
Pale green leaves	CULTURAL PROBLEMS: excessive watering, nitrogen deficiency (lower leaves)
Pale leaf veins	DISEASES: aster yellows
Purple spots on leaves	DISEASES: cherry leaf spot, shot hole
Red or purple leaves	DISEASES: black root rot complex, crown and collar rot, oak root fungus, peach leaf curl, strawberry leaf spot
Red, orange, or yellow spots on leaves	DISEASES: apple scab, bacterial leaf spot, downy mildew (colored spots on upper side, mildew underneath), fusarium wilt, needle cast, rusts
Scabby, black irregular patches on leaves	DISEASES: apple scab
Silvery leaves	PESTS: thrips (if black dots are present) DISEASES: peach leaf curl CULTURAL PROBLEMS: air pollution
Tan or white specks on leaves	PESTS: lace bugs, leafhoppers CULTURAL PROBLEMS: air pollution
Tiny dark spots on leaves	PESTS: leafhoppers, spider mites, thrips
Velvety spots on leaves	DISEASES: apple scab, black spot
White leaves	DISEASES: powdery mildew CULTURAL PROBLEMS: frost (see cold, winter injury)
Wilting leaves	PESTS: ants, borers, sawfly larvae, squash bugs, squash vine borers DISEASES: bacterial wilt, brown rot, club root, crown and collar rot, Dutch elm disease, fusarium wilt, oak root fungus, pythium root rot, rhizoctonia root and stem rot, verticillium wilt CULTURAL PROBLEMS: excessive watering, fertilizer burn, inadequate watering, leaf scorch, transplant failure
Yellowing leaves	PESTS: aphids, leafhoppers, nematodes, psyllids, scales, spider mites, whiteflies DISEASES: anthracnose, apple scab, aster yellows, bacterial wilt, black root rot, black spot, cherry leaf spot, club root, downy mildew, fusarium wilt, oak root fungus, peach leaf curl, powdery mildew, pythium root rot, rhizoctonia root and stem rot, ringspot viruses, sclerotium root rot, slime flux, verticillium wilt CULTURAL PROBLEMS: alkaline soils, excessive watering, inadequate watering, iron deficiency, leaf scorch, mechanical injury, nitrogen deficiency, salt damage, transplant failure
Yellow leaves with green spots or veins	DISEASES: downy mildew, verticillium wilt CULTURAL PROBLEMS: iron deficiency

EATEN LEAVES

MAJOR SYMPTOMS	POSSIBLE CAUSES
Yellow spots on leaves	PESTS: aphids, lace bugs, spider mites DISEASES: bacterial leaf spot, fusarium wilt, powdery mildew
Defoliation	PESTS: asparagus beetles, grasshoppers, gypsy moths, leaf rollers, mites, sawfly larvae, tussock moths CULTURAL PROBLEMS: inadequate watering
Large, ragged holes in leaves	PESTS: armyworms, birds, cabbage loopers (cabbageworms), cankerworms (see omnivorous loopers and inchworms), cutworms, fall webworms, grasshoppers, hornworms, Japanese beetles, Mexican bean beetles, oak moth larvae, (slime trail) slugs, (slime trail) snails, weevils DISEASES: bacterial leaf spot
Notched leaves	PESTS: leaf-cutting bees, weevils
Ragged edges of leaves	PESTS: earwigs, striped cucumber beetles
Round or angular holes in leaves	PESTS: striped cucumber beetles DISEASES: bacterial canker, bacterial leaf spot, cherry leaf spot, crown and collar rot, ringspot viruses, shot hole CULTURAL PROBLEMS: mechanical injury
Skeletonized leaves	PESTS: cabbage loopers (cabbageworms), Colorado potato beetles, elm leaf beetles, hornworms, leaf rollers, leaf skeletonizers, Mexican bean beetles, omnivorous loopers, pear slugs, sawfly larvae, slugs, snails, tent caterpillars, tussock moth caterpillars
Tiny puncture holes in leaves	PESTS: flea beetles, red spider mites
Torn leaves	CULTURAL PROBLEMS: wind

GROWTH ON LEAVES

MAJOR SYMPTOMS	POSSIBLE CAUSES
Froth on leaves	PESTS: spittlebugs
Gray or black mold or fungus on leaves	DISEASES: downy mildew, gray mold, late blight, peach leaf curl, sooty mold
Small galls on leaves	PESTS: gall mites, psyllids DISEASES: cedar-apple rust (on cedar and juniper needles), edema (lower leaf surfaces)
Sticky leaves	PESTS: aphids, leafhoppers, mealybugs, psyllids, scale, whiteflies
Tan or white bumps on leaves	PESTS: scales, in particular oyster shell scale
Watery blisters on leaves	DISEASES: anthracnose, bacterial leaf spot, edema (lower leaf surfaces), gray mold
Webs on leaves	PESTS: leaf rollers, spider mites, spruce budworms, tent caterpillars (large web nests)
White cottony mass on leaves	PESTS: mealybugs
White powder or mold on leaves	DISEASES: downy mildew (underside), late blight (underside), powdery mildew
Winding trails in leaves	PESTS: vegetable leaf miners, western tentiform leaf miners
Yellow, orange, or red blisters on leaves	PESTS: blister mites DISEASES: peach leaf curl, rusts

MALFORMED LEAVES

MAJOR SYMPTOMS	POSSIBLE CAUSES
Curled or rolled leaves	PESTS: apple aphids, leaf rollers, leaf skeletonizers, psyllids, thrips, weevils CULTURAL PROBLEMS: air pollution, leaf scorch
Distorted leaves	PESTS: aphids, gall midges, gall mites, leafhoppers, mealybugs, nematodes, psyllids, scale, webworms DISEASES: apple scab, aster yellows, downy mildew, edema, fireblight, mosaic virus, peach leaf curl, powdery mildew, ringspot viruses CULTURAL PROBLEMS: cold, iron or nitrogen deficiency, irregular water supply (see inadequate watering), leaf scorch
Small leaves	PESTS: nematodes DISEASES: root rots CULTURAL PROBLEMS: nitrogen deficiency

LAWNS

MAJOR SYMPTOMS	POSSIBLE CAUSES
Blackened roots	DISEASES: necrotic ringspot
Brown patches that lift up easily	PESTS: white grubs (scarab beetle larvae)
Curled blades	DISEASES: stripe smut
Dead blades	PESTS: white grubs (scarab beetle larvae), wireworms
Dead circles or arcs	PESTS: armyworms, pearl scale, sod webworms DISEASES: dollar spot, necrotic ringspot, patch disease, red thread CULTURAL PROBLEMS: dog urine, fertilizer burn or pesticide burn (see lawns with dead patches), inadequate watering, lawn scalping
Dead circles surrounded by dark green rings	DISEASES: fairy ring, patch disease CULTURAL PROBLEMS: fertilizer burn (see lawns with dead patches)
Discolored areas	PESTS: leafhoppers DISEASES: patch disease, pink snow mold, pythium blight, red thread, septoria leaf spot, slime mold
Discolored blades	PESTS: mites DISEASES: dollar spot, gray snow mold, septoria leaf spot
Disfigured lawn	PESTS: ants, gophers, moles, raccoons, skunks
Froth on blades	PESTS: spittlebugs
Mushrooms	DISEASES: fairy ring, oak root fungus (around tree base)
Pale green blades	DISEASES: stripe smut CULTURAL PROBLEMS: excessive watering, nitrogen deficiency
Ragged blades	CULTURAL PROBLEMS: lawn scalping, mechanical injury
Seedling failure	PESTS: armyworms, birds, cutworms, grasshoppers, millipedes, root maggots, slugs, snails, springtails, voles, wireworms DISEASES: damping off CULTURAL PROBLEMS: excessive watering, inadequate watering, transplant failure
Split blades	DISEASES: Stripe smut
Thinning lawn	CULTURAL PROBLEMS: iron deficiency, nitrogen deficiency, thatch, too much shade
Webbing and threads	PESTS: sod webworms DISEASES: dollar spot, pythium blight

BULB PLANTS

BULBS

MAJOR SYMPTOMS	POSSIBLE CAUSES
Yellow blades	DISEASES: edema, pythium blight, stripe smut
Bulbs fail to grow	PESTS: Japanese beetles, mites DISEASES: mosaic viruses CULTURAL PROBLEMS: excessive watering, inadequate watering
Decaying bulbs	PESTS: mites, nematodes DISEASES: bacterial soft rot, fusarium bulb rot CULTURAL PROBLEMS: excessive watering
Eaten bulbs	PESTS: gophers, mice, voles, other ground-dwelling animals
Holes	PESTS: borers, millipedes
Ooze	DISEASES: bacterial soft rot
White fungus	DISEASES: crown gall, fusarium bulb rot

LEAVES

MAJOR SYMPTOMS	POSSIBLE CAUSES
Black or brown spots	PESTS: nematodes, thrips DISEASES: bacterial leaf spot
Browning leaves	PESTS: aphids, leafhoppers
Chewed edges	PESTS: caterpillars, slugs, snails
Distorted leaves	PESTS: aphids, leaf rollers, mites, nematodes DISEASES: viruses
Holes	PESTS: caterpillars, Japanese beetles, slugs, snails, spotted cucumber beetles, weevils
Rust-colored pustules	DISEASES: rusts
White powder	DISEASES: powdery mildew
Wilting leaves	PESTS: borers DISEASES: bacterial wilt
Yellowing leaves	PESTS: aphids, borers, leafhoppers, mites, nematodes DISEASES: bacterial soft rot, fusarium bulb rot, mosaic viruses

FLOWERS

MAJOR SYMPTOMS	POSSIBLE CAUSES
Blossom rot	PESTS: borers DISEASES: gray mold
Bud drop	CULTURAL PROBLEMS: excessive watering, inadequate watering
Deformed blossoms	PESTS: nematodes DISEASES: aster yellows, crown rot
Holes in blossoms	PESTS: beetles, weevils
No blossoms	PESTS: mites, nematodes
White or brown stripes on blossoms	PESTS: thrips

FLOWERS

MAJOR SYMPTOMS	POSSIBLE CAUSES
Bleached blossoms	CULTURAL PROBLEMS: sunscald
Brown or black buds	PESTS: psyllids, rose midges
Brown spots on petals	DISEASES: camellia flower and petal blight
Browning blossoms	PESTS: thrips DISEASES: camellia flower and petal blight, fireblight
Damaged buds	PESTS: spotted cucumber beetles
Discolored blossoms	PESTS: thrips DISEASES: aster yellows, viruses
Distorted blossoms	DISEASES: aster yellows, mosaic viruses
Few or no blossoms	PESTS: budworms DISEASES: aster yellows, bacterial leaf spot CULTURAL PROBLEMS: inadequate watering, nitrogen deficiency, too much shade
Gray mold on blossoms	DISEASES: gray mold
Holes chewed in petals	PESTS: curculios, earwigs, grasshoppers, Japanese beetles, slugs, snails, spotted cucumber beetles
Lush foliage, small blossoms	CULTURAL PROBLEMS: too much nitrogen (see nitrogen deficiency), too much shade
Partially opened buds	PESTS: thrips
Seedling failure	PESTS: armyworms, birds, cutworms, flea beetles, grasshoppers, millipedes, root maggots, springtails, voles, wireworms DISEASES: damping off CULTURAL PROBLEMS: excessive watering, inadequate watering, transplant failure
Shriveled blossoms	DISEASES: brown rot of stone fruit CULTURAL PROBLEMS: inadequate watering
Small blossoms	PESTS: lace bugs CULTURAL PROBLEMS: inadequate watering, nitrogen deficiency

FRUITS, VEGETABLES

FRUITS

MAJOR SYMPTOMS	POSSIBLE CAUSES
Blackened fruit	DISEASES: fireblight
Brown spots	DISEASES: anthracnose, apple scab, bacterial leaf spot
Browning	PESTS: fruit flies DISEASES: brown rot of stone fruit, cedar-apple rust, shot hole CULTURAL PROBLEMS: blossom-end rot
Cracking	DISEASES: apple scab, bacterial leaf spot, peach leaf curl CULTURAL PROBLEMS: excessive watering, irregular watering (inadequate watering)
Crescent-shaped scars	PESTS: plum curculios
Decreased fruit crop	DISEASES: black root rot complex, peach leaf curl, red stele, ringspot viruses CULTURAL PROBLEMS: blossom drop, hardpan, inadequate watering, nitrogen deficiency
Disappearing fruit	PESTS: mice, opossums, raccoons, squirrels
Distorted fruit	PESTS: apple maggots, codling moths, sawflies, thrips DISEASES: apple scab, bacterial leaf spot, peach leaf curl, viruses CULTURAL PROBLEMS: irregular watering (inadequate watering)
Dried-out and shriveled fruit	DISEASES: bacterial wilt, brown rot of stone fruit

VEGETABLES

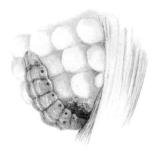

MAJOR SYMPTOMS	POSSIBLE CAUSES
Black spots with yellow halos on leaves	DISEASES: bacterial leaf spot
Corn ear galls	DISEASES: corn smut
Dark brown or black spots on leaves	DISEASES: early blight, late blight
Defoliation	PESTS: grasshoppers, hornworms, Japanese beetles, parsleyworms
Discolored leaves	PESTS: carrot rust flies DISEASES: aster yellows, club root, purple blotch, white mold
Discolored lesions on vegetables	DISEASES: early blight, (with odor) late blight
Distorted roots	PESTS: carrot rust flies DISEASES: aster yellows
Leaf holes	PESTS: cabbageworms, cucumber beetles, grasshoppers
Malformed vegetables	PESTS: blister mites, corn earworms, cucumber beetles DISEASES: aster yellows, potato scab
Nodules on root	PESTS: root knot nematodes
Ooze in roots	DISEASES: bacterial soft rot
Orange bumps on leaves	DISEASES: rusts
Plant wilting	PESTS: squash vine borers, wireworms DISEASES: bacterial wilt (sudden), club root (gradual), white mold CULTURAL PROBLEMS: inadequate watering
Small leaf galls	DISEASES: edema (lower leaf surface)
Tunnels in vegetables	PESTS: carrot rust flies, codling moths, corn earworms, wireworms
Water-soaked leaf spots	DISEASES: anthracnose, bacterial leaf spot, edema (lower leaf surfaces), purple blotch

MAJOR SYMPTOMS	POSSIBLE CAUSES
Fruit drop	PESTS: codling moths, fruit flies, leaf rollers, mealybugs, nematodes, sawflies DISEASES: anthracnose, apple scab, bacterial wilt, brown rot of stone fruit, peach leaf curl, powdery mildew CULTURAL PROBLEMS: inadequate watering, too hot, too little fertilizer (see fruit drop)
Irregular or scabby fruit skin	PESTS: thrips DISEASES: apple scab, potato scab, shot hole
Orange spots	DISEASES: rusts, including cedar-apple rust
Partially eaten fruit	PESTS: birds, cutworms, mice, opossums, raccoons, slugs, snails
Soggy areas	DISEASES: brown rot of stone fruit CULTURAL PROBLEMS: blossom-end rot
Tunnels and holes	PESTS: codling moths, cucumber beetles, curculios, earwigs, fruit fly maggots, leaf rollers, sawflies, wasps, wireworms
Undersize fruit	PESTS: whiteflies DISEASES: apple scab, powdery mildew, strawberry leaf spot, verticillium wilt, viruses CULTURAL PROBLEMS: irregular watering (inadequate watering), pollination problems (see blossom drop)
White or gray fuzzy growth	DISEASES: gray mold, powdery mildew
Wormy fruit	PESTS: apple maggots (see fruit flies), codling moths, oriental fruit moths, peach twig girdler borers

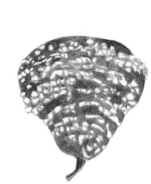

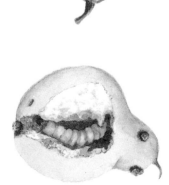

Encyclopedia of
DAMAGING AND
BENEFICIAL CREATURES

*H*ealthy landscapes support an amazing variety of life—not just plant life, but animals, including insects and creatures too small to see without a microscope. This chapter's photographs and descriptions help you identify more than 100 creatures that may appear in your garden—animals both helpful and harmful, from minuscule nematodes to deer the height of your fence. The pages that follow describe insects and their relatives; see pages 204–207 for animal pests.

Perfect gardens exist only in dreams. All landscapes have insects and animals that may be obstacles to your gardening goals. But while some are downright pests, other creatures are benign or even helpful to a garden.

Wise gardeners don't reach for the insecticide spray at the first nick on a leaf. They learn to positively identify the enemy first, a feat that may require some detective work. Sowbugs and pillbugs, for instance, often get blamed for eating holes in strawberries. In fact, these insects are just not very good at hiding; the gardener discovers them in daylight, innocently curled up in holes made by night creatures. Lifting a rock or a handful of mulch around your strawberry plants, you may discover the true culprit—a slug or snail—and then you can take action.

IDENTIFYING INSECT PESTS

The way to tell if a bug is "good" or "bad" is by observation. Get to know the plants in your landscape and look for damage. It often shows up first as torn, chewed, spotty, stippled, or twisted leaves; turn a leaf upside down and you may find the enemy. Other favorite hiding places are in cracks on tree bark or in the nodes or axils between branches and leaf petioles. Examine the creature closely, possibly with a magnifying glass. Then consult the following pages to identify it. Once you know what you're dealing with, you can consider the appropriate treatment.

INSECT LIFE CYCLES

The encyclopedia entries describe the life cycles of insect pests and suggest preventive measures that take these life cycles into account. For example, the wormy larvae that infest orchard fruits often spend the next phase of their life cycle on the ground. If you simply clear the ground beneath your fruit trees each autumn, you can significantly reduce infestations of codling moth and other fruit tree pests.

Insects grow through a process called metamorphosis: their form changes as they mature. Almost all begin life as an egg. The egg hatches into an immature insect called a larva, which grows by molting its rigid external skeleton. When this exoskeleton gets too tight, it splits open and the insect crawls out wearing its new shell. In *simple metamorphosis*, or incomplete metamorphosis, larvae, called nymphs, resemble small versions of the adult insects. They develop as they molt, growing wings and displaying other modifications such as new colors.

In *complete metamorphosis*, the young insect is a wormlike creature that does not resemble the adult. Moth and butterfly larvae are called caterpillars, beetle larvae are grubs, and fly larvae are maggots. Aggressive feeders, they do the most damage at this larval stage. When ready to mature, the insect pupates—that is, it encases itself in a protective shell, such as a chrysalis or cocoon. A pupating insect is called a pupa. After a dramatic transformation inside its casing, the insect emerges as an adult.

Insect development may be lengthy or fleeting: giant palm borers may remain in the grub stage for years, while fruit flies pass through their entire life cycle in just days.

Most insects have weak stages during which they're most vulnerable. As pupae, many insects are immobile and may be hand-picked or raked away. Hard-bodied bugs may resist some sprays as adults but are more easily killed as younger nymphs.

If you have annual or recurring problems with a certain pest, knowing its life cycle can help you choose the most effective time to attack it. Efficient, targeted spraying, when combined with preventive strategies over the course of a growing season, can help "break the cycle" of many recurring pests in your garden.

Creatures you may find in your western garden include (clockwise from top left) the western grape leaf skeletonizer; the damsel bug (a beneficial), the oak borer adult (a clearwing moth), and the California ground squirrel. The imported cabbageworm adult is shown at the top of this page.

Insect Larvae, in Various Guises

The larvae of three common groups of garden pests have distinctive forms, each with its own name. The caterpillar (left) is the larval form of moths and butterflies. The grub (below, left) indicates beetles are on the way. The maggot (right), which is legless, is the larva of a fly. Insects are generally most destructive to gardens during the larval stage of their life cycles.

Life History of an Insect

Squash bugs go through simple metamorphosis, hatching from eggs (inset, left), then molting through nymph stages until they attain wings and adult size (above). California oak moths also hatch from eggs (above, right), but they make a complete metamorphosis. Following the caterpillar stage, during which they cause the most damage by eating the leaves of oak trees (right), they form a pupa (below, right). After pupating, they emerge as adult oak moths (inset, right).

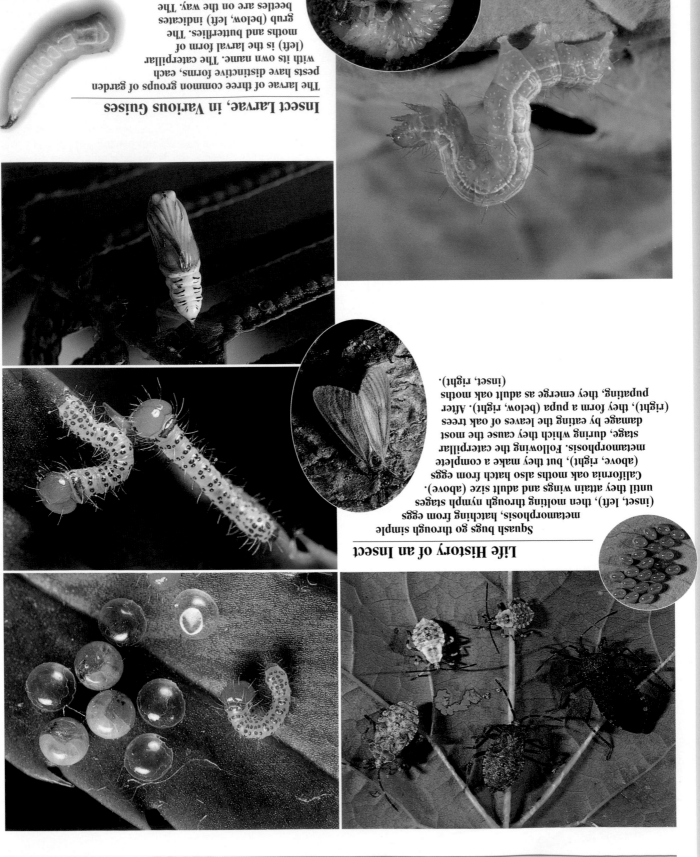

PREVENTING INSECT DAMAGE

The modern method for dealing with unwelcome garden guests is called Integrated Pest Management, or IPM (see "Solving Garden Problems," pages 27–71). IPM uses an assortment of strategies to manage harmful insects, from simple physical acts (such as hand-picking caterpillars off tomato plants) to an arsenal of pesticide sprays that are either botanically derived or chemically manufactured. An important goal of IPM is to use the least toxic and simplest method first, and only escalate to more stringent treatments if the severity of the problem warrants it.

In the flower garden, being alert to the first few pests and taking action can prevent a population explosion later. Good garden practices, such as weeding and wise watering, can help plants withstand minor attacks of sucking insects. A fertilizing schedule will help plants grow new leaves to replace foliage lost to chewing pests. Keeping landscape trees healthy and well irrigated is especially important, since many bark-boring beetles and moths are attracted to stressed trees.

Rotating crops in your vegetable beds can help reduce the numbers of the nematodes and soil-dwelling maggots that attack roots. Crop rotation deprives the second insect generation of the host plants it feeds on.

Integrated Pest Management accepts some loss. Wise gardeners learn to live with small depredations but are prepared to battle potentially big problems, especially those that, left unchecked, can kill valuable plants or ruin entire harvests.

PHYSICAL MANAGEMENT METHODS

For certain food crops, routine chores may include erecting barriers to keep pests away. Lightweight floating row covers, made from porous spun fibers that let in sunlight and rainwater, protect vegetables from flying pests such as whiteflies and cucumber beetles. Row covers work best when plants are young and small; remove them when flowers appear so that pollinating insects can find the blossoms. Other garden barriers include

- Mesh netting to keep birds from pecking fruits
- Copper stripping to deter slugs and snails (see page 189)
- Wire mesh or hardware cloth to wrap around tree trunks as protection from gnawing animals, and to place beneath raised beds and bulb plantings to deter moles and gophers
- Sticky tree-wraps to thwart tree-climbing pests, such as ants, bark beetles, and flightless moths
- Fencing to protect planting areas or the entire yard from deer, raccoons, and other troublesome animals

BIOLOGICAL MANAGEMENT TOOLS

Developed within the last century, biological controls have moved from agricultural applications to products the backyard gardener can readily buy and use.

Bacillus thuringiensis. A microbial insecticide applied in the form of a dust or spray, BT kills caterpillars and insect larvae but does not harm humans, other animals, birds, or treated plants. However, it is deadly to all caterpillars, including the larval forms of butterflies. If you want butterflies in your garden, use BT only on infested plants. The specialized strains of BT can kill Colorado potato beetles and elm leaf beetles. These helpful bacteria do not reproduce in a garden environment; to be effective, BT must be reapplied several times during the growing season.

Predatory and parasitoid insects. The larvae of tachinid flies are predators against soft-bodied insect pests. Tiny parasitoid wasps

are an efficient killer of the leaf-chewing larvae hardest to reach in the uppermost branches of backyard trees. Ladybug larvae, which look like small, crawly alligators, consume far more aphid pests than adult ladybugs do.

Don't expect beneficial insects to wipe out a pest population immediately or completely. When the pest population shrinks, beneficials starve or disperse to find other prey. Gardeners must tolerate a few insect pests to serve as a food source for new generations of beneficial insects.

If you release or encourage beneficial insects, you must refrain from using pesticide sprays or dusts that will kill them. You can apply a pesticide first, to reduce pest populations, before you try releasing beneficials. If you do, use selective pesticides that will kill only a narrow range of insect species, or use one that breaks down quickly and leaves no residue to harm beneficials.

Sticky traps. Traps make good controls for some flying insects, such as whiteflies, and are useful for monitoring populations of other pest insects, such as the codling moth in its flying adult stage.

Biological controls work only during certain parts of a pest insect's life cycle: for example, there's no point in spraying BT on adult moths; they will not ingest the microbe as caterpillars do. Releases of predators and parasitoids will be more cost-effective if they are timed to the proper season and target pest insects at vulnerable stages of their life cycles.

PESTICIDES

Insecticides work in many ways: they can kill insects outright or poison them when they feed on garden plants. Faster-acting insecticides (sometimes called knockdown insecticides) must come into physical contact with the pests, in order to stun or kill the insects by paralyzing them and penetrating their exoskeletons. Stomach poisons—including foliage sprays or dusts and systemic insecticides

Good Bug or Bad Bug?

Encountering this bug on a rosebush, you might assume it is a pest. But, in fact, it is the larva of the ladybug, a useful garden ally. These small creatures consume many more aphids than adult ladybugs do.

that are absorbed by the plant into all its tissue—become effective when sucking or chewing insects ingest them.

Botanical insecticides. Some of the oldest pesticides—such as pyrethrum, ryania, sabadilla, rotenone, and neem—are botanically derived. These still-effective killers are made from crude plant materials ground into a dust or wettable powder and mixed with water and sprayed. Pyrethrum and its more concentrated form, pyrethrin, are highly toxic to insects. Rotenone, ryania, and sabadilla are poisons that are sprayed or dusted onto leaves; after eating them, insects soon die or get too sick to feed. The toxins of botanical insecticides can also be harmful to bees, fish, and water sources. They can irritate human skin and mucous membranes, so use gloves and masks when applying them.

Neem is derived from the bark of a tree native to India, *Azadirachta indica,* and is not known to be toxic to birds, fish, animals, or humans. It disrupts the reproductive cycle of many insects. In the United States neem is labeled for use on ornamental plants and some vegetables.

Insecticidal soap sprays. Made from the concentrated mineral salts of fatty acids, these are most effective as a treatment against soft-bodied pests or bugs in their more vulnerable, immature nymph stages. Soap sprays are not effective against mites, scales, beetles, and bugs with hard body coverings, but they may injure or kill soft-bodied, flightless larvae.

Oils. These products kill insects, mites, and overwintering insect eggs and cocoons by smothering or breaking down their external membranes. Oil sprays are usually applied during winter, to destroy pests overwintering on tree bark. Lighter oils, also called summer oils, can be used in other seasons to kill mites and insects on citrus and other evergreens. Since all oils will magnify sunlight and can burn plant foliage, don't use them if the daytime temperature is expected to exceed 90°F.

Sulfur dusts and diatomaceous earth. These pesticides kill soft-bodied insects by irritating or piercing their exoskeletons so the insects dehydrate and die. In western gardens, diatomaceous earth is an effective barrier against snails and slugs. To be most effective, sulfur dusts should be reapplied after rain or irrigation. The sharp dust may irritate your eyes or lungs; wear protective goggles and a breathing mask when applying mineral products.

Synthetic pesticides. Synthetic products can be safe and highly effective when they are used properly, not as broad-spectrum palliatives but as tools targeted to specific insect pests. When you purchase any pesticide, read the label carefully. It will tell exactly which insect pests it works against (many chemical insecticides do not work against mites, since mites are not insects but arachnids). Chemicals recently labeled for home use include permethrin, a synthetic pyrethroid, and synthetic pheromone lures.

The following synthetics are among the most commonly used now in the West.

Diazinon and carbaryl. These pesticides kill on contact and are effective on many sucking insects as well as on chewing insect pests. They are moderately toxic to humans. Diazinon and carbaryl are generally recommended for ornamental trees and shrubs. Car-

---

PESTICIDES: HANDLE WITH CARE

Care should be taken whenever you use pesticides, particularly near edible crops. Be sure to read the labels on any product you bring into your garden and use it only as its label directs—it's against the law to do otherwise. Pesticide registrations change rapidly, and some products mentioned in this book may be removed from the lists of approved products or their label directions may be changed over time, as additional research becomes available. If you have questions concerning current regulations, consult your local nursery or cooperative extension office.

---

baryl also kills many beneficial insects, particularly beneficials that prey on mites. Spider mite infestations often occur after carbaryl is used, though modern product formulations may include a miticide to kill the mites as well. A single, well-timed application of carbaryl or diazinon may efficiently solve severe infestations of pests on ornamentals. Avoid frequent use where their runoff could contaminate nearby ponds, streams, creeks, or other waterways.

Malathion. This contact insecticide is highly toxic to both soft-bodied insects and harder-shelled beetles and bugs. Because it breaks down one to three days after application, it is less damaging to beneficial creatures than other insecticides are and may be used successfully as a targeted spray on infested plants. Among modern synthetics, malathion is about as dangerous to humans as pyrethrin is, but it is less toxic than rotenone. However, malathion can cause tissue damage to humans if it is absorbed through the skin, so wearing gloves, a breathing mask, goggles, and long clothing when applying it is recommended.

Acephate. A systemic insecticide that is absorbed through plant tissues, acephate effectively poisons many sucking and chewing insects, but it will also affect bees and beneficial insects that feed on nectar and pollen. Acephate and other systemics should not be used on food crops, only on ornamental landscape plants.

In the past, homeowners often looked for a one-size-fits-all spray that they could use to blanket their yards and kill everything that crawled. Today's gardener looks for pesticides that target specific problems, mitigate harm to beneficial creatures, and maintain a healthy landscape of varied insect life.

GETTING HELP

As a home gardener, you are not alone in your efforts to manage the pests that populate your landscape. Aid is as close as your local nursery, where qualified landscape professionals can often diagnose damage and recommend remedies. A nearby botanical or public garden may also offer a "plant doctor clinic" and problem-solving help.

One of the best sources of updated information on garden pest management is your local cooperative extension office (see page 50). Cooperative extension agents have on hand the latest research. Their offices may have free or inexpensive pamphlets; many offer a walk-in free service to identify pests and puzzling insects. Look for cooperative extension offices in the county government section of your phone book, under "Agriculture."

If you need help with pest control, choose the firm or individual with the best training, not just the best price. Modern landscape pest control professionals are trained in colleges and in certification programs administered by state agencies. Anyone who works on your property should be licensed and bonded and carry workers' compensation insurance. Find a firm that agrees with your attitudes about limiting toxicity. Establish a working relationship with a gardening professional who can be a partner in your effort to maintain a healthy home landscape.

ANTS

Soil pests, Leaf pests

⚡ Zones: All

 ost species of ants live in organized colonies in the soil, under rocks or trees, or in the crevices between paving stones. They are generally tiny—the largest species are just under an inch long—but all have six legs and elbowed antennae. Adult ants are winged during mating season and can be distinguished from termites by their narrow "waists" between body parts. In the garden, ants encourage and protect sap-sucking insects such as aphids, which produce honeydew, a sugary sap that ants like to eat. Honeydew-feeding ants can be identified by their swollen and somewhat transparent abdomens; columns of such ants marching up and down a tree trunk usually indicate an infestation by sap feeders as well. The small brown ant that often infests kitchens is the Argentine ant, a nonnative species that has supplanted some indigenous ant colonies in western cities.

Target: Anything sweet or greasy, such as honeydew, dropped fruits, or food scraps, attracts ants.

Damage: Ants may be tolerated in flower and vegetable gardens, since their tunnels help aerate soil, providing room for earthworms and roots and reversing the effects of soil compaction. On plants, they may only be eating nectar, as shown above. In lawns, the small mounds of soil they build can mar the look of your turf. Most ants do not eat vegetation; fire ants can shear ground covers, annuals, perennials, flowering bulbs, vegetables, and roses to ragged edges (see Notes). Ants on opening peony buds actually help the blossoms to open more fully, so they should not be discouraged. But ants encourage sucking insects and may also carry a pathogen from stalk to stalk on corn. In rainy seasons, Argentine ants often invade houses if their nests are submerged. Leaf-cutter ants are sometimes a problem in the Southwest.

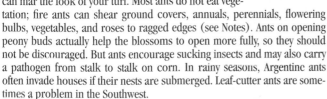

Fire ant with aphids

Life cycle: Winged males and females (queens) appear about once a year. After mating, the males die and the females lose their wings. Each female creates a nest and lays large numbers of eggs that turn into worker ants. The size of a colony can be many thousands, with several adult females in separate chambers. Populations swell during summer and fall, with some members migrating to form new colonies. Colonies overwinter in soil or garden debris or, sometimes, in houses.

Prevention: Monitor and manage populations of honeydew-producing insects such as aphids and whiteflies. Keep dining areas free of food scraps, especially in summer. Placing household ant traps near rows of developing corn may prevent the transmission of corn diseases by crawling ants.

Management: A variety of baited ant traps sold for indoor home use will keep down ant populations in the garden. To make your own, mix powdered boric acid (available in drugstores) with apple jelly. Boric acid is a stomach poison that ants will carry back to their colony and feed upon, then they will die. Boric acid is safe to use around food plants and is not toxic in small amounts, but if children or pets are a concern, put the bait in a covered, perforated container—for example, a flowerpot saucer, covered by an overturned pot. Place the traps on the soil surface near the plants (such as roses) most likely to be targeted by honeydew producers and also near your corn crop. Effective insecticide baits include both boric acid and avermectin, which prevents the queen ant from laying eggs, causing the colony to die out. Insecticides containing pyrethrin, diazinon, and carbaryl can be sprayed to kill large ant infestations around patios. When applying insecticide, always follow directions on the label.

✎ *Notes: Fire ants, common only in the southwestern states, are smaller than Argentine ants. These foliage eaters build hard mounds of soil up to 2 feet tall, shown above, right, and inflict painful stings when protecting their nests.*

There are two important species of fire ants, native and imported. The imported fire ant, native to Central America, has recently become a pest in Texas and Baja California. This aggressive, stinging ant is not easily controlled by pesticide sprays; consult your local cooperative extension office for the latest recommendations. In most cases, you will probably want to contact a pest control professional to get rid of these harmful insects.

The native species of fire ants is not aggressive and may be tolerated if the mounds are not near gardens, lawns, or homes. Commercial baited traps are effective on them. A southwestern home remedy considered effective enough to be recommended by cooperative extension agencies in Arizona is a mixture of fresh orange peels and water, whirled in a blender until it is the consistency of a thick syrup. This is poured into the center of the mound during the hottest part of a summer afternoon, so that volatile oils from the citrus peel may "gas" the underground chambers. The mound must be completely covered with the syrup, with as much as possible poured into the entrance hole.

APHIDS

LEAF AND STEM PESTS

✎ ZONES: ALL

Aphids (or aphides) are slow-moving, soft-bodied sucking insects that usually appear in clusters on the new growth of roses, perennials, and larger woody plants. More than 1,300 native species of aphids inhabit North America. They come in a wide range of colors, from black to pink to white and pale green, and measure $\frac{1}{16}$–$\frac{1}{4}$ inch long. Aphids are pear-shaped and usually wingless, with two tubes, called cornicles, at the posterior end. Woolly aphids, which are found on trees, are distinguished by white, wool-like tufts that grow on their backs. Large numbers of the woolly apple aphid on apple trees create the appearance of a cottony, waxy covering on the branches. Woolly apple aphids are shown above, right.

Target: Aphids feed on a wide variety of garden plants and on trees such as birch, cedar, linden, and maple. Woolly aphids are particular pests of apple, cotoneaster, and pyracantha. In warm-winter climates, cotton and green peach aphids feed on new growth of camellia and flowering plum. Black aphid is a common pest of artichoke plants and beans.

Damage: Although aphids in small numbers do little damage, they reproduce rapidly, so they should never be ignored. Both adults and immature nymphs damage plants by piercing the leaves and stems and sucking out sap and plant fluids. This weakens the plants and may leave them wilted, discolored, and stunted. Roses and other flowers will bloom poorly; artichoke buds may fail to develop or become deformed. Broad-leafed foliage may appear stippled or yellowed; the needles of heavily infested evergreens may grow out twisted and fall off. Any undigested sugars from the plant juices are excreted by aphids as honeydew, a sticky clear substance that attracts ants and also attracts an airborne fungus, sooty mold (see page 238). Dripping down from affected trees, honeydew and sooty mold can dirty cars, garden furniture, and paving. Some aphid species transmit viral diseases from plant to plant. On apple trees, the woolly apple aphid causes woody swellings on branch tips.

Life cycle: In cold-winter climates, aphids hatch from eggs at the end of May or June. Although the reproductive biology varies with the species, a common pattern is for females to give birth to live nymphs, with new generations appearing every two weeks until the fall. Literally born pregnant, the nymphs are able to reproduce without mating within a week of birth. As they grow, they molt, leaving cast-off transparent skins on leaves. Some nymphs mature to a winged form to lay the eggs that overwinter in the bark of trees. In warm-winter climates, some species of aphids produce live young through the year.

Prevention: These ubiquitous insects can be expected to show up every year. A preventive routine is to destroy ant colonies in flower beds; ants often "farm" aphids in exchange for feeding off their sweet honeydew. Reflective aluminum mulches can deter flying adult aphids from laying eggs. Natural enemies to be encouraged or introduced into the garden include the larval or immature forms of ladybugs and lacewings, syrphid flies, soldier beetles, and parasitoid wasps.

Management: Aphids usually appear as the weather begins to warm; they will first be noticed on plant tips, near opening flower and leaf buds. Monitor rosebushes and other susceptible plants with yellow sticky traps in spring, then apply management techniques while the insects are few. Small and even large infestations can be simply washed off plants with a stiff jet of water. Cradle tender plant tips and rosebuds in your hand as you rinse the pests away. Sticky honeydew and black sooty mold can be washed off with a mild soap-and-water rinse. These two methods are especially recommended for aphid attacks on edible plants. Releasing predator insects such as ladybugs and lacewings can be effective in reducing aphid infestations in spring, when their natural predators may not be sufficiently abundant to keep aphid populations down. To encourage the adult forms of aphid-hunting insects, interplant vegetables with nectar plants, such as flowering herbs. Soft-bodied aphids can also be killed by spraying plants with insecticidal soap or with the botanical insecticide neem, or by dusting leaves and stems with diatomaceous earth. Take care to apply these treatments to the undersides of leaves. Severely infested annuals may not recover from an aphid attack; it is perhaps best to dig these out and dispose of them.

Aphids on trees may be harder to reach with sprays and dusts, although hosing down foliage can help reduce damage. A good management technique that reduces recurring infestations of the green peach aphid on ornamentals and the woolly apple aphid on apple trees is applying a dormant-oil spray to branches and tree trunks during winter, to destroy overwintering aphid eggs. Dormant-oil sprays may also be used on rosebushes when plants are dormant. To kill large infestations, spray with a knockdown insecticide containing pyrethrin, diazinon, malathion, or acephate, applied according to label directions. To avoid killing off beneficials, limit your use of these insecticides and spray only infested plants.

 Notes: To control aphids on rosebushes, an old-fashioned treatment that works for many gardeners is underplanting roses with edible garlic, whose pungent leaves appear to repel or confuse aphids. On rosebushes, you may use a systemic insecticide labeled for roses, applied according to label directions. Since this type of pesticide enters the plant tissue, systemics should not be used on edible crops or on roses you plan to harvest for edible flowers or rose hips.

ARMYWORMS

LEAF AND STEM PESTS, VEGETABLE PESTS

✂ ZONES: ALL

Armyworms are caterpillars named for their habit of marching in troops, devouring vegetation in their path. They feed only at night or on overcast days. Common in vegetable gardens are the beet armyworm, which is greenish black, striped, and spotted; the western yellow-striped armyworm, shown above, which is purplish black with two long yellow stripes; and the fall armyworm, which is shiny brown, marked with black spots and a white Y-shape on the back of its black head. Full-grown caterpillars may be 1–2 inches long. All are the larvae of blue moths.

Target: Armyworms attack vegetable crops, including bean, beet, cabbage, corn, cucumber, lettuce, spinach, and tomato. Some species eat lawn grass. The fall armyworm is a particular pest of corn foliage, though it rarely attacks the ears.

Damage: The foliage of vegetables may be chewed or skeletonized; tomatoes and beans, gouged or pitted. Lawns may look ragged; heavy infestations may leave brown, bare patches. The edges of corn foliage may be ragged.

Life cycle: The adult moth lays pea-size, fluffy gray egg masses midsummer through fall on grassy weeds such as pigweed or nettle. (The moth of the yellow-striped armyworm often lays its eggs on the stakes supporting tomato plants.) Larvae hatch out small and pale green; they feed lightly during the autumn. They burrow into the soil to overwinter, then reappear in the spring to feed more aggressively. They burrow again into the soil to pupate, emerging later as winged adults. There are from one to several generations per year.

Prevention: To keep armyworms away from your vegetable garden, get rid of grassy weeds that may harbor eggs. You can also dig a steep-sided, 6-inch-deep trench around your vegetable garden; the migrating troops of armyworms will march in but can't climb out.

Management: A natural enemy of the armyworm to be introduced or encouraged in the garden is the trichogramma wasp, which parasitizes caterpillars. The bacteria *Bacillus thuringiensis* (BT) is effective against only smaller caterpillars; larger armyworms can be hand-picked. Armyworms can also be managed by spraying the larvae or the foliage of affected plants with the botanical insecticide neem or with an insecticide containing carbaryl or, for ornamentals, acephate. Be sure to follow all directions on insecticide labels.

ASPARAGUS BEETLES

LEAF AND STEM PESTS

✂ ZONES: ALL

Western species of asparagus beetles are about ¼ inch long and blue black or brown, with an enlarged rear section that is mottled with yellow to tan to orange markings. They are found on or near asparagus plants, as are their grubs, which are olive green to gray, with a black head and black legs. The spotted asparagus beetle is shown above.

Target: The asparagus beetle and its larvae attack only asparagus, though other plants, such as ferns, may be hosts.

Damage: Asparagus beetles chew tender new spears of asparagus. The chewed part of the spear grows more slowly and twists, so that spears emerge crooked from the ground. Spears may also look distorted, chewed, or scarred, with most damage during the harvest period in early spring. Later in the season, adults and larvae chew on stems and the ferny leaves of asparagus plants.

Life cycle: Adults overwinter in plant debris, flying in to feed just as asparagus shoots begin to sprout from spring soil. Adult females lay dark eggs that protrude horizontally from spear tips. Within a week, grubs hatch, feeding on asparagus stalks and leaves. After a few weeks, they burrow into the ground to form yellow pupae. There are two or three generations per year.

Prevention: Clean up garden debris in asparagus beds in the fall to eliminate overwintering adult beetles. Use floating row covers over asparagus beds in the spring to keep eggs off the spears.

Management: In a small garden, the easiest method of managing these pests is to hand-pick adult beetles and larvae. Natural enemies include birds, ladybug larvae, and spined soldier bugs, which eat the beetle's larvae and eggs. Adult beetles may be easily washed off the edible spears of asparagus plants with a jet of water. You can also wash off beetles found later in the season on the foliage of asparagus plants, or you can kill them by spraying with an insecticide containing rotenone or malathion. Spraying insecticide onto emerging spears is not recommended, as the insecticide may distort the spears. Spraying shortly after the harvest period can help reduce large populations of asparagus beetles and their larvae. Be sure to follow insecticide directions.

ASSASSIN BUGS

BENEFICIALS

✎ ZONES: ALL

The assassin bug is a slim insect, often brilliant red or black, with a ½-inch-long body, long legs, and even longer angled antennae. It crawls quickly like a spider. Its spiderlike gait is a good way to distinguish the helpful assassin bug, which eats other insects, from similar-looking sucking bugs, such as the squash bug. Look closely and you may see the beak with which the bug stabs its victims—hence its name. The adult form of the assassin bug, shown above, eating a leafhopper, has shiny clear wings, but it rarely flies, preferring instead to crawl on plants or wait motionless on tree bark for its insect victims to pass by.

Target: Assassin bugs help the gardener by feeding on smaller insect species and many insect pests, including sawfly lar-vae, aphids, and mites.

Damage: Assassin bugs do have a slight negative effect on the garden in that they also feed on smaller harmless or benefi-cial insects. In addition, if they are acci-dentally disturbed, some species will sting humans.

Assassin bug nymph

Life cycle: Adult bugs meet and mate in garden foliage, then lay barrel-shaped eggs in rows on the leaves of landscape plants. These hatch into immature nymphs, which are smaller, darker, and wingless. The nymphs gradually attain wings as they reach their full size. There are one or more generations per year.

Prevention: None is needed.

Management: No management of this insect is required, but to prevent your killing these beneficial bugs accidentally, you should avoid spraying botanical or chemical insecticides in the garden to kill other insect pests. Or spray very precisely, attempting to target just the pest-infested plant or plant part. Assassin bugs are rarely introduced into gardens, since there are many existing species in western states—40 in California alone. If your garden lacks assassin bugs, limiting the use of garden insecticides can help repopulate it.

BARK BEETLES

BARK AND BRANCH PESTS

✎ ZONES: ALL

Bark beetles are dark, shiny, hard-shelled beetles about ¼ inch long, the size of a rice grain, that live on and between the bark plates of trees. Bark beetle species include the ips or engraver, western pine, cedar, and cypress beetles. The larval stage is a white legless grub, ¼ inch or less, some with a black head. Shown above is a female mountain pine beetle lay-ing eggs.

Target: Bark beetles attack arborvitae, cypress, elms, fir, Monterey and other pines, redwood, and occasionally cedar. Homing in on a scent given off by stressed trees, bark beetles will fly long distances to attack trees suf-fering from drought or disease.

Damage: Larvae chew tunnels in the green cambium under bark, disrupt-ing nutrient flow; branches and trunks may be girdled and die. Conifers may ooze pitch mixed with sawdust (the frass, or insect excrement, from the tunnels) through holes in their bark. On cedars, small twigs die first and hang down. Infested pines lose their green color from the top down; all foliage eventually turns brown and dies. The tree may die.

Life cycle: Male adult beetles are attracted to stressed trees and often give off their own scent attractant to draw females to the feast. Females lay eggs within bark or into the ends of cut branches. Larvae tunnel through the cambium to feed and pupate under the bark, emerging through holes to fly as adults to other trees. There are from one to four generations per year.

Prevention: Keep landscape evergreens well irrigated and healthy. Do not leave cut branches or firewood near landscape trees, as adult beetles may emerge from the cut wood. To protect valuable landscape pines from the ips or engraver beetle, spray trunks in mid-February with an insecticide containing lindane or carbaryl, applied according to label directions.

Management: Irrigate and fertilize stressed trees so they can push out grubs by oozing pitch. Prune and discard infected branches; remove dead or dying trees.

✎ *Notes: Dutch elm disease, a fungus fatal to elms, is spread by the European elm bark beetle, an introduced pest now found in the Pacific Northwest and California. To repel the beetles, which are attracted to stressed or diseased trees, keep elms healthy. Remove dead branches, dying elms, and cut wood. Resistant varieties have recently been introduced.*

BEES

BENEFICIALS

✎ ZONES: ALL

As the primary pollinators of many flowers, vegetables, and backyard fruit trees, bees are important to the garden. European in origin, the honeybee was introduced to North America during the 1600s as a pollinator for apple orchards. This bee is about an inch long and has gold-and-black markings and two pairs of clear wings. The orchard mason bee, shown above, left, is a small, blue-black native. The native bumblebee, shown above, right, is a large, black, fuzzy bee with a yellow or reddish stripe on its middle. It is the primary pollinator of tomato, eggplant, and pepper plants. The humming sound made by bees is produced by the rapid movement of their wings as they hover to feed or to collect pollen.

Target: Honeybees, orchard mason bees, and bumblebees feed on pollen and nectar from the flowers of garden plants and flowering trees.

Damage: Bees are beneficial insects and should be tolerated. However, if disturbed, bees will sting humans. People who are allergic to bee stings may experience swelling, dizziness, or difficulty in breathing; in some cases, without quick medical attention, they may die. Sometimes bees are a nuisance when they build their nests in buildings or too near the garden.

Life cycle: Honeybees live in colonies around a dominant female, called a queen, who lays many thousands of eggs in her lifetime. These eggs hatch into sterile female worker bees. Some workers become males, or drones, which mate with the queen, then die. Other eggs bear new queens. When a honeybee hive becomes too crowded, thousands of the bees leave in a swarm, usually in late winter or early fall. While in search of their new nesting place, they may circle in a tight ball around the queen to rest upon a tree branch. During the summer, honeybees gather nectar and pollen and transform them into honey and wax in the hive. During the shorter, chillier days of winter, they retire to their hives to feed off stored honey. Bumblebees nest in the soil or sometimes in the soft duff of a compost pile. A bumblebee colony may be as small as a dozen bees, with a single queen that overwinters by hibernating underground. Orchard mason bees also roost in smaller groups, but they prefer the cavities of trees and other protected areas. Neither bumblebees nor orchard mason bees create usable honey or wax, but both are important as crop pollinators. All bees will sting, but unlike stinging wasps or yellow jackets, bees die after stinging, because the stinger and venom sac are ripped out when the bee flies away.

Prevention: When left alone during their foraging, bees will not sting. If you are concerned about allergic individuals, you can have hives removed by a professional beekeeper or pest control professional.

Management: In recent years, epidemics of viruses and mites have killed off large numbers of naturalized honeybees. Since this has left orchard fruits and other crops without pollinators, many gardeners and farmers are introducing the orchard mason bee as a substitute. To encourage bees to frequent your garden, plant nectar flowers and provide a water source. Tomato-pollinating bumblebees can be induced to nest if flowering lavender is planted near vegetable beds. To attract the orchard mason bee, purchase nesting boxes from orchard suppliers and hang them near backyard fruit trees. Bees may be killed if the flowers they feed on have been sprayed with pesticides; carbaryl is especially toxic to bees. To protect them, use only insecticides that degrade quickly, and apply them late in the evening, when bees are in their hives. If you are accidentally stung by a bee, apply wet mud to the wound to draw out the stinger—or scrape the stinger off your skin with a fingernail—then apply first aid. Persons who are allergic to bee stings should keep antihistamine first aid kits handy and seek medical attention immediately when stung. Swarms or hives should be removed only by a professional beekeeper or pest control professional.

✎ *Notes: The Africanized honeybee, also called the "killer bee," looks just like an ordinary honeybee but is smaller. It is, however, particularly aggressive; if disturbed, swarms of this honeybee will chase and attack humans and other mammals. The sheer volume of stings from a killer bee swarm can be fatal. Introduced from Africa to South America, this bee has traveled northward through Mexico and appeared in Arizona, Texas, New Mexico, and Southern California. The Africanized honeybee is expected to extend its range in summer migrations into the western United States, particularly as viruses and mites reduce naturalized European honeybee populations. Africanized bees are less susceptible to mites, and no controls are known to prevent their spread into warm-winter regions of the United States. They are extremely dangerous: they can be disturbed by the noise of a lawn mower several hundred yards away and can pursue humans for as much as half a mile, zeroing in on head and face. If these insects are known to be in your area, use extreme caution around any hives; swatting or killing a foraging bee releases an odor trigger that draws nearby bees to attack. If attacked, pull a shirt over your head to protect your face and eyes, and run away as fast as possible, seeking cover indoors or in a car. For more information, contact your local cooperative extension agent.*

BORERS (CLEARWING MOTHS)

BARK AND BRANCH PESTS

✄ ZONES: ALL

The wood-boring larvae of several western species of clearwing moth can be serious pests of landscape trees. The dirty-white larvae are often found under tree bark. Day-flying clearwing moths look like flies or small wasps, with two pairs of transparent wings below the head. They are black with markings that can be red, orange, or yellow. Common species include the ash borer, peach tree borer, sycamore borer, oak borer, sequoia pitch moth, and western poplar clearwing. Other wood-boring moth species include carpenter worm and pine bark borer.

Target: Individual borer species attack ash, birch, Douglas fir, lilac, oak, olive, pine, poplar, privet, sequoia, sycamore, and willow. The most frequently attacked trees are suffering from drought stress or other injury.

Damage: Tree borer larvae tunnel through and eat the bark, sapwood, and heartwood of branches and tree trunks. Their tunnels interrupt the flow of nutrients through branches, weakening the tree. Bark on birches or poplars may look roughened or bumpy, but the major damage will be dieback of branches, usually starting 5 to 10 feet above ground level. Holes may appear in bark, ringed with oozing sap or frass (insect excrement) that looks like sawdust.

Life cycle: Adult moths lay their eggs on tree trunks at various times during warm-weather months, depending on the species. The eggs hatch into larvae, which tunnel into the wood to feed. The mobile pupa may push through old holes to reach the bark surface, where it transforms into a moth, leaving behind the protrusion of a pupal skin. There is usually one generation per year.

Prevention: Since the moths are most attracted to trees suffering from stress, keep landscape trees healthy and well irrigated. Healthy plants can actually defend themselves by drowning the pests in sap or pushing them out of holes with oozing pitch.

Management: Water and fertilize trees, and prune affected branches, to help them recover from borer damage. Check with your local cooperative extension agent or a certified arborist regarding treatments for tree borers, including parasitoid wasps and beneficial nematodes that can be injected into tree trunks.

 Notes: The appearance of woodpeckers often indicates where borers are attacking a tree; these birds pull out and eat bark larvae.

BORERS, CHERRY BARK TORTRIX

BARK AND STEM PESTS

✄ ZONES: 1–4

Prevalent only in northern Washington state, the cherry bark tortrix may appear elsewhere if transported on host cherry trees. This orchard pest is the larval form of a small tortrix moth, but unlike other caterpillars in its family tree, it feeds not on foliage but on the soft green tissue of cambium under tree bark. The brown, ½-inch-long caterpillar may be discovered beneath loose bark on the branches of host trees.

Target: The cherry bark tortrix is a serious pest on ornamental cherry trees, including both Japanese and native cherry species. It also attacks edible cherry and other *Prunus* fruiting trees, such as almond, apricot, peach, and plum. Other deciduous trees may also be affected.

Damage: The caterpillar of the cherry bark tortrix tunnels beneath bark, eroding and feeding on the green cambium, which supports the vascular network of woody plants. Areas of branches where cambium is damaged—or eaten away entirely—die back permanently. Twigs, large limbs, and even trunks of trees may be girdled, and the tree may die.

Life cycle: The larval stage of this moth is longer than most; bark tunneling may go on for as long as a year, with the pest overwintering as a caterpillar beneath tree bark. Generations overlap, so adult moths, eggs, caterpillars, and pupae can be found on the same tree.

Prevention: Check for this pest by monitoring cherry trees for dieback; on affected trees, pull away loose bark to find the caterpillar itself or mined areas of cambium. Since the adult moth flies to host trees, sticky traps baited with food or pheromone lures may reduce populations. Check with your local cooperative extension agent for more information if you live where this pest is found.

Management: Prune off and destroy affected branches and branch tips. Since the caterpillar is protected beneath bark from pesticide sprays, no sprays are recommended for home use. In northern Washington, gardeners should check with their local cooperative extension agent for the latest information on managing this pest; strategies may include pheromone lure traps to capture adult moths.

BORERS, EUCALYPTUS LONG-HORNED

BARK AND BRANCH PESTS

✂ ZONES: 7–9, 14–24

This pest arrived from Australia in the 1980s, probably in a shipment of eucalyptus plants or eucalyptus foliage. The shiny black adult beetle, with a long body marked with two yellowish spots, is known for the long curving antennae that are as long as its 1-inch body. The antennae of the male have ridges or spines. The larval form is a dirty-white grub with a black spot on its head; it leaves a dark, smudged trail on the bark before tunneling inside the tree to feed.

Target: The eucalyptus long-horned borer targets only eucalyptus trees, which are also native to Australia.

Damage: Trees infested with borer larvae may exude large amounts of sticky sap. A single larva can create a tunnel several feet long within the woody part of a tree, feeding for several months by chewing woody plant tissues. Treetops, branches, or entire trees may be killed, although some species of eucalyptus may resprout from dead trunks.

Life cycle: Adult female beetles lay 3 to 30 eggs under the loose, peeling bark of eucalyptus trees or on felled logs. Each female may lay up to 300 eggs during warm-weather months. The eggs hatch in about two weeks and the larvae crawl around the bark a bit before burrowing into the wood. On a live eucalyptus tree, the larva feeds for about three months, enlarging the tunnel system as it grows. In dry logs or in colder climates, the process may take as long as nine months. Once fully grown, the larva pupates within the tree and emerges shortly after as an adult beetle. Generations may overlap, depending on the local climate.

Prevention: Certain species of eucalyptus—such as *Eucalyptus robusta*, called swamp mahogany—are resistant to the long-horned borer. Routinely removing felled logs, dead trees, and dead branches will help eliminate egg-laying sites.

Management: Natural enemies of the eucalyptus long-horned borer are being introduced from Australia to manage this new insect pest. Check with your local cooperative extension agent for information on their use and availability. Remove deadwood and felled logs immediately. In areas where the pest is commonly seen, plant only resistant types.

BORERS, GIANT PALM

BARK AND BRANCH PESTS

✂ ZONES: 7–13

Once thought to be nearly extinct in its native range around Palm Springs, the giant palm borer has appeared in recent years elsewhere in Southern California and in Arizona, transported in the bark of palm trees that are dug up and shipped. The whitish grub, which is about the size of a thumb (up to 2 inches long and ¾ inch wide), is rarely seen. It lives its life within the trunk of a palm tree. It is the immature form of a 2-inch-long black beetle.

Target: The giant palm borer attacks native western palms in the genus *Washingtonia*, although it has been found in nonnatives, such as date palms and Mexican fan palms.

Damage: The giant palm borer chews the woody interior of palm trees, making miles of frass-filled tunnels. This erodes the stability of the palm's central trunk, so that it may snap or break in wind or a storm. It is hard to determine if the tree has a borer within, unless you can find the evidence of sawdustlike frass, pushed out where new fronds are emerging as buds. Older trees may show a ¾-inch exit hole, shown above, an indication of the tree's fragility, which may have become dangerous.

Giant palm borer adult (top), larva (bottom)

Life cycle: The adult beetle emerges in midsummer, with peak activity during July. Adult females fly to the top of palm trees, burrow into the crown, and lay one or several eggs within the burrow. The larvae hatch and tunnel down into the tree, chewing away at the interior for three to nine years. The same tree may have more than one brood within its trunk. When fully grown, each grub pupates within the tree, then exits by a nickel-size hole as an adult beetle.

Prevention: Where the insect is known to be prevalent, you may be able to give a tree some protection by applying an insecticide at the crown to kill the adult beetles while they are active in June and July. Contact your local cooperative extension agent for pesticide recommendations.

Management: Before they break and cause injury or damage, remove damaged palms that show numerous exit holes. Keeping palms healthy may mitigate borer damage if the number of grubs per tree is small.

BORERS, PACIFIC FLATHEADED

BARK AND BRANCH PESTS

✂ ZONES: 1–9, 14–20

Common only west of the Rockies (excluding desert regions), the Pacific flatheaded borer in its adult form is a dark bronze hard-shelled beetle about ⅓ inch long. The larvae, found under the bark of affected trees, are twice the size, dirty white, with a flattened blobby triangle just below the head.

Target: The Pacific flatheaded borer attacks a wide variety of native and landscape trees, including manzanita, maple, mayten, and oak. Most affected are young or recently planted trees, or those that have been previously injured or have cracked bark from sunburn damage.

Damage: Damage to trees is caused by young larvae tunneling beneath the bark. Sap oozing from their tunnels may create darkened, wet-looking spots on tree trunks and branches. Later these bark areas may crack and expose the tunnels, which can be filled with sawdust. By tunneling, the larvae weaken branches and interrupt the flow of nutrients through the tree. Twigs and branches may be girdled and die back; small trees may die.

Flatheaded borer adult

Life cycle: Late spring to midsummer, adult beetles mate, and the females lay their eggs on damaged areas of trees, particularly in crevices where the bark has been cracked from sunburn damage or gouged accidentally by a string trimmer. The larvae feed on the outer wood, then burrow deeper to pupate and overwinter; they crawl out as adult beetles the following spring. There is one generation per year.

Prevention: Paint the trunks of young and newly planted trees with white paint to reflect sunlight and prevent sunburn damage. Keep trees well irrigated and fertilized. Prune off dead or dying branches when you notice them. Do not leave pruned limbs or cut firewood near young trees, as the beetles may lay their eggs there.

Management: Irrigate and fertilize affected trees to restore their vigor and help them overcome any dieback. Prune off dead or damaged branches. No chemical controls are recommended for this pest.

BORERS, PALO VERDE

BARK AND BRANCH PESTS

✂ ZONES: 10–13

Native to Arizona deserts, the palo verde borer is often discovered crawling around patios on summer nights, attracted by outdoor lighting. The dark brown beetle, 3–5 inches long, has long spined antennae that curve backward and a collar of spines behind its head. Although intimidating, the beetle does not bite. The immature form is a grub that lives in the soil around tree roots.

Target: The grub of the palo verde borer prefers to feed on the roots of nonnative landscape shrubs and trees, such as rose, privet, elm, cottonwood, citrus, and stone fruit trees, and tropical palo verdes, such as *Parkinsonia aculeata*, which is known as Jerusalem thorn or Mexican palo verde. Blue palo verde, *Cercidium floridum*, a native, appears to be resistant. Plants that are already stressed by disease or drought are usually the first to be attacked.

Damage: The larvae chew roots for years; healthy, well-irrigated trees seem to recover over time. When the grubs pupate and later emerge as adult beetles, they leave large holes in the soil under trees.

Life cycle: Adult beetles lay their eggs beneath trees; they appear to be attracted by scent or pheromone to trees that are drought stressed. After feeding underground for about three years, the grubs pupate in the soil and emerge as the ground heats up in late spring. The adults, which are nocturnal, can fly great distances. Generations may overlap in desert climates; several broods may infest the roots of the same tree.

Prevention: Plant resistant native varieties. In desert areas, rosebushes and introduced landscape trees should be kept healthy and well irrigated. Remove dying branches or diseased shrubs by early summer so the adult beetles are not attracted to the garden by a scent emanating from the plants.

Management: Since this pest attacks plants already suffering from drought or disease, the beetles' presence may indicate other problems you need to address. As native insects, beetles on patios may be left alone, but remove dying or diseased shrubs in the garden so they will not be attracted to lay eggs under sick trees.

✎ *Notes: Groups of holes beneath landscape trees may not indicate palo verde borers, since other desert insects, such as cicadas, make large holes as well.*

BORERS, PEACH TREE, AND PEACH TWIG GIRDLERS

BARK AND BRANCH PESTS, FRUIT PESTS

✍ ZONES: ALL

Two unrelated insects damage peach trees and other stone fruit trees. The peach tree borer, shown above, a 1-inch-long, pinkish caterpillar with a darker head, is common only in California. It is the larval form of a blue-black moth that looks like a large, dark fly. The peach twig girdler caterpillar, which is found near twig tips, is dirty white with a darker head. The adult form of the girdler is a small dark moth.

Target: Both pests attack apricot, nectarine, peach, plum, almond, and flowering cherry trees.

Damage: The larva of the peach tree borer tunnels around in the bark of a peach or plum tree, near the soil level. Small piles of sawdust near the crown or roots are telltale signs. Older trees can withstand some borer damage, but young or recently planted fruit trees may be girdled and die. The caterpillar of the peach twig girdler prefers the high life, nibbling new shoots, wilting leaf tips, and causing dieback from the tips of branches. The peach twig girdler may also enter ripening fruits later in the season.

Life cycle: The adult moth of the peach tree borer lays its eggs at the base of tree trunks in early summer. The hatching larvae feed upward into the wood, then leave the tree early the next spring to pupate in the soil near the roots of the tree. There is one generation per year. Peach twig girdlers, which may have two generations, overwinter as pupae on tree bark, within structures called hibernacula. These look like small, reddish brown chimneys of glued-together sawdust. The adult moths emerge from these structures, fly to seek mates, then lay their single eggs near leaf tips.

Prevention: Where peach tree borers are prevalent, examine trees yearly near the soil line.

Management: Check with your cooperative extension agent about sticky traps baited with pheromone lures and about introducing parasitoid wasps as a natural control for both pests. A yearly application of dormant-oil spray can kill more than 90 percent of peach twig girdlers overwintering on trunks; applying a light summer oil in midsummer may reduce the second generation as well. If you can find the holes of the peach tree borer, try sticking a metal skewer inside the hole to stab and remove the caterpillar.

BORERS, SHOT HOLE

BARK AND BRANCH PESTS, FRUIT TREE PESTS

✍ ZONES: ALL

The shot hole borer, a common pest of fruit trees, can be identified by a pattern on tree branches of small, pencil-point holes, shown above. Sap may be running out of the holes, which have been made by a black beetle so minute it is often hard to see. To determine if the damage has been caused by the shot hole borer, peel back the bark to look for galleries of holes running 1–2 inches lengthwise down the cambial layer. This is where the beetle has laid its eggs. The larval stage, which causes the damage, is a tiny worm the size of a pinhead.

Target: The shot hole borer most often attacks cherry, peach, and plum trees, particularly trees that are infrequently irrigated, already diseased, poorly pruned, or otherwise stressed. Almond, apple, and pear trees may also be affected.

Damage: Chewing through the cambial layer of tree branches, shot hole borers interrupt the flow of nutrients. In severe cases, branches may be girdled and die back. Since these beetles are attracted to trees that are already stressed, the appearance of shot holes usually means the tree has other, more serious problems.

Life cycle: Adult female beetles dig holes within the bark and lay their eggs in galleries on the cambium. The hatching larvae feed and pupate under the bark in sawdust-filled burrows 2–4 inches long. There may be one or two generations per year; the last generation overwinters inside as larvae and emerges as adult beetles the next spring.

Prevention: Keep fruit trees well irrigated and fertilized; routinely prune off dead or dying branches; correct any other disease or insect problems on the tree. Do not leave pruned limbs or cut firewood near fruit trees, as the beetles may lay their eggs there instead.

Management: Healthy fruit trees can withstand shot hole borers by exuding resinous sap, which drowns and kills the borer larvae. The sap oozing through trunk holes indicates that this cure is taking place. Irrigate and fertilize affected trees and prune off dead or infected branches. In early spring, spray the bark with an insecticide containing lindane, carefully following directions on the label since this pesticide may not be used on all trees.

BUDWORMS, TOBACCO OR GERANIUM

FLOWER PESTS

✽ ZONES: ALL

A close relative of the corn earworm (see page 164), the tobacco or geranium budworm is a striped caterpillar that may be greenish, tan, or reddish in color and up to ¾ inch long. If you find chewed foliage peppered with round black fecal pellets, check nearby plant stems for this caterpillar. It is the larval form of a native moth.

Target: Particularly troublesome in mild-winter climates, the tobacco budworm attacks calendula, garden penstemon, geranium, nicotiana, and petunia. Other annuals and roses may also be affected.

Damage: Tobacco budworms burrow into buds and feed from the inside. Buds of geranium, penstemon, or petunia may appear dried up or may not open, or the blossoms may open tattered and full of holes. This caterpillar also chews fully opened flowers and occasionally dines on leaves, leaving tiny black droppings on the plants.

Life cycle: Moths lay eggs singly on host plants. After caterpillars hatch, they tunnel into flower buds and feed for a few weeks before pupating. Sometimes the caterpillars pupate within the dried-up buds. Adult moths die in cold weather, but pupae may overwinter. There may be one or two generations per year.

Prevention: Ivy geraniums are resistant to the budworm moth. In warm-winter climates, raggedy, end-of-season petunias should be pulled up and thrown out to remove any eggs that may be sticking to the plant remains. Preventively spraying the microbial control *Bacillus thuringiensis* (BT) may protect established plantings of landscape-size geraniums.

Management: Remove dried-up buds and flowers that may harbor the caterpillars. BT will kill budworms if it can be dusted or sprayed on plants before the caterpillars enter the buds. You can also spray plants with an insecticide containing pyrethrin or carbaryl, but this too will be effective only when applied immediately after the eggs hatch. Once they enter the buds, the caterpillars will be protected from the spray.

CABBAGEWORMS

LEAF AND STEM PESTS

✽ ZONES: ALL

Several caterpillars are colloquially known as cabbageworms. The most common in gardens is the European or imported cabbageworm, shown above, the larva of a white butterfly often seen hovering around cabbage-family plants. The velvety light green larva grows to 1½ inches long. The native cabbage looper is about the same size, but, lacking legs in the middle of its body, it has a humpbacked gait like that of an inchworm. This is the larva of a nocturnal gray moth. Also common are the smaller, ¼-inch-long green caterpillars of the diamondback moth, which wriggle rapidly when disturbed. The cabbage maggot, the larval form of a fly, is ¼ inch long and white; it lives underground, feeding on plant roots.

Target: Cabbageworms attack cole crops, including broccoli, brussels sprouts, cabbage, cauliflower, and radicchio. Cabbage loopers also feed on the foliage of beet, carnation, lettuce, nasturtium, and spinach. The cabbage maggot attacks the roots of cole crops.

Damage: These caterpillars chew irregular holes in the leaves of cole crops, ruining edible foliage and florets. Plants affected by the cabbage maggot look yellowed and stunted; they wilt during the hot part of the day, even when they are watered.

Life cycle: Flying adults lay eggs singly on a leaf on or near host crops. The caterpillars hatch in a few days and begin to feed immediately. The larvae of imported cabbageworms, cabbage loopers, and diamondback moths pupate on the plant, wrapping themselves in a cocoon spun with white silk. Cabbage maggots pupate underground. There may be several generations per year. Diamondback moths overwinter as adults in garden debris.

Prevention: Shelter cole crops from egg-laying adults with floating row covers, especially in early spring. Crop rotation can reduce populations of cabbage maggots in the soil. Between crops, clear and till vegetable beds to remove lingering adult moths, eggs, or pupae.

Management: Hand-pick caterpillars and cocoons. Natural predators include trichogramma wasps, yellow jackets, and other wasps and lacewings. Spraying of cole crops with *Bacillus thuringiensis* (BT), as soon as you notice white butterflies, can minimize damage by cabbageworms and effectively manage even large infestations. You can kill the caterpillars with an insecticide containing rotenone, pyrethrin, neem, or carbaryl; follow directions in applying these products. Add beneficial nematodes to the soil to hunt and kill cabbage maggots.

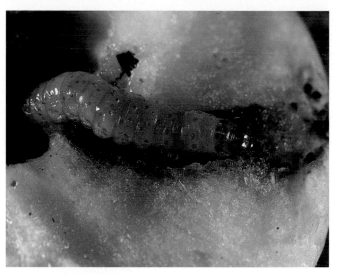

CARROT RUST FLIES

ROOT PESTS

✓ ZONES: ALL

The appearance of ⅓-inch-long, stiff white maggots in the roots of carrots is what introduces most gardeners to the carrot rust fly. The adult form is a ¼-inch-long fly with long yellow legs and a yellow head, sometimes found near the soil around plants in the carrot family.

Target: This maggot confines itself to carrot-family crops *(Apiaceae),* including celeriac, celery, cilantro, dill, parsley, and parsnip. Wild parsnip, wild anise, and Queen Anne's lace are weed hosts.

Damage: Maggots eat the root hairs of plants, then tunnel through roots. Carrot roots may be forked, deformed, or scarred with surface tracks or tunnels filled with mushy orange insect debris. Carrot tops usually do not appear damaged, but they look wilted. Parsley or celery may show yellowed or stunted tops.

Life cycle: This pest does most damage in early spring, although successive generations (two or three each year) may extend the problem into summer. The adult fly lays eggs in the crown or in the soil close to plants. The larvae hatch and enter roots. After three to four weeks, the maggots pupate. They may overwinter in the soil in pupal form.

Prevention: The first step in managing carrot rust flies is to remove nearby weed hosts, such as Queen Anne's lace, as well as overwintering carrots, parsley, and celery. To protect emerging carrots in the spring, place floating row covers over seedbeds, or spread wood ashes around plants to deter egg laying.

Management: Remove and destroy infected plants immediately. You can purchase beneficial parasitic nematodes targeted to the carrot rust fly. Water them into the soil of crop rows to kill the maggots. In the fall, till the soil thoroughly to destroy any overwintering pupae.

 Notes: A similar carrot pest found in Colorado and eastward is the beetlelike carrot weevil, whose white larval grub makes larger tunnels than those made by the carrot rust fly. The adult weevil, which has a snout and a hard brown shell, is about ¼ inch long. It hibernates in grass and weeds, such as plantain, over the winter, emerging in late spring. Row covers, weed removal, and beneficial nematodes are good controls for the grubs; the adult weevil may be killed with a pesticide containing rotenone. Be careful to follow directions on the pesticide label.

CODLING MOTHS

FRUIT AND NUT PESTS

✓ ZONES: ALL

This is usually the culprit found in spoiled fruit. The codling moth caterpillar is under 1 inch long, with a pink or whitish body and a dark brown head. It is often seen feeding in windfall apples or fruits still on the tree. The adult moth, gray brown with copper-brown bands, has a wingspan of less than an inch.

Target: The codling moth is a major pest of apple and pear orchards and is common on backyard apple, crabapple, pear, and quince trees. Caterpillars may also appear inside plums and walnut kernels.

Damage: Apple skins may be blemished with holes and dark spots, and the fruit tunneled and ruined with blackish fecal waste. Apples, pears, and walnuts may drop prematurely, with the caterpillar still inside.

Adult codling moth emerging from pupal skin

Life cycle: Shortly after bloom time in mid-spring, the adult moth lays single eggs on a small developing fruit or a nearby leaf. After hatching, the larvae tunnel into the fruit. They feed for several weeks, then crawl down the trunk (or take a ride on a windfall apple) to the soil where they pupate in a cocoon under loose bark or debris on the ground. There are two or more generations per year.

Prevention: Sanitation is key. Rake away fallen leaves and dropped fruit under the tree throughout the year to destroy cocoons.

Management: A combination of controls through the codling moth's life cycle is the most effective strategy. In early spring, adult moths may be lured into sticky traps with pheromone bait. The traps will help you recognize when the moths are in the egg-laying mood. Then you can introduce biological controls, such as parasitoid wasps, to kill caterpillars as they hatch. Wrap the trunks with sticky barriers to trap larvae as they crawl down. Rake away dropped fruit and leaves. For severe infestations, caterpillars may be killed by spraying with insecticides containing *Bacillus thuringiensis* (BT), malathion, or carbaryl, but the sprays will be effective only if the larvae are caught before they enter the fruit.

 Notes: A promising control used in commercial orchards is a targeted microbial pathogen, the codling moth granulosis virus (CMGV). This is not yet available for home use.

COLORADO POTATO BEETLES

LEAF AND STEM PESTS

✎ ZONES: 1–3

The adult Colorado potato beetle, shown above with grubs and eggs, is ⅓ inch long with showy, black-and-yellow-striped wing covers and an orange-and-black-spotted "vest" behind its head. This distinguishes it from other beetles that target potato plants. The immature or larval stage of the potato beetle is a humpbacked, articulated grub that is red with a row of black spots on each side.

Target: The potato beetle attacks the foliage of potato, tomato, eggplant, and related tomato-family plants such as tomatillo and ground cherry.

Damage: Both adult beetles and grubs feed voraciously on leaves and stems, leaving behind spots of black excrement. Large infestations can defoliate potato plants completely.

Life cycle: Adult beetles emerge from the soil in early spring to feed on young plants and lay eggs on the undersides of leaves. A single female may lay hundreds of eggs at a time. After a week, the eggs hatch and the larvae begin feeding for a few weeks, then burrow into the ground to pupate. Pupae may overwinter. There are one to three generations per year.

Prevention: In spring, floating row covers or a thick straw mulch can help prevent the adult beetles from reaching the plants and laying eggs. Strongly scented companion plants such as marigold, catnip, and tansy planted around potato and tomato seedlings may also keep the flying adults from identifying their target by smell.

Management: Adult beetles, egg clusters, and grubs can be hand-picked and destroyed by immersing them in soapy water. A dusting of *Bacillus thuringiensis* (BT) San Diego strain (also known as M-1 or *B. t. tenebrionis*) controls the grubs in the early stages. Natural predators of the larger grubs and beetles include birds, spined soldier bugs, and parasitic nematodes. To kill adult beetles and grubs, spray or dust plants with a pesticide containing pyrethrin, rotenone, neem, diazinon, or carbaryl. Be sure to follow the directions on those products. Remove plant debris and weeds from potato beds each fall, and till deeply between crops to expose and destroy any pupae.

 Notes: Native to Colorado, this insect has spread eastward and northward, farm by farm and garden by garden, wherever tomato and potato plants are widely grown.

CORN EARWORMS

FRUIT AND LANDSCAPE FLOWER PESTS

✎ ZONES: ALL

This pest changes from a tiny white caterpillar with a black head to one that is over an inch long, green or pink or dark brown, with rickrack stripes along its length. The adult form is a night-flying moth that migrates long distances.

Target: Besides corn, this caterpillar attacks the fruits of tomato, pepper, even bean and pea plants. A close relative of the tobacco and geranium budworm (see page 162), the corn earworm also feeds on garden flowers such as geranium, nicotiana, penstemon, petunia, and sunflower.

Damage: Earworm eggs and caterpillars may be found in the silks or tips of ripening corn; you can salvage the ear by cutting off the spoiled tip. On flowers, the buds and leaves will be chewed into holes; the plants may not bloom at all, or the blossoms may open tattered and ragged.

Corn earworm adult

Life cycle: The adult female moth lays domed, ridged white eggs singly on silks or leaf undersides. Caterpillars hatch and feed for several weeks, then crawl down to pupate in the soil. There can be up to seven generations per year, on various host plants. This pest will overwinter in the soil as a pupa in mild-winter climates. Where winters are snowy, the moth migrates to warmer zones.

Prevention: An old method that still works is to place 20 drops (about a teaspoon) of mineral oil on the tip of each ear when silks appear, to deter the egg-laying moth. Pinch the top of each ear with a rubber band to keep caterpillars out, or grow tight-husked varieties such as 'Country Gentleman'.

Management: Introduce or encourage beneficial insects, such as spined soldier bugs, lacewings, and trichogramma wasps. (Any eggs found on plants that are black, not white, have already been parasitized by the trichogramma wasp.) The biological control *Bacillus thuringiensis* (BT) does a good job of managing corn earworms on ornamentals such as petunia, when applied as a dust. Spray with an insecticide containing pyrethrum or carbaryl, according to directions on the label; target-spray directly onto the silks every two to five days, as long as the silks are still green. Tilling the soil between crops helps kill any overwintering pupae.

CUCUMBER BEETLES

LEAF AND STEM PESTS

✎ ZONES: ALL

The spotted cucumber beetle looks a bit like a ladybug (see page 175 to compare), but it may be recognized by the greenish yellow cast of its shiny, hard-shelled wing covers, which have a dozen black spots. The western spotted cucumber beetle is orange yellow with three rows of black spots. A third version is the western striped cucumber beetle, shown above. The most destructive, it wears black and greenish yellow stripes. All are about ¼ inch long. All have legged larvae that are slender and white, about ¼–½ inch long, with brown heads and brown patches on their first and last segments.

Target: Striped cucumber beetles attack cantaloupe, cucumber, muskmelon, and squash. The spotted species also feed on rosebushes, dahlias, and other garden plants.

Damage: The adult beetles chew holes in leaves and flowers and rip ragged lesions in stems, but they do the most damage to crops by spreading diseases, such as bacterial wilt and mosaic virus, via their mouth parts. The larvae of the spotted varieties also chew roots underground, which can kill off sprouted seedlings in a few days or can wilt and stunt the plants later in the season. On rosebushes, adult beetles chew leaves and flowers; they may transmit viral infections as they feed.

Life cycle: Adult cucumber beetles appear in late spring when the weather has warmed the soil. After mating, the females lay eggs in the soil around host plants. Larvae burrow into the soil and chew plant roots, then pupate after a few weeks. There are one to four generations per year, more in areas with warm winters. The beetles overwinter as adults, hiding and hibernating under cover of fallen leaves and garden debris.

Prevention: Some varieties of cucumber and squash are actually resistant to these flying pests. Floating row covers will keep out the adult beetles, but the covers should be removed when the flowers appear, to allow pollinating insects access to the plants.

Management: Natural controls include birds, tachinid flies, and humans who can hand-pick adult beetles off the leaves. For major infestations, spray plants with an insecticide containing rotenone, pyrethrum, malathion, or carbaryl, applied according to directions on the label. Tidy vegetable beds each fall to help reduce the adult beetle population.

CURCULIOS, PLUM

FRUIT AND FLOWER PESTS

✎ ZONES: 1–6

When disturbed, the curculio rolls up in a ball and plays dead. This small weevil with a long, curved snout is about ¼ inch long. Their grayish brown color makes curculios difficult to see on the branches of backyard orchard trees. But they cause noticeable damage to plum and apple fruit—a distinctive crescent- or mushroom-shaped scar. The larvae, seen only in spring, are grayish white legless grubs, ⅓ inch long.

Target: Plum curculios feed on fruit and nut trees, especially plum and stone fruit trees, and on blueberry plants.

Damage: Adult curculios chew holes in flower buds, blossoms, and green fruit. The larvae tunnel through fruits and nuts, leaving rotting brown interiors. Fruits and nuts are deformed and drop prematurely.

Life cycle: Adult curculios overwinter in fallen leaves and garden debris. In spring the females make a crescent-shaped incision in developing fruit and lay their eggs inside. After hatching, larvae feed for two to three weeks within the fruit. When the fruit drops, the larvae crawl out to pupate in the soil. Adults emerge from the soil from midsummer to late fall. There may be one or two generations per year.

Prevention: Clear fallen leaves and dropped fruits from under orchard trees on a regular basis, to reduce hiding places for adult curculios and to keep larvae from reaching the soil to pupate.

Management: Adult curculios can literally be knocked out of trees; place a cloth underneath and shake the branches, and they will fall in little balls onto the cloth where they can be gathered up and destroyed. You can also kill adult curculios by spraying tree branches with an insecticide containing pyrethrin, rotenone, malathion, or carbaryl, applied according to directions on the label. Spraying will be most effective if done right after petal drop, the time when adult curculios are most actively crawling on branches and beginning to lay eggs. Once the eggs and larvae are in the fruit, no amount of spraying will prevent fruit damage.

 Notes: Although plum curculio has appeared in the West, it is not a major pest here. An old farm remedy is to let chickens run in the orchard; they are good hunters of the weevils and they dig for the grubs.

CURCULIOS, ROSE

FLOWER AND FRUIT PESTS

⚡ ZONES: ALL

The rose curculio, which belongs to a different genus from that of the plum curculio, is a pest particular to rosebushes, although apple trees may be an alternate host. The rose curculio appears to be more prevalent in cold-winter climates. About the size of a ladybug, this ¼-inch-long weevil with a curved snout is colored black or rusty red. When disturbed, it will roll into a ball and drop onto the ground. The larvae are small, legless, and whitish. A clue to identifying this pest in the larval stage is a dried-up rosebud with a small hole bored into it.

Target: The rose curculio attacks the flower buds of garden roses. Oddly, the rose curculio is most attracted to roses that are yellow or white.

Damage: The adult weevil chews buds, leaves, stems, and canes of rose plants, riddling flowers and leaves with holes. Larva-infested rosebuds show bent pedicels, drop off, or die upon their stems.

Life cycle: Adult curculios emerge from the soil from midsummer to late fall to feed on rose foliage and flowers. They lay their eggs on developing flower buds. After hatching, the larvae tunnel into the buds to feed, then drop down to the soil where they may overwinter as fully grown larvae. Pupation takes place in the spring. There is usually one generation per year.

Prevention: Floating row covers may protect rosebushes from flying adults and may deter egg laying.

Management: Hand-pick adult pests by knocking them onto a cloth under the infested plant, then gather them up quickly and destroy them by immersing in soapy water. Prune off and destroy bent, dried rosebuds found on the plants. Till the soil around rosebushes to expose larvae and pupae to predators. Natural enemies include birds and beneficial soil nematodes, which can be introduced in the soil around rose plants to attack larvae and pupae. For chemical control of adult curculios, use a pesticide containing pyrethrin, rotenone, malathion, or carbaryl, applied according to label directions.

CUTWORMS

LEAF AND STEM PESTS

⚡ ZONES: ALL

Cutworms are the hairless caterpillar larvae of various species of night-flying moths. They come in various colors and may be up to 2 inches long. The cutworm feeds only at night but may commonly be found on the soil during the daytime, curled up into a C shape. Cutworms are particularly common in new gardens created from areas that had previously been lawn or a long-standing weedy patch. The black cutworm is shown above.

Target: Cutworms are so named because they chew seedlings and grass blades off at ground level. They will eat almost any type of grass, vegetable, or flowering plant.

Damage: Cutworms attack seedlings or recently transplanted garden vegetables or flowers, severing stems and leaving what's left of the young plants lying on the ground. In lawns, they can wreak havoc during spring and summer, causing small patches of sod to turn brown and die. Grass blades around the margins of the affected areas will show jagged holes along their edges. The entire lawn may look ragged.

Life cycle: The adult moths lay tiny white eggs in garden debris and soil. The caterpillars feed at night, retiring for the day to the cover of soil or a leaf. After feeding for several weeks, they burrow into the soil to pupate, then emerge as adult moths. There may be several generations per year and several moth species per garden.

Prevention: Before sowing seeds or transplanting seedlings, clear and till garden beds thoroughly to destroy any eggs, caterpillars, or pupae. To protect transplants, encircle each one with a stiff paper collar (a paper cup with the bottom cut out works well), pushed 1–2 inches into the ground and extending 1–2 inches above the soil level.

Management: Encourage or introduce natural predators, such as beneficial soil nematodes, parasitoid wasps, ground beetles, soldier beetles, predatory stinkbugs, and tachinid flies. Spreading diatomaceous earth around young seedlings may deter the caterpillars. Infested lawns may be treated with an insecticide containing diazinon or carbaryl and labeled for use on lawns. Apply according to directions on the label.

 Notes: To check for cutworms, go out at night with a flashlight to see if you can find the caterpillars feeding on grass stems or on seedlings.

CYPRESS TIP MOTHS

LEAF AND STEM PESTS

✎ ZONES: 1–3, 7–11, 14–24

Common only west of the Rocky Mountains, the cypress tip moth, also called cypress miner, can ruin the looks of landscape evergreens in both city and country. The pest form of this insect is the larva, a tiny, ¼-inch-long, dark-headed green caterpillar that can be found if you break apart an infected leaf tip and peer inside. The adult moth is slender and pear shaped when sitting and has a wingspan of ⅓ inch. It is dusty brown or gray, mottled with white bars or spots. The adult moths are often seen flying around host plants in late spring.

Target: The cypress tip moth affects soft-needled and scale-needled coniferous evergreens, including arborvitae, cypress, juniper, and redwood.

Damage: Tip moth caterpillars tunnel into the needles of evergreens, feeding on soft tissue within. Infested leaf tips turn yellow, then brown and dry. Damage is spotty throughout the plant, with brown foliage growing on the same branch next to healthy green needles. Young plants may die. Established evergreens usually regrow where the affected foliage is pruned off.

Life cycle: Adult moths fly to mate and lay eggs on host plants from April to June. The eggs hatch shortly afterward. The larvae bore into the rounded needles to feed and overwinter within the foliage. In spring they tunnel out to pupate in silvery white cocoons attached with silk between branch tips; shown above are damaged needles with exit holes. There is one generation per year.

Prevention: When selecting landscape junipers, choose varieties, such as Sargent juniper, that are resistant to cypress tip moth. Check with your local nursery for other resistant evergreens.

Management: Replace affected junipers with resistant varieties. Monitor existing plants for browned foliage tips; snap off some tips to see if you can find the green caterpillars hiding inside. To reduce populations of adult moths, prune off affected plant parts in late fall and early spring and remove any cocoons you see. If you shake a branch in late spring and quantities of adult moths fly up, you can kill them by spraying the branches with an insecticide containing malathion or diazinon, following label directions. Check the label to make sure your insecticide is registered for use on your evergreens, since certain sprays can permanently discolor conifer foliage.

DAMSEL BUGS

BENEFICIALS

✎ ZONES: ALL

Damsel bugs are dull gray or brown, very elongated in shape, and about ½ inch long. The juvenile or nymph stage looks much the same as the adult bug, but nymphs are smaller and darker and may have no wings or only wing nubs. Both adult damsel bugs and immature nymphs have long, jointed legs and angled antennae. Adults have four wings, which, when folded, make an X-like mark on their backs. Other plant-sucking insects also sport X-like markings on their backs; the beneficial damsel bugs and their nymphs may be distinguished from similar insects that are harmful to plants by their long, narrow heads. Damsel bugs and their nymphs also move quickly on plant parts to hunt their slower-moving insect prey. Adults may fly away when disturbed.

Target: Damsel bugs and their nymphs feed on aphids, leafhoppers, and small caterpillars.

Damage: Damsel bugs cause no damage to plants.

Life cycle: Adults lay eggs on a variety of host plants, including meadow grasses and weeds. The eggs hatch into nymphs that crawl around to hunt and that gradually attain wings after they molt. There may be several generations per year, depending on climate and species.

Prevention: No prevention measures are needed.

Management: No management is required. Many species of damsel bugs are native to western states. To attract them to your garden, consider adding ornamental grasses to a flower border or leaving a strip of lawn unmowed to create a mini-meadow. Such areas can provide egg-laying sites for succeeding generations during the growing season. If grasses or mini-meadows are impractical, you may be able to repopulate your garden with damsel bugs by limiting the use of pesticides in your garden. To protect these beneficial insects, be sparing in your use of knockdown or contact insecticides, which can kill the wingless nymphs along with their prey.

EARWIGS, EUROPEAN

SOIL PESTS, BENEFICIALS

✠ ZONES: ALL

These reddish brown insects measure ¾ inch long and are easily recognized by the pointy pincers on the tail end of their abdomens. Contrary to the old wives' tale and the modern horror film, earwigs do not crawl into people's ears and bore into their brains. Introduced from Europe in the early 1900s, the European earwig is now found throughout North America. Although they have wings, these insects rarely fly, preferring to run for cover with a quick, scurrying crawl when they are disturbed.

Target: Earwigs lodge in all garden plants, crawling out to feed at night on decaying plant remains. During the day they often congregate in dark, damp places in the garden, such as under rocks.

Damage: Earwigs are often blamed for creating damage in the garden that is often caused by another chewing pest. Young earwigs do like to nibble tender plant tips, so they can be destructive in the springtime. Mostly they are happy to be part of your garden's cleanup crew, helping to transform garden debris into useful humus. But large infestations may be a nuisance, as the insects can inflict a painful pinch.

Life cycle: Earwigs are active from spring through late fall; they hibernate through the winter. Adult females lay clusters of 20 to 60 eggs in the soil in the autumn or early spring, tending the nest until the eggs hatch and the insects emerge as immature nymphs that gradually attain size and wings. There is usually one generation per year.

Prevention: Keep the garden clean and remove earwig hiding places.

Management: To reduce populations in garden beds, make earwig traps by placing damp, loosely rolled-up newspapers on the ground near plants. The insects will crawl into the rolls, which you can then discard. Or fill a low-sided can, such as a cat-food can, with ½ inch of vegetable oil and place on the ground. Special earwig traps with poison bait are available at garden centers; place them near areas where earwigs are likely to be—in woodpiles, under wooden stairways or decks, near old wooden fences and arbors. For severe infestations, spray soil around plants with an insecticide containing diazinon in the late afternoon or evening, according to directions on the label.

ELM LEAF BEETLES

LEAF AND STEM PESTS

✠ ZONES: ALL

Found throughout North America, this beetle feeds on the leaves of elm trees both as a grub and as an adult. The adults are oval and about ¼ inch long; they have pale yellow wing covers with a lengthwise black stripe. The ½-inch-long grub is yellow with black stripes. Both are found on the undersides of elm leaves.

Target: The elm leaf beetle concentrates on trees in the elm family, *Ulmaceae*. European elms *(Ulmus)* are often hardest hit; American elms and Asian elms, such as zelkova, are less frequently attacked.

Damage: Adult beetles riddle foliage with holes; grubs skeletonize entire leaves. In the worst cases they defoliate branches or whole trees. Large grub populations chew so much foliage that a tree is weakened and becomes more susceptible to the elm bark beetle, which can carry Dutch elm disease.

Elm leaf beetle larvae

Life cycle: In spring, female elm leaf beetles lay rows of yellowish, teardrop-shaped eggs on the undersides of elm leaves. The larvae feed for several weeks, then drop to the ground to pupate in leaf mold. The bright yellow pupae are most often found near the tree trunk. There are one to five generations per year, more in warm-winter climates. In cold regions, the adult elm leaf beetle often overwinters in nearby buildings.

Prevention: Avoid planting European elms, if possible, and keep existing trees healthy and well irrigated to help them withstand a defoliating attack. Prune off dead or dying branches, which may provide a resting place for adult beetles. Dislodge pupae from tree trunks.

Management: Wrap sections of tree trunk with a sticky barrier to trap beetles and larvae that crawl on the bark. Native predators include several tiny parasitoid wasps and a black tachinid fly that lays its eggs in beetle larvae. The biological control *Bacillus thuringiensis* San Diego strain will kill both adult beetles and grubs but will not harm beneficial predators. Apply BT to the undersides of leaves every few days after you first notice the larvae. Heavy infestations may require banding or spraying with an insecticide containing acephate or carbaryl. For larger trees where spraying is impractical, elm trees may be injected through the bark with the systemic insecticide dicrotophos, a job that must be done by a professional.

EUROPEAN CRANE FLIES

LAWN PESTS

✎ ZONES: 1–6

Only one of the many kinds of crane flies is considered a pest. This species, the European crane fly, is largely restricted to the Northwest. Adult crane flies look like large, inch-long mosquitoes, but they don't bite. The larvae are legless, slim brown maggots, 1 inch long when fully grown.

Target: Crane fly larvae eat lawn grass and other grasses.

Damage: The crane fly in its larval stage damages lawns by eating the roots and blades of turf grass, causing large patches of lawn to turn yellowish brown. The damage is more noticeable in the spring. Usually the grass is not killed, and the lawn can recover once the larvae stop feeding.

Life cycle: In late summer or early fall, the European crane fly adults mate and lay eggs in lawns and other grassy areas. After the eggs hatch, the larvae move underground to feed on the roots of grass plants. At night, they come to the surface to chew leaf blades. They overwinter deep in the soil, then emerge to feed again in the spring. This round of feeding—and the damage it causes—is usually finished by mid-May. Then the larvae pupate over the summer before emerging as adults that die when cold weather arrives. There is usually one generation per year.

Prevention: Both birds and bats eat adult crane flies on the wing, so encourage these predators by placing a birdbath or bat house near your lawn.

Management: While lawn damage is not permanent, weeds may appear in affected spots. If large areas of lawn are turning sickly yellow brown and you determine that the lawn is heavily infested by crane fly larvae, you can kill many larvae with a pesticide labeled for lawn use that contains diazinon. Apply according to directions on the label. This treatment should be used only on affected areas while the larvae are active in spring or fall.

 Notes: To determine if crane fly larvae are infesting your lawn, drench suspect areas with water and cover them overnight with black plastic. Any crane fly larvae (brown maggots) present will be lying on the soil under the plastic the next day.

FLEA BEETLES

LEAF AND STEM PESTS

✎ ZONES: ALL

Flea beetles are shiny oval blue-black, brown, or bronze beetles about $\frac{1}{10}$ inch long. Some species have white or yellow markings. All jump like fleas when disturbed. The legless larvae are tiny and gray white. Flea beetles prefer hot, dry conditions.

Target: Adult flea beetles have an appetite for many garden vegetables, including beet, chard, eggplant, pepper, and radish; they also are attracted to marigold and nasturtium. The adults of one desert species have a fondness for corn; one species of larvae will attack potato tubers. Flea beetle larvae are particular pests of dichondra lawns.

Damage: Adult flea beetles chew leaves, leaving pits or small holes in foliage. While older plants can withstand some damage, seedlings may dry out and die from the many holes riddling their leaves. Jumping from plant to plant, flea beetles also spread plant diseases, such as early blight and bacterial wilt; tomatoes are often a victim. On dichondra lawns, the leaves of larva-infested plants turn brown around the edges, then entirely brown.

Tobacco flea beetle adult

Life cycle: Adult flea beetles overwinter in weeds and garden debris, and in warm-winter climates may gravitate to nasturtium vines left standing in the garden. In late spring they lay tiny white eggs under the soil around host plants. Larvae feed and pupate underground. There are one to four generations per year.

Prevention: Clean up the garden to remove havens for overwintering adults. To protect seedlings in spring, use floating row covers. Keep garden beds well irrigated in summer. Plant vegetables close together, so leaf cover keeps the ground moist and less attractive to egg-laying adults.

Management: Lightly misting the leaves of vegetables and ground covers under siege may make the foliage less attractive to flea beetles. To kill larvae in dichondra lawns, introduce parasitic nematodes to the soil. You can kill adult beetles by spraying with an insecticidal soap or with an insecticide containing rotenone or carbaryl, applied according to label directions. Tilling between crops will cut down the number of eggs, larvae, and pupae in soil.

FRUIT FLIES

FRUIT AND NUT PESTS

✂ ZONES: ALL

Adult fruit flies are smaller than houseflies. They are dark colored with lighter stripes and banded or spotted markings on their wings. In their immature stage, they are the white maggots found in fruit.

Target: Fruit flies attack fruit and nut trees as the fruits develop and ripen. Various species, such as walnut husk flies, apple fruit flies, cherry fruit flies, and the introduced pests known as Mediterranean fruit flies—or medflies—target specific types of trees. Caribbean fruit flies attack citrus. Apple maggots attack apples, crabapples, and hawthorn fruit. The Mexican fruit fly is shown above.

Damage: Infested fruits and nuts are decayed and wormy. Apple skins may be dimpled and pitted, cherries malformed and riddled with holes. Citrus fruits may have holes in the skins and rotted interiors.

Life cycle: Adult flies lay eggs under the skins of developing fruits or nuts. The larvae burrow into the fruit after hatching. Once fully grown, they eat their way out of the fruit, drop to the ground, and pupate in the soil during the winter, emerging as adult flies the next spring. Native species have one generation per year, but the Mediterranean fruit fly, where it is prevalent in California, may have as many as ten.

Prevention: Trap adult apple maggot flies and cherry fruit flies with sticky traps in the shape of red spheres; green spheres can be used to trap walnut husk flies. Remove dropped fruit daily or place a barrier such as plastic sheeting on the ground to prevent larvae from entering the soil to pupate.

Management: Placing red-colored sticky traps baited with fruit-flavored or pheromone lures in the branches of fruit trees can be very effective in managing many fruit fly species. However, timing is key. Check with your cooperative extension agent for information on the proper time to hang baited traps and which baits to get. Fruit flies on fruit trees may be sprayed with an insecticide containing malathion or carbaryl, according to directions on the label.

 Notes: In California, some locales have spraying programs to help control the Mediterranean fruit fly.

GALL-FORMING INSECTS AND MITES

TRUNK AND BRANCH PESTS, LEAF PESTS

✂ ZONES: ALL

Several hundred different species of wasps, aphids, adelgids, midges, mites, moths, and sawflies, some of them microscopic, create galls—distorted, sometimes colorful swellings on leaves, flowers, twigs, or branches of landscape trees. Galls may be green and rubbery like the ones found on the leaves of maple or honey locust (caused by flying midges) or on cottonwood leaf stems (caused by aphids), shown above, right; orange and woolly like those on the leaves of live oak (caused by a mite); or woody and hard like oak apple galls (created by oak gall wasps), shown above. Native plants in the landscape are most likely to sport galls created by indigenous insects. Ceanothus plants, for example, are prone to spindle-shaped galls along stems; willows may have reddish galls on their leaves. The fuchsia gall mite, first discovered on the West Coast in 1980, is an imported pest on fuchsias; it is often mistaken for a disease because of the way it distorts and twists fuchsia leaves and flower buds.

Gall wasp laying eggs

Target: Alder, beech, ceanothus, cottonwood, elm, fuchsia, grape, honey locust, linden, maple, oak, poplar, and willow are common hosts for gall-forming insects. On spruce trees, rubbery green or purple geometric-shaped galls are caused by an aphidlike native insect known as the spruce gall adelgid or Cooley spruce gall adelgid (see page 193).

Damage: Galls found on branches and leaves of deciduous trees are not known to harm the trees, although they may be unsightly. In severe cases, a number of galls on foliage may limit natural plant functions, weakening and stressing a tree or shrub. The damage caused by the fuchsia gall mite can be debilitating, because the leaves curl and distort so much that normal photosynthesis is disrupted and the weakened plant fails to bloom. However, infested plants will usually recover if further mite damage is controlled.

Life cycle: Adult gall makers either feed or lay one or more eggs in soft tissue on a leaf or on the thin bark of a tree branch. When the egg hatches, a larva that may be very tiny begins to feed on the bark or leaf tissue. Secretions from the digestive processes of the insects or larvae include a chemical that irritates the plant, which begins to protect itself by sealing off the intruder in bumpy, raised scar tissue. Gall shapes, which are quite specific depending on the insect involved, may appear at first like a bubble, blister,

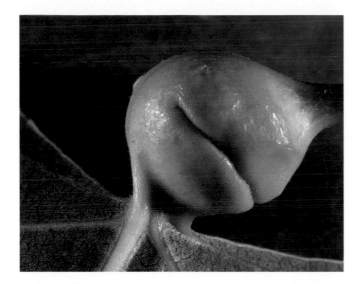

ball, or crownlike projection on a leaf or a twig. Depending on the species, larvae live from weeks to years within the gall, which increases in size over time. Eventually, the larvae break a hole in the gall casing and emerge to pupate nearby. Some species develop completely within their gall or pupate within it, then depart it as fully formed adults. There may be several generations per year, depending on the insect.

Prevention: Since many gall-forming insects are native to the West and many are winged in the adult stage, preventing gall makers from finding your garden is impossible. However, some varieties of honey locust, ceanothus, and fuchsia are resistant to gall-forming insects, such as the honey locust *Gleditsia triacanthos* 'Shademaster', ceanothus 'Blue Cloud', and fuchsia 'Mrs. Victor Reiter'. Check with your local nursery or cooperative extension office for names of other resistant varieties. Gardeners who grow fuchsias for exhibition may wish to routinely use a preventive spray with an insecticidal soap or with a miticide labeled for use on fuchsias.

Management: Where possible, replace affected plants with resistant varieties. Since the damage to landscape trees and shrubs is only aesthetic, prune off affected branches if you find the galls unsightly. Be sure to prune trees at the proper time of year so that branches and foliage will grow back normally. See the *Sunset Western Garden Book* for more information on pruning times for individual tree and shrub species.

Some gall-making insects on deciduous trees can be foiled by an oil spray. The spindle gall mite that disfigures the leaves of maple trees, for example, overwinters as an adult on maple tree bark and may be smothered by a dormant-oil spray, applied while the tree is leafless; apply this pesticide according to directions on the label. On honey locust trees, the honey locust pod gall midge can have up to seven generations per year, but its numbers can be reduced by spraying gall-dotted foliage with an insecticide containing carbaryl or malathion, applied according to directions on the label, during the period when adult midges are departing their galls.

Fuchsias attacked by the fuchsia gall mite should be pruned of all affected branches and the prunings should be discarded, not composted. To kill any remaining fuchsia gall mites, spray the rest of the shrub and the soil around it with a miticide that contains both acephate and hexakis and that is labeled for use on fuchsias. Apply according to directions on the label.

✎ *Notes: Oak apple galls, the rounded, woody galls that appear on oak trees, may persist for years after the intruder insect departs. Some gardeners feel they add character to branches. If you disagree, you can cut off the branch and give it to someone who does flower arrangements; dried branches with galls are often prized by arrangers for their unusual appearance.*

GRASSHOPPERS AND CRICKETS

LEAF AND STEM PESTS

✎ ZONES: ALL

There are more than 600 native species of grasshoppers (also called locusts). Adults are winged, 1–2 inches long, with enlarged hind legs. They can be brown, green, or yellow; the nymphs are smaller and have shorter wings. Crickets are smaller and nocturnal; males chirp in a high-pitched tone. Mole crickets, common only to the Rocky Mountains and interior Southwest, have a large head and front legs like shovels. Cicadas are wedge shaped, up to 2 inches long, with transparent wings and prominent red eyes. They develop underground for 2–4 years, as brownish nymphs, emerging in midsummer to molt a final time into adults.

Target: Grasshoppers chew grasses, corn, and grain crops; crickets chew foliage. Mole crickets tunnel in soil and feed on roots of warm-season grasses, leaving behind patches of dying grass.

Damage: Grasshoppers and crickets are usually not a problem, but in large numbers they can strip plants right to the ground, like the biblical hordes. They do the most damage to lawns in late summer and autumn. Female cicadas slit twigs to lay eggs, causing some dieback; feeding on roots and twigs may cause minor damage (see Cornus, page 84).

Life cycle: Grasshoppers and crickets usually overwinter as eggs in the soil or on weeds. Nymphs hatch out in midspring, molting their skins five or six times. Adults mate in the fall and die as the weather turns cold. House crickets may invade homes in the fall to reproduce.

Prevention: Clear nearby weeds before planting corn. Floating row covers can protect crops against flying grasshopper and cricket swarms. Seal openings around house foundations to prevent entry by crickets in fall.

Management: A biological control, *Nosema locustae*, targets only grasshoppers; it works best when used over large areas. Spraying lawn perimeters with an insecticide containing neem, malathion, diazinon, or carbaryl can help halt a feeding swarm. To manage mole crickets in lawns, drench the soil in affected areas with beneficial nematodes or with an insecticide that contains diazinon and is formulated for soil use. House crickets are often hard to find but if caught can be escorted outdoors or killed with an insecticide spray containing diazinon.

 Notes: The praying mantis and other beneficial mantids resemble grasshoppers slightly. While neither efficient nor discriminating predators of garden pests, these 5–7-inch-long insects make an interesting addition to the garden.

GROUND BEETLES

BENEFICIALS

✎ ZONES: ALL

There are many species of predatory ground beetles, ranging from pea-size to over an inch long. Shiny black, often with an iridescent sheen to their wing covers, they have knobby heads with small antennae and large, conspicuous jaws. While they can fly, they prefer to crawl and can move quickly on their medium-size legs. They live in burrows in the soil, emerging to hunt and feed at night. Often found crawling around potting sheds and compost piles, they will scurry off at a speedy run, when discovered, to hide. The larvae live underground and are rarely noticed; they also hunt insect prey.

Target: Small ground beetles hunt and eat other insects, caterpillars, soil maggots, and soil grubs. Some larger species, such as the one shown above, eat snail and slug eggs along with small snails and slugs; these ground beetles come equipped with long, narrow jaws, which they use to reach into snail shells to bite and pull out the snail that is hiding inside.

An insect-eating ground beetle

Damage: Despite the fearsome appearance of the larger ground beetles, they do not bite humans or damage plants. One species common to western states, known as the fiery searcher or Calosoma beetle, secretes a substance that when touched can irritate skin.

Life cycle: Ground beetles live quiet lives underground and in the shadows of garden structures, patios, and decks. The eggs are laid and hatched beneath the soil; the larvae tunnel around in search of soft-bodied prey, such as root maggots and cutworms. After pupating in soil or in the soft duff of decaying logs, they emerge as adult beetles to meet and mate. Depending on the species, there are from one to several generations per year.

Prevention: No preventive measures are needed.

Management: No management is required. When removing ground beetles that are inconveniently living in structures, prevent skin irritation by wearing gloves or trying not to touch the insects.

GYPSY MOTHS

LEAF AND STEM PESTS

✎ ZONES: POTENTIALLY ALL

A serious pest that has defoliated millions of acres in the eastern United States, the gypsy moth has gradually moved west since it was accidentally released in 1869 in Massachusetts. For an insect, it is quite a traveler, often laying egg masses on cars and trucks. The newly hatched caterpillars can float through the air on silken strands. The adult female moth is white with brown markings and has a wingspan of about 1¾ inches. The dark tan male moths are smaller. The caterpillars are distinctive: up to 2 inches long, hairy, and dark, with red and blue spots on their backs. Do not confuse them with tent caterpillars (see page 196).

Target: Gypsy moths attack many landscape trees, including coniferous evergreens, but especially oaks.

Damage: Gypsy moths can kill trees. Caterpillars cluster, chewing large holes in leaves; a heavy infestation can completely strip a tree or shrub. Conifers may die as a result of a single defoliation; broad-leafed and deciduous species can withstand two to three years of defoliation before dying.

Life cycle: Eggs overwinter in 1-inch-long, suedelike pouches stuck onto tree trunks. In spring, the larvae crawl up the bark to the leaves, feeding until midsummer, then crawl back down to form mahogany-colored pupae in the cracks of bark. Adults emerge in late July or August. After mating, the females are too heavy with eggs to fly, so they crawl up trees or other rough-surfaced objects to lay egg masses. There is one generation per year.

Prevention: Sporadic sightings of gypsy moths have occurred in the West. Be careful not to introduce the pest: when traveling from eastern states, check vehicles and camping gear for egg pouches; when moving west, examine hoses, lawn mowers, and garden furniture.

Management: Hand-pick and destroy egg masses and caterpillars. (Wear gloves: some people are allergic to gypsy moths.) Wrap tree trunks with sticky barriers to prevent adult females from climbing up to lay eggs, and to trap larvae traveling down. Encourage or introduce natural predators—assassin bugs, spined soldier bugs, parasitoid wasps, tachinid flies. The BT strain *Bacillus thuringiensis kurstaki* will kill the larvae when they are still small. Kill larger caterpillars with insecticide sprays containing neem, carbaryl, or acephate, applied according to label directions.

HORNWORMS, TOMATO AND TOBACCO

LEAF AND STEM PESTS

✔ ZONES: ALL

Green with diagonal white stripes, hornworms are giant-size caterpillars, up to 5 inches long, with a single prominent horn at their rear end. They are the larval stage of an even larger grayish brown sphinx moth with a 4–5-inch wingspan. The caterpillars are often hard to see at first because they cling to the undersides of leaves and stems, and their green color provides good camouflage. You can track them by the black pellets of excrement found where they feed. The tobacco hornworm is shown above.

Target: Hornworms relish eggplant, pepper, potato, tomato, and other tomato-family plants. The hornworm is also attracted to garden flowers, such as datura, nicotiana, and petunia.

Damage: Hornworms are rapacious chewers of leaves and stems, devouring foliage and stripping stems bare. Once they have eaten all the leaves of a tomato plant stem, they will move on to eat the green or ripening tomatoes as well. The buds, leaves, and flowers of flowering plants may be chewed to tatters.

Life cycle: Female moths lay pale green eggs like smooth round balls on the undersides of the leaves of host plants, one egg per leaf. The hatching larvae feed for three to four weeks, growing in size. They enter the soil and form brown, shiny, 2-inch-long pupae, each with a handlelike projection at one end. Later, they emerge from the soil as adult moths. There may be from one to four generations per year.

Prevention: To protect tomato plants in the garden, rotate them to clean the soil each year. To expose and destroy pupae, till soil well before planting. Floating row covers can protect crops when the moths are most active, typically in June or July.

Management: In small gardens, hand-pick caterpillars. *Bacillus thuringiensis* (BT) is effective only on smaller larvae, but when combined with the introduction of braconid wasps, it can provide good management through the season. Other natural enemies include birds and the larvae of the green lacewing. Hornworm caterpillars can be killed with an insecticide containing pyrethrin, rotenone, neem, or carbaryl. Apply all insecticides according to directions on the label.

 Notes: A hornworm with small white cocoons sticking out of its back has been parasitized by a wasp. Remove it from your plant and let the wasps hatch to finish it off.

JAPANESE BEETLES

LEAF AND STEM PESTS, FLOWER PESTS

✔ ZONES: POTENTIALLY ALL

Native to Japan, the Japanese beetle is a major pest in the eastern United States that is gradually moving westward. Sporadic sightings have occurred in California and other western states. The body of the ½-inch-long, oblong adult beetle has a distinctive metallic green sheen. The wing covers are copper colored. The larvae, which dwell in soil, are white, C-shaped grubs that can measure up to 1 inch long. Adults feed on flowers and foliage during the day; they can fly as far as 5 miles at a clip.

Target: This beetle feeds on a variety of fruiting and ornamental flowering plants, including fruit trees, grapevines, rosebushes, annuals, perennials, and bulbs. The grubs chew the roots of grasses and garden plants.

Damage: The voracious adult Japanese beetle dines singly or in crowds, chewing leaves until they are skeletonized and eating away at flowers until they are mere shreds. Defoliation of entire shrubs is not uncommon. The grubs are serious pests of lawns, creating brown dead patches that spread during the season.

Life cycle: Adult beetles fly, feed, and mate from June to August. Through the summer, female beetles burrow into the soil to lay eggs. The eggs hatch and the larvae feed on roots. When the soil warms up in spring, the grubs move upward to feed on roots once again. The larvae pupate in May or June, emerging from the soil as adults shortly after. There is a new generation every one to two years.

Prevention: Use care to avoid bringing infested plants or soil into the West from eastern states.

Management: No management is needed where the pest is not found. Hand-pick beetles off plants if you see them, drowning them in soapy water. Spraying the foliage of roses with the botanical insecticide neem appears to deter beetles from feeding on rosebushes. Yellow target traps treated with a food or pheromone lure are effective; empty the trapping bag periodically to prevent a dead-beetle smell. Larvae in lawns may be killed by introducing parasitic nematodes. Kill adult beetles by spraying with a pesticide containing rotenone, pyrethrin, carbaryl, or, for ornamentals, acephate, applied according to directions on the label. Diazinon granules labeled for lawn use, watered in well and applied according to label directions, kill many grubs.

LACE BUGS

LEAF AND STEM PESTS

 ZONES: ALL

Most species of lace bugs are whitish or pale brown, 1/8 inch long, boxy in shape, with transparent, lacy wings. Wingless nymphs, which may have spines, are darker than mature bugs. Both cling to the underside of leaves, sucking sap. The bugs rarely fly; instead, they move with slow, sideways movements.

Target: Lace bugs are attracted to many ornamental trees and shrubs, especially ash, azalea, ceanothus, cotoneaster, poplar, rhododendron, and sycamore. Different species attack specific host plants only.

Damage: As these pests suck nutrients from leaves, the dry, dying areas of foliage lose chlorophyll and appear speckled, splotched, or stippled with bleached-looking spots. Excrement left by feeding insects on the undersides of leaves looks like hard, black spots. Landscape trees usually show damage in summer, dropping their leaves prematurely. Flowering shrubs lose vigor and may bloom poorly.

Life cycle: Adult lace bugs lay egg clusters within leaf veins. Nymphs of most western species hatch in late spring, maturing through molts. Some species lay eggs on the undersides of evergreen leaves and hide them underneath excrement spots that remain over winter. Other species overwinter as adults, hiding under loose plates of tree bark. There are several generations per year.

Prevention: Trees and shrubs infested one year may be sprayed the next, to smother overwintering eggs and emerging nymphs. Use light horticultural oil on the undersides of leaves during early spring.

Management: Pluck off and destroy any heavily infested leaves. Lace bugs may be washed off with a jet of soapy water or killed by spraying with insecticidal soap spray or contact insecticides containing pyrethrum, malathion, diazinon, carbaryl, or acephate. It is important to spray the undersides of leaves, where these pests congregate. Always apply insecticides according to directions on the label. Severe infestations on broad-leafed evergreens, such as ceanothus or azaleas, may be abated by using a systemic insecticide during late spring when the nymphs are feeding.

 Notes: If you use insecticidal soaps or spray pesticides, spray before or after the bloom period to avoid ruining open blossoms.

LACEWINGS

BENEFICIALS

 ZONES: ALL

Lacewings fit their name. They are flying insects with lacy, netted wings that extend in a graceful oval beyond their slim bodies. Green lacewings measure about an inch long, including their long antennae; they have pale green wings, distinct legs, and copper-colored eyes. The brown lacewing, shown above, is half the size of the green species. The immature or larval form of both the brown and the green lacewing is shaped like an alligator, 1/2 inch long, with visible legs and pincers on its mouth end. In this form it is often called an aphid lion. Larvae can be spotted or striped and may be green or brown.

Target: Lacewing larvae devour aphids, leaf-hoppers, mites, thrips, mealybugs, whiteflies, psyllids, and other smaller insects. Winged adults do not eat insects; they feed only on nectar, pollen, and honeydew from garden flowers.

Damage: Lacewings and their larvae cause no damage to plants.

Brown lacewing larva (top) and green lacewing larva (bottom)

Life cycle: Green lacewings lay their oval white eggs singly, balanced on a threadlike stalk attached to a trunk or stem. After hatching, the larvae crawl to hunt aphids and other small, soft-bodied insects. They feed for a week or two, then spin a spherical pupa and attach it with silk to a tree trunk or to the underside of a leaf. Winged adults emerge in about five days to mate and lay eggs; they die when the weather gets cold.

Prevention: No preventive measures are needed.

Management: Beneficial lacewings can be introduced into the garden. They are usually purchased as eggs that are ready to hatch. Three or more releases, spaced a week apart, may be necessary to establish a large enough population to effectively reduce aphids and whiteflies. To encourage adult lacewings to come to your garden, plant nectar sources such as buddleia, coneflower, lychnis, milkweed, native buckwheats, and yarrow.

 Notes: You should not use pesticides that kill soft-bodied insects while you are introducing purchased lacewings to the garden. To maintain good populations of native lacewings, avoid or limit your use of pesticides in garden areas.

LADYBUGS

BENEFICIALS

✎ ZONES: ALL

The colorfully spotted ladybug, or ladybird beetle, is a welcome guest in gardens. Most of the several western species are about ¼ inch long. Their rounded, shiny wing covers may be red with black spots, or spotted or solid orange, brown, yellow, or black. Some species have no spots at all. The immature or larval form looks like a small, six-legged alligator about ¼ inch long, with a roughened or corrugated hide and markings of orange and black spots or stripes. The convergent ladybird beetle is shown above.

Target: Adult ladybugs and ladybug larvae hunt and feed on aphids, mites, and other soft-bodied insects. They are often introduced into gardens for this purpose, although recent research suggests they are less effective than lacewings for insect pest control.

Damage: Ladybugs cause no plant damage. In the eastern United States, one species of ladybug has a tendency to swarm and by the thousands invade houses. Although they are harmless, this can be a nuisance.

Life cycle: Female beetles lay clusters of elongated orange eggs on a variety of host plants. These hatch into the larvae that immediately begin to hunt and feed on aphids and other prey. After pupating on host plants, ladybugs fly to mate and seek food sources. There may be from one to several generations per year.

Prevention: No prevention measures are needed. Window and door screens may be the most effective barriers against the swarms of ladybugs that invade homes.

Management: Ladybugs are commercially sold as beneficial insects by mail-order firms and at garden centers, usually as bags of adult beetles or larvae. The convergent ladybird beetle, native to Colorado, is the species most often sold. Released ladybugs may fly off rather than settle down to the business of eating aphids. A strategy to retain them is to wet down garden foliage with water or a diluted sugar-water solution before releasing them, since captured ladybugs are often thirsty. Releasing ladybugs at ground level in the cooler temperatures of late evening may also help. To increase populations of ladybugs native to your region, avoid or limit spraying of insecticides within your garden space. Most pesticide formulations, from insecticidal soaps to chemical preparations, will also kill ladybugs and their larvae.

LEAF-CUTTING BEES

LEAF AND STEM PESTS

✎ ZONES: ALL

Leaf-cutting bees can best be identified by the damage they leave behind: precise circles or ovals in foliage, their edges as clean as if they had been cut with a small pair of scissors. The bees themselves are small and hairy, and either black, green, purple, or blue. Their wings have a metallic sheen. Several different species can be found across North America.

Target: Leaf-cutting bees seem to prefer the foliage of roses, although any tree or shrub that has a shiny, firm leaf may be cut.

Damage: Affected foliage is cut from the edges in scalloped, circular, or oval patterns that are about ¼ inch in diameter. Bees may also cut circles out of rose petals. The edges of the cuts become dry and turn brown. While they are unsightly, the cuts do not affect the health of rosebushes or other plants, but the damage may ruin the foliage of roses earmarked for cutting or exhibition. These bees are docile and rarely sting humans.

Leaf-cutting bee

Life cycle: Leaf-cutting bees live in small colonies, gathering pollen and nectar during the warm months and hibernating during the winter season. Female worker bees cut foliage with their mouth parts and then use the material to construct their nests, which are built on the ground under cover of weeds or garden debris, under house shingles, or in woodpiles.

Prevention: In home gardens, leaf-cutting bees can be tolerated, since they are important pollinators for legumes and many garden plants. You can eliminate potential nesting sites around rosebushes by clearing away weeds and leaf debris. To avoid further damage to the foliage of roses intended for competitive exhibition or for sale as cut flowers, cover plants with floating row covers when you first notice evidence of leaf-cutting bee damage.

Management: No controls are recommended for this native insect and useful pollinator.

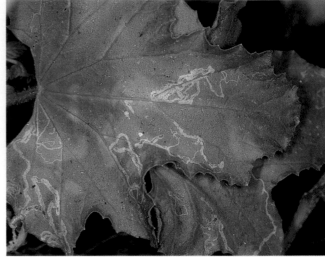

LEAFHOPPERS

LEAF AND STEM PESTS

✄ ZONES: ALL

There are some 2,500 species of these small, wedge-shaped insects. Many leafhoppers are handsomely colored and patterned, while others are camouflaged green to blend in with foliage. When disturbed, they run sideways; as the name implies, they also leap from plant to plant, although adults can fly. Adults are ¼ inch or smaller. The wingless nymphs are smaller still. The grape leafhopper is shown above.

Target: Some leafhopper species savor just one kind of plant, while others enjoy a broad menu. Noticeably affected plants include apple, aster, bean, beet, carrot, eggplant, grape, and potato. The rose leafhopper attacks rosebushes and apple trees.

Damage: Both adults and nymphs suck plant juices, making leaves look bleached or mottled with whitish spots. Sometimes the leaves turn brown and curl up at the edges, a condition called hopperburn that is often found on potato plants. Black excrement specks may ruin grapes and apples (however, they can be scrubbed or peeled from apple skins). Severe infestations cause stunting and leaf drop in flowers and vegetables. Certain species transmit plant diseases: for instance, curly top virus is spread by the beet leafhopper.

Life cycle: Adult leafhoppers lay yellowish, curved eggs in the stems or leaf veins of host plants. These hatch into feeding nymphs, which reach full size within one month. There may be one to six generations per year; the rose leafhopper has two per year. Leafhoppers overwinter as eggs in cold-winter climates; in warm-winter climates, some species overwinter as adults, hiding in weeds and garden debris.

Prevention: Clear weeds and brush to remove cover for overwintering adults and eggs. Use floating row covers to protect potato and carrot and other susceptible crops.

Management: Lure leafhoppers to yellow sticky traps, or wash them off with a stiff jet of water or a spray of insecticidal soap. Natural predators to be encouraged or introduced into the garden include birds, green lacewings, and parasitoid wasps. Apply an oil spray during the dormant winter season to kill overwintering eggs of the rose leafhopper. For severe infestations on edible crops, apply insecticides containing pyrethrum, neem, rotenone, malathion, or carbaryl—according to label directions—especially to the undersides of leaves.

LEAF MINERS

LEAF AND STEM PESTS

✄ ZONES: ALL

The name "leaf miners" is a catchall term for certain moth, beetle, and fly larvae that tunnel between the upper and lower surfaces of leaves, leaving a near-transparent trail behind. Each species produces its own characteristic pattern, but specific identification usually isn't necessary. On vegetables, the most common leaf miners are the larvae of tiny black flies with yellow markings.

Target: Various species of leaf miners attack evergreen holly and other ornamental trees, perennials, annual flowers, and vegetables. A similar creature is the cypress tip miner, which feeds on cypress, juniper, redwood, and other evergreens (see page 167).

Damage: Leaf miners do the most damage on leafy edible crops such as chard, lettuce, and spinach, which may be ruined. On ornamental plants such as holly, the foliage may be unsightly. However, the damage is slight unless there is a severe infestation, in which case the loss of chlorophyll can result in a weakened plant.

Leaf miner larvae exposed

Life cycle: Adults lay eggs under the leaf surface, usually on the underside of the foliage. Larvae hatch and feed on the soft tissue between the leaf ribs. After feeding, leaf miners drop off the leaf to pupate underground or under cover of plant debris. There can be several generations per year, depending on the species.

Prevention: To protect edible leafy crops, use floating row covers to prevent adult insects from laying eggs on the foliage. To prevent larvae from pupating near plant roots, lay a plastic mulch under leafy crops and keep your vegetable beds well weeded during the growing season. Tilling the soil between crops helps destroy pupae. Parasitoid wasps, natural enemies of leaf miners, lay their eggs on larvae or near leaf miner egg sites.

Management: Pick off and destroy infected leaves. Since the larvae are protected under the leaf cuticle, insecticide sprays are not effective and in fact should not be used, as they may harm the tiny parasitoid wasps that prey on leaf miners. Leaves that show only small or interrupted trails are a good indication that native wasps are on the prowl.

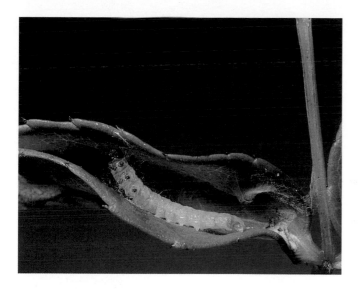

LEAF ROLLERS

LEAF AND STEM PESTS

⚡ ZONES: ALL

The name "leaf roller" is given to many different species of caterpillars that roll foliage around themselves as they feed, creating shelter from predators such as birds. The caterpillars spin sticky webbing as they roll, attracting dust and dirt, which also helps conceal them.

Target: Some species of leaf rollers target specific plants, while others enjoy a varied diet. The fruit-tree leaf roller, found throughout North America, is a thin, light green caterpillar with a black spot on its head; it feeds on apple trees as well as on aspen, buckeye, maple, oak, poplar, and willow. When disturbed, it wriggles vigorously and tries to escape by dropping to the ground on a thread of silk. The adult form is a brown moth.

Damage: Leaf rollers rarely do enough damage to hurt garden shrubs and flowers. The fruit-tree leaf roller is an exception, because it feeds on new growth. The new leaves appear ragged or stunted, and the tree or plants beneath are covered with silken threads. In severe infestations, an entire tree may be defoliated and weakened, although it may produce a second crop of spring leaves. Some leaf rollers eat and scar fruits.

Life cycle: Adults lay masses of eggs on host plants, which hatch out as caterpillars and begin to feed, sometimes moving from leaf to leaf as they grow. Fruit-tree leaf rollers pupate within rolled leaves or attached to bark with a brownish silk cocoon, emerging as adults two weeks later. There is one generation per year. Other leaf rollers usually have two or three generations and overwinter as eggs or as pupae.

Prevention: Natural enemies of leaf roller caterpillars include birds and parasitoid trichogramma wasps, which can be encouraged or introduced to the garden. Dusting ornamental plant foliage with *Bacillus thuringiensis* (BT) on a routine basis may kill some leaf rollers as they hatch.

Management: Pick off and destroy infested leaves. Where the fruit-tree leaf roller is a problem, apply dormant-oil spray during the winter when the trees are leafless, thoroughly covering the branches with oil to smother and kill any egg masses.

LEAF SKELETONIZERS

LEAF AND STEM PESTS

⚡ ZONES: ALL

Skeletonizers are named for their habit of chewing plant tissue between the upper and lower leaf surfaces. The leaf, instead of looking chewed, is ghostly pale and translucent between the ribs when it should be solid and green. Leaf skeletonizers are the larval form of several insect species that are also called casemakers: their other calling card is a cigar-shaped cocoon with a ribbed, boxy shape.

Target: The oak ribbed casemaker feeds on both deciduous and live oak; the oak leaf skeletonizer feeds on the leaves of oak and chestnut. A different species known as the birch skeletonizer attacks only birch; yet another species, shown above, attacks only apple-family fruiting trees, such as apple, crabapple, hawthorn, and sometimes cherry.

Damage: On oak leaves, damage by the oak ribbed skeletonizer first appears as brown patches when the young larvae hatch and feed within the leaf. As they grow, they begin to chew the undersides of leaves as well, attaching themselves to the underleaf surface with rounded webbing. Eventually, leaves turn translucent between the veins. The lack of chlorophyll in the affected leaves and the numbers of larvae present are usually not extreme enough to damage the health of the tree.

Life cycle: Flying adults lay eggs on leaves of host plants; these hatch and the larvae chew their way through the leaf cuticle, then feed on the green tissue of the leaf as they attain their full size of about ¼ inch. Once full grown, they spin a white silk cocoon that is pea size, cigar shaped, and often ribbed. The white cocoons can be found on leaves, tree bark, nearby plants, and garden structures. There are two generations per year of most species; the birch skeletonizer produces only one generation per year.

Prevention: No preventive measures are known.

Management: No controls are usually needed, since the damage to trees is generally superficial. To reduce populations of skeletonizers, remove and destroy leaves that show "window" damage or cocoons. You can treat a severe infestation of the oak ribbed casemaker on deciduous or evergreen oak trees by spraying the undersides of the leaves with an insecticide containing carbaryl, applied according to label directions, in the spring and again in midsummer.

MAGGOTS, ONION AND ROOT

ROOT PESTS

✎ ZONES: ALL

The onion maggot and other root maggots in the genus *Delia* live in the soil and chew at the root hairs of plants or make tunnels through root crops such as onions and garlic. Usually shiny white, the maggots are about ⅓ inch long and may have a blunted head. The adult form is a dark gray fly that looks like a housefly.

Target: Onion maggots infest onion-family crops, such as garlic, leek, onion, and shallot, shown above. Related species attack the roots of vegetable seedlings in early spring.

Damage: Onion bulbs are gouged with holes. These openings often provide entry to the bacteria that cause soft rot, which ruins onions with a powdery, blackish bloom that collapses the entire bulb. On the surface, onion tops may look wilted, yellowed, or stunted. Harvested onions may rot in storage.

Life cycle: This pest does most damage in the cool, wet weather of early spring, although successive generations (two to three each year) may extend the problem through the summer. The adult fly lays clusters of white eggs at the base of young plants. When the larvae hatch, they burrow into the roots. After three to four weeks, the maggots pupate and may overwinter in the soil in pupal form as a brown, cylindrical case about the size of a grain of rice.

Prevention: Placing floating row covers or cheesecloth over seedbeds in early spring will prevent the flies from laying eggs in sprouting crops. Crop rotation may help as well.

Management: Remove and destroy infected plants immediately. You may purchase beneficial nematodes that prey on the onion maggot and water them into the soil; keep the soil around the roots moist so the nematodes will remain active. In the fall, till the soil throughly to expose and destroy any overwintering pupae. To clean soil of onion maggots, treat planting areas with an insecticide registered for soil use and containing diazinon or chlorpyrifos. Apply according to directions on the product label.

MAPLE MOTHS

LEAF AND STEM PESTS

✎ ZONES: POTENTIALLY ALL

Two moths that attack maples are common to the eastern United States and sometimes appear on specimen maples brought into the West from those regions. The maple trumpet skeletonizer, shown above, native as far west as Michigan, attacks only maples during its immature or larval stage. This caterpillar often rolls up leaves with silk to make a hiding place. An unrelated species also seen in caterpillar form is often called the maple leaf cutter, for its habit of trimming bits of foliage and wrapping them with silk to form a protective covering while feeding. A variety of other caterpillars also feed on maple foliage; these rarer insect pests may be considered part of a group affecting landscape maples and the unique and often costly maple varieties used for Japanese gardens and bonsai.

Target: Maple moth caterpillars are found on maple, both container plants and landscape trees.

Damage: Large holes are cut or chewed in foliage; branches of small trees may be defoliated completely. Leaves may be rolled up with webbing to hide the caterpillar inside. Bonsai specimens may be weakened and fail to thrive.

Life cycle: Caterpillars appear in late spring or early summer, chewing buds, feeding on foliage, and moving around the branches until they reach full size. The maple skeletonizer overwinters as a pupa, in a cocoon tied with silk to branches or trunk bark. The maple leaf cutter pupae overwinter beneath the soil; it is during this period that they are most likely to be transported to locations outside of their natural range. Adult moths emerge in spring to mate and lay eggs on host plants. There is one generation per year.

Prevention: Check maples for signs of leaf damage. In addition, look for rolled-up leaves or leaves that may be tied together with webby silk, where a caterpillar may be hiding. The slim brown caterpillars may also travel unnoticed on leaf twigs; you can locate them by running your fingers along the branches.

Management: Hand-pick and destroy caterpillars and cocoons. Caterpillars on maple trees may also be killed by spraying foliage with the microbial insecticide *Bacillus thuringiensis* (BT). To avoid killing off desirable butterfly larvae, apply BT only to infected maple trees.

MEALYBUGS

LEAF AND STEM PESTS

✓ ZONES: ALL

Common on house plants, these sap-feeding aphid relatives are also found outdoors in warm climates. Their bristly gray coats make them look like powdery or cottony fluff when they mass in colonies on leaves and stems. Their waxy coating is a shield that protects them from most pesticide sprays. Citrus mealybugs are shown above.

Target: Mealybugs feed on the soft green tissue of house plants. They also favor cacti, succulents, citrus, and other landscape ornamental plants. Annual and perennial flowers may be affected.

Damage: Mealybugs in large colonies weaken plant tissues by sucking plant juices. Leaves may be stunted, distorted, discolored, spotted, or yellowed. Mealybugs excrete a sugary honeydew when they feed, and this honeydew attracts not only ants but also a sooty mold fungus that appears as black sticky goo on leaves and stems.

Life cycle: Small numbers of mealybugs quickly become large colonies, since each adult female may lay up to 600 eggs at a time. The eggs are usually laid beneath leaves in a white cottony sac. Nymphs hatch in about ten days and crawl to feeding sites, usually in the crotches between leaf petioles and stems. Overlapping generations feed in the same colonies; there may be several generations per year. Mealybugs overwinter as eggs or adults in warm climates; they proliferate quickly indoors in cold-winter areas.

Prevention: Controlling ants around cactus or succulent plants is a good strategy, since ants often cultivate mealybugs in exchange for honeydew.

Management: Natural predators to encourage or introduce in the garden include green lacewings and ladybugs, particularly a ladybug species known as the mealybug destroyer. Spray branches and leaves of citrus trees with a light horticultural oil. Choose a cool or overcast day to apply the oil spray; during hot, sunny weather the oil may burn the leaves. For severe infestations on citrus, apply an insecticide containing pyrethrum, neem, malathion, diazinon, or, for ornamentals, acephate. Always apply insecticides according to directions on the label.

 Notes: The mealybug destroyer is a black-and-orange ladybug native to Australia, often sold commercially to control mealybugs in greenhouses. To thrive, these beneficial insects need warm temperatures and high humidity, so their usefulness in the garden is limited to warm months and warm-winter areas. They do not survive cold winters.

MEXICAN BEAN BEETLES

LEAF AND STEM PESTS

✓ ZONES: 6–24

Mexican bean beetles are found throughout North America except for the Northwest, and everywhere they are prevalent they can be serious pests on garden bean crops. Closely related to ladybugs, they resemble these helpful insects in size and shape, but the bronze or coppery sheen of their wing covers gives them away. Adult bean beetles have rows of black spots on their backs. The immature or larval form is ⅓ inch long and yellowish, with rows of spines on the back.

Target: Mexican bean beetles attack most varieties of bean plants.

Damage: Adult bean beetles and their larvae feed on the undersides of leaves, chewing away leaf tissue and leaving skeletonized stems behind. Bean pods may also be chewed. Heavily infested plants may die. The worst damage occurs in July and August.

Life cycle: Bean beetles overwinter as adults in garden debris or in wooded areas. In spring, females emerge to feed lightly and lay eggs in a yellowish cluster on the undersides of bean leaves. After hatching, the larvae feed for two to five weeks, then pupate on the leaves. Adults are plain yellow when they first emerge from pupa. Their spots appear later, after voracious feeding in late summer.

Prevention: Choose from the varieties of American natives or European species that are resistant to the Mexican bean beetle. Use row covers in spring to shield bean plants from egg-laying adults. Check the undersides of the leaves on young bean plants for yellow egg masses. In the fall, clean up garden debris and brush in nearby wooded areas to remove havens for adult beetles.

Management: Place a cloth beneath bean plants and shake the plants; the beetles will drop off onto the cloth and can be gathered up and destroyed. Hand-pick and destroy adult beetles, larvae, and egg masses. Natural predators to encourage or introduce include toads, birds, spined soldier bugs, and parasitoid wasps. If bean crops are severely or repeatedly infested, spray plants with an insecticide containing rotenone, pyrethrum, malathion, or carbaryl. Apply according to directions on the label, and be sure to spray the undersides of leaves, where the insects congregate. To avoid killing off ladybugs and other beneficial insects, target your spraying only to affected bean plants.

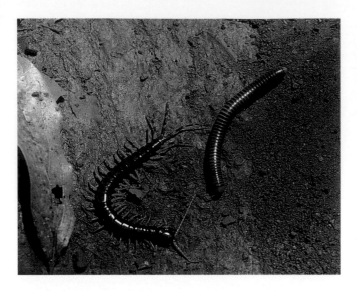

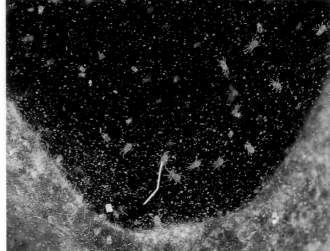

MILLIPEDES AND CENTIPEDES

SOIL PESTS, BENEFICIALS

ZONES: ALL

Centipedes, shown above, left, look like 1-inch worms with many feet. They are brown and somewhat flattened; with one pair of legs per segment, they run fast. They hunt at night, seizing and paralyzing smaller insect prey with venomous claws, and hide during the day under logs and stones or in damp debris. Millipedes, shown above, right, have hard-shelled, cylindrical, and segmented bodies, with two pairs of short legs per segment. They can measure up to 2 inches long and may be black, pink, or gray brown. Most coil up when disturbed. They too prefer a damp environment.

Target: Centipedes are beneficial soil dwellers that gobble up insects, baby snails, and slugs. Millipedes benefit gardens by feeding on decaying plant material, helping to create humus. They may eat fallen fruit.

Damage: Centipedes do not eat plants but occasionally bite humans (it hurts like a bee sting). Millipede feeding may damage fallen fruit; some species can irritate the skin when touched. Both can be a nuisance when they invade homes or gardens in large numbers.

Life cycle: Centipedes and millipedes overwinter underground, as adults. In the spring, they lay clusters of translucent eggs in or on the soil. These hatch into nymphs that are smaller versions of the adults. There is one generation per year.

Prevention: Fruits that ripen on the ground, such as strawberries, can be protected by mulching the soil surface around plants with dry straw or diatomaceous earth. To prevent centipedes from entering your home, eliminate damp areas around house foundations.

Management: You can swat indoor invaders or spray with an insecticide labeled for indoor use and containing pyrethrin. To minimize millipede damage in garden beds, sprinkle diatomaceous earth or ashes between the rows. These materials irritate the millipede's many feet but make an effective barrier only if replaced when wet. For serious infestations, treat the soil with an insecticide containing diazinon labeled for soil use, and apply according to directions on the label.

 Notes: Despite their name, millipedes do not have 1,000 legs, but they may have as many as 400. Centipedes found in North America typically have about 30 legs. Some centipedes found in the tropics can have several hundred legs and reach 12 inches long.

MITES

LEAF AND STEM PESTS, FLOWER PESTS

ZONES: ALL

Mites are common throughout North America and native to the continent, although some pest species have been introduced accidentally from overseas. They are not insects; rather, as their eight legs imply, they are closely related to spiders. Variously colored—they may be red, black, green, or yellow—these tiny creatures are about the size of a pinpoint and are nearly invisible, except when clustered together to feed. They are usually identified by the damage they cause. If you suspect mites are responsible for plant damage, hold a piece of white paper under the affected foliage and tap the plant. The disturbed mites will drop onto the paper, looking like specks of pepper, then try to crawl away. The spider mite, shown above, is also a common pest on house plants, where it makes a cottony web between leaf stems.

Target: While some mites, such as clover mites and citrus bud mites, are host specific, spider mites and rust mites attack a variety of annuals, perennials, vegetables, shrubs, trees, and potted plants. Severe mite infestations usually coincide with periods of dry, hot weather and tend to occur on plants that have not been well irrigated.

Damage: Mites in hordes suck juices from leaves, stems, and flower buds. On landscape plants and vegetables, the affected foliage or flowers may appear dull colored and on closer inspection may look stippled, spotted, bleached, yellowed, twisted, or deformed. On tomatoes, potatoes, petunias, and other members of the family *Solanaceae*, greasy yellow to bronze-colored leaves are a sure sign of the tomato russet mite. On all plants bothered by mites, the foliage, buds, and stems eventually dry out and turn brown. Webbing may appear between stems and leaf petioles or on flower buds. Heavily infested plants become weak because the flow of water and nutrients to and from their leaves is disrupted; smaller plants and even young trees may die.

Life cycle: Small numbers of mites quickly become serious infestations, since these pests can produce a new generation every three to seven days in warm, dry climates or in protected areas such as greenhouses. In cold regions, mites overwinter as adults or as eggs on the bark of host plants. During their immature or nymph stage, tiny mites often start out with six legs, then grow another two as they reach full size.

Prevention: Dry air encourages mites to breed and multiply, so to prevent a mite population explosion, irrigate plants in the garden and in containers regularly. It is particularly important to provide moist-air environments to susceptible tropical and semitropical plants that naturally prefer a higher

humidity, such as citrus and tomato plants. Hose off landscape shrubs and trees now and then during dry summers to remove dust from foliage and to keep the plants healthy. Since spider mites often hitch a ride on commercially grown plants, check any plants you purchase from a garden center or nursery for webbing and other signs of infestation.

Management: Check leaves of susceptible plants for early signs of mites, especially in dry-weather periods. Succeeding generations of mites tend to spread from the undersides of leaves, near the leaf ribs, then to stem nodes and leaf surfaces. At this point the damage is usually easier to see, but the infestation is also more severe and thus harder to control.

Mites can be sprayed off foliage with a stiff jet of water. Ladybug larvae are natural predators; native predatory mites may be purchased as well. On edible plants such as tomato, dusting the foliage with sulfur dust will kill many mites. This treatment will be most effective if you are careful to dust the undersides of leaves. Following up the treatment by thoroughly irrigating the soil around plants to provide a moist-air environment will discourage new attacks. Some insecticidal soaps are formulated for mite control (and are labeled as such) and can be used on vegetables and plants to manage small infestations. Bedding plants and flowering annuals that are heavily infested are best torn up and thrown out.

Tomato russet mites, magnified

On citrus and deciduous trees and shrubs, spraying with horticultural oil in late winter may smother mites and overwintering eggs. Be sure to cover all the branches and bark with the spray. Lighter oils (known as summer oils) can be used on evergreens and citrus at other times of year to control mites, but these should not be used if daytime temperatures will exceed 90°F, because oiled foliage may burn in high heat. If the affected plant is a broad-leafed ornamental or conifer, check the label of the oil spray to make sure it can be safely used on the plant; some oils will discolor the foliage of evergreens.

Since mites are not insects, insecticides generally do not kill them. In some cases mites have evolved a resistance to pesticides, although these sprays may still kill off beneficial insects, such as ladybug larvae. Miticides containing a combination of synthetics can be effective against mites on ornamental shrubs. Consult the label on the container to be sure the pesticide is labeled for use on the type of plant that is infested, and always apply insecticides according to the directions on the label.

 Notes: Predatory mites, which feed on greenhouse thrips and other mite species, are sometimes available through insectaries. Native predatory mites can be as small as a speck of pepper, so their good work usually goes unnoticed.

NEMATODES

ROOT PESTS, BENEFICIALS

✀ ZONES: ALL

Nematodes are not insects but microscopic worms less than $\frac{1}{16}$ inch long. There are two basic types: root nematodes live in the soil and feed on plant roots, and foliar nematodes live in stems and leaves. Some are the gardener's friend, beneficial because they attack harmful insect pests. Virtually invisible to the naked eye, nematodes may be found wherever there is moist, rich soil. They move from garden to garden by hitching a ride on transplants, garden tools, water, ants, and shifted earth.

Target: Root and foliar nematodes are attracted to particular plant hosts. The most troublesome species afflict the roots of tomato, shown above, and other vegetable crops.

Damage: Nematode damage often looks like a plant disease. Leaves may turn yellow and become wilted or stunted. When plants are pulled out of the ground, roots may look stunted and show lumpy nodules. Unlike the nodules produced by beneficial, nitrogen-fixing bacteria on the roots of legumes, nematode nodules can't be flicked off with a fingernail. Firmly attached, the nodules shelter the nematodes and help them siphon off nutrients and water. These activities weaken the host plant.

Life cycle: It takes nematodes about one month to hatch from their gelatinous egg mass and become fully formed adults. Generations are continuous throughout the year, although nematodes are most active in warm soil. They overwinter as eggs or as adults, depending on the climate.

Prevention: Some varieties of tomato are resistant to root nematodes.

Management: Remove and destroy infected plants, along with their roots. Natural enemies of nematodes include a soil fungus that can be encouraged by digging in organic matter such as leaf mold. Planting Mexican marigold *(Tagetes)* throughout flower and vegetable beds appears to inhibit soil nematodes, but soil solarization and crop rotation are more effective. For severe cases, consult a pest control professional about soil fumigation. No chemical controls available to home gardeners will kill nematodes.

 Notes: Certain beneficial nematodes, available for purchase, attack some 400 varieties of borers, caterpillars, and insect root pests by parasitizing soil grubs or releasing bacteria that kill insect larvae. To apply, mix the nematodes with water and spray the soil or target plants, or inject them into plant stems with a syringe. Repeat applications every two to three weeks if needed.

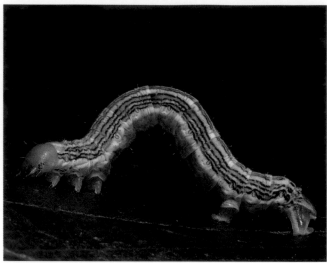

OAK MOTHS

LEAF PESTS

✄ ZONES: 6–9, 14–17

Also known as the California oak worm, the larva of the oak moth causes visible damage to oak trees through the West. The larvae are striped black and yellow and at full size are 1 inch long. The adult moth, which may be tan or gray, has a 1-inch wingspan and noticeable veining on its wings. The oak moth is most common along the coast near San Francisco and Monterey bays.

Target: The oak moth is attracted only to oak trees and prefers to lay its eggs on the coast live oak, *Quercus agrifolia.*

Damage: Larvae chew oak leaves from late winter through early fall, making holes and eventually defoliating branches. The damage worsens through warm weather; entire trees may be defoliated by September. Healthy trees and deciduous oaks usually bounce back from infestation, although landscape trees will look terrible while defoliated. Stressed evergreen oaks and young transplants may die with repeated defoliation.

Life cycle: There are two generations per year. Adult moths lay their tiny round eggs in groups of two or three dozen on oak leaves in June and July and in October or November. After hatching, the larvae overwinter as caterpillars, and their feeding becomes more aggressive as they reach full size. The shell-like pupae resemble dried leaves but are white or yellow with black marks; they may be attached to bark, leaves, or twigs.

Prevention: Since the insect is native and flies to target trees, infestations cannot be prevented.

Management: Check leaves for caterpillars and chewing damage in the summertime. Small populations of this native caterpillar do not harm healthy oak trees, so an insecticide treatment may not be needed in most years. If you see more than two dozen caterpillars on a branch, you may wish to spray with an insecticide. Smaller larvae can be killed by spraying or dusting the undersides of leaves with *Bacillus thuringiensis* (BT), although this bacterial control is not very effective on full-size caterpillars. Hand-pick or kill the larger caterpillars by spraying them with an insecticide containing carbaryl or acephate, applied according to label directions. Large trees may need to be treated by an arborist or a pest control professional.

OMNIVOROUS LOOPERS AND INCHWORMS

ROOT PESTS

✄ ZONES: ALL

The omnivorous looper, shown above, gets part of its name because it folds into a rounded loop as it walks. The full-grown omnivorous looper is a slender, 1-inch-long caterpillar, yellow, green, or pink, with black stripes along the sides and a golden head. The adult form is a tan night-flying moth. There are several species in the West. Inchworms are hairless green or brown caterpillars.

Target: Omnivorous loopers are found on deciduous trees, including buckeye, chestnut, elm, ginkgo, maple, willow, and fruit trees. Inchworms are commonly a pest on fruit trees.

Damage: Loopers and inchworms feed on the edges of foliage, chewing through the soft parts of a leaf surface, leaving a thin membrane that browns with age. Sometimes these caterpillars spin silk to tie leaves together and feed within. Tree health is not affected, but specimen ornamentals look unkempt. On fruiting trees, large colonies of inchworms may defoliate branches and chew into the skin of fruits.

Life cycle: Adult moths of the omnivorous looper fly to lay barrel-shaped eggs in clusters on the undersides of leaves. The hatched caterpillars feed for about six weeks, then spin a small brown or white cocoon that is attached to a leaf with white webbing. After a short time, adult moths emerge. There may be as many as five generations per year. The eggs of the inchworm are laid in spring or fall by female moths that climb up tree trunks. The eggs hatch about the time new growth appears on twigs, and the inchworms feed for three to four weeks before they lower themselves to the ground on a silken thread to pupate in the soil. Inchworms have one generation per year.

Prevention: Check tree foliage now and then for caterpillars or cocoons. Protect trees from inchworms by wrapping sticky barriers around the trunks in spring and fall to trap wingless adult females that will be laying eggs.

Management: Hand-pick and destroy caterpillars and any leaves that hold cocoons. Apply dormant-oil spray while orchard trees are leafless, to smother overwintering inchworm eggs. Omnivorous loopers and inchworms can be controlled by spraying or dusting leaves with the microbial insecticide *Bacillus thuringiensis* (BT). Repeated applications may be necessary; apply according to label directions.

ORIENTAL FRUIT MOTHS

ROOT PESTS

✀ ZONES: ALL

The oriental fruit moth is an imported pest whose larvae feed on tree fruits. The larva, shown above, is ½ inch long, dirty white or pink, with a brown dot of a head. The adult form is a narrow-winged, night-flying moth with a ½-inch wingspan.

Target: The oriental fruit moth concentrates on trees in the genus *Prunus,* which includes almond, apricot, cherry, nectarine, peach, and plum trees.

Damage: Early in the season, the larvae of the oriental fruit moth chew new leaves and twigs, causing young shoots to wilt and die back. Later generations enter developing fruits and create wormy tunnels as they bore toward the pit, often leaving gummy castings behind. Damaged fruits are usually those found on top branches.

Life cycle: The adult moths fly to lay tiny disks of eggs on host trees. After hatching, the larvae munch on new growth or enter green or ripening fruits, feeding for about two weeks. The larvae then spin a cocoon to pupate either on the tree or in debris on the ground. Adult moths emerge about a month later. There may be as many as seven generations per year, more in warm-winter climates.

Prevention: Sticky tent traps baited with pheromone lures are used in commercial orchards to monitor and trap adult moths, while other pheromone treatments that disrupt mating have been in use for more than a decade in California. Colorado has seen limited success with the mass release of a parasitic mite. These controls are not currently available for home use, but contact your local cooperative extension agent for updated information.

Management: Spraying is not recommended for home fruit trees, since larvae already ensconced in twigs or fruits are well shielded from pesticide treatments. Dormant-oil sprays are also ineffective against the eggs of the oriental fruit moth. To capture adult moths, hang sticky traps baited with pheromone lures in the top branches of host fruit trees. Pruning off wilted leaf tips and clearing the ground beneath fruit trees when you first notice the pest may reduce the damage to fruits from later generations during the growing season.

PARSLEYWORMS

LEAF PESTS

✀ ZONES: ALL

The parsleyworm is a 2-inch-long, brightly colored caterpillar. A pair of orange horns protrude to frighten off enemies when the parsleyworm is disturbed, but it does not sting or bite. One of the biggest caterpillars you are likely to find in the backyard, it is technically a pest on carrot-family crops *(Apiaceae)*. However, you might want to leave it alone so it will metamorphose into its adult phase—a large and brilliant black-and-yellow swallowtail butterfly. This butterfly is common throughout North America.

Target: The parsleyworm gets its name because it is usually found on garden parsley. It feeds on carrot and related plants, such as anise, celery, cilantro, dill, fennel, parsnip, Queen Anne's lace, water hemlock, and yarrow. The adult butterfly feeds only on flower nectar.

Anise swallowtail

Damage: The caterpillar eats leaves and stems but produces only minor damage.

Life cycle: In cold climates, this insect overwinters as a pupa and in warm climates as an adult butterfly. Female swallowtails lay round, pale green or cream-colored eggs the size of pinheads on the leaf tips of host plants. Small brown larvae hatch out, feed, and develop into caterpillars. After feeding, the caterpillar attaches itself to a plant stem to rest as a chrysalis, which looks a bit like a dried leaf, before emerging as a butterfly. There are two to four generations a year.

Prevention: No preventive measure is known. This species, native throughout the United States, is too widespread to avoid. Fortunately, the damage it produces is minor enough that it is welcome in most gardens.

Management: Hand-pick the caterpillars. Instead of killing them, you may wish to move them to an expendable host plant, such as a stand of wild anise. Birds will pick off the caterpillars, although they may not eat them (parsleyworms that feed on anise have a licorice taste birds do not like).

✐ *Notes: To encourage swallowtail butterflies in your garden, provide water and nectar plants (such as butterfly bush and lantana) as well as carrot-family hosts. Since the microbial insecticide* Bacillus thuringiensis *(BT) will kill butterfly larvae, limit your use of this pesticide in your garden if you want to encourage swallowtails.*

PEARL SCALE (GROUND PEARLS)

TURF PESTS

✎ ZONES: 10–13, 18–24

Ground pearls are scale insects that infest the roots of turf grass in the southeastern United States and occasionally are discovered as grass-root pests in warm-winter regions of Arizona and California. One of many pests that cause circular dead patches in lawns, they can be identified if you pull up and inspect the roots of grasses still alive on the edges of the damaged areas. Pearl scale looks like whitish, pearly cysts or nodules on grass roots. The nodules are less than $\frac{1}{16}$ inch wide. Do not confuse the cysts with the larger white nodules found on the roots of clover in lawn; these are created by nitrogen-fixing bacteria and benefit the soil by pulling down nitrogen in a form plants can use as fertilizer. Nitrogen-fixing nodules occur only on the roots of clovers and leguminous plants, not on grasses.

Target: Ground pearls attack only warm-season grasses used for turf in southern zones: Bermuda grass, centipede grass, St. Augustine grass, and zoysia grass.

Damage: The extremely tiny scale insect attaches itself to grass roots and begins siphoning off water and nutrients. The grass plant responds by forming a cyst or gall around the insect, but nonetheless the grass gradually weakens, turns brown, and dies. Lawn browning gradually extends to large, intersecting circular patches as the infestation continues.

Life cycle: Small infestations can become big ones with parthenogenetic creatures like ground pearls—the females do not need males to produce the young. The immature insects overwinter underground within the protection of cysts, then emerge in May as mature breeding females that crawl through the soil to new feeding sites on fresh grass. There may be one or two generations per year.

Prevention: No preventive measure is recommended where the pest is not found. When buying warm-season grasses as sod, check the roots for signs of scale cysts.

Management: None is required where the pest is not found. If you positively identify pearl scale in your warm-season grass lawn, remove and dispose of the affected sod and surrounding grass. Watering in beneficial nematodes on your lawn during April and May may provide some control if the nematodes can attack the scale insects when they have emerged from their cysts.

PHYLLOXERA

ROOT PESTS

✎ ZONES: 7–11, 14–17

While many people think phylloxera is a grapevine disease, it is actually an insect related to the aphid. Nearly microscopic, phylloxera can usually be identified by blistery galls on grape leaves, shown above, and nodulelike galls on grapevine roots. Although native to much of North America, it is mainly a problem in the grape-growing regions of California. However, transmission of the pest through infected rootstocks may cause it to appear elsewhere in gardens.

Target: Grape phylloxera attacks grapevines; related species of this insect attack the leaves of hickory, pecan, and walnut trees, leaving telltale galls on the foliage.

Damage: Phylloxera is a serious pest of grapevines, attacking roots and weakening the vine's ability to take up water and nutrients. Entire plants may be stunted or dwarfed, or may die back; leaves may be distorted with galls. Also known as the root louse, phylloxera travels underground from plant to plant and can infest an entire vineyard.

Life cycle: When vines and trees have leafed out in late spring, phylloxera leave their galls to lay eggs on twigs. The hatching broods crawl down to the roots and onto other host plants. There are several generations per year in California.

Prevention: Some grape varieties are resistant to this pest. Grape varieties grafted on native American rootstocks can withstand this pest better than European grape varieties. When purchasing grape plants, ask for certified pest-resistant rootstocks.

Management: Natural predators of phylloxera include ladybugs, which can be encouraged or introduced into the garden. Once vines are infested, keeping plants well watered and fertilized may offset some of the root damage. Severely infested plants should be dug up and destroyed. Later, more resistant varieties may be planted in a different part of the garden, away from the affected soil.

 Notes: The phylloxera species that attacks hickory, pecan, and walnut trees does not attack grapes. To control leaf damage on nut trees, apply a dormant-oil spray while trees are leafless during winter, to smother any phylloxera or eggs that may be on tree trunks.

PILLBUGS AND SOWBUGS

SOIL PESTS, BENEFICIALS

⌁ ZONES: ALL

These dark gray, crawling crustaceans with segmented backs and wavy antennae are often confused. Here's how to tell them apart: sowbugs, shown above, right, have two tail-like appendages on their rears; only pillbugs, shown above, left, will roll up into a round, tight ball when disturbed. While adapted to dry land, both are related to crabs and crayfish; neither is classified as an insect. They rest in dark, moist places during the day and venture out at night to feed on decaying plant matter. Plentiful in moist, organic soils, sowbugs and pillbugs can be a nuisance to gardeners who have no reason to fear them.

Target: Pillbugs and sowbugs are often wrongly blamed for chewing holes in strawberries and flowers, since daylight finds them curled up in a hole that was already chewed by snails, slugs, or nocturnal insects. They prefer to munch on decaying vegetation, which is why they are often found near damaged fruits or foliage.

Damage: Colonies of pillbugs and sowbugs perform a useful function in the garden by breaking down plant debris into humus. When their numbers are high, they may nibble on the tender tips of foliage at ground level.

Life cycle: Like kangaroos, females carry their young in a pouch on their bodies. The immature pillbugs and sowbugs are smaller, paler versions of their elders. There are from one to three generations per year.

Prevention: Pillbugs and sowbugs in your fruits or vegetables usually signal the presence of a different chewing pest. Keeping fruits off the ground with a rough mulch or with a heat-attracting black plastic mulch can keep them away from damaged crops that could be partly salvageable.

Management: Instead of killing sowbugs or pillbugs, move them to the compost pile where they will happily feed on decaying vegetation and where their efforts can be more appreciated. If you find individuals that are bright blue or grayish black, this indicates they have been infected with a virus that usually keeps their populations well in check.

PINE TIP MOTHS

LEAF AND STEM PESTS

⌁ ZONES: ALL

The adult form of the pine tip moth has rust red wings with silver gray markings and a 1-inch wingspan. Various species are common throughout North America. The larvae are minute and rarely seen, as they hide within the tips of pine needles.

Target: Pine tip moths are attracted mainly to two-needle or three-needle pines, such as Japanese red pine, Monterey pine, and shore pine. Some, including Japanese black pine and Torrey pine, appear to be resistant.

Damage: The larvae of pine tip moths feed on or in new needles on the branch tips of pine trees. Needles turn yellow, reddish, or brownish, and shoots may be distorted. Branches with new shoot growth may die back. Webbing and oozing pitch often appear on the damaged shoots. Young or recently pruned trees are most susceptible to damage.

Life cycle: Adult moths appear at the same time that native pines put out their first shoots of soft, new growth—which can be as early as January in California. After mating, females lay eggs one at a time on the tips of pine branches. Eggs hatch in one to two weeks, and the larvae tunnel into needles and buds, feeding within for about three weeks before pupating. In snowy climates, the pine tip moth overwinters as a pupa in leaf litter underneath pine trees; there is one generation per year. In warmer climates there may be up to four generations per year, with succeeding generations pupating in cocoons near leaf tips.

Prevention: Plant resistant varieties of pine when possible. Consult with your cooperative extension agent, arborist, or local nursery expert about resistant species.

Management: Prune and destroy affected branch tips from October through January. In late fall, clear leaf litter under trees to remove pupae. Natural predators include native parasitoid wasps that usually provide adequate control for landscape trees. For infestations on valuable specimen pines or bonsai, spray the trees monthly during the growing season with an insecticide containing acephate or chlorpyrifos, applied according to label directions, to break the generational cycle.

PSYLLIDS

LEAF AND STEM PESTS

✄ ZONES: ALL

The several species of these small winged insects are sometimes called jumping plant lice. The greenish or brownish adults are no more than 1/10 inch long and have antennae and clear wings that fold into a triangular shape; they jump up when disturbed. The smaller, wingless nymphs, shown above with green adults, are nearly immobile and often have a white, waxy coating.

Target: Psyllids are usually host specific. In the garden, the favorite feeding sites for psyllids of foreign origin are host plants originally from South America, New Zealand, or Australia, such trees and shrubs as acacia, boxwood, eucalyptus, eugenia, laurel, magnolia, and pepper. The pear psyllid is a serious pest of orchard pear trees and also attacks ornamental pear.

Damage: Adults and nymphs suck plant juices, weakening foliage. Leaves may turn yellow, curl up, and die, or they may look blasted and brown. Honeydew excreted from pear or eucalyptus psyllids encourages a sticky black fungus called sooty mold, which further disfigures and weakens stems and leaves. On pear trees, beads or droplets of honeydew may disfigure fruit. Trees and shrubs fail to thrive.

Life cycle: The cycle varies with the species, but there can be many as five or six overlapping generations in a year. These pests overwinter as adults in warm climates and as eggs in cold zones.

Prevention: To control psyllids, clear away weeds and plant debris, particularly in the fall, to remove hiding places for adults.

Management: You can kill overwintering adults on deciduous pear trees by applying a dormant-oil spray while trees are leafless. Eggs and nymphs are usually impervious to insecticides, although nymphs may be destroyed by dusting leaves with diatomaceous earth or sulfur, which penetrates their skin coatings. Adult psyllids may be killed by spraying leaves repeatedly with a pesticide containing acephate.

RED HUMP CATERPILLARS

LEAF AND STEM PESTS

✄ ZONES: ALL

The festive-looking red hump caterpillar is chunky, 1 inch long, and yellow with black and white stripes and spiny black warts all over its back; when older, it has a large lacquer red bump located two segments from the head end. The adult form is a brownish gray moth.

Target: Native to most of North America, the red hump caterpillar has a variety of deciduous host trees, from aspen and birch to walnut and willow. It is an occasional pest on fruit trees, significant only when found on young saplings of, for example, walnut and plum trees.

Damage: Red hump caterpillars feed in large groups. Slow-moving, they may attack only a single branch of a tree, but they can succeed in defoliating that branch completely. Infested branches are usually at the top of a tree; the first evidence of damage may be a pile of droppings on the ground below. Young fruit or nut trees are most harmed by defoliation. Larger landscape trees can easily recover the next year.

Life cycle: Adult moths first appear in late spring, and females lay shiny round eggs in clusters of 25 to 100 on the undersides of leaves. After hatching, the caterpillars feed on leaves, taking several weeks to reach full size. Then they drop to the ground and pupate in a hard, reddish brown shell on or just under the soil. There can be one to three generations per year.

Prevention: From May to July, periodically inspect leaves on new or recently planted trees for egg masses or caterpillars.

Management: Hand-pick leaves that hold egg masses. Hand-pick caterpillars and either remove them to other host plants or kill them by dropping them into soapy water. Natural predators include two species of native parasitoid wasps. Insecticide sprays are not recommended, as they will also kill the beneficial wasps. If the infestation is severe, dust or spray the affected leaves with *Bacillus thuringiensis* (BT).

 Notes: The wasps that parasitize the red hump caterpillar feed on nectar. They can be attracted with native flowering trees such as ceanothus or toyon.

ROSE MIDGES

FLOWER PESTS

✿ ZONES: 7–11

If the rosebuds on your rosebushes are turning black before they open, the culprit may be a relatively new pest in the West called the rose midge. Although native to eastern North America, the rose midge has been discovered by rose growers in parts of California, Washington, and Oregon. The insect itself is a tiny fly; the larvae, which cause the damage, are white and less than $\frac{1}{12}$ inch long.

Target: The rose midge attacks the flowers of roses, although it may have alternate host plants.

Damage: While other insects, such as rose curculios and rose slugs, also feed on and harm budding roses, damage from the rose midge is more severe, causing unopened rosebuds to turn black and shrivel up on the stem. The foliage and the stems around the affected buds will also turn black. If you inspect closely, you may find larvae feeding on plants. These pests are most active in spring and summer. A large infestation at this time can ruin all the roses in a garden. Rose midge damage is shown above.

Life cycle: Adult flies lay their eggs in the buds, leaves, and growing tips of rose canes. After hatching, the larvae feed in groups on leaves and rosebuds, then drop to the ground to pupate among debris at the base of plants. There can be several generations per year.

Prevention: Be alert to the presence of rose midges in your area. Experts at your local rose society or public rose garden may have up-to-date information about this pest.

Management: If you discover rose midges on your garden roses, prune off and destroy blackened buds and canes. Lay sheets of black plastic underneath the plants to prevent larvae from reaching the ground to pupate. Clear away leaf litter, weeds, or any debris where the larvae or adults may hide.

SAWFLIES

LEAF AND FRUIT PESTS

✿ ZONES: ALL

Related to bees and wasps, sawflies are named for the way the females use their egg-laying organs to saw slits in plant hosts. Adult sawflies have transparent wings and look like wasps, but they don't have a "waist" or a sting. It is their larvae that cause damage to foliage and to fruits. Many species are native throughout North America, including cherry and conifer sawflies, rose slugs, bristly rose slugs, and pear slugs, shown above. Larvae of the slug type do look like little slugs, complete with a slimy coating. Other types resemble small caterpillars. The bristly rose slug has a shiny black or pale green body and legs. Conifer sawflies have the largest larvae; they may spin webs or silky nests on the needles of evergreens.

Target: Sawflies are host specific, each species attacking a narrow range of plants. Plantings of cherry, pear, pine, and rose may be affected, along with alder, elm, and willow.

Rose slug

Damage: On pear and cherry trees, pear slug larvae chew and skeletonize the foliage, starting with new growth, then moving on to older leaves. On roses, rose slugs may chew holes in the leaves or lightly skeletonize the foliage; flower buds may also be infested and chewed. On conifers, webbing or silks appear on the needles; later, the needles turn brown or drop off.

Life cycle: Sawflies lay eggs in slits they cut in the green tissue of host plants. After hatching, the larvae feed for several weeks, then pupate in the soil. Many species overwinter as pupae; depending on the species, there may be one or several generations per year.

Prevention: No preventive measures are recommended.

Management: Sawflies have a large number of natural enemies, including birds, predaceous beetles, viruses, and native parasitoid wasps, which are usually able to manage this pest. Larvae on rosebushes and cherry and pear trees can be hand-picked, washed off the leaves, or killed by spraying with insecticidal soap. Dusting leaves with wood ash will also kill rose and pear slugs, and may control sawfly larvae that attack conifers. No chemical insecticides are recommended for home use.

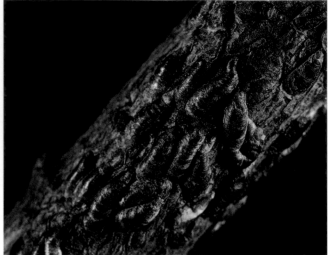

SCALES

BARK AND BRANCH PESTS, LEAF AND STEM PESTS

✄ ZONES: ALL

Scale insects look more like a disease than a pest, because they appear as a crusty, fuzzy, or bubbly growth on leaves, stems, branches, and tree bark. Look closer and you will notice they are individual rounded bumps, each one hard, waxy, or fuzzy. This insecticide-resistant coating protects a tiny, wormlike creature within. Varying in size, shape, and color, scales cling, immobile, like barnacles on their host plants. Remotely related to aphids and mealybugs, scales are just as ubiquitous. Most scales are classified as either "soft" or "armored." So-called soft scales have leathery or waxy coatings; armored scales have stiff, lacquered coatings. Soft scales produce honeydew as a byproduct of their feeding, and this may be seen as a sticky substance on leaves and stems. Common scales in the West with descriptive names are oyster shell scale, an armored scale shown above, right; white cottony cushion scale; black scale; brown soft scale, shown above, left; sycamore scale; oleander scale; snow scale; and calico scale.

Target: Scales attack the foliage of many evergreen plants, including citrus, cymbidium orchid, cypress, pine, and even cactus; other species live on the bark, branches, and leaves of deciduous landscape trees, such as aspen and willow.

Damage: Immobile for most of their life, scale insects suck plant juices from underneath their protective coatings. On conifers, needles and shoots that are covered by scale may turn a sickly yellow or brown. On other evergreen plants, leaves may turn yellow or grow weakly. Infested twigs and bark may be covered with black sooty mold fungus. Unless there is a heavy encrustation, scale damage to a plant is minimal, although leaves and stems will look rough, spotted, sticky, and unsightly.

Life cycle: Scales lay eggs under their protective shells. The tiny offspring, called crawlers, travel short distances on the host plant to settle in. Once they attach their mouth parts—which provide both a sucking tool and an anchor—and start feeding, they begin to create their protective covering. They remain in one place and move again only to mate. The males of some species, such as cottony cushion scale, leave their shells to spin cocoons. After pupating, they emerge winged and fly to mate with wingless females. Armored scales usually have several generations per year, so a small infestation may quickly become a large, unsightly mess. Soft scales have only one generation per year.

Prevention: Many naturally occurring predators and parasites, including lacewing larvae, predaceous beetles, and a microscopic wasp, control or limit scale populations. Unless a valuable plant is in jeopardy, do not routinely spray plants such as citrus and orchid with insecticides, because this will kill off the scale's natural enemies. Dust on leaves inhibits scale enemies, so periodically hosing down plants that are susceptible to scale can help reduce scale problems, especially during dry summers. Since ants may cultivate or farm scales for their sweet honeydew, placing household ant traps around susceptible plants may reduce the occurrence of scales.

Management: If only one tree or only a few plants are infested, removing scales by hand can be far more effective than using an insecticide. Since their sturdy armor protects them quite well, the spray is more likely to kill beneficial predators. Remove and destroy scales by scraping them off leaves and bark with a nail file or your fingernail. On trees, you can rub them off with a plastic scouring pad from the kitchen. Scales have many natural enemies, including lacewing larvae and beetles that attack them in the crawler stage; some beneficial wasps pierce the hard shells and lay eggs within to parasitize the scales. If you see scales that appear to have a hole at the top, these are likely to be empty shells that have been successfully parasitized. Check with your cooperative extension office or garden center for more information about buying and releasing beneficial wasps.

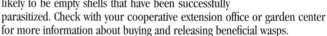

Scale with sooty mold

A treatment for deciduous fruit trees is to spray the bark and branches with a light horticultural oil during the winter season when the trees are leafless. This can be very effective against soft scales, such as the cottony cushion scale that affects apple trees. The oil will smother the insects as they hatch and begin to crawl in early spring. Repeated spraying may be needed if the winter is warm and rainy.

Spraying insecticides is not recommended to get rid of scales, as this treatment rarely removes or even inconveniences the pests. However, if you are lucky enough to spot scales in their crawler stage, you can kill them by spraying with insecticidal soap or with an insecticide containing diazinon. Always apply insecticides according to directions on the product label. Sometimes it is possible to detect when some species of tree scale are in the crawling stage by wrapping sticky tape traps around branches. Check the traps for evidence of crawlers (a hand magnifier may be required), and begin your spraying program when the crawlers have appeared. If you find scales with holes that indicate parasite activity, refrain from spraying to allow the beneficial insects to do their job.

SLUGS AND SNAILS

LEAF AND STEM PESTS, FLOWER PESTS

✎ ZONES: ALL

These pests are mollusks, not insects, and are closely related to shellfish such as clams and oysters. Snails have shells; slugs do not. Both travel by extending the length of their bodies along a patch of slippery, silvery slime. Native species range from the common garden slug, a 1-inch brown slug found in damp places, to the banana slug, a denizen of redwood forests that grows to 6 inches long and has a rubbery yellow skin. One of the most despised pests of western California is the European brown snail *(Helix aspersa),* shown above, the same snail served in French restaurants as escargot. Released intentionally by a French entrepreneur near the cities of San Francisco and San Jose shortly after the gold rush, the European brown snail is now found up to the snow line. It has become a serious crop pest of orange groves in Southern California.

Target: Slugs and snails eat any and all garden plants. They seem to especially relish basil, delphinium, hosta, marigold, and leafy garden vegetables. Only herbs with stiff, highly scented foliage, such as lavender, rosemary, and sage, appear to be unpalatable to these voracious feeders.

Damage: Snails and slugs have toothlike jaws that rasp large, ragged holes in leaves and flowers. Seedlings and new transplants may be eaten entirely, with just a slime trail left behind to tell the tale. The European brown snail will also climb up citrus trees to chew foliage and rasp holes in the skin of oranges, grapefruits, and lemons. These pests feed at night and on overcast or rainy days, hiding under cover when the sun shines. They are most active during warm, rainy springs.

Life cycle: Every slug and snail has both male and female sex organs, so after mating, any individual can lay clusters of up to 80 small gelatinous eggs in soft soil. After hatching, snails and slugs may take from a few months to a few years to reach their full adult size. Once grown, they may lay eggs up to six times per year. Native snails adapted to cold-winter areas hibernate in topsoil. During hot seasons or droughts, snails can seal themselves up with a membrane and stay dormant for up to four years.

Prevention: The first step to managing snails and slugs is to eliminate any daytime hiding places near your vegetable and flower beds. Boards, stones, bricks, unused flowerpots, and ground covers in shady places are favorite haunts of snails and slugs. To protect newly planted seedlings in vegetable beds, surround the beds with copper stripping 3–4 inches high. Snails and slugs will not cross copper; something in their slime reacts with this metal to give the gastropods a small electric shock. Do not lay the copper flat on the soil; keep it vertical, like a little fence. It can be stapled to raised beds, wrapped around citrus tree trunks or flowerpots, or curled into a collar to protect individual plants. Wood ashes, crushed eggshells, and diatomaceous earth irritate the bodies of slugs and snails and thus also make good barriers. During rainy springs, hunting, hand-picking, and laying bait traps for snails and slugs early in the season may prevent a population explosion of these gastropods later on.

Management: Use copper stripping, wood ashes, crushed eggshells, or diatomaceous earth as snail barriers around beds and individual plants. During overcast or rainy days, hand-pick snails (you can also hunt them at night, with a flashlight) and destroy them by crushing them in a paper bag and tossing their remains into the compost pile. Follow slime trails to find their hiding places—brown snails often hang upside down from the undersides of flower boxes or attach themselves to the wood of decks or stairs. Encourage in your garden natural enemies of snails and slugs: birds, toads, salamanders, and predaceous ground beetles. Chickens and ducks are also efficient snail hunters.

Dishes baited with beer will lure banana slugs and garden slugs to their deaths; commercial snail baits poisoned with metaldehyde are the most effective against the European brown snail, which is less attracted to beer. Metaldehyde kills snails slowly; larger brown snails may not die but will be immobilized and can then be picked off by the gardener or by birds in daylight. Granular snail baits will be more effective if you wet the ground first; read product labels carefully before applying. However, heavy rain or water on the pellets usually dissolves them before snails can get them. Set out poison baits in the late evening and try to clear them in the morning, since many formulations can be poisonous to birds and pets. You can also set poison bait within a flowerpot turned on its side, where the snails and slugs will find it. Metaldehyde poison in the form of a caulky paste lasts longer through rainy weather and makes a good barrier when snaked along the edge of paving or garden paths.

Sprinkling salt on snails and slugs does kill them, but salt is bad for the soil and can be chemically harmful to growing plants.

✎ *Notes: In some California counties gardeners can get permission to release a predator snail, called the decollate snail, which hunts and kills the European brown snail. Since the decollate snail also preys upon native forest species of ecological importance, its release is restricted at this time to Imperial, Los Angeles, Riverside, San Bernardino, San Diego, Santa Barbara, Tulare, and Ventura counties in California. Release in other counties and other states is illegal. Check with your local cooperative extension agent for more information.*

SOLDIER BEETLES

BENEFICIALS

ZONES: ALL

Soldier beetles have elongated reddish bodies with leathery-looking black wing covers. About ¾ inch long, they usually have reddish heads with waving black antennae. Adult soldier beetles are sometimes mistaken for fireflies; they do look similar to the flickering favorites of children, but they do not have a phosphorescent tail. While the red-and-black version is most commonly seen in gardens, there are several western species of different coloration, with bodies and wing covers that are tan, orange, or completely black. Occurring naturally throughout North America, particularly in areas with shrubby brush and chaparral, all the soldier beetles are helpful in the garden as insect predators. When disturbed, the adults will often curl their heads under their bodies and drop to the ground. Their larvae, which live underground, are rarely seen.

Target: Adult soldier beetles attack and feed on aphids and soft-bodied insects. The adults also feed on pollen and nectar from flowers. The tiny soldier beetle larvae attack smaller soil-dwelling insects.

Damage: Soldier beetles and their larvae, beneficials all, do no damage to plants—they are garden helpers.

Life cycle: Soldier beetles lay their eggs in clusters on the soil. Once hatched, the larvae burrow into the soil to feed on underground prey until they pupate. These insects may overwinter as eggs or as pupae; there may be several generations, depending on the species.

Prevention: No preventive measures are recommended.

Management: No management of these insects is required. Interplanting nectar flowers among vegetable crops and providing a water source may help to attract adult soldier beetles to your garden. You can also purchase these beneficials in packages to be released once the weather has warmed. After you release purchased insects, refrain from using insecticides, or limit insecticide use, to help establish succeeding generations of soldier beetles during the growing season. Follow the same practice if you want to encourage naturally occurring species in your garden.

SPINED SOLDIER BUGS

BENEFICIALS

ZONES: ALL

The spined soldier bug, a beneficial stinkbug (see page 194), is a dull gray or brown, peppered with black spots, and has a triangle etched on its back. Adults are about ¾ inch long; nymphs are small, dark, and flat. Both adults and nymphs have long, daggerlike mouth parts, which they fold under their bodies when they are not using them to stab and suck the juices of other insects that are their primary food.

Target: The spined soldier bug is usually introduced into gardens to manage infestations of the Mexican bean beetle, but it also feeds on just about any type of insect larvae or insect eggs it can find on a leaf surface. It attacks more than 100 garden pests, including gypsy moths, Colorado potato beetles, corn earworms, cabbage loopers, and armyworms. The spined soldier bug shown above is attacking a cabbage webworm.

Damage: Adult spined soldier bugs do no damage to plants. As young nymphs, immature bugs may suck plant juices, but after their first molt they become predators instead.

Life cycle: Each female soldier bug may lay up to 40 clusters of about 30 bronze-colored eggs each on garden plants. The eggs hatch as nymphs that develop into adults in a few weeks. A growing season may see several succeeding generations, their numbers waxing and waning according to how much insect prey is available. Since the adults can fly, they will often leave an area where prey has been depleted.

Prevention: No preventive measures are recommended.

Management: Spined soldier bugs may be purchased as beneficials in nymphal or adult form. Annual releases may be required to control Mexican bean beetles outside of the spined soldier bug's normal range, which is mainly east of the Rocky Mountains. After you have introduced purchased bugs into your garden, either refrain from using pesticides or limit their use to help establish succeeding generations during the growing season. Since this predator insect is not selective in its choice of prey, releases of the spined soldier bug should be weighed against the danger it poses to other beneficial insects and whether the seriousness of the infestation warrants the release of this predator.

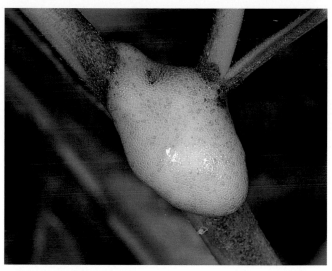

SPINY ELM CATERPILLARS

LEAF AND STEM PESTS

✠ ZONES: ALL

The spiny elm caterpillar, shown above with white eggs of parasitoid tachinid flies attached, is a crawler rarely seen by gardeners, since it usually lives and feeds in the topmost branches of host trees. About 1 inch long, it is dark brown or black with bristly tufts of black spines. A closer look reveals a row of orange spots down the middle of the back, and tiny white dots on each leg segment. This is the larval form of one of North America's most beautiful butterflies, the mourning cloak, which has large, velvety, purple-brown wings.

Target: The spiny elm caterpillar is host specific and feeds mainly on the foliage of elms and elm-family plants, such as zelkova. It is also found on hackberry, poplar, and willow trees.

Damage: Spiny elm caterpillars feed in groups, chewing ragged holes in foliage. The group generally works on a single branch at a time, until it is completely defoliated. Since top branches are usually affected, damage tends not to be noticed until the branch is quite bare. There is no long-term damage to affected trees, and most gardeners are happy to host the young of this butterfly. You should use gloves if you handle the caterpillar; the spines can cause a slight sting.

Life cycle: Adult butterflies lay ribbed orange eggs in massed groups on leaves, twigs, or branches in the topmost part of the tree canopy. After hatching, the larvae feed in groups for a few weeks; then each forms a dark gray or blackish chrysalis, which may be attached to a twig. Butterflies emerge from these pupae, or the insects may overwinter as pupae on the tree. There are usually two generations per year, although in Southern California both caterpillars and adult butterflies may be spotted year-round.

Prevention: No preventive action is recommended.

Management: No management is required, although you can prune off the infested branches if you cannot tolerate the caterpillars. Use gloves to relocate caterpillars to other host trees. To attract adult mourning cloaks, plant your garden with nectar-producing flowers and with elm or poplar trees where they can lay their eggs.

SPITTLEBUGS

LEAF AND STEM PESTS

✠ ZONES: ALL

The sudsy white foam, shown above, that appears on the stems of flowering perennials and annuals in the springtime is produced as a protective covering by the immobile nymphs of the spittlebug. These small triangular insects can be green or brown—although you may not be able to tell which, since they are well hidden by their foam as they suck sap from garden plants. The adult insects, which are oval and brownish, produce no foam and are quite mobile. They hop or fly from plant to plant. Spittlebugs are found across North America, but are noticed more in gardens than in the wild. They are related to cicadas, which may explain why spittlebugs are more of a problem in some years than in others.

Spittlebug

Target: Spittlebugs usually appear on annuals, perennials, herbs, and the foliage of spring bulbs. Two species common in the West are known to congregate on the branches of fir, hemlock, juniper, and pine trees.

Damage: Don't be alarmed if you find this insect in your garden: although they are sucking insects, spittlebugs rarely damage garden plants. You can wash off the frothy bubbles if you don't like the way they look.

Life cycle: In the spring, spittlebug nymphs hatch from overwintered eggs and begin feeding. They reach maturity in a week or two, then their spittling days are over. There may be one to three generations per year.

Prevention: No preventive action is required.

Management: No management of this insect is needed, since the unsightly effect does not last very long. If you can't tolerate the foam, you can easily wash it off plants with a jet of water from a garden hose.

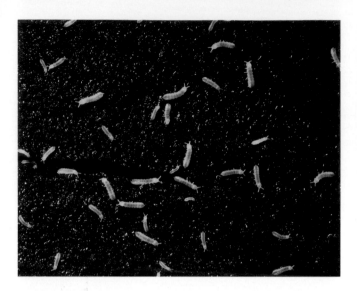

SPRINGTAILS

SOIL PESTS, BENEFICIALS

ZONES: ALL

Less a pest than a nuisance, springtails live in soil and lawns. These grayish or blue-black insects are less than ¼ inch long and have a tiny forklike appendage on their rear. This is not a fang or a stinger; instead it enables them to jump into the air when threatened. Attracted to damp places, they often jump or fall into swimming pools and garden fountains. Springtails are usually found in damp soils, in potted plants, and on the soil beneath sod lawns.

Target: As beneficial insects, springtails gobble up micro-organisms beneath the soil and help turn decaying plant matter into useful humus.

Damage: Most springtails feed on decaying plant matter, but a species that affects lawns will chew on the root hairs of grasses, especially if the grass is very soggy. Recently laid sod lawns may not thrive if this insect is prevalent, as the grass may be unable to resist fungus infections, such as rust, that also attack damp turf. When the sod is lifted up, clusters of springtails may jump up from the damp soil.

Life cycle: Successive generations appear throughout the year.

Prevention: Since these tiny pests love a damp environment, letting garden soil dry out between waterings generally keeps them underground. When setting new sod lawns, be sure the soil underneath is well graded and fast draining.

Management: Small populations of springtails should be tolerated, as springtails have a role in the garden as beneficial soil builders. The presence of springtails in potted plantings usually means the pots are being overwatered. Adjusting irrigation schedules will also keep down populations in lawns. Where lawns are severely infested, drench the turf and soil below with a pesticide labeled for lawn and soil use that contains diazinon. Always apply pesticides according to directions on the product label.

SPRUCE BUDWORMS

LEAF AND STEM PESTS

ZONES: ALL

Spruce budworms are caterpillars that attack evergreen conifers, especially spruce and fir. These pests are 1¼ inches long and reddish brown with raised spots. The adult is a gray moth with brown markings and a wingspan of ½ inch. The moth and its larval form are common in North America, but they are rarely seen in southwestern states.

Target: Spruce budworms appear on fir, hemlock, larch, and spruce.

Damage: In spring and summer, budworm larvae chew the tender tips of new growth on evergreens, covering the needles as they feed with a silky webbing that binds them together and creates a hiding place from predator birds. Webbing will appear on affected needles by midsummer. Large sections of a tree may turn brown and die back.

Life cycle: Budworm epidemics are cyclical, with severe outbreaks every ten years or so. Females lay clusters of pale green eggs near branch tips in late summer. After the eggs hatch, the larvae are quite small; they retire to crevices in bark to spin a silk case where they hibernate over the winter. As the weather warms in spring, the larvae begin feeding heavily, burrowing into needles and buds. After about a month, they pupate on the tree and then emerge as adult moths. There is one generation per year.

Prevention: No preventive measures are needed in most years. Landscape firs and spruces should be monitored in early summer for the presence of webbing on new growth. If you hear of an outbreak in your area, you may prevent infestation by treating buds on susceptible evergreens with the microbial insecticide *Bacillus thuringiensis* (BT). Repeated applications may be required if the moths are in your neighborhood.

Management: Hose off webbing and pry apart wrapped needle bunches, then kill the exposed larvae by dusting or spraying with BT, or treat the branches with an insecticide containing acephate or carbaryl, applied according to label directions.

SPRUCE GALL ADELGIDS

LEAF AND STEM PESTS

ZONES: ALL

The Cooley spruce gall adelgid appears in the West where native stands of spruce are common; it is rare in the southern half of North America. Adults are winged. The nymphs, which cause the distinctive gummy, green, pineapple-shaped galls, are minute and rarely seen.

Target: Norway, white, black, and red spruce *(Picea)* are affected by the Cooley spruce gall adelgid in its nymphal form. Douglas fir *(Pseudotsuga menziesii)* is an alternate host.

Damage: On the leaf tips of infected spruce trees, needles become slightly enlarged and turn reddish brown, shown above. After the needles fall from infested stems, the stems become rubbery, flattened or pineapple-shaped galls. The galls may be green or purple and can be ½ – 3 inches wide. The galls are caused by chemicals secreted by the nymph as it sucks plant juices from needle tips; the tree reacts by forming an enclosure around the offending insect. The galls turn brown and may persist for many years. On Douglas fir, needles may be discolored or may drop.

Life cycle: This pest has a complicated lifestyle, alternating between two different hosts, spruce and Douglas fir trees. Winged adelgid adults lay eggs on either tree. Nymphs that hatch on spruce trees in the spring begin sucking plant juices, which then create the gall. By midsummer, the nymphs within the galls molt and exit as winged adults, which migrate to Douglas fir. They settle into cones or needle tufts, produce white cottony stuff to make a nest, then give birth to a new generation of nymphs. These nymphs feed on Douglas fir until some develop wings, which they use to migrate back to spruce trees.

Prevention: Since these pests fly, spruces cannot be protected. Do not plant Douglas fir and spruce trees close together, as this provides the ideal habitat for this pest.

Management: To encourage replacement growth and reduce the numbers of new adults that will emerge, prune infested foliage while the galls are still green. Wash the cottony deposits off Douglas firs with a jet of soapy water. Natural predators to be encouraged or introduced into the garden include ladybugs and lacewings. Insecticide sprays are not recommended for home gardens, and oil sprays should not be used on spruces, since they will discolor the foliage.

SQUASH BUGS

LEAF AND STEM PESTS

ZONES: ALL

Squash bugs are true bugs; they belong to a group that includes stinkbugs, harlequin bugs, and tarnished plant bugs. The almond-shaped adults are dark brown or black and about ½ inch long. From under the wings, a squash bug's orange-toned body protrudes a bit, looking like edging. The nymphs are smaller and yellowish green with red heads. Both nymphs and adults hide on the undersides of leaves; they can run quickly on their long legs. When they are caught and crushed, their bodies emit a foul odor.

Target: Squash bugs attack plants in the cucurbit family, feeding on cucumber, gourd, melon, pumpkin, and squash. Some squash varieties are resistant, including 'Butternut', 'Early Summer Crookneck', 'Improved Green Hubbard', and 'Table Queen'.

Damage: Both nymphs and adult squash bugs suck plant juices. At first, leaves may show spots that turn yellow and then brown; then the stems of affected plants wilt and blacken. Infested plants are weakened, and younger plants may die. The outsides of squash may show signs of feeding by adult bugs.

Life cycle: After overwintering as adults in garden debris, squash bugs fly to lay clusters of shiny, reddish brown eggs on the leaves and stems of cucurbits. Nymphs group together to feed, eventually growing into the darker adults. There is one generation per year.

Prevention: Plant resistant varieties. Check the undersides of transplanted or newly sprouted squash plants for egg masses; pick off affected leaves and destroy them. Tidy vegetable beds each fall to get rid of weeds and plant debris where adult squash bugs could overwinter. Crop rotation can be helpful (see page 40).

Management: Clean up weeds and plant debris each fall, to prevent adult squash bugs from overwintering. Nymphs and adults can be killed by spraying the undersides of leaves with insecticidal soap. For severe infestations, spray the undersides of leaves with an insecticide containing rotenone, applied according to label directions.

SQUASH VINE BORERS

LEAF AND STEM PESTS

ZONES: 1–5

Common east of the Rocky Mountains but sometimes found in the West, the squash vine borer is the larval form of a large moth that is orange and black with clear wings. The caterpillars can be found within the stems of squash vines; if you slit a stem lengthwise with a knife, you may find a fat white worm about 1 inch long.

Target: The squash vine borer usually attacks winter squash. Occasionally it is found in zucchini plants and in cucumber and melon vines. Butternut squash varieties are usually resistant to this pest.

Damage: The borer tunnels through squash vine stems, disrupting the flow of water and nutrients. Vines suddenly wilt and collapse, even though the plants may be well irrigated. Bubbly, greenish yellow frass, or insect excrement, may appear near holes in the stems. The wilted plants usually die.

Life cycle: The adult female moth appears on squash plants in late spring and lays its eggs on the vines in June and July. When the eggs hatch, the larvae bore into plant stems and feed for four to six weeks. Then they crawl out of the stems and into the ground to pupate over the winter. There is one generation per year.

Prevention: To protect squash plants from flying adults, cover crops with floating row covers. Remove the covers when flowers appear, to allow access by pollinating insects. Crop rotation and early planting is helpful, too.

Management: Insecticides are useless once the borer has retreated inside a vine stem. If only parts of a vine are affected, you may be able to save the remaining crop by cutting away the wilting portions. If you notice frass around a hole, slit the vine near the hole to locate the borer and destroy it. You can also try to kill the borers by injecting beneficial parasitic nematodes into squash stems with a garden syringe. After harvest, pull up old vines, destroy crop debris, and till the soil to kill resting pupae.

STINKBUGS

FRUIT AND FOLIAGE PESTS

ZONES: ALL

Stinkbugs, lygus bugs, and harlequin bugs are colorful winged insects with flattened bodies; they often have markings that appear brightly lacquered, etched, or engraved. But what really distinguishes these true bugs is that all of them give off an offensive odor when threatened or crushed. Quite variable in color, stinkbugs have long legs, long antennae, and shield-shaped bodies with a raised triangle on the back. The backs of the slender and yellowish lygus bugs also carry the distinctive triangle. Harlequin bugs, found in southern regions, have shiny red-and-black markings on their backs. The rough stinkbug, a useful predator of orchard pest insects, is steely gray and dusted with white specks. Adult forms of all these bugs measure less than ½ inch long. The green stinkbug is shown above.

Target: Stinkbugs and lygus bugs attack a variety of fruits from tomatoes to berries to pears and plums, while harlequin bugs are usually found on broccoli, cabbage, radish, and leafy greens.

Damage: These bugs insert their strawlike mouth parts into fruits and foliage to suck out plant juices. Affected fruits and leaves are usually spotted, blemished, yellowed, or distorted. The damage is worse on strawberries and tomatoes, which may show "catfacing"—a deformity in which fruits look gnarled, creased, or twisted.

Life cycle: Adults overwinter in weeds or leafy debris, then in the spring lay barrel-shaped eggs in groups of ten, in an egg mass about the size of a grain of rice, on or in a leaf or stem. When nymphs emerge, they crawl quickly to feeding areas on nearby fruits, then over a few weeks transform into winged adults without a pupal stage. There may be three or four generations per year.

Prevention: Floating row covers offer some protection to strawberries and vegetable crops. Remove broad-leafed weeds and debris that could harbor adult bugs, especially in the spring when populations build.

Management: Adults attacking foliage can be hand-picked and destroyed, or killed by spraying with insecticidal soap. Remove catfaced strawberries and tomatoes before they ripen, to encourage a later crop. In orchards, release parasitoid wasps or tachinid flies, which attack stinkbug eggs and nymphs. Chemical controls are not recommended for home use; check with your cooperative extension agent for information on pesticides suitable for severe infestations.

SYRPHID FLIES

BENEFICIALS

✔ ZONES: ALL

Syrphid flies are native to North America and occur naturally in gardens, although gardeners may not notice them or may confuse them with other insects. Look for them among your garden flowers: syrphid flies have golden, yellow-banded bodies. They look a bit like bees, but they have only one set of transparent wings, which they use to hover in midair over blossoms. In this adult form they feed only on flower nectar and pollen. However, in their immature or larval form—maggots with small fangs—they feed on other insects, particularly preying on aphids.

Target: Larvae of syrphid flies hunt and feed on soft-bodied insects, such as aphids, mealybugs, and scale insects in the crawling stage. They use their fangs like hooks to impale and carry off prey, then drain them of fluids, leaving a skin behind.

Damage: Syrphid flies and their larvae do no damage to plants.

Syrphid fly larva eating aphids

Life cycle: Adult flies lay their eggs near colonies of aphids and other prey. The larvae hatch and feed on their victims as they hatch. There may be more than one generation per year.

Prevention: No preventive action is needed.

Management: Management is not required. To attract adult syrphid flies to your garden, provide a source of water for the adult flies and plant nectar flowers near crops. Winged adult males often establish territories and "routes" on certain plants when they are in flower, waiting for females but chasing off other males and other nectar-gathering insects. Intercropping rows of flowers, flowering herbs, and food plants can help create a welcoming environment for syrphid flies. To allow them free rein in your garden, limit the use of both botanical and chemical insecticides, which can kill the larvae of these beneficial insects.

 Notes: Some species of syrphid flies are commonly called hover flies.

TACHINID FLIES

BENEFICIALS

✔ ZONES: ALL

Tachinid flies resemble houseflies. They are gray and bristled and may be seen perched on flowers or buzzing around the ground. The adult flies feed only on flower nectar, but their immature or larval forms parasitize many other insects. Native to North America, these flies occur naturally in gardens. The tiny larvae look like spined green maggots.

Target: Tachinid fly larvae parasitize grasshoppers, armyworms, cutworms, stinkbugs, and smaller larvae of beetles. Individual tachinid fly species attack only certain types of insect pests.

Damage: Tachinid flies and their larvae do no damage to plants.

Life cycle: Adult flies lay their eggs near colonies of their prey. Some species lay their eggs on the bodies of caterpillars and beetles; when the fly larvae hatch, they eat their way through the living prey. When they reach full size, fly larvae drop to the ground and pupate in the soil. There may be one or several generations per year, depending on the species.

Prevention: No preventive measures are needed.

Management: Management of this insect is not required. Many species are native to the West. To attract adult tachinid flies to your garden, plant nectar flowers near crops. Intercropping rows of flowers, flowering herbs, and food plants can help create a welcoming environment for tachinid flies. To allow tachinid flies free rein in your garden, limit the use of both botanical and chemical insecticides—which can kill these beneficial insects and their young—on flowering plants.

TENT CATERPILLARS

BARK, BRANCH, AND LEAF PESTS

✎ ZONES: ALL

The western tent caterpillar, the larval form of a brown-gray moth, is hairy, wrinkly, and up to 3 inches long. It is orange and black, with white dashes along its side. A forest species is blackish blue.

Target: Tent caterpillars attack many trees and shrubs. They are pests primarily on fruit trees, such as apple, cherry, and crabapple.

Damage: Caterpillars build gauzy nests in the crotches and forks of tree branches. The caterpillars leave these nests during the day to feed on foliage. Entire branches and large portions of severely infested trees may be defoliated.

Life cycle: Adult female moths crawl up tree bark to lay orange-brown egg masses that may encircle branches and twigs. The first crop of caterpillars hatches in early spring, spins webbing for nests, and feeds until early summer. The full-grown caterpillars then drop to the ground or lower themselves on silken threads to pupate in leaf litter. These pests overwinter as egg masses on twigs. There may be one to several generations per year.

Prevention: Check tree bark in the winter and remove egg masses if you see them. Also check wooden garden structures. Natural predators that can be introduced or encouraged in your garden include birds, ground beetles, spined soldier bugs, tachinid flies, and parasitoid wasps.

Management: Spray or dust the tent area with the microbial control *Bacillus thuringiensis* (BT), which will kill the caterpillars. Caterpillars and their webs can also be removed by hand, but wear gloves since many people are allergic to these pests. For severe infestations, spray trees with an insecticide containing diazinon, carbaryl, or malathion, applied according to directions on the label.

THRIPS

LEAF AND STEM PESTS

✎ ZONES: ALL

Thrips attack many ornamental landscape plants and spread virus diseases from plant to plant. Adult thrips look like tiny elongated flies. They are light or dark brown, only $\frac{1}{20}$ inch long, with two pairs of narrow, feathery wings. (The banded greenhouse thrips is shown on page 197.) The smaller and wingless nymphs are light green or pale yellow. There are many kinds of thrips. Although hard to see without a magnifier, thrips can be identified by the damage they cause: silvery or bronzy stippled foliage where they feed. Thrips damage is similar to that caused by mites (see page 180), without the webbing characteristic of mite damage. Mites cannot be well controlled by insecticides that can kill thrips.

Target: Thrips attack vegetables, annuals, perennials, bulbs, and landscape shrubs such as rhododendron and laurel. They also go after roses, cacti, and succulents. Flower thrips, the most abundant species, cluster on buds, flowers, and new tip growth. In the vegetable garden, bean, onion, pea, and tomato may be attacked. Citrus, pomegranate, and pepper trees are targets of citrus thrips. Thrips may infest greenhouses to feed on seedlings and potted house plants.

Damage: Thrips and their nymphs chew and suck plants vigorously, scraping away the chlorophyll on leaves where they feed. The surface of damaged leaves often looks silvery or bronzy, with a pattern of dots or spots where the chlorophyll is missing. Leaves may also be stippled, streaked, spotted, or stunted. Flowers and leaf buds may fail to open normally, appearing twisted, stuck together, or discolored. Although the insects may be hiding in a flower bud or leaf axil or under a leaf, the telltale black specks of excrement indicate that they are around. Infestations are likely to crest during hot, dry weather.

Life cycle: Like aphids, some kinds of thrips can reproduce without mating, so a small infestation quickly becomes a large problem. Immature nymphs molt one or more times before developing wings. The life cycle takes about two and a half weeks to complete. In warm climates reproduction is continuous; in cold climates, thrips overwinter as eggs laid within plant tissues by the winged adults.

Prevention: Dry plants are more likely to be attacked by thrips, so keep plants properly irrigated. The leaves of shrubs such as rhododendron should be periodically hosed off. If thrips have been a problem in your vegetable garden, rinse off the leaves of crops every three days to discourage the insects.

Management: Thrips that attack vegetables, annual flowers, and non-woody perennials should be treated differently than thrips that infest ornamental woody shrubs and trees. For example, a patch of heavily infested annuals is probably best torn out and discarded, to prevent the insects' multiplying in your yard. To keep populations down early in the season, lay shiny aluminum foil mulches in beds to disorient egg-laying adults. (Remove foil when the weather gets hot so plant foliage doesn't burn.) Yellow or blue sticky traps set at foliage level will catch flying adults. You can make your own sticky traps by coating with oil or petroleum jelly a piece of yellow cardboard or a board painted yellow. Encourage or introduce into your garden beneficial insects, such as parasitoid wasps, soldier beetles, and especially the green lacewing, whose larvae will hunt and kill nymphs. Thrips nymphs can also be killed by dusting the undersides of infested foliage with sulfur or diatomaceous earth. You can often kill thrips by spraying them with insecticidal soap or pesticides that contain pyrethrum, rotenone, neem, diazinon, or malathion. Apply according to label directions.

The species of thrips that infests ornamental trees and shrubs can be harder to kill, since the insects hide within new leaf buds or flower buds. Insecticide sprays will not reach them there, though the sprays may mar the appearance of flowers and damage unfurling leaves. Spiders are useful natural predators against thrips on shrubs because hunting spider species will crawl into buds to reach their prey. Releasing lacewings and parasitoid wasps may also provide some control. Later in the season, you can kill the thrips on leaves of ornamental landscape plants by spraying foliage with insecticidal soap.

If a valuable collection of landscape plants (a rhododendron hedge or an entire rose garden) is endangered by thrips, prune and discard infected plant parts in the early spring to reduce the population of thrips on woody shrubs and trees. However, you may lose a year's growth or the current year's floral show. Prune branches well below the damage and just above dormant buds. Avoid shearing off only the infested leaf tips or terminals on woody perennials, trees, and shrubs: the resulting fast new growth just attracts more thrips. After pruning, new growth may be slow but should recover uninfested if all affected plant parts have been removed. (Check Sunset's *Pruning* on pruning specific plants.) Discard prunings rather than putting them in your compost heap or woodpile, where thrips may continue to breed.

After spring buds and blooms mature, you can treat severe infestations on ornamental trees and shrubs by spraying the undersides of leaves with an insecticide containing pyrethrum, rotenone, neem, diazinon, malathion, or acephate, applied according to label directions. Systemic insecticides should not be used on edible crops, but a systemic pesticide labeled for roses may be applied to control thrips on rosebushes if rose petals or rose hips will not be eaten.

TUSSOCK MOTHS

LEAF AND STEM PESTS

✐ ZONES: 3–7, 14–24

The colorful caterpillar of the western tussock moth, the larval form of a brownish moth, is slender and over an inch long. Prominent tufts of bristled hairs sprout from either side of its body, and its back is covered with red, blue, and yellow spots. Adult male moths are winged, but adult females are wingless or may have only wing buds, so they crawl rather than fly. The moth is usually found along the western coast, from British Columbia to Southern California. The rusty tussock moth is a day-flying reddish moth that is black and brushy as a caterpillar.

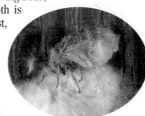

Wingless adult female tussock moth

Target: Hosts for this caterpillar include most deciduous fruiting trees, nut trees, oak, and manzanita. Douglas fir and needle and broad-leafed evergreens may also be affected.

Damage: The western tussock moth caterpillar appears in large numbers every seven to ten years and is rarely a serious pest in the off years. The caterpillars chew leaves, usually defoliating trees from the top down. Later in the season the caterpillars may sample and scar apples or other fruit.

Life cycle: Adult moths emerge from cocoons on trees in late spring or early summer. The wingless female produces a pheromone to attract flying males. After mating, the female lays several hundred tiny eggs on a branch, in a mass about the size and shape of a pumpkin seed. These egg masses remain over the winter, emerging as caterpillars in early spring, to feed and then pupate in fuzzy brown cocoons on tree trunks.

Prevention: Naturally occurring predators, such as small parasitoid wasps, usually keep the western tussock moth in check. Fruit and nut trees can be treated with a dormant-oil spray while the trees are leafless, to smother and kill overwintering egg masses.

Management: The caterpillars, egg masses, and cocoons may be picked off by hand and either destroyed or moved to other host plants. Wear gloves when hand-picking the caterpillars, since the bristles can sting or irritate skin. Large periodic infestations of western tussock moths can be controlled by spraying or dusting trees with the microbial control *Bacillus thuringiensis* (BT) or by spraying with an insecticide containing acephate (for ornamentals only) or carbaryl, according to directions on the label.

SPIDERS

and Other Arachnids

While they are often indiscriminate in their appetites, spiders and other arachnids may be considered beneficial insects because they hunt and eat other, smaller insects. But a small group of arachnids is dangerous to humans and worth knowing about—if only to give them a wide berth whenever you see them.

Most homes, gardens, and woodlots harbor many species of spiders. Not classified as insects, they are more closely related to lobsters and crabs. Arachnids have eight legs, which they use to move quickly when chasing after prey. Home and garden spiders may be active or passive hunters; some species chase their quarry and inject them with a paralyzing venom, while other kinds spin broad webs to trap their victims as they fly by or tumble in. Jumping spiders, lynx spiders, and wolf spiders are hunters that may be commonly seen in western states, as is the daddy longlegs spider often found haunting ceilings and moldings in the home. Outdoors, hunting spiders rest in leaf debris and establish hunting areas under shrubs and hedgerows and around rows of vegetable crops and bedding annuals. Each spider can be counted on to consume several insects a day. Some of the larger daddy longlegs have also been observed to kill and feed on small slugs and snails.

Lynx spider

HAZARDOUS TO HUMANS

Of the few spiders that pose real dangers to humans, the most poisonous are the black widow spider and the brown recluse, which is also called the violin spider. Fortunately, these spiders are well marked and easy to identify. The black widow spider is shiny black, about half an inch long, with a distinctive red hourglass shape on its rounded abdomen. The brown recluse is a dull brown spider of about the same size, with a mark shaped like a violin, in darker brown, on its back.

A third spider with a venomous bite is the hobo spider, also called the aggressive house spider. This small brown spider may be recognized by its web, which is thick, with a funnel-shaped opening. However, there are other less threatening spiders that make funnel-shaped webs.

If poisonous spiders are attacked or disturbed, they will bite humans. Their venom can cause the victim to have a serious allergic reaction. The bite of the black widow spider can be toxic and perhaps even fatal, if medical attention is not sought promptly. The bites of the hobo spider and brown recluse spider do not heal; instead they ulcerate the skin. The venom of all these spiders can damage internal organs in humans and animals. If a person or pet is bitten by any spider or other arachnid, apply ice to the wound to slow the spread of the venom, and seek medical attention immediately.

To prevent being bitten by a spider, leave webs alone if possible, and use care when working in garden areas where these poisonous species congregate. Rockeries, crawl spaces under gazebos and garden structures, dark corners of potting sheds, and stacked woodpiles and compost piles are usual nesting places of black widow, brown recluse, and hobo spiders. Wear gloves when clearing out these areas, to avoid spider bites. Black widow spiders seem to be fond of nesting in the metal ground boxes that shield drip irrigation valves or outdoor lighting wires; use caution and gloves when opening lids of these boxes to inspect valves or wires.

Spotlight on the Black Widow Spider

The eggs of the black widow spider are enclosed in an egg sac suspended in the web (top). This spider can be readily identified by the red hourglass-shaped mark on its abdomen (bottom).

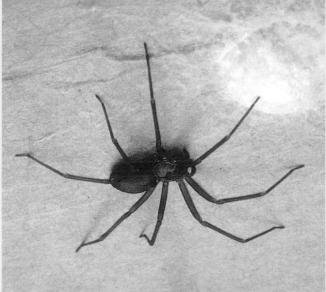

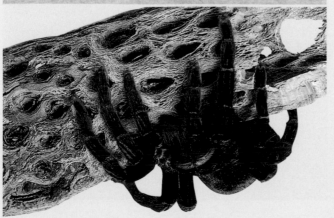

Living with Arachnids

Tarantulas (top) and scorpions (bottom) live in desert regions and rarely bother humans. But gardeners need to be wary of the brown recluse spider (center), found throughout the West. It nests in human habitations such as garden structures and house foundations, and its poisonous bite can be serious.

In southwestern states such as Arizona, Nevada, and desert California, gardeners must add to their daily chores that of looking out for scorpions and tarantulas. Shaking out garden boots or rustling a corner of the potting shed may surprise a small scorpion, which will sting if it can't scurry away to cover. Desert species range in length from 1 inch to several inches—about the size of a fist. The larger desert arachnids tend to be nocturnal hunters, but they may also be found in the daytime, sunning on rocks or resting in the shade of desert trees, depending on the time of year.

Life cycles of arachnids can be a fascinating study—at a distance, of course. Scorpions, tarantulas, and spiders fight with each other for territory; some species, such as the black widow, devour their competitors and even their mates. They reproduce by laying eggs, which hatch into small crawlers that then molt into larger sizes. Some web-spinning spiders are so small when they hatch that they can be carried along by wind on a single silken thread, to relocate far from their original nest. This process, called ballooning, is common to most species; spiders traveling in the air have been found as high as several thousand feet up in the atmosphere, and by this method of transport they may be carried hundreds of miles, even across oceans. Arachnids usually produce one generation per year. Many species are highly visible in the autumn, when they leave the reduced cover of fading vegetation to find winter shelter indoors. Other species die with the approach of cold weather, the next generation safely overwintering as eggs, protected by silken pouches tied to leafy debris or to high positions on garden structures. In the garden, lacy webs should be left intact, to glitter with morning dew or—better yet—to serve the purpose for which they were constructed, to catch flying insects. Spider silks are generated by special organs called spinnerets, which are found beneath the abdomens of the smaller land species of spiders.

Many types of large and small spiders have organs that paralyze or poison insect prey. Emboldened by the venom they carry, spiders, tarantulas, and scorpions will attack much larger creatures and fiercely fight until they or their victims succumb. Unlike stinging bees, which die after they sting, spiders, tarantulas, and scorpions can repeatedly bite or stab their victims with their stingers, injecting more venom each time. In desert habitats, scorpions may also kill lizards, mice, and other small mammals.

To control spiders in the home, you can squash them or spray individuals with pesticides containing diazinon, which will kill them; follow directions on the label, and be sure the pesticide is labeled for indoor use. You can kill individual scorpions by crushing them with a shovel or spade if they pose a danger. If you find large numbers or nests of these dangerous pests, call a professional exterminator. In wild areas, leave scorpions and tarantulas alone, and do not attempt to collect them as pets.

TICKS IN WESTERN STATES

Other members of the arachnid group that cause trouble in gardens are centipedes (see page 180), mites (see page 180), and ticks. Ticks are parasites that feed on the blood of animals, including human beings. Common in wooded areas, ticks drop down from leafy perches to hitch a ride on mice, deer, or other mammals, attaching themselves under the fur and sucking blood through jawlike mouth parts. Fully engorged with blood, a tick may expand its abdomen by six to ten times, and at this point it may be noticeable in a pet's coat.

Tick

Ticks also attach themselves to people. Some wild ticks carry diseases, including Lyme disease (an inflammatory disease that began in the East but has also sprung up in wooded areas of the West) and Rocky Mountain spotted fever. Welts or wounds shaped like bull's-eyes, fever, and muscle aches signal the initial stages of diseases borne by ticks. When in areas where deer are prevalent, wear long pants that extend to the top of your socks, and check equipment, clothing, and skin afterward to detect ticks. To remove a tick from a human or an animal, coat the pest with heavy cooking oil. The tick will react by pulling out of its host. At this point, you can remove the tick with tweezers. Do not attempt to burn or pull out a tick from the skin; the mouth parts can break off and remain embedded, causing an ulcerated wound and further exposure to diseases.

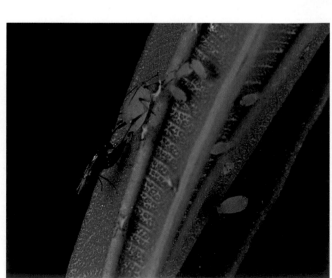

WASPS, HORNETS, AND YELLOW JACKETS

BENEFICIALS

✓ ZONES: ALL

Wasps, hornets, and yellow jackets, like honeybees, have a role in the garden as useful pollinators of fruit, nut, and vegetable crops. Left alone, they do no damage, and in fact many species of wasps and yellow jackets are helpful because they prey on harmful garden insects. Since many types of wasp do sting humans, though, it is worthwhile to recognize them, if only to give them a wide berth, along with the insects we call hornets and yellow jackets. These closely related species all have two sets of clear wings and a noticeably defined "waist" between their body parts.

Yellow jackets live in large colonies, often in underground burrows or hollow logs; they may be seen gathering in garbage piles. Their shiny yellow bodies are banded with brown or black. They tend to feed in clusters; single yellow jackets may forage ahead as scouts in the manner of honeybees. Wasps and hornets generally cluster in nests built on trees or garden structures; wasp nests are often elaborate constructions of mud, or they may be made of a papery substance. Wasps may be yellow, brown, black, or blue; they range in size from microscopic to 1½ inches in total length. Some species of solitary wasps build small individual nests of wood or mud on trees or structures. Some of the predatory wasps, also called hunting wasps (such as mud daubers or sand wasps), build nests in holes in the ground or in sandbanks near a water source. Braconid wasps, shown above, left, and ichneumon wasps, shown above, right, which are native western species, are black and very slender, with transparent wings. They parasitize prey such as caterpillars by laying eggs within the bodies of a larval host. The smallest wasps, although barely visible to the naked eye, make up several species of garden beneficials that may be introduced to manage other insect pests (see Notes).

Target: Wasps, hornets, and yellow jackets are primarily nectar feeders. Certain wasps chew wood to make the stuff of nests, but they are not considered damaging to structures or trees. Hunting wasps feed on other insects, sometimes capturing their prey and consuming it while in flight. Predatory paper wasps, parasitic braconid wasps, and those in the genera *Encarsia* and *Trichogramma* prey on caterpillars and smaller insects—for instance, flies, airborne beetles, and winged bugs. Yellow jackets will attack other insects and are attracted to food debris, such as rotting meat and leftover cans of sugary soft drinks.

Damage: If their nests are not inconveniently located, wasps and their relatives should be tolerated as beneficial insects and useful pollinators of garden plants. While parasitoid wasps do not sting, larger wasps, hornets, and yellow jackets will sting humans if they or their nests are threatened. Wasps, hornets, and yellow jackets do not lose their stingers when they attack, so—unlike bees—they can sting repeatedly. Yellow jacket stingers also release a signature chemical that draws other yellow jackets to attack. Some people are allergic to wasp, hornet, or yellow jacket stings.

Life cycle: Adult mated females, called queens, overwinter in nests or other protected places. In spring, they begin a new nest to produce off-spring—winged workers that construct and maintain the nest and procure pollen and nectar for food. The queens will use their nests for one season only. With the exception of colony queens, in most species all the insects die with the advent of freezing weather. There is usually one generation per year, but several broods from the same queen.

Prevention: No preventive measure is recommended. Removing leftover food and garbage after meals can help keep yellow jackets out of picnic areas.

Management: Nests in inconvenient places, such as backyard trees or the eaves of a home, should be removed by a pest control professional. If you are stung, apply ice to reduce swelling. If an allergic reaction develops, see a doctor immediately.

Notes: Some of the most helpful flying insects in the garden are the parasitoid wasps, usually so small that five or six could fit on the head of a pin. Many species inhabit gardens naturally. To attract them, plant nectar flowers and provide a water source. Encarsia and Trichogramma wasps are commonly available to some gardeners in packages; they may be released into the garden to help manage pest insects such as whiteflies, scales, beetles, and a variety of harmful larvae. Since these tiny wasps can fly, they can effectively attack orchard pests, such as codling moth larvae, that may be unreachable in tall trees. They are quite specialized—certain species attack only certain insect pests—so they can be effective as a targeted management for harmful orchard insects. The life spans of these tiny wasps are brief, so weekly releases are recommended.

For more information on obtaining and using wasps as beneficials, contact your cooperative extension office or garden center. If you will be releasing beneficial wasps into your garden, refrain from spraying insecticides or limit insecticide use until the wasps are well established.

WEEVILS

LEAF, STEM, AND FRUIT PESTS

ZONES: ALL

Weevils are snouted, chewing insects that feed on a variety of landscape plants. Of more than a thousand species, only a few are serious garden pests. One of these, the black vine weevil, shown above, is about ⅓ inch long. Like most weevils, it crawls quickly on jointed legs. The larvae are white, legless grubs. A long-snouted ½-inch weevil called the billbug is a pest in southwest lawns: its white ½-inch larvae chew roots, leaving irregular brown patches and whitish sawdustlike excrement. They can be distinguished from other lawn grubs because they are legless.

Target: The black vine weevil damages broad-leafed evergreens such as azalea and rhododendron, as well as blueberry plants and grapevines. It may also attack hemlock and liquidambar trees. Other weevils attack Douglas fir, iris, lilac, pine, roses, strawberries, and yew. Billbugs are usually a problem only on warm-season grasses, such as Bermuda grass and zoysia.

Damage: Weevil larvae feed on roots. Damage is often so gradual it goes unnoticed, but if their roots are constantly chewed, plants may fail completely. Adult weevils at night feed on leaves, flowers, and bark.

Life cycle: Adults emerge from the soil in spring to mate and feed. Females lay their eggs in the soil near the base of host plants. After hatching, the larvae enter the soil to feed on roots throughout the fall. Most weevils overwinter in the soil as grubs and emerge again to feed more heavily in the spring before pupating. There is one generation each year.

Prevention: Check purchased rhododendrons and azaleas for healthy roots and bark; the white larvae of black vine weevils are often introduced on the roots of newly transplanted shrubs.

Management: Natural predators include chickens, other birds, spiders, ground beetles, and beneficial soil nematodes. You can trap adult weevils by wrapping sticky tape or loose burlap around the trunks at the base of shrubs; any weevils that hide beneath the burlap during the day can be shaken out over a bucket of soapy water, which will kill them. Adult weevils can also be killed by spraying with an insecticide containing rotenone, neem, pyrethrum, or acephate (for ornamentals only), applied according to directions on the label. Spray at dusk, when weevils are most active. Dying plants should be dug up, roots and all, and destroyed to prevent the spread of this pest. Billbugs in lawns can be managed by watering in beneficial soil nematodes, which feed on the larvae. Treating lawns with an insecticide that contains diazinon and is labeled for soil and lawn use also kills many grubs.

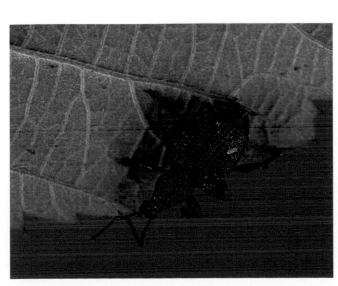

WEBWORMS

LEAF AND STEM PESTS, TURF PESTS

ZONES: ALL

Found throughout the United States and Canada, webworms are a group of caterpillars that create loose, dirty-white or brown webs or tents on shrubs and trees. Unlike the tent caterpillar, which makes its nest close to the trunk, the webworm makes its nest on the outer ends of branches. The yellowish caterpillars are about 1 inch long, with stripes and hairy projections along their backs. The adult form of most species is a white moth with a 1 – 1½-inch wingspan, sometimes with black wing spots.

Target: The species of webworm attack various and specific host plants. Garden plantings most likely to be affected are albizia, cotoneaster, honey locust, mimosa, and fruit trees. Rosebushes may also be affected.

Damage: The silken tents of this caterpillar get bigger as the caterpillars within broaden their feeding range. The webbing is unsightly, and a large infestation can defoliate portions of a tree.

Life cycle: Adult moths emerge in late spring or early summer to lay their rounded eggs in large masses on the undersides of tree leaves. The eggs hatch in about ten days, and the caterpillars begin making tents to shield themselves as they feed. Later in the season, the caterpillars spin brown cocoons, which may be attached to tree trunks or hidden among leaf litter on the ground. These pests overwinter as cocoons.

Prevention: Inspect garden trees regularly for webworm tents and egg masses, destroying any you find.

Management: Remove tents or prune off heavily tented branches. Break up tents with a jet of water, then spray or dust with the microbial control *Bacillus thuringiensis* (BT), which will kill the caterpillars. Spray severely infested trees with an insecticide containing diazinon, carbaryl, or malathion, applied according to directions on the label.

Notes: The sod webworm is the larva of a night-flying tan moth that drops its eggs onto grass plants. When the eggs hatch, the larvae build web-lined tunnels underground but close to the soil surface. The larvae eat grass blades. In hot periods of summer and autumn, affected areas of turf turn brown in patches. Beneficial soil nematodes, BT, and insecticides containing diazinon or chlorpyrifos that are labeled for lawn or soil use are good controls against the sod webworm. Affected lawns usually recover from webworm damage.

WHITEFLIES

LEAF AND STEM PESTS

ZONES: ALL

Like aphids, whiteflies appear suddenly in hordes, sucking sap from the leaves of vegetables and flowering plants. The immature form is a nearly transparent wingless nymph; when feeding it excretes honeydew, a sticky sweet substance that attracts ants. Adults look like tiny white moths; they typically feed together and fly up in a cloud when disturbed. Whiteflies are found year-round in warm climates but only during summer months in colder zones. Warm, still air is the perfect environment for whiteflies, making greenhouses a favorite haunt. A mixture of nymphs and adults is shown above.

Target: Whiteflies attack many annuals, perennials, vegetables, and fruits.

Damage: By sucking plant juices, whiteflies weaken plants and stunt their growth. Affected foliage may be stippled yellow, then may curl and turn brown. The honeydew excreted by adults and nymphs attracts sooty mold fungus, which turns leaves a sticky black. Some whiteflies transmit viruses from plant to plant.

Life cycle: Adult whiteflies lay minuscule eggs on the undersides of leaves. Nymphs hatch out within a day or two, then begin to feed. As they molt, nymphs lose their legs and antennae, becoming nearly immobile as they transform into pupae, which appear transparent, oval, and fringed when viewed under a microscope. Winged adults emerge shortly thereafter. There are many overlapping generations each year.

Prevention: To keep whiteflies off crops such as lettuce and strawberries, lay a shiny, reflective mulch beneath planted rows. Seeing the sky reflected in the mulch, whiteflies are disoriented and do not land. Remove the foil when the weather gets hot, or some foliage may burn. Floating row covers also provide some protection.

Management: Natural enemies, which can be encouraged or introduced in the garden, include lacewing larvae and parasitoid wasps. Pesticides should be avoided, as they will kill these beneficial insects. For small infestations, use yellow sticky traps, hand-pick infested leaves, or hose down leaves with soapy water. Whiteflies and nymphs can also be killed by spraying with insecticidal soap or a pesticide containing pyrethrum, neem, malathion, or, for ornamentals only, acephate, applied according to directions on the label. Be sure to spray the undersides of leaves.

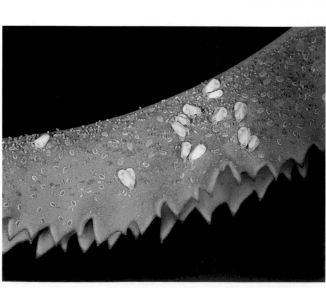

WHITE GRUBS

SOIL PESTS

ZONES: ALL

Several scarab-beetle larvae that infest lawns and grassy areas are grouped together under the catchall name "white grubs." Adult beetles in this group include the flying June bugs—grub shown above—that buzz around window screens during the summertime, destructive Japanese beetles, and chafers (such as the rose chafer). Generally the larvae are white with brown heads and stoutly rounded, with three pairs of legs. They usually lie immobile in the soil, curled up in the shape of the letter C.

Target: White grubs are pests of lawn grasses.

Damage: Living underground beneath lawns, white grubs chew up the roots of grasses. Unable to take up water or nutrients, impaired grass blades turn brown and die. Later in summer, you will see large brown patches of dead turf. The areas of dead grass or sod will be rootless and may be pulled up easily, like a carpet. Raccoons and skunks, searching for the grubs as food, may do this job for you. A lawn often torn up by nocturnal animals may indicate the presence of many grubs.

Life cycle: Adult beetles lay eggs on grass blades in the summer. The larvae hatch and burrow underground to feed. They usually remain within 3 inches of the soil level and may sometimes emerge at night to chew the green parts of grass blades. Most species move deeper into the soil as winter approaches, hibernating as grubs through the colder seasons. When warm weather returns, the larvae feed more vigorously before pupating. Adults emerge to meet, mate, and migrate in late spring.

Prevention: Prevention of white grubs is nearly impossible, as the adult beetles often fly great distances to lay eggs in grassy areas. Removing grassy weeds close to lawn areas may help by limiting resting places for adult beetles on the move. Installing beneficial soil nematodes into the soil before lawns are newly seeded or sodded may provide some protection.

Management: Promising new treatments for grub-infested lawns include spraying lawns and perimeter plants with the botanical insecticide neem, which apparently disrupts the reproductive cycles of Japanese beetles, and drenching affected turf areas with beneficial soil nematodes, which will attack or parasitize the grubs underground. Many grubs are resistant to soil drenches of chemical insecticides. Check with your local cooperative extension agent or turf professional for current recommendations.

WINTER MOTHS

LEAF AND STEM PESTS

⚡ ZONES: 1–5

Very few pests, aside from certain species of cutworms and loopers, are active in winter. Winter moths are one of the exceptions. Native to Asia and Europe, the winter moth was first noticed in western North America in the late 1970s and has since appeared in Washington, Oregon, and southern Canada. The male has a wingspan of 1½ inches; female moths are the same size, but wingless. Both are pale brown. The caterpillar, shown above, is about 1 inch long, thick, and greenish, black striped on top and yellow striped along the side. It crawls in a looping motion, like an inchworm.

Target: Winter moth caterpillars feed on deciduous ornamentals and fruit trees and shrubs such as maple, blueberry, cherry, and apple; broad-leafed evergreens, including azalea, evergreen oak, and rhododendron; and understory plants growing in oak groves.

Damage: The caterpillars chew leaves and stems, girdling twigs and defoliating branches. Branch dieback may occur. Trees and shrubs may be seriously defoliated before the caterpillars are noticed and controlled. Young or recently transplanted shrubs suffer the most; established trees can withstand some defoliation.

Life cycle: Adult moths emerge from the soil in autumn and winter. The wingless females crawl up trunks of host plants and wait for the flying males to approach them; then they lay eggs in clusters. The caterpillars hatch in late winter to early spring as broad-leafed evergreens begin to put forth new growth. The caterpillars feed until early summer, then drop to the ground to pupate. There is one generation per year.

Prevention: No prevention is required where the caterpillar is not found. To protect landscape oaks and specimen rhododendrons, wrap their trunks in sticky tape barriers to trap adult females crawling up the trunk. Where this pest has been sighted, gardeners should regularly check trees during the winter.

Management: Hand-pick and destroy caterpillars. In autumn, remove mulch and leaf debris from underneath broad-leafed evergreens and live oaks, and till the soil lightly to expose any pupae. To kill the caterpillars, spray affected foliage with the microbial insecticide *Bacillus thuringiensis* (BT). State agencies in Oregon and Washington have released two winter moth parasitoids—the tachinid fly and a beneficial wasp—to manage this new pest without sprays. Contact your local cooperative extension agent for the latest recommendations.

WIREWORMS

SOIL PESTS

⚡ ZONES: ALL

Wireworms, the shiny, reddish brown larvae of click beetles, are jointed and rounded like earthworms, but they have hard shells instead of soft bodies. Reaching a length of about 1½ inches, wireworms can move quickly in the soil using the three pairs of legs that are right behind their head. They are usually found in rich, organic soils or in garden beds created from areas that formerly were lawns. The adult form is a night-roaming dark beetle.

Target: Root crops such as carrot and potato are occasionally attacked by wireworms.

Damage: In their natural meadow environments, wireworms cause little trouble. In garden beds, they may nibble on seeds and emerging seedlings or burrow into the soft tissue of potatoes, sweet potatoes, and carrots to ruin these root crops.

Life cycle: In spring or summer, adult click beetles lay eggs in the soil. Within a month, the worms hatch out and begin to feed on organic matter they find underground. Some species of wireworms mature in a single year, while other types may spend up to six years underground before they pupate. Generations may overlap, as both adults and larvae overwinter underground, often at a depth of 10 inches or more.

Prevention: Till garden beds deeply before planting root crops. Rotate crops when planting carrot, potato, or other root crops.

Management: Pesticides are not usually needed and may be overkill for this soil-dwelling pest. Till soils to a depth of at least 10 inches, and practice crop rotation to keep the wireworm populations down. Soil solarization may be helpful. For severe worm infestations, a pesticide that is formulated and registered for soil use and that contains diazinon may be applied according to label directions.

Fine Feathered Friends?

House finches (top) and the white-crowned sparrow (bottom) are usually welcome in gardens, but like the common starling (center), even they can be nuisances when they descend in large groups. Protect new plantings and fruiting bushes with mesh netting, tucking the ends of the mesh into the ground so birds don't get trapped inside.

ANIMALS

and Animal Pests

The gradual loss of wilderness to urban development means that, more than ever, birds, reptiles, and mammals large and small are likely to be part of your gardening life. Displaced animals learn quickly to hide and adapt to civilized surroundings, where their food source may be an easy buffet of goodies from your garbage pail or vegetable patch. The damage caused by insect pests can seem minimal compared with the depredations of a single night's raid by a raccoon.

Many mammal pests prefer to feed after dusk or in the early morning, so you may not see them close-up. But most of these pests cause distinctive kinds of garden damage to help you pinpoint the culprit. Birds, for example, will often peck bites out of fruits and vegetables just before harvest; deer chew foliage and bark at a higher level than rabbits do.

Healthy gardens support a wide variety of insects, which in turn attract birds and animals that feed on insects. If you enjoy seeing wildlife in your own backyard, you can plant a habitat garden, with water sources and native food plants, to encourage birds and animals to come by. But if wild guests become too much at home, you may need to use barriers and repellents to redirect them, away from prized garden plants or food crops.

THE ANIMALS OVERHEAD

We like to see birds in our gardens: they're helpful insect eaters, and they add beauty and song. But at certain times of year, flocks of even small birds can cause damage, when they swoop down to devour newly spread grass seed or to strip fruits and decorative berries from vines and bushes.

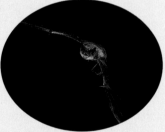

The little brown bat (Myotis lucifugus)

The most effective deterrent to such bird attacks is protective barriers. Cover newly seeded areas and ripening crops with floating row covers or wire mesh screening. To protect small beds, poke brushy twigs into the ground where you have planted the seeds; this maze of branch bits acts as a barrier. When the seedlings are large enough, you can remove the twigs. Bushes, grapevines, and orchard trees can be draped with mesh bird netting. "Scarecrows" made from shiny reflective tape or suspended pie tins also help keep birds away.

If you live near the coast or by a major waterway, fishing birds may be attracted by the decorative koi in your garden pond. Removable metal grates are recommended to protect pond fish.

Native bats should be encouraged in the garden; they feed on mosquitoes and night-flying insects, and some desert species are important pollinators of night-flowering cacti. However, since bats can carry rabies, nesting sites inconveniently close to houses and patios should be removed by a pest control professional.

Like birds, tree squirrels are seldom a problem unless they attack orchard crops. To protect walnuts, other nuts, and fruits, wrap sticky barriers around tree trunks to deter squirrels from climbing. Plant nut trees away from garden structures and house roofs, and prune the trees so that their lowest branches are at least 6 feet from the ground. Squirrels can easily jump anything less than 6 feet. To keep squirrels away from seeds in flower borders or bird feeders, dust the seeds with finely ground cayenne pepper (use gloves to avoid burning your hands). Although birds cannot taste the hot pepper, squirrels can.

UNDERGROUND INHABITANTS

Several small native pests live in burrows they dig through the soil. All are active in the daytime, feeding on green plants and their roots. They can damage turf grasses, flower bulbs, tubers, and the soft green foliage of annuals, perennials, and recently transplanted shrubs.

Pocket gopher

If you find uprooted and chewed plants, look around for earth mounds that indicate burrow entrances or for 2–6-inch-wide holes in the ground. Moles and pocket gophers always plug their holes with clods or loose soil; active ground squirrel and chipmunk burrows are left open, although chipmunk burrows may be well concealed under rock ledges, logs, or shrubs. Ground squirrels, common in the West, resemble tree squirrels, but when frightened they will retreat to a burrow, while tree squirrels will climb. Ground squirrels can transmit diseases to humans, so removing them from your yard should be a priority. The bucktoothed, brown-furred pocket gopher is a well-known western pest. These creatures are energetic: a single animal can tunnel through 2,000 feet of garden space, leaving dead plants and unsightly soil mounds in its wake.

Moles are insect eaters, damaging gardens indirectly by uprooting lawn grass, flower bulbs, vegetables, and border flowers as they tunnel in search of food. Well-irrigated, fluffy, and organic soils attract moles. Entrances to their tunnels are distinctively marked with volcano-shaped mounds of excavated soil. Their narrow, shallow tunnels often appear as ridges 3–5 inches wide under the surface of a lawn. (Mole ridges in lawns may be repaired by tamping down the damaged area, then irrigating thoroughly to help roots recover.)

You may be able to keep tunneling pests out of your garden by surrounding your yard with underground fencing, such as a barrier of hardware cloth or chicken wire, buried 3–4 feet underground and extending 1 foot above the soil level. Alternatively, line raised beds with wire fencing to prevent these pests from tunneling up. To protect newly planted perennials and shrubs, set their root balls into wire cages in the soil; tulips, lilies, and other bulbs may also be planted above a protecting layer of wire mesh. Where moles are common, protect lawns and flower beds by installing galvanized wire mesh 8–12 inches below the soil level before you install new sod or plants.

Chipmunks and ground squirrels are harder to keep out, although domestic cats and dogs may be a good deterrent in a garden setting. Flooding burrows with water may force some tunneling animals aboveground, where you can dispatch them with a shovel if you are comfortable with the direct approach. Trapping is the best method for getting rid of moles. For information on traps and poisoned baits, consult your local cooperative extension agent; or hire a pest control professional.

VOLES, MICE, AND RATS

Voles, also called meadow mice, are small rodents that nest in shallow burrows in soft earth or leaf mulches. Widespread in the West, they usually appear in gardens cyclically, whenever a rise in their populations causes them to move from wild areas. They are about 7 inches long, with rounded ears and chisel-like teeth; they eat seedlings, chew up ground covers, and gnaw tree bark. Other rodents that appear in western gardens include natives such as white-footed mice (also called deer mice) and kangaroo rats and introduced pests such as house mice. These creatures seldom cause plant damage, feeding instead on the dropped seeds of flowering plants and ornamental grasses and on spilled seeds from bird feeders. Rats, which are undesirable neighbors because they pose a health problem to humans, tend to dwell in structures but may also make their nests in trees or beneath dense ground covers.

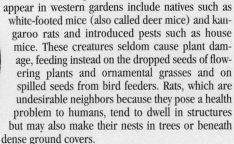

Deer mouse

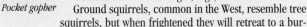

Pests, Aboveground and Below

Moles (inset) create a series of tunnels (above) as they search for grubs and earthworms among the roots of grass lawns and garden plants. Folk remedies such as chewing gum, castor beans, and so-called gopher plant will not remove them; try wire mesh barriers or trapping instead. Squirrels (below) can be kept out of nut trees if you prune limbs high and wrap sticky barriers around tree trunks.

Who Will Get Your Harvest?

Check fencing and apply scent repellents around your garden perimeter as beans, corn, and fruit crops mature: animals such as armadillos (top), rabbits (center), and opossums (bottom) have a knack for appearing just as fruits and vegetables ripen. As an extra step, drape bird netting around lettuces and harvest-ready crops.

To rid your yard of rodents, eliminate their favorite nesting sites by removing weeds and brushy debris, especially on the edges of wooded areas. Pull mulches away from the bases of trees and shrubs. Wrap young tree trunks with wire mesh to prevent chewing damage. Cats, conventional mousetraps, and mousetraps with anticoagulant baits may be used to keep down populations of mice and voles.

To deter rats, eliminate garbage and other food sources, and remove overgrown vines and ground covers that may be nesting sites. Spring traps and baited traps will kill rats. For advice on combating large infestations, contact your local cooperative extension office or health department.

ROVERS, WILD AND DOMESTIC

Skunk

A smart pest is the worst pest—and sometimes nothing seems smarter than the wily raccoon, opossum, rabbit, or skunk that has figured out a way into your vegetable patch. Even urban dwellers fairly often see these displaced wild creatures in city backyards. Raccoons and skunks are often quite bold, entering your garden to snatch fruits and vegetables right in front of your eyes; armadillos and opossums engrossed in chewing on flowers or vegetable stalks may also be undeterred by humans if they have adapted to the area. Roaming neighborhood cats and dogs may fall into this pest category if they habitually get into your garden and cause damage by digging.

Trapping wild animals is a job best left to pest control professionals, but sturdy fencing and a large, loud dog are good deterrents to these animals. For fencing, choose ¾-inch mesh or chicken wire, and bury it 1 foot below the soil level. Fence heights should be at least 3 feet high to keep out skunks, woodchucks, rabbits, and dogs.

Climbing animals—such as raccoons, opossums, and cats—may be kept out if you extend the top of a wire fence outward 1½ feet above the top fencepost: the unsupported wire won't bear the weight of animals trying to climb and they will fall back to the ground. Or instead of fencing your entire yard, you might encircle certain plantings—for instance, roses, fruit trees, and raised vegetable beds—with wire mesh cages.

Another strategy is to make your backyard inhospitable to these animals. Commercial odor repellents are useful but need to be applied frequently. Setting backyard lighting and sprinkler systems to turn on briefly at random intervals, especially at night, may annoy raccoons and other night feeders, but discuss this option with neighbors before installing such a system. An electronic garden scarecrow hooks up to your outdoor hose and by an electronic eye and motion sensors detects an animal intruder. Then it releases a stiff stream of water in a spray targeted at the intruder. Humane and completely automatic, such products provide a technological edge against intelligent hunting animals.

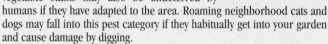

Cairn terrier

Domestic cats and dogs can do as much damage to gardens as wild animals, and they are often harder to control or exclude. Fences can keep out neighborhood dogs, but your own canine may need to be trained to avoid certain areas. If you can, give Rover a fenced-in area for playing. Dog urine will cause yellowing patches on grass, but lawns can be restored by sprinkling the affected areas with horticultural lime and deeply watering the patches to reverse the effects of the acidic salts in dog urine.

Cats are usually attracted to the soft earth of newly seeded beds, which they will use as litter boxes. To keep cats from digging, cover the soil with a layer of green grass clippings. Replace the clippings when they dry out, until the seedlings are large enough. Placing wire fencing directly on the soil, so that plants will grow through its holes, is also effective.

Familiar Garden Marauders

Deer and raccoons will make your garden a regular dining stop unless you bar their way with fencing, supplemented if necessary with a variety of visual and odor repellents and noisemakers.

DEER

As wild vegetation becomes less available in summer droughts or winter snows, deer will move into gardens to forage, chewing at the bark of trees if they can't find anything else to eat. They appear mainly at dawn and dusk, often in groups.

Fond of many flowering plants, these graceful animals will sample just about any bit of greenery. What they will or won't eat depends on how hungry they are. How-ever, there are a number of plants that deer generally avoid. If your garden is subject to heavy

Mule deer

depredation, you may find it's easier to switch to some of these plants (see list, page 109).

Deer may be deterred by odor repellents, if you change the type of repellent frequently, since deer get used to smells. Physical barriers, such as cages around fruit trees or rosebushes, work better, and yard fencing is the best defense. Since deer can jump, fencing should be at least 8 feet high on level ground, higher on slopes. As an alternative, try two parallel 4-foot-high fences, spaced 4–5 feet apart. This creates a baffle with no room for jumping and allows you to establish smaller plants between the fences. Wire mesh fences should be used, not fence boards or wire strands, since deer can wiggle through gaps as narrow as 12 inches.

OCCASIONAL INTRUDERS TO BE AWARE—AND WARY—OF

From time to time, western gardens are visited by large animals that, while they do not qualify as pests, do present obstacles to gardening. In Rocky Mountain areas, elk are sometimes glimpsed in backyards; they are usually just passing through on their way to more remote wild areas. Mountain lions, bears, coyotes, and sometimes even bob-cats do turn up in suburban gar-dens, and these carnivorous predators will attack humans as well as pets.

If confronted by one of these preda-tors, you may be able to scare the ani-mal off by waving your arms rapidly and shouting loudly, to convince the predator that you are no easy prey. Seek shelter in a car or house; turn on a smoke alarm, or make other loud noises to scare away animals in your yard.

Mountain lion

All sightings of mountain lions or bears should be reported to your state wildlife or game department, so it can monitor wild predator populations. This agency will also offer advice and take appropriate action to manage dangerous animals that have wandered too close to human residences.

Sometimes a smaller animal becomes a menacing intruder. Any wild animal—if cornered—can be dangerous. Ground squirrels, raccoons, skunks, opossums, and rabbits have sharp teeth and claws, and even voles and mice will bite. Alive or dead, such animals should not be touched with bare hands, since they may carry diseases. If any animal frequenting your garden becomes troublesome, give it a wide berth and contact your local animal control office, state wildlife department, or a pest control profes-sional to remove it.

When you must deal with wild animals, from birds to big cats, it may help to remember that they exist as a vital part of the ecology of our west-ern states. Native species can be expected to appear where human-made landscapes help supply their needs for food, water, nesting sites, and shel-ter from predators. While gardeners may sometimes have to adopt defen-sive techniques, making room for animal life often adds pleasure and interest to outdoor living and can help maintain a healthy balance of nature in your own backyard.

Encyclopedia of
PLANT DISEASES AND
CULTURAL PROBLEMS

To help you diagnose the causes of damage on plants in your garden, this chapter describes 60 different diseases that commonly affect plants in the West. Photographs and descriptions of symptoms will aid in the all-important task of identifying the problem. By following the prevention techniques and management methods described in the pages that follow, you can keep your garden disease free. Since cultural problems—such as improper watering methods and soil deficiencies—sometimes produce symptoms easily mistaken for evidence of disease, this chapter also explains 28 cultural conditions that can prevent plants from thriving, with guidelines for correcting them.

PLANT DISEASES

A plant disease is a plant health problem caused by pathogens. Plant pathogens are disease-producing microscopic organisms—fungi, bacteria, and viruses—many thousands of which exist.

TYPES OF PLANT PATHOGENS

Fungi. Fungi are microscopic and predominantly multicelled organisms that lack the green pigment chlorophyll. Most plants nourish themselves by taking in water, nutrients, and sunshine. Through the functioning of chlorophyll, they transform these materials into food for existing tissues and building blocks for new tissue. Without chlorophyll, fungi cannot supply themselves with food, so they feed on organic matter—including but not limited to plants.

These parasites normally multiply by means of microscopic spores, the fungal equivalent of seeds, which are produced by their fruiting bodies in massive quantities. One infected leaf may give off 100 million spores. Spores are disseminated by wind, rain, tools, machinery, garden watering, insects, or handling. They may land on the soil rather than on a plant, but they do not necessarily die; some types of spores can survive in soil for a long time—even indefinitely—despite quite adverse conditions. When they come in contact with condensed moisture on a plant that is a suitable food source, the spores germinate. This results in the growth of hyphae, threadlike structures that are a fungus's vegetative body, where its growth takes place.

The hyphae, forming a mass or network called mycelium, feed on the plant tissue and produce symptoms that vary depending on the specific fungus and the plant affected. Among these symptoms are rotting fruit, curled leaves, mildew and molds on plant tissues, and stunted and wilted plants.

Bacteria. Bacteria are single-celled organisms. Like fungi, they cannot create their own food supply, so they feed on organic matter, including but not limited to plants. Unlike fungi, plant pathogenic bacteria must remain inside a plant host or plant debris in order to survive. They do not produce spores, but they multiply extremely rapidly by division. Each cell increases in size until it divides into two new cells, which then go through the same process. This means that there are huge numbers of bacteria in the ooze coming out of a single stem infected with a disease such as bacterial wilt.

Bacteria, in order to multiply, require both moisture and warmth. In a dry climate, therefore, they may not present a serious problem. However, garden watering creates the moisture that bacteria need. Anything that comes in contact with them—insects, garden equipment, people, splashing rain, plants—can disseminate the bacteria. When bacteria land on a susceptible plant, they enter through a wound or natural opening and begin to feed. Pathogenic bacterial feeding may cause symptoms such as galls, water-soaked leaf spots, scabs, and wilted plants.

Viruses. Smaller than bacteria, viruses are not alive. They are not organisms and do not have the ability to grow or replicate on their own. Instead, they can only reproduce by entering host cells and using the cellular machinery to replicate, or copy, themselves. These activities can seriously disrupt the normal functioning of the infected host cells. The result is often a plant disease with symptoms such as abnormal growth of plant parts, spots or discoloration on leaves, damaged fruit, or stunted plants.

Plant diseases and cultural problems common to western gardens are (clockwise from top left) heart rot, affecting ornamental and fruit trees; bacterial leaf scorch, here shown on Japanese maple; and a mosaic virus.

Viruses are commonly spread by vectors, which are plant-feeding insects, such as aphids, leafhoppers, and thrips. But infected seed and pollen can also introduce a virus into a plant. Or a virus can enter through any opening—a pruning cut, for instance, or a broken twig.

PREVENTING DISEASES

Plant diseases result from the combination of three factors: the pathogen itself, a susceptible plant, and a favorable environment. You can break up this disease-producing trio by any of three methods.

Exclude the pathogen. Try to keep the pathogen out of the garden. Gardeners may inadvertently introduce some disease-causing organisms into their gardens. To avoid collaboration with diseases, use certified disease-free seed. Examine nursery plants before purchasing them, and reject any that have obvious problems. Check out gift plants as well. Keep your tools clean, and if you borrow tools, disinfect them before use (as described at right).

Plant resistant varieties. A plant's genetic makeup determines its susceptibility or resistance to plant diseases. In "Problem Solving by Plant Type" (pages 72–137), you will find lists of the diseases to which common plants of the West are susceptible, and in the following encyclopedia entries you can learn about the conditions in your garden favor a disease and a plant you plan to use is susceptible to that disease, look for a resistant variety. If there are no resistant varieties, reconsider your choice of that plant. Your garden will be healthier—and you will be happier—if you match your selection of plants to your garden's conditions.

Create a discouraging environment. Aim for creating an environment unfavorable to diseases. Avoid placing closely related annuals, including vegetables, in the same area every year. A three-to four-year crop rotation will starve out many plant pathogens that would otherwise increase each year (see pages 40 and 41).

Be scrupulous about spacing plants correctly, following their particular planting directions. Plants placed too close to one another block air movement and allow moisture to remain on plants longer, which can encourage the development of diseases.

Do not overwater or water from overhead late in the day. Do not plant in areas with poor drainage; excess water encourages seed decay, root rot diseases, and damping off.

Analyze your soil to be sure you are providing the proper growing medium for your plants. Fertilize plants adequately.

MANAGEMENT OPTIONS

If a disease does develop in your garden, remove as much of it as you can and limit its potential for spreading. As a last option, you may choose to apply a chemical treatment.

Remove the diseased material. Remove as much as possible of the infected parts of the plant. The three basic pruning tools for this task are hand shears, hand loppers, and a pruning saw. Use the appropriate tool for the type of pruning you will be doing; if you use the wrong one, you may damage the plants or the tool itself.

In general, cut well below the diseased part of the plant and just above a bud or stem. At such points, a callus, or protective tissue, will grow over the cut surface. To cut back to a bud, make an angled cut with the higher end of the cut above the bud and the lower end opposite it. To cut back to a stem, place the blade close to the stem; slant the shears so the cut is slightly angled (see illustration below).

For more detailed information on pruning tools and techniques for specific plants, consult the Sunset book *Pruning*.

Control the spread of the disease. Avoid working in the garden when the plants and soil are wet. Plant pathogens transfer easily in such conditions.

Keep your garden weed-free. Disease pathogens may overwinter in weeds; eliminating the weeds can break the life cycle of a pathogen and help manage it. Removing weeds also improves air circulation, minimizing conditions that encourage disease.

Disinfect pruning tools used on infected plants after each cut, so plant pathogens are not transferred. Disinfect by dipping these tools into a solution of 1 part household bleach to 9 parts water.

Discard infected plant debris promptly to reduce the likelihood that the pathogens will survive and spread. Bag the debris or place it in a securely fastened trash container to prevent windblown organisms from re-entering your garden. Many kinds of infected debris (but not all; see individual disease descriptions) can be composted if you use a method that produces high temperatures. However, don't attempt composting if you don't have the time for maintenance; unattended compost piles can be an overwintering site for many plant pathogens.

Using chemical treatments. Fungicides and bactericides may be used to destroy, diminish, or prevent some plant pathogens. Always read the container label on any pesticide you are considering for use, and use only as specified. When in doubt about a chemical treatment, ask a garden center consultant or a cooperative extension agent for current options. New products are constantly being researched and developed—a recently introduced formulation may be the best for your needs.

PESTICIDES: HANDLE WITH CARE

Care should be taken whenever you use pesticides, particularly near edible crops. Be sure to read the labels on any product you bring into your garden and use it only as its label directs—it's against the law to do otherwise. Pesticide registrations change rapidly and some products mentioned in this book may be removed from the lists of approved products or their label directions may be changed over time, as additional research becomes available. If you have questions concerning current regulations, consult your local nursery or cooperative extension office.

POSITIONING PRUNING SHEARS

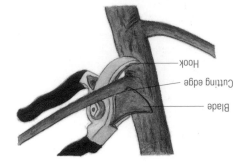

Blade
Cutting edge
Hook

To make a proper close pruning cut, hold pruning shears with the blade closest to the stem or plant part that will remain. Too long a stub results when you reverse the position and place the hook closest to the plant. Note that the shears are also slanted to produce a slightly angled cut.

ANTHRACNOSE

FUNGUS

ZONES: ALL

The disease of anthracnose, which results from infection by fungi, appears early in the growing season. The many genera and species of anthracnose fungi are specific to plant type. Anthracnose causes considerable tree defoliation, but it seldom kills plants. Anthracnose-damaged leaves can look burned, much like leaves affected by hot-weather scorch (see Leaf Scorch, page 248); however, leaf scorch browns leaf margins rather than spots the leaves.

Target: Many herbaceous and woody plants. Crop plants include cane berries (such as raspberry), lettuce, pepper, strawberry, and tomato. Trees include ash, elm, maple, oak, and sycamore.

Symptoms: Anthracnose symptoms depend on the affected plant. In general, the anthracnose fungi cause sunken spots of gray or tan to dark brown on leaves, stems, fruit, or twigs. The spots, which can be watery at first, may have spore masses—like light pink slime, or pink or tan mounds—in their centers. The spots may enlarge to cover the leaf. Leaves may wither and drop. You will see dead twigs and branches.

On tomatoes and peppers, small, circular water-soaked spots increase as fruit approaches maturity. As the spots darken and deepen, they often have concentric markings. In warm weather, the spots soon penetrate and spoil the fruit. On black raspberries, circular sunken spots, initially purplish, form on the lower canes. Later, the spot centers turn gray. As the canes age, the sunken spots develop raised margins. Berries ripen unevenly.

Prevention: Wetness encourages these fungi. If your area receives plentiful rainfall during the growing season, find out what plant varieties are resistant locally. Grow vining plants on trellises or poles to keep them dry. Use mulch to decrease splashing of rain or sprinkler water. Avoid overhead watering, or do it in the morning to give plants a chance to dry. (Water anytime if you can avoid wetting foliage.) Give plants sufficient space for good air circulation. Trim tree overhangs to increase sunlight for sun-loving plants. Pruning the previous season's growth on trees may help.

Management: Prune and destroy affected plant parts; trim affected twigs and branches. Rake fallen leaves. Fungicides containing lime sulfur, Bordeaux mixture, or chlorothalonil may be applied. The fungicide you choose and the time you apply it depend on the affected plant. Consult your cooperative extension agent for application information and additional options.

APPLE SCAB

FUNGUS

ZONES: ALL

Apple scab, the most prevalent apple disease in the world, is severe in all coastal states. *Venturia inaequalis,* the fungus that causes it, thrives in cool, moist weather. This fungus overwinters on dead apple leaves on the ground. Spores carried by spring winds quickly infect developing young twigs, foliage, flowers, and fruit. In only six hours of wetness at 70°F, the fungus can infect fruit around the bloom. Visible infections occur one to two weeks later. Mature fruit and leaves are much less susceptible to apple scab infection than immature fruit, leaves, and twigs.

Target: Apple and crabapple trees

Symptoms: Initially, dark olive green or blackish irregular patches, scabby and sometimes blistered, develop on upper leaf surfaces. Velvety spots may enlarge and join, covering the entire leaf undersurface. Leaves become twisted, puckered, and yellow. Infected leaves may fall early; severely affected trees may lose all leaves. On fruit exteriors, olive brown scabby patches appear, then develop a white rim around a dark, velvety center. The rim later disappears, and the centers may become raised, corky, and tan. Severe attacks result in small, distorted, and possibly cracked fruit that drops early. Cracks in the fruit allow fruit-rotting organisms into the apple. Scab fungus spores may also infect mature apples, which can develop blackish scab lesions during storage. These lesions are sometimes referred to as pinpoint scab or storage scab.

Prevention: Plant resistant apple varieties. In cool, damp coastal areas, try heirloom varieties, which may be scab resistant. Prune trees to increase air circulation and reduce the amount of wettable foliage. Rake up and discard fallen leaves and fruit.

Management: To manage scab infections and protect new growth, apply fungicides early and thoroughly. The most critical period is from the breaking of cluster buds until leaves are fully expanded. Apply fungicides containing triforine, sulfur, lime sulfur, or captan, always according to directions on the label. Once scab appears on fruit trees, it cannot be cured. Remove scabby shoots and fruits. Discard all fallen leaves. Infected fruits look unsightly, but unless they are infected very early, they can be used.

ASTER YELLOWS

PHYTOPLASMA

✂ ZONES: ALL

Aster yellows—also known as lettuce white heart, potato purple top, potato late break, celery yellows, western aster yellows, strawberry green petal, and California aster yellows—is a severe problem for 170 species of flowering plants as well as many vegetables. Although aster yellows is present in plants throughout the growing season, its symptoms become most noticeable in warm weather; it is seldom seen at temperatures below 50°F. Aster yellows is caused by phytoplasmas, bacteria that do not have cell walls. Phytoplasmas are smaller than bacteria but larger than viruses. The phytoplasmas multiply in leafhoppers, the insect vector, which then transmit aster yellows to plants when feeding. The phytoplasmas that cause aster yellows may overwinter on weeds.

Target: Annuals, perennials, bulbs, and vegetables

Symptoms: On flowers—such as asters, chrysanthemums, and delphiniums—foliage yellows and leaf veins become pale. New leaves are distorted. Older leaf edges may turn brown. Flowers are nonexistent, or small and deformed, often turning greenish yellow. Bulb tops may be killed, and plant growth is usually stunted. Gladiolus may have many thin, weak leaves that turn yellowish green. Flower spikes are twisted and deformed. Flowers often remain green. The plant is generally small and spindly.

On vegetables, symptoms vary. The older outer leaves of carrots become reddish or purple. New leaves are yellow and smaller than usual. Many tiny leaves grow from the root top. Carrot roots are distorted and small; dense tufts of hairlike rootlets may grow from the main root. Affected carrots taste bitter. Celery stems curl and twist. Lettuce is stunted and may not form a head. The heart leaves, which may be pale yellow to white, fail to develop normally—they look like short, thickened stubs. The plant at left above has aster yellows.

Prevention: Leafhoppers tend to avoid shaded plants, so you can protect garden beds from leafhoppers by using floating row covers over plants. Promptly remove and discard infected plants.

Management: You can't eliminate aster yellows, but you can keep the disease under control. Start by uprooting and destroying infected plants. Remove any weeds, particularly dandelions, plantains, and thistles, that may be carrying the disease or harboring leafhoppers. If infestations are severe, control the leafhoppers.

BACTERIAL CANKER

BACTERIA

✂ ZONES: ALL

The bacterium causing bacterial canker, *Pseudomonas syringae,* is normally present on plant surfaces, and it generally causes no problems for healthy plants. However, with favorable growing and weather conditions, it invades plants through wounds, leaf scars, and buds, killing the tissues. The wounds can be caused by frost damage, mechanical injury, or early pruning. Trees weakened by unfavorable soil pH and poor nutrition are more susceptible. This disease is most serious on sweet cherry trees and young trees.

Target: Almond, cherry, peach, and other stone fruit trees

Symptoms: Irregularly shaped, brown, water-soaked cankers appear in early spring on the bark of tree trunks or branches. The cankers may expand to encircle entire branches. As the tree leafs out, a brown, sour-smelling substance may emerge from the canker margins. Leaves may not appear in spring or may wilt on affected branches as weather becomes warmer. New tree shoots often appear at the rootstock. When the disease is severe, trees may die.

Prevention: Plant tolerant varieties or rootstocks, if available. Tolerant cherry varieties include 'Corum' and 'Sue'. Avoid planting stone fruit trees in sandy or shallow soils that may have nematodes; nematode feeding weakens trees, making them more vulnerable to disease (for more information on nematodes, see page 181). If the tree is to go into a spot with shallow soil over hardpan, break through the hardpan before planting. Fertilize regularly, but don't use a nitrogen-containing fertilizer in late summer or fall. Keep trees adequately watered. Use a protective covering if the temperature drops to freezing during bloom or early fruit growth.

Management: Once bacterial canker takes hold, it is difficult to manage; prevention is the key. In summer, prune out infected twigs and branches, cutting a few inches below the infected site. Sterilize shears after each cut with rubbing alcohol, shellac thinner, or 1 part bleach to 9 parts water (note that bleach tends to rust tools quickly). Although materials containing copper are not always effective, you can try them to manage bacterial canker; spray in fall at the time of the initial leaf drop. Discuss other options with a garden center consultant or cooperative extension agent.

✎ *Notes: Citrus is affected by a form of* Pseudomonas syringae, *as is apple, but the resulting diseases differ.*

BACTERIAL LEAF SPOT

BACTERIA

✎ ZONES: ALL

Bacterial leaf spot and stem rot, caused by *Pseudomonas* and *Xanthomonas* bacteria, is a common flower and vegetable disease. Damage caused by the *Xanthomonas* bacteria is shown above. Leaf spot bacteria, which can live in plant debris for three to six months, spread via garden equipment or splashing water. Mild, wet spring weather favors progression of the disease, as does rapid plant growth.

Target: Geranium, poinsettia, brussels sprouts, celery, cucumber, and other flowers and vegetables

Symptoms: Symptoms vary, depending on the pathogens at work and the affected plant. On brussels sprouts and other brassicas, tiny black to purplish spots surrounded by yellow halos appear on outer leaves. These spots eventually grow together to form light brown, papery areas. On celery leaves, a water-soaked spot appears, then becomes bright yellow. The center of the spot gradually turns brown, with a yellow halo. On poinsettias, dull, grayish brown, slightly water-soaked spots appear on leaves. The spots may develop a yellow halo, and heavily infected leaves may drop prematurely. On geranium cuttings, a black rot may develop at the cutting base. Leaves may have slightly sunken, ¼-inch dark spots. Leaves may remain on the plant or may drop. Blue-black rotting occurs on many or all stem parts. The stems may partially recover and produce new leaves at the terminals. If an infected stem is cut open, a thick yellow liquid may ooze from the cut surface; it is filled with millions of bacteria.

Prevention: Inspect plants regularly to detect the disease early. Avoid sprinkler or overhead irrigation in the seedbed once the crop has germinated. Do not handle transplants when they are wet. If possible, plant only in dry weather.

Management: Remove small plants that are infected. Prune infected branches and stems from larger plants. Do not replant the area with susceptible crops the following year. Shred diseased crop residue and spade it under to hasten breakdown of infected plant material. Disinfect cutting tools after use. Bacterial leaf spot organisms are not easily managed by the home gardener; ask a cooperative extension agent or garden center consultant for advice.

BACTERIAL SOFT ROT

BACTERIA

✎ ZONES: ALL

Any diseased, weak, or over-ripe fruit or vegetable is susceptible to bacterial soft rot, which also can infect some healthy plants. The bacteria *(Erwinia)* overwinter in infected plant debris and soil, entering plants via wounds. Enzymes produced by the bacteria break down plant cells. At high temperatures, the damage progresses rapidly—the disease is severe in warm (80–85°F), moist conditions.

Target: Fruits, especially melons; vegetables, particularly broccoli, carrot, celery, cruciferous vegetables, lettuce, onions, and potatoes; cacti; flower bulbs and rhizomes

Symptoms: Small, water-soaked areas appear on foliage, stems, some underground vegetables, bulbs, and rhizomes, and then rapidly enlarge. Plant tissue rots, becoming soft and mushy. The affected parts may collapse, appear sunken, and smell bad. Bacteria and cell debris may ooze through growth cracks; the sticky ooze dries and may turn brown, gray, or tan. Foliage on infected plants may yellow, wilt, and die, and the plant may eventually die. Bulbs and rhizomes are filled with a smelly, thick white ooze; foliage easily pulls away, and the plant usually dies. When bulbs or rhizomes are lifted for dividing, empty shells may be all that remains. Once a bulb is infected, it may die within five days of the initial infection. On potatoes, a slimy, smelly decay appears in tubers and can cause complete rot within ten days.

Prevention: Good garden and storage practices are the key to preventing bacterial soft rot disease. Plant only healthy plants, in well-drained soil, leaving ample space between them to promote good air circulation. Avoid overwatering and overhead watering, and do not use stagnant water sources. Control pest insects. Wait until potato vines yellow before digging.

Management: On cactus, cut out the diseased area with a knife, removing about ½ inch of healthy tissue around the rot. This disfigures the plant but may stop the rot from spreading and save the plant. Remove and discard all bulbs and plants showing signs of decay. There is no cure for many of the bacterial soft spots. Seek information on additional options from your cooperative extension agent.

BACTERIAL WILT

BACTERIA

✎ ZONES: 1–9

The bacterium *Erwinia tracheiphila* causes this disease of plants in the cucumber family. It overwinters in the bodies of the striped and the 12-spotted cucumber beetles and is transmitted to the plant via beetle feeding—or later in the season, via grasshopper feeding. As beetles chew on affected leaves, which they seem to prefer, their mouth parts become contaminated with bacteria that they then carry to unaffected plants. An entire plant can be infected within two weeks. However, infection occurs only if there is a film of water on leaf tissue. The problem is greater in areas with moderate rainfall and daily temperatures of 52–60°F. If the beetles are eliminated, so is the bacterium.

Target: Cucumber, cantaloupe, pumpkin, squash, white gourd; however, watermelon is not affected

Symptoms: Dull green flabby patches appear on leaves, followed by sudden wilting and shriveling of foliage. Stems shrivel and dry but do not turn brown. If you cut a wilted stem near the plant's base, bacteria ooze out in white sticky masses. If you touch this ooze with a knife or other utensil and withdraw it slowly, the white ooze strings out in a fine thread. Affected plants may die. Partially resistant plants may be dwarfed, with excessive blooming and branching, wilting during the day but partially recovering at night. Fruit wilts and shrivels.

Prevention: Control carrier beetles early in the season. Avoid overhead watering. Do not overwater or crowd plants. Cover cucurbits with floating row covers to prevent cucumber beetles and grasshoppers from feeding on the plants. Clean up and destroy plant debris to eliminate sites where carrier beetles can overwinter. Rotate cucurbit plants with less susceptible crops (see page 40).

Management: There are no chemical or other cures for the disease once it takes hold. Promptly remove and discard affected plants.

 Notes: Bacterial diseases are often categorized according to their symptoms. For example, bacteria that penetrate a plant's water-conducting system are known as wilts. Bacteria that may stimulate growths at a plant's base are called crown galls. Bacteria that kill plant tissue are called blights.

BLACK ROOT ROT COMPLEX

FUNGUS

✎ ZONES: ALL

Black root rot decays the roots of strawberry plants. The plants most vulnerable to infection are those weakened by drought stress, root-lesion nematodes, frost injury, or crowns buried too deep. Plants growing in sterile but saturated soil may also develop black root rot. Plants may be infected at any growth stage. The disease is caused by any of several different soil-inhabiting fungi, including *Coniothyrium fuckelii, Hainesia lythri, Idriella lunata, Pyrenochaeta, Pythium,* and *Rhizoctonia fragariae.* Some of these organisms are native soil fungi, surviving indefinitely in soil. If soil is heavy and waterlogged, black root rot fungi are especially prevalent. Resting spores may be transferred to plants via running or splashing water.

Target: Strawberry

Symptoms: Leaves are smaller than normal. They wilt in warm weather, turn yellow, then red, then brown, and eventually they die. Fruiting of strawberry plants slows, then stops. If you dig up an affected plant, you may see unhealthy-looking roots that lack new lateral growth or an entire root that has turned black. Sometimes only the outer root layer is affected, while the inner core stays a normal pale yellow. Roots affected by black root rot differ from those with red stele (see page 232) in that they do not have the red core discoloration typical of red stele.

Prevention: Grow strawberries as annuals, and do not replant strawberries on the same spot for at least two years. Select resistant varieties from certified strawberry stock grown under controlled conditions that protect plants from contracting specific communicable plant diseases; check the certification tag or label. Do not buy plants with darkened or black roots; take only those with white healthy roots. Keep soil pH between 5.5 and 6.5. Root strawberry runners in a well-drained, soil-less mixture or in soil known to be free of black root rot. Place plants at the proper depth, being careful not to injure roots. Keep roots from getting dry, but do not overwater. Clean up plant debris after harvest.

Management: Plants with black root rot do not recover. Remove and destroy all infected plants. Do not place them in a compost pile.

BLACK SPOT

FUNGUS

ZONES: ALL

Black spot is a significant and well-known rose disease caused by *Diplocarpon rosae,* a fungus that overwinters on rose canes and fallen leaves. It thrives in warm, moist environments. Spores spread to other plant parts via splashing rain or overhead watering.

Target: Rose

Symptoms: The disease initially appears on young leaves as black circles with irregular margins. These spots, which are fungus colonies, grow to about ½ inch wide and may be surrounded by a yellow halo. The irregular margin differentiates rose black spot from other leaf spots, and from spotting caused by cold or chemicals. Leaves may turn yellowish and drop. In severe cases, roses lose most or all of their leaves. A new crop of leaves may appear, only to be lost again. A third crop may start by late summer. In cold areas, the plant may die from winter stress. Flowers are small and fewer in number. This fungus can also show up as dark blisters on rose stems. Few infections affect canes.

Prevention: Planting resistant varieties is the best prevention. Roses resistant to black spot in one area may have less resistance in another area, due to fungus variations. Avoid planting your favorite susceptible varieties next to one other to prevent the fungus from transferring via splashing rain or watering. Give roses maximal sun and good air circulation. Water during hours of full sun so leaves can dry before nightfall; avoid overhead watering. Pruning to remove crossing branches in the plant center helps reduce lingering moisture. Remove all old leaves. After the season ends, clean the planted area thoroughly.

Management: Once black spot appears, it is difficult to control. Pruning roses into dormancy in the winter and removing all the leaves, as well as raking up all fallen leaves, is the best management for black spot. Applying a thick mulch in early spring reduces water splashing that transfers fungus spores. If the canes are infected, prune them back to two buds. Remove and discard diseased foliage during dry weather to avoid transferring spores while handling. If a favored plant continually develops black spot in one location, try moving it to a sunnier place with better air circulation. Fungicides are ineffective in managing this fungus unless they are used frequently in early spring. In spring or at the first appearance of black spot, you can spray leaves thoroughly with fungicidal soap, wettable or liquid sulfur, or chlorothalonil.

BROWN ROT OF STONE FRUIT

FUNGUS

ZONES: ALL

In the western United States, brown rot is the most common and most destructive blossom and fruit disease of almonds and stone fruits. The fungus overwinters in rotted fruit on the ground, in dried rotted fruit remaining on the tree, and in infected twigs. In spring, wind and rain carry spores to healthy fruit tree buds. Flowers can be infected from the time buds open until petals fall; most fruit rot develops the month before harvest. Brown rot is most severe in mild, moist weather.

Target: All stone fruit trees, including almond, apricot, cherry, peach, and plum

Symptoms: Brown rot is initially noticed as a browning and wilting of blossoms and leaves. Dead blossoms may remain on trees for a long time. After causing flower decay, the fungus grows down into nearby twigs, producing brown, sunken cankers that may ooze with a gummy substance. During moist weather, small, rotting brown circles appear on mature fruit and spread rapidly to cover it. Light brown or gray powdery fungus spores, sometimes in concentric rings, soon cover the rotted surfaces. Fruit eventually shrinks, darkens, and dries out. It sometimes drops, but often it remains on the tree—such fruits are known as mummies. Ripe fruit can also develop brown rot in storage.

Prevention: Plant resistant varieties. Maintain good garden-cleanup practices. Emphasize insect management. Avoid wetting blossoms.

Management: Inspect trees before growth begins in spring; promptly remove and destroy affected parts to help prevent the spread of the disease. Prune out mummies, damaged twigs, and any branches with gummy cankers. Do not place the debris in a compost pile unless you are using the rapid composting method. Thin trees to encourage good air circulation. Depending on the season, you can manage the disease by using a fungicide containing captan, chlorothalonil, or triforine; there are dormant, early-blossom, full-bloom, and petal-fall treatments. Ask a garden center consultant or cooperative extension agent for information. Always apply fungicides according to directions on the label.

Notes: A brown rot of citrus fruit—a different disease—is caused by a Phytophthora *fungus.*

CAMELLIA FLOWER AND PETAL BLIGHT

FUNGUS

ZONES: ALL

Infection by the fungus *Ciborinia camelliae* begins any time after camellia flowers begin showing color. This fungus attacks only flower parts, not leaves, stems, or roots. Hard brown or black fungus bodies (sclerotia) develop in the base of old infected flowers. These fungus bodies later produce mushroomlike growths, which in turn produce spores that cause new petal infections. The fungus, which can survive at least five years in the soil, is spread by wind to new flowers. Germination occurs when there is condensed moisture on the foliage. In an attempt to prevent the spread of this serious and widespread pathogen, some states may quarantine shipments or gifts of camellias or require that they be certified free of this disease.

Target: Camellia

Symptoms: Small tan or brown spots appear on petals, then enlarge, and eventually may cover entire petals—after a few days, the entire flower may be brown. Darkened veins give a netted appearance to the brown coloration. Dark brown to black fungus bodies, an inch or more in diameter, are visible in the flower base after the flowers fall to the ground.

Prevention: To avoid introducing camellia blight into the garden from contaminated soil, buy bare-root plants, those without attached soil. On plants in containers, pick off and destroy all flower buds before planting. On existing plants, always rake up old leaves, flowers, and other plant debris throughout the garden, but especially under camellias. Avoid overhead watering, or water only at times when plant leaves will dry quickly.

Management: Remove and discard diseased camellia flowers, buds, and flower and leaf debris. Carefully remove any existing mulch, replacing it with a fresh mulch at least 4 inches thick. Spray with a fungicide containing captan or chlorothalonil. Always apply fungicides according to directions on the product label.

 Notes: Camellias can also suffer from weather injury. The effects differ from camellia flower and petal blight in that spots caused by weather are lighter and usually limited to the outer edges of the flowers.

CEDAR-APPLE RUST

FUNGUS

ZONES: ALL

The *Gymnosporangium* fungi that cause rust diseases require specific alternate hosts each year. Cedar-apple rust lives on apple trees one year and species of red cedar and juniper trees the next.

Target: Apple, crabapple, hawthorn, red cedar, mountain ash, quince, and upright junipers

Symptoms: In spring or early summer, a small, greenish brown swelling may appear on a host cedar tree or on juniper needles and stems. By fall, the swelling enlarges into a hard brown gall about $1\frac{1}{2}-2$ inches across. Although unsightly, these brown galls covered with small circular depressions do not damage the tree. However, the following spring, during wet, warm weather, the galls absorb water, swell up, and display orange jellylike horns up to 1 inch long. The spores produced by these horns may infect apple trees up to 4 miles away. The galls eventually die but may remain on the cedar or juniper for more than a year. From mid- to late spring, tiny yellow spots appear on fruit and upper leaf surfaces of infected apple trees. These spots slowly enlarge and turn orange, spotted with minute black dots. During summer, spores appear within tiny brown, cuplike, fringed growths on lower leaves. The wind blows these spores back to cedars and junipers, restarting the infection cycle. Infected apples may have a large concave area with raised orange rust spots, sometimes in concentric rings. Fruit, which may be small and irregular, may drop early.

Prevention: Plant rust-resistant species. Resistant apple varieties include 'Freedom', 'Liberty', and 'Priscilla'; varieties of juniper are Chinese and savin. If possible, remove alternate hosts from the immediate growing area.

Management: No chemical management is available to the home gardener for cedar-apple rust or other alternate-host rusts. Remove and discard galls and infected fruit and leaves. Rake and discard fallen leaves. Ask your cooperative extension agent about other options.

 Notes: A similar disease called Pacific Coast pear rust lives on pears and the incense cedar. Although its life cycle is similar to that of cedar-apple rust, galls do not form on cedars. However, you will see orange jelly masses on cedar scales. 'Bartlett' is a resistant pear. Other rusts requiring alternate hosts include cedar-quince rust and cedar-hawthorn rust.

CHERRY LEAF SPOT

FUNGUS

ZONES: ALL

Cherry leaf spot, also called shot hole or yellow leaf, is one of the most destructive leaf diseases of cherries, particularly in coastal areas. Spores of the fungus *Blumeriella jaapii* overwinter in fallen cherry leaves. In spring, the rain or wind carries them to cherry trees. The resulting infection decreases the nutrition available to the tree, resulting in reduced crops of poor-quality cherries. The spore infection may continue past the summer harvest, but older leaves are less susceptible. Cherry leaf spot is worst during warm, wet weather. If leaf drop is severe, weakened trees may be further damaged by winter cold, bringing lower fruit yield in subsequent years and possible tree dieback or death. The defoliation also predisposes the tree to sunscald damage.

Target: Cherries, sweet and sour

Symptoms: Many tiny purplish to brown irregular or circular spots appear on upper leaf surfaces. These spots enlarge, and the tissue dies. A toxin that causes leaf yellowing and then defoliation, usually by midsummer, is produced in infected leaves. In severe infections, spots appear on leaf stems and fruit. During warm, wet weather, whitish specks appear on leaf undersides, then become raised, creamy bumps, directly beneath the colored spots above. The spot centers may dry, separate from healthy plant tissue, and fall out, leaving a shot hole pattern. Defoliation before fruit ripening may decrease fruit yield, and the remaining fruit may be soft and watery.

Prevention: Select the proper cherry tree for your climate and soil. Immune cherry trees are not available, but there are partially resistant sour cherry varieties, such as 'Meteor' and 'Northside' (also resistant to brown rot fungi). Sweet cherries tend to be more resistant than sour cherries. Water and fertilize the trees properly, and prune to improve air circulation and fruit quality.

Management: Complete management of cherry leaf spot is not possible in the season in which the disease appears. You can partially manage this disease if you begin at petal fall. Spray with a fungicide containing captan, chlorothalonil, or sulfur. Rake and discard fallen diseased leaves; do not use them as mulch. Prune plants to increase air circulation. Always apply fungicides according to directions on the label.

CLUB ROOT

FUNGUS

ZONES: ALL

Club root fungus causes abnormal cell growth and division within the root. Affected roots may become oddly club shaped. Because these damaged roots cannot supply water or nutrients to the plant, young plants will not grow well. In later stages of the disease, rotting of the roots spreads millions of fungus spores into surrounding soil, and from there they spread via watering or garden tools to other plants.

Target: Cabbage, cauliflower, and most other cruciferous crops

Symptoms: There are many types of club root fungus, and symptoms may vary in different regions and climate zones. Initial symptoms—leaf wilting and some leaf yellowing—usually occur on a hot, sunny day. The plant may recover from wilting at night, only to droop again as the next day warms up. If you pull out the plant, you will see swollen, thickened roots in a gnarled mass. Younger plants attacked by the club root fungus may die. Mature plants can survive, but the crop produced is not worth harvesting.

Prevention: Purchase certified disease-free seedlings and resistant varieties. If disease-free seedlings are not available, inspect seedling roots and reject those that appear abnormal.

Place seedlings in sterilized soil or soil where club root has not appeared before; do not plant cruciferous vegetables in infected soil for at least seven years. If you add manure, be sure it did not come from areas where animals could have fed on diseased plants. All planting areas should be well drained. Club root is most common in acid soils; as a preventive, add ground limestone and hydrated lime to soil, bringing it to a pH of 7.2.

Management: An infected plant cannot be cured. Dig up and discard the whole plant, including the root system. Clean tools after using them in infected soil, as the fungus that causes club root can survive long periods in the soil even without a host plant present.

✎ *Notes: Root swelling can also be caused by diseases other than club root fungus.*

CORN SMUT

FUNGUS

⚹ ZONES: ALL

Common smut infection is most likely to occur in these situations: when soil is high in nitrogen; when plants have been injured by hail, blowing sand, insect damage, or careless use of garden tools; when summer temperatures are 80–90°F; or when there is moderate rainfall as corn ears mature. The spores, which spread from plant to plant via watering, wind, and manure, can affect just a few ears or an entire crop. Where they germinate, the spores form galls that look like puffballs, tumors, or boils. Overwintering in soil, garden refuse, and manure, the spores can live up to seven years, waiting for a host and suitable weather conditions.

Target: Corn

Symptoms: Damage from head smut appears on any aboveground part of the corn, after the corn ears and tassels have formed. The kernels and cobs are replaced by pale greenish white or sometimes black-covered galls, particularly on sweet corn. Smut-infected plants are small, their corn ears quite disfigured. While some galls are pea size, others may grow to 6 inches wide.

Prevention: Many corn varieties are resistant to head smut. Ask your local nursery or cooperative extension office about the varieties most successful in your area. Keep plants adequately watered; even resistant varieties can show smut symptoms if summers have been very hot and dry. Eliminate galls before they open and release spores to infect more corn plants. Discard galls; do not place in a compost pile. Clean up corn debris after harvest, and discard debris if corn smut has appeared in the last several years. Do not use any manure fertilizers on corn, as they may transmit the fungus. Rotate crops so that corn isn't planted in the same area each year.

Management: There are no chemical controls for common corn smut or head smut. Call your cooperative extension agent for advice if your crop has a severe problem.

 Notes: Other names for corn smut are boil smut, corn goiter, and corn-soot. In some areas, even in gourmet restaurants in the United States, the galls of common corn smut are prized as food.

CROWN AND COLLAR ROT

FUNGUS

⚹ ZONES: ALL

Crown and collar rot is a disease of tree roots and crowns caused by *Phytophthora cactorum* and other *Phytophthora* species. This is a serious disease of apple and other orchard trees. Infection is common in plants that are constantly wet at the soil line between spring and fall. Fungus oospores, or resting spores, survive in soil, organic debris, or infected plant tissues. During wet weather, plants become infected. Movement within the roots is greatest in the period between pink bud and shoot growth.

Target: Apple and other orchard trees

Symptoms: Leaves on one or several branches turn to purple, yellow, or bronze. Bark reddens. Leaves wilt, and new leaves are smaller than normal. Fruit may appear only on upper branches. If you scrape away soil at the tree base, you may find dead bark. The growing layer of tissue underneath the bark, the cambium, which is normally white or light green, becomes brown to black. A distinct margin may be visible between healthy and infected portions of the wood cambium. Because this is a tree-base problem, the tree may be completely girdled by the fungus before the condition is noticed. A mature tree can continue on in a weakened condition or it may die; a young tree may decline rapidly and die.

Prevention: While there are no truly resistant varieties, some crops have moderate to high resistance. Consult your cooperative extension agent for advice. Plant trees on an elevated area to help keep them dry even during heavy rainfall. Keep sprinklers from constantly wetting trunks, and avoid overwatering. Be careful not to wound the tree crowns. If an injury does occur, keep it uncovered and open to air circulation for the rest of the growing season.

Management: In summer, examine crowns of susceptible trees for collar rot. Scrape off any diseased tissue and move soil away from the trunk, leaving the crown exposed to air until late fall. Once infection progresses, no chemical management is available.

CROWN GALL

BACTERIA

ZONES: ALL

Crown gall may seriously harm plants, as well as deform them and make them unattractive. It can invade your garden via diseased nursery stock and spread by contaminated pruning tools. The bacterium *(Agrobacterium)* enters plants through open wounds and stimulates abnormal cell growth, which forms the galls, often during summer months. Galls usually appear at the crown but also may form lower in the roots and are occasionally seen on aboveground parts. The galls interrupt the flow of both water and nutrients through the plant. Sometimes the galls crack, creating an opening through which secondary organisms may enter and damage the plant. Soil can be infested with crown gall bacteria for several years.

Target: Ground covers, perennials, shrubs, vines, roses, berries, and fruit, nut, and ornamental trees

Symptoms: Galls—hard, rough, whitish, irregularly shaped, tumorlike growths—appear near the soil line and on stems and roots. The galls range from the size of a pea to that of a baseball. Larger galls may split open. On young trees, the galls may initially be soft, spongy, or wartlike, but they become brown and woody with age. Plants with many galls may weaken and grow slowly; leaves may turn yellow.

Prevention: Consult your cooperative extension agent or a garden center consultant for information about resistant plants. Inspect nursery stock before buying, and reject any plant with gall symptoms, including suspicious bumps. If crown gall has occurred in your garden in the past, do not place susceptible, healthy new plants in that area. Be careful not to wound plants when planting them or cultivating around them. Control insects, especially those that may damage plants around the soil line.

Management: Remove and destroy infected smaller plants and seriously affected and declining trees with large galls surrounding the crowns. When pruning and grafting, use only disinfected tools (disinfect with a solution of 1 part bleach and 9 parts water). Solarizing for five weeks helps kill any bacteria in the soil.

CYTOSPORA CANKER

FUNGUS

ZONES: ALL

Cytospora canker is caused by *Leucostoma* and *Cytospora* fungi. These fungi are vigorous invaders of tree wounds. Insects, rodents, mechanical damage from picking ladders, sunscald, or winter injury may have been responsible for the wounds. The fungi overwinter in infected stems and stem debris and are transmitted by rain, wind, and insects in the spring. The disease damages the tree by clogging its water- and nutrient-conducting channels. The damage is particularly severe on weakened trees and after very cold winters. The canker damage caused by these fungi is compounded by other fungi that invade the infection sites and produce rapid wood rot.

Target: All stone fruit and pome fruit trees; spruce trees; especially deciduous trees, including aspen, cottonwood, mountain ash, and Siberian elm

Symptoms: The trees' reactions to fungus invasion vary widely. Dead twigs are usually the first visible sign. On closer inspection, you can see raised oval or elongated gummy cankers that girdle or nearly girdle the leaf stems below the dead twigs. Leaves droop above the stem infection and become discolored; the discoloration ranges from shades of green to shades of brown. The leaves remain attached, sometimes through the winter. On trees with smooth bark, the canker surfaces have raised, barely visible, pinhead-size pimples. Amber to orange, hairlike spore tendrils arise from the cankers in humid weather. Initially small cankers will enlarge. In late fall, calluses may form at canker margins, as the tree tries to wall off the infection. Branches and even whole trees may be killed quickly. Those that are not killed look unhealthy and are said to be in a condition known as perennial canker.

Prevention: There are no resistant varieties. Take special care not to wound trees during the growing season. Manage pest insect populations. Paint the southwest side of the tree with white latex paint to avoid winter injury. Prune only in dry weather and as late as possible in the dormant season. Avoid excessive nitrogen fertilization.

Management: Remove dead branches, cutting at least 12 inches below the bark discoloration. Paint cutting wounds with disinfectant solution. Avoid overhead watering. Spray with a fungicide containing chlorothalonil, captan, or triforine. Always apply fungicides according to directions on the label.

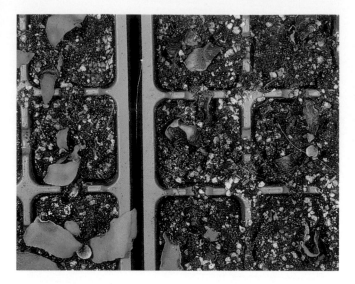

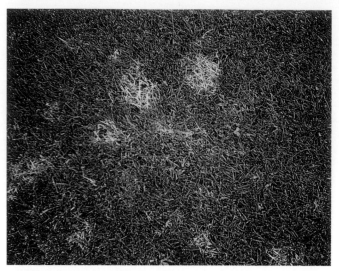

DAMPING OFF

FUNGUS

ZONES: ALL

Damping-off disease, also called seed and seedling rot, is caused by various fungi, including botrytis, *Fusarium* spp., *Phytophthora, Pythium,* and *Rhizoctonia solani.* Varying amounts and types of these fungi are normally present in soil; they attack young plants when encouraged by cold soil, damp soil with a high nitrogen level, crowding, shade, high humidity, or cloudy days. Container plants grown in garden soil rather than potting mix are more susceptible to damping off than those planted directly in the ground. The disease frequently kills young seedlings just as they emerge from the soil. Older seedlings are resistant to attack.

Target: Vegetable, flower, and grass seedlings

Symptoms: Seedlings may not emerge, or if they do, they may grow to about 1 inch high and then suddenly wilt and fall over. You may not see them go, but there will be gaps in planting areas where they have disappeared. Seedlings may have discolored or water-soaked lesions at the soil line where fungi have rotted the stems.

Prevention: For container planting, use new flats or pots, or thoroughly wash and disinfect old containers before using. Use a pasteurized potting soil for containers. Be sure that the seed packet is stamped for use in the current year; fresh seed is less likely to incur damping-off disease. Try seeds treated with a fungicide. Be careful to plant seeds at the correct depth, and do not overwater them. Scatter a thin layer of sand or perlite on the soil surface to keep seedlings dry at the soil line. Thin seedlings so they are not crowded together and give them ample light. Add fertilizer only after seedlings have formed their first true leaves. Delay planting seeds in the garden until soil warms up; seedlings will be stronger and grow faster.

Management: As soon as you see signs of damping off, stop watering and allow the soil to dry slightly around the plants. However, do not let soil around seedlings dry completely or the seedlings will die. If seedlings are in cold frames or flats, give them as much air and light as possible—the better the growing conditions, the less likely damping off will continue. Treatment varies with the specific fungus causing damping-off disease. Contact your cooperative extension agent for treatment advice.

DOLLAR SPOT ON LAWNS

FUNGUS

ZONES: ALL

Warm, wet weather, 60–85°F in May and June, and fall weather with cool nights encourage this disease, which is caused by the fungus *Sclerotinia homeocarpa.* Most prevalent in lawns lacking nitrogen and in underfertilized, compacted, poorly drained soils, the disease—also called small brown patch—spreads via shoes or garden equipment. Lawns usually recover on their own over a period of several months if watering, aeration, and fertilization are improved.

Target: Many lawn grasses, especially Bermuda, creeping fescue, fine-leafed bent grass, and Kentucky bluegrass

Symptoms: Small round brown spots appear in lawn and later become straw colored. Initially measuring 1–2½ inches wide, they sometimes coalesce to form bigger, irregularly shaped patches that cover large areas and possibly the entire lawn. Leaf blades have tan blotches with reddish brown margins. Dieback from leaf tips often occurs. A white cobwebby fungus growth, which can be seen in early morning before the dew dries, may cover dying leaf blades.

Prevention: Plant resistant varieties such as 'Arlington' or 'Pennpar' bent grass; 'Pennlawn' creeping fescue or 'Jamestown' Chewings fescue; or bluegrass 'Columbia', 'Majestic', 'Parade', 'Vantage', or 'Victa'. Fertilize regularly with a balanced lawn fertilizer containing nitrogen. Water deeply and infrequently to encourage a deep, strong root system—and only in the morning, so the lawn has a full chance to dry during the day.

Management: If dollar spot develops, do not walk on affected parts of the lawn. The grass will recover quickly if treated promptly. Keep deep watering to a minimum: only in the morning, once or twice a week. Disinfect garden equipment, including mowers, after using on infected areas. Improve soil aeration and apply a fertilizer containing nitrogen if there is a nitrogen deficiency. Rake thatch and discard. With severe infestations that do not clear up after a few months, remove the entire lawn and reseed with resistant grasses. If the problem is severe and continuous, spray with a fungicide containing chlorothalonil.

DOWNY MILDEW

FUNGUS

✎ ZONES: ALL

Downy mildew is caused by fungi of the genera *Bremia, Peronospora,* and *Plasmopara*. These fungi must survive on living tissue, so they rarely kill infected cells or their host plants. But affected plants may be unsightly, stunted, and poorly fruiting. Downy mildew fungi overwinter on infected plant debris, weeds, and existing plant parts. High humidity, cool temperatures, fog, drizzle, and heavy dew encourage the development and spread of the disease; it is rare in arid and semiarid climates.

Target: Alyssum, bachelor's button, beet, cane berries, crucifers, grape, lettuce, onion, pansy, pea, rose, snapdragon, spinach, and others

Symptoms: Symptoms vary considerably, depending on the causative fungus and the plant type; each downy mildew fungus is host specific. Alyssum leaves become slightly deformed, ranging from puckered to curled. A whitish to grayish mold grows in puckered areas on the leaf undersides. Plants are stunted and unsightly. On cane berries, small, conspicuous, irregularly shaped patches appear on the upper leaf surface. These patches change from yellow to deep wine red. Stems show red streaking. Fruits dry and shrivel, a condition called dryberry disease. Berries may split, appearing to be two berries on one pedicel (the stalk that supports the fruiting organ). The leaves, shoots, and tendrils of grapevines become brown and brittle. Grapes may be covered with a white cottony growth or may shrivel and discolor. On lettuce, older leaves are attacked first. Upper leaf surfaces have light green or yellowish areas; undersides are patched with a downy substance. Affected parts turn brown and centers of infected areas may die. The upper leaf surfaces of pansies turn yellow. A light gray-brown, feltlike growth, shown above, appears on the undersides of the leaves. Purplish red to dark brown irregular spots show up on rose leaves. Leaflets are yellow but may contain a "green island." The leaves may drop if the infection is severe.

Prevention: Plant disease-free seeds and healthy, disease-resistant plants. Do not take cuttings from roses with symptoms of the disease. Water in the morning and remove debris from around plants.

Management: Remove and discard infected plants and plant parts.

DUTCH ELM DISEASE

FUNGUS

✎ ZONES: ALL

The fungus causing Dutch elm disease, *Ophiostoma ulmi,* is spread via the feeding of infected elm bark beetles. Initially the infected beetles feed in upper sections of a tree. The fungus multiplies and spreads through the tree, producing a toxin that interferes with the tree's water-conducting system. Symptoms begin in late spring.

Target: American and European elm trees

Symptoms: There are two forms of Dutch elm disease: an acute form and a slower, chronic form. In the acute form, water-deprived leaves suddenly wilt, sometimes so rapidly that leaves dry, curl, and fall while still green. Trees with the acute disease may die within a few weeks. In the chronic form, symptoms are gradual. Infected trees leaf out late in the season. Starting near the tree top, one or more branches may be covered with yellowing leaves, and their bark may have small holes. Many leaves drop off. Infected twigs and branches may be ringed with brown dots just under the bark—these are the clogged water-conducting tubes. Infected trees may linger for more than a year but eventually die. Get positive identification of Dutch elm disease by checking with a cooperative extension agent.

Prevention: An individual can do little to prevent Dutch elm disease: plant only resistant elms and keep them healthy with proper watering and fertilizing. Otherwise, prevention must be a community program, because elm bark beetles can fly a considerable distance. Contact your cooperative extension agent for advice.

Management: Early detection is the key to ultimate control. Inspect susceptible elms each spring and late summer, promptly removing and destroying any infected trees. Elm bark beetles feed only on healthy wood, but they breed in dead or dying wood. Therefore do not save the logs for firewood nor the wood chips for mulch; strip off the bark on tree stumps below ground level and destroy it. If one of a group of trees becomes infected, consult a professional arborist. You may need to remove all of them.

 Notes: This disease is not of Dutch origin; it was first studied in Holland, about 1918. In 1930, the disease reached the United States via elm burl logs imported for furniture veneer. It spread quickly and has threatened the existence of the native American elm.

EARLY BLIGHT

FUNGUS

✎ ZONES: ALL

Heavy dews, frequent rains, and warm air temperatures usually accompany severe outbreaks of early blight fungus (also known as alternaria blight and alternaria leaf spot). The fungus, *Alternaria solani,* affects both old and new plants; it is most severe toward the close of the growing season. Poorly fertilized potato and tomato plants are particularly susceptible, as are heavily loaded tomato vines. The disease is more frequent when plants are watered from overhead and less frequent in well-fertilized, well-managed soil. Spores can survive in plant debris for at least a year.

Target: Potato, tomato, eggplant, and wild plants related to the tomato

Symptoms: Small, dark brown to black spots, oval or irregularly shaped, appear on potato and tomato leaves. Leaf tissues around the spots may turn yellow, and the entire leaf may yellow. Ridged concentric rings in the lesion center form a bull's-eye. The lowest, oldest plant leaves are infected first; they droop, dry out, and later die. The tubers are not affected as frequently as its leaves are. Tuber lesions appear as brown to black sunken spots, less than ½ inch wide. On tomatoes, mature fruit develops dark, leathery, sunken spots near the stem. The spots, which may become quite large, may have concentric ridges like those on infected leaves.

Prevention: Use seed potatoes certified disease free by the state department of agriculture. For other species, plant resistant varieties. Rotate potato and tomato crops with crops that do not get early blight. Avoid overhead watering and watering during cool, cloudy weather. Keep plants healthy by fertilizing properly; thin them to allow light and air to reach all plant parts. Handle carefully when harvesting to reduce bruising injuries through which the fungus can enter. Clean up and destroy all harvest debris. Eliminate weeds.

Management: Remove and destroy leaves as soon as you see spots. Rake and burn dry vines of affected plants after harvest. Throw out infected tubers; do not compost. You may be able to spray with a fungicide containing chlorothalonil, but it is best to consult your local cooperative extension office before considering chemical management. Some fungicides are for regional use only.

EDEMA

VARIOUS CAUSES

✎ ZONES: ALL

Edema is a physiological disorder that is often mistaken for a pathogen-caused problem. Although scientists are not certain of all the causes of edema, we do know that it can result from injury—from insect feeding (particularly by thrips and aphids), from windblown soil particles, and from chemical applications. The problem usually occurs with a combination of environmental conditions, such as high soil moisture, low light levels, and high relative humidity. However, edema is also seen in very dry areas.

Target: Indoor and outdoor plants, including annuals, vegetables, and perennials. Outdoors, begonia, camellia, geranium, and ivy are most often damaged. Other plants include eucalyptus, hibiscus, privet, and yew.

Symptoms: Edema most frequently occurs during late winter and early spring. Watery blisters or small galls—from just a few to many—appear on leaves, primarily on lower leaf surfaces. Blisters may harden and turn brown, yellow, or rust colored. Affected leaves may turn yellow and drop. On camellias, leaf undersides may develop brown, corky, roughened swellings. On foliage plants, these lesions, which may be concentrated near leaf margins, may be lighter in color than surrounding leaf areas. On tomatoes, edema shows up as very small, clear, watery, and sometimes numerous blisters. As the blisters dry, they turn opaque and usually reddish brown. On cabbage and cauliflower, the disorder usually begins on lower leaf surfaces. Initially a few watery blisters appear, then turn dark brown, yellow, or rust. They may be mistaken for a rust or bacterial infection.

Prevention: Plant several vegetable varieties, instead of just one or two, as varieties differ in susceptibility. Provide good drainage; water plants early in the day so soil can drain and does not remain saturated at night. Be sure plants have adequate light. Fertilize regularly with a fertilizer recommended for the plant type. Control insects. Harvest crops before the heavy fall rains that saturate the soil.

Management: Manage insect populations, such as aphids and thrips. Do not overwater plants.

FAIRY RING

FUNGUS

ZONES: ALL

From late spring to early autumn, fairy ring mushrooms can disfigure a lawn. The disease is especially a problem in acid soils and in areas where there is buried wood, such as tree parts and construction residue. As the mushroom fungus multiplies, its white underground growth, or mycelium, becomes so dense and tough that water cannot penetrate the lawn. Starved and thirsty as weather warms up, grass around the mushrooms initially begins to die. However, the dying mycelium provides nutrition to the grass above it, which turns green again. Fairy rings may be small or several hundred feet wide. They expand about 1–2 feet per year.

Target: All lawn grasses

Symptoms: Fairy ring damage appears in a target pattern: a brown area surrounded by a wide circle of dark grass. Small, tan mushrooms appear within or just outside the grass circle. Sometimes there is an inner circle of dark green grass as well. The grass in these circles may be greener than any other grass in your lawn.

Prevention: Rake or pick all mushrooms as soon as they appear in a lawn, before the mushroom caps open up and release spores. On new home sites, remove old tree roots and stumps, as well as wood left over from construction, before installing a new lawn.

Management: No grass varieties are resistant. Use a grass fertilizer containing nitrogen to try to revitalize the fairy ring center. Use a lawn aerator to break up mycelia and bring water to the lawn roots. Repeat aeration weekly. Water and mow more often. There is no chemical control for fairy ring. Contact your local nursery or cooperative extension office about new management measures or techniques that may have been developed for use in your growing zone.

 Notes: Although fairy ring mushrooms generally are not poisonous, children and pets should not eat them, or any mushrooms that appear in your lawn. Be extremely cautious about removing all mushrooms. Place them in a plastic bag, seal it securely, and discard it safely.

FIREBLIGHT

BACTERIA

ZONES: ALL

The fireblight bacterium is very destructive, particularly if temperatures average above 60°F daily and the weather is wet during the blooming season. The bacteria multiply quickly within the host plant: a single fireblight bacterium can cause massive bacterial damage, eventually killing a previously healthy tree. Some apple and pear rootstocks are so susceptible to fireblight that an infestation there may cause an entire tree to collapse without other symptoms appearing.

Target: Apple, pear, pyracantha, and others

Symptoms: In early spring, infected blossoms and leaves suddenly shrivel, turn blackish brown, and die. The young twigs wilt from the tips back, appearing black and twisted, as if they have been through a fire. Damaged bark is an abnormal dark brown to purplish color and appears sunken. Tree branches develop ovoid sores or cankers, which initially appear dark, sunken, and dry. Then in warm, moist spring weather, a thick liquid oozes from the cankers. Within the liquid are infective fireblight bacteria that spread to other target plants via insects, birds, squirrels, and splashing rain. Fruit may have black spots or may turn entirely black.

Prevention: Plant varieties that are fireblight resistant. Control vector insects, such as leafhoppers, ants, aphids, and fruit tree bark beetles. If fruit trees are a mainstay in your garden, don't plant other susceptible trees—hawthorn or mountain ash, for instance—nearby. Avoid growing fruit trees in heavy, poorly drained, or acid soil. Lush new growth is particularly susceptible, so avoid overfertilizing.

Management: Although there is no cure for fireblight, you can take certain helpful measures. In spring and summer, prune infected twigs and branches at least 12 inches below any evidence of the disease. Repeat pruning in the fall. Discard cuttings; do not compost.

FUSARIUM BULB ROT

FUNGUS

ZONES: ALL

This destructive fungus, *Fusarium oxysporum,* attacks both growing plants and bulbs in storage. The disease usually enters a planting or storage site via infected bulbs, corms, soil, or tools, and infects stored bulbs through wounds or abrasions in the bulb tissue. Plants in the ground are infected through their roots and then decay in the ground. The disease particularly attacks trumpet daffodils, daffodils forced for indoor use in winter, and Madonna lilies. Bulb rot is prevalent in warm climates where temperatures rarely drop below freezing; it is worst when soil temperatures reach 60–70°F. It persists in the soil indefinitely.

Target: Cyclamen, daffodil, dahlia, freesia, gladiolus, iris, lily, narcissus, onion, tulip, and other bulbs and corms

Symptoms: Leaves turn yellow, and the plant is stunted and dies prematurely. When dug up, affected bulbs may have few or no roots and often fall to pieces. Flower bulbs in storage develop a chocolate, bluish gray, or purple-brown spongy decay easily visible if you pull away the outer fleshy bulb scales. White fungal strands sometimes grow on the bulbs. Corms affected by this fungus show small, reddish brown lesions, more often on the lower half of the corm. These lesions enlarge in storage, and the entire corm may become a hard, dry, brownish black mummy.

Prevention: Purchase fusarium-resistant varieties of bulbs; reject any that show rot or are soft when pressed. Do not plant healthy bulbs in an area where diseased plants have previously grown; rotate planting beds from year to year. When digging up bulbs for storage or transfer, be careful not to bruise them, and dry them rapidly.

Management: There is no treatment for fusarium bulb rot. Discard all diseased plants, bulbs, and bulb remnants, as well as the soil surrounding any infected bulb for 6 inches in each direction.

 Notes: Species of this fungus also cause basal rot and fusarium brown rot of corms.

FUSARIUM WILT

FUNGUS

ZONES: ALL

The *Fusarium oxysporum* fungi overwinter in soil; some species survive in soil indefinitely. They can be transmitted by seed, contaminated soil and other growing media, garden equipment, running irrigation water, plant roots, or other vegetative parts. High soil temperatures—about 82°F—and air temperatures above 70°F favor these wilt diseases.

Target: Annuals, perennials, and vegetables, such as basil, cyclamen, dahlia, marigold, melon, spinach, squash, and tomato

Symptoms: Initially plants wilt in warm weather, partially recovering in the evening. Wilting intensifies as the season goes on. Leaves may turn yellow, and on cantaloupe and tomato, leaves appear scorched; lower leaves are most strongly affected at first, as shown above. Lightly infected plants may be stunted and produce fewer leaves; severely infected plants may wilt and die—either gradually, or suddenly with heat stress. If you cut across the stem of an infected plant, you may see dark or discolored fungus-clogged vascular tissue. A mildewy growth may appear on cantaloupe stems near the crown of the plant. On dying watermelon vines, you may see a pinkish white cottony growth near ground level on the stems. Infected asparagus stalks are yellow and stunted.

Prevention: Plant varieties that are resistant to fusarium wilt; obtain transplants grown from treated seed. In garden catalogs, look for seed packets with an F noting fusarium resistance. Plant seeds in sterile soil or potting mix, in new pots or in used pots that have been thoroughly cleaned and disinfected. Fertilize and water adequately to promote vigorous plant growth. Practice crop rotation with long intervals.

Management: Inspect plants at least once a week, and remove and discard infected plants as soon as infection is visible. Do not use diseased plants as mulch or in compost. Chemical management may be difficult for the home gardener; for current options, ask your cooperative extension agent.

 Notes: Resistant cantaloupe varieties include 'Classic', 'Durango', 'Easy Rider', and 'Gold Star'. Fully or partially resistant spinach varieties include 'Jade' and 'Spookum'. For tomatoes, try 'Better Boy', 'Carmen', and 'Merced'.

GRAY MOLD

FUNGUS

 ZONES: ALL

Gray mold fungus, *Botrytis cinerea,* is the most damaging rot of strawberries, but it attacks other plants as well. This fungus easily invades weak and damaged plant tissue, including blossoms; flowers are very susceptible during bloom, while berries are attacked at all stages of development. Gray mold spores survive in plant debris and are spread through the air during the whole growing season, from spring to early fall. Spores may also spread via splashing water or contact with infected plant parts. Cool temperatures, high humidity, and standing water on plants favor the disease, as do close plant spacing and overhead watering. Gray mold is more severe if crops are not rotated.

Target: More than 240 annuals and perennials; bean, strawberry, and tomato plants

Symptoms: Water-soaked lesions appear on leaves, stems, blossoms, or fruit. In advanced stages of the disease, lesions may be covered with gray spore masses, shown above. Fruit is unsightly. Tomatoes develop faint, pale halos, 1–3 inches in diameter, white on immature fruit and yellow on ripe fruit. Strawberries soften and rot.

Prevention: Create good air circulation by spacing plants properly. If possible, orient crop plants in the same direction as the prevailing winds. Irrigate on the ground rather than from overhead. Mulch with pine needles, straw, or plastic to keep fruit off the ground. Harvest small fruits every few days when ripe.

Management: Remove and discard all dead or infected plant parts. There is no chemical control available for gray mold on tomatoes. On annuals and perennials, spray with a fungicide containing chlorothalonil. For strawberries, use a fungicide containing captan. Apply all fungicides according to directions on the label.

✎ *Notes: The symptoms of this disease may resemble damage from frost, but you can distinguish this disease from frost damage by the gray mold that covers the affected areas in moist conditions.*

HEART ROT

FUNGUS

 ZONES: ALL

Heart rot is usually an old-age disease, one of nature's ways of recycling old trees. The disease is caused by various fungi that normally rot dead wood, such as fallen trees. However, when wounds—caused by insects, mechanical injury, and weather damage—provide an entrance, heart rot fungi may also invade the heartwood of living trees. Healthy trees may stop the infection by producing cells that wall off the invading fungi, but older trees that have many wounds may have little resistance to decay-causing organisms. Decay spreads throughout the heartwood, weakening affected branches, which are then brought down by rough weather. The fungus spores are spread by the wind.

Target: Ornamental and fruit trees

Symptoms: Yellowish to brown mushroomlike or woody growths may appear on the tree bark exterior; invisible beneath them is internal decay, shown above inside a stump. When the growths are hard, they are called conks. They may remain on affected trees for many years. During storms, branches may fall from the tree. The wood in the area of the break looks discolored and may be spongy.

Prevention: Promote the health and longevity of your trees with good gardening practices, including adequate fertilization. Water appropriately, making certain water gets down to the tree roots. Avoid wounding trees.

Management: Once conks appear on tree trunks, it is too late to do anything about heart rot; no chemical management is possible. Where practical, after a decayed branch has cracked and fallen, cut off the remaining stub, flush with the trunk or a larger branch. If the disease appears on large, specimen, or prized trees, consult a professional arborist to determine the extent of the decay. If the decay is severe, the entire tree may have to be removed for safety reasons. It's always a good idea to have a professional arborist examine large older trees that are located adjacent to residences or to anything else that might be damaged by falling trees or limbs.

JUNIPER TWIG BLIGHT

FUNGUS

✎ ZONES: ALL

Also known as phomopsis twig blight, juniper twig blight disease is caused by *Phomopsis juniperovora*. This fungus can enter the tree through wounds or through healthy tissue. Older, mature foliage is resistant to infection, but new growth is susceptible, especially when moisture and humidity are high. Excessive pruning or shearing in summer stimulates new, succulent foliage that is prone to infection. Plants grown in too much shade are also highly vulnerable. The spores are spread by overhead watering, insects, tools, and splashing rain. The black spore-producing structures overwinter on dead needles.

Target: Juniper, arborvitae *(Thuja)*, false cypress *(Chamaecyparis)*

Symptoms: In the spring, needles, twigs, and smaller branches turn dull red or brown, then ash gray. Tiny black dots, which are the fruiting bodies of the fungus, may appear on needles and stems after the needles have dried and turned gray. Small gray lesions often girdle branch tips, generally on the final 4–6 inches of branches, and kill the foliage beyond the diseased tissue. Repeated blighting in early summer can result in abnormal bunches of shoots that together resemble a broom. Young trees or shrubs may be stunted, with discolored foliage, and trees under five years of age are often killed.

Prevention: Grow resistant varieties. Plant susceptible trees in sites with good air circulation and appropriate amounts of sunlight. Avoid wounding the twigs. Keep plants as dry as possible consistent with good growth; avoid watering during evening hours. Do not overfertilize.

Management: Prune out and destroy affected twigs and branches. Use a fungicide spray containing thiophanate-methyl at two-week intervals in spring, beginning when growth starts. Additional fungicide applications may be needed after pruning or shearing. Always apply fungicides according to directions on the label.

 Notes: Juniper twig blight damage sometimes resembles drought damage. However, the change from healthy tissue to damaged tissue is gradual with drought damage, whereas plants infected with this blight show a sharp change.

LATE BLIGHT

FUNGUS

✎ ZONES: ALL

Late blight results from infection by *Phytophthora infestans;* the Latin name means "potato destroyer." This is the fungus responsible for the Irish potato famine of the mid–nineteenth century. Infected tomato and potato plant parts harbor the fungus, which overwinters in compost piles or garden debris, including infected potato tubers. Spores, dispersed by the wind, germinate when they encounter condensed moisture on susceptible plants.

Target: Tomato and potato

Symptoms: Small, dark, water-soaked spots appear on potato and tomato leaves and stems. Under cool, moist conditions, they rapidly enlarge, forming purplish black lesions, shown above. In humid areas, a white or gray mold may appear on the leaf undersides. On green tomatoes, gray-green, water-soaked, sunken spots form. They expand, join, and darken, causing the fruit to be malformed. Potato tuber skin is initially discolored from brown to purple. Later, a brownish dry rot with an unpleasant odor sets in. In cool, wet weather, late blight may advance rapidly, ruining an entire field of potatoes or tomatoes in a few days.

Prevention: There are potato and tomato varieties with some resistance. Use certified disease-free potato seed. Keep tomato and potato growing areas as separate as possible. Space and stake tomato plants to provide good air circulation. On potatoes, regularly apply protectant fungicides containing mancozeb every seven days, starting when shoots are 6 inches high; continue treating vines as long as they are green. Potatoes planted in early spring and harvested before fall wet weather are more likely to escape severe infection. Eliminate tomato and potato volunteer seedlings. Avoid overhead irrigation. Remove and destroy tomato and potato plant debris at the end of the season.

Management: Remove and destroy infected leaves of tomato or potato as soon as they show spots. Do not dig potatoes infected with late blight until at least 14 days after vines have been killed by frost or herbicide; do not harvest potatoes when soil is wet. Do not hold potato seed over from one year to the next or put rotten potatoes on the compost pile. In early spring, spray tomatoes with fungicides containing Bordeaux mixture or copper ammonium carbonate. Be sure to follow label directions for these products. The late blight fungus has developed fungicide resistance; check with your cooperative extension agent for advice on the best solution in your area.

LEAF SPOT, STRAWBERRY

FUNGUS

ZONES: ALL

The fungus that is the causal agent, *Mycosphaerella fragariae,* over-winters on old infected leaves. A long rainy season and temperatures over 50°F favor its development in spring and fall; however, it may occur in moist summers. This fungus can also infect strawberries with black seed disease. There are many other leaf spot diseases—some caused by bacteria (see page 213)—that attack a wide range of plants.

Target: Strawberry

Symptoms: Initially leaves are red or purplish, gradually becoming grayish. Tiny fungus spots with a whitish center and red margin scatter widely over the leaf surface, fruitstalks, runners, and berry caps. Fruit is small. Berries attacked before ripening may never fully ripen and are inedible. Strawberry caps may die, making berries unsightly, or the entire plant may die. Plantlets growing from infected plant runners are weak and may produce a small crop. Black seed disease may cause unripe berries to develop one to ten brownish black, hard, leathery spots. The fruit does not rot, but it discolors under the spot.

Prevention: Plant varieties that are resistant to most forms of leaf spot, such as 'Apollo', 'Headlines', 'Klonmore', 'Midland', 'Northwest', 'Ogallala', 'Surecrop', and 'Totem'. Moderately resistant varieties include 'Blakemore', 'Darrow', and 'Hood'. Set healthy plants in well-drained soil.

Management: After harvesting June-bearing plants, remove their foliage and mow them about ½ inch above the crown. This reduces fungi overwintering on old leaves. Do not mow everbearing strawberries, but do remove foliage. Clean up and discard plant debris at the season's close. Spray with a fungicide containing captan. You may need to spray both upper and lower leaf surfaces. The fungicide treatment may have to be repeated at seven- to ten-day intervals, stopping several days before harvest, according to directions on the label. Avoid overhead watering.

 Notes: Several diseases infect strawberries, including armillaria root rot, Sclerotinia sclerotiorum, verticillium wilt, black root rot complex, gray mold, powdery mildew, red stele, and various viral diseases. As some may occur simultaneously, try to identify the problems before using fungicides. For help in identifying the disease, take an infected plant in a sealed plastic bag to a cooperative extension agent or a garden center consultant.

NEEDLE CAST

FUNGUS

ZONES: ALL

Needle cast disease, which is caused by a variety of fungi, is most severe on young pine trees. It affects the parts of trees that are more frequently shaded. On pine, the disease is occasionally called tar spot. Needle cast is shown above on Douglas fir.

Target: Pine, Douglas fir, true fir, and spruce trees

Symptoms: When older trees develop needle cast, it tends to be on the lower branches only. The needle tips on the prior year's growth begin changing color in winter. By early the following spring, the needles may have become completely brown, or they may have developed brown bands or brown spots with yellow margins. Infected trees look scorched or burned. The infected needles may fall, leaving only new green needles. In severe cases, the branch tips die back. If this happens for several consecutive years, the tree may die. On pine, tiny black structures like long pimples develop on the midribs of dead needles. These structures, which may have cracks down their centers, release fungus spores during summer rains. The spores can travel as far as 300 feet to land on other needle-bearing trees.

Prevention: When you plant susceptible trees, space them so they get good air circulation, and avoid planting in low-lying areas with poor water drainage. If possible, remove any buildings or trees that are shading specimen pines. Control weeds around the bases of trees. If needle cast has proved a problem in the past, spray specimen pines with a fungicide containing chlorothalonil in the early spring as the new growth comes out. Be sure to follow directions on the product label.

Management: Cleaning up fallen infected needles helps reduce the number of infectious spores. On Douglas fir, pine, or spruce, if necessary, you can apply a fungicide containing chlorothalonil. Always apply fungicides according to label directions.

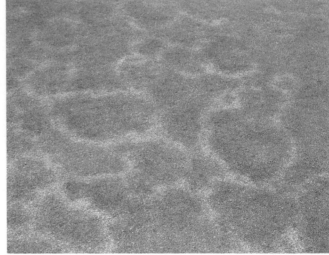

OAK ROOT FUNGUS

FUNGUS

ZONES: ALL

This disease is caused by an *Armillaria* fungus, a native parasite often found in tree roots on newly cleared land. It can live many years in old tree roots and stumps. The fungus breaks down root tissue and eventually girdles plants. Infected plants may die rapidly or may linger for years. Infection is most severe in heavy, poorly drained soil.

Target: About 700 species of woody and herbaceous plants, including black and red raspberry, grape, oak, rose, stone fruit and nut trees, strawberry, and willow

Symptoms: On infected plants, the initial symptoms are a decline and dieback in which the leaves turn yellow, wilt, and die. On blackberries, leaf damage may occur on only one side of the plant or in just one or two canes; few berries are produced. During fall and winter wet weather, clumps of honey-colored mushrooms, 2–5 inches in diameter, may appear on the crowns of infected plants or on nearby soil if roots are near the surface. White fans of feltlike fungus grow on an infected plant's crown and roots between the bark and the wood at ground level and just below it.

Prevention: Avoid placing susceptible plants in locations where oak root fungus is known to have occurred or where *Armillaria* fungi are likely to be present, such as on old orchard sites. When you clear trees, shrubs, or brush from a new planting site, remove and destroy all roots larger than 1 inch in diameter. Plant resistant species. Use sound cultural practices. Provide good drainage.

Management: No fungicide management is available. When plants are severely affected by oak root fungus, remove them and replant with a resistant species, such as catalpa, cedar, fig, liquidambar, madrone, magnolia, maple, pecan, and some varieties of pear and plum. If the tree is a prized one that you would prefer not to replace, consult a professional arborist when you first notice symptoms.

 Notes: Alternate names for oak root fungus are armillaria root rot, mushroom root rot, shoestring fungus, and honey mushroom.

PATCH DISEASES

FUNGUS

ZONES: ALL

Brown patch is one of the most prevalent lawn diseases in warm, humid areas. Yellow patch, shown above, which is active when temperatures are cool and moist, is more common in the Pacific Northwest. Take-all patch is a wet-weather disease, most severe on bent grass. Initially, infected patches tend to be just a few inches in diameter, but they can expand to several feet wide. Both shoots and roots are killed. Weeds may invade the patch center where the lawn has died. Patch fungi may overwinter in plant debris.

Target: All lawn grasses

Symptoms: Brown patch appears as brown, irregularly shaped or circular areas in a lawn. The margin of each affected area may be surrounded by a darker grass ring. This is where the fungus is advancing most actively. Crowns and roots are generally intact. After a few weeks, the centers of affected areas may recover somewhat, giving them a doughnut appearance. Yellow patch symptoms include yellowing or light brown patches that recur in the same locations year after year. Their first appearance is during the fall months, and they may be visible through a mild winter. Turf tends to recover if the weather stays dry. Take-all patch shows as circular reddish brown patches that later become brown or gray.

Prevention: Plant resistant varieties of grass, in mixtures of two or more varieties for best results. Maintain good garden practices, including fertilizing according to label directions for the type of lawn grass planted. Avoid excess fertilizer, as lush growth makes the grass more susceptible to injury. Provide good drainage. Water only in the morning, and do not overwater. Raise mower height in summer, since close mowing leaves the grass vulnerable. Rake off mowed grass and excess thatch. To prevent take-all patch, keep soil pH below 5.5.

Management: For brown patch, use a fungicide containing propiconazole or chlorothalonil. For yellow patch, spray affected areas with wettable sulfur. Apply all treatments according to directions on label. Water well before and after treatment, so fungicides penetrate to the depth of the grass roots.

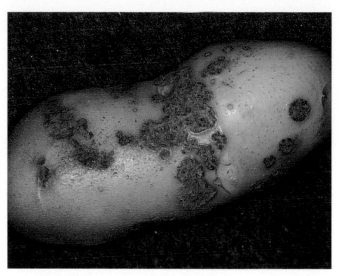

PEACH LEAF CURL

FUNGUS

ZONES: ALL

 Peach leaf curl is one of the worst diseases infecting peach trees. It usually occurs when springtime weather is cool and wet. The spores of the fungus *Taphrina deformans* overwinter on peach tree bark, having been carried there by wind or rain. In the spring, rain carries the spores to developing buds. At the end of the season, a grayish white powdery fungus forms on the leaf surfaces. This blows onto the bark, setting the stage for the next year's life cycle of peach leaf fungus.

Target: Peach and nectarine

Symptoms: New leaves are abnormally thick, and they pucker and curl as they grow. Yellow or reddish blisters appear on the leaves, later turning a powdery white. Entire leaves may turn red, yellow, or pale green and develop a white covering. In early summer, the leaves shrivel, turn black, then fall. A second crop of leaves may form after the first ones drop from the tree. Infected trees are weak and as a result become vulnerable to other diseases. Fruit may not appear; if it does, it may be misshapen, cracked, and covered with raised, wrinkled lesions of varying shapes. Such deformed fruit will drop before it is ripe. Several years of peach leaf curl defoliation will weaken the tree severely and may cause considerable reduction in the fruit crop. It rarely kills the tree.

Prevention: Plant resistant varieties of trees. If you have had problems with peach leaf curl in earlier years, use a dormant-season fungicide containing lime sulfur spray or Bordeaux mixture after the last leaf has fallen in autumn and again before the trees leaf out in spring. Do not wait until the buds open before beginning a spray program.

Management: There is no cure for infected leaves. Remove and destroy them; do not put them in the compost heap.

Notes: Peach leaf curl has afflicted peach trees in the United States for more than 100 years.

POTATO SCAB

BACTERIA

ZONES: ALL

Potato scab, which results from infection by *Streptomyces scabies*, a bacterium, is often called common scab. The disease may be introduced initially via infected seed pieces; it is transmitted by insects, the gardener's handling, and wounds from tools, as well as through breathing pores in the tuber skins during rapid growth. Most damage occurs when air temperatures are between 75°F and 85°F and the soil is dry. The disease is encouraged by a soil pH of 5.7–8.0; damage increases markedly if pH is raised by adding wood ashes or lime. The bacteria will survive in the soil indefinitely, withstanding temperature and moisture extremes. Bacteria also survive on infected tubers remaining in the garden.

Target: Potato

Symptoms: Potato scab infection begins with tiny black specks on tubers. The specks expand rapidly, forming conspicuous, circular, brown corky pits, or scabs, that may eventually join to cover most of the tuber. Usually scabs are only superficial, although occasionally pitted scab may occur, with lesions that may be ½ inch deep. Leaves and stems are not affected by potato scab.

Prevention: Use seed potatoes certified as resistant to scab. Grow russet varieties, which are generally less affected than smooth-skinned varieties. Because scab is seldom a serious problem in acidic soils, test and correct the soil to pH 5.0–5.5, using sulfur or acid-forming fertilizers. In the desert Southwest, where soil pH can rarely be changed, good irrigation practices are the most important prevention measure. In all zones, water regularly, especially in the first two weeks as plants emerge and tubers form. Do not fertilize with manure from animals that have fed on scabby potatoes, as scab bacteria can pass intact through the digestive tracts of plant-eating animals. Instead, use commercial fertilizer recommended for the specific vegetable, because nutrient deprivation encourages the infection. If you have had a scab problem before, plant potatoes in the same garden area only once every three years.

Management: No chemical management is available for potato scab fungus. Increase soil acidity with acid-forming fertilizers.

Notes: Affected potato tubers are edible once the scabs have been removed.

POWDERY MILDEW

FUNGUS

ZONES: ALL

There are many different powdery mildew fungi. On fruit trees, the fungus spores overwinter in dormant buds. In spring, the buds begin opening, the fungus begins to grow, and spores are released—one infected leaf can give off 100 million spores—to travel on the wind to young leaves. Powdery mildew is most common in plants that are not getting enough light or air circulation. It thrives in areas where cool nights follow warm days.

Target: Apple, bean, clematis, dahlia, grape, hydrangea, lilac, pansy, pea, peach, potato, pumpkin, rhododendron, rose, squash, strawberry, tomato, and maple, oak, and sycamore trees

Symptoms: A white or gray powdery fungus appears on plant foliage and flowers (not on woody parts). You may first see round white spots scattered on upper leaf surfaces; these spots expand until they merge, covering both sides of the leaves. Infected leaves turn yellowish green to brown. New growth may be stunted, curled, and distorted. Plants may continue do all right, or they may decline. Infected blossoms may not set fruit; if fruit does appear, it may be covered with the powdery fungus. Fruit drops early or is dwarfed.

Prevention: Plant resistant varieties; consult your cooperative extension agent for advice on plant selection. Give plants sufficient light and good air circulation. Water plants from underneath rather than above, to be sure that leaves stay dry.

Management: Reduce nitrogen fertilizer. Try a regular routine of spraying with jets of water to wash off fungus spores, and prevent the dry conditions that encourage the fungus to spread in the wind. Trim or cut back trees and shrubs that may be blocking sunlight. You may partially control the disease by using fungicides containing thiophanate-methyl or triforine. Always apply fungicides according to directions on the label. Powdery mildew fungus spores die at 30°F or below. In the fall, discard infected flowers of annuals and leftover produce. If plants have chronic powdery mildew and are not thriving, consider moving them.

PURPLE BLOTCH

FUNGUS

ZONES: ALL

Injury caused by other fungi, or by sand or dust during windstorms, often makes onions, garlic, and shallots susceptible to infection by *Alternaria porri*. This fungus overwinters on infected bulbs and on dead, diseased onions in the garden or field. Most infection takes place between 77°F and 81°F when weather is rainy or dew is heavy. Almost no infection occurs below 55°F. 'Sweet Spanish' onions are particularly susceptible.

Target: Onion, garlic, shallot

Symptoms: A small, whitish or yellowish, water-soaked sunken area with a purple center develops on leaves. The area enlarges, turning brown, then purple. During moist weather, the damaged area may be gradually covered with a brownish black, powdery fungus. Leaves with large spots turn yellow, wither, and are blown over by the wind. Onion bulbs may decay around harvesttime. Decay appears initially as a watery rot around the onion neck, accompanied by a yellowish to wine red discoloration. Onion tissues progressively dry, then develop a papery texture. Although damaged plants are seldom killed, they may be inedible.

Prevention: Plant tolerant varieties. Destroy old onion debris. Handle and harvest plants carefully.

Management: Clean up and destroy any diseased onions. When you see the initial blotches, spray with a fungicide containing chlorothalonil. Repeat as directed on the label. Pay particular attention to label instructions regarding the safety of spraying close to harvest.

 Notes: To prevent infection while onions are in storage, let bulbs complete their growth, with the yellowing tops falling over naturally. When tops have died down, carefully pull out all the onions. Let them sun-dry for about ten days, hanging where they will get good air circulation, as in nets. Be sure all outer leaves and skins are thoroughly dry before storing onions; a fan will hasten drying. Handle bulbs gently to prevent the entry of rot organisms. Low humidity and storage temperatures at 32–45°F are optimal conditions.

PYTHIUM BLIGHT

FUNGUS

✔ ZONES: 1–7, 17

Pythium blight, also called cottony blight or grease spot, is caused by a fungus. Although it most often occurs on new lawns, all lawns can suffer from pythium blight if growing conditions are not adequate. Overwatered lawns and those that drain poorly are particularly vulnerable to pythium blight fungus. Grass that has become dense and lush may also develop this disease. Pythium blight is worse in hot, 85–95°F, humid weather. The disease spreads rapidly via watering, mowing, and foot traffic (infected blades mat together when walked on). Grass affected by pythium blight can die within 24 hours.

Target: Lawns, particularly bluegrass and ryegrass

Symptoms: Lawns damaged by pythium blight display varying symptoms. In the spring or fall, you may see areas of thin, yellowing grass growth. In summer, affected areas quickly wilt and turn light brown. Originally only a few inches wide, these areas will expand at a variable rate to form patches up to 10 feet in diameter or streaks about 1 foot wide. Early in the morning, a white or gray threadlike coating may be visible on the grass.

Prevention: Seed lawn grasses in late fall to avoid hot, humid weather. To prevent recurring infections, use good garden practices. Water management is key to reducing the potential for pythium blight. Avoid excess watering during warm weather and watering late in the day. Provide good surface and beneath-surface drainage when installing turf. Aerate the lawn to improve air circulation. Remove excessive thatch. Fertilize according to the specific needs of your lawn type; do not overfertilize.

Management: Pythium blight fungus is hard to manage because it spreads so rapidly. Severely damaged areas do not recover, but damage can be minimized by encouraging strong plant-root growth and reducing plant stress. If cultural controls, such as water, fertilizer, and aeration, do not slow down the disease process, you may have to reseed or resod the lawn. Unfortunately, there are no resistant varieties, although bluegrass/fescue mixes tend to recover more rapidly.

PYTHIUM ROOT ROT

FUNGUS

✔ ZONES: ALL

Because the fungus spores may swim short distances through soil water to attack the roots of susceptible plants, *Pythium* and *Phytophthora* are sometimes called water molds. Water molds are most active in warm soils (55–80°F), but they can survive in dry, cold soils while they wait for favorable conditions. Lawns and flower beds that are frequently watered often have pythium root rot problems, as do areas with heavy, poorly drained soils. Very wet conditions increase the damage. Water molds often cause damping-off disease (see page 220) in seedlings and young plants.

Target: Lawns; azalea, geranium, rhododendron, and other ornamental plants

Symptoms: Symptoms develop over several weeks to several months. Young leaves turn yellow and wilt. Affected plants may be stunted and may flower prematurely, or the entire plant may wilt and die, even though the soil is moist. Plant stems or trunks show a dark discoloration close to ground level. If you peel back the stem covering or bark at the plant's base, you may see a distinct margin between the dark diseased plant tissue and the white healthy tissue.

Prevention: Do not overfertilize plants. Keep the soil moist; do not allow plants to dry out, but do not overwater them. Diminish the water needs of susceptible plants by placing those that are in containers in a more shaded area and by creating shade for ground-growing plants. Improve plant drainage or use raised beds. If drainage cannot be improved, use plants that are resistant to root rot, such as American arborvitae (*Thuja occidentalis*) and Pfitzer juniper.

Management: No chemical management is possible. Remove and discard diseased plants.

 Notes: The symptoms of rhizoctonia root and stem rot (see page 233) may on some plants look similar to those of pythium root rot. But Rhizoctonia *fungi often favor well-drained, fertile soils, whereas* Pythium *tends to prefer soils that are poorly drained. Like pythium root rot, drought stress causes wilting, but drought stress can be alleviated by watering. Watering may increase the severity of pythium root rot.*

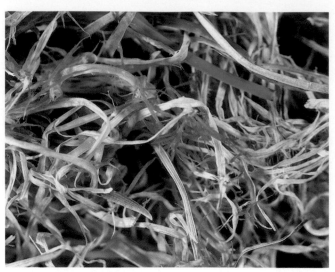

RED STELE

FUNGUS

✔ ZONES: ALL

Red stele, also called brown core rot, is caused by the *Phytophthora fragariae* fungus. *Phytophthora* infections, of which there are many types, are the major cause of strawberry damage. A resistant strawberry variety in one field may be susceptible in another field to a different type of this fungus. The fungus can survive many years in soil, becoming active in cool, wet weather; it remains active through the winter months. It spreads more rapidly in heavier soils or where drainage is poor. It attacks plant roots soon after fall rains begin, destroying fine feeding roots first before moving into the stele, or plant core.

Target: Strawberry

Symptoms: Slightly infected plants fail to thrive but may still produce fruit. Severely infected plants are stunted, and the youngest leaves may develop a bluish tinge and a dull rather than glossy finish. Older leaves of severely infected plants may dry out and turn red, orange, or yellow. Little or no fruit is produced on severely infected plants, which may wilt and die in the first dry period. If you pull up an affected plant, you can see the damage. Lateral roots are destroyed, giving the main roots a "rattail" appearance. The stele of diseased strawberry roots is tinged pink to red in winter and spring; this discoloration gradually turns cinnamon brown, as shown above. The outer cortex, instead of remaining the normal pale yellow, becomes white. Eventually the entire stele turns black. After May, you may have to cut the roots lengthwise to see the diseased core.

Prevention: Use only certified disease-free plants. Place plants in well-drained soil that never has standing water, not even in winter, and that has never been infected by red stele disease. Use raised beds 15 inches high to improve drainage. Resistant varieties, such as 'Hood', 'Rainier', and 'Totem', are available, but even these may be infected if especially virulent types of red stele fungus are in the soil.

Management: Remove and discard infected plants. Once the red stele fungus enters a growing area, it is worthless for strawberries for at least ten years. Start again with new strawberries in a new planting area.

RED THREAD ON LAWNS

FUNGUS

✔ ZONES: ALL

Once known as corticium red thread, red thread fungus (*Laetisaria fuciformis*) appears from late fall through winter and into early spring. It is most common in wet climates, particularly coastal areas, when the temperature ranges between 60°F and 80°F. It tends to turn up following heavy rains. The fungi live on diseased grass and in soil; they are prevalent in poorly aerated soil and in lawns lacking nitrogen. The disease is more severe in perennial ryegrass (*Lolium perenne*), red and Chewings fescue (*Festuca rubra*), and bent grass (*Agrostis*); hardy fescue is resistant. Although unsightly, red thread fungus seldom kills lawns.

Target: Grasses, especially bent grass, some fescues, and perennial ryegrass

Symptoms: Tiny, pale pink to red, branching, jellylike fungus strands appear on patches of grass 2–5 inches wide. The strands seem to be tying or matting the grass blades together. Short pink "horns," 1/8–2 inches long, protrude from the tips of diseased grass blades. These fruiting bodies are a sure indication of infection by this fungus. They become brittle and then break into pieces, spreading the fungus. The affected lawn areas later turn whitish to tan as the grass dies.

Prevention: Plant resistant lawn varieties, such as bluegrass 'Adelphi', 'Birka', or 'Touchdown'. Aerate the lawn if the soil is heavy or compacted. Fertilize the lawn regularly to improve the resistance of the grass to fungus damage, using a fertilizer that supplies all three major nutrients—nitrogen, potassium, and phosphate. Do not fertilize late in the season when the weather is very cool. Prevent drought stress by watering deeply and infrequently. Prune nearby trees and shrubs to increase light and to improve the movement of air around the lawn.

Management: Collect and remove all grass clippings from the infected areas. Fungicide treatment is not necessary or recommended; some fungicides can actually increase the severity of the disease.

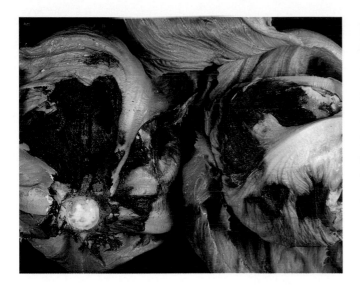

RHIZOCTONIA ROOT AND STEM ROT

FUNGUS

 ZONES: ALL

The fungus *Rhizoctonia solani* can be found in most soils, its many pathogenic strains causing a variety of diseases. The fungi that cause rhizoctonia root and stem rot enter the plant through the root system or the main stem at the soil line. The infection moves into other stems and the lower leaves, then progresses up the plant. This fungus thrives in warm, moist, fertile conditions and in aerated, well-drained soils.

Target: Ornamentals such as calendula, carnation, geranium, poinsettia, and sunflower; vegetables such as bean and lettuce

Symptoms: All the leaves may turn pale and wilt, sometimes suddenly. The lower leaves and stems may rot. Upper portions of affected plants wilt and die, and the stems may decay. If you remove the plant from the ground, you may find that the roots are very dark and perhaps badly rotted, even if it has been planted in soil with good drainage.

Prevention: Provide moisture as needed, but avoid overwatering.

Management: If all the leaves are wilted, remove and replace the plant. Less severely affected plants can be saved by decreasing irrigation. Diminish your plants' water needs by placing container plants in a shaded spot, and by creating shade for plants growing in the ground. The following year, use a fungicide containing thiophanate-methyl. If you have a container plant that will grow from cuttings and that has a healthy top, consider removing the top and rooting it in a sterile medium. Discard the infected soil, and wash the pots thoroughly, disinfecting them in a mixture of 1 part household bleach and 9 parts water for about 30 minutes.

✎ *Notes: The symptoms of rhizoctonia root and stem rot and pythium root rot are similar. However,* Pythium *fungi most often appear in heavy, poorly drained soils.* Rhizoctonia solani *fungus attacks seedlings as well as grown plants. It is also one of the fungus species that causes damping off.*

RINGSPOT, PRUNUS NECROTIC

VIRUS

 ZONES: ALL

Prunus necrotic ringspot virus (PNRSV) has many strains that produce a variety of viral diseases with several names—some that are regional and some that change over the years. The diseases are called almond calico, apple mosaic, cherry rugose mosaic, rose mosaic, necrotic ringspot, tatter leaf peach ringspot, and recurrent ringspot. The symptoms, which are also quite varied, depend on climate, the number of viruses involved, and the degree of tolerance of the host species. The virus is easily transmitted by grafting and budding. It also spreads via infected pollen in some *Prunus* species.

Target: Almond, apple, cherry, peach, and plum trees

Symptoms: Trees initially develop shock symptoms; these are followed by chronic symptoms. On previously uninfected trees, shock symptoms may include yellowing, misshapen, or dying leaves, and stunting of overall growth. These symptoms may be visible on the entire plant or on just a portion of it. Chronic symptoms afflict the leaves with yellowing, pale rings, brown dying spots, and then multiple small round holes. In late spring, careful inspection of sweet cherry trees may reveal brown or black dying spots covering entire branches. The cherry rugose mosaic strain of PNRSV produces turned-up or "boating" leaf tips, delay in fruit maturity for up to three weeks, and leaves that are thicker and stiffer than normal ones. Trees infected with the rugose mosaic strain may bear no crop at all or only a very light, late-maturing crop. On almond trees, PNRSV causes almond calico, which shows up as a yellow mottling or striping on leaves.

Prevention: Purchase healthy, virus-free trees from a reputable nursery. Make a point of using good gardening practices, including providing adequate water and appropriate fertilizer.

Management: There is no treatment for PNRSV. However, plants may continue to produce fruit and live with the disease for an indefinite period. But those infected with the rugose strain infection may have to be removed.

ROSE MOSAIC VIRUS

VIRUS

✎ ZONES: ALL

Rose mosaic is the most common viral disease of roses. It is caused by several viruses, including prunus necrotic ringspot virus and apple mosaic virus. It has no known insect vector—that is, it is not known to be transmitted by insects—but spreads instead by infected rootstocks or infected budwood, usually at the nursery where roses are budded. Cuttings from infected plants may also be infected. Plants can be infected for a long time without showing symptoms, then suddenly develop severe symptoms, often in early spring with new growth.

Target: Rose

Symptoms: Symptoms vary considerably, depending on the time of year, temperature, and type of virus infecting the plant. Leaves may develop a yellowing zigzag pattern, as well as ringspots and mottles. New leaves may be distorted. Although symptoms are often evident in spring and early summer, they may not be visible on leaves produced in the summer. Some infected roses may not show any discoloration or leaf pattern change at all. Plants that are infected may grow slowly, and may be more sensitive to winterkill. Flowering is normal.

Prevention: Buy healthy roses, certified as virus-free.

Management: Prevention is the only management for this mosaic virus disease. Do not buy plants exhibiting rose mosaic symptoms. Do not propagate infected plants.

 Notes: Roses may be afflicted with several other viral diseases—including rose rosette, rose ring pattern, and rose leaf curl. Rose rosette symptoms include wrinkled or bright red leaves, witches' broom (broomlike clusters forming a swelling or knot), and excessive thorniness. The symptoms of rose ring pattern virus are similar to those of rose mosaic. Roses with rose leaf curl may have small spring leaves, easily detachable leaflets, yellow vein flecking, and pointed shoots that have a broad base. Management is the same as for rose mosaic virus.

RUSTS

FUNGUS

✎ ZONES: ALL

There are at least 4,000 types of rust diseases. Rust is present, in varying species, throughout most of the world. Most strains infect only specific plants. The fungi can overwinter on living leaves, in stems, and in plant debris. The spores become active in moist weather, or after rain or overhead watering, when they are spread by wind and splashing water. Some may travel as far as 300 miles on the wind, although most are more limited. The spores also may spread via the gardener's handling when the plant is wet.

Target: Lawns; pine and true fir trees; hawthorn, oregon grape, fuchsia, geranium, hollyhock, rose, snapdragon, sunflower, asparagus, onion, snap bean and dry bean, fig, pear, blackberry, and other plants

Symptoms: Rust initially appears as powdery pustules or pimples on the undersides of lower leaves. These pustules are usually orange yellow to rusty brown but may be purple, red, white, or black. Each pustule contains millions of microscopic spores; if you touch one, you will find an imprint of rust-colored spores on your finger. As the disease progresses, upper leaf surfaces may be spotted with yellow, then completely yellow. Severely infected plants are small and misshapen. Fruit is of poor quality and may drop from the tree early.

Prevention: Seek out the current selection of resistant varieties, as rust fungi have attacked some of the resistant varieties of the past. Give each plant maximum air circulation. Remove rust-infected leaves as they occur. Clean up plant debris in the vicinity. Try not to water from overhead; if it's necessary to water from overhead, do so during full sun hours so plants can dry fully before dusk.

Management: Chemical controls vary with the affected plant. Among successful fungicides are those containing propiconazole.

 Notes: Early agricultural writings mentioned rust. The ancient Romans held ceremonies praying to the sun god Apollo, who was in charge of making plants ripen, to shield their growing fields from dreaded rusts and other diseases. In the late 1800s, a new rust disease attacked the main coffee-growing plantations in Ceylon. Planters started growing tea instead of coffee, and the English became a nation of tea drinkers.

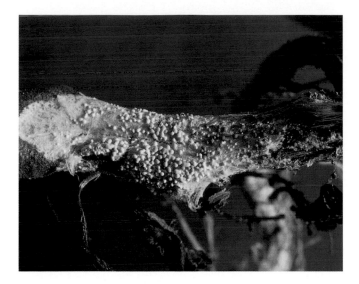

SCLEROTIUM ROOT ROT

FUNGUS

ZONES: 9–23

This disease, also known as southern root rot, is caused by the fungus *Sclerotium rolfsii*. It is most common in warm, moist soils deficient in nitrogen. The fungi overwinter in affected plant parts or in soil, where they can survive for many years.

Target: Wide range of hosts that includes most flowering annuals and perennials; vegetables such as carrot; and all bulbs and rhizomes, including daffodil, iris, and tulip

Symptoms: On daffodils and tulips, the bulb surface is covered with a coarse white fungus growth. Small, reddish brown fungal bodies (sclerotia) may appear within this growth. Leaves of tulips turn red, wilt, and die. Rhizomatous iris show a gradual dieback at the tips of the outer leaves. The iris leaves rot at their base near the soil line. The disease progresses toward the clump center of the iris, and the plant usually dies. While the fungus does not affect rhizomes directly, white, fanlike fungus mats are found within the bases of the leaves. With bulbous irises, infection usually begins at the bulb tip, but it may also begin elsewhere. Infected plants are stunted, with yellowing leaves; the outer leaves may yellow before the inner ones do. Bulbs may become soft and crumbly, or they may rot completely away, with only the husk and attached fungus bodies remaining. Stems and leaves may rot just above the bulb. The bulb may die.

Prevention: Plant disease-free bulbs in uninfested soil. Do not allow bulbs to become overcrowded.

Management: Chemical management is not appropriate in the home garden. For current options available to you, ask a garden center consultant or cooperative extension agent. Remove and discard all infected bulbs and plants. Remove the soil surrounding any affected plant and for 6 inches beyond. Discard plant debris. Do not replant susceptible bulbs in the same soil for at least three years.

SEPTORIA LEAF SPOT

FUNGUS

ZONES: ALL

Septoria leaf spot, also known as tip burn, tip blight, and tip scorch, is caused by *Septoria* fungi. The fungi overwinter in infected plants and debris. During spring and fall rainy seasons, spores ooze from the infected areas and are carried by splashing water or garden tools to healthy plants. These fungi thrive in cool, moist weather; the disease usually declines during hot summer months. Septoria leaf spot is worse when grass is unmowed, underfertilized, or overly long.

Target: Cool-season grasses and Bermuda grass

Symptoms: Spots develop near the tips of individual grass blades. These spots are initially grayish green before fading to a pale yellow and then to whitish gray. On the infected areas, which may be up to an inch long, are black or brown spots, the fungus fruiting bodies. An entire lawn may appear gray with a mass of burned leaf tips.

Prevention: No truly resistant lawn grass varieties are currently available, so use seed mixtures of two or more disease-tolerant varieties. Get advice from a local nursery consultant or cooperative extension agent on selecting the varieties best suited to your site. Disease-tolerant varieties of bluegrass include 'Bensun', 'Bonnieblue', 'Bristol', 'Columbia', 'Flyking', 'Glade', 'Majestic', and 'Parade'. Avoid watering the lawn at night. Limit nitrogen fertilizer through fall and winter. Use good lawn maintenance practices, including mowing at the recommended height for the grass type, adequate deep watering, and regular fertilization as recommended for the grass variety. Aerate the lawn if needed.

Management: Frequent mowing will remove most of the diseased blade tips. Mow the lawn 1½–2 inches tall and discard the clippings. Remove excess thatch in early spring, aerate the lawn, and improve drainage as necessary. If cultural management is not fully effective, fungicide management is possible; apply a fungicide containing chlorothalonil. Fungicide treatment may need to be repeated at intervals of seven to ten days, as long as the rainy weather that favors the disease continues. Always apply fungicides according to directions on the label.

SHOT HOLE

FUNGUS

ZONES: ALL

S hot hole is also known as peach blight, California peach blight, and coryneum blight. The spores of the fungus *Wilsonomyces carpophilus,* which causes shot hole, overwinter on twigs and buds of infected plants. Symptoms appear during the growing season, as fungal spores disperse with splashing rainfall or irrigation water and attack leaves, buds, blossoms, fruit, and twigs. Weakened plants are more likely to show shot hole symptoms. The disease is most severe following warm, wet winters and extended spring rains.

Target: Fruit trees, especially peach and nectarine; almond, apricot, and ornamentals in the genus *Prunus*

Symptoms: The initial infection appears as round purplish spots, about ¼ inch wide, forming on young leaves, twigs, and developing fruit. Microscopic dark fungus specks appear in the brown centers of the spots. On leaves, the spots eventually fall out, producing the characteristic "shot hole" look. In severe infections, large parts of leaves disappear, and leaves may fall from the tree prematurely. Fruit buds may be killed by the fungus. On maturing fruit, the spots become scablike and later drop off, leaving corky lesions. A clear gummy discharge may ooze from spots on fruit. On trees less than a year old, there are small, reddish, slightly sunken circles on fruiting wood; they may badly damage it. On trees two to four years old, rough cankers develop, reaching 3 inches long.

Prevention: Ask your cooperative extension agent about resistant varieties. Peach varieties 'Lovell' and 'Muir' reportedly are blight tolerant. Keep sprinkler irrigation aimed low so it doesn't wet tree leaves or fruit. Give trees appropriate fertilization and air circulation.

Management: You cannot eliminate shot hole fungus during the current growing season, but you can take measures to minimize future problems. At the first signs of shot hole fungus, remove and destroy infected buds, blossoms, twigs, and fruit. After the leaves fall, inspect buds and twigs. Remove and destroy any part with a varnished appearance. Clean up fallen leaves and fruit, which may harbor the fungus. If sanitation measures are not effective enough, you can use chemical management during leaf fall in the autumn and petal fall in the spring. Discuss current options with a garden center consultant or a cooperative extension agent. Always follow directions on product labels regarding plant type and appropriate use.

SLIME FLUX

BACTERIA

ZONES: ALL

S lime flux, also called wetwood, is a bacterial disease occurring primarily during the growing season from April to August or September. It may be stimulated by environmental stress, such as very warm weather or drought. The bacterium *Erwinia nimmipressuralis* infects the tree's heartwood, causing fermentation in tissues. This produces intense sap pressure, which forces the fermented sap out of wounds, cracks, and other tree openings, a symptom called flux. It is not usually a serious disease.

Target: Ornamental trees, including birch, elm, maple, poplar, and willow; fruit and nut trees, including pistachio

Symptoms: Sour-smelling sap oozes from the tree trunk. As the slime is exposed to air, it becomes darker and dries on the bark, causing unsightly gray or black streaks, which may enlarge and thicken. Bacteria and yeasts working within the flux cause it to become increasingly foul smelling with age, and insects are attracted to it. Where the flux drips onto a lawn, it can cause dead spots. The amount of flux increases markedly when the tree is growing rapidly. You may see wilting and scorched leaves if the tree is also suffering from water stress.

Prevention: Be careful not to wound trees with tools. If a tree is in a situation where it may suffer damage at the base, erect a small barrier around it for protection. Maintain trees in good health, and fertilize and water them adequately.

Management: There is no cure for slime flux. The flux might stop by itself, but it also might continue for years. Slime flux causes interior wood to be discolored and wet. Remove any loose bark you find, to allow the wood to dry out. Since this disease indicates a weakened tree, subject to decay, you should consider the tree hazardous. Diseased limbs and those that hang over houses or driveways should be removed for safety. When pruning infected trees, disinfect tools with a solution of 1 part bleach or alcohol and 9 parts water. Homeowners were once advised to insert drainage pipes into the tree just below the oozing wounds, to deflect the sap from the tree. Recent studies indicate that when done by nonprofessionals, such an intrusion into the tree increases the damage.

SLIME MOLD

FUNGUS

ZONES: 4, 5, 15–17

Slime molds are caused by any of several types of fungi. Because these fungi are nonparasitic, they are harmless, but they use leaf blades as support for their reproductive processes. The spores are spread by the wind. Slime molds are most likely to appear abruptly, following lawn watering. They are more common during cool, humid, or wet weather, particularly in the fall, but they also appear in spring and summer after heavy watering or rains. Cool coastal areas are most commonly affected.

Target: All grasses and many other small plants

Symptoms: This fungus initially makes a sudden appearance as a gray, watery white, or yellowish white slimy growth that crawls over plants. You can easily rub it off the plants if you don't mind slimy stuff all over your hand. After a few days, the growth moves up onto any nearby plant parts and changes into pinhead-size balls of purple brown, black, white, or bluish gray. This phase is easier to spot than the slime phase. A profusion of these globular or spherical balls may cover grass patches ranging from a few inches to several feet wide. The balls, composed of fungus spores, feel powdery when you rub them between your fingers. When these balls break, masses of fine, dark spores are released. An abundance of the powdery spores covering the grass may block the sunlight and turn the grass yellow.

Prevention: Preventing thatch buildup on your lawn may help.

Management: In most instances, these unsightly molds will disappear if left alone. If you wish to remove them, sprinkle with a strong water spray during dry weather, rake them away, or sweep the area with a broom. Chemical management is not necessary or useful.

 Notes: Parasitic fungi feed on living plants and as a result may cause varying degrees of injury. But nonparasitic fungi are harmless to plants because they feed only on decaying organic matter.

SNOW MOLD

FUNGUS

ZONES: 1–9, 14–17

There are several different varieties of snow mold. Tiny brown spots on leaves and crowns of infected lawn grasses may be evidence of gray snow mold, which is more prevalent in the Pacific Northwest. Fungal spots with a pinkish cast may be evidence of pink snow mold. Pink snow mold is actually fusarium patch; gray snow mold is typhula blight. Snow molds appear as white-gray, tan, yellowing, or pinkish circular patches of grass. These diseases get their names because they often appear with the melting of a deep snow or occur at the edges of a snowbank. While active beneath the snow, snow mold may also appear when weather is cold and moist or after a heavy rainfall. Both gray and pink kinds may occur in the same area at the same time, often intermingled. Both are prevalent in high elevation and mountain areas. When only grass blades are attacked by snow mold fungi, the patches are unsightly but the affected grass usually survives. When crowns are attacked, the grass may die.

Target: All lawn grasses

Symptoms: The discoloration may spread from a few inches to a few feet wide. Close inspection in the morning or during damp weather may reveal a cottony fungus growth on leaf blades. Grass blades look as if they are stuck together. Infected patches sometimes enlarge and join, forming much larger patches.

Prevention: Plant lawn grasses that are known to have some resistance to snow mold and those that are winter-hardy. Consult your cooperative extension agent for local advice on resistant strains of lawn grass. Poor drainage, fast fall growth, and an abundance of thatch favor the snow mold fungi. To avoid drainage problems, aerate the lawn regularly. To regulate growth, mow closely and avoid fertilizing during fall months. Keep thatch to a minimum to avoid buildup of a water-holding mat. In spring, remove melting snow from lawn as soon as practical, then rake the lawn well.

Management: Fungicide management of pink snow mold is not recommended for home lawns. For gray snow mold, use a fungicide containing propiconazole or chlorothalonil. Always follow directions on the container label. If damage is severe along north-facing exposures, reseed or resod.

SOOTY MOLD

FUNGUS

✏ ZONES: ALL

Sooty molds are also called black molds. These unsightly molds are caused by several species of fungi. More than one sooty mold fungus may appear on the same plant at the same time, feeding on the honeydew of numerous insects. Fungus growth takes place from spring through early fall. Splashing rain or water may spread the fungus to unaffected plants.

Target: Ground covers, trees, shrubs, vines, annuals, and perennials

Symptoms: Sooty mold usually appears as a dark brown-black powdery fungus growth covering leaf surfaces and twigs. It can also look like a thin dark film or like black spots. In severe cases, the fungus almost completely covers a leaf's surface. Although the fungus is considered fairly harmless because it does not feed on plants, extremely heavy infestations can block sunlight from reaching the leaves, which may yellow and fall prematurely.

Prevention: Control scale, aphids, mealybugs, whiteflies, and other honeydew-excreting insects, as well as ants.

Management: On small plants, wipe or wash off the molds with a small sponge and water. On large trees, use a hose-end sprayer to wash off mold. No chemical management is needed for the sooty mold, but something may be required to get rid of the insects that attract the fungi.

 Notes: Some sap-sucking insects do not fully digest plant sap. The undigested portion is excreted as a sweet, sticky liquid called honeydew. Honeydew may appear anywhere such insects land, including buildings and windowsills. In addition, honeydew attracts both flies and wasps. If copious amounts of honeydew form on trees, sidewalks and other surfaces below may become coated with honeydew and with the sooty mold that follows it. Ants add to the sooty mold problem by collecting and tending honeydew-excreting insects, such as aphids, scale, and mealybugs. Stroking the bodies of these insects, they milk them for the honeydew, which they take back to the ant nest to be used as food. Ants will also transfer honeydew-excreting insects from plant to plant.

STRIPE SMUT ON LAWNS

FUNGUS

✏ ZONES: 1, 4–6

Stripe smut is caused by the *Ustilago striiformis* fungus, which overwinters in diseased plants as mycelium (the mass of interwoven threads that make up the vegetative body of the fungus) and in infested soil as spores. Germinating spores attack grass crowns and rhizomes. Once the fungus penetrates the plant's exterior, it usually spreads through the entire plant. Debilitated, the grass dies during the next bout of hot weather. Lawns that have been heavily watered and fertilized are most susceptible to stripe smut. Damage is worse during the spring and fall months, when temperatures are cool (50–68°F); however, the disease may appear anytime from April to November. Hot, dry weather usually halts stripe smut. Spores can be seedborne—i.e., carried in contaminated seed—or may enter the garden via new plants from infected soil or contaminated machinery, including mowers and dethatchers.

Target: Grass, particularly bluegrass and bent grass

Symptoms: Leaf symptoms first appear as narrow, parallel, yellow-gray leaf streaks. Single blades or patches of grass ranging in width from a few inches to more than a foot may be affected. The grass turns pale green to yellow to brown. Growth slows, so that grass in the infected areas is shorter than the surrounding healthy grass. The leaf blades darken, turning gray, then black; the leaf lesions then burst open, displaying masses of spores. The leaf blades curl, wither, and begin splitting into thin strips from the tips of the blades downward.

Prevention: Use treated seed, disease-free sod, and resistant grass varieties. Resistant varieties of Kentucky bluegrass include 'Adelphi', 'Bensun', and 'Sydsport'. Water lawn deeply but infrequently and do not overfertilize it. Rake and discard thatch.

Management: Stripe smut is difficult to eliminate. However, some control is possible with fungicides containing thiophanate-methyl or propiconazole. Always apply fungicides according to directions on the product label.

VERTICILLIUM WILT

FUNGUS

✂ ZONES: ALL

More than 200 plant species are infected by the fungi *Verticillium dahliae* and *V. albo-atrum*. Plants may contract verticillium wilt through infected seed, plant debris on the soil, or direct contact. Infections may occur anytime during the growing season. The fungi multiply in plants during cool, moist seasons but become obvious in warm, dry weather when plants are stressed. Verticillium wilt damages plants by affecting their water-conducting mechanisms. It is more common on herbaceous plants than on woody ones; on woody plants, it usually affects young trees early in the bearing season. Overfertilization with nitrogen may favor fungus damage. Infested soil can harbor the fungi for many years, and in some instances they may be impossible to eradicate. Many weeds are susceptible and also harbor these fungi.

Target: Sunflower; rose; fruits such as strawberry, melon, and cane berries; tomato; and ornamental, fruit, and nut trees, including maple, cherry, peach, olive, and pistachio

Symptoms: Scattered branches on trees may die. Fruit and flowers may be stunted or may not appear at all. The plant may survive for weeks to years with the infection. On roses, leaves turn yellow. If only a few canes are affected, they may die back or grow normally the next season. On sunflowers and many herbaceous plants, the wilting starts with the lower leaves and progresses up the stem. The tissue between leaf veins turns yellow, then brown, giving the leaves a mottled appearance. Severely infected plants may be stunted.

Prevention: Choose resistant plant varieties. Control weeds. Avoid excessive irrigation, severe pruning, or other measures that promote heavy leaf growth. Do not plant susceptible crops in old vegetable gardens. In areas where verticillium wilt is present, grow susceptible crops in containers with pasteurized soil. Use nitrogen fertilizer at minimal rates, sufficient only to provide normal growth. If possible, practice crop rotation with long intervals, or solarize soil (see page 54).

Management: Prune out dead branches to improve the appearance of affected trees.

 Notes: Resistant trees include birch, dogwood, sycamore, and conifers. In seed catalogs, look for the letter V, which indicates Verticillium *resistance. Resistant tomatoes include 'Better Boy', 'Merced', and 'Toy Boy'.*

WALNUT BLIGHT

BACTERIA

✂ ZONES: ALL

Walnut blight is a common disease on walnut trees; early-blooming varieties are the most susceptible. The bacterium *Xanthomonas arboricola juglandis* overwinters on cankers, infected tree buds, and infected nuts. In early spring, a thick, shiny fluid containing millions of bacteria is exuded from the infected plant parts. The disease spreads to buds, shoots, flowers, and developing walnuts through rain. Frequent and lengthy rain, from just before bloom to about two weeks afterward, may result in severe outbreaks of walnut blight. Nuts are most susceptible at this time. The infection can continue to spread to healthy nuts throughout the summer if wet weather persists. If nuts are infected before their shells harden, the bacteria may enter the kernels.

Target: Walnut trees

Symptoms: The infection initially appears as reddish brown leaf spots and black, slightly depressed lesions on stems. Infected young leaves and buds of catkins (slender flower clusters) turn dark brown or black and may quickly die. Leaves may be distorted. On nuts, the infection causes black slimy spots of varying sizes. The bacteria penetrate the husk, the shell, and sometimes the edible meat, causing it to shrivel and blacken. If the infection occurs late in the season, black rings appear on walnut husks. Most nuts fall prematurely, but others reach full size with husk, shell, and kernel blackened and destroyed.

Prevention: Plant late-blooming varieties, such as 'Hartley' and 'Vina'. 'Howe' is a resistant variety in some areas. Consult your cooperative extension agent for information on resistant varieties in your growing area.

Management: If possible, prune out all diseased twigs and branches. When the catkins start to shed pollen, then again when the nutlets begin appearing, apply a fungicide containing basic copper sulfate or Bordeaux mixture. Be sure to follow directions on the product label. A later spraying may be necessary if rains persist.

 Notes: In California, strains of the bacteria that are resistant to copper products are widespread; they may be developing in the Pacific Northwest as well.

WHITE MOLD

FUNGUS

✺ ZONES: ALL

White mold, also called sclerotinia rot and watery soft rot, results from infection by the fungus *Sclerotinia sclerotiorum*. It overwinters as small black structures (sclerotia) attached to decomposing infected plant parts. It may also survive several years in soil. In early spring or fall, the sclerotia produce small, cup-shaped fruiting structures, resembling tiny mushrooms, which release spores into the air. The sclerotia also produce vegetative strands that can infect many plants. Moist, cool conditions favor infection. White and gray mold (*Botrytis cinerea*) can occur simultaneously.

Target: Bean, carrot, lettuce, marigold, sunflower, tomato, zinnia, and many other plants

Symptoms: Symptoms vary on different types of plants. On snap beans, most infections occur near the ground as a result of fallen, infected blossoms. If fungi invade the main stem, most leaves will yellow and wilt. On the types of beans that are often dried, such as pinto beans and red kidney beans, rapid wilting and plant death may occur if fungi invade stems near the soil line. Lesions on dry infected stems and vines are beige to white; stem surfaces may be papery. The lesion color, sclerotia, and white mold growth distinguish white mold from pythium blight on these beans. On carrots, the disease is sometimes called cottony soft rot for the cottony white growth on the surface of soft lesions on the carrot root. On tomatoes, affected stems may turn a tan color. They are also covered with a white cottony fungus growth dotted with hard black fungal sclerotia. In general, water-soaked lesions appear on plant stems, leaves, and pods. You may also see a fluffy white fungus embedded with hard black fungal sclerotia.

Prevention: Choose plant varieties that do not produce excessive foliage near ground level. Do not grow any very susceptible hosts, such as lettuce, in the same place every year; rotate them with plants—such as onion— that are not susceptible. Position plants so that air circulates between rows. Do not overwater.

Management: Management measures will not work once the infection is moderate to severe. No fungicide for white mold is currently available for home garden use. Since sclerotia are near the soil surface, solarization treatment may reduce their numbers.

WITCHES' BROOM

VARIOUS CAUSES

✺ ZONES: ALL

The numerous causes of witches' broom include fungi such as *Taphrina wiesneri* on cherry trees, bacteria, viruses, phytoplasmas, mistletoe, dodder, chemical damage, and insect attack; shown above is witches' broom caused by the honeysuckle aphid. On potato, the cause is a phytoplasma transmitted by several leafhopper species and by potato seed pieces. On hackberry, the cause is believed to be a powdery mildew combined with a mite. On cherry trees, fungus spores from diseased plants blow onto buds, germinate, and penetrate the branch. The spores stimulate the branch to develop abnormal growths year after year. Once a branch is infected, it will remain infected, and the leaves on the "broom" will be diseased every year. Although witches' broom is unsightly and weakens the affected branches, it may not seriously damage the entire plant. However, it may be accompanied by a disease or an insect that can cause considerable harm.

Target: Rose; ornamental shrubs, such as lilac and rhododendron; vegetables, such as potato; and trees, including cherry

Symptoms: On cherry trees, individual branches sprout long slender branches in large broomlike clusters from a swelling or knot. These "brooms" have few flowers, and leaf out earlier than normal branches. Affected leaves are thick and reddish, with a white fungus growth on the leaf undersides. At the base of the broom is a common stem that may be much thicker than the branch to which it is attached. On potatoes, stunted plants have multiple and highly branched stems; leaves, which have yellow margins, roll up. Tubers are plentiful but quite small. In general, shoots on the broom quickly die and turn brown. Branches are weak and easily damaged.

Prevention: Prevention depends on the causative agent, which may be difficult for the home gardener to identify. Consult your cooperative extension office for help in diagnosing the problem.

Management: If the area is unsightly and accessible, prune out infected branches at least 12 inches below the brooming. There is no general chemical management of this disease.

Encyclopedia of
CULTURAL
PROBLEMS

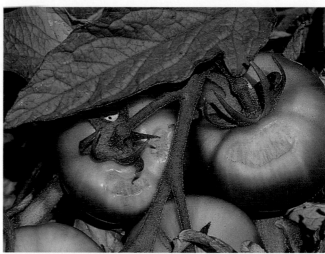

Tomatoes exposed to excessive sunlight

Cultural problems are defined as causes of plant damage that are related to the environment of the garden and to the gardening techniques—or lack of them—used there. Soil type, soil nutrient content, water management, weather conditions, air pollution, careless practices, and garden sanitation are important aspects of gardening that can affect plant health. Cultural problems may cause damage to the plants or they may make the plants vulnerable to insects and disease pathogens that tend to attack weakened plants.

This chapter on diseases includes these cultural problems because, at first glance, the damage they cause may appear to be the result of a disease. Identifying the type of problem you confront in your garden can be difficult and puzzling, especially if there is no visible evidence of a disease or an insect. One way to distinguish among causes is to look for patterns. A uniform pattern—say, wilting on all plants in a bed—suggests a cultural problem. A nonuniform pattern—all the hollyhocks are affected but none of the other flowers is—indicates a plant-specific disease or pest.

Another way to differentiate a cultural problem from one caused by a pathogen is to apply the remedy for the cultural problem. If this does not resolve the problem, you need to seek another cause. Starting with the cultural solution is a good idea because it often involves simply improving the care you give your plants, such as being more precise in applying fertilizer. Moreover, a large proportion of plant problems are caused by cultural conditions or can be ameliorated by improved plant care, so your chances of returning the plant to health are quite high when you focus first on the potential cultural cause.

Here's an example of how cultural problems can affect your garden. You planted a bit later than the seed packet recommended, you didn't have time to amend the soil with organic matter, and you haven't fertilized, but those lapses haven't seemed to make too much difference—your tomato crop appears bountiful. Then suddenly the temperature soars over 90°F for several days. It's too hot and windy to garden, you're busy, and so you just let the tomatoes cope—they need good heat to develop anyway, don't they? As the temperatures return to normal, you go out to the garden, thinking of your aunt's recipe for fried green tomatoes. Unfortunately, you're met with an unwelcome culinary surprise: on every plant, leaves have shriveled and wilted. The edges of the leaves look burned. The tomatoes have blistered, sunken areas. A black mold is growing on some of the blistered areas, and the fruit is rotting underneath. Watering the plants does not help.

What's at fault? An opportunistic plant fungus is clearly at work here, but the basic problem is cultural practices.

Planting according to the instructions on a seed packet ensures that the plants will grow in the weather best for that variety. Soil additions, such as organic material, not only create a crumbly, porous soil that is helpful for strong root growth, but also provide nutrients that strengthen a plant's resistance to disease and other problems. Fertilizer provides additional nutrients, enabling a plant to become and remain healthy.

In adverse weather conditions, plants need help. Extra water, shade, or a cooling mulch—all good general gardening practices—might have prevented or diminished the sunscald your tomatoes have suffered.

Most cultural problems can be avoided by adherence to good gardening practices, such as those described in chapters 2 and 3. Simply monitoring the garden is one of the most important techniques. Make it a point to inspect the garden often, at least several times a week. Initially you may notice only obvious problems, but as you become more aware of what to look for, you will learn to recognize early trouble signs.

Talk to neighbors and friends to learn the types of problems that typify the area and the steps for dealing with them that have proved most helpful. Other resources are the staff at local garden centers, the experts at cooperative extension offices, native plant societies, and societies dedicated to specific plants (roses or succulents, for instance)—all these can provide useful information about the challenges of your area and the cultural techniques that can help you garden successfully.

AIR POLLUTION DAMAGE

Sulfur dioxide, peroxyacetyl nitrate (PAN), ozone, ethylene, and nitrogen dioxide are the air pollution components most troubling to plants. These chemicals are breakdown products of gases released into the air by trucks, cars, and industrial processes. Air pollution problems are worse during the warm weather of mid- to late summer. Plants in urban areas suffer most from air pollution, but polluted air has followed businesses and heavy traffic to the suburbs, making those areas less healthy for plants as well. Even in the mountains, trees may be pollution damaged and therefore more vulnerable to insect attack. Air pollution affects plants via leaf pores, which absorb pollutants that disrupt cell membranes. Ozone damage is shown above.

Symptoms: In response to air pollution, the tissue between leaf veins turns grayish green to pale brown or light tan. Leaves may curl, then drop. Upper leaf surfaces may develop white to tan flecks. On some plants, both the upper and the lower leaf surfaces are affected. Pine trees and other conifers may have blotched needles. The tips of new needles may abruptly turn reddish brown or gray, and needles may drop. Fruit may fall prematurely from fruit trees.

Pollution damage slows plant growth. Repeated attacks weaken the plant, and it may eventually die. On the West Coast, PAN causes a silvering or bronzing on lower leaf surfaces. Leaf damage may show up as raised bands across the leaf, with healthy leaf tissue between the bands. Rapidly growing leaves are most prone to PAN damage.

Prevention: While we all can—and should—take individual steps to reduce air pollution in general, the damage caused by environmental pollutants cannot be completely prevented at this time. If your area has a definite problem with air pollution, ask your cooperative extension office or local garden center about plants that are resistant to pollutants.

Management: Before attributing all plant damage to air pollution, check for other factors that may cause leaf, blossom, or bark damage—for instance, insects, nutrient deficiencies, lack of water, soil problems, and diseases. Fertilize and water injured plants to encourage their recovery.

ALKALINE SOILS

Soil is measured in terms of acidity and alkalinity, on a scale of pH 1–14. A neutral pH is 7.0. At one end of the scale are low pH numbers, which indicate acid soils. At the other end are alkaline soils, those with a pH of more than 7.0. Alkalinity is caused by too much calcium, sodium, and other alkaline substances in the soil. It may result from lime that leaches from cement or brick walkways or patios. Soil is usually alkaline in areas that receive less than 20 inches of rain per year, with desert areas the most extreme example. Soil pH often determines what nutrients are available for plant use. Above a pH of 8, some nutrients, such as manganese, iron, copper, and zinc, become less available to the plant. This in turn affects the ability of plant roots to absorb water and other nutrients. Most plants grow well between pH 6 and 6.8.

Symptoms: Plants growing in soil that is too alkaline for their needs may develop yellow areas between the veins on their newest leaves. Older plants usually remain green, unless the plant has been growing for some time in soil that is too alkaline. Plants needing a high-acid soil content, such as azaleas and rhododendrons, may show deficiency symptoms even when the pH is slightly acid.

Prevention: Test soil pH, either with a kit from a garden center or through a commercial service. Test across the entire planting area, rather than at just one spot, as pH may vary from one place in your garden to another. Select plants, such as natives, that grow well in alkaline soils. For other plants, correct the soil pH, or use raised beds or containers with purchased soil or soil-less mixes. Add organic material before planting. Consult your cooperative extension agent for advice about your soil.

Management: Correct soil pH to 6–6.8 if possible. Use a fertilizer that encourages an acid soil reaction, such as one designed for azaleas, camellias, rhododendrons, or hydrangeas. Use a mulch, such as peat, decomposed pine needles, or any decomposed organic matter. If you have been adding lime to the soil, reconsider. An overabundance of lime will change soil from acid to alkaline.

BLOSSOM DROP

Plants are sensitive to temperature variations during pollination in spring, and this may cause the blossoms of vegetables, trees, flowers, or fruit-producing plants to fall rather than produce fruit. For example, the optimal temperature range for peppers and eggplant is 58–85°F; pollination will not occur if night temperatures fall below 58°F, and blossoms may fall if the temperature rises above 85°F. Flowers that have not been properly fertilized will form fruit, but it will be imperfect. Pollination problems may be the result of low temperatures or rain deterring bees, or a lack of necessary pollenizer plant varieties.

Bean blossoms may fall if the temperature remains over 85°F. Hot winds exacerbate the problem. Tomato flowers are usually self-pollinating. Successful pollination requires optimal soil fertility, moisture, temperature, and humidity. If night temperatures fall below 55°F for more than four nights in a row, tomato flowers may fall off unfertilized. Freezing temperatures may cause fruit tree blossoms to drop. Flowers may also drop when the temperature rises above 90°F during the day or 75°F at night.

Symptoms: Blossoms fall. Little or no fruit appears on the plant. Fruit that does appear may have a rough skin or may be misshapen.

Prevention: Select plant varieties that cope best with your garden conditions. Avoid planting eggplant, tomatoes, and peppers too early in spring. If nights are cold, plant in the warmest area of your garden. Use a protective covering to warm the air around plants. Where summer temperatures are very high or where hot, dry winds are common, avoid planting midsummer beans. Fertilize according to directions on the label for the specific crop; do not overfertilize. Give adequate water.

Management: There is no control for this problem once it occurs. However, if air temperature stays warm and stable, plants that lose blossoms early in the season may still provide a full fruit crop and the plants may do well. Watering when temperatures are warm will cool plants and help reduce blossom loss. Decrease fertilization, following instructions on the fertilizer label for the specific plant. Gentle shaking may help tomato pollination: tap the flowers lightly on a warm, sunny day between 10 A.M. and 2 P.M. Discard misshapen and rough-skinned fruit that may slow down later production.

BLOSSOM-END ROT

Blossom-end rot has multiple causes, all stemming from a plant's inability to utilize calcium in the soil. Soil calcium is available to the plant only when soil is evenly moist, so the most common causes of this disorder are drought and extreme variation in soil moisture—going consistently from soaked to very dry and back again. This variation may result from the weather or from watering practices—or both. Other causes of calcium deficiency include a soil mineral imbalance, root damage, heavy soil resulting in an inadequate plant root system, temperature swings, and high soil salt content.

This disorder in tomatoes, peppers, squash, and watermelon often appears on immature fruit but can also appear on ripe fruit. Blossom-end rot frequently affects plants in sandy or dry soil.

Symptoms: A soggy-looking sunken area develops on the blossom end (opposite the stem end) of affected fruits, often at earliest fruit set. This damaged area becomes dark brown or black, and leathery. It may be flat or concave. As the rot develops, the damaged area enlarges and eventually may cover half the fruit. Mold caused by fungi may appear on the rotting area, which adds to the damage.

Prevention: Plant resistant varieties in well-drained, good garden soil or raised beds. Place 3–5 inches of mulch around your plants, especially tomatoes, as blossom-end rot occurs more frequently in staked tomatoes without mulch. Mulches also will help maintain a consistent soil moisture. Avoid damaging roots when cultivating; don't dig more than 1 inch deep within a 1-foot radius of the plant. Regular but infrequent deep waterings are better than frequent light waterings. However, do not let plants dry out completely; soil should be moist. Avoid using high-nitrogen fertilizers or fresh manure soil amendment; manure, which can have a high salt content, should be at least partially decomposed when used.

Management: If the water or soil in your area contains too much salt, water more thoroughly to help leach salts through soil. Correct any soil drainage problems in your garden. If improving garden practices does not halt blossom-end rot, have your soil tested for a mineral imbalance.

COLD, WINTER INJURY

Even warm-weather areas can be subject to sudden cold spells. Tender plants, seedlings, and plants raised indoors and brought out too early in spring are most susceptible to freezing injuries. Sudden cold temperatures above freezing can result in discolored leaves that may die. Tree branches heavily coated with snow or ice may fall due to the extra weight. Strong winds increase injuries. Alternating freezes and thaws can cause more problems than the frost itself. Frozen plant sap expands upon thawing, destroying the cell walls of plants. Repeated freezing temperatures alternating with thaws bring waterlogged soil and subsequent root damage.

Symptoms: Freezing temperatures cause leaves to wilt and appear water soaked. Shortly afterward, leaves and stems turn black. Evergreen trees, with their winter leaf load, are most susceptible to limb drop caused by snow and ice. Tree bark may develop longitudinal cracks, often on the south and southeast sides, or bark can split completely around the trunk. These cracks are caused by expansion and contraction of the wood during sudden cold-spell temperature changes.

Prevention: Put in plants adapted to your climate zone. Or in the fall bring indoors the tender plants that won't survive your winter; you can also place them in a greenhouse or protected porch. In the spring, start seeds indoors and wait until frost danger is gone before planting them outside. Before placing house plants or greenhouse plants outdoors in spring, harden them to outdoor conditions by placing them for several days in a shady or partially shady area outdoors. Wait until consistent spring warmth before pruning evergreen trees or shrubs. Fruit tree and deciduous tree pruning is usually done during the dormant season. Keep plants in good condition with adequate fertilization, water, and garden placement appropriate for their light needs. Use a protective mulch. Shape hedges to avoid snow buildup. If sudden, very cold weather is forecast, protect sensitive plants with hay, burlap, cardboard, or heavy paper coverings. Remove any thick snow covering from vulnerable plants and tree branches. Frost-damaged flowers, leaves, and vegetables should be removed immediately, as they create a favorable environment for insect and fungus entry.

Management: Once winter damage has been done, it cannot be remedied. Shelter plants to prevent further damage. Maintain good gardening practices to restore plant health.

FLOWERING PROBLEMS

To produce flowers, plants need appropriate light and growing conditions. Plants that require full sunlight will not bloom well, or at all, in shaded situations. Plants with inadequate light are often leggy or spindly. Overcrowded plants will be smaller than normal, producing smaller flowers or no flowers. Plant bloom is also keyed to seasonal sunlight and air temperatures. Sometimes unusually cool and cloudy weather delays or prevents bloom.

Flowering can be affected by the plant's normal cycle. All plants, including bulbs and corms, need to reach a minimum age or size before they will flower. Biennial plants (those with a two-year life span) seldom bloom their first year; expect blooms the second year under good garden conditions. Some plants slow down flower production when older faded blossoms are left on the plant—these blooms form seeds, diverting plant energy from flowering.

Another cause of poor flowering or nonflowering can be over- or underfertilizing. All plants need nitrogen to grow and flower properly, but excess amounts bring lush leaf growth at the expense of flowers.

Symptoms: Apparently healthy plants with leaves that look normal fail to produce flowers or produce flowers that are quite small.

Prevention: Research the planting time, blooming time, light requirements, and optimal garden conditions of your plants. When planting seeds, follow the information on the seed packet. Purchase only large, healthy bulbs or corms; while undersized bulbs and corms may eventually reach blooming size, some cannot withstand adverse weather conditions.

Management: Thin out overcrowded plantings. Remove old flower heads. If garden conditions seem adequate, yet plants are not blooming their first season, wait until second season maturity before taking action. If light conditions are the problem, move the plant to a more satisfactory environment. When transplanting, handle it carefully, taking up as much of the root system as possible. Water immediately, and keep the ground slightly moist until vigor is restored. Transplant perennials and biennials early in the growing season so that plants attain good root growth before winter. Fertilize according to directions on the container label. Always check for insect and disease conditions before transplanting and several times a week afterward.

FRUIT DROP

Some fruit normally drops every year in a natural thinning process that adjusts the tree's load to its nutrient capacity. Although sometimes called June drop, it doesn't always occur in June. Normal fruit drop occurs in pome fruit trees—those bearing fruit with a core with small seeds, such as apple and pear—and in citrus. These fruit trees generally produce a heavy, mature fruit crop one year, then undergo a substantial fruit drop the following year, resulting in a normal light crop. Fruits containing the weakest or fewest seeds are usually the first to fall. Fruit drop may be preceded by blossom drop (see page 243).

Abnormal fruit drops can result from a number of factors. Large quantities of fruit may drop when the tree is under stress from overwatering, underwatering, high heat, extreme cold, or rapid changes in air temperature and moisture. Unusual spring frosts can freeze and kill developing young fruit. Excessive fruit drop may also be caused by improper fertilization.

Fruit may develop to the size of a pea, then fall off if the flowers have not been pollinated. Pollinators could be deterred by rain and cold weather. Or perhaps the open land whose plants and trees provided them with food and shelter has been developed—paved over or covered with new houses. Pollinators may also be killed by pesticide use in the vicinity or by predators. Two mites are currently killing off the wild honeybees in some areas. To find out whether this is a problem in your area and what you should do about it, contact your cooperative extension agent.

Symptoms: Large amounts of young, newly formed fruit drops from a tree that does not appear to have insect or disease problems. Fruit drop continues until the fruit has grown to ½–1 inch in diameter.

Prevention and management: If unusual spring frosts cause stress or if pollinators are routinely deterred by spring rains, consider planting later-blooming trees. Plant trees that do not require an insect pollinator; if they need a tree pollinator, be sure you have the correct one. Try to avoid stress in trees by protecting them from frost. Give them adequate water, and supply extra water if the weather has been particularly warm or windy. Use a general fruit tree fertilizer containing nitrogen, but avoid overfertilization. Maintain the tree in a healthy condition.

FRUITING PROBLEMS

Certain fruit trees—such as nectarine, apple, pear, peach, and Japanese plum—tend to produce a lot of small, often poorly flavored fruit if trees are not thinned or pruned adequately. When fruit-bearing wood is not pruned during the dormant season, the tree may set many more fruits than it can nutritionally support to full size, so most fruit fails to develop. Some fruit trees tend to overbear even when properly thinned or pruned. A normal variability in color, quality, and size can occur on large trees, where the amount of sunlight reaching fruit on foliage-shaded inner branches is different from that reaching fruit on outer branches. Smaller fruit can also result from poor pollination.

Symptoms: A tree that displays no sign of pests or disease produces many small fruits.

Prevention: Buy self-fertile fruit trees, which will produce a crop without a pollinating cultivar nearby. During the dormant season, prune the tree properly. During the fruiting season, thin to balance the distribution of fruit. This helps prevent overloaded branches from breaking. It also diminishes the alternation of heavy and light crops from year to year, a problem with some pome fruit trees (those having a core with small seeds, such as apple and pear).

Management: Thinning practices vary, depending on the tree. On mature trees, thin immature fruits, about four to eight weeks after bloom, when they are about the size of a nickel. Remove unhealthy, malformed, or damaged fruits first, then reduce the number that remain, leaving only the largest fruits. Apples should have a single fruit every 6 inches along branches. For early peaches, leave 6–8 inches of space between fruits. For late peaches, thin after the June fruit fall, leaving 5 inches of space between fruits. Thin Japanese plums to one fruit every 4–6 inches. Thin pears at midsummer, leaving one fruit per cluster, unless crop is light—then leave two fruits per cluster. You do not need to thin cherry, persimmon, or orange trees unless overloading is so severe it threatens to break branches. If you are planting a fruit tree that needs cross-pollination or one that is not reliably self-fertile—many sweet cherries, apples, and pears fall into this category—be sure to select the correct pollenizer. Ask a garden center consultant for advice.

HARDPAN

Hardpan is a soil layer, often hidden under topsoil, that allows very little water to pass through. In desert soils, it is usually caused by a caliche (calcium carbonate) layer where soils have not weathered and the soil particles have been cemented together by minerals. In other areas, the soil particles in the hardpan layer are cemented together by iron and aluminum compounds. At times this very compacted soil seems to hold water like a bucket, as shown above. Hardpan, usually within a foot of the soil surface and as much as 3 feet deep, is immediately evident when you try to dig through it. Because plant roots cannot penetrate the hardpan, they are restricted to the shallow soil layer above it. This limits their ability to obtain nutrients and to obtain a firm ground hold. The shallow soil above the hardpan can retain only small amounts of water, so plants wilt rapidly in hot, dry weather.

Symptoms: Trees and shrubs grow slowly and may fail to thrive. Trees, particularly large ones, may fall over when heavy rains combine with wind. Fruit trees may have a limited harvest.

Prevention: Determine if hardpan is present in your target planting area by digging down 2–3 feet deep. Avoid planting large trees and shrubs in hardpan areas. Instead use raised beds for vegetables and flowers and aboveground containers for smaller trees and shrubs.

Management: Water affected plants frequently, but do not overwater. Profuse watering can drown the plants, by overfilling soil pores and eliminating oxygen from the hardpan-confined root zone. The longer the air supply is cut off, the more damage occurs. Repeated instances may result in permanent plant damage. While it is not always an easy task, you can penetrate hardpan. Some gardeners try to remove it entirely, but this isn't necessary. Creating a drainage channel often allows root growth and adequate water flow. Around mature plants, use a crowbar, jackhammer, or power post-hole digger (these can be rented) to punch holes in the hardpan, about 4 feet apart. Fill the drainage holes with prepared soil or good surface soil.

IRON DEFICIENCY

Called a minor nutrient because only small amounts are necessary to plant growth, iron aids in production of the green plant pigment chlorophyll, as well as in plant enzyme functions. Iron and other trace elements may be present in soil but in a form the plant cannot use. If the soil is too alkaline, with a pH over 7.5, some minerals may form compounds that are not sufficiently soluble. Overly alkaline soils can result from lime leached from patio or driveway brick. Soggy, poorly aerated soils also delay or deter mineral release. In soil deficient in trace elements, the early leaves of a plant get whatever is available. Once the minerals are utilized by these plant tissues, they cannot be reused by new leaves, which then suffer the most severe damage.

Symptoms: Lack of iron causes leaves to lose their green color, starting at the outer edge and progressing inward (this is a condition called chlorosis; see page 91 under Rhododendron, Azalea). Leaf veins usually remain green. The newest leaves, located at stem tips, are the most affected. In plants with severe iron deficiency, the newest leaves are very small and may turn completely white or bright yellow. Older leaves remain green. On fruit trees, the crop may be small and fruit flavor may be poor.

Prevention: Test soil pH before planting in any area. Many garden centers have kits for soil testing; or you can consult your cooperative extension agent for advice. If possible, correct the soil pH to the recommended levels before putting in plants. With susceptible plants, adding organic matter before planting will also help. Check your garden's drainage and improve it as needed. Use mulches to increase soil water retention. Avoid overwatering or underwatering. For most plants, regularly use a slow-acting, all-purpose fertilizer as recommended on the label.

Management: Apply chelated iron according to directions on the product label. Recheck soil pH after all treatment. If the soil is high in lime, add sulfur or organic matter. When incorporating any additives, remember that feeder roots are close to the soil surface. Work carefully, preferably at shallow levels, to avoid further plant stress.

LAWN SCALPING

When a lawn mower is set to cut too low, it exposes the lower parts of the grass blades to sunlight, which burns them. If grass-blade bases are damaged, the affected lawn area may die; however, the grass will usually recover with proper lawn care. Overgrown grass may present similar symptoms even if mowed at the appropriate height: mower cutting exposes the lower grass segments to sudden bright sun, and they burn. Scalping may also result from thatch (see page 253); thatch accumulation gives the lawn a spongy texture that causes the mower to bounce, scalping the lawn in spots. Mowing just after a rain worsens this problem.

Symptoms: Yellow patches appear on grass a few days after mowing. Several days later, the patches may turn tan or brown and die. The grass usually is not permanently affected, although the abnormal coloration may remain for a week or two.

Prevention: Adjust mower blades to the appropriate height for the specific lawn type. Keep mower blades sharpened. Mow often enough so that mowing does not remove more than a third of the grass-blade height. If the grass is overgrown, adjust the mower height to half the grass height and lower it gradually over the next few mowings. If lawn surface is irregular, level the high spots: cut an H-shape across the bump, roll the resulting two sod flaps back, scrape off raised soil, and level the bump. Roll back the cut lawn pieces, making certain the area is not too low—it should be level. Keep the area moist until the cut places heal. If the lawn is spongy from thatch accumulation, do not mow immediately after lawn watering or rain. Remove excess thatch using dethatching equipment available at garden centers. Do not remove it all at once. The best time to dethatch warm-season grasses is early spring. Dethatch cool-season grasses in early fall.

Management: Proper lawn care brings faster and healthier remedial growth after lawn scalping.

LAWNS WITH DEAD PATCHES

Chemicals such as gasoline, fertilizers, pesticides, and hydrated lime may burn grass if accidentally spilled or applied improperly. Dog urine contains salts that burn lawns. Blade death from such causes may take up to five days to become visible. Lawns suffer the most damage from these materials during hot, dry weather.

Symptoms: Dead or dying grass patches, round or irregular, appear in lawn. If caused by dog urine or fertilizer, as shown above, each spot may be encircled by a ring of dark green grass. Damage depends on the amount spilled, the intensity of the damage-causing agent, and the lawn condition at the time damage occurs.

Prevention: Store chemicals in their original containers with their original instructions. Apply fertilizers, pesticides, and hydrated lime according to directions on the product label. Never combine chemicals unless the manufacturer specifically recommends doing so. Water immediately and thoroughly after fertilizer application, so the product does not rest on the plant surface for an extended time. Water deeply, so the fertilizer gets down into the grass root zone. Fill spreaders and sprayers on an unplanted surface, such as a driveway, rather than on the lawn. Water the grass regularly to minimize the odor that attracts dogs.

Management: Problems can be minimized and sometimes prevented if the damaging material is immediately cleaned up. If the material is water soluble, water the area thoroughly, as much as six times longer than you ordinarily would. If the damaging material is not water soluble—such as gasoline or weed oil—inundate the area with a mixture of water and dishwasher soap, which will cut through the gasoline and oil. Then water heavily. Some substances, such as pre-emergence herbicides, cannot be eliminated from the soil after an accidental spill. You must replace the top layer of soil in the affected area and overlap slightly into unaffected parts of the lawn. To combat dog urine, try to keep dogs off grass. Since dogs tend to return to the same elimination areas, try a commercial chemical repellent to disguise prior aromas. As with other lawn chemicals, apply according to directions on the label.

Notes: When you water after a spill, be careful not to splatter spilled material. If any gets on your clothes or body, wash it off immediately.

LEAF DROP

Leaf drop has many causes. One is lack of water because of sparse or inadequate watering; another is disease or insect feeding that damages or kills roots. Excess water, including water puddling inside a container, may decrease the air available to the plant roots. Leaf drop may also be due to inadequate light.

However, leaf drop can be a normal phenomenon. Deciduous trees drop their leaves in fall, although in a tree that is weak from disease, insect pests, or poor cultural conditions, leaf drop can occur by midsummer. The foliage of evergreen plants has a life span of one to four years; leaf drop may occur every year or every second or third year. Hollies tend to lose their leaves in late winter, while pine trees and other conifers drop needles at various seasons, depending on the species. Many western trees drop old leaves in the spring as new leaves form. Normal leaf drop also occurs when new growth shades older, interior growth.

Symptoms: All or part of the plant may wilt. Lower, older needles or leaves turn yellow, brown, or reddish, then drop. Or many leaves of all ages and sizes suddenly may turn orange or red and drop. Leaf dropping may progress until only stems are left on the plant. The problem may develop over a few days, several weeks, or longer. Insect or disease damage may be visible. Leaves on apparently healthy trees may fall off.

Prevention: Provide water, fertilizer, and light that are adequate and appropriate for the plant type.

Management: If the soil of container plants is soggy and plant leaves have fallen or are mostly yellow, you may need to transplant carefully to good potting soil. Give supplemental light and adequate fertilizer for the plant type. Make sure in-ground plants have good drainage and aerated soil. Fertilize according to plant needs. Look for insect or disease symptoms, and treat as appropriate. No management is necessary for seasonal leaf drop.

 Notes: Anthracnose, a disease of trees such as ash and syca-more, causes major leaf drop in late spring (see page 211). Other diseases causing leaf drop include apple scab (see page 211), black spot (see page 215), and cherry leaf spot (see page 217).

LEAF SCORCH

Leaves are cooled by water evaporation, or transpiration, from their surfaces. If the amount of water getting to the leaves is less than the amount the plant transpires, leaves dehydrate and may die. Anything that disrupts the balance between water input and water output can cause leaf scorch. Conditions that decrease water uptake include fewer roots due to recent transplanting, diseases such as root rot, salt burn on young plants, and frozen soil. Drying winds, drought, and too much sun increase water loss. When water balance is disrupted, the greatest loss usually occurs at leaf margins and sometimes at leaf tips.

Symptoms: Browning leaf margins are the primary symptom of leaf scorch. Entire leaves may wilt. Damage usually occurs first on newer leaves. On trees, the damage is most severe on youngest branches, with many leaves dropping during late summer. Trees do not usually die from leaf scorch.

Prevention: Select only plants adapted to your climate zone. Place shade-loving plants in appropriately shaded situations. Keep plants adequately watered, wetting the entire root system; during very hot, dry weather, keep plants moist by gently sprinkling them several times a day. Apply a mulch around plants to conserve moisture. Leach salts from soil with very heavy watering. Protect plants from strong winds. Cover shade-loving plants during extremely hot weather with newspaper or other temporary shelter. If freezing temperatures are expected, keep soil moist. Prevent plant diseases and control damaging insects.

Management: Leaves damaged by leaf scorch do not recover. Proper watering reduces further damage, as does adding mulch and providing shade. Inspect affected plants for disease or physical injury (see page 250), and treat appropriately.

 Notes: Overheated leaf cells also cause a condition called leafburn, which is different from leaf scorch in that the damage appears as dead patches in the center of the leaf. Leaves damaged by leafburn also do not recover. The name leaf scorch is also applied to a disease; see Nerium, page 88.

LIGHTNING INJURY

When severe thunderstorms occur, lightning damage is a possibility. Although there may be no outward signs of electrical shock, trees may die suddenly from burned roots or internal damage. Or trees may immediately show external damage ranging from moderate to severe. Tall trees growing in open areas or along riverbanks are most susceptible to lightning damage. In some instances, deep-rooted species and decaying trees may be more prone to lightning injury than shallow-rooted species or healthy trees.

Symptoms: Trees may burst into flames during an electrical storm. Tops of trees or branches may explode, leaving a jagged stub. A piece of bark may be burned or stripped from the entire length of the tree. Part or all of the tree suddenly may turn brown and die.

The fronds of palm trees may suddenly droop around the trunk, beginning with the lower fronds. Frond color may remain green initially, but change rapidly to yellow and then to brown. About two weeks after the lightning damage, most fronds will have drooped or fallen off. The central bud area wilts and bends over. A reddish fluid may be seen along the trunk. No pests or signs of diseases are visible on the dying fronds.

Prevention: If your area is prone to thunderstorms, water your trees well, especially during droughts, to prevent or reduce damage by increasing the overall health of the trees. Do not plant trees that will attain considerable height, such as palms. Select trees that are less susceptible to lightning injury, such as birch, beech, and horse chestnut. Consult a professional arborist about lightning protection for valuable old trees in thunderstorm areas.

Management: Some trees, including palms, may recover from lightning strike. To help a tree in this process, remove all loose and injured tree bark. Water well, and fertilize adequately for the tree variety. Remove dead trees so they do not become a safety hazard.

 Notes: Plants other than trees also may be damaged by lightning. Trellised crops are vulnerable: lightning can hit trellis wires and go completely down the plant row. The plants will turn brown and may die.

NITROGEN DEFICIENCY

Plants need nitrogen at all times, but they require particularly large quantities when plant growth is rapid, from early spring through early summer. When nitrogen is deficient, plants move nitrogen from older leaves to new leaves, thereby damaging the old leaves. Most soils require additional nitrogen to support healthy plant growth. Commercial fertilizers provide nitrate nitrogen, which is readily available to plants. It acts quickly and is effective in both cold and warm soils. Organic nitrogen—found in blood meal, cottonseed meal, fish meal, fish emulsion, and manure—must be decomposed by soil micro-organisms before it is available to plants. Decomposition speed depends on soil temperature and moisture. Dormant plants and slow-growing plants require less nitrogen.

Symptoms: Plant growth is slow and plants are spindly. Older, lower leaves, which are affected first, may turn yellow but remain hanging on the plant, or they may drop. New leaves and blossoms may be smaller than normal. In very severe nitrogen deficiency, leaf undersides of some plants may turn bluish purple.

Prevention: Use a fertilizer containing nitrogen according to directions on the label for the specific plant. A synthetic nitrate fertilizer is most effective if applied in frequent, light feedings, unless formulated as a timed-release product that replaces nitrogen automatically throughout a specified time period. When adding organic material to soil, be sure it is properly composted, add it a little bit at a time, and supplement with additional nitrogen fertilizer; these steps are necessary because organic material increases microbial activity in soil, reducing the amount of nitrogen available for plant use. Dried-blood and fish meals are the organic materials highest in nitrogen content. Make certain that mulches have nitrogen content—a heavy mulch lacking nitrogen may cause nitrogen depletion in nearby plants. The rhododendron shown above has been mulched with bark, which is low in nitrogen, resulting in a nitrogen deficiency.

Management: Use a commercial fertilizer containing nitrogen according to directions on the label. Water the fertilizer in adequately.

 Notes: Overfertilization with nitrogen results in lush vegetative growth that is very attractive to aphids and increases humidity, perhaps leading to plant diseases such as powdery mildew or gray mold.

PHYSICAL INJURY: ANIMAL, HUMAN, AND MECHANICAL

Injury from construction activities or lawn mowers, motor vehicle impact, animal digging and gnawing, or foot traffic may affect plant roots, stems, and bark. Such damage disturbs water and nutrient movement through the plant. Bark wounds to more than a quarter of the trunk diameter will slow tree growth past that point. Disease fungi may invade damaged areas, further weakening the plant. Although a tree may not appear to be within a construction site, its roots reach as far as—sometimes even farther than—the edge of the drip line (the line directly under the tips of the outermost branches).

Symptoms: The plant may wilt, and leaves may turn yellow, then brown. Wounds or cankers may appear on any part of the plant. Blade ends of lawn grasses may be ragged and dead at the tips. There may be holes, surrounded by sap or sawdust, in a tree trunk or its branches. Tree bark may appear chewed by animals. Overall plant growth is poor. If mechanical damage is severe, the plant may die.

Prevention: Be careful not to wound plants while transplanting them or cultivating around them. Keep lawn mower blades sharp to avoid tearing grass blades. Place barrier fencing or other plant guards around garden areas or large vulnerable plants to protect them from lawn mowers and to deter animal digging and gnawing and casual foot traffic. Reroute garden pathways away from susceptible areas, or create new pathways for pedestrian shortcuts. During construction, fasten scrap wood around tree trunks or set up temporary fencing around trees, shrubs, and other plantings that could be harmed. Discuss with construction personnel the need to take care around plants. Consult your local department of fish and game, wildlife, or animal control to find out what regulations apply to coping with animals, both domestic and wild, that invade your yard.

Management: Keep an injured plant adequately watered to speed its recovery. Fertilize if necessary. During hot weather, reduce water evaporation from leaves by providing shade. Thin tree branches to decrease the possibility of breakage and to reduce the tree's nutrition needs.

SALT DAMAGE

Salt damage to plants is most prevalent in arid and semiarid growing areas, but it can occur anywhere. Salt accumulation in soil may come from fertilizers (including manure), soil composition, and deicing salts. Salt spray from a nearby ocean or other salt-water source is carried by wind. Normally, adequate rainfall or garden watering washes the salt through the soil layers and away from the plant root zone. But at least 30 inches of rain each year is necessary to leach salt through soil and away from plant roots. If rainfall diminishes or if garden watering is sparse or erratic, salt remains in the soil. Irrigation water often adds to the problem in arid areas, as it may itself be salty. When hot weather evaporates the water quickly, the salt is left behind. High salinity in your soil reduces your planting choices.

Symptoms: Leaves may yellow. Salt deposits in leaf tips or margins cause them to turn a dark brown that looks like a burn. Leaves may drop. Plant growth slows or stops. A dark or white crust may form on the soil.

Prevention: All garden areas need good drainage. If low spots in the garden tend to accumulate water and drainage is poor, fill these areas with commercial soil before placing plants. In areas with continual salt-water intrusion, plant salt-tolerant plants. Consider putting in windbreaks if sea-spray salt is the problem. Water adequately and thoroughly. Fertilize according to container directions, and do not overfertilize with commercial fertilizers. Avoid using fresh manure, which has a high salt content. Ask the local water district about the salt content of the water. If problems cannot be prevented, consider container gardening for susceptible plants, using purchased water. Consult your local garden center or cooperative extension office for advice on how to cope with salinity in your area.

Management: Increase the amount of water the garden receives by at least 50 percent. Improve garden drainage. Installing drain tiles, although expensive, is a long-lasting method of improving garden drainage. Create furrows so irrigation water can move through root zones, carrying salt with it.

SEED SPROUTING FAILURE

Seeds may fail to sprout well for a number of reasons. Heavy garden watering or rainfall may have washed seeds away or buried them too deep, or the gardener may have placed them too deep. Seeds sown far below the surface will suffocate from lack of oxygen.

In addition to oxygen, seedlings need water to sprout. Without it, seed coats do not soften enough to permit the seedling to break through, or if the seedling does emerge, it may be weak and therefore vulnerable to damping-off organisms. Seeds placed in dry soil will not germinate. Too-shallow planting speeds the effects of soil drying. When soil has a crust, water fails to penetrate even when applied sufficiently. Tiny seedlings cannot push their way through crusted soil. Soil temperature is also a factor; each plant has its own preferred sprouting temperature.

In addition to problems in soil, air, and water conditions, several soil-dwelling fungi attack and kill emerging seedlings. Birds may nip seedlings as they emerge.

Symptoms: Seedlings fail to germinate or sprout.

Prevention: Loosen soil before planting, using soil amendments as necessary. Purchase seed varieties appropriate for your garden soil and site, and plant them properly, at the correct time of year, according to the seed packet. Make certain the packet bears a current date; seeds lose viability after a year. Place seeds at the recommended depth and distance apart. Keep soil slightly moist, watering gently with a fine hose spray. The tiny root systems of seedlings have no protection against even short periods of drought; in hot, sunny weather you may have to water more than once a day. Take protective measures against birds: place floating row covers, netting, or rustproof chicken wire over newly seeded areas. Be sure the covering is high enough that birds cannot reach the seedlings through it; anchor the edges. Eliminate weeds, since weed seeds may attract some birds. Prune trees near newly seeded areas, opening up their canopies to discourage communally roosting birds.

Management: You can check whether seeds have failed to germinate by digging up a few and looking at the stems. Seeds may be protected during the germination process by coating them with a fungicide containing captan. Follow directions on the product label. It is also possible to order treated seed.

SHADE

Maintaining a healthy lawn or low-growing plants in shade is difficult, whether the shade is cast by trees, fencing, roof overhangs, awnings, or neighboring buildings, or whether morning fog restricts sunlight to a few hours a day. Shade blocks out sunlight needed for proper plant growth, flowering, fruiting, and general health. The trees that provide the shade can cause another problem: shallow-rooted trees may absorb many of the nutrients and water intended for nearby plants.

Symptoms: Grass growing under trees becomes thin and spotty; it may die out altogether. Leaf blades are thin and dark green. Moss and algae may grow on the soil. Sun-loving plants fail to thrive; they become spindly, they form lush foliage with few if any flowers, or they may even die. Diseases that thrive in shade, such as powdery mildew, may appear.

Prevention: When planting shade trees in lawns or near other plantings, keep in mind their size at maturity, and choose trees that cast filtered shade. Keep trees pruned to let light reach plants. Select plants that are tolerant of partial or full shade, and don't overplant. Select shade-tolerant grasses, and seed lawns in the fall, so the grass has a chance to get established before the deciduous trees leaf out in spring. Or plant shade-tolerant ground covers in lieu of lawn. Water more heavily under trees so there is an ample supply for both trees and the plants underneath. Some plant consultants recommend fertilizing trees with soil injections instead of applying tree fertilizer directly on the plants below; if you're considering this option, discuss it with a garden adviser. Set mowing height for shaded grass higher than for grass that is in full sun. Rake up fallen leaves regularly so they do not block light to plants under trees.

Management: If plants in shaded conditions do not thrive, prune overhead trees. If plants do not improve, move them to better light. Water well after moving. Reseed faltering lawns with shade-tolerant lawn varieties. If shade is a severe problem and alternative plantings are not feasible, consider using an attractive bark or stone mulch instead of lawn grass or other plants.

✎ *Notes: A lawn needs about 50 percent of the sunlight passing through a tree to achieve good growth.*

SOIL COMPACTION

Continual foot and vehicle traffic—even the temporary weight of heavy-duty construction equipment—will press the top 2–4 inches of soil down into a compacted mass. The tightly packed soil particles leave little space for air or water. Roots are deprived of oxygen and cannot penetrate the compacted soil to reach areas where oxygen is available. Water penetrates compacted soil slowly, causing puddling and runoff, which in turn result in water-stressed plants. Clay and some loamy sand soils are more prone to compaction than other types.

Symptoms: Leaves turn yellow and do not grow as large as usual. Plants are stunted and may die. Plants may get a number of diseases, especially root and crown rots.

Prevention: Create walkways to direct foot traffic around planted areas. Protect plants by placing barriers—such as fencing—to keep traffic off garden areas, or install raised beds for planting. If vehicles or heavy equipment must be temporarily driven across the garden area, make certain the soil is as dry as possible.

Management: Aerate and remediate compacted soil. On lawns, use a lawn aerator to poke 3-inch-deep holes at least 3 inches apart; air and water will then be able to reach plant roots. If large areas are badly compacted, you may need to use a rotary tiller. Organic matter—such as peat moss, well-aged manure, or compost—should be added during tilling. If the compaction was caused by construction equipment, as sometimes occurs during new home construction, professional aid may be required to loosen the soil to a depth of 2 feet or more. If possible, create walkways that reroute foot traffic away from landscaping. If traffic is inevitable, put in stepping-stones, or cover the area with at least 4 inches of gravel or rocks. You can also plant a ground cover that is fairly tolerant of light to medium foot traffic.

SUNLIGHT, EXCESSIVE

Some plants will not thrive if they get too much sunlight. Plants that are grown in low light conditions will easily develop sun damage—bleaching or burning—if moved abruptly to a sunnier location. Indoor or porch plants moved directly outdoors in the spring or summer are especially prone to overexposure. Even cacti and other sun-loving plants can develop sun damage if suddenly moved from a low light area to a high light area. While sun damage may occur with damage from wind (see page 255) or inadequate watering (see page 255), the three are not synonymous. Sun bleaching and burn, shown above, are caused by light and heat breaking down chlorophyll, the green pigment of plants. Too much exposure to sunlight also results in leaf scorch (see page 248) and sunscald (facing page). In very sensitive plants, such damage may cause plant death.

Symptoms: Plants subjected to too much sun develop faded yellowish white, yellow, pale green, or brown leaves on the section of the plant facing the sun. Leaves may become brittle. Growth may be poor. The damage is worse if the plant is allowed to dry out. Plants may wither and die.

Prevention: Grow shade-loving plants in appropriate light situations. Provide temporary shade, such as cardboard set at a protective angle for small outdoor plants, or burlap on frames for larger plants. Water adequately for plant needs—for plants in containers, this may mean watering as often as twice a day during heat waves. Sprinkle lawns during the hottest part of the day. Wrap the trunks of newly transplanted trees—especially those with smooth, thin bark—with tree-wrapping paper or burlap to prevent sunscald. Do not move sun-tolerant plants abruptly from low light areas to sunnier areas; place them in partial shade for several days so they can adjust. When selecting new plants, choose native plants and others that are adapted to local growing conditions.

Management: Move plants suffering from too much exposure to a shadier spot. Water well after moving; prune off badly damaged leaves to improve the plant's appearance.

SUNSCALD

Overexposure to sun causes sunscald. The problem commonly occurs when young trees are moved from a protected situation, such as a shaded nursery, to an open garden site. Trees that have been shaded have thin and tender bark. If exposed to sudden intense sunlight, tree bark cells heat up rapidly. Since they are not adapted to very high temperatures, they are easily injured or killed. Sunscald may also occur on cold, clear winter days with sudden, intense sunlight. Recently pruned or transplanted trees are more susceptible to sunscald, as are young trees and species with smooth, thin bark. Sunscald may also occur on shade-loving plants, such as camellias, rhododendrons, and hazelnut trees. Dry soil conditions intensify sunscald problems.

Symptoms: Bark turns dark brown, splits open, and dies. The splits form patches or long cracks, usually on the southwest side of the tree. The damaged bark and wood may be invaded by decay organisms, which enter the wood and cause canker formation, diminishing the tree's general health. Young trees may die from sunscald damage. On shade-loving plants, sunscald causes leaf centers to turn a bronze color. Severely affected areas turn brown and die. Flowers may appear bleached.

Prevention: Transplant in cool, overcast weather. Use burlap or tree-wrapping paper, available at plant nurseries, to wrap trunks and major branches of recently transplanted trees. Painting the tree trunk with white-wash is an alternative. Place shade-loving plants in appropriate sites. Water immediately after transplanting, and do not let plants get too dry. Consult your cooperative extension agent for advice on preventing sunscald.

Management: Unless there is major damage, trees suffering from sunscald will usually recover, given proper care. Fertilize to encourage new growth, following container recommendations for the variety of tree. As the transplanted tree takes hold and adapts, its bark will eventually thicken to withstand differing sunlight conditions. Water regularly, deep enough to reach tree roots. Shade-loving plants affected by sunscald should be moved or protected from sun.

THATCH

Thatch is a layer of intermingled dead roots, partially decomposed grass stems, and debris that has accumulated below the grass blades and above the soil surface. A thatch layer of $\frac{1}{4} - \frac{1}{2}$ inch thick is normal. Deeper thatch stops water and fertilizer from reaching the soil and grass roots. It may also harbor plant pathogens and pest insects; pest and disease management becomes more difficult because chemical solutions cannot penetrate the thatch. Thatch builds up when the lawn is overfertilized or overwatered, or when the soil is too acid or compacted. Some grass varieties—bent grass, Bermuda, fine fescue, Kentucky bluegrass, St. Augustine, and zoysia grass—form more thatch than others. Perennial ryegrass seldom forms heavy thatch layers. To determine if your lawn has a thatch problem, cut and lift a few 2-inch-deep grass plugs. If the stringy feltlike material between the grass and soil surface is more than $\frac{1}{2}$ inch thick, there is too much thatch.

Symptoms: Large patches of grass suddenly go dormant during summer heat and drought. Grass thins out, and weeds may appear in the thinning portions. The lawn feels spongy. When the lawn is mowed, particularly just after a rainfall, the mower bounces, sometimes enough to cause scalped spots in the lawn. Diseases such as necrotic ringspot, summer patch, spring dead spot, and leaf spot are more likely to occur in heavily thatched lawns. Fungicides seem to be ineffective. The thatch layer is more than $\frac{1}{2}$ inch thick.

Prevention: Rake lawns regularly. Practice core aeration (see page 98).

Management: Thatch may have accumulated over many years and should not be removed all at once. Instead, dethatch annually (see page 98) until the problem has been corrected—in early spring to early summer for warm-season grasses, in early fall for cool-season grasses. Avoid dethatching while lawn is turning green. A dethatching machine may be available from garden-equipment rental outlets, or a professional garden service can do the job. Obtain dethatching instructions before using the machine, as you could damage the lawn if you use it improperly. Remove thatch debris, then fertilize and water to hasten lawn recovery. Consider replanting with perennial ryegrass or other grass varieties less prone to heavy thatching.

TRANSPLANT FAILURE

Even with careful handling and good all-around conditions, transplanted plants may lose leaves, flowers, or buds after being moved. Damage to the hairlike water-absorbing rootlets at the bottom of the plant's root system will decrease the amount of water taken in by the plant. The plant wilts due to water stress, even though the ground around it is wet. The plant is losing water at the same time, so in hot, dry weather, the plant suffers even more.

Symptoms: Recently transplanted seedlings or mature plants die or fail to thrive. Flower buds drop off before opening, and older flowers may also fall. Double-flowered plant species may produce only single flowers. Leaves yellow and droop and may drop. The plant may wilt during daylight hours, even though the soil seems adequately watered.

Prevention: Lack of water is the major cause of transplant failure. Plant as quickly as possible after purchasing plants or digging them up. Transplant on cooler or cloudy days, in the early morning or late afternoon. Dig holes at least twice as wide as the full root system; amend the soil according to local recommendations. Be as gentle as possible when digging up plants or taking them out of their containers. Try not to disturb the soil around the roots. If root disturbance occurs, and plants are older or very large, prune the foliage by one-third to decrease the amount of water needed to survive. Water immediately after transplanting, making certain that roots are fully wetted, and continue to water diligently, not allowing soil to dry. Protect newly installed plants from cold, heat, or drying. In very hot weather, shade transplants with white shade cloth or floating ground covers for a week. If extra caution is necessary, instead of transplanting seedlings, plant them where they are to grow. Or purchase or grow plants in individual peat pots that go directly into the ground without disturbing the root system; scoring the pot will help roots penetrate it.

Management: Plants suffering from transplant shock often recover if their root zones get adequate water, with no dry periods, and if they're temporarily protected from drying winds and too much sun. Be alert for snail and slug damage on the already weakened plant.

WATERING, EXCESSIVE

Overwatering is a very common cause of plant problems. Heavy and poorly drained soils are particularly susceptible to getting waterlogged. Roots growing in waterlogged soil may die because they cannot absorb the oxygen they need to function normally. They obtain it from pores, tiny air spaces in soil. During irrigation, water pushes the air out of the soil pores. The pores refill with air as water drains through the soil, evaporates up through the soil surface, and is absorbed by plant roots. However, if water is constantly reapplied and if it cannot drain well, the soil pores remain filled with water and the soil may become compacted. The longer the air is cut off, the greater the root damage. The dying roots decay and cannot supply the plant with nutrients and water.

Irregular watering, such as heavy soaking after a dry period, can cause fruit to crack, may encourage weeds and disease problems, and may prevent uniform crop growth.

Damage caused by overwatering is frequently misdiagnosed as pest damage. However, pest damage rarely causes roots to concentrate near the surface of the soil. Or, damage could be caused by a downspout located too near a plant (shown above).

Symptoms: Plants are stunted, slow growing, and weak, and they may die. Leaves are greenish yellow; fruit cracks. Roots concentrate just under or just above the soil surface, where soils dry out faster and oxygen is more available. Plants suffer from leafburn or leaf scorch (see page 248). Water-soaked spots or pale green blisters form on stems and leaves due to plant cell edema. Root rot diseases appear.

Prevention: Test your soil's water-holding capacity and drainage potential. Design your watering system and prepare soil to promote even water distribution and good drainage. Water to meet plant needs, and be careful not to overwater. Adding large amounts of organic matter to heavy soil will help loosen it, allowing more air and water to enter. Where soggy soil cannot be prevented, use bog or other plants tolerant of wet soil, or create raised beds. Consult your local garden center or cooperative extension office for advice on plant selection.

Management: Allow soil, especially clay soil, to dry partially between waterings, so air can get into it. If soil drains poorly, take steps to improve its drainage.

WATERING, INADEQUATE

Plants suffer more from improper watering than from any other problem. Water is stored in plant cells, which are kept filled by pressure exerted by the water. As water evaporates from the cells—faster in warm weather—cell water needs to be replaced. If watering or rainfall isn't sufficient, the entire plant's metabolism is disturbed. This can in turn encourage weeds and disease and prevent uniform maturation of fruits.

A soggy ground surface does not necessarily mean sufficient water has been applied. The water may have run off, rather than penetrating soil to the proper depth. In clay and compacted soils, water penetrates very slowly. Sandy soil retains very little water.

Symptoms: With mild water deficiency, plants are usually slow growing and stunted. Under long-term water stress, plants may permanently wilt or stop growing; they may have diminished crops and discolored leaves, flower buds, and flowers. Plants may eventually die. Bare spots may appear in ground covers. Water-stressed plantings may show the effects of weeds, insect pests, and diseases.

Prevention: In low-rainfall zones and in gardens requiring low water maintenance, use drought-tolerant plants. Create good drainage conditions. Improve soil with organic additives, and use mulches to slow evaporation. If the water-retaining layer of soil is shallow (perhaps above a layer of hardpan—see page 246) and cannot be deepened, water more frequently or use shallow-rooted plants, such as annuals. Water whenever the top 2 inches of soil feel just barely moist. Keep sprinkler heads in good repair so they do not become clogged and leave some spots dry. Drip irrigation systems are very useful with sandy soils.

Management: Start providing adequate water, and do not let drought stress recur. Badly damaged plants may not survive; however, try letting them recuperate before giving up on them. If water from sprinklers tends to puddle or run off, turn them off for an hour or so and reapply.

 Notes: Damage caused by underwatering is frequently misdiagnosed as pest damage. But plants suffering from temporary drought stress usually recover within 24 hours of receiving adequate water and remain healthy as long as watering is sufficient. Pest damage is not alleviated by irrigation. However, pests, especially spider mites, tend to home in on drought-stressed plants.

WIND DAMAGE

Wind causes leaves to lose moisture more rapidly than a plant's root system can replace it. Wind is most likely to cause damage when it occurs with heat or very dry cold. Dry or frozen soil aggravates the problem because such soil does not provide replacement water. Boughs damaged by injury, disease, or insects may be brought down by even moderate winds. Wind may also dash sand against plant parts, damaging them. Young or newly transplanted plants with limited root systems are quite susceptible to wind damage.

Symptoms: Leaves or entire plants wilt. Leaf scorch from winds may make young and exposed leaves brown and dry, especially around the leaf margins and near the tips. Asparagus spears may grow crookedly, particularly in areas where windblown sand damages tender shoots. The leaves of bramble plants, such as blackberry and raspberry, may be torn by the plant's thorns. In high winds, apparently healthy tree branches break and fall. Branches may also drop in the middle of the day during a hot spell. Leaning trees, or those pushed by the wind, can pull loose and fall over with part or all of the roots attached.

Prevention: Plant trees adapted to your climate zone, particularly those that have strong rather than brittle wood. Select native plants; they are often well adapted to local wind problems. Place tall plants or fencing to serve as windbreaks. Do not plant brambles too close together, and stake or trellis bramble canes. Water and fertilize regularly to maintain plant health. Mulch after plants are dormant to reduce the depth of frost penetration into the soil. Deep-water trees to encourage deep rooting. Brace or cable trees—you may need a professional arborist for this. In areas with high winds, prune back some branches to reduce the tree's wind load.

Management: Tip and margin browning caused by wind damage cannot be corrected. Pick off damaged leaves if they are unsightly, and give plants a deep watering. Plants may recover when the wind or heat diminishes.

Encyclopedia of
WEEDS

A longside the many types and varieties of plants that thrive in the West grow numerous and equally various weeds. To help you identify the weeds invading your garden, the most troublesome are pictured and described in the pages that follow. For each weed you will find detailed information on the environments that favor its development; its life cycle, means of reproduction, and habit of growth; and its usual size, foliage, flowers, fruits, and seeds. Each entry also lists techniques for successful management of the weed: methods of preventing its appearance in the first place, physical ways of getting rid of it, and chemical treatments that have proved effective against it.

Weeds are plants growing where human beings, especially gardeners and farmers, do not want them to grow. Our reasons for designating certain plants as weeds vary considerably. Such plants may be robbing more desirable plants of water, nutrients, and sunlight—as purslane or sowthistle do in the vegetable garden. They may be poisonous or otherwise harmful to people or domestic animals—like poison hemlock or puncture vine. Other plants, such as rampant Algerian ivy, may undermine buildings and fences. Some grow so quickly they seem to take over parts of the garden overnight; knotweed and quack grass can do this. Or they detract from the beauty of other plants—for example, crabgrass in lawns, or field bindweed among roses.

Plants such as dock, oxalis, spurges, and thistles are weedy anywhere they grow. Some plants are unwelcome in certain locations and invited into others. Yarrow that invades a lawn is a weed, but when used as a ground cover in a hot, dry part of the garden, the same plant becomes a pleasing ornamental.

Many weedy plants can be useful. Members of the carrot, mustard, and sunflower families nourish or shelter beneficial insects or butterflies. Weeds feed wildlife as well; even the dreaded poison oak is important to the deer, birds, and rabbits that eat its berries. And humans eat blackberries and the leaves of chicory, lamb's quarters, mustards, and purslane. Weeds can prevent erosion, covering bare soil that otherwise would wash or blow away. When they die and decompose, weeds add humus to the soil.

Most weedy plants share certain characteristics. Weeds are most likely to grow where the soil has been disturbed by cultivation or by repeated close mowing, compaction, or overuse of herbicides. Annual species, biennials, and many perennials produce enormous numbers of seeds that often remain dormant in the soil for many years, germinating when conditions are right. Many weeds have developed effective means of dispersing seeds, such as the airborne parachutes of dandelions. And the root systems of many perennials can grow again even when severed from the parent plant.

These adaptive strategies suggest ways gardeners can stop weeds before they get started. Try to avoid unnecessary digging or disturbing of the soil. Or cover bare soil right away with an organic mulch or landscape fabric. Ground cover plantings around shrubs and trees are a living mulch, blocking the light that weeds need to take hold. Be careful about inadvertently introducing weed seeds or roots through contaminated topsoil or compost, containers of nursery plants, or seed for wild birds or poultry.

To decide what to do about weeds growing in your garden, you need to know exactly which weeds you have. Some weeds, especially perennials, can be a serious threat to the garden and should be dispatched at once, while others are fairly benign and can perhaps be tolerated or dealt with less urgently. Correct identification of weeds is essential to using herbicides, as most herbicides do not control all species of weeds. If you cannot identify a weed from the descriptions and photographs that follow, take a sample to a local nursery or cooperative extension office.

MANAGING WEEDS

In most garden situations, physical management of weeds will take care of the problem over time. Hand-weeding or hoeing is the first line of defense, especially against annual or biennial weeds. If you remove these persistently for several years, before they set seed, the numbers of weeds in your garden will decline significantly. In mild-winter zones of the West, winter annual weeds—such as annual bluegrass and mustards—are a special problem. They grow quickly in early spring, setting seed while the weather is still cool, often before gardeners are thinking about weeding.

Perennial weeds are more difficult to manage once they have grown past the seedling stage, because they develop extensive root systems, rhizomes, bulbs, or tubers that aid in reproduction. Pulling them usually does not remove all their underground structures, and the weeds are able to resprout from fragments left behind. Instead, dig these weeds out, removing as much as possible of the root

This sampler of weeds contains (clockwise from top left) perennial jubata grass (often called pampas grass), a weed in wildlands; chickweed, a broad-leafed annual that thrives in cool weather; horsetails, nonflowering plants related to ferns; and poison oak, a shrub or vine that causes severe skin irritation.

system—a process that you may need to repeat several times.

Perennial weeds can also be killed by repeatedly mowing or cutting the tops, although this method may take several seasons to work. Another strategy involves smothering perennial weeds. After clearing the top growth, lay down a thick mulch of cardboard, newspaper (at least three dozen sheets thick), or black plastic. Overlap these materials so weeds can't grow through the cracks. A top layer of bark chips dresses up the area. Leave this smothering mulch in place for at least a full growing season—a year or more for tough weeds.

You can safely put leafy annual or biennial weeds on the compost pile, if they do not yet have flowers or seeds. The top growth of perennial weeds—before seeding—can also be composted. However, roots of perennials and any weeds with seeds should be tossed in the trash rather than composted; even a very hot compost pile may not destroy them.

Preventing seeds already in the soil from germinating is an important weed-control strategy. After clearing an area of visible weeds, cover the soil with a permanent mulch of ground bark, straw, compost, or other organic materials, or inorganic materials like landscape fabric or black plastic. In hot-summer areas, you can effectively kill seeds of many annual and some perennial weeds by solarizing the soil (see page 54). Another method, presprouting, is performed before planting vegetables, perennial beds, or new lawns. Add needed soil amendments, till the soil, water, and then let the weed seeds germinate. When they are only a few inches high, scrape the weeds away, and sow or transplant the lawn or new plants, disturbing the soil as little as possible to avoid bringing more weed seeds to the surface.

PESTICIDES: HANDLE WITH CARE

Care should be taken whenever you use pesticides, particularly near edible crops. Be sure to read the labels on any product you bring into your garden and use it only as its label directs—it's against the law to do otherwise. Pesticide registrations change rapidly and some products mentioned in this book may be removed from the lists of approved products or their label directions may be changed over time, as additional research becomes available. If you have questions concerning current regulations, consult your local nursery or cooperative extension office.

USING HERBICIDES SAFELY

Chemical herbicides are not recommended for food gardens; they are a last resort for weed management in home ornamental gardens. Besides questions about the risks they pose to health and the environment, many of these materials can damage desired plants when they drift through the air or run off in irrigation and rainwater. Some persist in the soil for long periods, injuring later plantings. Often the process of deciding on an appropriate herbicide, reading the label, mixing the spray, applying it, and cleaning up afterward takes more effort than simply pulling or digging the weeds. If you decide to use herbicides, read pages 56–62 on safe use of these products. Always read labels carefully so as to know how to use the chemical safely—sites and uses for which it is intended, time of year and the plant-growth stage at which it is best applied, and quantities to be used.

Herbicides are classified by when in the course of the weed's life cycle they are applied and by what types of plants they kill. Pre-emergence herbicides (such as oryzalin and pendimethalin) inhibit the growth of seeds and very young seedlings; they are often sold in combination with fertilizers. Postemergence products, which kill or damage growing plants, are subdivided into contact and translocated types. Contact herbicides (such as herbicidal soap) kill only the plant parts on which they are sprayed; regrowth may still appear from roots or unsprayed buds. Contact herbicides are most effective on young or annual weeds. Translocated, or systemic, herbicides (including fluazifop-butyl, glyphosate, and triclopyr) are absorbed by various parts of a plant and move to growing points throughout it. While they are most effective on perennial weeds, they are typically slower to show effectiveness.

Herbicides are selective or nonselective. Selective herbicides kill only certain types of plants. Products containing dicamba, MCPP, or MCPA are used in lawns because they kill broad-leafed weeds, but not grasses; however, spray drift from these herbicides can injure nearby shrubs and trees. Nonselective herbicides kill or injure any plant they touch. Glyphosate, a widely used nonselective herbicide effective on many persistent perennial weeds, should be applied to actively growing vegetation. Apply glyphosate carefully; a few misdirected drops can kill or harm desired plants. Using a paintbrush, rag, or special droplet applicator helps you control the placement of glyphosate.

Broad-leafed Seedling

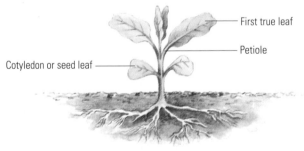

First true leaf

Petiole

Cotyledon or seed leaf

Grass-collar Region

Leaf blade

Ligule

Auricle

Leaf sheath

Grass Culm (jointed stem)

Leaf blade

Node

Leaf sheath

Internode

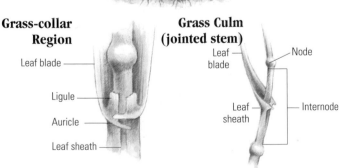

Types of Spreading Stems

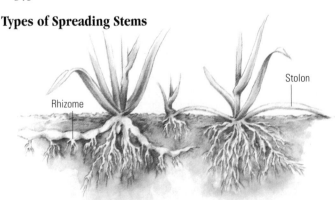

Rhizome

Stolon

ALGAE

SEVERAL SPECIES AND FAMILIES

MICROSCOPIC ORGANISMS

✓ ZONES: ALL

Algae are microscopic organisms lacking roots, stems, or leaves. They grow in ponds and in overly wet, shaded lawns and other damp spots in the garden. In ponds, algae turn the water an unattractive pea green, especially in newly filled ponds and also in early spring as the water warms. On land, algae show up as slimy or scummy areas ranging in color from green to black.

Life cycle: A diverse group of organisms containing one-celled, colonial, and filamentous forms that reproduce by cell division, fragmentation, or spores

Management: In ponds, the key to reducing growth of algae is maintaining an ecological balance. Algae thrive in ponds where ample sunlight coincides with high levels of dissolved nutrients in the water. Reduce the nutrients in the water by preventing runoff from fertilized areas of the garden. You can also give pond fish less food; in a balanced pond, fish can often survive primarily on naturally occurring nutrients with little or no additional food. Adding submerged or oxygenating plants—such as anacharis, cabomba, and vallisneria—is also helpful: they compete with algae for dissolved nutrients and carbon dioxide. These plants are available from companies that sell plants and supplies for ponds. Plan to add one submerged or oxygenating plant for each square foot of pond surface. As they grow larger in spring, the leaves of water lilies shade the water, reducing the growth of algae. Special dyes intended for ponds also help by darkening the surface of the water, which slows the growth of algae by cutting the amount of sunlight that reaches them. Aeration by means of a waterfall, a fountain, or even a trickling hose adds needed oxygen, as do mechanical or biological filters. To manage algae on land, loosen the soil to reduce compaction, improve drainage, and prune nearby vegetation so more sunlight reaches the ground.

As a last resort, chemical algicides provide temporary management, but some formulations are unsafe for fish and others harm aquatic plants. It is vital that you read the label of these products carefully. For chemical control of algae on land, spray with wettable sulfur in early spring, and once again a month later.

ANNUAL BLUEGRASS

POA ANNUA (POACEAE)

ANNUAL GRASS

✓ ZONES: ALL

Annual bluegrass germinates and grows during the cool weather of fall, winter, and early spring, forming a bright green tuft of softly textured, 2–10-inch leaves with curved, prowlike tips. When held up to the light, the young seedling leaves of annual bluegrass show transparent white lines on both sides of the midvein. Pyramidal clusters of small whitish flowers appear throughout the growing season, giving a white haze to infested lawns. The seeds mature from May through July. With the arrival of hot, dry weather the clumps die, leaving unsightly brown patches in lawns. Annual bluegrass also grows in vegetable beds, where it is troublesome to winter and early spring crops, in flower and shrub borders, between paving stones, and in orchards, as well as in lawns. It especially favors wet, poorly drained, and compacted soil.

Life cycle: Usually an annual, but there are perennial forms; spreads by seed

Management: Pull or dig annual bluegrass when the plants are young, before seeds form. To discourage establishment of annual bluegrass in lawns, maintain a thick turf of desirable grasses by improving drainage, avoiding overwatering, and fertilizing appropriately. An organic mulch, such as ground bark or compost, will prevent this weed from growing in vegetables and ornamentals. Solarize to kill seeds before planting vegetable gardens or a new lawn.

If chemical control is necessary, in late summer apply a pre-emergence herbicide containing dithiopyr (for lawns) or pendimethalin or oryzalin (for lawns, shrubs, and ground covers). Check the label to be sure the particular product is safe for your type of lawn. Carefully spot-treat clumps of annual bluegrass in lawns or the garden with a product containing glyphosate. Take care not to get this chemical on desired plants.

✎ *Notes: One of the most widely planted cool-season lawn grasses, Kentucky bluegrass* (Poa pratensis), *is a perennial relative of annual bluegrass. Its leaves also have the characteristic tip shaped like a boat prow or canoe. Another perennial relative, rough-stalked bluegrass* (P. trivialis), *is very tolerant of shade and damp soil. This species is sometimes included in seed mixtures for planting in such conditions, although it can become weedy.*

BAMBOOS

PHYLLOSTACHYS, PLEIOBLASTUS, SASA, AND OTHER GENERA *(POACEAE)*

GIANT GRASSES

✔ ZONES: 4–24, DEPENDING ON GENUS AND SPECIES

While bamboos can be dramatic and useful plants in the landscape, some species spread rapidly and invade other plantings, or creep unbidden under a fence from a neighboring garden. All bamboos have woody stems (culms) divided into sections or internodes by joints (nodes). Leafy branches grow from buds in the upper nodes. Bamboos spread by underground stems (rhizomes) that give rise to new vertical shoots. The rhizomes of running bamboos (those listed above and others) can grow varying distances from the parent plant before sending up new shoots. These bamboos form large groves and can be difficult to manage. Clumping bamboos (*Bambusa* and other genera) are the safest bet for most home gardens, as their rhizomes will extend only a short distance from the main clump.

Life cycle: Perennials that reproduce by rhizomes; the canes usually live for several years

Management: You can get rid of unwanted bamboo in several ways. You can cut off all the shoots at ground level, and repeat as they sprout again, cutting the new shoots before they reach 2 feet. This method will eventually starve the roots, but it takes patience and time. You can also dig out the entire clump. Cut back the stems to make it easier to get at the roots. Using a mattock and spade, remove all of the rhizomes. Generally, the rhizomes do not grow deeply in the soil, but they may be widespread, and any left behind will resprout.

To combine mechanical and chemical controls, cut the stems almost to the ground. Then with an ax, chop vertical gashes in the stumps. Immediately spray or paint glyphosate on the cut stumps. This method requires less of the chemical than spraying the entire plant would. You are also less likely to accidentally damage nearby desired plants. Expect some regrowth that will require repeating this treatment.

 Notes: To contain running bamboo so that it does not become a weed, install a barrier around the root, 1½ feet into the soil. Poured concrete or strips of galvanized metal are effective. You can also plant running bamboo in large containers, such as bottomless oil drums or flue tiles, sunk into the ground.

BARLEY, WILD

HORDEUM MURINUM LEPORINUM (POACEAE)

ANNUAL GRASS

✔ ZONES: ALL

Also known as hare barley, common foxtail, and farmer's foxtail, this grass is found in vegetable and ornamental gardens, lawns, orchards, and vineyards, and along roadsides. It is a winter annual, its seeds germinating from November to March; the plant matures in late spring or summer. The seedling's hairy foliage gives it a velvety look, but older leaves are smooth and dull green. As it matures, wild barley forms a branching plant, 6–39 inches tall. The stems at the lower nodes often bend downward, and the plant takes on a prostrate form in mowed lawns. The leaf blades are ⅛–⅓ inch wide and 2½–6 inches long. At the base of each leaf blade, a well-developed auricle—an ear-shaped lobe or appendage—clasps the stem. Foxtail-shaped flowering spikes, 2–3 inches long and often tinged red, may be partially covered by the uppermost leaf sheath. The spikelets—flower groups—are 1½–3 inches long and tipped with stiff bristles, or awns. These long, sharp awns, which can injure animals, are a distinctive feature of wild barley.

Life cycle: Annual that reproduces by seed

Management: Pull or hoe wild barley when the plants are young. Managing this plant requires weeding early in the season, as it germinates in winter and can mature, setting seed, by late spring; you need to remove it before it sets seed to avoid future infestations. A mulch, kept in place throughout the year, will prevent seeds of wild barley already in the soil from germinating. Soil solarizing during the heat of summer will kill seeds of this weed.

If chemical control is necessary, use a pre-emergence herbicide containing oryzalin around the turf grasses and ornamentals listed on the product label; apply in fall before germination. Do not use oryzalin on cool-season lawns. Apply a selective herbicide for grasses containing sethoxydim on young wild barley plants. Nonselective herbicides, including herbicidal soap, and products containing glufosinate-ammonium or glyphosate are effective on young plants. Take care not to get these chemicals on desirable plants.

BARNYARD GRASS

ECHINOCHLOA CRUS-GALLI (POACEAE)

ANNUAL GRASS

✔ ZONES: ALL

Barnyard grass, also called Japanese millet, cockspur grass, or water-grass, is a vigorous warm-season annual. In mowed lawns it grows only a few inches tall, but in the garden it can reach 4–5 feet. The seedling plant has a flattened reddish stem and gray-green leaves. The coarse, upright stems of the mature plant retain the reddish tint at the base. The light green leaf blades are about ½ inch wide and lack the membrane (auricle) and the fringe of hairs (ligule) that many other grasses have at the junction of the leaf blade and the stem. Erect or drooping flower heads, 2½–4 inches long, are usually reddish to dark purple with bristlelike projections (awns). Seed heads, which may also have a purplish cast, are crowded with relatively large seeds. Barnyard grass germinates in spring, growing in vegetable gardens, ornamental beds, and lawns. It sets seed and dies by fall.

Leaf bases of barnyard grass

Life cycle: Annual that reproduces by seed

Management: In vegetable and ornamental gardens, hoe or hand-pull barnyard grass while the plants are small; as they mature they develop an extensive, fibrous root system that is difficult to remove. And since a single plant of barnyard grass can produce as many as 1,000,000 seeds, it is essential to remove this weed before it sets seed. A thick mulch prevents germination of the seeds; solarization effectively kills them. In lawns, improve cultural conditions so the turf is thick enough to resist weed infestations.

If chemical management is necessary, a late-winter application of a pre-emergence herbicide containing dithiopyr, oryzalin, or pendimethalin will prevent germination of barnyard grass in turf. Check the label to be sure the particular herbicide is safe for your type of lawn. Oryzalin is also labeled for pre-emergent use around many ornamentals. For postemergent control, use a selective herbicide containing fluazifop or sethoxydim. Spot-treat with a product containing herbicidal soap or glyphosate, taking care not to get this chemical on desired plants.

BELLFLOWER, CREEPING

CAMPANULA RAPUNCULOIDES (CAMPANULACEAE)

BROAD-LEAFED PERENNIAL

✔ ZONES: 1–9, 14–24

Creeping bellflower—also known, fittingly, as rover bellflower—is sometimes planted as an ornamental. However, it easily escapes from its allotted spot in the garden, spreading aggressively by seed and deep-seated creeping rhizomes to infest areas near and far. Its adaptability to sun or shade and to many soil types makes it a serious pest in lawns, gardens, meadows, and fencerows. Creeping bellflower grows 2–4 feet tall. Its smooth, upright, and often purplish stem exudes a milky sap when broken. Heart-shaped, pointed leaves, 1–3 inches in length, grow on long stems from the base of the plant; the larger upper leaves clasp the stem. The leaves are somewhat rough to the touch and have conspicuous veins. Pretty, bell-shaped purple flowers, about 1 inch long, nod from one side of the upper stem in late summer.

Life cycle: Perennial that reproduces by seed and by creeping rhizomes

Management: Once established, creeping bellflower is difficult to eradicate, especially if it has crept in and around other perennials and shrubs. Dig out the plants, getting as much of the root system as possible. Then cut down new shoots as they appear until the remaining roots are exhausted and they stop resprouting. To manage a large patch of creeping bellflower, cut down all vegetation and cover the area with a mulch of black plastic topped with organic matter, such as chopped tree trimmings. Leave the mulch in place for at least one growing season.

For chemical control in lawns, spray with a product containing dicamba. Spot-treat creeping bellflower with a product containing glyphosate, taking care not to get this product on desired plants. Repeat treatments will probably be necessary.

✎ *Notes: Another ornamental campanula, Serbian bellflower (Campanula poscharskyana), is also quite vigorous, although not as invasive as creeping bellflower. Serbian bellflower is a spreading, many-branched, leafy plant that grows 1 foot tall or taller. Its star-shaped blue-lilac flowers appear in spring and early summer. While it can quickly spread into and over more delicate plants, it has shallow roots, so it can be pulled or dug out of the garden fairly easily.*

BERMUDA GRASS

CYNODON DACTYLON (POACEAE)

PERENNIAL GRASS

✠ ZONES: 8, 9, 12–24

Also called devil grass or dogtooth grass, Bermuda grass is frequently planted as a lawn grass in warm climates. However, it can also be a troublesome weed in other kinds of lawns, in orchards, and in beds of flowers, shrubs, and vegetables. Bermuda grass reproduces from underground stems (rhizomes), aboveground runners (stolons), and seed. So many possibilities make it an aggressive competitor with other plants. Both the rhizomes and the stolons root at the nodes, forming new plants that spread to make a dense mat of wiry stems and short, 1–4-inch bluish green leaves. A fringe of white hairs is visible where the leaf blade joins the stem. The flower head of Bermuda grass is composed of three to seven slender, 1–2-inch-long spikes radiating from a single point at the tip of the stem. (In contrast, the flower spikes of crabgrass can arise from several points on the stem, and they are attached to the main stem by a short stalk.) Seeds are produced throughout the summer, and they germinate readily in warm soil.

Life cycle: Perennial that reproduces by stolons, rhizomes, and seed

Management: If you have a Bermuda grass lawn, prevent its spread into other parts of the garden with a deep barrier or edging. Dig up stray clumps before they form sod, taking care to remove all of the underground stem, as it can generate new shoots. Repeated pulling and digging are generally necessary to stop Bermuda grass. To kill the root system, leave it exposed to dry in the sun. To avoid spreading this weed, take care not to transport soil containing roots or rhizomes to other parts of your garden. Mulches will slow growth, but eventually Bermuda grass grows through most of them. Solarization (see page 54), if carried out during the hottest part of summer, over a period of at least six weeks, kills the seed of Bermuda grass and rhizomes that are not too deeply buried. Weeder geese can be used to slow the spread of Bermuda grass and other weedy grasses in gardens and orchards.

For chemical control of Bermuda grass, use a selective herbicide containing fluazifop or sethoxydim. Spot-treat actively growing plants with a product containing glyphosate. Take care not to get this chemical on desired plants.

BINDWEED, FIELD

CONVOLVULUS ARVENSIS (CONVOLVULACEAE)

VINING BROAD-LEAFED PERENNIAL

✠ ZONES: ALL

Field bindweed is a persistent pest in vegetable and ornamental gardens, orchards, and lawns throughout the West, particularly in clay and loam soils. This weed's many common names—including wild morning glory, cornbind, creeping Charlie, creeping Jenny, and greenvine—attest to its troublesome nature. The 1–4-foot-long vining stems of field bindweed crawl over the ground and twine over and around any plants they encounter. The extensive root system can penetrate 10 feet into the soil, producing many underground stems, or rhizomes, which give rise to new plants. New plants also grow from seeds. The seedling leaves are large and rounded, with a notch on the end. The first true leaves are spade shaped. As the plant matures, the leaves usually become arrow shaped, although they vary in size and shape depending on soil fertility and moisture. Flowers are white or pink funnels that open in the morning and close in the afternoon.

Life cycle: Perennial that reproduces by rhizomes and seed

Management: Field bindweed is difficult to manage. If pulled, the stems break off, but regrowth occurs from the roots and rhizomes. The seeds can sprout even after lying dormant in the soil for 50 years. Therefore, remove young plants as soon as you see them, before they have a chance to form a perennial root system or to bloom and set seed. Digging out as much of the root system of established bindweed as possible slows down growth somewhat. Repeatedly digging out the roots can eventually control bindweed, but you must be persistent. Solarization kills seeds of bindweed but is not an effective way to control the deeply buried root system.

An herbicide containing trifluralin may provide pre-emergent control around many ornamentals. For postemergent control in lawns, use an herbicide containing MCPA and dicamba. Spot-treat bindweed with a product containing glyphosate. These chemicals are most effective when the weed has a few flowers but has neither reached full bloom nor set seed. Repeated treatments are usually needed to destroy the entire root system. If bindweed is twined around desirable plants, detach it before treating with herbicide. Avoid applying nonselective herbicides such as glyphosate to desired plants.

BLACKBERRY

RUBUS, VARIOUS SPECIES (ROSACEAE)

ARCHED BRAMBLES

 ZONES: 4–17

Several species of blackberries or brambles are pests in various parts of the West. 'Himalaya', a blackberry that has escaped from cultivation, is the most vigorous, thriving in the mild, moist climates of northern California and western Oregon and Washington. With semierect canes that can grow 20–30 feet in a single season, this blackberry quickly forms a dense thicket if not checked. The greenish or reddish stems are studded with sharp thorns and have five angles. Mature leaves are compound, with three or five leaflets that have toothed edges. Five-petaled white or pink flowers appear in large terminal clusters in spring, followed by tasty, shiny black fruits in midsummer. The rhizomes (underground stems) spread rapidly, sending up shoots to form new plants. Birds enjoy the berries and scatter the seeds, sowing blackberries in pastures, along roads, and in gardens, where they turn up in lawns, paths, flower beds, shrub borders, and ground covers.

Life cycle: Plants are perennial; the canes sprout and grow the first year, then flower, fruit, and die the next year

Management: Pull young plants in spring, before they have time to develop a perennial root system. To kill established clumps, repeatedly prune back the stems as they sprout. This will eventually exhaust the roots, and they will die. Mowing or cutting back the stems to ground level in summer and digging out the roots with a shovel and pickax slows down growth more effectively, although some canes will still sprout again from rhizomes left in the soil. More cutting and digging will then be needed. Cover cleared areas with a dense mulch—cardboard, black plastic, or several layers of landscape fabric, topped with bark or chopped tree debris—for at least one season, to prevent any remaining rhizomes from sprouting.

To use both mechanical and chemical controls, cut stems to the ground and apply glyphosate to the stubs as soon as possible after cutting. Spot-treat any new shoots with glyphosate as they appear. Or you can spray triclopyr or glyphosate on mature leaves. With either herbicide, take care to avoid contact with nearby desirable plants. Do not spray fruiting plants in areas where berries could be picked and eaten.

BRACKENFERN, WESTERN

PTERIDIUM AQUILINUM PURESCENS (POLYPODIACEAE)

PERENNIAL FERN

 ZONES: 1–9, 14–24

Western brackenfern is a large, coarse fern found around the world. The species listed here, sometimes called bracken or brake, is native throughout the western United States and Canada. (A second, similar species, *Pteridium aquilinum latiusculum*, is also found in Colorado and Wyoming.) Brackenfern often grows in gardens in or near open woodlands on sandy, acid soil. Although useful as a tall ground cover or screen in untamed areas of the garden, brackenfern can become a tough, invasive weed. The fronds of brackenfern are leathery in texture, much divided, and hairy on the underside. Brown spores are found along the undersurface edge of each frond. The fronds, which emerge directly as a single stem, without branching, from creeping, woody rhizomes, grow from 2 feet to as tall as 7 feet under the ideal conditions of moist soil and partial shade. The deeply rooted rhizomes spread widely.

Life cycle: Perennial that reproduces by creeping rhizomes and by spores

Management: Simply pulling up fronds of brackenfern does not control it, because more fronds will soon unfurl from the tough, deeply buried rhizomes. Try to dig out as much of the rhizome as possible. Digging probably will need to be repeated several times as new fronds sprout from missed pieces of rhizome. Since brackenfern prefers to grow in acidic soil, changing the pH of your garden soil to make it more alkaline discourages this weed. Have the soil tested to learn exactly how acid it is and how much lime is needed to approach a neutral pH (see soil pH, page 36). Working plenty of compost into the soil also helps neutralize the pH.

For chemical control, apply a product containing glyphosate to actively growing fronds, or cut off the fronds and apply the herbicide to the cut stems. Take care not to get this chemical on desired plants. Herbicides containing dicamba are also effective; apply carefully to avoid damaging nearby broad-leafed ornamentals.

Notes: Do not gather and cook the young fronds as you would fiddleheads; the fronds of brackenfern slowly poison humans who ingest them. The fronds are also a cumulative poison in horses and sheep.

BROMES

BROMUS, VARIOUS SPECIES *(POACEAE)*

ANNUAL GRASSES

 ZONES: ALL

Several bromes are weedy grasses in the West. Two of the most wide-spread are downy brome *(Bromus tectorum),* shown above, and fox-tail brome *(B. rubens).* Both are found in vegetable gardens, ornamental beds, orchards, and vineyards, and along roadsides. Downy brome, also called cheatgrass or downy chess, germinates and grows in the cool seasons. Leaf sheaths and flat leaf blades are densely covered with soft hair. Downy brome grows 4–30 inches tall. The inflorescence (flowering part) is dense, soft, and drooping, with slender branches, nodding spikelets, and often a purple cast. Foxtail brome, also known as red brome or foxtail chess, grows 6–18 inches tall, with narrow leaves covered with short, dense, soft hairs. The flowering heads are erect and compact, with sharp, bristly awns. The heads are green at first, but they become reddish with age. When dry in summer, large stands of this grass can be a serious fire danger.

Life cycle: Annuals that reproduce by seed

Management: Hoe or pull out bromes by hand when they are young. Try to remove them before they set seed to reduce future infestations. Mow taller weeds in late spring, especially in areas where there is danger of fire. Mulch around vegetables and ornamentals to reduce germination of brome seeds.

If chemical control is necessary, use a pre-emergence herbicide containing trifluralin. Growing brome plants can be controlled with herbicidal soap or an herbicide containing glyphosate; these are most effective when the plants are young. Take care not to contact desired plants.

 Notes: The long stiff awns of ripgut brome (B. diandrus) *can injure domestic animals and are also uncomfortable for humans who brush up against these bristlelike projections. An annual growing 1–3 feet tall, this brome has flat leaf blades with somewhat hairy sheaths. The ligule (upward projection where the leaf blade joins the sheath) is a thin membrane. The flower head is open and drooping and has fewer flowers than downy or foxtail brome. Management is the same as for other bromes.*

BROOMS, SCOTCH AND SPANISH

CYTISUS SCOPARIUS, SPARTIUM JUNCEUM (FABACEAE)

SHRUBS

 ZONES: VARY BY SPECIES

Introduced as ornamentals, these shrubs have escaped from cultivation and taken over large tracts of wild land in California and the Northwest, crowding out desirable native plants. They are well adapted to grow in dry areas with poor, rocky soil. Scotch broom *(Cytisus scoparius,* Zones 4–9, 14–22) is an evergreen woody shrub that grows up to 10 feet tall. Its many upright, wandlike stems are often leafless. When young, the stems generally are hairy, with five green ridges. As they mature, the hairs fall off, and the stems become tan in color. A profusion of golden yellow, sweet pea–shaped flowers appears in spring and early summer. Flattened brown or black seedpods follow; each of these holds five seeds and has white hairs on the margins only. The seeds can remain viable in the soil for many years. Spanish broom *(Spartium junceum,* Zones 5–24), shown above, grows 6–10 feet tall, forming an erect evergreen shrub of many green, almost leafless stems without ridges. Fragrant, bright yellow flowers bloom in spring and summer. The seedpods are hairy.

Life cycle: Shrubs that reproduce by seed

Management: Pull young broom plants by hand, removing as much of the roots as possible. To remove older plants, use a sharp mattock to cut out the roots. If the stems are cut with a saw, they usually resprout. Or use a weed-pulling tool designed to remove woody shrubs; it is found in specialty tool catalogs. At the bottom of a wooden handle, this tool has a clamp that grips the stem of the plant. Once the stem is caught in the grip, you rock the tool back and forth, pulling up the plant, roots and all. Goats will eat broom and can also help clear large infestations.

If chemical control is necessary to manage large stands of broom, use a product containing triclopyr, taking care not to get this translocated herbicide on desired broad-leafed plants.

 Notes: There are many colorful and less aggressive forms of Scotch broom that are safer to plant in the home garden, especially near wild lands.

BURCLOVER

MEDICAGO POLYMORPHA; ALSO CALLED M. HISPIDA (FABACEAE)

BROAD-LEAFED ANNUAL

ZONES: ALL

Also known as California burclover, this weed is actually a native of the Mediterranean region. In the West, it grows in lawns, vegetable and ornamental beds, and orchards and can also be troublesome in gravel paths and driveways. The spiny burs or seedpods bother animals, getting tangled in their fur. The seeds of burclover germinate in spring. The plant has weak stems, up to 2 feet long, that are usually prostrate, although they sometimes grow upright when supported by a dense population of other plants. Leaves are compound, each with three parts or leaflets. The wedge-shaped leaflets of burclover have toothed margins, an indented tip, and often a reddish tinge. All the leaflets grow from the same point at the end of the leafstalk. The bright yellow flowers, which look like small sweet peas, grow in clusters of two or three on the ends of short stalks. Flowers appear from April to September; the seedpods mature in August and September. The spiral coils of the seedpods give them a rounded appearance. Their two rows of sharp prickles help distinguish burclover from the closely related black medic *(Medicago lupulina)*, page 283, which has seedpods that are hairy but not spined.

Seedpods of California burclover

Life cycle: Annual that reproduces by seed

Management: Hoe or hand-pull burclover from garden beds and lawns before it sets seed. Laying down a thick mulch will help prevent any seeds that are already in the soil from germinating in flower and vegetable beds. Maintain a dense lawn through proper fertilization and watering to prevent the germination and growth of burclover. Flaming—using a special hand-held flamer fueled by propane or kerosene (see page 54)—is an effective way to control burclover in gravel driveways and paths.

If chemical control is necessary, you can use a pre-emergence product containing isoxaben around the ornamentals that are listed on the label. For postemergent treatment, use a product containing MCPP, MCPA, and dicamba on lawns. You can spot-treat burclover with a product containing glufosinate-ammonium or glyphosate; take care not to get these chemicals on desired plants.

BUTTERCUP, CREEPING

RANUNCULUS REPENS (RANUNCULACEAE)

BROAD-LEAFED PERENNIAL

ZONES: 1–11, 14–24

Creeping buttercup is a low-growing weed found in lawns, vegetable gardens, ornamental beds, and orchards, and especially in damp, poorly drained areas. Introduced from Europe as an ornamental, this plant, like its showier double-flowered form, *Ranunculus repens* 'Pleniflorus', is now considered a weed in most locations. A vigorous plant with thick, fibrous roots and hairy stems that root at the lower nodes, creeping buttercup can spread several feet in a season. The leaves are hairy and deeply cut, with toothed margins. The bright yellow flowers appear in spring on 1–2-foot-high stems and are followed by greenish seed heads.

Life cycle: Perennial that reproduces by seed and by rooting at the nodes of creeping stems

Management: In lawns, dig up creeping buttercup, roots and all. Or cut off the tops of the plants repeatedly, until the roots stop resprouting. Improve drainage to help prevent the establishment of creeping buttercup, which flourishes in perpetually moist soil. If improving drainage is not possible, consider planting a ground cover that is tolerant of damp soils instead of trying to grow lawn grass. In garden beds, mulch to prevent seeds from germinating. To manage established creeping buttercup in garden beds, remove the top growth and, for one season, cover the roots with plastic or cardboard topped with organic mulch.

If chemical control is necessary, use a product containing MCPP, MCPA, and dicamba for postemergent control in lawns.

Notes: Other buttercups that sometimes occur as weeds in western gardens include tall buttercup and roughseed buttercup. Tall buttercup (R. acris) is a perennial growing as tall as 3 feet, with hairy, deeply lobed, narrow leaves and yellow or cream-colored flowers. Roughseed buttercup (R. muricatus) is an annual or a sometimes short-lived perennial, usually less than a foot tall, with smooth leaves and bright yellow flowers. Management of these buttercups is the same as for creeping buttercup.

CELERY, WILD

CICLOSPERMUM LEPTOPHYLLUM (APIACEAE)

BROAD-LEAFED ANNUAL

ZONES: 7–13

Wild celery can be a troublesome weed in lawns and in vegetable and ornamental gardens. It is found along roadsides and in orchards as well. This annual is also known as marsh parsley and wild parsley, and is sometimes listed as *Apium leptophyllum*. Seeds of wild celery germinate from late fall to early summer; the plants mature, producing new seed, from late spring until late summer. The light green leaves of the seedling plant are long, narrow, and needlelike. As the plant matures, it becomes very branched and grows either prostrate, only a few inches high, or partially erect, with curving branches that can reach 2 feet high. The dark green stems and leaves are smooth. The long-stalked lower leaves are 1½–4 inches long and are divided into small segments. The leaves on the upper part of the plant are smaller, without stalks, and divided into narrow, linear segments. Typical of the carrot family, the flowers of wild celery occur in a flat cluster, or umbel. The individual flowers are white and very small. They are followed by an egg-shaped fruit containing two seeds.

Life cycle: Annual that reproduces by seed

Management: Pull wild celery plants when they are young. The taproot is easier to remove if the soil is damp. To prevent later problems, be sure to get rid of this weed before it sets seed. A mulch around vegetables and ornamentals will prevent seeds already in the soil from germinating.

If chemical control is necessary, you can use a pre-emergence product containing isoxaben around the ornamental plants that are listed on the label. To control wild celery plants, spot-treat with herbicidal soap, or use a product containing glyphosate, taking care not to get this chemical on desired plants.

 Notes: The celery grown as a vegetable, Apium graveolens, *has escaped cultivation and become a weed in some regions, particularly in moist areas. It is an upright plant with smooth, dark green stalks and leaves. In the wild it is smaller, more open, and coarser looking than celery grown in a vegetable garden.*

CHICKWEED

STELLARIA MEDIA (CARYOPHYLLACEAE)

BROAD-LEAFED ANNUAL

ZONES: ALL

Chickweed, also known as common chickweed, starwort, starweed, and satin flower, is a low-growing succulent weed found in lawns and gardens, both vegetable and ornamental. Generally, it grows most vigorously in the cool weather of fall, winter, and spring, then sets seed and dies when hot weather arrives. But it sometimes lives through the summer in cool, shaded gardens. Chickweed has slender stems with many branches and a line of white hairs on one side of each branch. The leaves are smooth and pointed, ¼–1 inch long, bright green on the upper surface and paler on the underside. Starry white flowers appear from midwinter to early spring, borne on slender stalks that rise from the base of the leafstalks.

Life cycle: Annual that reproduces by seed and by creeping stems that root at the nodes

Management: Chickweed is easy to pull when the plants are young. As they develop and spread by rooting at the leaf nodes, pulling is less successful because it is difficult to get out all of the roots. Keeping lawns healthy and growing thickly—through proper fertilization, watering, and mowing—helps prevent the growth of chickweed. In flower and

Mouse-ear chickweed

vegetable gardens, a thick mulch will prevent germination of chickweed seeds. Before planting new gardens or lawns, solarize to kill the seeds.

If chemical control is needed, in fall to late winter use a pre-emergent containing oryzalin or pendimethalin on lawns or around the ornamentals listed on the label. For postemergent control on lawns, use a product containing MCPP, MCPA, and dicamba. Spot-treat chickweed with a product containing herbicidal soap or glyphosate. Be especially careful not to get glyphosate on desired plants.

Notes: Although mouse-ear chickweed looks similar to common chickweed, it is a perennial plant belonging to a different genus, Cerastium vulgatum. *Its small rounded leaves are hairy and look like mouse ears. Manage this plant by pulling or digging out the entire weed before it sets seed. Chemical controls include postemergence herbicides containing MCP or dicamba for outbreaks in lawns or glyphosate among ornamentals.*

CHICORY

CICHORIUM INTYBUS (ASTERACEAE)

BROAD-LEAFED PERENNIAL

 ZONES: ALL

Chicory, also called blue daisy, coffeeweed, or succory, is found along roadsides, in fencerows, ornamental gardens, and vegetable gardens, and sometimes in lawns, especially in alkaline soil. It tolerates dry conditions. Chicory grows from a tough, deep, woody taproot. The basal rosette of 3–8-inch-long leaves resembles that of dandelion, but chicory's leaves are rougher and hairy. From the rosette grow 1–3-foot branched stems, with smaller, clasping leaves. The leaves, stems, and roots of chicory contain a bitter-tasting, milky juice. The flower heads are borne in the axils of the upper leaves. Chicory flowers, which appear in midsummer, are daisy-like, up to 1½ inches wide, and usually a pretty sky blue but occasionally purple or white. The flowers close in the afternoon.

Life cycle: Perennial that reproduces by seed and pieces of the taproot

Management: Pull or cut young chicory plants as soon as you see them. Older plants are more difficult to remove. Dig up the plant, getting as much of the taproot as possible. It may sprout again, but after you pull or cut it several times, chicory usually does not regrow. In any case, be sure to remove the plants before they set seed. If there are many chicory plants growing in your garden, cut them back to the ground and cover the area with a thick mulch, such as black plastic or cardboard topped with an organic mulch. Leave the mulch in place for a full growing season.

If chemical control is needed, use a product containing dicamba, MCPP, or triclopyr. Take care not to get any of these products on desired broad-leafed plants.

 Notes: Chicory is a weed with a useful side. Its thick roots have traditionally been dried, roasted, and ground to serve as a pleasantly bitter-tasting coffee substitute. The young leaves, which also taste somewhat bitter, can be added to spring salads or cooked as a vegetable. From the wild form of chicory, gardeners have selected and cultivated the plant now known as radicchio. Endive, curly endive, and escarole are closely related vegetables.

CLOVER, WHITE

TRIFOLIUM REPENS (FABACEAE)

BROAD-LEAFED PERENNIAL

 ZONES: ALL

White clover, also known as white Dutch clover, is a weed in vegetable and ornamental gardens. Common in lawns, it is considered by some to be a weed there, because it detracts from the overall smoothness of a grass lawn and it attracts bees. Others feel it contributes to a good lawn because, like other legumes, it can capture nitrogen from the air and add it to the soil, providing for its own nitrogen needs and contributing significantly to the needs of the lawn grasses. In addition, white clover is more drought tolerant than most grasses.

White clover has branching stems that grow close to the ground, rooting at the joints. Under open conditions, white clover may grow up to 12 inches tall, but it remains much shorter in mowed lawns. The leaves are compound, divided into the three leaflets characteristic of clovers. Each leaflet of white clover is marked by a white crescent. The round flowering head is made up of a cluster of small white flowers, which may turn pink and droop as they age.

Life cycle: Perennial that reproduces by seed and by rooting at the nodes of creeping stems

Management: To reduce infestations of white clover in lawns, follow good lawn management practices, including providing sufficient nitrogen fertilizer and water to help the lawn grasses compete with the clover. Mowing the grass at its tallest recommended height helps shade out white clover. In vegetable and ornamental beds, cultivate to remove young plants. Pull or dig older plants before they set seed. A mulch not only helps prevent germination of white clover seeds, but also loosens the soil, so that it is easier to pull weeds. If you want white clover in your lawn, install a barrier or curb to prevent it from spreading into nearby ornamental beds.

Chemical control of white clover is often only partially effective. Treat clover growing in lawns with a product containing dicamba. In other areas, spot-treat clover with a product containing glyphosate. Take care not to get this herbicide on desired plants.

 Notes: Several annual clovers, including hop clover (Trifolium dubium) and subterranean clover (T. subterranean), are weeds that may appear in fall, winter, and early spring. Pull or hoe these clovers before they set seed.

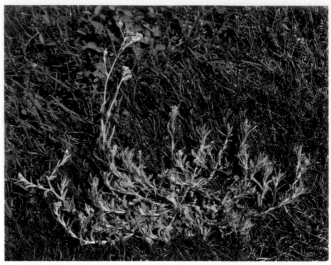

CRABGRASS

DIGITARIA, VARIOUS SPECIES *(POACEAE)*

ANNUAL GRASSES

✎ ZONES: ALL

Probably the most infamous of annual summer weeds, crabgrass infests lawns, vegetable and ornamental gardens, orchards, and vineyards. This weed, also referred to as large crabgrass and hairy crabgrass, thrives in hot, damp areas. Seeds germinate in early spring, as soon as the first few inches of the soil remain at 50–55°F for three to seven days. The young plant's first true leaf is flat, pale green, and covered with coarse hairs. A membranous sheath is on the inside of the leaf blade. Tufts of hair at the junction of the stem and leaf blade distinguish this crabgrass from other annual grasses. As crabgrass grows, it branches from the base; joints often root where the stems touch the soil. The inflorescence (flowering part), which appears in mid- to late summer, is made up of 3 to 11 slender branches that arise near the tip of the stem. A single plant is capable of producing more than 8,000 seeds. Smooth crabgrass *(Digitaria ischaemum)*, shown above, is quite similar to large crabgrass, but it is smaller overall and not hairy.

Life cycle: Annuals that reproduce by seed and by roots growing from swollen joints in the stems

Management: Pull crabgrass from vegetable gardens and flower beds before it sets seed. In lawns, crabgrass is especially vigorous if the soil is compacted or low in fertility, or if the lawn is overwatered or sparse. Help the turf grow more thickly by proper fertilization and aeration. As crabgrass has shallower roots than lawn grasses, you can dry out the crabgrass roots by watering the lawn deeply but not frequently. Solarization will partially control crabgrass.

For chemical control in lawns and on ornamentals listed on the label, use pre-emergence herbicides such as dithiopyr, pendimethalin, or trifluralin. Apply in late winter to early spring, depending on when crabgrass germinates in your zone. (Check with local nursery personnel or your cooperative extension agent to obtain this information.) For postemergence control in ornamentals, use a product containing fluazifop or sethoxydim. For postemergence control in lawns, use a product containing methanearsonic acid. Nonselective herbicides containing glufosinate-ammonium or glyphosate also kill crabgrass. Take care not to get these products on desired plants.

CUDWEED

GNAPHALIUM, VARIOUS SPECIES *(ASTERACEAE)*

BROAD-LEAFED ANNUALS OR BIENNIALS

✎ ZONES: ALL

Several species of cudweed, most native to the United States, crop up as weeds in lawns and garden beds, especially in poor soils lacking organic matter. Some cudweeds are aromatic, with a pungent or sweet scent. The white, woolly stems are useful dried as everlastings. Cotton batting plant *(Gnaphalium chilense, G. stramineum)*, like other cudweeds, looks white, silky, and hairy. If unmowed, it can grow from 6 inches to 2½ feet tall, with long, narrow leaves and clusters of small, inconspicuous greenish yellow flower heads at the ends of the stems. Sparsely branched purple cudweed *(G. purpureum)* grows 4–24 inches high. When young, its leaves are covered with a dense coating of white woolly hairs, but the leaves become greener and smoother as they age. Brownish or purple flower heads appear on the stem or at the base of

Cudweed seedling

the leafstalks. A third species, lowland cudweed *(G. palustre)*, is a low-growing plant, to 12 inches high, with a dense, spreading growth habit. It has dense tufts of woolly hair along the stems and in the leaf axils. The flower heads are small, borne at the ends of branches and in the leaf axils.

Life cycle: Annuals or biennials that reproduce by seed

Management: Spotting these white, woolly plants among lawn grasses and other plants is easy, so it is not difficult to find them and pull them up before they set seed. In vegetable and ornamental beds, a thick mulch will help prevent existing seeds from growing. Improving the soil by adding compost will deter growth of this weed. Fertilize lawns to thicken the turf grass, making it less hospitable to weeds.

If chemical control is necessary, spot-treat cudweed in lawns with a selective postemergence herbicide containing dicamba or MCPP.

CUPGRASS, SOUTHWESTERN

ERIOCHLOA GRACILIS (POACEAE)

ANNUAL GRASS

 ZONES: 8, 9, 12, 13, 18–24

Southwestern cupgrass, also called summergrass or wiregrass, is native to southern Arizona and is also found in much of California in gardens, orchards, and vineyards. The seeds of this summer annual grass germinate throughout spring. The plant matures from June through August. Southwestern cupgrass has hairless stems, but the sheath (the lower part of the leaf that surrounds the stem) has short hairs. The leaf blades of this grass are flat and smooth, about ½ inch wide and 2–5 inches long. When mature, southwestern cupgrass is 1–4 feet tall. The bright green stems have two to five conspicuous nodes or joints, where rooting sometimes occurs. The flowering portion of this grass is hairy, 2–6 inches long, and sparsely branched. Greenish or purple flower groups (spikelets) are arranged in two rows on one side of the branch. A dark, cuplike ring at the base of each spikelet gives the grass its common name, cupgrass. Abundant seed is produced and shed by late summer.

Life cycle: Annual that reproduces by seed and occasionally by rooting at stem nodes

Management: As with other annual weeds, it is important to prevent future problems by removing southwestern cupgrass before it produces seed. Hoe or pull plants in spring and early summer. Mulching around vegetables and ornamentals will prevent seeds already in the soil from germinating.

If chemical management is necessary, use a pre-emergence herbicide containing trifluralin, pendimethalin, or oryzalin around the ornamentals listed on the label. To control young southwestern cupgrass plants, use an herbicidal soap. A product containing glyphosate will kill the weed, but take care not to get this nonselective herbicide on desired plants.

Notes: In the seedling stage, southwestern cupgrass resembles barnyard grass. However, southwestern cupgrass has a fringe of hair at the base of the leaf blade that is absent in barnyard grass. The stems and leaf sheath of barnyard grass are flattened and purplish, while those of southwestern cupgrass are bright green and rounded.

DALLIS GRASS

PASPALUM DILATATUM (POACEAE)

PERENNIAL GRASS

ZONES: ALL

Dallis grass grows in low, wet areas, flourishing in warm, sunny weather, but will tolerate drought once established. Though found in vegetable and ornamental beds, orchards, and vineyards, dallis grass is especially troublesome in lawns. Its coarse, flat stalks are noticeable among finer-textured lawn grasses, and it regrows quickly after mowing. A clumping grass, dallis grass grows from a hard, knotty base. It reproduces by seed, which germinates in spring, and by rhizomes. Its dark green foliage is similar to other grasses, which makes the seedling plant difficult to identify. However, as the plant matures, a firm, membranous ligule (projection) shows up at the base of the leaf where it joins the stem. The leaf blades have only a few hairs at the base of the upper surface. If unmowed, dallis grass can grow almost 5 feet high. The branched flowering heads are 6–16 inches long. Dallis grass seed matures in fall.

Dallis grass flowering head

Life cycle: Perennial that reproduces by seed and rhizomes

Management: In lawns, hand-weeding is effective, especially if done before the grass has produced seed. Dig out as much of the rhizome as possible. As this will leave a fairly large open space susceptible to further weed infestations, it is a good idea to cultivate the area, add compost, and sow lawn seed. Keep the area watered until the seeds germinate and are growing well. If dallis grass is a persistent problem in your lawn, you probably should take steps to improve the drainage. In garden beds, cultivate to remove dallis grass seedlings. Dig out larger plants before they set seed. Mulch to prevent seeds already in the soil from germinating.

If chemical control is necessary, apply a product containing trifluralin or dithiopyr as a pre-emergence herbicide in the kinds of lawns and among the ornamentals listed on the labels. To treat dallis grass during the growing season, choose a product containing methanearsonic acid; several treatments may be necessary. A product containing glyphosate can be used to spot-treat clumps of dallis grass in gardens; take care not to get this herbicide on desired plants.

DANDELION

TARAXACUM OFFICINALE (ASTERACEAE)

BROAD-LEAFED PERENNIAL

ZONES: ALL

One of the most familiar weeds of lawns and gardens throughout the West, dandelion is especially troublesome in the Northwest and mountain states. The newly sprouted light green seed leaves (cotyledons) of dandelion unite at the base, forming a shallow cup. As the plant matures, a deep taproot forms. The leaves arise from the taproot, forming a rosette; shallow to deep lobes etch the edges of the leaves, which end in sharp points. Both leaves and flower stems exude a milky, bitter-tasting juice when torn. Bright yellow flowers appear from spring until frost, followed by circular balls of seeds that are dispersed by wind.

Life cycle: Perennial that reproduces by seed and by sprouting root crowns and pieces of taproot

Management: In lawns, the presence of dandelions indicates that the turf is thin and undernourished. To discourage dandelions, thicken the lawn grasses by overseeding, proper fertilization, watering, and mowing. Pull dandelions from lawns and gardens when they are young, before they produce a taproot and before they set seed. Once the taproot has formed, you must remove all of it when attempting to get rid of dandelions; new plants can sprout from even a small piece. A special dandelion weeder with a forked blade and a short or long handle (also known as an asparagus knife or a fishtail weeder) is effective at popping the taproot out of moist soil (also useful with other taprooted weeds, such as curly dock). Using this kind of weeder minimizes soil disturbance, leaving less ground open for further weed colonization. In gardens, maintaining a year-round mulch helps prevent dandelion seeds from germinating.

For chemical control in lawns, use a selective postemergence herbicide containing MCPA, MCPP, or dicamba in spring or fall. Spot-treating with a product containing glyphosate will partially control dandelions in gardens. Take care not to get this chemical on desired plants.

 Notes: Young dandelion leaves are edible, imparting a refreshingly bitter flavor to spring salads; they are also tasty as cooked greens. Cultivated forms have been selected for larger, thicker leaves to be used at the table. Seed is available in packets from vegetable seed companies.

DICHONDRA

DICHONDRA MICRANTHA; ALSO CALLED *D. CAROLINENSIS*, OR *D. REPENS* (CONVOLVULACEAE)

BROAD-LEAFED PERENNIAL

ZONES: 8–10, 12–24

In areas with warm winters, dichondra is sometimes planted as a substitute for grass lawns, although it is subject to damage by flea beetles. Dichondra is better used as a small-scale ground cover, especially between stepping-stones in a walk or terrace. Dichondra spreads by slender stems that creep along the ground, rooting freely at nodes and forming a dense mat of foliage. Because it spreads by both runners and seed, however, dichondra can invade nearby flower and shrub beds, as well as other ground covers, especially in rich moist soil. Dichondra can also become a pest in grass lawns. Dichondra has smooth kidney-shaped leaves, $1/4 - 1/2$ inch wide. In sun the leaf stems remain short, but in shade they may grow 6 inches tall. The flowers are small and inconspicuous, growing in the leaf axils (the juncture of leaf and stem).

Life cycle: Perennial that reproduces by rooting surface runners and by seed

Management: To prevent dichondra planted as a ground cover from creeping into nearby ornamental or shrub borders or into other ground covers, install a barrier, such as a brick or wooden edging. Landscape fabrics—special materials that are permeable to air and water but that restrict weed growth—can help prevent dichondra and other weeds from establishing themselves in ornamental beds. Cover the fabric with an organic mulch, such as bark chips, shredded bark, or compost, to improve its appearance and make it last longer. You can pull out unwanted mats of dichondra by hand or rake out the shallow-rooted runners. Some resprouting may occur from runners you have missed or from seeds buried in the soil.

For chemical control of dichondra that has become a weed in a grass lawn, spray with a selective postemergence herbicide containing MCPA, MCPP, and dicamba. Products containing glyphosate are sometimes effective at controlling dichondra in gardens; take care not to get these herbicides on desired plants.

DOCK, CURLY

RUMEX CRISPUS (POLYGONACEAE)

BROAD-LEAFED PERENNIAL

ZONES: ALL

Curly dock, also known as sour dock, yellow dock, and narrowleaf dock, is a tenacious weed that grows from a thick, fleshy taproot. It is found in lawns, vegetable and ornamental beds, orchards, and vineyards. The weed grows 2–5 feet tall in the open garden, but remains a low rosette of leaves in frequently mowed lawns. The seeds of curly dock germinate from early spring into summer. Leaves of the seedlings are often reddish with darker brown or reddish spots on the upper surface. As the plant grows, it produces lance-shaped, curly-edged, bluish green leaves, 3 inches to 1 foot long. Erect stems grow from the base; they are slightly ridged and usually reddish. The small, green-tinged flowers form dense clusters at the top of the stems from May until frost. The seeds are enclosed in brown, papery, smooth-edged, winglike structures, which are spread by wind or water. A curly dock plant can produce as many as 40,000 seeds; once buried, these remain viable for up to 80 years.

Life cycle: Perennial that reproduces by seed and by regrowth of pieces of taproot and crown

Management: In lawns and gardens, dig out young plants, removing as much of the root as possible. You can kill large plants by cutting the top growth every week or two until the roots die and they stop resprouting. Be sure to get rid of curly dock before it sets seed. In garden beds, mulch to prevent germination of seeds already in the soil.

For chemical control in lawns, use a postemergence product containing MCPP, MCPA, and dicamba. For nonselective control, use a product containing glyphosate, taking care not to get it on desired plants. Repeated treatments may be necessary.

 Notes: Broadleaf or bitter dock (Rumex obtusifolius) *is a weed in moist areas of the West. Although similar to curly dock, it has broad, flat, heart-shaped leaves and small spines on the winglike structures of the seed. Management is similar to that for curly dock.*

DODDER

CUSCUTA, VARIOUS SPECIES (CUSCUTACEAE OR CONVOLVULACEAE)

ANNUAL PARASITE

ZONES: ALL

Startling when first encountered in the garden or in the wild, dodder is a leafless parasitic plant that lacks chlorophyll. Its yellow to bright orange stems twine over host plants, creating a mass of smothering growth. Several species of dodder occur in the West, some infesting vegetable crops, alfalfa, and hay, others parasitic on shrubs. Dodder, a flowering plant, produces seeds that germinate from late winter through summer. The small seedling has a threadlike stem, which swings about slowly and twines upon any support it encounters. If the support is not a suitable host, the seedling dies. If it is a suitable host, dodder produces wartlike suckers that penetrate the stem of the host, drawing in nourishment. The lower part of the seedling withers and dies, losing contact with the soil, and the dodder plant becomes entirely parasitic, weakening or killing the host plant. Dodder grows rapidly, producing branches that soon attach to neighboring plants. Clusters of cream-colored flowers appear from July to October.

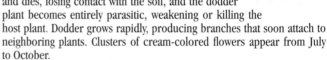
Dodder flowers

Life cycle: Parasitic annual that reproduces by seed

Management: There is no reliable way to remove dodder from infested branches, as even the smallest piece left behind will grow again. Therefore, cut away the entire branch, dodder and all, and burn it or place it in the trash; do not compost dodder. Sometimes the only way to get rid of dodder is to remove the entire host plant. It is important to remove dodder before it sets seed. The seeds are fairly long-lived in the soil: some may sprout several years after removal of plants that have gone to seed. A thick mulch will prevent most dodder seeds from germinating.

There are currently no chemicals for managing dodder registered for homeowner use.

ENGLISH DAISY

BELLIS PERENNIS (ASTERACEAE)

BROAD-LEAFED PERENNIAL

✷ ZONES: ALL

Aplant that is sometimes grown as an ornamental in flower borders, English daisy has escaped cultivation and turns up unbidden in lawns and ornamental gardens, and in spaces in sidewalks and between pavers. Some gardeners welcome the little white flowers of English daisy in their lawns and meadows, while others regard it as a pest. English daisy prefers moist soil and cool weather; in hot climates it dies back with the arrival of summer, leaving brown patches in lawns that persist until the cool weather of fall brings regrowth. The seeds of English daisy germinate in spring, producing light green, rounded seed leaves (cotyledons) about ¼ inch long, with very short stalks. The mature leaves are 1–2 inches long, dark green, and spoon shaped; the edge of the leaf may be smooth or scalloped. The plant grows as a low rosette with fibrous roots. The flower stalks rise above the leaves, up to 8 inches tall, each bearing one white or pinkish daisylike flower, about an inch wide. Flowers are most abundant in late spring and in fall.

Life cycle: Perennial that reproduces by seed

Management: Pull or dig English daisy plants from lawns. This is easiest if the plants are young and the soil is moist. Mow the flower heads of English daisies frequently to prevent their forming seed. English daisy is more likely to be a problem in turf that is thin and stressed due to lack of nutrients. Fertilize, as recommended for your type of lawn, to thicken the turf and crowd out weeds. In garden beds, dig up English daisies before they set seed, as they can reproduce abundantly.

This weed is difficult to manage with chemicals, but you can use a selective postemergence herbicide containing dicamba. Repeat treatments are usually necessary.

 Notes: Selected, ornamental forms of English daisies are sold in containers at nurseries and in seed packets. These have fully double flowers of pink, rose, red, or white.

FESCUE, TALL

FESTUCA ARUNDINACEA (POACEAE)

PERENNIAL GRASS

✷ ZONES: ALL

Tall fescue is a clump-forming grass that was once added to lawn seed mixtures as a nurse crop because it is fast growing. However, since it is coarser looking than other kinds of turf grass, it is mostly considered a weed in lawns. Tall fescue can also invade other areas of the garden, becoming a weed in vegetable and flower beds. When mowed, tall fescue grows as a flat, spreading clump, with stiff leaf blades up to ⅓ inch wide that form a 90-degree angle with the stems. The leaves, which may be flat or rolled, have prominent ridges on the upper side and tiny stiff hairs along the margins. When tall fescue is growing in lawns, the flower stalks lie flat. If unmowed, tall fescue produces leaves 10–28 inches long and seed stalks up to 4 feet tall. The inflorescence is branching, with a purple tinge. Meadow fescue *(Festuca elatior)* is a similar clumping grass that has also been included in lawn seed mixes.

Life cycle: Perennial grass that reproduces by seed

Management: Remove clumps of tall fescue from lawns by cutting under the root crown with a sharp shovel. This grass does not spread by runners, so digging out the clumps usually gets rid of it. If the digging leaves large empty spots, incorporate compost into the soil; plant grass seed, or lay sod. In gardens, dig out tall fescue, removing the plants before they set seed, to prevent later problems. A thick mulch will prevent any seeds already in the soil from germinating.

If chemical control is necessary, use a product containing sethoxydim—a selective herbicide that controls grasses—around the broad-leafed ornamentals listed on the label. Or use a nonselective herbicide containing glyphosate, taking care not to get the chemical on desired plants.

 Notes: Forms of tall fescue chosen for their finer leaves are planted as lawns, especially for athletic fields and play areas. Tall fescue is also grown as an animal-forage crop.

FIDDLENECK, COAST

AMSINCKIA MENZIESII INTERMEDIA (BORAGINACEAE)

BROAD-LEAFED ANNUAL

✎ ZONES: ALL

Coast fiddleneck, also known as rancher's fireweed, fingerweed, yellow forget-me-not, and yellow tarweed, is an annual weed that grows during the cool seasons and flowers in late spring. Native to many areas of the West, this weed may appear in vegetable and ornamental gardens, as well as in orchards and vineyards. Coast fiddleneck has an upright growth pattern, with hairy stems that are usually 1–2½ feet tall, although they can reach 3½ feet in good soil with plenty of moisture. Both stems and leaves are rough and bristly. The leaves are lance shaped, 1–4 inches long, alternating on the stems. Bright orange-yellow flowers, about ½ inch long, are arranged on one side of the flower stalk, which is coiled at the tip like the neck of a fiddle, giving the plant its common name. The leaves and seeds of coast fiddleneck are toxic to livestock.

*Coast fiddleneck
flower head*

Life cycle: Annual that reproduces by seed

Management: Coast fiddleneck is fairly easy to pull, especially when the plants are young. However, the sharp, bristly plant hairs are irritating, so be sure to wear gloves. To prevent future infestations, destroy the weeds before they set seed. A thick mulch of straw, sawdust, or other organic material will help prevent the germination of seeds already in the soil. Solarize before planting to destroy seeds of coast fiddleneck.

If a large infestation makes chemical management necessary, use a pre-emergence herbicide containing pendimethalin on turf and around labeled ornamentals. For postemergent control, use a product containing glyphosate, taking care not to get this herbicide on desired plants.

✎ *Notes: Several other western native plants are closely related to coast fiddleneck; all have the characteristic flower stalk with a curled top. Douglas fiddleneck (Amsinckia douglasiana) is about the same size as coast fiddleneck, but it has spoon-shaped leaves and slightly larger flowers. Tarweed fiddleneck (A. lycopsoides) is common in open, disturbed soil; the petals of its individual flowers are arranged somewhat differently. Management of these is the same as for coast fiddleneck.*

FILAREE, REDSTEM

ERODIUM CICUTARIUM (GERANIACEAE)

BROAD-LEAFED ANNUAL OR BIENNIAL

✎ ZONES: ALL

Related to geraniums and cultivated cranesbills, redstem filaree—also called storksbill—is found in gardens, orchards, vineyards, and pastures in many areas of the West. This weed may grow as a rosette, flat to the ground, or it may take a more upright form, to 2 feet high, when growing among other plants. The leaves are distinctive, divided into narrow, feathery, toothed segments. Both the leaves and the stems are hairy. Umbrella-like clusters of small purplish pink flowers are carried on long leafless stems. The flowers are followed by long, needlelike seedpods. At maturity, the pods separate into five parts, each containing one seed. The seeds are unique. Each seed has a tightly twisted, hairy tail, 1¾ inches long. When wet, the tail uncurls and can drive the seed into the soil. The seeds germinate in winter or early spring, and the plant matures in early summer.

Life cycle: Annual or biennial that reproduces by seed

Management: Hoe or pull young plants of redstem filaree. Dig or pull larger plants before they set seed, to prevent future infestations. Mulch around garden plantings to prevent seeds that are already in the soil from germinating. Redstem filaree can also be controlled by soil solarization.

If chemical control is needed, use a pre-emergence herbicide containing oryzalin, pendimethalin, or isoxaben around the plants listed on the product label. Spot-treat redstem filaree in lawns with a product containing MCPA, MCPP, and dicamba. Spot-treat redstem filaree plants in gardens or paths with herbicidal soap. Or you can use a product containing glyphosate, but take care not to get this chemical on desired plants.

✎ *Notes: Two other weedy filarees may appear in western gardens. The leaves of broadleaf filaree (Erodium botrys) are deeply lobed, but not finely divided like redstem filaree. The tail on the seed is longer, up to 5 inches. Whitestem filaree (E. moschatum) is usually larger than redstem or broadleaf filaree, with fleshy whitish to light green stems; the tail on its seed is about ½ inch long.*

FOUNTAIN GRASS, CRIMSON

PENNISETUM SETACEUM (POACEAE)

PERENNIAL GRASS

ZONES: 8–24

Widely grown as an attractive ornamental, crimson fountain grass has escaped from cultivation, especially in Southern California and parts of Arizona. It self-seeds freely and threatens to crowd out native plants; it can also become a pest in ornamental gardens. Seeds of crimson fountain grass germinate in spring. The leaves of the seedlings are light green and rather stiff. The grass grows quickly, sending up many stems to form a dense, rounded clump up to 4 feet tall. The leaf blades, $1/8$–$1/4$ inch wide, feel rough to the touch. The showy purplish pink flowers emerge in late spring or early summer, borne on 3–4-foot stems, held just above the foliage clump. This grass dies back in winter, even in mild climates.

Life cycle: Perennial that reproduces by seed

Management: Gardeners living near wild areas should avoid planting crimson fountain grass, as eradicating the plant is very difficult once it invades a population of native plants. To prevent its spread within a garden, cut the plumes before the seeds mature. Dig out seedlings and larger plants before they flower. A thick mulch will help prevent germination of seeds already in the soil.

For chemical control, cut back the grass to the ground. When new growth has reached about 4 inches, treat with glyphosate, taking care not to get the herbicide on nearby desirable plants.

 Notes: A selected cultivar of crimson fountain grass, known as purple-leaved fountain grass (Pennisetum setaceum 'Rubrum', P. s. 'Cupreum'), *does not set viable seed and therefore is not a pest in the garden or in wild areas. However, another relative, feathertop* (P. villosum)—*also known as white-flowering fountain grass—has naturalized widely in areas with mild winters. This fountain grass grows 1–2 feet tall, with bright blue-green leaves and bristly foxtail-like flowers. The flowers are greenish white when they emerge in mid- to late summer, maturing to creamy white. As with crimson fountain grass, feathertop should not be planted near stands of native vegetation.*

FOXTAILS, ANNUAL

SETARIA, VARIOUS SPECIES (POACEAE)

ANNUAL GRASSES

ZONES: ALL

Foxtails are annual grasses that grow in lawns, vegetable and ornamental gardens, orchards, and vineyards. Seeds of both yellow foxtail *(Setaria pumila,* also called *S. glauca)* and green foxtail *(S. viridis),* shown above, germinate from early spring into summer. The seedlings are difficult to differentiate from other annual grasses. As they mature, plants of yellow foxtail grow 1–3 feet tall, with upright stems. The leaf blades are smooth, $1/8$–$3/8$ inch wide, with a spiral twist. Distinct long hairs grow at the base of the leaf. The seed heads are dense, bushy spikes, 1–5 inches long, with yellowish to reddish brown bristles and relatively large seeds. Green foxtail grows 6–32 inches tall. Its angled stalks bend downward at the lower joint. The leaf blades lack the hairs at the base that are characteristic of yellow foxtail. Green foxtail, shown above, also has a smaller seed head, with pale yellow to purplish bristles and smaller seeds than does yellow foxtail; both plants flower and set seed from July to September.

Life cycle: Annuals that reproduce by seed

Management: Dig or pull foxtail plants before they set seed, removing the entire plant, roots and all. If parts of the crown remain in the ground, they will reroot, and you will need to weed again. Improving the quality of turf through regular fertilization and adequate irrigation discourages annual foxtails. In garden beds, a thick mulch prevents foxtail seeds from germinating. Solarize beds before planting to kill seeds.

If chemical control is needed, in late winter to early spring apply a pre-emergence herbicide containing dithiopyr, pendimethalin, or oryzalin to lawns or around ornamentals listed on the label; a pre-emergent containing trifluralin is also suitable for control around many ornamentals. For spot control in lawns, except those planted in St. Augustine grass, centipede grass, or carpetgrass, use methanearsonic acid. In ornamental beds, spot-treat foxtails with a selective postemergence herbicide containing sethoxydim or with a nonselective product containing herbicidal soap, glufosinate-ammonium, or glyphosate, taking care not to get these chemicals on desired plants.

GOOSEFOOT, NETTLELEAF

CHENOPODIUM MURALE (CHENOPODIACEAE)

BROAD-LEAFED ANNUAL

✂ ZONES: ALL

Nettleleaf goosefoot, a native of Europe that is also known as sowbane and swinebane, is now common in gardens, orchards, and vineyards, and along roadsides in the West. Growing 1–3 feet high, this weed is coarse and bushy. The 1–2-inch-long leaves are dark green and somewhat fleshy, with a mealy texture. The pointed, irregular teeth around the edges of the leaves form the outline of a goose's foot. The small, greenish flowers are borne in spikes at the tips of the branches or between the branches and the main stem. Seeds germinate in late winter, and the plants flower in fall. Nettleleaf goosefoot is a host for the beet leafhopper, an insect that transmits curly top virus; the virus attacks many vegetable crops, including beets, beans, tomatoes, squash, and melons.

Life cycle: Annual that reproduces by seed

Management: Like most other annual weeds, nettleleaf goosefoot is easy to hoe or pull when the plants are young. Be sure to remove them from the garden before they set seed. A mulch around vegetables, ornamentals, and trees will prevent germination of seeds already in the soil. Solarize newly prepared planting beds to kill seeds of this weed.

If chemical control is necessary, use a pre-emergence herbicide containing oryzalin or trifluralin to prevent seeds from germinating. Spot-treat growing plants with herbicidal soap or a product containing glufosinate-ammonium, taking care not to contact desirable plants.

✎ *Notes: Other goosefoots may appear in western gardens. Jerusalem-oak goosefoot* (Chenopodium botrys) *is a fragrant annual weed that grows 8–24 inches tall with many upright branches. The entire plant is covered with small glandlike protuberances and short hairs. The flowers are borne in clusters on long terminal stems. Tasmanian goosefoot* (C. pumilo), *also an annual, is a dark green branching plant that grows close to the ground. It has the hairs and glandlike protuberances of Jerusalem-oak goosefoot, but Tasmanian goosefoot's inconspicuous flowers appear at the base of the leafstalks.*

GOOSEGRASS

ELEUSINE INDICA (POACEAE)

ANNUAL GRASS

✂ ZONES: 4–24

Also known as silver crabgrass, wiregrass, and crowfoot, goosegrass is a tough summer annual, most often found in sparse lawns and in paths where the soil is compacted. Seedlings emerge in spring when the soil has warmed, several weeks later than crabgrass. Seedlings are light green, with a thin, papery appendage (ligule) at the base of the leaf blades. The mature plant can grow to 3 feet in height, but it stays much lower in mowed lawns. The leaf blades are flat or folded, 1/8–1/3 inch wide, with soft, whitish hairs that extend to the sheath. The flattened stems are pale green or silver at the base; the blades are darker green. Unlike crabgrass, goosegrass does not root at the stems but instead grows in tufts. The inflorescence, like that of crabgrass, forms a whorl of fingerlike spikes at the tip of the stem. Sometimes one or two spikes appear just below the tip of the stem. Goosegrass can flower and set seed even when closely mowed.

Life cycle: Annual that reproduces by seed

Management: Pull or dig goosegrass before it sets seed. In lawns, improving the growing conditions to favor lawn grasses will discourage goosegrass. Aerating the soil to reduce compaction is especially important. Overseed after aerating the lawn. If a part of the lawn is subject to heavy traffic and continual compaction that leads to weediness, consider replacing the lawn with a path. In garden beds or in preparation for a new lawn, solarize to kill goosegrass seeds.

If chemical control is necessary for management in lawns, apply a pre-emergence herbicide containing dithiopyr or pendimethalin in early spring. A pre-emergent containing oryzalin can be used in warm-season lawns as well as around ornamentals listed on the label. A selective post-emergence herbicide containing fluazifop controls goosegrass; it is most effective if applied when the weed is under 8 inches tall. Nonselective products containing herbicidal soap, glufosinate-ammonium, or glyphosate can be used to spot-treat goosegrass. Take care not to get these chemicals on desired plants.

GROUND CHERRY

PHYSALIS, VARIOUS SPECIES *(SOLANACEAE)*

BROAD-LEAFED ANNUALS AND PERENNIALS

✔ ZONES: ALL

Relatives of tomatoes and potatoes, ground cherries appear in vegetable and ornamental gardens, orchards, and vineyards. Several weedy species similar in overall habit and in fruit are found in the West. Wright ground cherry *(Physalis acutifolia)*, shown above, has a bushy habit of growth, reaching 5 feet in good soil. Its leaves are variable, ranging from 1½–5 inches long and ⅓–2½ inches wide, with lobed or wavy edges. This ground cherry has whitish flowers, which develop into the typical fruit, a round berry about ½ inch in diameter, enclosed by a papery husk with dark purple veins. Lanceleaf ground cherry *(P. lancifolia)* grows to a height of 2–2½ feet, forming an upright, branching plant. The toothed leaves are smaller than those of Wright ground cherry; the flowers are yellow. A perennial, Virginia ground cherry *(P. virginiana)*, grows 1–2½ feet tall, with branching stems. Its leaves are oval, 2–3 inches long, with wavy edges, and its flowers are yellow. Unlike the annual ground cherries, this plant produces stout, wide-spreading roots.

Life cycle: Annuals that reproduce by seed and perennials that reproduce by seed and rootstocks

Management: Ground cherries produce many seeds, so it is important to remove them from the garden before the fruits mature. Pull or dig out the entire plant; dig out as much of the roots of perennial ground cherry as possible. A mulch around vegetables and ornamentals helps prevent germination of seeds already in the ground.

These weeds are difficult to manage with chemicals. A postemergence herbicide containing dicamba is effective on some species of ground cherry. Products containing glyphosate, a nonselective herbicide, can be used; take care not to contact desired plants.

✎ *Notes: Related plants frequently grown in gardens include Chinese lantern plant (P. alkekengi), a spreading perennial that is often grown as an annual, and edible ground cherry (P. peruviana), a plant that produces sweet, seedy yellow fruits. Tomatillo (P. ixocarpa) is grown for its fruits, which are picked when green and tart and are used in Mexican cooking. Tomatillo has escaped cultivation and become weedy in many areas of the West.*

GROUND IVY

GLECHOMA HEDERACEA (NEPETA HEDERACEA) (LAMIACEAE)

BROAD-LEAFED PERENNIAL

✔ ZONES: ALL

Ground ivy can be an effective ground cover in shady, moist locations, but it can also spread quickly and widely beyond its allotted area. Also known as gill-over-the-ground, creeping Charlie, and runaway robin, ground ivy can become a pest in lawns, garden areas, and orchards. A trailing plant with the squarish stems and characteristic odor of the mint family, ground ivy forms dense patches of greenery. Its 1½-inch-wide leaves, in opposite pairs, are bright green, slightly hairy, and scalloped around the margins. In spring and summer, small trumpet-shaped blue flowers appear in the leaf axils (where the leaves join the stem). The plant grows only 3 inches tall, but the trailing stems or stolons reach 1½ feet or more, rooting at the nodes as they grow. Broken pieces of the stem also root, forming new plants.

Ground ivy in bloom

Life cycle: Perennial that reproduces by seed and by stolons

Management: If you want to grow ground ivy as a ground cover, you will need to contain its spread with an edging of bricks, wood, or other barrier. If ground ivy has invaded a lawn, pull or dig it out as soon as possible; raking helps remove the stems, which have shallow roots. You usually need to weed out ground ivy several times over the course of one or two growing seasons, as bits of stolons left behind will resprout. Fertilize the lawn to help it compete with this weed, and take care not to overwater. In gardens, pull or rake ground ivy, repeating as necessary. Once the top growth is removed, landscape fabric, covered with a mulch, will prevent its return.

If chemical control is necessary to remove a stubborn patch of ground ivy in lawns, use an herbicide containing MCPP, MCPA, and dicamba, following directions on the label. Spot-treat ground ivy in ornamental beds with a product containing glyphosate, taking care not to get this nonselective herbicide on desired plants.

GROUNDSEL, COMMON

SENECIO VULGARIS (ASTERACEAE)

BROAD-LEAFED ANNUAL

ZONES: ALL

Common groundsel—also known as grimsel, bird-seed, and (like several other weeds) ragwort—is an annual native to Eurasia. It appears at the edges of lawns, among shrubs and perennials in ornamental gardens, and in vegetable gardens, orchards, and vineyards. Seedlings of common groundsel are tiny rosettes of sharply notched, dull green, red-tinged leaves. The mature plant varies in height from 4–24 inches, usually with branching stems that are ridged and succulent; under crowded conditions the plant may form a single stem, rather than branching. The lower leaves are purplish on the underside, 1–4 inches long and ½–1½ inches wide, with jagged margins. Upper leaves are smaller and clasp the stem. Many small, yellow, cylindrical flower heads cluster together, surrounded by black-tipped bracts at the base. The flower heads mature into puffball seed heads, which separate, allowing the wind to disperse the seeds. Seeds are able to germinate as soon as they ripen; thus common groundsel can produce several generations in a single year.

Life cycle: Annual that reproduces by seed

Management: To reduce later problems, hoe or pull common groundsel before the plants set seed. They can also be killed by flaming. Mulch to prevent seeds already in the soil from germinating. Before planting a new ornamental or vegetable bed, solarize the soil to destroy seeds.

If chemical treatment is necessary, a pre-emergence product containing oryzalin, used around ornamentals listed on the label, will help suppress the weed. Spot-treat with glyphosate, taking care not to get this herbicide on desired plants.

 Notes: Woodland groundsel (Senecio sylvaticus) is also an annual, with flowers that are similar to those of common groundsel. It grows to 3½ feet tall and has a disagreeable odor when it is crushed. Another relative, tansy ragwort (S. jacobaea), occurs in parts of California, Oregon, Washington, and Idaho. A biennial or short-lived perennial, this weed grows 1–3½ feet tall and is erect, forming a single stem that branches at the top. Deeply lobed leaves give the plant a ragged appearance. The daisylike flowers are bright yellow. Tansy ragwort is very toxic to cattle and horses.

HENBIT

LAMIUM AMPLEXICAULE (LAMIACEAE)

BROAD-LEAFED ANNUAL, SOMETIMES BIENNIAL OR SHORT-LIVED PERENNIAL

ZONES: ALL

Henbit, also known as dead nettle, bee nettle, or giraffe head, occurs as a weed in lawns and garden beds, especially in areas with rich soil. Seeds of henbit usually germinate in fall. The plants grow slowly over the winter, becoming most obvious in spring. Henbit grows 12–16 inches high, with the square stems typical of the mint family. The stems lie close to the ground at the base, where they may root at the nodes, then curve upward. The coarsely toothed leaves are paired, opposite one another; lower leaves have long stalks, while the upper leaves clasp the stem. The small, slender, purplish red flowers appear in clusters in the axils (where the leaves join the stem) of the upper leaves in spring. The blooms are tubular, ½–⅔ inch long, with two lips; the upper has short hairs on the back, and the lower has spots on the middle lobe.

Bud of the henbit flower

Life cycle: Annual that reproduces by seed and stolons; sometimes a biennial or short-lived perennial

Management: Henbit is relatively easy to pull by hand, and you can greatly reduce the number of plants in your lawn and garden by weeding in late winter and early spring. Keep the lawn grass healthy and growing vigorously to crowd out henbit seedlings. Be sure to pull or dig henbit plants before they set seed. Remove plants from the garden after pulling them, as they may reroot if left in contact with the soil. Mulching will prevent seeds already in the soil from germinating. Before planting new lawns or garden beds, solarize to kill seeds of henbit.

If control with chemicals is necessary, use a pre-emergence herbicide containing pendimethalin, trifluralin, or oryzalin on turf and ornamentals listed on the label; do not use oryzalin on cool-season grasses. To treat plants of henbit in lawns, use an herbicide labeled for control of broad-leafed weeds in lawns, such as a product containing MCPP, MCPA, and dicamba. In gardens, spot-treat henbit with herbicidal soap or a product containing glyphosate. Be especially careful to keep spray or drift from glyphosate from contacting desired plants.

HORSETAILS

EQUISETUM, VARIOUS SPECIES *(EQUISETACEAE)*

PERENNIAL PTERIODOPHYTES

✎ ZONES: ALL

Rushlike survivors of the Carboniferous Age, several species of horsetails are native to North America and occur as weeds in the West. Common scouring rush *(Equisetum hymenale),* shown above, produces slender, hollow, bright green stems, up to 4 feet tall, with distinctive black and ash-colored rings at each joint. Horsetails are nonflowering plants related to ferns: conelike spikes at the end of each stem bear spores.

Common scouring rush is the species most often planted in gardens, but it may easily escape its allotted area, becoming a pest in lawns and garden beds. Smooth scouring rush *(E. laevigatum)* has shorter, narrower stems and may also appear as a weed, especially in sandy, wet soils. It often enters the garden from nearby ditches or other wild areas. Field horsetail *(E. arvense)* has two types of mature plants, fertile and sterile. The 2–12-inch-tall fertile plants are single stemmed and topped by spore-bearing cones. The sterile plants' many jointed branches radiating from joints of the main stem give them a bushy look, somewhat like a

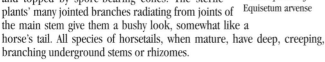

Sterile plants of Equisetum arvense

horse's tail. All species of horsetails, when mature, have deep, creeping, branching underground stems or rhizomes.

Life cycle: Perennials that reproduce from spores and creeping rhizomes

Management: If you decide to plant horsetails, confine them to a container to prevent their escape. In open ground, root-prune the plants frequently, cutting back unwanted shoots. If horsetails have spread into your lawn or garden, dig out as much of the root system as possible. When new sprouts appear, cut them off, and dig up the roots again. With persistence the weed can be controlled, but it takes several seasons. After clearing as much of the growth as possible, spread a mulch of landscape fabric or cardboard, topped with organic matter, to discourage further growth.

Horsetails are difficult to manage with chemicals. A product containing MCPA, MCPP, and dicamba will give partial control, but the horsetails usually return.

HORSEWEED

CONYZA CANADENSIS (ASTERACEAE)

BROAD-LEAFED ANNUAL

✎ ZONES: ALL

Horseweed, which is also known as mare's tail, is a summer annual that is native to North America. It is found in gardens, vineyards, and orchards, and along roadsides throughout the West, mainly in dry areas. The seeds of this weed germinate from fall through spring, producing a seedling plant that forms a low rosette of dull green leaves covered with soft, short hairs. As the plant matures, it sends up a rough stem that grows to 7 feet tall and that branches near the top, fanning out in a shape that resembles a horse's tail. The leaves are bristly and crowded closely along the stem. The lower leaves are spatulate in shape, and the leaves farther up, along the stem, are lance shaped or linear. Many small flower heads form across the top of the plant. The individual flower heads have greenish white "petals," or outer ray flowers, and yellowish center, or disk, flowers. Horseweed blooms in summer, producing seeds that float away on white bristles in late summer and fall.

Life cycle: Annual that reproduces by seed

Management: The young rosettes of horseweed are easily pulled or hoed. Be sure to remove the plants before they set seed, to prevent later problems. A mulch around vegetables and ornamentals will prevent seeds already in the soil from germinating. As seeds of horseweed can easily blow in from wild areas or pastures, it may appear again after you have removed the weed from your garden. Solarizing the soil kills the seeds of horseweed.

If chemical control is necessary, use a pre-emergence herbicide containing isoxaben around ornamentals that are listed on the label. A nonselective postemergence herbicide containing glufosinate-ammonium or glyphosate is effective on horseweed; take care not to get these chemicals on desirable plants.

✎ *Notes: Horseweed contains a terpene, a chemical substance that may be irritating to the throat and skin of some people, as well as to the nostrils of horses.*

IVIES, ENGLISH AND ALGERIAN

HEDERA HELIX, H. CANARIENSIS (ARALIACEAF)

EVERGREEN WOODY VINES

ZONES: ENGLISH IVY: ALL; ALGERIAN IVY: 8, 9, 12–24

Ivy is widely planted in the West as a ground cover and as a climbing vine for fences and walls. However, as many gardeners have discovered, ivy is an aggressive spreader that can quickly invade areas beyond its allotted territory, smothering small plants in its path. Ivy spreads by trailing branches that root at the nodes as it grows along the ground, or it develops aerial rootlets that cling to walls, fences, or trees. English ivy *(Hedera helix)* has dull, dark green leaves 2–4 inches wide at the base and equally long, with three to five lobes; there are many varieties. Algerian ivy *(H. canariensis),* shown above, has shiny, rich green leaves 5–8 inches wide, with three to five shallow lobes. The leaves of the variegated form are edged with yellowish white. Both ivies have a mature phase that appears when the vine has grown vertically for several years. The vine then develops stiff branches with unlobed leaves, and it flowers and produces fruit. Algerian ivy is usually more vigorous than English ivy, though both can be weedy, and both can harbor rodents.

Life cycle: Evergreen woody vines that spread by roots forming at nodes on the branches and by seed

Management: To remove English or Algerian ivy growing as a ground cover, mow it close to the ground with a heavy-duty mower. Then dig up the roots, removing as many as possible. As ivy is deep rooted, expect regrowth from roots you have missed, and further digging. Once the area is clear of top growth, to prevent further growth, cover it with a double layer of landscape fabric, black plastic, or cardboard, topped with bark or chopped tree debris, for at least a full growing season. To control ivy growing vertically, cut and pull it down in sections. Dig out the roots, repeating until they stop sprouting.

If chemical control is necessary, use a product containing dicamba, taking care not to get it on desired broad-leafed plants. Products containing glyphosate provide some control; take care not to get this nonselective herbicide on any desired plants.

JOHNSONGRASS

SORGHUM HALEPENSE (POACEAE)

PERENNIAL GRASS

ZONES: 2–24

Johnsongrass is a tough, spreading perennial grass that can be troublesome in vegetable and ornamental beds, orchards, and vineyards, and especially in rural gardens. This grass reproduces from seed or from its thick, white, fleshy underground stems (rhizomes), which are segmented and break apart easily. With stems growing 2–8 feet high, johnsongrass has a coarse, leafy appearance. Its leaf blades are ¼–1 inch wide and bright green, with a conspicuous white midvein that breaks when the leaf is folded over. The large reddish purple flowering top, 6–22 inches long, is made up of branches bearing many shiny spikelets; it droops with age.

Life cycle: Perennial grass that reproduces by seed and by spreading rhizomes

Management: Repeated mowing helps manage johnsongrass by preventing seed formation and weakening the roots. But digging out whole plants is more effective. Remove as many of the rhizomes and as much of the root system as possible. Any roots remaining in the soil will sprout, making repeated digging necessary. Rotary-tilling or disking is not recommended, as the machinery breaks the rhizomes into short segments, spreading the weed rather than eliminating it; this is why johnsongrass is a serious agricultural pest. Cover cleared areas with a double layer of landscape fabric, black plastic, or cardboard, topped with bark, for at least one growing season to prevent regrowth from remaining rhizomes. Mulch also prevents germination of seeds. Soil solarization kills seeds of johnsongrass and rhizomes that are shallowly buried, but deep rhizomes survive.

If chemical control is necessary to prevent germination of seeds of johnsongrass, use a pre-emergence herbicide containing trifluralin around ornamentals listed on the label, or an herbicide containing oryzalin or pendimethalin around turf and ornamentals listed on the label; oryzalin can be used only on warm-season turf grasses. Growing plants can be controlled with a selective herbicide containing sethoxydim or fluazifop; these chemicals are most effective if applied when the weeds are small. Or use nonselective herbicides containing glyphosate, taking care to avoid contact with or drift onto desirable plants.

KIKUYU GRASS

PENNISETUM CLANDESTINUM (POACEAE)

PERENNIAL GRASS

✎ ZONES: 8, 9, 14–24

A native of tropical Africa, kikuyu grass is an introduced species in the West. It is sometimes planted in gardens and parks along the California coast as a turf grass because it grows quickly, stays green year-round, and requires little maintenance. However, it has escaped cultivation and has become a serious pest in gardens and orchards. Kikuyu grass grows rapidly, making a low mat of coarse, wiry leaves and stems that spread both by rhizomes (underground stems) and stolons (horizontal, above-ground stems). The stolons are white and the thickness of a pencil, with short internodes. They may grow a foot or two over sidewalks and up shrubs, trees, and telephone poles. The yellowish green leaves grow 1–6 inches long and about ¼ inch wide, terminating in a sharp point. Both leaves and stems are covered with fine hairs. Flowers are inconspicuous, but they produce filamentous anthers (threadlike stalks that bear the anther in a stamen); these appear above the surface of the grass in early morning, giving it a whitish cast.

Life cycle: Perennial grass that spreads by rhizomes, stolons, and seed

Management: If you plant kikuyu grass as turf, contain its spread with a barrier made of concrete, bricks, or wood. Dig out unwanted plants in your garden, removing as much of the root system as possible. This stubborn grass will continue to sprout from rhizomes left in the ground, making it necessary for you to repeat the digging. To prevent resprouting by kikuyu grass, cover cleared areas with landscape fabric, black plastic, or cardboard, topped with bark or chopped tree trimmings, for at least a full growing season.

There are few chemical controls for kikuyu grass. Spray the plants, preferably when they are young, with an herbicide that contains glyphosate, taking care that this chemical does not contact desirable plants.

KNOTWEED, JAPANESE

POLYGONUM CUSPIDATUM (POLYGONACEAE)

DECIDUOUS BROAD-LEAFED PERENNIAL

✎ ZONES: ALL

S ometimes planted as an ornamental in untamed or naturalistic parts of gardens, Japanese knotweed has escaped from cultivation, becoming a weed of roadsides, pastures, and gardens. This tough, vigorous plant forms large clumps of reddish brown, stout, wiry stems, growing 4–9 feet high each year. The woody stems, which die back in fall, have swollen nodes or joints, giving the plant its common name of bamboo or Mexican bamboo (though it is not related to true bamboo). The large, 2–6-inch-long leaves, nearly heart shaped with a narrow pointed end, are borne on short stalks. Greenish white flowers in large plumelike clusters appear at the ends of the stems and in the leaf axils in late summer and fall.

Life cycle: Perennial that reproduces by spreading rhizomes

Management: Getting rid of Japanese knotweed requires persistence. Cut the stems to the ground, repeating as new shoots appear. As substantial food reserves are stored in the extensive system of rhizomes (underground stems), Japanese knotweed can continue to send up new shoots for months or even several growing seasons. If possible, let the area infested with this weed go dry during the summer to help slow it down.

For chemical control, spot-treat whole plants or cut stems with an herbicide containing glyphosate. This is most effective in late summer when Japanese knotweed has just begun to flower. Take care not to get this non-selective herbicide on desirable plants.

✎ *Notes: A lower-growing form of Japanese knotweed,* Polygonum cuspidatum compactum (P. reynoutria), *is sometimes planted as a perennial ground cover. Growing 10–24 inches high, with showy clusters of pale pink flowers in late summer, it spreads by creeping roots and can become a nuisance near more delicate plants if not cut back frequently or confined by a barrier. Another relative,* P. capitatum, *is also a vigorous ground cover, growing about 8 inches tall and spreading to 20 inches, with pink flowers over much of the year. You must also confine this polygonum to check its invasive roots, or plant it in areas you do not plan to cultivate.*

KNOTWEED, PROSTRATE

POLYGONUM ARENASTRUM; ALSO CALLED P. AVICULARE (POLYGONACEAE)

BROAD-LEAFED ANNUAL

ZONES: ALL

Prostrate knotweed, also known as common knotweed, doorweed, or knotgrass, grows in lawns and vegetable and ornamental gardens, especially in areas with compacted soil. It also appears in cracks in sidewalks and driveways. This weed germinates from late winter to midspring, quickly forming a spreading, low-growing plant with wiry stems 1–3 feet long. The stems are swollen at the joints, with many branches. There is a silvery, papery sheath where the leaves emerge from the joints; leaves are bluish green, narrow, and about ½–1 inch long and ⅜ inch wide. Tiny white or pink flowers appear in clusters in the leaf axils in summer and fall. Prostrate knotweed somewhat resembles another low-growing weed, spotted spurge, but it lacks the purple spots found on the leaves of spurge, nor does it have the milky juice found in spurge.

Life cycle: Annual that reproduces by seed

Management: Aerating, fertilizing, and providing adequate irrigation for lawns will help prevent the establishment of prostrate knotweed. If the soil in parts of your lawn remains compacted due to constant traffic and thus is prone to weed infestation, consider replacing the turf with a permanent path. Pull or hoe prostrate knotweed from lawns and gardens; the weeds are not difficult to pull when young, especially if the soil is damp. Mulch to prevent the germination of prostrate knotweed seeds in flower and vegetable gardens.

For chemical control of the weed in lawns and around ornamentals, use a pre-emergence herbicide containing oryzalin or pendimethalin in late winter; do not use oryzalin on cool-season lawn grasses. Be sure the species of the plants you want to protect are listed on the label of the herbicide. Spot-treat prostrate knotweed in lawns with a selective herbicide for broad-leafed weeds containing MCPP, MCPA, and dicamba. Spot-treat this weed in other areas, such as in sidewalk cracks, with a product containing glyphosate, taking care that this nonselective herbicide does not contact desired plants.

 Notes: Silversheath knotweed (Polygonum argyrocoleon) looks similar to prostrate knotweed. Also an annual, silversheath knotweed grows in a more upright fashion. It has fewer leaves, and its flower spikes are rose colored.

KOCHIA

KOCHIA SCOPARIA TRICHOPHYLLA (CHENOPODIACEAE)

BROAD-LEAFED ANNUAL

ZONES: ALL

Kochia, also known as Mexican fireweed or burning bush, is sometimes sown as a summer annual because of its handsome shrubby form and bright red fall color. It is well adapted to hot, dry soil and even alkaline conditions and has naturalized in many areas of the West. It is a pest in newly seeded lawns, around the edges of lawns, and in ornamental and vegetable gardens, cultivated fields, pastures, and orchards. Kochia grows 1–6 feet high, with stems that have many branches. Kochia is sometimes planted in the garden as a small annual hedge; its branching habit of growth means it can be sheared. The narrow leaves, arranged alternately on the stems, are lance shaped and ½–2 inches long. The margins have a fringe of hairs; the undersurface of the leaves is also hairy, the upper surface usually smooth. The small, petal-less green flowers of kochia are inconspicuous, forming short spikes in the leaf axils (where the leaves join the stem). Flowering begins in midsummer and continues into fall. Where adapted, kochia grows quickly, with a taproot that penetrates deeply into the soil.

Life cycle: Annual that reproduces by seed

Management: Kochia seedlings emerge from March through May. Hoe or pull them as soon as possible, before they form a deep taproot. Larger plants can be mowed or cut. To prevent future problems, remove kochia plants before they set seed. A mulch of shredded bark, compost, shredded leaves, or chipped tree trimmings around vegetables and ornamental plants will prevent seeds of kochia already in the soil from germinating.

For chemical control, use a pre-emergence herbicide containing trifluralin in sites listed on the label. Treat young kochia plants in lawns with a product containing MCPP, MCPA, and dicamba, applied according to directions on the label. Nonselective herbicides—including herbicidal soap or products containing glyphosate or glufosinate-ammonium—applied according to directions on the label will also kill kochia. Take care not to contact desired plants.

LAMB'S QUARTERS

CHENOPODIUM ALBUM (CHENOPODIACEAE)

BROAD-LEAFED ANNUAL

ZONES: ALL

A common weed in vegetable and ornamental gardens, orchards, and vineyards, and along roadsides throughout the West, lamb's quarters is also called fat hen, white pigweed, and wild spinach. The seeds of this weed germinate from early spring through autumn. The seed leaves (cotyledons) are easy to recognize: on top they have a mealy texture and are dull green; on the underside they are bright purple. The white mealy texture or powder is also found on the leaves of mature plants, especially on the undersides. This characteristic helps distinguish this weed from pigweeds (species of *Amaranthus*), which have smoother leaves. The ½–4-inch-long leaves of lamb's quarters are triangle shaped; some have smooth edges, others are lobed or wavy edged. Lamb's quarters grows 1–6 feet tall, depending on the fertility of the soil, with a main stem bearing many branches. The flowers, which are greenish, small, and mealy, grow in clusters at the tips of the stems.

Life cycle: Annual that reproduces by seed

Management: Lamb's quarters is fairly easy to pull, especially when young. Remove the plants from the garden before they set seed, as the seeds are very long-lived; seeds of this plant found in a 1,700-year-old archaeological site in Denmark survived and germinated. Mulch around vegetables and ornamentals to prevent seeds already in the soil from germinating. Solarization is also effective in managing lamb's quarters.

A number of pre-emergence herbicides are effective around ornamentals, including oryzalin, pendimethalin, and trifluralin; use as directed on the label. Spot-treat plants with herbicidal soap or a product containing glufosinate-ammonium or glyphosate, according to directions on the label. Take care not to get these chemicals on desirable plants.

 Notes: Small, tender leaves of lamb's quarters can be cooked like spinach. The strongly scented leaves of a close relative, epazote, or Mexican tea (Chenopodium ambrosioides), are sometimes used to flavor Mexican dishes, especially beans.

LONDON ROCKET

SISYMBRIUM IRIO (BRASSICACEAE)

BROAD-LEAFED ANNUAL

ZONES: 8, 9, 11–13, 18–24

London rocket, or desert mustard, is a native of Europe that has become a widespread winter annual weed in parts of the West. It is found along roadsides, and in winter vegetable gardens, ornamental gardens, orchards, and vineyards. The seeds of London rocket germinate throughout the cool season, from October to March. The seed leaves are light green with long stalks. The first true leaves have indented margins, a feature that helps distinguish London rocket from a similar weed, shepherd's purse; the first true leaves of shepherd's purse are usually not indented or lobed. The leaves on mature London rocket plants are 3–8 inches long and deeply divided, with a large terminal lobe. The plant grows 1½–4 feet high, with many leafy branches. The small yellow flowers, much like the flowers of other weeds in the mustard family, are borne in small clusters on slender stalks at the ends of the stems in early spring. As the slender 1½–2½-inch seedpods mature, the flower stalks grow longer.

Life cycle: Winter annual that reproduces by seed

Management: Hoe or pull London rocket plants as soon as you spot them in the garden. Getting rid of this weed before it flowers and sets seed will help prevent future infestations. A mulch of compost, shredded bark, or other organic material will prevent seeds that are already in the soil from germinating. Install landscape fabric around shrubs to control London rocket, as well as many other weeds. Solarization (see page 54) will kill seeds of London rocket.

If chemical control is necessary, use a nonselective herbicide that contains herbicidal soap, glufosinate-ammonium, or glyphosate; apply only to weeds, as these products will harm desirable plants as well. Always apply chemicals according to the directions on the label.

MALLOWS

MALVA PARVIFLORA, M. NEGLECTA (MALVACEAF)

BROAD-LEAFED ANNUALS OR BIENNIALS

✔ ZONES: ALL

Little mallow *(Malva parviflora)*, shown above, is also known as mallow, or cheeseweed, because the fruit resembles a round of cheese. A widespread weed in the West, it infests lawns, vegetable and ornamental gardens, orchards, and vineyards. The seeds germinate from November to April, depending on climate. The seed leaves (cotyledons) are smooth, reddish brown, and pear shaped, with reddish stalks. The plant grows quickly, becoming bushy and branched, and ranging from a few inches to 2½ feet in height. The rounded leaves grow on 1–6-inch-long stalks and are 1–5 inches wide. The leaves have five to seven lobes and a distinctive folded or accordion-like appearance. The pinkish white, five-petaled flowers are borne singly or in small clusters in the leaf axis. The fruits turn from green to brown as they mature, separating into sections, each containing a seed. Common mallow *(M. neglecta)* is quite similar, but its flower petals are longer and the fruits more rounded and smoother than those of little mallow.

Flower of little mallow

Life cycle: Annuals or biennials that reproduce by seed

Management: In lawns, fertilize and water to promote dense growth of grasses and to crowd out mallow and other weeds. In gardens, hoe or pull mallow plants when they are young. As they mature, mallows develop a long, tough taproot. To remove older plants, cut the taproot below the crown (the area where the branches originate) with a sharp hoe or clippers. Mulch to prevent germination of seeds already in the soil. Solarize new beds to kill seeds of little mallow.

If chemical control is necessary, use a pre-emergence herbicide containing oryzalin or isoxaben to control mallow in lawns and around ornamentals listed on the product label. Do not use oryzalin on cool-season grasses. To control mallow growing in lawns, use a product containing MCPP, MCPA, and dicamba. Spot-treat young mallow plants with an herbicide containing glufosinate-ammonium or glyphosate, taking care not to get these chemicals on desired plants.

MEDIC, BLACK

MEDICAGO LUPULINA (FABACEAE)

BROAD-LEAFED ANNUAL OR SHORT-LIVED PERENNIAL

✔ ZONES: ALL

Black medic—also known as black clover, trefoil, or yellow trefoil—is a low, trailing plant that grows in lawns and in flower and vegetable gardens, as well as in orchards and meadows. Seeds of black medic germinate in March and April. The four-angled, hairy stems branch from the taproot, trailing 1–2 feet along the ground. The compound leaves have three parts or leaflets; each finely toothed leaflet is about ½ inch wide. The central leaflet has a longer stalk than the other two. Clusters of small, bright yellow flowers appear in May and June, followed by the seedpods in August, or later in frequently mowed lawns. The curved seedpods are kidney shaped and hairy but do not have the prickly spines of the seedpods of burclover, a close relative.

Life cycle: Annual or short-lived perennial that reproduces by seed

Management: Hoe or hand-pull young plants before they set seed. Older plants develop a fairly tough taproot; dampen the soil to make it easier to pull them. A thick mulch will help prevent existing seeds in the soil from germinating. Good lawn management, especially applying adequate nitrogen fertilizer, will help prevent the growth of black medic. Soil solarization can kill black medic seeds if high temperatures are achieved; this method of control is most effective in zones with hot summers.

Black medic seed pods

If chemical treatment is necessary to control plants of black medic, apply a postemergence herbicide containing MCPP, MCPA, and dicamba on lawns. Spot-treat black medic with a product containing herbicidal soap, glufosinate-ammonium, or glyphosate. Be especially careful not to apply these chemicals to desired plants.

✎ *Notes: Black medic is sometimes planted as a forage crop in pastures with thin, poorly drained soil, and as a cover crop, dug into the soil before seeds are set. Like other members of the legume or Fabaceae family, black medic takes nitrogen from the air and puts it into the soil through the action of root bacteria.*

MILKWEEDS

ASCLEPIAS, VARIOUS SPECIES *(ASCLEPIADACEAE)*

BROAD-LEAFED PERENNIALS

✺ ZONES: ALL

Several species of milkweed may be pests in western gardens, orchards, fields, and roadsides. All are perennial herbs that grow from deep roots or rootstocks. Their clustered flowers attract butterflies. Milkweed leaves exude a sticky latex when broken. Many species of milkweed are poisonous to livestock. Showy milkweed *(Asclepias speciosa)*, which is native to much of the West, is a pale green or gray-green plant, growing 2–4 feet high. The soft, woolly leaves are oval, 4–7 inches long, with prominent veins. The purplish pink flowers are followed by narrow pods containing the seeds; each seed is attached to silky fibers that carry it away on the wind. Although common milkweed *(A. syriaca)*, shown above, is an eastern native, it is found in parts of the West, especially on the eastern slope of the Rocky Mountains. This milkweed grows 3–6 feet high, with a stout, unbranched stem. The leaves are 4–8 inches long and marked with deep veins. Clusters of fragrant pink or white flowers appear in summer, followed by large, hairy seedpods. Mexican whorled milkweed *(A. fascicularis)* is found at lower altitudes in the West. An erect plant, 2–4 feet tall, it has linear leaves 2–4 inches long and only about ½ inch wide. The flowers are white or greenish, sometimes with a purple tint. The seedpods that follow are long and narrow.

Milkweed seeds emerging from pod

Life cycle: Perennials that reproduce by seed and by creeping rootstocks

Management: Regular mowing in lawns or open fields will eventually control established colonies of milkweed. In garden beds, hoe or chop the stems of milkweed at or below soil surface, repeating as they grow again. Also hoe or pull any seedlings that appear. Be sure to get rid of milkweed before seeds form, to avoid later problems.

For chemical control, apply a product containing glyphosate when milkweed is flowering. Take care not to get this chemical on desired plants.

MISTLETOES

PHORADENDRON, VARIOUS SPECIES *(VISCACEAE)*

PARASITIC EVERGREEN SHRUBS

✺ ZONES: 7–17

Mistletoes are parasitic plants that grow on woody plants, taking nutrients and moisture from their hosts. Two species of large-leafed mistletoe *(Phoradendron)* are found in the West. Big leaf mistletoe *(P. macrophyllum)* infects many trees, including alder, ash, birch, black walnut, box elder, California buckeye, cottonwood, locust, mesquite, and fruit and nut trees. Oak mistletoe *(P. villosum)* attacks only oaks. These mistletoes have green or gray-green stems and leaves; the leaves are oval shaped and thick and firm in texture. Small sticky white or pinkish berries are spread by birds or by humans working in infected trees. Mistletoe plants can grow to 3 feet high, forming a dense rounded clump attached to the host tree. Mistletoes can kill branches of a tree, seriously weakening it, especially if it is already stressed by disease or lack of water.

Life cycle: Parasitic evergreen shrubs that reproduce by seed

Management: Prune out the branch of the infested tree, at least 1 foot below the place where the mistletoe is attached. If the mistletoe is attached to the trunk of the tree or to a main branch that is too large to prune, cut the mistletoe flush with the trunk or branch. This will slow the spread and growth of the mistletoe, but it will grow back. To prevent regrowth, wrap the cut area with several layers of landscape fabric or black polyethylene and tie it with flexible tape. This keeps light from reaching the parts of the mistletoe that are still in the tree; however, even under these conditions it may take several years for the mistletoe to die. If the covering becomes detached, be sure to replace it.

For chemical control, use a product containing the plant growth regulator ethephon, applied according to the directions on the label.

✎ *Notes: Some species of trees are somewhat resistant to mistletoe. The list includes Chinese pistache* (Pistacia chinensis), *crape myrtle* (Lagerstroemia), *ginkgo, golden rain tree* (Koelreutia paniculata), *liquidambar, persimmon, sycamore, and conifers.*

MORNING GLORIES

IPOMOEA, VARIOUS SPECIES *(CONVOLVULACEAE)*

ANNUAL VINES

ZONES: 7–24

Several annual morning glories are pesky weeds in parts of the West, twining around desired plants, choking or smothering them. Tall morning glory *(Ipomoea purpurea)*, native to tropical America, is sometimes grown as an ornamental. It has escaped to become a weed in gardens, orchards, and vineyards. This morning glory's heart-shaped leaves have no lobes and are 3–4¾ inches long and 1½–3 inches wide at the base; they are covered with short hairs. Its typical morning glory flowers come in white, pink, purple, or blue. The stems grow 5–13 feet long. Another escaped ornamental, Japanese morning glory *(I. nil)*, shown above, grows vigorously to 15 feet or more with twining, angled stems. The 1–3½-inch-long leaves have three lobes; the large flowers are light blue or purple. Native to tropical America and the southwestern United States, red morning glory *(I. coccinea)* has become a pest in desert regions of the Southwest. It has reddish, ridged stems. The leaves are 1½–2½ inches long, heart shaped on some plants and deeply lobed on others. The narrow, trumpet-like flowers are scarlet red.

Life cycle: Annual vines that reproduce by seed

Management: Hoe or pull seedlings as soon as you spot them. If morning glories have grown large enough to twine around other, more desirable plants, carefully untangle them and pull out the roots. To prevent future infestations, remove morning glories before they set seed. A mulch around vegetables, flowers, and other plants will prevent seeds already in the soil from germinating.

For chemical control, use an herbicide containing oryzalin or isoxaben as a pre-emergent in landscapes around labeled ornamentals. Apply according to the directions on the label. While products containing glyphosate or triclopyr will kill morning glory, it is difficult to apply them to a vining plant without harming desirable plants. Applying these chemicals to mature leaves with a paintbrush is the safest method.

MOSSES

MANY GENERA AND FAMILIES

NONFLOWERING, NONVASCULAR, ROOTLESS PLANTS

ZONES: ALL

While moss is sometimes valued by gardeners as a soft and beautiful ground cover in wooded locations, Japanese-style gardens, and shaded rock gardens, moss growing in lawns or on pathways is usually considered a weed. Moss, as it appears in gardens, is a collection, or mat, made up of thousands of tiny, rootless plants. Generally no taller than 2 inches, moss forms a green, velvety cover over the soil, rocks, or paths. Moss is most likely to invade shaded lawns planted in acidic soil that is compacted and overly wet.

Life cycle: Nonvascular plants that reproduce from stem pieces and spores

Management: Changing your existing soil conditions is the best way to eliminate moss permanently from lawns. Have the soil analyzed to determine its pH level; add lime as recommended by the soil testing laboratory to raise the pH to a level less hospitable to moss. Aerate the lawn to improve drainage. If water continues to puddle on the lawn, you may need to install a permanent drainage system. Prune trees or shrubs, if possible, to let in more sunlight. You can remove patches of moss from lawns or garden beds by raking or digging them up; however, they will grow back if the underlying problems with the soil are not remedied. Remove moss from the flat surfaces of brick or concrete paths with a wide spatula or flat shovel.

For chemical treatment of moss in lawns or on structures, use a product containing potassium salts of fatty acids, applied according to the directions on the label. Or treat moss with 3 tablespoons of copper sulfate for every 1,000 square feet of lawn. These chemicals will not destroy the moss permanently; in time it will grow back unless the cultural conditions that favor it are changed.

Notes: If getting rid of moss in a lawn proves very difficult, consider planting a ground cover that is adapted to the existing conditions or purposefully cultivating a "lawn" composed of mosses.

MUGWORT, CALIFORNIA MUGWORT

ARTEMESIA VULGARIS HETEROPHYLLA, A. DOUGLASIANA (ASTERACEAE)

BROAD-LEAFED PERENNIALS

✎ ZONES: ALL

California mugwort *(Artemisia douglasiana)*, a native plant also known as Douglas's mugwort, western mugwort, or wormwood, is found in pastures and along roadsides. It also appears in gardens, where it may have been planted as an herbal or native plant or may have spread from a nearby wild area. A closely related and similar mugwort *(A. vulgaris heterophylla)*, which is native to Europe and Asia, is also sometimes planted in gardens. Its leaves are more toothed than those of California mugwort. Both mugworts are invasive plants, spreading widely and quickly by their extensive, running rootstocks. Western mugwort grows 3–7 feet high, with erect leafy stems, woody at the base, that rise from the rootstocks. The 2–6-inch-long leaves are variable in shape: the lower leaves have three to five deep notches or lobes, and the upper leaves have few or no notches. Leaves, dark green on the upper side and whitish green and mealy underneath, have a strong odor reminiscent of sage. Long flowering branches appear in summer, bearing clusters of greenish flowers on short stalks.

Life cycle: Perennial herbs that reproduce by seed and by rootstocks

Management: Eliminating mugwort—and other plants with spreading rootstocks—demands patience. Cut off the stems and dig out as many of the roots as possible. In a few weeks new shoots will appear from pieces of root left behind; cut back these shoots and dig out the roots again. Cover cleared areas with a mulch of landscape fabric or thick cardboard to help suppress any remaining roots. Mulch also prevents seeds of mugwort from germinating.

If chemical control is necessary, first cut back the stems of mugwort. When the plant regrows to flowering stage, treat it with a product containing glyphosate. Repeat treatments may be necessary. Take care not to get this chemical on desired plants.

 Notes: A relative of mugwort, silver king artemisia (A. ludoviciana albula), *also native to the West, is sometimes planted as an ornamental. However, it also spreads by running rootstocks and can be invasive, especially in good soil.*

MULLEINS

VERBASCUM, VARIOUS SPECIES (SCROPHULARIACEAE)

BROAD-LEAFED BIENNIALS

✎ ZONES: ALL

Mulleins form a large group of plants that includes favorites for the flower border and also weeds of gardens, orchards, and roadsides. Common mullein *(Verbascum thapsus)*, shown above, also called Aaron's rod or blanket leaf, is a weed found in dry soil that is low in fertility. The plant produces a large, thick rosette of furry, gray-green leaves the first year. In its second year, common mullein sends up a single, stout, erect stem, 1–6 feet tall. Leaves alternate along the lower part of the stem; the closely spaced flowers are borne on 1–3-foot-long terminal spikes at the top of the stem. The yellow, five-lobed flowers are held tightly to the spike, without stalks, and are followed by woolly, egg-shaped capsules holding a multitude of tiny dark brown seeds. A single plant of common mullein can produce as many as 200,000 seeds. Moth mullein *(V. blattaria)* produces in the first year a rosette of smooth, dark green leaves with shallow teeth. In spring of the second year, a slender, dark green, 1½–5-foot-long flower stalk shoots up. The flowers are about an inch wide, usually yellow, but in some forms they bloom pale pink or

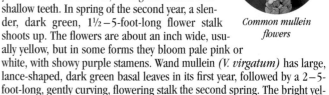

Common mullein flowers

white, with showy purple stamens. Wand mullein *(V. virgatum)* has large, lance-shaped, dark green basal leaves in its first year, followed by a 2–5-foot-long, gently curving, flowering stalk the second spring. The bright yellow flowers with reddish centers are ¾–1 inch across.

Life cycle: Biennials that reproduce by seed

Management: Try to pull, hoe, or dig out mullein plants during the first year, before they have a chance to flower and set seed. Be sure to dig out the taproot, which may resprout if not removed completely. Mulch around vegetables and ornamentals to prevent seeds already in the soil from germinating.

For chemical control, spot-treat mullein with a product containing glufosinate-ammonium or glyphosate. These herbicides are most effective on seedlings or young plants. Take care not to get these chemicals on desired plants.

MUSTARDS, WILD MUSTARDS

BRASSICA, VARIOUS SPECIES *(BRASSICACEAE)*

BROAD-LEAFED ANNUALS

ZONES: ALL

Wild mustards are familiar weeds in the West, appearing in gardens, orchards, and vineyards. Most are winter annuals, sprouting in fall, growing slowly over winter, and bursting into a sea of yellow flowers in spring. One species, called charlock or wild mustard *(Brassica kaber)*, grows 1–3 feet tall, with erect stems that have stiff hairs on the lower portions. The leaves are 2–8 inches long, 1–4 inches wide; the lower leaves have lobes, and the upper ones are toothed. The four-petaled flowers are followed by 1¼–2-inch-long seedpods. Black mustard *(B. nigra)* is often taller, up to 8 feet high. Its leaves are 2–10 inches long, 1–6 inches wide, sometimes with stiff hairs, and similar in shape to those of wild mustard. Its seedpods are less than an inch long and are carried close to the stem; the pods of wild mustard are larger and spreading. A third weed, birdsrape mustard *(B. rapa)* grows 1–4 feet tall. From roots that look like a small turnip, it sends up smooth stems with large lower leaves, up to a foot long, and smaller, pointed upper leaves that clasp the stem. The seedpods of this mustard are 2–3 inches long and spread out from the stem.

Life cycle: Annuals that reproduce by seed

Management: In lawns, increase the vigor of the grass by correct fertilization and overseeding in fall. Pull or hoe mustards when they are young. The plants are easy to pull from moist soil. To prevent future problems, be sure to remove them before they set seed. As these weeds often crop up in fall-planted vegetables, solarize vegetable beds in summer, before planting, to kill mustard seeds.

If chemical control is necessary, use a pre-emergence herbicide containing isoxaben in fall to kill mustard seeds in the ornamentals listed on the label. Products containing MCPP, MCPA, and dicamba are effective on mustard plants. Products containing herbicidal soap will control young mustard plants. Or apply a nonselective herbicide containing glufosinate-ammonium or glyphosate, taking care not to get these chemicals on desired plants.

 Notes: The young leaves, flower buds, and flowers of these mustards are edible; they give a peppery flavor to early spring salads.

NETTLE, STINGING

URTICA DIOICA (URTICACEAE)

BROAD-LEAFED PERENNIAL

ZONES: 1–9, 14–24

The painful welts caused by the stinging hairs of this weed are familiar to hikers and many gardeners in the West. Preferring moist, shaded sites, stinging nettle infests shrub borders, orchards, vineyards, riverbanks, and roadsides. It grows 2–9 feet tall, spreading widely by underground stems or rhizomes. The four-angled stems often branch from the base; they have both stinging hairs and stiff bristles. The coarsely toothed leaves, 2½–5 inches long, grow in pairs along the stem. The undersides are densely covered with stinging hairs. Spiky clusters of whitish green flowers are borne on slender branches at the base of the leafstalks in summer. Male and female flowers occur in separate clusters.

Life cycle: Perennial that reproduces by seed and by creeping underground stems or rhizomes

Management: Wear gloves and long sleeves when working around this weed. Mow or cut it, repeating when new growth appears. Eventually the roots will stop growing, but this may take several seasons. Digging up the roots and removing as many of the rhizomes as possible will control stinging nettle more quickly. Or, once the top growth is cleared, cover the area with a thick mulch, such as a double layer of landscape fabric or cardboard, topped with bark, for at least one growing season.

Burning nettle seedlings with first true leaves

If chemical control is necessary, treat stinging nettle with a selective herbicide for broad-leafed weeds, such as a product containing MCPA or dicamba. Or you can spot-spray with a product containing glyphosate, taking care not to get this nonselective herbicide on desired plants.

Notes: Burning nettle or small nettle (Urtica urens) *is a summer annual weed found in coastal and some inland counties of California, Oregon, and Washington. This sparsely branched plant grows 5–24 inches tall from a slender taproot and has toothed leaves, ½–2 inches long, with stinging hairs that irritate and blister the skin like stinging nettle. Burning nettle can be controlled around ornamentals listed on the label with a pre-emergence herbicide containing isoxaben.*

NIGHTSHADES

SOLANUM, VARIOUS SPECIES (SOLANACEAE)

BROAD-LEAFED ANNUALS OR SHORT-LIVED PERENNIALS

ZONES: ALL

Several nightshades—close relatives of tomatoes, potatoes, and egg-plant—are weedy pests in gardens, fields, orchards, and vineyards. The foliage and berries of nightshades contain toxic alkaloids that are harmful to animals and humans. Black nightshade *(Solanum nigrum)*, shown above, also known as deadly nightshade or garden nightshade, is probably the most common species in gardens. A variable plant, it grows from 6 inches to 2½ feet tall, with branching stems that may stand erect or lie on the ground. The leaves are egg shaped, with smooth or wavy margins. The white or pale blue flowers are the shape of tomato flowers. The small berries are carried in bunches, dull green when young, maturing to black. Black nightshade is usually an annual, but if undisturbed it can live for several years in warm climates. Hairy nightshade *(S. sarrachoides)* is similar to black nightshade, but it has spreading foliage that is hairy and somewhat sticky to the touch. Its flowers have white petals, and the green to yellowish berries are half enclosed by the calyx (leaflike parts at the base of the flower). An annual, hairy nightshade grows 2½ feet high. Cut-leaf nightshade *(S. triflorum)* grows flat on the ground, with branches 1–2 feet long. The small, hairy leaves are deeply lobed. White flowers are followed by greenish berries.

Life cycle: Annuals or sometimes short-lived perennials—all reproduce by seed

Management: Pull or hoe nightshade plants when they are young, making sure to get rid of this pest before the berries and seeds form. Mulch to prevent seeds that are already in the soil from germinating. Solarization is effective in killing seeds of nightshades.

If chemical control is necessary, use a pre-emergence herbicide containing isoxaben. Spot-treat nightshade plants with an herbicide containing glufosinate-ammonium or glyphosate, taking care not to get these chemicals on desired plants.

NUTSEDGES, YELLOW AND PURPLE

CYPERUS ESCULENTUS, C. ROTUNDUS (CYPERACEAE)

PERENNIALS

ZONES: 2–24

Although nutsedges resemble grasses, they have solid stems that are tri-angular in cross section; in contrast, the stems of true grasses are hollow and round. Nutsedge leaves grow from the base in groups of three; grass leaves grow in sets of two. Nutsedges thrive in waterlogged soil but will tolerate drought. Yellow nutsedge *(Cyperus esculentus)*, shown above, grows 6–30 inches tall, with true leaves that rise from the base of each stem. Leaflike bracts radiate out below the flower cluster of spreading yellowish brown spikes. The flowering stem is about as long as the basal leaves. Purple nutsedge *(C. rotundus)* grows 1–2 feet high; its basal leaves are generally shorter than the flowering stem. Flowers are purplish brown. (In mowed turf, flower stalks are usually not produced.) Both nutsedges reproduce by seed but also by abundantly produced underground rhizomes and "nutlets" (tubers), which allow them to spread rapidly. The edible nutlets of yellow nutsedge taste a bit like almonds, giving rise to one of the plant's alternate names, earth almond (another name for this plant is chufa). The globe-shaped nutlets are smooth and brown; just one nutlet grows at the end of each rhizome. By contrast, the bitter-tasting nutlets of purple nutsedge are oblong and grow in a chain along the rhizomes.

Life cycle: Perennials that reproduce by seed, rhizomes, and tubers

Management: Remove nutsedges when they are young—with fewer than five leaves or less than 6 inches tall. Older and taller plants are mature enough to produce the nutlets from which they can regrow. When the plant is dug or pulled, the nutlets break off, remaining in the soil to sprout and start a new plant. To suppress nutsedges, remove as much of the weed as possible, and cover the area with several layers of landscape fabric or with cardboard. Top with chipped bark or tree trimmings. Leave the cover in place for at least one growing season. Yellow nutsedge can be partially eliminated by soil solarization, but solarization has little effect on purple nutsedge. Bringing the nutlets to the surface and allowing them to dry helps control purple nutsedge but is not effective on yellow nutsedge.

For postemergence chemical control, you can use a nonselective product containing glyphosate, but only when plants are very young. This herbicide will not affect any nutlets that have become detached from the treated plant. Take care not to get the chemical on desired plants.

 Notes: Try to prevent introducing nutsedges into the landscape by purchasing clean mulch, topsoil, and plants.

OAT, WILD

AVENA FATUA (POACEAE)

ANNUAL GRASS

✔ ZONES: ALL

Wild oat is an annual native to Europe that occurs in gardens, orchards, and vineyards, as well as along roadsides and in fence-rows. This weed adapts to many different types of soil. It is abundant in pastures and grazing land, where it makes an excellent feed for animals. The seed of wild oat germinates from late fall through early spring, and the plant matures, producing the next generation of seed, in late spring to late summer. Viewing this weed from above shows that the soft, succulent young leaves of wild oat twist counterclockwise. The mature plant, which grows 1–4 feet tall, has several stems rising from the base. Leaf blades, rough to the touch, are ⅛–½ inch wide and 4–12 inches long. The flower cluster, or inflorescence, is a drooping, open panicle, 6–16 inches long, made up of spikelets (flower groups) about 1 inch long. The spikelets contain two or three seeds with awns that are bent at the center when mature.

Life cycle: Annual that reproduces by seed

Management: Pull, hoe, or dig wild oat in early spring, when the plants are small. Remove them before they set seed; once in the soil, seeds of wild oat can remain dormant for up to ten years, making management difficult. Mulching around vegetable and ornamental plants will prevent the oat seeds from germinating. Solarization (see page 54) is also an effective way to kill seeds of wild oat.

If chemical control is necessary, in fall use a pre-emergence product containing EPTC, oryzalin, or trifluralin around the ornamentals listed on the label. Products containing fluazifop-butyl or sethoxydim are selective postemergence herbicides for grasses growing among broad-leafed ornamentals. A nonselective herbicide containing glyphosate or glufosinate-ammonium will kill wild oat, but take care not to get these chemicals on desired plants.

 Notes: Cultivated or domestic oats (Avena sativa) *are similar in appearance to wild oat, except that the awn on their seed is straight, rather than bent.*

ONION AND GARLIC, WILD

ALLIUM TRIQUETRUM, A. VINEALE (LILIACEAE)

PERENNIALS

✔ ZONES: VARY BY SPECIES

Wild onion, or onion lily *(Allium triquetrum),* shown above, is a pesky weed of gardens and lawns primarily in Zone 17, although it is found in other areas with cool summers. Native to the Mediterranean, this onion is sometimes cultivated as an ornamental for its pretty white flowers. However, it spreads rapidly by both seeds and bulbs. Appearing in fall, wild onion leaves are flat with a prominent ridge on the underside; both leaves and bulbs are edible, with a strong onion flavor. Flower stems grow at least a foot tall and are triangular in cross section; they carry nodding clusters of bell-shaped white flowers, followed by black seeds enclosed in a roundish pod. After flowering in spring, the aboveground parts of wild onion die back, but the seeds and bulbs remain, ready to sprout in fall.

Wild garlic (*A. vineale,* Zones 1–9, 14–17) grows from a cluster of bulbs covered with a papery sheath, like cultivated garlic. The leaves are hollow and round, pointed at the tip. Wild garlic sends up a solid, 3-foot flowering stem in spring or summer, topped with a terminal cluster that usually contains small bulbils rather than flowers. The bulbils fall to the ground, sprouting in fall or spring to form new plants. The original bulbs also sprout again.

Life cycle: Perennials that reproduce by bulbs and seed

Management: Dig up the whole plant to get rid of the bulbs of wild onion and garlic—any bulbs left in the ground will eventually sprout. Be sure to remove these plants before they set seed. Cover cleared areas with a thick mulch, such as cardboard or black plastic, topped with bark chips, for at least a full growing season. Landscape fabric helps prevent the growth of these weeds.

If chemical control is necessary, use a selective herbicide containing dicamba. Or use a nonselective herbicide containing glyphosate, taking care not to get this chemical on desirable plants. Even with repeated applications, herbicides provide only partial control of these weeds.

OXALIS

OXALIS, VARIOUS SPECIES *(OXALIDACEAE)*

BROAD-LEAFED PERENNIALS

⚡ ZONES: VARY BY SPECIES

Two species of oxalis are persistent perennial weeds in many areas of the West. Yellow oxalis (*Oxalis corniculata*, all zones), also called creeping wood sorrel, is found in lawns, gardens, and greenhouses. This plant's spreading stems, 2–12 inches long, initially grow from a single taproot. The stems soon root at the joints, eventually invading large areas. The green or purplish compound leaves are made up of three heart-shaped leaflets carried at the tip of 1–2-inch stalks. The small, ¼–⅓-inch-long yellow flowers have five petals. They are followed by cylindrical seed capsules; when the seeds are ripe the capsules burst open, shooting seeds as far as 10 feet away. Cape oxalis (*O. pes-caprae*), shown above, also known as Bermuda buttercup, was introduced from South Africa as an ornamental and has escaped to become a weed in Zones 8, 9, and 12–24. It

Yellow oxalis or creeping wood sorrel

sprouts in fall, sending up long-stalked leaves directly from its base. Clusters of showy, yellow, funnel-shaped flowers, up to 1 inch across, appear in late winter. Cape oxalis has a deep rootstock that produces numerous small bulbs.

Life cycle: Perennials that reproduce by rooting at stem joints and by seed, or by small bulbs.

Management: Pull or dig small plants of yellow oxalis before they form seeds. To manage cape oxalis you need to get rid of the bulbs. Dig the whole plant in late winter, sifting through the soil to remove as many of the small bulbs as possible. Solarization will help manage cape oxalis. Both kinds of oxalis can be suppressed, although not completely exterminated, by covering a cleared area with landscape fabric or cardboard, topped with mulch, for at least a full growing season.

For chemical control, use a pre-emergence herbicide containing oryzalin or pendimethalin on lawns and around the ornamentals listed on the label. Spot-treat oxalis in gardens with glyphosate, taking care not to get this chemical on desired plants.

PAMPAS GRASS, JUBATA GRASS

CORTADERIA SELLOANA, C. JUBATA (POACEAE)

PERENNIAL GRASSES

⚡ ZONES: 4–24

Two related species of *Cortaderia*, a native of South America, appear in the West. Although both are frequently referred to as pampas grass, their growth habits differ significantly. Jubata grass (*C. jubata*), shown above, also known as purple pampas grass, has become a serious weed along the California coast, crowding out sensitive native plants and threatening coastal ecosystems. This grass usually grows 9–12 feet tall, but it has been known to reach 15 feet under ideal conditions. Dense, mounding clumps of sharp-edged leaves are surmounted by flower spikes that rise 6–9 feet above the foliage. These fluffy, loose plumes—pink, red, purple, or yellowish—produce prodigious quantities of seeds, which germinate and grow quickly in bare sandy soil or in cleared forestland.

True pampas grass (*C. selloana*) may reach 20 feet in height. Its white, beige, or pink flowering plumes are only slightly taller than the saw-toothed grassy leaves. Pampas grass is less invasive than jubata grass, because both male and female plants must be present for viable seed to form, and many pampas grass plants available for sale are female. However, male plants have been sold by nurseries, and pampas grass has spread by seed, both within gardens and into wild areas. Many gardeners and horticulturalists feel that pampas grass, like jubata grass, should not be used in landscaping, and that existing plants should be removed, at least from gardens that are near wild lands.

Life cycle: Perennial grasses that reproduce by seed or by slowly spreading roots

Management: Pull or dig out all volunteer seedlings of jubata grass and also of pampas grass, as they could be male plants. Removing large jubata or pampas grass plants is a major undertaking. Wearing protective clothing (goggles, long-sleeved shirt, boots, and gloves), cut back the sharp foliage; a weed cutter fitted with a blade attachment is helpful. Then, with a sharp ax or mattock, dig out all the aboveground portions of the stem.

For chemical control, treat with an herbicide containing glyphosate, taking care not to get this nonselective herbicide on desired plants.

PIGWEEDS

AMARANTHUS, VARIOUS SPECIES *(AMARANTHACEAE)*

BROAD-LEAFED ANNUALS

✺ ZONES: ALL

Several species of pigweed are found in western gardens. One of the most common is redroot pigweed *(Amaranthus retroflexus)*, shown above, also called rough pigweed, green amaranth, or careless weed. This coarse, branching, upright plant can grow as tall as 7 feet, but it is more likely to grow to 1–3 feet. The lower stems and the taproot are reddish. The leaves are oval, 1–3 inches long, with wavy margins and distinct veins on the underside; they are borne on stems ½–1½ inches long. Both the stems and leaves are covered with short, rough hairs. Dense flower spikes grow at the ends of the stems and from the leaf axils, containing many inconspicuous flowers. Smooth pigweed *(A. hybridus)* is similar, reaching 7–8 feet in height, with smooth, deep green leaves and stems. Its flowering stem is longer and more slender than that of redroot pigweed. Prostrate pigweed *(A. blitoides)* forms a low mat of 6–24-inch, smooth, branching stems. The leaves are oval, about ½ inch wide, light green, sometimes reddish underneath. The flower spikes are borne in the leaf axils rather than at the end of the stems. Tumble pigweed *(A. albus)* makes a rounded, bushy, branching plant 6–36 inches tall. The stems are light green; the oblong, 1–2-inch-long leaves are light green on top and can be reddish on the underside. When the plant is mature, the main stem breaks easily, releasing the plant to tumble away in the wind, scattering seed. All pigweeds are prolific seed producers; a single plant of redroot pigweed can produce more than 100,000 seeds.

Life cycle: Annuals that reproduce by seed

Management: Pull or hoe pigweed seedlings when they are small. Older plants are more likely to scatter seeds, and they are also more difficult to pull out. Mulch to prevent seeds already in the soil from germinating. Solarization is effective in managing pigweeds.

If chemical control is necessary, several pre-emergence herbicides can be used, including products containing oryzalin, pendimethalin, or trifluralin. Spot-treat pigweed in lawns with an herbicide containing MCPP, MCPA, and dicamba. In gardens, treat with products containing glyphosate or glufosinate-ammonium, taking care not to get these chemicals on desired plants.

PLANTAINS, BROADLEAF AND BUCKHORN

PLANTAGO MAJOR, P. LANCEOLATA (PLANTAGINACEAE)

BROAD-LEAFED PERENNIALS

✺ ZONES: ALL

Two species of plantain are found throughout the West in lawns, gardens, and roadsides, often in compacted soils that are low in organic matter. Broadleaf or common plantain *(Plantago major)*, shown above, can grow up to 16 inches tall, but it usually remains shorter, especially in areas that are mowed or walked on. Forming a rosette, the thick leaves are dark green, 2–7 inches long, and somewhat egg shaped. Their short, V-shaped stem grows from the base of the plant; parallel veins mark the leaves from end to end. The flower stem is leafless, rising 4–16 inches from the base of the plant. It curves upward, topped with a dense spike crowded with many small, greenish white flowers. Buckhorn plantain *(P. lanceolata)*, also called narrowleaf plantain, grows up to 18 inches tall, with leaves 3–10 inches long and less than 1½ inches wide. The leaves are covered with soft hairs and have three to five prominent veins that run the length of the leaf blade. The flowering stalks are 6–20 inches tall, ending in dense spikes of small flowers with prominent white stamens.

Life cycle: Perennials that reproduce by seed

Management: To reduce infestations of plantains in lawns, keep the lawn thick by consistent fertilization. Aerate the lawn to improve drainage; or if the area is very wet, install a drainage system. Adding plenty of organic matter, such as compost, before planting new lawns or garden beds helps reduce the numbers of this weed. In vegetable and ornamental gardens, dig out plantains before they set seed. As they can regrow from pieces of their fibrous rootstalk left behind in the soil, it is important to remove as much of the roots as possible; a dandelion weeder is helpful. Mulch to prevent seeds already in the soil from germinating.

If chemical control is necessary, use a pre-emergence herbicide containing isoxaben around the ornamentals listed on the label. A selective herbicide containing MCPP, MCPA, and dicamba can be used on plantains growing in lawns. Spot-treat plantains in gardens with a product containing glyphosate, taking care not to get this chemical on desired plants.

POISON HEMLOCK

CONIUM MACULATUM (APIACEAE)

BROAD-LEAFED BIENNIAL

✿ ZONES: ALL

Poison hemlock is found in gardens, orchards, and vineyards, especially near pastures and streams, in many parts of the West. It is a biennial—sprouting from seed one year, blooming and dying the next. Poison hemlock grows 3–10 feet tall from a fleshy white taproot. The stems are erect, extensively branched, and hollow between the leaf nodes. They are marked with purplish dots (*maculatum,* the species name of poison hemlock, means spotted). The large leaves, divided and toothed, resemble those of parsley, which is related to poison hemlock. The long stalks of the lower leaves clasp the main stem, while the upper leaves have short or no stalks. The foliage smells musty when crushed. Poison hemlock produces many umbrella-shaped flower clusters borne on stems ¼ – ¾ inch long. The white flowers give the plant a lacy look. Flowers appear in spring and summer, followed by small oval fruits, each containing two seeds that are scattered in late summer and fall. The seeds germinate in winter or very early spring, producing a seedling plant that looks much like a parsley seedling, having narrow light green cotyledons (seed leaves), which are followed by deeply cut true leaves.

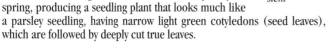

Poison hemlock stem

Life cycle: Biennial that reproduces by seed

Management: Pull out young plants; they are easier to pull if the soil is moist. Mow or cut older plants before they set seed. They will sprout again from the taproot, requiring repeated mowing until the root dies. Or, after mowing or cutting the tops to the ground, cover with a thick mulch of cardboard or landscape fabric, topped with chopped tree trimmings or bark chips. Mulching also prevents seed already in the soil from sprouting.

If chemical management is necessary, cut back the plants. When new growth appears, treat it with a product containing MCPA, MCPP, and dicamba, or with a product containing glyphosate. Take care not to get these chemicals on desirable plants.

 Notes: All parts of this plant are poisonous. Humans have been poisoned by mistaking poison hemlock leaves for parsley or the seeds for anise.

POISON IVY AND POISON OAK

TOXICODENDRON RADICANS, T. DIVERSILOBUM (ANACARDIACEAE)

DECIDUOUS SHRUBS OR VINES

✿ ZONES: VARY BY SPECIES

Poison ivy, which is found east of the Cascade Range and the Sierra Nevada, and poison oak, which is familiar to gardeners and hikers in areas west of the mountains, are toxic plants. A resin on their leaves, stems, fruits, and roots causes severe contact dermatitis in most people. These plants are spread by birds, who eat the fruits and disperse the seeds. Poison oak and poison ivy can appear in gardens as low shrubs, or they can twine around trees or other shrubs, developing an extensive root system before they are noticed.

Poison ivy *(Toxicodendron radicans),* shown above, usually grows as a bushy shrub, up to 3 feet tall in the variant common in the West. In the eastern United States it is typically a trailing or climbing vine. The stems grow from branched, creeping horizontal rootstocks, which can spread several yards from the parent plant, sending up new shoots. The leaves, arranged alternately on the stem, are compound and borne at the end of a stalk. Each leaf is composed of three shiny, oval, pointed leaflets, which are often reddish when young, becoming glossy dark green in summer. The edges may be smooth, toothed, or lobed. Clusters of small greenish flowers appear in summer, followed by round, ridged, cream to yellow fruits that are ¼ inch wide. The foliage turns bright orange to scarlet in fall.

Poison oak *(T. diversilobum),* shown on page 293, grows as a dense, leafy shrub in open or partially shaded areas; in deeper shade it becomes a vine, climbing with aerial roots. Like poison ivy, it has extensive creeping horizontal rootstocks. Its leaves are also compound, made up of three leaflets, although at first glance the leaflets look like individual leaves. The central or terminal leaflet has a stem or petiole, but the side leaflets do not have distinct stems. In contrast, the leaves of true oaks are not compound; they grow singly, with each leaf on a distinct stem. The margins of the leaflets of poison oak are scalloped, toothed, or lobed.

Poison oak leaves in early spring

The new growth is tinged red, usually becoming shiny green in summer, then turning scarlet in fall. In spring the plant develops clusters of small white flowers, which develop into waxy, white berries. The berries are important food for birds and are also eaten by deer, rabbits, and other wildlife.

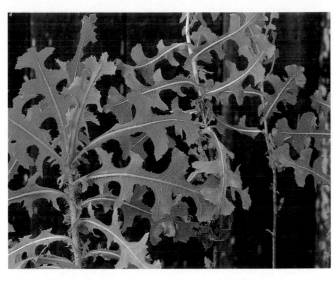

Life cycle: Deciduous shrubs or vines that reproduce by creeping horizontal rootstocks and by seed

Management: How much poison ivy or poison oak is present and where it is growing will affect your decisions on how to manage it. A few small plants in the garden can be grubbed out physically. Wear protective clothing—tightly woven long-sleeved shirt and pants, and washable cotton gloves over thick plastic gloves. Carefully cut and remove the top growth, then dig out the roots to a depth of 8 inches. Do not compost the stems or roots; wrap and put them in the trash, or bury them deeply in the ground. This can be done in winter when the plants are leafless, but be careful—the stems contain the toxic resin and are still dangerous. Never burn poison ivy or poison oak, as inhaling the smoke can cause severe injury. Wash your clothing separately after contact with poison ivy or poison oak. Also wash your tools carefully, including the handles. Rinse the tools in alcohol, then dry and apply oil to prevent rust.

For larger stands of these weeds, goats can provide effective management. There are commercial companies that provide goats for this purpose. Ask your cooperative extension office or local nurseries for help in finding such companies.

For chemical control, spray the foliage of actively growing plants with a product containing glyphosate or triclopyr. Glyphosate is most effective when applied after the berries have formed. As these herbicides will kill any other plants they contact, take care not to get them on desired plants. Glyphosate can also be applied to the cut stems of poison ivy or poison oak; this must be done immediately after cutting to be effective.

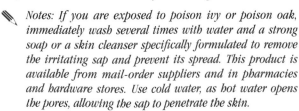 *Notes: If you are exposed to poison ivy or poison oak, immediately wash several times with water and a strong soap or a skin cleanser specifically formulated to remove the irritating sap and prevent its spread. This product is available from mail-order suppliers and in pharmacies and hardware stores. Use cold water, as hot water opens the pores, allowing the sap to penetrate the skin.*

PRICKLY LETTUCE

LACTUCA SERRIOLA (ASTERACEAE)

BROAD-LEAFED ANNUAL OR BIENNIAL

ZONES: ALL

Prickly lettuce, also called wild lettuce or china lettuce, is found in gardens, orchards, and vineyards, and along roadsides, especially in areas with dry soil. When the seedling first sprouts in winter or spring, its seed leaves (cotyledons) are about ⅓ inch long and less than ⅙ inch wide, with a few bristles on top; bristles also appear on the midveins on the underside of the leaf. The leaves exude a milky juice when broken or pulled from the crown. The main stem of prickly lettuce grows 1–5 feet tall from a deep taproot. The lower part of the stem is quite prickly or bristly, but it is nearly smooth toward the top. The light green leaves alternate along the stem, with the leaf blades clasping the stem. They are somewhat twisted at the base and may point north and south (prickly lettuce is also sometimes called compass plant). Varying in length from 2 to 10 inches, the lower leaves are usually lobed, and soft hairs scatter the top. The underside of the leaf is distinctive, with a prominent whitish midvein lined with curved prickles. The upper leaves are smaller and generally not lobed. The inflorescence (flowering head) is spreading and branched. The individual flower heads are ⅛–⅓ inch across, yellow, and often drying to a bluish color. The seeds, tufted with white hairs like a dandelion seed, float away on the wind.

Life cycle: Annual or biennial that reproduces by seed

Management: Pull or hoe seedlings of prickly lettuce. Dig or pull larger plants before they set seed. Mulch around vegetables and ornamentals to prevent seeds already in the soil from germinating.

If chemical control is necessary, use a pre-emergence herbicide containing isoxaben around ornamentals listed on the label. Spot-treat prickly lettuce with a product containing glufosinate-ammonium or glyphosate, taking care not to get these chemicals on desired plants.

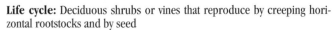 *Notes: Prickly lettuce is sometimes confused with annual sowthistle* (Sonchus oleraceus). *But the midribs on the undersides of the leaves of prickly lettuce have curved prickles, while the undersides of annual sowthistle leaves are smooth. Although prickly lettuce is not edible, it is related to salad lettuce,* Lactuca sativa.

PUNCTURE VINE

TRIBULUS TERRESTRIS (ZYGOPHYLLACEAE)

BROAD-LEAFED ANNUAL

✓ ZONES: ALL

Puncture vine—with its sharp, thorny burs that poke into tires, paws, and bare feet—is familiar to gardeners and bicyclists over much of the West. This weed, also called caltrop or burnut, is found in lawns, gardens, orchards, and vineyards, and along roadsides. Puncture vine germinates in spring and grows rapidly, forming a dense low mat 5–15 inches in diameter. Its reddish, trailing stems are covered with bristly hairs. The tiny, hairy leaves are divided into five to eight pairs of oblong leaflets. Yellow five-petaled flowers are borne singly in the leaf axils (where the leaf joins the stem) and usually open only in the morning or on cloudy days. When mature, the burs break apart into separate sections, each having two sharp spines and containing two to four seeds. The seeds can remain dormant in the soil for many years, making control difficult.

Puncture vine

Life cycle: Annual that reproduces by seed

Management: Hoe or dig puncture vine plants when they are small, cutting below the crown to prevent regrowth. Be sure to get rid of this weed before it sets seed, to avoid the thorny burs as well as future infestations. Mulch to prevent seeds already in the soil from germinating. Remove puncture vine from lawns, then improve the soil and sow grass seed in the bare spots to prevent more weeds. Keep turf thick and weedproof with proper watering, fertilization, and mowing height.

If chemical control is necessary, use a pre-emergence herbicide containing trifluralin or pendimethalin around the lawn grasses and ornamentals listed on the label. In lawns, treat puncture vine with a selective herbicide containing dicamba or methanearsonic acid. Always apply herbicides according to directions on the label. In garden areas other than lawns, use herbicidal soap on young plants, or use a product containing glyphosate. Take care not to get glyphosate on desired plants.

✎ *Notes: Since 1961, puncture vine has been managed in some areas through the release of imported weevils that feed on its seeds and stems. These weevils are best suited to warm climates and are most effective in large gardens or on farms. They can be purchased from companies specializing in beneficial insects.*

PURSLANE

PORTULACA OLERACEA (PORTULACACEAE)

BROAD-LEAFED ANNUAL

✓ ZONES: ALL

Purslane, sometimes called pusley or wild portulaca, is a low-growing summer annual found in gardens and orchards, between stepping-stones, and in cracks in pavement. It thrives in moist conditions but can also withstand considerable drought. The seeds germinate in late spring, after the soil has warmed. The seed leaves (cotyledons) are teardrop shaped, succulent, and tinged with red. As the plant matures, it produces many branched stems, 6 inches to 3 feet long, that form a prostrate mat. The stems may turn up at the ends, clothed with smooth, shiny, succulent leaves. Five-petaled yellow flowers appear in the leaf axils, opening when the sun shines. Globe-shaped seedpods filled with small black seeds follow the blooms. A single plant can produce more than 50,000 seeds, making management difficult.

Purslane seedlings

Life cycle: Annual that reproduces by seed and by stem fragments that root in damp soil

Management: Purslane is easy to pull or hoe. Pieces of stem can reroot easily, so be sure to remove them from the garden. Also remove plants that have begun to flower, as they can ripen seed even after they have been pulled from the soil. Mulch to prevent seeds already in the soil from germinating. Purslane seeds can be killed by soil solarization (see page 54), but only if high temperatures are achieved.

For chemical control, use a pre-emergence herbicide containing oryzalin or pendimethalin. Treat purslane plants growing in lawns with a product containing dicamba, an herbicide that acts selectively on broad-leafed weeds. Always apply herbicides according to directions on the label. In gardens, spot-treat young plants with an herbicidal soap. Or use a product containing glyphosate or glufosinate-ammonium, taking care not to get these nonselective herbicides on desired plants.

✎ *Notes: Purslane leaves and stems are edible, with a tart, lemony flavor. They are used in both French and Mexican recipes in salads, soups, pork stew, and egg dishes. Seed for strains of purslane with extra-large leaves is sold by specialty companies.*

QUACK GRASS

ELYTRIGIA REPENS (POACEAE)

PERENNIAL GRASS

✀ ZONES: 1–9, 14–24

Quack grass is an aggressive perennial weed that invades lawns and vegetable and flower gardens, as well as orchards and vineyards. It is also called couch grass or devil's grass, and is sometimes listed by the botanical name *Agropyron repens.* Quack grass can grow as tall as 3 feet, but it stays much lower in mowed areas. The ¼–½-inch-wide leaf blades are flat, thin, pointed at the tip, and green to blue green in color. Small grasping auricles—earlike projections—clasp the stem at the base of each leaf blade. The seed heads, which are dense spikelets resembling wheat, are borne on erect stalks in summer. Quack grass produces an extensive mass of long, slender, yellowish white, branching rhizomes (underground stems) that can spread laterally 3–5 feet. The rhizomes are able to penetrate through hard soil and into roots and tubers of other plants, such as potatoes and bearded iris.

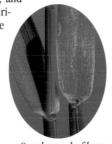

Quack grass leaf bases showing auricles

Life cycle: Perennial that reproduces by seed and by rhizomes

Management: Because it can reproduce readily from even small pieces of rhizome left in the soil, quack grass is difficult to manage. However, before planting, you can thoroughly dig the area and remove all visible pieces of root to slow down its growth for a few years. Watch carefully for any new sprouts and remove them immediately. Quack grass can also be suppressed by cutting back the top growth and covering the area with a mulch of black plastic. Leave the cover in place for at least one year. In lawns, frequent close mowing reduces the nutrient reserves in the roots of this weed. If the infestation is severe, it is usually best to kill the lawn and weeds with an appropriate herbicide and replant.

If chemical treatment is necessary, use selective herbicides containing fluazifop-butyl or sethoxydim; these will suppress quack grass and most other grasses. Always apply herbicides according to directions on the product label. You can apply a nonselective herbicide containing glyphosate in spring when quack grass has 6–10 inches of new growth, although you must take care that this chemical does not get on desired plants.

RAGWEEDS

AMBROSIA (ASTERACEAE)

BROAD-LEAFED ANNUALS AND PERENNIALS

✀ ZONES: ALL

Several plants known as ragweed are found in the West in gardens, at the edges of fields, and along roadsides. All produce copious amounts of pollen carried by the wind, causing hay fever in susceptible people in late summer. Common ragweed *(Ambrosia artemisiifolia),* shown above, is an annual that grows up to 4 feet high. Its leaves and upright, branched stems are blue green and covered with fine hairs. The feathery and fernlike leaves are 2–4 inches long. Greenish male flowers grow on terminal spikes, producing pollen. Western ragweed *(A. psilostachya),* which is somewhat similar in appearance, is a perennial with a running rootstock or rhizome. It grows 1–4 feet tall, with aromatic, grayish green stems and leaves that are covered with short white hairs. The feather-shaped leaves are 1¼–4¾ inches long. Greenish flowers are borne on terminal spikes. Giant ragweed *(A. trifida),* an annual, may grow taller than 10 feet in moist sites but is shorter in dry areas. Its leaves are quite different: large, 2½–12 inches long, and shaped like hands, usually with three lobes but sometimes five. Both the leaves and stems are rough. The flower clusters are often more than 6 inches long.

Life cycle: Annuals and perennials that reproduce by seed; perennial western ragweed also spreads by running roots

Management: Young ragweed plants can be controlled by pulling or hoeing. Pull, cut, or mow older plants before they flower and set seed. Be sure to remove the roots of western ragweed, as it can grow from pieces left behind in the soil. Mulching prevents ragweed seeds already in the ground from germinating.

For chemical control, use a pre-emergence herbicide containing isoxaben or oryzalin around the plants listed on the label. Treat ragweed plants with a selective herbicide containing MCPP, MCPA, and dicamba or use a nonselective herbicide containing glyphosate. Take care not to get this chemical on desired plants.

✎ *Notes: Although goldenrod is often blamed for hay fever because its showy flowers appear at the same time as ragweed's, its pollen is too heavy to become airborne. Ragweed is the true culprit.*

RUSSIAN THISTLE

SALSOLA TRAGUS (CHENOPODIACEAE)

BROAD-LEAFED ANNUAL

✄ ZONES: ALL

Russian thistle, also called tumbleweed, common saltwort, and wind-witch, is found in much of the West, especially in arid regions. It is sometimes listed by the botanical names *Salsola iberica* and *S. kali* or *S. tenuifolia*. Growing 6 inches to 5 feet in height, Russian thistle is a rounded bushy plant, with slender, stiff branches often striped with purple. The seedling plant has ¼ – ½-inch-long fleshy leaves that resemble pine needles. The threadlike leaves reach ⅓ – 2 inches in length and develop a spiny tip with age. The whitish, petal-less flowers are inconspicuous, blooming in clusters at the bases of the leaves. At maturity the whole plant becomes grayish brown, stiff, and woody. It breaks away from the soil and is blown away, scattering seeds, which germinate from late winter to early summer, depending on climate and soil moisture. Russian thistle is a host to the beet leafhopper. This insect transmits curly top, a virus that affects beets, tomatoes, and other vegetable crops.

Russian thistle flower with spiny bracts

Life cycle: Annual that reproduces by seed

Management: Hoe or pull Russian thistle plants when they are young. Be sure to remove them from the garden well before they set seed to prevent later problems. A mulch will prevent seeds already in the soil from germinating. Russian thistle can be managed by soil solarization.

If chemical control is necessary, use a pre-emergence herbicide containing trifluralin around the ornamentals listed on the label. To control Russian thistle plants, use a selective herbicide for broad-leafed weeds that contains dicamba. Or use a nonselective product containing herbicidal soap (most effective on young plants), glufosinate-ammonium, or glyphosate. Take care not to get these chemicals on desired plants. Always apply herbicides according to directions on the label.

✎ *Notes: Russian thistle came to North America from Russia in the late 1800s as an impurity in flax seed. It has spread rapidly, infesting cropland and rangeland in many regions.*

SANDBURS

CENCHRUS (POACEAE)

ANNUAL GRASSES

✄ ZONES: ALL

Sandburs are troublesome weeds: their sharp, stiff spines can penetrate shoes and bicycle tires, as well as injure animals. They grow in lawns, gardens, orchards, and vineyards, and along roadsides throughout the West, especially in sandy soils. Long-spine sandbur *(Cenchrus longispinus)*, shown above, grows 4 – 24 inches tall, with weak stems that usually trail on the ground, forming a mat. The flat stems are enclosed by the lower part of the leaf, or sheath. The upper part of the leaf may enclose the flower head and burs. The 2 – 6-inch-long leaf is flat, pointed at the tip, and sometimes twisted. At maturity, the 1 – 3-inch-long flower spike bears 10 to 30 burs. The burs, yellowish green when young, age to light brown; they have flat, spreading ⅛ – ¼-inch-long spines. Field sandbur *(C. incertus,* also listed as *C. pauciflorus)* looks similar but has slightly smaller burs. Sandburs have been reported to produce more than 1,000 seeds per plant. The seeds are spread when the burs attach to clothing or the fur of animals.

Life cycle: Annuals that reproduce by seed

Management: The root system of sandburs is fairly shallow, so they are easy to dig or pull, especially when young. Be sure to get rid of sandburs before they set seed. To discourage this weed (and others) in lawns, fertilize and water properly to thicken the turf. Mulch around vegetables and ornamentals to prevent germination of seeds already in the soil.

If chemical management is necessary, use a pre-emergence herbicide containing pendimethalin, trifluralin, or oryzalin to prevent the germination of sandbur seeds in the turf grasses and ornamentals listed on the product label. Selective herbicides for grasses, such as products containing fluazifop-butyl or sethoxydim, can be used around the ornamentals listed. Always apply herbicides according to directions on the label. Use a product containing herbicidal soap on young sandbur plants. A nonselective herbicide containing glyphosate or glufosinate-ammonium will control sandburs, but take care not to get these chemicals on desired plants.

SCARLET PIMPERNEL

ANAGALLIS ARVENSIS (PRIMULACEAE)

BROAD-LEAFED ANNUAL

 ZONES: ALL

Scarlet pimpernel, also known as poor man's weatherglass, common pimpernel, and shepherd's clock, is an annual that pops up in lawns and flower and vegetable gardens, as well as orchards and vineyards. In mild-climate zones, its seed can germinate and the plant can mature at any time during the year. In colder areas it grows in spring, summer, and fall. It is actually one of the prettiest weeds. The dark green seed leaves (cotyledons) are triangular in shape. The true leaves are oval to triangular and pointed, with small dark spots on the undersides. Their length varies from ¼ to 1 inch, depending on soil moisture. Usually the leaves are opposite one another on the stem, but sometimes three leaves grow from one node. Scarlet pimpernel grows 4–12 inches high, with many branching, four-angled stems. The flowers are borne on long, delicate stalks that grow from the base of the leaf. While usually salmon colored, the showy five-petaled, ½-inch-wide flowers are occasionally brick red, blue, or white. They open only on sunny, clear days and close at the approach of bad weather—thus the common name "poor man's weatherglass." Smooth, round seed capsules follow the flowers. When mature, the capsules split around the middle, spilling out many shiny brown seeds.

Life cycle: Annual that reproduces by seed

Management: Scarlet pimpernel is not a real threat to other plants in the garden, except for young vegetable seedlings. If it is troublesome, you can easily pull or hoe this plant, as its root system is shallow. To prevent future infestations, remove the plants before they set seed. Mulching around vegetables and ornamentals will prevent seeds already in the soil from germinating. Scarlet pimpernel can be managed by soil solarization.

If chemical control is needed, use a product containing herbicidal soap on young plants.

 *Notes: You can distinguish scarlet pimpernel from a similar weed, common chickweed, by comparing the leaves. The seedling leaves of scarlet pimpernel are darker green and lack the prominent midrib of chickweed. And the true leaves of scarlet pimpernel have small dark spots that chickweed leaves lack.*

SHEPHERD'S PURSE

CAPSELLA BURSA-PASTORIS (BRASSICACEAE)

BROAD-LEAFED ANNUAL

ZONES: ALL

Shepherd's purse, also called lady's purse or pepper plant, is a common winter annual weed in lawns, gardens, orchards, and vineyards throughout the West. The seed germinates from November through March, producing a seedling with small, pale green seed leaves with tiny glossy dots. The first true leaves are a silvery grayish green; their leaves do not have indented margins. (In contrast, the first true leaves of London rocket, a similar weed, do have indented margins. This difference disappears as the plants mature: the later leaves of shepherd's purse are indented.) Shepherd's purse grows 2–20 inches tall with slender, erect stems sprouting from the basal rosette. The deeply indented lower leaves grow on stalks; the upper leaves are without stalks and clasp the stem. Small white flowers with four petals appear in spring, alternating along the upper ends of the stems. The characteristic seedpods or capsules that follow are triangular or heart shaped—something like a little purse—and are attached by a stalk to the main stem. A multitude of tiny orange-brown or reddish seeds fill these capsules.

Life cycle: Annual that reproduces by seed

Management: In lawns, dig out shepherd's purse early in the season, when the plants are young. Fertilize the lawn to thicken it and prevent the weed from establishing itself. In gardens, pull or hoe this weed when it is small, before seeds form. Kill seeds by solarizing the soil (see page 54) before planting winter vegetable crops. Mulch will prevent seeds already in the soil from growing.

If chemical control is necessary, use a product containing dicamba, a selective herbicide for broad-leafed weeds, on shepherd's purse plants growing in lawns. Always apply herbicides according to directions on the label. Spot-treat young plants with herbicidal soap. A nonselective herbicide containing glyphosate will kill shepherd's purse, but care must be taken not to get this chemical on desired plants.

 Notes: As with many members of the mustard family, the young leaves of shepherd's purse can be served in salads or cooked as greens.

SORREL, RED

RUMEX ACETOSELLA (POLYGONACEAE)

BROAD-LEAFED PERENNIAL

✿ ZONES: ALL

Red sorrel, also known as sheep sorrel, occurs in lawns, gardens, and fields, and along roadsides. While common to areas with poorly drained, acidic soil, it also adapts to other soil types and to dry conditions. Young plants grow as a low rosette of leaves. As they mature, thin, upright, 4–16-inch-tall stems appear, branching near the top. Several stems may grow from a single crown; the plants spread by shallow but extensive woody, underground rootstocks to form clumps or patches. The arrow-shaped lower leaves are thick and 1–3 inches long. The upper leaves are usually thinner and smaller. Both the leaves and stems of red sorrel have a sour taste, something like that of cultivated sorrel. The flowers are carried on slender upright stalks near the top of the plants. Red sorrel is dioecious: the orange-yellow male flowers are borne on separate plants from the red-orange female flowers. Red sorrel is related to curly dock (see page 271), a taller weed that grows from a thick taproot.

Life cycle: Perennial that reproduces by creeping rootstocks and by seed

Management: In lawns, pull or dig out red sorrel, removing as much of the shallow, spreading root system as possible. To help prevent the return of this weed, fertilize the lawn, and aerate to improve drainage. Have the soil tested to determine its pH; if necessary, add lime to make the soil less acid. In gardens, hoe or pull red sorrel, taking care to get out the roots. If regrowth occurs from roots left behind, you will need to do more cutting and digging. After you clear an area, apply a thick mulch of landscape fabric or cardboard to smother the remaining roots and to prevent seeds already in the soil from germinating.

If chemical control is necessary, apply an herbicide containing dicamba, which is selective for broad-leafed weeds, to lawns. Always apply herbicides according to directions on the label. Spot-treat red sorrel with a product containing glyphosate, taking care not to get the chemical on desirable plants.

SOWTHISTLES

SONCHUS OLERACEUS, S. ASPER (ASTERACEAE)

BROAD-LEAFED ANNUALS

✿ ZONES: ALL

Sowthistles are common weeds in western gardens, orchards, and vineyards; they sometimes grow in lawns as well. These weeds are summer annuals, germinating in spring and maturing by late summer or fall in most areas. They have stout taproots, hollow stems, and a milky sap that oozes out when a leaf or stem is broken. The yellow flower heads look like those of dandelions; they are followed by fluffy seeds, spread by the wind. Annual sowthistle *(Sonchus oleraceus),* shown above, also called colewort or hare's lettuce, grows 1–4 feet tall. The lower leaves, which are attached to the stem by stalks, are 2–14 inches long. The upper leaves are smaller, lack stems, and clasp the stalk. Most of the bluish green leaves are deeply lobed with toothed margins; the terminal lobe is shaped like a broad arrow. Spiny sowthistle *(S. asper)* has upright stems 1–4 feet high. The leaves are dark green. The lower leaves are deeply lobed with spiny margins and short stalks. The upper leaves clasp the stem, without stalks; they are jagged, rather than lobed, and edged with sharp, stiff prickles. Stems and upper leaves may have a reddish tint, especially in areas of low moisture.

Life cycle: Annuals that reproduce by seed

Management: Pull sowthistle plants when they are young, making sure to remove them before they flower; sowthistle seeds may mature even after the plants have been pulled from the soil. When pulling larger plants, try to remove the taproot, as new shoots can grow from it. Mulching around vegetables and ornamentals will prevent sowthistle seeds already in the soil from germinating. Soil solarization manages sowthistles.

If chemical control is necessary, use a pre-emergence product containing isoxaben around the plants listed on the label. Always apply herbicides according to the label directions. Spot-treat sowthistle plants with herbicidal soap while they are young. A product containing glyphosate or glufosinate-ammonium will kill this weed. Take care not to get these nonselective herbicides on desired plants.

SPEEDWELLS

VERONICA, VARIOUS SPECIES (SCROPHULARIACEAE)

BROAD-LEAFED ANNUALS

ZONES: ALL

Speedwells are close relatives of veronicas, perennials prized for summer flowers. However, two annual speedwells can be pests in western gardens, invading lawns and vegetable and ornamental beds. Persian speedwell *(Veronica persica),* shown above, germinates in late winter or early spring, setting seed and dying by early summer. It is a branched plant with slender stems that spread over the ground, forming a low mat. The oval or rounded leaves are toothed around the edges; most leaves are attached to the branch with short stalks, but some are without stalks. Pretty, four-petaled violet blue flowers with dark stripes and white centers appear on slender stalks in the leaf axils. Heart-shaped seed capsules follow the blooms. Persian speedwell, which is native to Europe, may have been introduced in the United States as an ornamental. Purslane speedwell *(V. peregrina)* is native to North America. Its seed germinates in spring, and the plant matures by midsummer. An erect, branching plant 2–12 inches tall, this weed has narrow oblong leaves, ¼–1 inch long, rounded at the tip and usually with smooth margins. Minute, four-petaled white flowers are borne in the leaf axils. The seed capsule is similar to that of Persian speedwell.

Life cycle: Annuals that reproduce by seed

Management: Persian and purslane speedwells are easy to hoe, pull, or dig out when young; take care to remove them before they set seed. A thick mulch will prevent seeds already in the soil from germinating. Soil solarization manages speedwells.

If chemical control is necessary, use a pre-emergence product containing isoxaben around the ornamentals listed on the label. Spot-treat speedwell in lawns with a product containing MCPP, MCPA, and dicamba. Spot-treat young plants with herbicidal soap. Or use a product containing glyphosate, taking care not to get this chemical on other plants.

 Notes: A perennial called creeping speedwell (V. filiformis), *which forms mats and spreads by creeping roots and seeds, is troublesome in lawns, especially in western Washington. This speedwell can eventually be controlled through persistent weeding.*

SPOTTED CAT'S EAR

HYPOCHAERIS RADICATA (ASTERACEAE)

BROAD-LEAFED PERENNIAL

ZONES: 4–6, 14–17

Although European in origin, spotted cat's ear, also known as false dandelion, is now established in many areas of North America, including Northern California and west of the Cascades in Washington and Oregon. This weed is found in lawns and garden beds, as well as along roadsides. Growing from a fleshy taproot up to 2 feet long, spotted cat's ear has a basal rosette of oblong or lance-shaped leaves that usually lie flat on the ground. The leaves are 2–12 inches long, lobed or toothed, and hairy; they have prominent midribs. The flower-bearing stem, which is leafless and usually branched, rises 8–30 inches above the basal leaves. A single bright yellow flower head, an inch across, appears at the end of each stem. The one-seeded fruits are attached to a circle of feathery, grayish white hairs that allow the seeds to be spread by the wind. Seeds germinate in spring and the plant grows over the summer, maturing in late fall. This weed is a perennial, which means the parent plant reappears each spring, along with new seedlings.

Life cycle: Perennial that reproduces by seed and pieces of taproot

Management: Young plants of spotted cat's ear can be pulled or hoed in spring. You need to dig out larger plants to remove the taproot. In lawns, mow, water, and fertilize properly to thicken the turf, preventing the establishment of weeds. Mulch to prevent seeds from germinating in gardens.

If chemical control is needed, use a product containing MCPA, an herbicide that acts on broad-leafed weeds, to manage spotted cat's ear growing in lawns. Always apply herbicides according to directions on the label. A product containing glyphosate will also kill this weed; take care not to get this nonselective herbicide on desired plants.

 Notes: Smooth cat's ear (Hypochaeris glabra) *is an annual relative of spotted cat's ear. The flower head of smooth cat's ear is almost hidden by the green leaflike structures— bracts—at its base, so that it seems to be not fully open. In contrast, spotted cat's ear has showy yellow flower heads.*

SPURGES

CHAMAESYCE, VARIOUS SPECIES *(EUPHORBIACEAE)*

BROAD-LEAFED ANNUALS

 ZONES: ALL

Spotted spurge and petty spurge, sometimes listed as species of *Euphorbia*, are annual weeds found in many areas of the West. Their stems exude a milky juice when cut. Spotted spurge *(Chamaesyce maculata)*, shown above, is a particularly aggressive weed because it produces large quantities of seed and can set seed within a few weeks of germination. Flourishing in hot weather, it grows from a shallow taproot, forming a low mat of branching stems in lawns, cracks in pavement, and gardens. The ¼–¾-inch oblong leaves have the characteristic reddish brown spot on the upper side. Clusters of tiny pinkish brown flowers bloom at the base of the leafstalks, followed by seed capsules only ¹⁄₁₆ inch long. Petty spurge *(C. peplus)* is usually found in moist shade among shrubs or in flower beds. This weed grows 4–18 inches tall with stems that branch from the base. The yellow green, roundish, and somewhat crinkled leaves are attached to the stem by short stalks—except for the leaves just below the flowers, which are heart shaped and without stalks. The tiny, greenish yellow flowers have no petals.

Life cycle: Annuals that reproduce by seed

Management: Hoe or pull out spotted and petty spurges early in the season, before they bloom and set seed. Mulch prevents seeds already in the soil from germinating. A vigorous, well-fertilized lawn competes well against spotted spurge.

If chemical control is necessary, use a pre-emergence product containing isoxaben, oryzalin, or pendimethalin in the turf and around the ornamentals listed on the label. Spot-treat spurge plants with herbicidal soap when they are young. A selective herbicide for broad-leafed weeds containing MCPP, MCPA, and dicamba can be used to control young spotted spurge plants in lawns. Always apply herbicides according to directions on the product label. For spurge growing in cracks in pavement, apply a product containing glyphosate or glufosinate-ammonium, taking care not to get these chemicals on desired plants.

 Notes: Creeping spurge (C. serpens) is an annual that is becoming common in some areas. Its smooth, roundish leaves are less than ½ inch long. The stems root at the nodes, forming a prostrate mat.

STARTHISTLE, YELLOW

CENTAUREA SOLSTITIALIS (ASTERACEAE)

BROAD-LEAFED ANNUAL

 ZONES: ALL

Yellow starthistle, a weed native to southern Europe, has invaded pastures, fields, and roadsides, spreading into garden beds and lawns in many areas of the West. It is toxic to horses, causing "chewing disease," a nervous syndrome that can result in death from starvation. Seeds of yellow starthistle germinate in fall through early spring, and the plant matures and sets seed in summer. The seedling leaves are tongue shaped. The first true leaves are dull green and lobed; the distinctive whitish color of foliage and stems appears later in the plant's life cycle. Yellow starthistle reaches 1–3 feet in height, with rigid, spreading stems that branch from the base. The basal leaves are 2–6 inches long, with several deep lobes. Leaves on the stems are narrow; the leaf blades clasp the stem, forming winglike structures. The uppermost leaves are small and sharply pointed. Bright yellow flower heads, an inch across, appear singly at the ends of branches; they have sharp ridged spines, up to ¾ inch long, at the base.

Life cycle: Annual that reproduces by seed

Management: In lawns, dig out yellow starthistle. Fertilize and water to improve the condition of the lawn and thereby discourage weeds. In gardens, hoe or dig out yellow starthistle when the plants are small, taking care to remove them before they set seed. Mulching around vegetables and ornamentals will help prevent seeds already in the soil from germinating. The seeds of this weed can be killed by solarization.

If chemical control is necessary, treat yellow starthistle with a product containing dicamba, an herbicide that acts selectively on broad-leafed weeds. Always apply herbicides according to directions on the label. A nonselective herbicide containing glyphosate will kill yellow starthistle, but it may also kill plants that you want to keep; take care not to get this chemical on desirable plants.

 Notes: The starthistle weevil, Bangasternus orientalis, a beneficial insect that feeds only on yellow starthistle, may somewhat reduce the population of this weed in infestations of an acre or more—on one property or several neighboring ones. This biological control is most effective against larger infestations; without a constant source of food, the weevils either starve or migrate elsewhere.

THISTLES

CIRSIUM, CARDUUS (ASTERACEAE)

BROAD-LEAFED ANNUALS, BIENNIALS, AND PERENNIALS

✱ ZONES: ALL

A number of thistles are objectionable weeds in the West, invading gardens, orchards, vineyards, and roadsides. Canada thistle *(Cirsium arvense),* shown above, is a tough perennial that grows from deep, widespreading horizontal roots to form extensive colonies. Leaves are oblong or lance shaped, with spiny-toothed margins. The ridged stems, 1–4 feet tall, branch near the top and bear clusters of ³/₄-inch-wide purple flower heads in summer and fall. Bull thistle *(Cirsium vulgare)* is a biennial that produces a rosette of deeply lobed and toothed leaves in the first year. The second year, flowering stems 2–5 feet tall appear, bearing many spreading branches and topped with clusters of four or five showy rose purple flowers. Canada thistle leaves are smooth on top and smooth or hairy underneath; the leaves of bull thistle are prickly on top and cottony below. Seeds of Italian thistle *(Carduus pycnocephalus),* an annual weed, germinate in spring; the plant blooms and dies by midsummer. Its leaves are deeply lobed with spiny teeth. The flowering stem is 1–6 feet tall and has narrow, spiny wings. The 1-inch flowering heads are reddish purple. Musk thistle *(Carduus nutans)* is a biennial or winter annual with deep green, spiny-margined leaves that have lighter green midribs. The leafy stems grow up to 6 feet tall, and carry solitary 1½–3-inch-wide dark rose or white flowers with distinctive bracts (small leaflike structures) at the base.

Bull thistle flower

Life cycle: Annuals, biennials, and perennials that reproduce by seed; Canada thistle also reproduces by creeping roots

Management: Hoe or dig out thistles before they set seed, removing as much of the root system as possible. To weaken the roots, cut or mow new shoots as they appear. It may take several seasons to kill the roots of the perennial Canada thistle.

For chemical control, use a selective herbicide for broad-leafed weeds that contains MCPP, MCPA, and dicamba. Or use a nonselective herbicide containing glyphosate. Check the label for the best time to apply glyphosate—either rosette or flowering stage of plant growth—for the kind of thistle you have. Take care not to get this chemical on desired plants. Repeated treatment may be necessary. Always apply herbicides according to directions on the label.

VETCHES, COMMON AND HAIRY

VICIA SATIVA, V. VILLOSA (FABACEAE)

BROAD-LEAFED ANNUALS

✱ ZONES: ALL

These vetches are often planted as cover crops for their contribution of nitrogen to the soil and for their use as hay and forage. However, they have escaped from cultivation and become weeds in gardens, orchards, and vineyards, and along fences and roadsides. The seeds of common vetch *(Vicia sativa),* shown above, germinate in early winter, and the plant matures in spring. This branching, twining plant climbs on shrubs, trees, and fences and insinuates itself among perennials in flower beds. Growing 1–2½ feet tall, it has compound leaves that are made up of five to seven pairs of oblong leaflets arranged on each side of a stalk. The stalk ends in a slender, coiling tendril that helps the plant climb. Showy pink or reddish flowers resembling sweet peas appear singly or in clusters of two in the leaf axils. The flowers are followed by soft, hairy, twisted brown seedpods, 1½–3 inches long; each contains 5 to 12 round seeds. Hairy vetch *(V. villosa)* has hairy stems up to 6 feet long and hairy leaves. The compound leaves, which are smaller than those of common vetch, have 10 to 20 narrow leaflets and end in a tendril. The flower clusters are made up of 10 to 20 purplish red flowers, arranged on one side of the stalk. The seedpod is small, ³/₄–1 inch long.

Life cycle: Annuals that reproduce by seed

Management: As with other annual weeds, you need to pull vetch before it sets seed. The stems twine around other plants and tend to break off when pulled, making it difficult to remove the whole weed at once. Landscape fabric or a thick mulch around vegetables and ornamentals will help prevent seeds already in the soil from germinating.

If chemical control is necessary, use a selective herbicide for broad-leafed weeds that contains MCPA or dicamba. Or use a nonselective herbicide containing glyphosate, taking care to protect desired plants from this chemical. Always apply herbicides according to directions on the label.

✎ *Notes: The seedpods of vetch resemble those of peas, but vetch contains toxic substances and should never be eaten.*

VIOLETS

VIOLA (VIOLACEAE)

BROAD-LEAFED ANNUALS AND PERENNIALS

✎ ZONES: ALL

Sweet-smelling violets can be charming garden plants, but they can also be pests if they spread out of control, invading lawns or garden beds planted with more delicate perennials. They are most likely to be troublesome in moist, shaded areas of the lawn or garden. The familiar sweet violet *(Viola odorata),* a perennial, has dark green heart-shaped leaves, toothed on the margins, on a mounding 6–10-inch-tall plant. The fragrant short-spurred flowers are usually deep violet but sometimes bluish rose or white. Sweet violet spreads by long leafy stolons, or runners. The perennial Labrador violet *(V. labradorica),* shown above, is lower growing, only about 3 inches high, with roundish, 1-inch leaves tinged with purple. The tiny lavender blue flowers appear in spring. This violet spreads aggressively by runners and by seeding. Field violet *(V. arvensis),* also known as wild pansy, is an annual with prostrate or erect branching stems growing 2–15 inches tall and coarsely toothed, egg-shaped leaves. This violet has showy cream-colored flowers. Another annual violet, Johnny-jump-up *(V. tricolor),* grows 6–12 inches tall with oval, deeply lobed leaves. The purple-and-yellow flowers appear in spring. Both annual species self-sow prolifically.

Life cycle: Annuals and perennials that reproduce by seed; perennials also reproduce by runners

Management: To curb perennial sweet violet and Labrador violet, confine these spreaders with a barrier of wood or brick. To get rid of them, dig them out, removing as much of the roots as possible. Cut down or dig up new shoots as they appear, until they stop resprouting. Pull up annual violets before they set seed. A thick mulch will prevent seeds of all of these violets from sprouting, and will suppress the roots of the perennial kinds.

If chemical control is necessary, spray an herbicidal soap on young plants. Use a product containing glyphosate on older plants, taking care not to get this chemical on desired plants.

WILLOWWEED, PANICLE

EPILOBIUM BRACHYCARPUM (ONAGRACEAE)

BROAD-LEAFED ANNUAL

✎ ZONES: ALL

Panicle willowweed, also called panicle willowherb, is an annual native to the West. It occurs in the wild in grassland and dry open woodland and along roadsides. It can be a weed in gardens, orchards, and vineyards. The seeds of panicle willowweed germinate in spring, and the plant matures, setting seed in mid- to late summer. If germination happens in the cool weather of early spring, the seed leaves (cotyledons) are small, rounded, and reddish green. Seeds that germinate later, in warmer weather, produce dark green seed leaves. During the early stages of growth, this plant is quite leafy. The leaves, which alternate on the stem, are narrow, about ½–2 inches long, with shallow teeth. Very small leaves (fascicles) appear at the base of each leaf. Before panicle willowweed reaches maturity, it sheds its leaves, leaving the angular stems bare and peeling. Mature height ranges from only 8 inches to over 6 feet. Clusters of small white to rose purple flowers are carried on thin stalks. The flowers have four petals, each split deeply in the middle. The seedpods are ¾–2½ inches long and very narrow. They split open, exposing the small seeds, which have soft tufts of hair that enable them to float away on the wind.

Life cycle: Annual that reproduces by seed

Management: As panicle willowweed produces many seeds that are scattered far and wide, you will need to pull or mow the plants before they set seed. Mulching around vegetables and ornamentals will prevent seed already in the soil from germinating. The seeds of this weed are killed by solarization.

If chemical control is necessary, use herbicidal soap; this product is most effective on young plants. Or use a product containing glyphosate, taking care not to get this chemical on desired plants.

✎ *Notes: A related plant, fireweed* (Epilobium angustifolium), *is a perennial that is common in much of the West. It grows from spreading rootstocks and seeds and can have stems as tall as 9 feet. Its leaves, up to 8 inches long and lance shaped, are not shed early in the season. The showy rose or purple flowers are borne on long spikes at the ends of the stems.*

WITCHGRASS

PANICUM CAPILLARE (POACEAE)

ANNUAL GRASS

✄ ZONES: ALL

Witchgrass, also called tickle grass, tumble panic, or witches' hair, is a common weed in gardens, lawns, orchards, and vineyards. This bushy, branching grass germinates from seed in spring and grows 1–2 feet high. Although similar to crabgrass seedlings, witchgrass seedlings have narrower leaf blades and silky hairs on the lower part of the leaf blade (sheath) that encloses the stem. Mature witchgrass plants are covered with hairs swollen at the bases. The light green leaf blades are 1/8–9/16 inches wide and 2–8 inches long. The ligule (an appendage at the base of the leaf blade) is a fringe of hairs. The flowering head is large, 6–16 inches long, with slender, spreading branches, each bearing a single shiny seed at the tip. The whole head breaks off at maturity and blows about, scattering seed.

Witchgrass sheath with hairs (left); ligule (right)

Life cycle: Annual that reproduces by seed

Management: Witchgrass is shallow rooted, so it is fairly easy to hoe or pull. Be sure to remove this weed before its seeds form. Mulch will prevent seeds already in the soil from germinating.

If chemical control is needed, apply a pre-emergence product containing pendimethalin or oryzalin over the lawn grasses and ornamentals that are listed on the label. Selective postemergence herbicides for grasses—containing fluazifop-butyl or sethoxydim—will control this weed. Always apply herbicides according to directions on the label. You can also use a nonselective herbicide containing glyphosate or glufosinate-ammonium; take care not to get these chemicals on desired plants.

 Notes: Two annual grasses closely related to witchgrass are also found in gardens in the West. Fall panicum (Panicum dichotomiflorum) grows up to 3 feet tall, with an upright or spreading habit of growth. Its leaf blades are smooth, with a prominent white midrib. The flower head is more compact than that of witchgrass. Texas panicum (P. texanum) grows 20 inches to 5 feet tall, with some lower stems rooting where the nodes touch the soil. The leaves are velvety.

YARROW, COMMON

ACHILLEA MILLEFOLIUM (ASTERACEAE)

BROAD-LEAFED PERENNIAL

✄ ZONES: ALL

Common yarrow, also known as milfoil, is a native found in the wild in many plant communities, including open forest, sagebrush, and meadows. In gardens, common yarrow and named garden varieties derived from it, such as 'Rosea' and 'Fire King', are often planted as drought-tolerant ground covers. However, this tough plant sometimes invades lawns, as well as beds planted in more delicate perennials; its spreading rhizomes make it difficult to remove. The presence of yarrow in lawns may indicate that the soil is acidic and infertile. Common yarrow grows 2–4 feet tall if left unmowed; in lawns, it adapts to mowing and grows as low rosettes of foliage. The aromatic 2–6-inch-long leaves are lance shaped in outline and finely divided, giving the plant a feathery appearance. Both stems and foliage are covered with fine hairs. If yarrow is not mowed, flat-topped clusters made up of many individual flowers appear throughout the summer at the ends of the stems. The flowers are most often white in the wild form of yarrow, but pinkish or yellow forms may occur. Named varieties have red, salmon, or rose pink flowers. Seeds are produced from late summer through fall.

Life cycle: Perennial that reproduces by seed and spreading rhizomes

Management: In lawns, dig out yarrow, getting as much of the root system as possible, repeating if new growth appears. To help prevent re-infestation in lawns, have the soil tested; if it is overly acidic, add lime as recommended by the testing laboratory. Thicken the turf through fertilization and proper watering to help it compete with weeds. To keep a ground cover of yarrow from spreading into other areas, install a barrier of wooden strips or bricks. In gardens, hoe or dig out yarrow. Once an area is cleared, cover it with a dense mulch of cardboard or black plastic, topped with bark chips, for at least one growing season.

If chemical control is necessary, use a selective herbicide, labeled for broad-leafed weeds and containing dicamba. A nonselective herbicide containing glyphosate will kill yarrow, but take care not to get this chemical on desired plants. Always apply herbicides according to directions on the label.

Green lacewing

RESOURCE DIRECTORY

*H*ere *is information on a variety of resources, which should help make easier the job of planning, creating, and maintaining a healthy garden. You'll find a host of mail-order suppliers, many of which specialize in IPM products and tools; state pesticide agencies, for the last word in pesticide safety; and a listing of cooperative extension offices, which are ready to help with plant and pest identification or with management issues.*

MAIL-ORDER SUPPLIERS

These days there seems to be an ever-increasing number of garden-related products available through the mail. Not uncommon in the product lines of the mail-order suppliers are IPM products and tools, as well as disease- and pest-resistant plant varieties and native seeds and plants. Western suppliers are well represented in the list that follows. Call or write to these companies for current catalog prices. Addresses and phone numbers are subject to change.

GENERAL PRODUCTS AND SERVICES

A&L Western Laboratories, Inc.
1311 Woodland Avenue, Suite 1
Modesto, CA 95351
(209) 529-4080; fax (209) 529-4736
http://www.al-labs-west.com
A&L tests soil samples by mail. Send a 1-pint sample taken from the top 6 inches of earth for pH, nematode, and pesticide content analysis. The S3C package suits most home gardeners.

Arbico
Box 4247 CRB
Tucson, AZ 85738
(800) 827-2847
Carries a full line of row covers, pheromone and other traps, hand lenses, beneficial organisms, natural chemical controls, sprayers and dusters, and soil care products.

Beneficial Insectary
14751 Oak Run Road
Oak Run, CA 96069
(800) 477-3715; fax (560) 472-3523
e-mail: bi@insectary.com
Specializes in beneficial insects.

BioLogic
Box 177
Willow Hill, PA 17271
(717) 349-2789
Produces a biological insecticide made from beneficial nematodes called the Scanmask®.

Biological Control of Weeds
1418 Maple Drive
Bozeman, MT 59715
(406) 586-5111
Supplies beneficial insects and information on weed management.

Bountiful Gardens
18001 Shafer Ranch Road
Willits, CA 95490
(707) 459-6410
e-mail: bountiful@zapcom.net
Primarily a seed supplier, but also sells natural chemical pest and weed management tools.

Gardener's Supply Company
128 Intervale Road
Burlington, VT 05401
(800) 444-6417

Apple maggot trap

Carries a full line of row covers, pheromone and other traps, hand lenses, beneficial organisms, natural chemical controls, sprayers and dusters, and soil care products.

Gardens Alive!
5100 Schenley Place
Lawrenceburg, IN 47025
(812) 537-8650; fax (812) 537-5108
e-mail: 76375.2160@compuserve.com
Supplies products for pest and weed management, such as traps, beneficial insects, repellents, natural chemical controls, sprayers and dusters, and row covers.

Floating row cover over turnips

Gempler's
211 Blue Mountain Road
Box 270
Mount Horeb, WI 53572
(800) 382-8473; fax (800) 551-1128
Supplies pheromone and other traps and lures; weed management fabrics and mats; repellents, sprayers, and protective equipment; and beneficial organisms.

Great Lakes IPM
10220 Church Road Northeast
Vestaburg, MI 48891
(517) 268-5693; fax (517) 268-5311
Supplies pheromone and other traps, beneficial organisms, row covers, and netting.

Harmony Farm Supply & Nursery
Box 460
Graton, CA 95444
(707) 823-9125; fax (707) 823-1734
Carries a full line of row covers, pheromone and other traps, hand lenses, beneficial organisms, natural chemical controls, sprayers and dusters, and soil care products.

Integrated Fertility Management (IFM)
333 Ohme Gardens Road
Wenatchee, WA 98801
(800) 323-3179
Carries a full line of row covers, pheromone and other traps, hand lenses, beneficial organisms, natural chemical controls, sprayers and dusters, and soil care products.

Nature's Control
Box 35
Medford, OR 97501
(503) 899-9751
Supplies natural pest controls ranging from predatory nematodes to Snail Barr® copper stripping.

Nitron Industries, Inc.
Box 1447
Fayetteville, AR 72702-1447
(800) 835-0123
Specializes in organic enzymes, beneficial organisms, fertilizers, foliar sprays, soil conditioners, and sprayers and applicators.

Peaceful Valley Farm Supply
Box 2209
Grass Valley, CA 95945
(916) 272-4769
Carries a full line of row covers, pheromone and other traps, hand lenses, beneficial organisms, natural chemical controls, sprayers and dusters, and soil care products.

Planet Natural
Box 3146
Bozeman, MT 59772
(800) 289-6656; fax (406) 587-0223
e-mail: ecostore@mcn.net
http://www.planetnatural.com/
Supplies natural pest, disease, and weed controls, as well as gardening tools and other products.

Ringer Corporation
9555 James Avenue South, Suite 200
Bloomington, MN 55431
(612) 703-3300; fax (612) 887-1300
Supplies natural chemical controls, fertilizers, and soil and lawn care products.

Rocky Mountain Insectary
Box 152
Palisades, CO 81526
Supplies beneficial insects.

Sterling International
Box 220
Liberty Lake, WA 99019
(800) 666-6766; fax (509) 928-7313
e-mail: sterling@rescue.com
http://www.rescue.com
Sterling's RESCUE!® is a reusable and disposable trap for a variety of insect pests. Also supplies dog and cat repellents.

Tumblebug
2029 North 23rd Street
Boise, ID 83702
(800) 531-0102
The Tumblebug® is a rolling composter.

Worm's Way
7850 Highway 37 North
Bloomington, IN 47404-9477
(800) 274-9676; fax (800) 316-1264
http://www.wormsway.com
Supplies a variety of items such as fertilizers, insect traps, plant protectors, and composters.

NATIVE PLANT AND SEED SPECIALISTS

Abundant Life Seed Foundation
Box 772
Port Townsend, WA 98368
(360) 385-5660; fax (360) 385-7455
e-mail: abundant@olypen.com

A High Country Garden
2902 Rufina Street
Santa Fe, NM 87505
(800) 925-9387; fax (505) 438-9552

Desert Moon Nursery
Box 600
Veguita, NM 87062
(505) 864-0614

A healthy newborn

Garden City Seeds
778 Highway 93 North
Hamilton, MT 59840
(406) 961-4837; fax (406) 961-4877
e-mail: seed@juno.com

Great Basin Natives
Box 114
Holden, UT 84636
(801) 795-2236

Greenlee Nursery
257 East Franklin Avenue
Pomona, CA 91766
(909) 629-9045; fax (909) 620-9283

High Altitude Gardens—Seeds Trust
Box 1048
Hailey, ID 83333
(208) 788-4419; fax (208) 788-3452

Inside Passage
Box 639
Port Townsend, WA 98368
(800) 361-9657; fax (360) 385-5760
e-mail: inspass@whidbey.net

Sunflower and seeds

Joy Creek Nursery
20300 Northwest Watson Road
Scappoose, OR 97056
(503) 543-7474

Las Pilitas Nursery
Las Pilitas Road
Santa Margarita, CA 93453
(805) 438-5992; fax (805) 438-5993

Native Seeds/SEARCH
2509 North Campbell Avenue
Box 325
Tucson, AZ 85719
(602) 327-9123

Northwest Native Seed
915 Davis Place South
Seattle, WA 98144
(206) 845-1504

Valley Nursery
Box 4845
Helena, MT 59604
(406) 458-3992

STATE PESTICIDE AGENCIES

Each western state has an agency dedicated to pesticide regulation. These agencies maintain databases on the pesticides they register and can be contacted for information on specific products and how to use them correctly. Agencies are listed alphabetically by state.

Environmental Services Division
Arizona Department of Agriculture
1688 West Adams Street
Phoenix, AZ 85007
(602) 542-3578

California Department of Pesticide Regulation
1020 N Street, Room 100
Sacramento, CA 95814-5624
(916) 445-4300

Division of Plant Industry
Colorado Department of Agriculture
700 Kipling Street, Suite 4000
Lakewood, CO 80215-5894
(303) 239-4140

Division of Agricultural Resources
Idaho Department of Agriculture
Box 790
Boise, ID 83701-0790
(208) 332-8605

Agricultural Sciences Division
Montana Department of Agriculture
Box 200201
Helena, MT 59620-0201
(406) 444-2944

Bureau of Plant Industry
Nevada Division of Agriculture
350 Capitol Hill Avenue
Reno, NV 89502
(702) 688-1180

Bureau of Pesticide Management
Div. of Agricultural & Environmental Services
New Mexico State Dept. of Agriculture
Box 3005, MSC-3AQ
Las Cruces, NM 88003-0005
(505) 646-2133

Plant Division
Oregon Department of Agriculture
635 Capitol Street Northeast
Salem, OR 97310-0110
(503) 986-4635

From top: 'Lettuce Leaf' basil, 'Opal' basil, and 'Greek Miniature' basil

Division of Plant Industry
Utah Department of Agriculture
Box 146500
Salt Lake City, UT 84114-6500
(801) 538-7180

Pesticide Management Division
Washington State Department of Agriculture
Box 42589
Olympia, WA 98504-2560
(360) 902-2010

Technical Services
Wyoming Department of Agriculture
2219 Carey Avenue
Cheyenne, WY 82002-0100
(307) 777-6590

National Pesticide Telecommunications Network
(800) 858-7378
US Environmental Protection Agency's pesticide hotline.

OTHER ORGANIZATIONS AND WEB SITES

When it comes to pest, disease, and weed management, there are a number of organizations and Web sites that promote the use of the least toxic products available. Some of these groups require membership, while others provide information free of charge.

ORGANIZATIONS

Bio-Integral Resource Center (BIRC)
Box 7414
Berkeley, CA 94704
(510) 524-2567
Promotes the least toxic methods of managing pests.

Biological Urban Gardening Services (BUGS)
Box 76
Citrus Heights, CA 95611-0076
(916) 726-5377
e-mail: bugslrc@cwia.com
Promotes ecologically sound landscape horticulture through the reduced use of potentially toxic pesticides and fertilizers. Also provides information on alternatives through its quarterly newsletter.

National Coalition Against the Misuse of Pesticides (NCAMP)
701 E Street Southeast, Suite 200
Washington, DC 20003
(202) 543-5450
e-mail: ncamp@igc.apc.org
http://www.ncamp.org or **www.csn.net/ncamp**
Promotes alternatives to highly toxic pesticides and provides information about the hazards associated with pesticide use.

Northwest Coalition for Alternatives to Pesticides (NCAP)
Box 1393
Eugene, OR 97440
(541) 344-5044
e-mail: info@pesticide.org
http://www.efn.org/~ncap/
Works to reduce pesticide use by providing information on alternatives for many pest problems.

Pesticide Action Network (PAN)
North American Regional Center
116 New Montgomery Street, Suite 810
San Francisco, CA 94105
(415) 541-9140; fax (415) 541-9253
e-mail: panna@panna.org
Provides information about the hazards of misusing pesticides and about ecologically sound alternatives.

Pesticide Watch
116 New Montgomery Street, Suite 530
San Francisco, CA 94105
(415) 543-2627
e-mail: pestiwatch@igc.apc.org
Seeks to reduce pesticide use and to promote alternative methods of managing pests and diseases.

Washington Toxics Coalition
4516 University Way Northeast
Seattle, WA 98105
(206) 632-1545
e-mail: wtc@igc.apc.org
Provides information about pesticides and their alternatives.

WEB SITES

California Department of Pesticide Regulation
http://www.cdpr.ca.gov/docs/label/m4.htm
Lists pesticides registered for use in the state of California.

National IPM Network
http://www.colostate.edu/Depts/IPM/index.html
Links to many other IPM sites.

Washington State University Gardening in Western Washington
http://gardening.wsu.edu
Covers ecology, composting, integrated pest management, and more.

Snail

COOPERATIVE EXTENSION SERVICES

The cooperative extension service is organized by county or region. Your local horticultural agent, often a native plant specialist, is a valuable resource.

Aquilegia McKana hybrid

ARIZONA

Apache   (520) 337-2267
Cochise   (520) 384-3594
Coconino   (520) 774-1868
Gila   (520) 425-7179
Graham   (520) 428-2611
Greenlee   (520) 359-2261
La Paz   (520) 669-9843
Maricopa   (602) 470-8086 ext. 310
Mohave   (520) 753-3788
Navajo   (520) 524-6271
Navajo Nation   (520) 871-7406
Pima   (520) 626-5161
Pinal   (520) 836-5221
Santa Cruz   (520) 761-7849
Yavapai   (520) 445-6590
Yuma   (520) 329-2150

CALIFORNIA

Alameda   (510) 567-6812
Amador   (209) 223-6482
Butte   (530) 538-7201
Calaveras   (209) 754-6477
Colusa   (530) 458-0570
Contra Costa   (510) 646-6540
Del Norte   (707) 464-4711
El Dorado   (530) 621-5502
Fresno   (209) 456-7285
Glenn   (530) 865-1107
Humboldt   (707) 445-7351
Imperial   (619) 352-9474
Inyo-Mono   (619) 873-7854
Kern   (805) 868-6200
Kings   (209) 582-3211
Lake   (707) 263-2281
Lassen   (530) 257-6363
Los Angeles   (213) 744-4851
Madera   (209) 675-7879
Marin   (415) 899-8620
Mariposa   (209) 966-2417
Mendocino   (707) 463-4495
Merced   (209) 385-7403
Modoc   (530) 233-6400
Monterey   (408) 759-7350
Napa   (707) 253-4221
Nevada   (see Placer)

Orange   (714) 708-1606
Placer   (530) 889-7385
Plumas   (530) 283-6270
Riverside   (909) 683-6491
Sacramento   (916) 875-6913
San Benito   (408) 637-5346
San Bernardino   (909) 387-2166
San Diego   (619) 694-2845
San Francisco   (415) 871-7559
San Joaquin   (209) 468-2085
San Luis Obispo   (805) 781-5940
San Mateo   (650) 726-9059
Santa Barbara   (805) 934-6240
Santa Clara   (408) 299-2635
Santa Cruz   (408) 763-8040
Shasta-Trinity   (530) 224-4900
Sierra   (see Plumas)
Siskiyou   (916) 842-2711
Solano   (707) 421-6790
Sonoma   (707) 527-2621
Stanislaus   (209) 525-6654
Sutter-Yuba   (530) 822-7515
Tehama   (530) 527-3101
Tulare   (209) 733-6363
Tuolumne   (209) 533-5695
Ventura   (805) 645-1451
Yolo   (916) 666-8143

A Rocky Mountain garden

COLORADO

Adams   (303) 659-4150
Alamosa   (719) 589-2271
Arapahoe   (303) 730-1920
Archuleta   (970) 264-5931
Baca   (719) 523-6971
Bent   (719) 456-0764
Boulder   (303) 444-1121
Chaffee   (719) 539-6447
Cheyenne   (719) 767-5716
Conejos   (see Alamosa)
Costilla   (see Alamosa)
Crowley   (719) 267-4741
Custer   (719) 783-2514
Delta   (970) 874-2195
Denver   (303) 640-5273
Dolores   (970) 677-2283
Douglas   (303) 688-3096
Eagle   (970) 328-8775
El Paso   (719) 636-8920
Elbert   (719) 541-2361
Fremont   (719) 275-1514
Garfield   (970) 945-7437
Grand   (970) 724-3436
Gunnison   (970) 641-1260
Huerfano   (719) 738-2170
Jackson   (970) 723-4298
Jefferson   (303) 271-6620
Kiowa   (719) 438-5321
Kit Carson   (719) 346-5571
La Plata   (970) 247-4355
Larimer   (970) 498-7400
Las Animas   (719) 846-6881
Lincoln   (719) 743-2542
Logan   (970) 522-3200
Mesa   (970) 244-1834
Mineral   (see Alamosa)
Moffat   (970) 824-6673
Montezuma   (970) 565-3123

Montrose   (970) 249-3935
Morgan   (970) 867-2493
Otero   (719) 254-7608
Ouray   (see Montrose)
Park   (719) 836-4289
Phillips   (970) 854-3616
Prowers   (719) 336-7734
Pueblo   (719) 583-6566
Rio Blanco   (970) 878-4093
Rio Grande   (see Alamosa)
Routt   (970) 879-0825
Saguache   (see Alamosa)
San Miguel   (970) 327-4393
Sedgwick   (970) 474-3479
Summit   (970) 668-3595
Teller   (719) 689-2552
Washington   (970) 345-2287
Weld   (970) 356-4000 ext. 4465
Yuma   (970) 332-4151

IDAHO

Ada   (208) 377-2107
Adams   (208) 253-4279
Bannock   (208) 236-7310
Bear Lake   (208) 945-2265
Benewah   (208) 245-2422
Bingham   (208) 785-8060
Blaine   (208) 788-5585
Bonner   (208) 263-8511
Bonneville   (208) 529-1390
Boundary   (208) 267-3235
Butte   (208) 527-8587
Camas   (208) 764-2230
Canyon   (208) 459-6003
Caribou   (208) 547-3205
Cassia   (208) 678-9461
Clark   (208) 374-5405
Clearwater   (208) 476-4434
Custer   (208) 879-2344
Elmore   (208) 587-2136
Fort Hall   (208) 238-3777
Franklin   (208) 852-1097
Fremont   (208) 624-3102
Gem   (208) 365-6363
Gooding   (208) 934-4417
Idaho   (208) 983-2667
Jefferson   (208) 745-6685
Jerome   (208) 324-7578
Kootenai   (208) 667-6426
Latah   (208) 883-2267
Lemhi   (208) 756-2824

Sunset on the Lembi Mountains of Idaho

Lewis   (208) 937-2311
Lincoln   (208) 886-2406
Madison   (208) 356-3191
Minidoka   (208) 436-7184
Nez Perce   (208) 799-3096
Oneida   (208) 766-2243
Owyhee   (208) 896-4104
Payette   (208) 642-6022
Power   (208) 226-7621
Teton   (208) 354-2961
Twin Falls   (208) 734-9590
Valley   (208) 382-3249
Washington   (208) 549-0415

MONTANA

Beaverhead   (406) 683-2842
Big Horn   (406) 665-1405
Blackfeet Res.   (406) 338-2650
Blaine   (406) 357-3200
Broadwater   (406) 266-3419
Carbon   (406) 962-3522

Cascade   (406) 454-6980
Chouteau   (406) 622-3751
Custer   (406) 233-3370
Daniels   (406) 487-2861
Dawson   (406) 365-4277
Deer Lodge   (406) 563-8421 ext. 231
Fallon/Carter   (406) 778-2883 ext. 40
Fergus   (406) 538-3919
Flathead   (406) 758-5553
Fort Belknap Reservation
    (406) 353-2205 ext. 484
Gallatin   (406) 582-3280
Garfield   (406) 557-2770
Glacier   (406) 873-2239
Granite   (406) 859-3771
Hill   (406) 265-5481 ext. 33
Judith Basin   (406) 566-2270
Lake   (406) 676-4271
Lewis and Clark   (406) 447-8346
Liberty   (406) 759-5625
Lincoln   (406) 293-7781
Madison/Jefferson   (406) 287-3282
McCone   (406) 485-2605

Montana (continued)

Mineral   (406) 822-3545
Missoula   (406) 721-4095
Musselshell/Golden Valley
   (406) 323-2704
Northern Cheyenne Reservation
   (406) 477-6498
Park   (406) 222-4156
Phillips   (406) 654-2543
Pondera   (406) 278-4054
Powder River   (406) 436-2424
Powell   (406) 846-3680
Prairie   (406) 635-2121
Ravalli   (406) 375-6245
Richland   (406) 482 1206
Roosevelt   (406) 787-5312
Rosebud/Treasure   (406) 356-7320
Sanders   (406) 827-4394
Sheridan   (406) 765-2310
Silver Bow   (406) 723-8262 ext. 226
Stillwater   (406) 322-5334
Sweetgrass   (406) 932-5146
Teton   (406) 466-2491
Toole   (406) 434-5351
Valley   (406) 288-8221 ext. 41
Wibaux   (406) 795-2486
Yellowstone   (406) 256-2828

Nevada

Southern counties   (702) 222-3130
Western counties   (702) 784-4848

Fall colors in the Ruby Mountains of Nevada

Spuria irises and tawny gaillardia in a New Mexico garden

New Mexico

Bernalillo   (505) 243-1386
Catron   (505) 533-6430
Chaves   (505) 622-3210
Cibola   (505) 287-9266
Colfax   (505) 445-8071
Curry   (505) 763-6505
De Baca   (505) 355-2381
Dona Ana   (505) 525-6649
Eddy   (505) 887-6595
Grant   (505) 388-1559
Guadalupe   (505) 472-3652
Harding   (505) 673-2341
Hidalgo   (505) 542-9291
Lea   (505) 396-2819
Lincoln   (505) 648-2311
Los Alamos   (505) 662-2656
Luna   (505) 546-8806
McKinley   (505) 863-3432
Mora   (505) 387-2856
Otero   (505) 437-0231
Quay   (505) 461-0562
Rio Arriba   (505) 753-3405
Roosevelt   (505) 356-4417
San Juan   (505) 334-9496
San Miguel   (505) 454-1497
Sandoval   (505) 867-2582
Santa Fe   (505) 471-4711
Sierra   (505) 894-2375

Socorro   (505) 835-0610
Taos   (505) 758-3982
Torrance   (505) 384-2416
Union   (505) 374-9361
Valencia   (505) 865-9561

Oregon

Baker   (541) 523-6418
Benton   (541) 757-6750
Clackamas   (503) 655-8631
Clatsop   (503) 325-8573
Columbia   (503) 397-3462
Coos   (541) 396-3121 ext. 240
Crook   (541) 447-6228
Curry   (541) 247-6672
Deschutes   (541) 548-6088
Douglas   (541) 672-4461
Gilliam   (541) 384-2271
Grant   (541) 575-1911
Harney   (541) 573-2506
Hood River   (541) 386-3343
Jackson   (541) 776-7371
Jefferson   (541) 475-3808
Klamath   (541) 883-7131
Lake   (541) 947-6054
Lane   (541) 682-4243
Lincoln   (541) 265-4107
Linn   (541) 967-3871

Malheur   (541) 881-1417
Marion   (505) 588-5301
Morrow   (541) 676-9642
Multnomah   (503) 725-2000
Polk   (503) 623-8395
Sherman   (541) 565-3230
Tillamook   (503) 842-3433
Umatilla   (541) 278-5403
Union   (541) 963-1010
Wallowa   (541) 426 3143
Wasco   (541) 296-5494
Washington   (503) 725-2300
Wheeler   (541) 763-4115
Yamhill   (503) 434-7517

UTAH

Beaver   (435) 438-6451
Box Elder   (435) 734-2031
Cache   (435) 752-6263
Carbon   (435) 636-3200
Davis   (435) 451-3402
Duchesne   (435) 738-2435
Emery   (435) 381-2381
Garfield   (435) 676-8826
Grand   (435) 259-7558
Iron   (435) 586-8132
Juab   (435) 623-1791
Kane   (435) 644-2551
Millard   (435) 743-5412
Morgan   (435) 829-3472

Piute   (435) 577-2901
Rich   (435) 793-2435
Salt Lake   (435) 468-3183
San Juan   (435) 587-3329
Sanpete   (435) 835-2151
Sevier   (435) 869-9262
Summit   (435) 336-4451
Tooele   (435) 882-9170
Uintah   (435) 781-5452
Utah   (435) 370-8464
Wasatch   (435) 654-3211
Washington   (435) 652-5814
Wayne   (435) 836-2662
Weber   (435) 399-8203

WASHINGTON

Adams   (509) 659-3209 ext. 214
Asotin   (509) 243-2018
Benton   (509) 786-5609
Chelan   (509) 664-5540
Clallam   (360) 417-2279
Clark   (360) 254-8436
Columbia   (509) 382-4741
Cowlitz   (360) 577-3014
Douglas   (509) 745-8531
Ferry   (509) 775-5235
Franklin   (509) 545-3511
Garfield   (509) 843-3701
Grant   (509) 754-2011 ext. 412
Grays Harbor   (360) 249-4332

Island   (360) 679-7327
Jefferson   (360) 379-5610
King   (206) 296-3900
Kitsap   (360) 876-7157
Kittitas   (509) 962-7507
Klickitat   (509) 773-5817
Lewis   (360) 740-1212
Lincoln   (509) 725-4171
Mason   (360) 427-9670 ext. 395
Okanogan   (509) 422-7245
Pacific   (360) 875-9331
Pend Oreille   (509) 447-2401
Pierce   (206) 591-7180
San Juan   (360) 378-4414
Skagit   (360) 428-4270
Skamania   (509) 427-9427
Snohomish   (206) 338-2400
Spokane   (509) 533-2048
Stevens   (509) 684-2588
Thurston   (360) 786-5445
Wahkiakum   (360) 795-3278
Walla Walla   (509) 527-3260
Whatcom   (360) 676-6736
Whitman   (509) 397-6290
Yakima   (509) 574-1600

WYOMING

Albany   (307) 721-2571
Big Horn   (307) 568-2278
Campbell   (307) 682-7281
Carbon   (307) 328-2642
Converse   (307) 358-2417
Crook   (307) 283-1192
Fremont   (307) 332-1044
Goshen   (307) 532-2436
Hot Springs   (307) 864-3421
Johnson   (307) 684-7522
Laramie   (307) 633-4383
Lincoln   (307) 886-3132
Natrona   (307) 235-9400
Niobrara   (307) 334-3534
Park   (307) 587-2204 ext. 248
Platte   (307) 322-3667
Sheridan   (307) 674-2980
Surlette   (307) 367-4380
Sweetwater   (307) 352-6775
Teton   (307) 733-3087
Uinta   (307) 789-3277
Washakie   (307) 347-3431
Weston   (307) 746-3531

Balsamroot on Dog Mountain, Washington

INDEX

Note: Plants are listed under their common names, unless they have none or are more commonly known by their botanical names. Page references in **bold type** indicate encyclopedia entries. Encyclopedia entries for pests and beneficials, diseases and cultural problems, and weeds always show a photograph; a number of plants are illustrated as well. Page references in *italics* indicate other illustrations.

PHOTOGRAPHY CREDITS

For pages with 4 or fewer photographs, each image has been identified by its position on the page: Left (L), center (C), or right (R); top (T), middle (M), or bottom (B). On other pages, photographs are identified by their position in the grid (shown right). Photographs on the back cover are designated as "back".

L	LC	RC	R
1	1	1	1
2			
3			
4			

William D. Adams: 153 TR; 185 R; 206 BR, ML; 218 L; 243 L. **Walt Anderson:** 49; 180 L; 256 BL; 263 R; 273 L, M; 274 L; 286 BR; 292 TL. **Art Antonelli:** 157 L. **Max E. Badgley:** 24; 51 BR; 174 BR, TR; 181 BL; 184 L; 304 L. **Tom Bean:** 14 B. **Leann Beeman-Simms:** 75 CT; 80 R. **Paul M. Bowers:** 58 T. **Marion Brenner:** 6 TR; 25; 84 L; 89 TL; 109 C4; 110 L; 308 T. **Lisa Butler:** 89 BL. **Ralph S. Byther:** 167 L; 177 R; 193 L; 211 R; 212 R; 213 R; 216 R; 217 L; 219 R; 220 L; 221 L; 222 R; 224 L; 225 L; 226 L; 227 L, R; 232 L; 233 L; 235 R; 236 L; 237 L; 238 R; 242 R; 250 L; 253 L. **R. Calentine/Visuals Unlimited:** 221 R. **James L. Castner:** 148 BR; 150 R4; 156 B; 165 R. **David Cavagnaro:** 26 TR; 28 B; 125 M, T; 127 TL; 128; 133 BL; 136 M. **Walter Chandoha:** 126 T; 130 B; 306 TR. **Jack K. Clark:** 109 L. **Sharon J. Collman:** 70 L; 75 CB; 154 R; 169 L; 187 L, TR; 191 L; 201 L. **Patrick Cone:** 309; 310 B. **Ed Cooper:** 8 BL, BR, TL, TR; 16 B; 18 R; 21 T; 58 M. **Crandall & Crandall:** 28 C; 51 TL; 53 R; 60; 96 R; 107; 116; 124 R; 149; 304 R. **Rosalind Creasy:** 34 B, T; 35 B, T; 126 M; 132 R; 137 B. **D. Cudney:** 109 R1; 257. **Claire Curran:** 87 L; 93 R; 109 C2; 112 BL; 114 M; 115 L, M. **David M. Dennis/ Tom Stack & Associates:** 199 MR. **Alan & Linda Detrick:** 122 L; 130 M; 134 BL, M. **William Dewey:** 109 C3. **James F. Dill:** 150 L1, L2; 178 L; 183 L; 192 R. **Ken Druse:** 48. **Clyde Elmore:** 266 BR; 268 L, TR; 269 BR; 270 R; 272 L, R; 276 TR; 278 R; 297 L; 298 L, R. **Thomas E. Eltzroth:** 52 R; 117 BL, BR; 215 L; 216 L; 230 L; 234 L, R. **Craig Engle:** 90 L. **William E. Ferguson:** 32 T; 63 L, R; 96 L; 155 R; 156 R; 158 L; 166 L; 172 BL; 173 R; 177 L; 182 L, TR; 183 BR, TR; 184 R; 186 R; 189 L, R; 191 BR; 192 L; 199 BR; 205 BR, MR; 206 BL; 207 TL. **Charles Marden Fitch:** 45 BL, BR; 153 TL; 172 R; 194 L; 199 TR. **Flame Engineering, Inc.:** 54 R. **John Gerlach/Tom Stack & Associates:** 108 BR. **Marion Gilsenan:** 28 T. **David Goldberg:** 18 L; 39; 43 BL; 51 TL; 54 L; 62; 68 L, R; 72 TR; 75 T; 76 T; 82 T; 84 R; 85 M; 92 M, R; 93 M; 99 L, R; 106; 111 M; 112 R; 127 BL, R; 131 L; 135 L; 208 BR; 244 R; 245 L; 248 R; 251 L; 254 L; 255 L; 256 BR, TL; 260 R; 261 R; 262 L; 263 L; 265 BL; 268 BR; 271 L; 278 TL; 279 L; 281 L; 283 BR; 285 L; 288 R; 289 L; 290 R; 293 L; 295 TL; 302 R. **Mick Hales:** 20 R. **Ali Harivandi:** 231 L; 247 R; 253 R; 261 TL; 269 TR. **Phil Harvey:** 246 L. **Saxon Holt:** 19 T; 26 BR; 38 L; 50; 53 L; 64 T; 73; 121; 124 L; 135 R; 243 R; 281 R; 300 R; 302 L. **James Frederick Housel:** 58 B; 88 M. **Sandra Ivany:** 118. **A.L. Jones/Visuals Unlimited:** 219 L. **Suzanne Kores/Fairchild Tropical Garden:** 66. **Dwight Kuhn:** 40. **Eric LaGasa:** 158 R; 203 L. **David Langston:** 159 R, TR. **Weldon Lee:** 207 BL. **Dr. Lyon:** 178 R. **Ray Maleike:** 225 R; 248 L; 249 R; 252 L; 254 R. **Allan Mandell:** back BR; 17 M, T; 26 TL; 311. **Charles Mann:** back BL; 6 BL; 9 TL; 22 B, T; 23 B, T; 52 T; 71; 93 L; 108 TL; 109 C1; 111 R; 114 R; 126 B; 310 T. **David McDonald:** 85 T; 89 R; 113 R. **Joe McDonald/Tom Stack & Associates:** 204 R. **Charles W. Melton:** 32 M; 47 BL; 97; 160 BL, TL; 170 L; 194 R; 199 L; 204 TL; 206 TL, TR; 207 TR. **William T. Molin:** 259 L; 260 L; 266 L; 269 L; 275 R; 276 L; 279 R; 283 TL; 284 R; 291 L. **Glen M. Oliver/Visuals Unlimited:** 160 R. **Jerry Pavia:** 10; 46 BL, BR; 72 TL; 76 BC, BL; 91 R. **Joanne Pavia:** 306 TL. **Pamela K. Peirce:** back RC; 20 L; 36 TR; 37 R; 42 TL, TR; 44 R; 52 L; 64 BL, BR; 81 L, R; 82 B; 83 B, M; 86 L, M, R; 87 R; 88 L, R; 90 R; 91 L; 113 BL; 115 R; 123 L; 133 R, TL; 134 BR, TL; 135 M; 136 R; 163 L; 164 TR; 170 TR; 176 BR; 181 TL; 187 BR; 196 R; 201 R; 208 TL; 223 L, R; 226 R; 241; 244 L; 245 R; 247 L; 251 R; 252 R; 256 TR; 259 R; 262 R; 265 TL; 266 TR; 274 R; 275 L; 277 L; 280 R; 283 BL; 285 R; 287 BR; 288 L; 289 R; 290 BL; 291 R; 294 BR, TR; 297 R; 300 L; 301 R. **Rod Planck/Tom Stack & Associates:** 67 T. **Norman A. Plate:** 11 T; 29 R; 38 R; 44 L; 47 TL, TR; 61; 65 ML, MR; 111 L; 113 TL; 119 R; 120 TL, TR; 132 L; 137 TL. **Rob Proctor:** 308 B. **Jay Pscheidt:** 211 L; 214 R; 218 R; 232 L; 233 R. **Ed Reschke/ Positive Images:** 122 R. **Susan A. Roth:** 14 T; 80 L; 82 M; 85 B; 90 M; 92 L; 123 R; 132 M; 136 L; 137 R; 214 L. **Janet Sanchez:** 286 TR; 299 L; 305. **Science VU/ Visuals Unlimited:** 217 R. **Wendy Shatill/Tom Stack & Associates:** 205 BL. **Richard Shiell:** back TR; 36 BL; 43 BR; 45 TR; 67 B; 72 BL; 108 BL; 131 M, R; 148 BL, TL; 205 TL; 207 BR; 240 R; 250 R; 264 R; 271 BR; 276 BR; 284 TL; 286 L; 287 TR; 290 TL; 292 BR, TR; 294 TL; 296 BL; 301 BL, TL; 303 R. **Malcolm C. Shurtleff:** 220 R; 228 R; 230 L; 231 R; 235 R; 236 R; 237 L; 242 L. **Steve Sibbett:** back LC;

69; 228 L; 239 L, R. **John J. Smith:** 265 R; 267 L, R; 284 BL; 295 R; 299 R; 270 L. **Superstock:** 21 B. **Dan Suzio:** 150 L3, R1, R2, R3; 198 BL; 278 BL; 280 L. **Dean G. Swan:** 261 BL; 264 L; 273 R; 277 BR, TR; 283 TR; 292 BL; 295 BL; 296 R; 303 BL, TL. **Randy Tatroe:** 26 BL. **Michael S. Thompson:** 6 BR, TL; 9 B, TR; 15; 16 T; 17 B; 29 B; 31; 36 TL; 42 BL, BR; 72 BR; 74; 76 BR; 87 M; 91 M; 112 TL; 117 T; 119 L; 120 B; 125 BL; 130 T. **Larry Ulrich:** 19 B; 22 L; 108 TR. **Greg Vaughn/Tom Stack & Associates:** 30 B. **VISIONS-Holland:** 125 BR. **Washington State University:** 161 L. **Andy Wasowski:** 46 TR. **Darrow M. Watt:** 11 B; 65 T; 306 BL. **William J. Weber/Visuals Unlimited:** 164 BR. **Ron West:** back TL ; 30 T; 32 B; 51 BL; 63 M; 65 BL, BR; 70 R; 75 B; 148 TR; 150 L4; 151; 153 B; 154 L; 155 L; 156 L; 157 L; 159 L; 161 R; 162 L, R; 163 BR; 164 L; 165 L; 166 R; 167 R; 168 BR, L, TR; 169 BR, TR; 170 BR; 171 L, R; 172 TL; 173 L; 174 L; 175 BR, L, TR; 176 L, TR; 179 L, R; 180 R; 181 R; 185 L; 186 L; 188 BR, L, TR; 190 L, R; 191 R; 193 R; 195 BL, R, TL; 196 L; 197 BR, L, TR; 198 R, TL; 200 L, R; 202 L, R; 203 R; 204 BL, ML; 205 TR; 208 TR; 213 L; 215 R; 222 L; 229 L, R; 238 L; 246 R; 271 TR; 282 L, R; 287 L; 293 TL; 294 BL; 296 TL; 307 B. **Doug Wilson:** 34 BR; 84 M; 110 R; 114 L. **Kent Wood:** 249 L; 255 R. **Tom Woodward:** 7; 27; 209. **Cynthia Woodyard:** 83 T. **Tom Wyatt:** 37 L; 100 L, R; 101 L, M, R; 102 L, R; 103 L, R. **Thomas A. Zitter:** 208 BL; 212 L; 224 R; 240 L.

DESIGN CREDITS

Our thanks to the garden and landscape designers who allowed their work to appear in this book, including:

Barbara Blossom Ashmun: 26 TL. **Catherine Clemens:** 71. **Billie Gray:** 14 T. **Harland Hand:** 2; 18 L. **Carrie Nimmer:** 23 T. **Jana Olson Drobinsky:** 25. **Jonathan Plant and Associates:** 48. **Suzanne Porter:** 6 TR.

ACKNOWLEDGMENTS

Our thanks to the following entomologists, pathologists, and weed science specialists for their contributions to this book:

William W. Allen (Professor Emeritus, Environmental Sciences, Policy, and Management, University of California, Berkeley); K. George Beck (Bioagricultural Science and Pest Management, Colorado State University); Sharon J. Collman (Department of Entomology, Washington State University); Whitney Cranshaw (Bioagricultural Sciences and Pest Management, Colorado State University); Clyde L. Elmore (Weed Science Program, University of California, Davis); Dave T. Langston (Extension Specialist, Department of Entomology, University of Arizona); Rex E. Marsh (Professor Emeritus, Department of Wildlife, Fish, and Conservation Biology, University of California, Davis); William T. Molin (Department of Plant Sciences, University of Arizona); Mary W. Olsen (Extension Specialist, Department of Plant Pathology, University of Arizona); Robert Parker (Department of Crop and Soil Sciences, Washington State University); Laura Pickett Pottorff (Cooperative Extension, Colorado State University); Jay W. Pscheidt (Extension Specialist, Department of Plant Pathology, Oregon State University); Robert Raabe (Department of Plant Biology, University of California, Berkeley).

Special thanks to Bill Nelson at Pacific Tree Farms, Chula Vista, CA.

If you would like to order copies of any of our books, call Leisure Arts, distributor for Sunset Books, at 1 (800) 526-5111, or check with your local bookseller.